W9-BNU-821

BARBARIANS WITHIN THE
GATES OF ROME

BARBARIANS within the GATES of ROME

A Study of Roman Military Policy and the Barbarians, ca. 375–425 A.D.

Thomas S. Burns

Indiana University Press
Bloomington and Indianapolis

The paper used in this publication meets the minimum
requirements of American National Standard for Information
Sciences—Permanence of Paper for Printed Library Materials,
ANSI Z39.48-1984.
Manufactured in the United States of America

Library of Congress Cataloging-in-Publication Data

Burns, Thomas S.
Barbarians within the gates of Rome : a study of Roman military
policy and the barbarians, ca. 375–425 A.D. / Thomas S. Burns.
p.   cm.
Includes bibliographical references and index.
ISBN 0-253-31288-4
1. Rome—Army—Recruiting, enlistment, etc.   2. Germanic peoples—
Employment.   3. Rome—History, Military—30 B.C.–475 A.D.
I. Title
U35.B79   1994
937'.08—dc20
94-12788

2 3 4 5   00 99 98 97 96 95

**To
my
friends**

CONTENTS

Preface
xi

Introduction
xiii

1
Valentinian, Valens, and the Battle of Adrianople
I

2
Theodosius in Action
43

3
Concluding the Gothic Wars
73

4
Barbarians and Civil War
92

5
Stilicho's Transalpine Recruitment Areas
112

6
Four Generals
148

7
Alaric and Stilicho: Working Together
183

8
The Sack of Rome
224

9
The Settlement of 418:
Constantine, Constantius, Athaulf, Wallia, and Rome
247

Conclusion
280

Emperors and Principal Usurpers, 284–455
285

Chronological Outline
287

Notes
293

Bibliography
378

Index
408

LIST OF ILLUSTRATIONS

1. "Hut-type" coin of Constans   *12*

2. Tetrarchic medallion from Lyon   *14*

3. Typical urban defenses in the Thracian area in late antiquity   *21*

4. Gold ingot from Feldioara, Romania   *51*

5. The insignias of *Comites sacrarum largitionum* from the *Notitia dignitatum*   *66*

6. Obelisk base of Theodosius the Great (erected in the Hippodrome in Constantinople)   *90*

7. Depiction of *villa rustica* from the era of the Principate   *113*

8. Late Roman farmstead near Weßling, Germany, in the era of Valentinian I   *124*

9. Types of late Roman "onion-topped" fibulae   *125*

10. Siliqua of Constantine III   *127*

11. Depiction of Goldberg near Türkheim in the era of Valentinian I   *136*

12–13. Frauenberg near Weltenburg   *141*

14. Depiction of a late Roman soldier from Straubing-Azlburg   *142*

15. Two-layer sardonyx cameo showing Emperor Honorius and Empress Maria   *160*

16. Both panels of an ivory diptych with Stilicho, Serena, and Eucherius   *222*

17. Solidi of a) Honorius, b) Galla Placidia, and c) Priscus Attalus   *248*

18. Solidus of Constantius III   *250*

LIST OF MAPS

1. Dioceses and Provinces of the Roman Empire in the Fourth and Fifth Centuries A.D. — 6

2. Late Roman Balkan Roads and Provinces — 20

3. Production and Discovery Sites of Gold Ingots — 51

4. Roman Frontier and Hinterland, Lauriacum to Singidunum — 97

5. The Late Roman Danube-Iller-Rhine Frontier and Hinterland — 120

6. Hilltop Fortifications beyond the Upper Rhine and Danube Rivers — 131

7. Late Roman Greece — 157

8. The Rhine and Late Roman Gaul — 211

9. Northern Italy and the Late Roman Alpine Passes — 226

10. Provinces of Late Roman Iberia — 252

11. Late Roman Iberia — 253

PREFACE

THIS BOOK BEGAN its slow gestation during the summers of 1978 and 1979 in Passau, Germany. I was then involved as historian and co-director of the excavation of a Valentinianic watchtower (ca. 370) with Prof. Helmut Bender, now a professor for Roman provincial archaeology at the Universität Passau. We were very fortunate to be digging on the Roman frontier at that time, for much was happening in late Roman history and archaeology. Archaeologists working on Roman sites along the upper Danube were turning up increasing amounts of very dark pottery that was clearly non-Roman. Ever since, I have attempted to identify those Roman policies in effect ca. 375–425 which aimed to control Roman-barbarian interactions along the frontiers, and to understand the long-term results of those policies. The era of Theodosius and his dynasty is a difficult one to explore, but early on I became convinced that explanations for any of its many crises had to be sought in a much wider context than any recently surveyed. The decade and a half since this study began has produced an avalanche of new archaeological data and historical interpretation, but no major reassessment of Roman policy toward the barbarians during the final, epochal years of the Western empire. This book is an attempt to satisfy that need.

There are many people to thank for their advice and encouragement over the years of work on this book. Several scholars in Germany and America were particularly helpful and read drafts of chapters and ultimately most of the entire book in one form or another. We discussed ideas repeatedly but those in this book remain my own. So I thank Prof. Helmut Bender, Universität Passau, Prof. Gunther Gottlieb, Universität Augsburg, Prof. Bernhard Overbeck, Staatliche Münzsammlung München, and Dr. Mechtild Overbeck for their patience, advice, and good humor. Closer to home I owe thanks to Prof. Herbert W. Benario, Prof. Patrick N. Allitt, and Prof. John Juricek of Emory University, and Prof. John W. Eadie, Michigan State University. Early ideas for many chapters were offered first at symposia at the University of Sheffield and the University of Nottingham, England; the Janus Pannonius University, Pécs, Hungary; at the Universität Passau and the Universität München, Germany; McGill University, Canada; University of California at Santa Barbara; Rutgers University; and the University of the South. I thank all those institutions for inviting me to present my ideas. Finally I owe special thanks to Ms. Patricia Stockbridge for her courage under fire as she put the manuscript into final form.

I also wish to acknowledge my debt to individuals and institutions for the use of illustrations: Prof. Dr. Bernhard Overbeck and the Staatliche Münzsammlung München for illustrations 1, 4, 10, and base map for map 3; Dr. Helmut Bender for illustrations 8 and 11; Dr. Erwin Keller for illustration 9; Prof. Dr. Konrad Spindler for illustrations 12 and 13; Prof. Dr. Thomas Fischer for illustrations 7 and 14; Dr. Jochen Garbsch for the base map for map 5; Dr. Pierre Bastien for illustration 2; St. Martin's Press, Inc. (from *Bulgaria in Antiquity. An Archaeological Introduction* by R. F. Hoddinott. Copyright 1975 by R. F. Hoddinott. Reprinted with permission of St. Martin's Press, Inc.) for illustration 3; Hirmer Verlag GmbH for illustrations 6, 15, and 16; and Dumbarton Oaks for illustrations 17 and 18, copyright 1993 by Dumbarton Oaks, Trustees of Harvard University, Washington, D.C.

INTRODUCTION

THIS BOOK is designed to explain when, how, and why the Romans began a policy of allowing large, unified, and potentially troublesome groups of barbarians onto Roman soil. For generations modern historians have called this Rome's "federate policy" from the relationship it had to a treaty or *foedus*. Historians have searched almost as long for a single explanation or event that forced the Roman emperors into making this fateful decision, this epoch-changing mistake. No such solution is offered here. No one Roman defeat or victory accounts for Rome's employment of barbarians at the end of the fourth century and in the early decades of the fifth. Nor were all barbarians in the Roman army deployed in the same way, such as in the cavalry, for example. Nor did any government pursue anti-barbarian or pro-barbarian policies. Nonetheless there is a line leading from the Roman defeat near Adrianople in 378, through the "non-event" of the Sack of Rome in 410, to the settlement of the Goths and their allies in Aquitaine in 418. The path is strewn with the litter of failed efforts to recruit new troops into the Roman army in sufficient numbers. In its endeavors to raise and maintain the army, Rome faced daunting problems in its role of paymaster and provisioner.

Even before 378, finding high quality men willing and able to serve was a formidable challenge, usually met by enrolling the sons of veterans in the frontier provinces and by encouraging barbarians to enter Roman service from settlements near the frontiers. Germanic recruits were already commonplace during the profound crisis of the third century that had resulted from the combination of usurpation and foreign invasion. By turning consistently to the barbarians beyond—and ultimately to those within the frontiers of the Empire—the Roman army merely followed the path of least resistance and maximum success. Small decisions built upon one another, none seemed unusual or revolutionary, but during the half century explored here the pace of experimentation quickened. New uses of barbarian recruits did not mean that the old ones were abandoned. They were not. The result in any one province or diocese—the civilian administrative units of the late Empire that also held military significance—from our vantage point looks a bit like a patchwork quilt. This book examines the creation of that compound design. It is also a study in the Roman decision-making processes that resulted from the flow of local and regional information up the chain and the corresponding strategic decisions moving downward through the administrative hierarchies.

The Roman army's needs for manpower were as varied as its missions. Had there been major sources of young men other than the Germanic barbarians, Roman generals could have enjoyed the luxury of earlier times, when specialized units of barbarians were regularly assigned functions peculiar to their prior experience and training. Even at the end of the fourth century, some units were still employed in tasks for which their native skills had prepared them well, but these units seem to have been exceptions. Roman soldiers, their ethnic identities submerged in the army, were needed in garrisons along the frontiers, in units guarding highway junctions and bridges, as individuals in elite regiments and regular units, and ultimately in groups accountable only to their kings. Typically Roman soldiers in the late Empire served in small detachments, but occasionally in larger ones. Just as the needs for barbarian recruits varied, so too did the terms of their service, for barbarians were used as the commanding generals or local officers saw fit.

Rome was the recruiter, and as such generally could dictate where and how new soldiers were assigned to duty stations, how much they drew as pay, and when they might be discharged with a pension. Therefore no single pattern of service, either in length or location, existed that could not be modified. During the roughly half century to be explored in this book, barbarian soldiers of diverse backgrounds will be seen in roles ranging from imperial guards to quasi-farmer soldiers. Some native leaders were recruited as officers; most men served as common soldiers. Roman policy was to recruit from whatever resources were available and assign units and individuals according to need and circumstance. The book ends shortly after the settlement of the Goths in Aquitaine in 418. Constantius, who would share the purple for a few months before his death in 421 as Constantius III, was then the Roman commander-in-chief. He, not the freshly minted Gothic kings, was still able to call the tune.

The manpower crisis was not primarily a result of the decline in the general population. That decline appears beyond statistical proof, but must lie behind many of the imperial edicts and the archaeologically demonstrable fact that in the transalpine regions urban civilization had often all but vanished. The edicts in question repeatedly point to the obstruction of imperial recruiters by the wealthy landowning classes. This was particularly troublesome in the core provinces of the Mediterranean world, where villa-based agriculture still flourished with the labor of slaves and semi-dependent workers. The need for agricultural labor in the Mediterranean provinces competed with the military requirements along the frontiers. Rome had to find steady sources of new soldiers not subject to the demands of the landowners, who might best be taxed anyway. Geographically this meant concentrating recruitment efforts upon the frontier regions. Rome was very much able to recruit there, for it still controlled all the material means used to reward loyalty, at first money and precious metals but increasingly, after 395, supplies. Rome nevertheless had to struggle for resources.

The basic equation for the Roman army during this period was the balance between the availability of recruits and the means to pay them. The fact that Rome controlled the reward system for military service did not mean that it always got what it paid for, or even that it was able to pay. There were many non-military demands upon the state's budget, all impossible to calculate. For example, the cost of operating the imperial post, the expenses associated with travel and the court, and the direct and indirect costs of the emperor's religious policies, to name but a few, drew heavily upon the imperial coffers. The progressive modification of the military pay and provisionment system toward local resources, especially land and food, had profound and largely unanticipated results, which sent ripples of change throughout the society of the Western Empire. No region was immune. The army was the largest expense and the one which the emperors probably felt, however naively, that they could control.

The central focus of this book is always the Roman army. Little attempt is made to explore the complex political and social evolutions that were concurrent with the military events described. Occasionally, however, political forces convulsed so dramatically as to alter military planning. During such crises, political intervention was short-term—typically only for a specific operation—rather than a sustained intrusion into the basic dynamic of military life.

The relative rarity of outright political intervention into military affairs was due in part to the peculiar political situation brought about by the abrupt death of the last great warrior emperor, Theodosius I, in 395. Neither of his young sons, Honorius nor Arcadius, could ever assert military command over their leading generals or political advisers. Arcadius died in 408, again leaving the East in the hands of a minor, his son Theodosius II, and his advisers. Honorius's death in 423, five years after the deployment of barbarian auxiliaries under their native leaders in Aquitaine in 418, changed nothing.

The commanding general in the West, the *magister peditum*, made all essential military decisions. Outside the chain of command he was usually referred to as the *magister utriusque militiae* (the commanding general of both branches of the army, the infantry and cavalry, a title officially used primarily within the Eastern army).[1] The command situation never really changed in the West. Although the Germanic barbarians, especially the Gothic speakers, are central participants in many chapters, this is not a book about Gothic society, or the reestablishment of Visigothic kingship with Alaric, or any single barbarian group. Roman policy was to break any pre-existing groupings apart or find safe ways to build upon them. Only when the social and political aspects of the barbarian societies had a manifest effect upon the Roman military are they included, for always the primary goal is to better understand Roman military policy.

The concentration of military planning as well as its execution in the hands of the generals meant that the aristocracy and the professional court-iers, from whose hands so much of our information about these times de-rives, were even more isolated from the military than was usual in late antiquity. Other defects in our literary sources tend to heighten still further the sense of a sharp change in the direction of military affairs—a diver-gence from tradition that this book seeks to minimize. Ammianus Marcel-linus, indisputably the last great historian of the Roman Empire, was only partially an exception.[2] He wrote around 395 of the events leading up to the accession of Theodosius the Great a few months after the death of the emperor Valens in the great battle that took place not far from Adrianople on 9 August 378. Ammianus was a veteran himself, a retired officer who never made it to the top and never won personal acceptance among the top levels of the Roman aristocracy. While there is no dearth of courtly gossip and intrigue in his history, the extant portions provide a soldier's view of the Empire. Ammianus Marcellinus was the last Roman historian to un-derstand the army as an insider.

The historiographic problems become extraordinary after the end of Ammianus's account. There is not a single extant Roman history for the years 378–425 written by a contemporary, unless we choose to abandon the traditional definition of what comprised history. Such materials, how-ever, did exist once upon a time and were exploited by other writers, often carelessly. There is nonetheless a surprisingly large assortment of relevant accounts, some even written at the time of the events they narrate. Modern historians are always concerned to discover the nature and limits of their sources, a matter of special concern to those who attempted to portray the four decades following the accession of Theodosius. Here the sources offer layers of intrigue and prejudicial editing hinting at what might have been had fate left them whole, or not unlike a fine wine well past its prime.

The Roman army existed in a real landscape of roads, forts, and command systems. The physical realities of military life sometimes emerge from the traces left behind and discovered in excavations or by chance in their native soil. Archaeology has revealed a wealth of details about army camps, support systems, and military deployments. As a result, the overall military establishment and the outlines of major changes are becoming clear. Recent advances in dating that do not rely exclusively upon coins have allowed the substantiation of the last phases of the Roman occupation of ancient sites with much greater confidence than just a decade ago. Much, however, remains unclear. The details at particular locations sometimes remain in dispute, occasionally even among archaeologists working on the same site. There are often significant differences from one province or diocese to the next, which perhaps reflect the different decisions made by local and regional commands in accordance with general policy. Upon occasion, a single archaeological discovery can truly transform our understanding. Unlike the ancients themselves, we cannot take their physical environment for granted.

Coins had a very long lifetime of service. The fact that common Roman bronze coinage in the West ended with the last mintings of Theodosius the Great does not allow us to conclude that sites where the last coins are Theodosian ceased to exist after Theodosius. Archaeology and numismatics do not often provide the solid chronological framework historians seek, but they do give us much to think about in regard to physical setting and at times can offer direct and compelling specific information that forces a reinterpretation of theories based exclusively upon literary material. The dating of archaeological and historical materials is crucial to archaeological and historical theories of explanation. Innumerable otherwise persuasive explanations have been exploded by a single erroneous date. Even with the best modern methods, scholars continue to differ over dates and—as a result—over what happened and why. The reader is therefore urged to take the time to explore major scholarly debates over dating as they appear in the text and notes.

I have tried to provide the reader with a view through the eyes of the generals making the decisions, and this means providing data about troop availability and the logistical supports in place to move those men to the points of engagement. Generals did not make decisions without information. They would have tried to know about the current state of the fortifications and units under their commands. The principals in our drama were all experienced veterans with years of service behind them: the emperor Theodosius; Stilicho, a member of the imperial family through marriage and the guardian of Honorius; Alaric; and finally Alaric's successors to the

Gothic kingship and the *magister militum* Constantius. Many others entered upon center stage briefly and most of these were military men too. Galla Placidia, Honorius's half-sister, held no command at all but cast her imprint upon three decades nonetheless.

Not even Ammianus Marcellinus concerned himself with providing his readers with details of supply and recruitment. He either took them for granted or, more likely, appreciated the fact that the canons of the Roman historical discipline did not provide for such discussion. The ancient reader expected explorations of character, particularly that of the emperor, for divine favor on the Empire was thought to take this into account. Today we deplore such simple moralistic causation. Another aspect of ancient historical writing that we tend to dismiss is the literary power of juxtaposing stereotypes to engage the reader in moral judgment.

Edward Gibbon and the *philosophes* of the so-called Age of Enlightenment, whose ideas about society and government are still so much a part of our western cultural heritage, rarely let slip a chance to see history move as a result of the collision of basic human characteristics personified in individuals or ethnic groups. In this they learned lessons from the ancient authors—lessons perhaps unintended by their Latin and Greek teachers. One of the most enduring of all ancient stereotypes was that of the barbarian. Already honed to precision in Greek literature, the technique of using the "barbarians" as foils to the civilized Romans had a long history that bridged the transition to the Christian Roman world of late antiquity. The intellectual abstraction "barbarian" influenced every literary source cited in this study whether pagan or Christian. The intensification of military recruitment among the barbarians in the decades following the battle of Adrianople sharpened the literary criticism of alleged favoritism shown the barbarians in the "Roman army." For some authors any general, even Theodosius himself, committed a singular transgression of Roman morality whenever he relied upon "barbarians." Several Christian writers saw the age as a prelude to the Apocalypse. The combining of the canonical concern with the private morality of public people and the traditional avenues of social criticism conveyed in the contrast of "Roman and barbarian" is another aspect of this period this study aims to elucidate.

The ramifications of the so-called federate policy were never so negative to contemporaries as they were to Edward Gibbon and his modern followers.[3] The term federates or *foederati* itself appears first around the time of the settlement of the Goths in Aquitaine.[4] Employing federates was not then regarded as a threat to imperial survival, nor was the term confined or even primarily used to describe large groups of barbarians under their native leaders. The survival of the Empire was unquestioned by all but a few religious hopefuls seeking immediate entry through heaven's gates. The earthly gates of Rome remained open and guarded. The challenge for some was at once both simpler and more complex than pondering divine plans for humankind: to provide a structure and mechanisms within the traditional framework to manipulate, harness, and absorb the new immigrants into a Roman society that was progressively less comfortable with its classical pluralisms.

Despite their penchant for hiding complex procedural and legal issues beneath a few seemingly all-encompassing laws, Roman policies were based much more upon what had worked before and in trust won by deeds. Such trust was won in the course of generations rather than by a signature on a treaty or the word of an individual. Most, if not all, of the legislation usually associated with the establishment of the barbarians upon Roman soil derived from the need to billet and move Roman troops and the practice of receiving barbarian peoples into the Empire—*receptio*. Particularly relevant are the procedures worked out and codified during the reign of Valentinian I (364–75) and his brother Valens (364–78), although the interpretation of this corpus of laws remains in dispute. Later legislation provided timely instruction upon the earlier edicts and reveals just how much the Romans living under Honorius regarded the barbarian problem as a continuation of various military concerns already of considerable antiquity by 400. Throughout the four decades following the Roman defeat at Adrianople no Roman political or military leader appeared to despair of the Empire's survival. Theodosius, Stilicho, and finally Constantius III remained confident that they controlled the situation. Roman policy makers, including Valentinian, Valens, Theodosius, Stilicho, and Constantius, consistently decided to expand the sphere of trust and interaction with the Germanic peoples. Finally, under pressure of circumstances to no one's liking, Theodosius and his successors moved to accept and provide for the barbarians as a revitalizing auxiliary system within the territorial instead of merely within the diplomatic and conceptual framework of the *Imperium Romanum*. The shift in policies was gradual and complex. Their actions will speak for themselves.

Reference to the Chronological Outline at the back of the book should also help. Whenever possible I have tried to hold to a straight chronological presentation. This is difficult, however, when trying to explore the contexts of general developments on local and regional levels. In these instances the presentation is typically regional and within that region chronological. At times we must follow developments week by week as the sources permit. During the half century explored in this book, Rome took many baby steps

rather than one giant leap along the path of finding a place for barbarians
in the Roman army. After fifty years had passed, Rome reached a new pla-
teau—one small step at a time—in harnessing the energies of the Germanic
barbarians within the Empire. Only a careful chronological presentation
can recapture the painstaking slowness of Roman policy changes when
each decision followed so logically from the preceding one.

The question of "grand strategy" invariably arises since the 1976 publication of *The Grand Strategy of the Roman Empire* by E. N. Luttwak.[5] What
might pass as a change in grand strategy in regards to the barbarians is really
not that at all. Although Theodosius the Great was the most important emperor of this period, he never articulated a change in policy. The same stages
in evolution took place even under usurpers. We can see it in the Balkans
and on the Rhine, in Gaul and the German provinces, not always in syn-
chronization but marching to the same tune. The concept of grand strategy
presupposes that the Romans rationally assessed their defensive problems
and then set about creating a system to solve them. Rather, it seems, Diocletian (284–305) and Constantine (307–337), for example, had a finite resource base in revenue and manpower with which to accomplish the defense of the Empire at a time when most frontier provinces were still trying
to preserve an important civilian component. The civilians are the ones
whose interests they best served by erecting stout walls around towns, securing the roads, and in general cultivating the rule of law. By the time this
book opens, Rome had accumulated an impressive array of military assets—garrisons, supply depots, walled fortifications, and so forth—in excess
of local military needs. In the last half of the fourth century emperors
and their generals devised strategies based upon these assets. Towns had
dwindled.

When Valentinian I died in 375, he bequeathed a different type of frontier environment to his successors than had Constantine the Great in 337.
In the interval civilians had left the frontier provinces in great number and
those who remained were deeply enmeshed in a highly militarized world.
In 375 the Roman army could operate with little regard for civilian values.
They could allow large areas of the provinces along and behind the frontier
to fend for themselves for long periods. They no longer had to face strong
civilian criticism for allowing barbarian bands to strike into the interior.
The barbarians themselves were part of the frontier society. Military tac-
ticians could employ what appears to have been a defense-in-depth because
of the nature of the frontier provinces. In other words, the Romans used
the system as if it had been so designed, even though it had not. Probably
no military strategist would have commissioned the building of so much

defensive redundancy into a system, but when crisis came they knew how to use it. The same can be said for Roman policy toward the barbarians, but that will take the rest of this book.

The maps are essential in seeing situations unfold from the perspective of the commanders. The other illustrations reveal some of the archaeological, numismatic, and topographic details relevant to the narrative. The battle of Adrianople in 378, the death of Theodosius in 395, and the "Sack of Rome" in 410 provide convenient mileposts in the study. The settlement of 418 in Aquitaine is a logical end. Taking into account a few years on either side of these events yields almost precisely a half-century of accelerating change, fifty years that forever altered the Western Empire and as a result Western Civilization. The first task is to set our feet upon bedrock, and in late antiquity that is almost always provided by Ammianus and the reign of Valentinian I and his brother Valens.[6]

BARBARIANS WITHIN THE
GATES OF ROME

VALENTINIAN, VALENS, AND THE
BATTLE OF ADRIANOPLE

THE BATTLE OF Adrianople is generally regarded as a disaster from which Roman power never recovered.[1] Contemporaries Ammianus Marcellinus, Jerome, Orosius, and others seem to leave no room for doubt about that. For the secular Ammianus, the events of 9 August 378, a dry and dusty day indeed, marked a check to the relentless and basically successful reassertion of Roman dominance depicted in the rest of his extant work.[2] Because he did not wish to continue his history into the reign of Theodosius, the emperor under whom he wrote, Ammianus ended just months after the defeat. But, since his is the last major Latin history of the Empire, by ending when he did, Ammianus unintentionally elevated the significance of the defeat beyond what even he himself believed to be the case. Virtually all early historians writing up through the Enlightenment fell into the trap created by the absence of any subsequent account that even approached the depth of Ammianus's history. Some still find the transition from Ammianus to most fifth-century Western authors difficult to accept without recourse to themes of historical decline. Christians like Jerome, Ambrose, and Orosius expressed a sense of profound despair, punctuated by the expectancy of the end of the world. Greek authors, although perhaps slightly less powerful in their imagery than was Jerome, nonetheless also reflected the extraordinary sense of crisis surrounding the defeat and the three decades of turmoil resulting from it.

Whatever the distortions in our sources (and many of our authors after all were quite removed from these events in time and circumstance), there is no reason to doubt that the defeat at Adrianople was the worst setback to Roman arms since before the days of Diocletian's tetrarchy (284–305). Still, a reversal on the battlefield need not have inspired major changes in military policies. Moreover, to erect upon the fragile literary sources claims that the battle precipitated a new Roman approach to the barbarians and, indeed, to Rome's very ethos—specifically the origins of the "federate policy"—

would be rash. This chapter will explore the events leading up to the Battle of Adrianople, the battle itself, and the military policies and realities that provided the context for the entire episode.

The Roman Army in Action

Valentinian and his brother Valens (364–75, Valens alone to 378) expended much of their energies addressing problems along the frontiers, repeatedly instilling respect for Roman arms by exacting a high cost in barbarian blood. They took important steps in the employment and payment of new types of troops, many of Germanic stock and often led by native-speaking leaders. Many soldiers of barbarian origins reached generalships during the reigns of Valentinian and Valens. The policies and other military actions implemented under these imperial brothers established precedents for later developments that are traditionally thought to have arisen only after 378.

Valentinian and Valens pursued an aggressive strategy of keeping the barbarians off balance through brutal preemptive campaigns across the Rhine and Danube.[3] The origins of their policy went back at least to the era of Diocletian and Constantine but took definitive form under Constantius II (337–61) and his Caesar in the West and later challenger, Julian (Caesar from 355, emperor 360–63).[4] In the West Valentinian and in the East Valens took and held the initiative from 364 to 378.

When Valentinian I suffered a fatal stroke in 375 while rebuking the Quadic ambassadors, Roman policy toward and defenses against the barbarians were clear and potent. Many of the events of the half century following Valentinian's death relate directly to his reign, particularly to his successes against the barbarians and the refinement of the Roman frontier system to manage them. Much of the defensive system of forts and strongpoints were begun in the era of the tetrarchy or before, and Valentinian only needed to bring them into line with his defensive policies. Early in their reigns Valentinian and Valens each faced challenges to their rule from combinations of barbarian invasions and armed usurpation, and in each case neither could afford to be unforgiving to the leaders whose swords had been raised against them. Rebelling soldiers and invading barbarians fared better once they submitted themselves for judgment.

The welcoming of barbarians fleeing the Huns between 376 and 378, which culminated in the great battle just outside Adrianople, graphically illustrates Valens's understanding and execution of these policies. However, without knowing how the system really worked, even the great struggle against the Goths is difficult to reconstruct from the extant accounts. Before the arrival of the Huns on the lower Danube (ca. 375), there were two incidents that foreshadowed Rome's responses to barbarians and internal rebellion—the two often difficult to separate—later and elsewhere. One was the combination of rebellion and barbarian invasion in the East centered around the rebel Procopius (365–66); the other was the unrest on the Rhine and in Britain in 367–69, which also witnessed invasion and usurpation, this time that of a certain Valentinus.[5]

One of Valens's first crises after ascending the throne was suppressing a revolt among some followers of the Constantinian dynasty that had ended with the death of Julian in 363. The revolt of Procopius in 365 and its cast of participants also brought out many aspects of the barbarian-Roman relationship and revealed the system of defense as it was intended to work. Procopius revolted upon learning of the elevation of Valentinian and subsequently that of Valens, but his army came to him because of the barbarians. Very early in 365 Valens moved eastward to address matters on the Persian frontier. Persia had controlled the area since the demise of Julian's campaign against it and his successor Jovianus (363–64) had ceded five of its provinces to Persia by treaty.[6] Valens ordered his brother-in-law Petronius, recently elevated to the patriciate from his legionary command, to press the sons of veterans into the service which legally they owed. His order was posted at Beirut in the province of Syria on 13 April 364.[7] While passing through Bithynia, Valens learned that a Gothic invasion of Thrace was imminent and dispatched two of his legions back to Thrace. Procopius found these two legions in Constantinople and rallied them to his side. His revolt had begun.[8] Procopius set off after Valens, winning new adherents along the way and dispatching a message to the Goths on the Danube.[9]

After some successful initial skirmishes, Procopius clashed with Valens at Thyatira in Asia Minor. There many of Procopius's men under the command of Gomoarius defected back to Valens, the legitimate emperor. Gomoarius had pursued a long and successful military career since coming into Roman service sometime prior to 350. He had also achieved a certain fame for betraying would-be usurpers. Procopius's revolt had turned Valens's army back toward Constantinople from its base in Antioch, forcing the emperor to abandon, at least for the time being, the idea of launching a campaign against Persia. Valens was again in Antioch in 376.

Usurpation had been a major concern from 350 onward, and each incident was slightly different. These rebellions often reveal indirectly the routine handling of Germanic recruits. In January 350 Magnentius assumed the purple after overthrowing Constans. Magnentius had risen through the ranks. He was a *laetus*, perhaps born at Amiens of a Romano-British father and Frankish mother. Ironically, his mother had probably settled in the Empire as one of the numerous barbarians whom Constans's father, Constantine the Great, had established there to help defend the lower Rhine. The archaeological data from this area point to an almost completely Germanized society from around midcentury. Here German settlers and non-Germanic indigenous peoples created a uniform culture, dominated by warrior elites serving as *laeti* in the Roman army.[10]

At the moment of his rebellion Magnentius, *comes rei militaris*, commanded two palatine legions serving with the emperor. Magnentius, a usurper against the house of Constantine, nonetheless tried to defend himself by making the traditional usurper's claim that he was overthrowing a tyrant. For the first six months of his usurpation he sought acceptance from Constans's brother and co-emperor Constantius II, but failed. On the first of March 350, Vetranio, Constans's *magister peditum*, also revolted, apparently to hold Illyricum for Constantius II (337–61). Constantius defeated Magnentius at the strategic Illyrian city of Mursa (Osijek) in 351 and again in Gaul two years later.[11] Vetranio, apparently betrayed by one of his junior officers, Gomoarius, soon abdicated in favor of Constantius II and accepted a pension.[12] The events of 350 foreshadowed the course of many usurpations that were to follow over the next half-century. Usurpation against an emperor of an established dynasty was a very risky venture. It was best to try to interest him in a joint rule first.

Constantius had rewarded Gomoarius's loyalty in 360 with the office of *magister equitum* in Gaul under his Caesar Julian—Gomoarius probably also acting as a highly placed watchdog for his benefactor. Upon his elevation to the purple, Julian, himself a member of the imperial family and husband to Constantius's sister Helena, removed Gomoarius from his command and apparently sent him back to Constantius in the East. He noted that as a young officer Gomoarius had turned against usurpers before, specifically Vetranio (December 350).[13] When next we see Gomoarius, shortly after Julian had rebelled against Constantius, he is at the head of a group of *laeti*, farmer-soldiers serving under Roman supervision, ordered to block the advance of Julian's forces by holding the Succi Pass in the Haemus Mountains.[14]

This was in 361. The Empire was fortunate that Constantius died before civil war could begin. Then in 366 Gomoarius appears as a principal general supporting the rebel Procopius, but, typically enough, he soon returned once more to the true emperor, taking his troops with him.[15] The Succi Pass was a key strongpoint in securing the central Balkan highway and played an important role in the wars against the Goths in the following decades. The use of *laeti* under Roman command is clear in this incident in 361 as well. Gomoarius was not executed after his return to Valens, contrary to some accounts, but must have retired shortly thereafter.[16]

Finally, on 26 May 366, Procopius's other leading general, his *magister* Agilo, defected and abetted the capture and execution of Procopius himself.[17] His severed head gradually made its way through the Balkans to Valentinian in Gaul, the sight of it disarming the last of his supporters along the way.[18] Agilo happened to be of Alamannic blood, though this was not a factor in the conflict. For that matter, Valens relied upon Vadomarius, formerly a prince of the Alamanni, to besiege Procopius's supporters in Nicaea, because he was particularly skilled in siege warfare.[19] He would have had to have learned this as a Roman soldier. The highly successful careers of Agilo and Vadomarius, both Alamannic in origin, were relatively commonplace in the Roman army at this time for the very best officers regardless of origins. Men of genuine distinction could move from the ranks, including those of units clearly raised from barbarians kept together because of their special capabilities, into the officer corps and even to the rank of general. For example, Vitalianus rose from a common soldier in a *numerus* of Eruli to the imperial guard and held comital rank in Illyricum against the Goths.[20] In Ammianus's account alone there are countless ways to see the merging of Germanic and Roman customs that were resulting from the recruitment of successive generations of peoples on both sides of the frontiers; for example, the use of the barbarian war cry, the *barritus*, by the Roman army to hail Procopius emperor while invoking Jupiter in their oath of loyalty to him.[21] More significantly for barbarian–Roman relations, some 3,000 Goths arrived belatedly on the Danube. They were on their way to assist the usurper, who had acclaimed himself the heir to Julian and hence to the emperor with whom they had concluded an agreement of cooperation. Unknown to them the Romans had already taken measures against Procopius's rebellion in Asia Minor and had finalized plans to contain any related military threat which might arise in Thrace.

The Romans were always watchful of the barbarians north of the Danube, perhaps especially those opposite the vital diocese of Thrace (see map 1). At the onset of his revolt in 365 Procopius forced Valens's *praefectus praetorio Orientis* (the praetorian prefect of the Orient[22]), Nebridius, to issue a false order to Julius, *comes rei militaris* for Thrace. The Thracian commander was instructed to report at Constantinople and convey news on recent stirrings among the barbarians.[23] Those in rebellion had little difficulty executing their ruse since reconnaissance of barbarians was clearly an important and routine function of the regional command. Besides, everybody

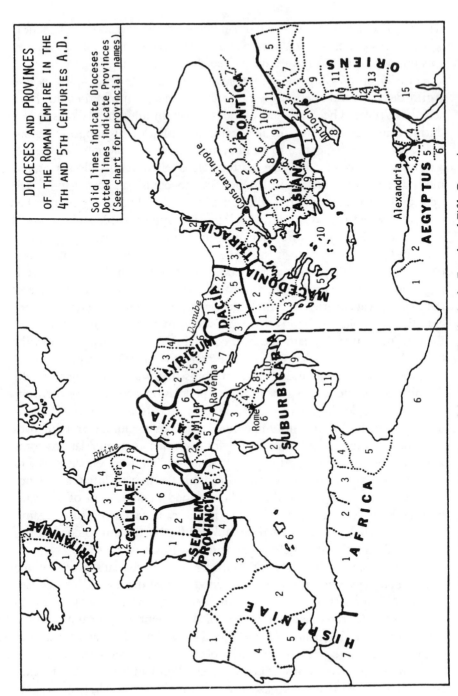

Map 1 Dioceses and Provinces of the Roman Empire in the Fourth and Fifth Centuries A.D.

(Key to Map 1)

Western Division

Britanniae
1. Valentia
2. Britannia II
3. Flavia Caesariensis
4. Britannia
5. Maxima Caesariensis

Galliae
1. Ludgunensis III
2. Ludgunensis II
3. Belgica II
4. Germania II
5. Ludgunensis Senonia
6. Ludgunensis I
7. Belgica I
8. Germania I
9. Maxima Sequanorum

Septem Provinciae
1. Aquitanica II
2. Aquitanica I
3. Novem Populi
4. Narbonensis I
5. Viennensis
6. Narbonensis II
7. Alpes Maritimae

Hispaniae
1. Gallaecia
2. Carthaginiensis
3. Tarraconensis
4. Lusitania
5. Baetica
6. Insulae Balearum
7. Tingitania

Africa
1. Mauretania Caesariensis
2. Mauretania Sitifensis
3. Numidia
4. Africa
5. Byzacena
6. Tripolitania

Italia
1. Alpes Cottiae
2. Aemilia
3. Raetia I
4. Raetia II
5. Liguria
6. Venetia et Histria
7. Flaminia et Picenum

Suburbicaria
1. Corsica
2. Sardinia
3. Tuscia et Umbria
4. Valeria
5. Picenum Suburbicarium
6. Roma
7. Campania
8. Samnium
9. Bruttii et Lucania
10. Apulia et Calabria
11. Sicilia

Pannonia (to ca. 400); Illyricum (after ca. 400)
1. Noricum Ripense
2. Noricum Mediterraneum
3. Pannonia I
4. Valeria
5. Savia
6. Pannonia II
7. Dalmatia

Eastern Division

Dacia
1. Moesia I
2. Dacia Ripensis
3. Praevalitana
4. Dardania
5. Dacia Mediterranea

Macedonia
1. Epirus Nova
2. Macedonia
3. Epirus Vetus
4. Thessalia
5. Achaea
6. Creta

Thraciae (? Thracia)
1. Moesia II
2. Scythia
3. Thracia
4. Haemimontus
5. Rhodope
6. Europa

Asiana
1. Hellespontus
2. Phrygia Pacatiana
3. Phrygia Salutaris
4. Asia
5. Lydia
6. Pisidia
7. Lycaonia
8. Caria
9. Pamphylia
10. Insulae
11. Lycia

Pontica
1. Bithynia
2. Honorias
3. Paphlagonia
4. Helenopontus
5. Pontus Polemoniacus
6. Galatia
7. Armenia I
8. Galatia Salutaris
9. Cappadocia II
10. Cappadocia I
11. Armenia II

Oriens
1. Isauria
2. Cilicia I
3. Cilicia II
4. Euphratensis
5. Mesopotamia
6. Syria
7. Osrhoene
8. Cyprus
9. Syria Salutaris
10. Phoenice
11. Phoenice Libanensis
12. Palaestina II
13. Arabia
14. Palestina I
15. Palestina Salutaris

Aegyptus
1. Libya Superior
2. Libya Inferior
3. Aegyptus
4. Augustamnica
5. Arcadia
6. Thebais

knew that trouble with the Goths was on the horizon. The order made sense also since Julius probably anticipated taking command of the two legions that Valens had ordered to his assistance in Thrace. With Julius lured out of the way, the rebels were able to welcome Thrace into the rebellion.[24] There were fewer loyalist troops than normal on hand, not even their commander. In response to the loss of Thrace Valentinian ordered Aequitius, his *magister militum* in Illyricum, to close the three key passes leading north and westward out of Thrace and then secure the trunk road leading through Philippopolis toward Constantinople in order to establish a safe passage to assist Valens against Procopius's supporters in Thrace if need be.[25] Aequitius had only limited forces available and was unable to open Philippopolis, which he left in rebel hands. Nonetheless, Valentinian did not hesitate to go beyond his sphere and order limited military action in Thrace—that is, in the prefecture of the Orient, his brother's to administer. The prefecture was the largest civil administrative unit in the Empire. At its head stood the *praefectus praetoris* or praetorian prefect. Beneath him in the hierarchy were the vicars (*vicarii*) of the diocese and the provincial governors (*praesides*).[26]

When Valentinian divided the Empire with Valens, he retained as his own subordinates the praetorian prefect of Italy with Africa and Illyricum and the praetorian prefect of the Gauls. Valens governed with the aid of the praetorian prefect of the Orient alone.[27] When a major invasion required the concentration of all available forces, the prefecture was typically the unit at which the emperor himself took charge. This had long been the case and remained so under Constantius II, Valentinian I, and Valens, and it would remain so.[28] Occasionally we can glimpse the tension and rivalry between prefects, the highest ranking civilians, and the leading generals.[29] The prefects were responsible for coordinating the civilian government's resources with the army's needs and movements as the emperor saw fit. Praetorian prefectures served the needs of the emperors and were not barriers to cooperation. On the other hand, since any major movement of troops required very substantial advanced preparations of the type best done by the prefects, armies did not casually cross these administrative boundaries. The pass defenses Aequitius strengthened were: an unspecified one along a route through Dacia Ripensis, the Succi Pass in the Haemus Mountains, and the Acontisma Pass blocking the southern approach through Macedonia along the via Egnatia between Thessalonica and Amphipolis.[30] Therefore, even if the Goths had arrived in time to link up with the rebels, Valens and Valentinian had the situation well in hand. The rebellion had been contained within Thrace.

Gothic leaders, ignorant of the demise of Procopius and of Roman

preparations, dispatched a force in response to a written request for assistance from the usurper. Procopius had demanded that the Goths live up to
their treaty commitments to his dynasty, specifically the house of Constantine, of which he was the sole surviving heir. By the time the Goths got
to the frontier, Valens had restored its effectiveness. With little effort the
frontier army stopped and disarmed the Goths,[31] whereupon "Valens resettled them in some towns on the Danube, ordering that they be put under
surveillance, but not in chains."[32] Whether or not the Goths would actually
have invaded without the letter from Procopius is unknowable. Invade they
did, and invaders had to be punished. Those Goths who surrendered were
lucky; a life of slavery could have been their fate, but instead they were
distributed to the garrisons along the frontier. The army command manifested little concern that they might betray their units to their old comrades
still living across the Danube. Thus did the system work. The effective administrative unit of response was the diocese, where the invaders were
slowed or contained until sufficient counterforces could deploy against
them. Although it was a civilian administrative unit, the diocese contained
all the logistical support necessary for a successful military campaign. If the
diocese failed, the *magister militum* (master of soldiers) responsible for the
entire army command with the emperor's consent had to mount a relief
effort by mobilizing available manpower from elsewhere. In this case, the
diocese of Thrace was not the primary area of rebellion and essentially held
its own with some strategically significant but tactically inconsequential
assistance from the Western command in Illyricum.[33] A usurper's head rode
a pike through the streets; Roman troops and barbarians once loyal to him
now again served Rome.

The West faced an even graver situation. Shortly after ascending the
throne in 364, Valentinian gave affront to certain Alamannic ambassadors
seeking a renewal of their treaty status with Rome and the payment of the
customary "gifts" due them. Valentinian's response was apparently not up
to previous standards, and the Alamanni lost little time in testing the new
emperor in battle. For at least a decade afterward Alamannic raids across the
frontiers were the principal military problem confronting the West. By 367
Britain was in chaos as well. Perhaps because Ammianus wrote under Theodosius the Great, the career of Theodosius, the emperor's father, occupies
a considerable portion of those books which concern these campaigns in
Ammianus's *History*, most especially Theodosius's suppression of the combination of invasion and rebellion in Britain (367–68). It is easy to overes-
timate the importance of Britain at this time and of Theodosius's actions
there.[34] Nonetheless, the details Ammianus provides allow for an extraor-

dinary glimpse of the workings of the Roman army and the approach of the emperor and his senior generals to a widespread military crisis that occupied the Roman army for about a decade. Although these troubles took place at almost exactly the same time that his brother was engaged against Procopius and the Goths, Valentinian himself had no illusions about the higher priority that needed to be assigned to the Alamanni: "Procopius is only my own and my brother's enemy; the Alamanni are truly the enemies of the entire Roman world." Nonetheless, he did send a few troops to secure Africa and ordered his *magister* Aequitius to position himself to be able to provide support for Valens in Thrace.[35] The current troubles in Britain went back to early in 367 or 366.

With most of the army tied down against the Alamanni, Jovinus, the *magister equitum* in Gaul (362–69) charged with the Alamannic wars, ordered Severus, *comes domesticorum* (the commander of the household troops, perhaps only the corps of officer cadets) to hasten to Britain.[36] News of the magnitude of the problem must have reached Jovinus soon after Severus's departure, and Jovinus recalled him and his men before they could board ship. Both of the principal commands in Britain had lost their generals. Nectaridus, perhaps count of the Saxon Shore, *comes litoris Saxonici*, if we dare use the later terminology of the *Notitia dignitatum*, was dead.[37] The rebels had taken the commander of the frontier garrisons, the *dux (? Britanniarum)*, Fullofaudes, captive.[38] Jovinus determined that a larger force was necessary and set about personally to see to it, probably meaning that he rushed off to see Valentinian who was either at Reims or elsewhere in northern Gaul throughout much of 366 and 367. Once the emperor was so gravely ill at Amiens that he raised his young son Gratian to the purple to secure his succession.[39] One result of the crisis in Britain was the appointment of Theodosius, the father of the future emperor, as *comes rei militaris* to rid it of rebellion. Severus evidently did not disgrace himself by his hasty about-face, since in this same year (367) he was promoted to *magister peditum*. At the same time Jovinus held the consulship with Valentinian's newly proclaimed co-emperor Gratian, as a reward for his conduct of the Alamannic wars.[40] Realizing the magnitude of the problem in Britain, Jovinus pulled units out of the Alamannic campaign and placed them at Theodosius's disposal. Soon four elite units of the *auxilia palatina* (perhaps 1,500 men) joined up as well and were also transferred to Britain via Boulogne and Richborough.[41]

Like virtually every victorious general in the late Empire, Theodosius, having achieved victory with a few thousand men still needed elsewhere, could ill afford not to extend an open hand to defeated troops, barbarian or

Roman. For his success, in 369 Valentinian made Theodosius *magister equitum* (369–75), succeeding Jovinus, but by then Theodosius was fighting the Alamanni in Gaul,[42] where some Franks and Saxons had also apparently joined in invading.[43] Later Theodosius served against some Sarmatians in the Balkans (372) and distinguished himself in Africa against the rebel Firmus (373). Shortly afterward he was executed (375 or 376) at Carthage under mysterious circumstances, but not before taking Christian baptism.[44] Barbarians and an internal armed usurpation—the Roman army clearly gave some assistance to Valentinus—had wreaked havoc in Britain and tested the Roman army's ability to wage war beyond the diocesan level. Thanks to its superior logistical system, continental troops were rushed into battle and peace was again imposed on the island.

Theodosius made his way to London with the first units to cross the Channel, routing disorganized rabble along the way. After the demise of their generals the Roman army had ceased to resist the rebels effectively and many had deserted. Nothing much had hindered the rebels—a combination of barbarians, deserters, and outright followers of Valentinus—in the countryside. Some towns, their defenses in decay, had fallen and were retaken in the following spring, but other towns like Richborough and London held for the government. The rebels had rustled large numbers of cattle and had taken whatever else was at hand as booty. In 368, once his four units of palatine forces arrived, Theodosius pressed his campaign, "restored many towns and fortifications, which had fallen into disrepair during the long period of peace,"[45] and reestablished defenses with guards and garrisons on the frontiers.[46] Theodosius also defeated and captured the rebel Valentinus, an exile from Pannonia then in Britain, around whom some of the Roman deserters had rallied.[47] Theodosius handed Valentinus over to Dulcitius, the *dux* he appointed to replace Fullofaudes, for execution.[48] Fullofaudes, whether or not liberated, disappeared from history. Theodosius also requested that Valentinian appoint Civilis as *vicarius* of the diocese of Britain.[49] An amnesty allowed most deserters to return to the army.

The emperors Valentinian and Valens expected swift decisive action against barbarians and rebels and got it. They contained the threat, defeated the rebels, and allowed the survivors to serve the Empire. Usurpers were summarily dealt with and "tranquility restored." Victory was celebrated over barbarians. Indeed the mints at Antioch, Alexandria, and elsewhere struck bronze coins of Valens or Valentinian on the obverse with the emperor seen dragging a captive with his right hand and holding the *labarum* in his left, standard iconography of victory.[50] Earlier, Constans and Constantius II had issued especially evocative "hut-type" bronze pieces in which a bar-

Illustration 1. "Hut-type" coin of Constans

barian emerging from a hut under the watchful eyes of a Roman soldier was brought into civilization (see illustration 1).[51] Technically the Romans received (granted *receptio* to) the subdued barbarians.

Just as Constantius had done, Valentinian pressured defeated barbarians beyond the frontiers to provide young men to serve in the Roman army. All recruits served as Rome wished, although sometimes temporary deals seem to have been struck. Upon occasion Valentinian made some of their chiefs military tribunes in the Roman army. Some of these new officers soon found themselves commanding troops far distant from their homes, but others did not leave the theaters in which they were recruited.[52] Constantius was able to honor a plea not to send some youths too far from home, since he found use for them in the general area of the Iron Gates, but he was not obligated to do so if he was willing to face the probable rebellion of their families.[53] In all cases the standard procedure for admitting any new recruit was applied—*receptio*, the formal act of receiving immigrants. This included the *dediticii*, literally those who had "surrendered," and those who volunteered for Roman service.

Dediticii remained a special legal category well into the fifth century. They probably still could not become citizens or leave wills or inherit through one. The recently defeated and the new volunteers were processed and disappeared into the ranks of Roman soldiers. *Dediticii* were fully free and owned slaves. *Dediticii* was not a military term. No military units of *dediticii* appear in the sources. The status of *dediticii* was solely a legal category for individual recruits.[54] By the late Empire most are thought to have derived from defeated barbarians. They served in all units of the Roman army, and as far as their commanders were concerned their legal restrictions probably were relevant only in that they could not make a will, something Roman soldiers were granted special flexibility in doing. They were different in this regard only from other barbarian soldiers serving Rome. Whatever their legal status, new recruits formally beseeched the commanding officer for imperial permission to enter through their personal supplication, swore oaths of loyalty, and agreed to serve Rome. The same procedure applied to all recruits forcibly obtained or peacefully recruited as a matter of routine. The emperor or his representative might integrate them into existing units, sometimes in the neighborhood, or order them about like any other new soldier.[55] Some served as *coloni* (semi-dependent farmers) on vacant lands, perhaps with a militia-type responsibility for defense. The process was old already to Constans (337–50); so too was the symbolism.

Perhaps the most remarkable commemoration of the process of *receptio* discovered to date is the so-called tetrarchic medallion of Lyon, long actually thought to portray Valens and Valentinian because of its supposed representation of their policies (see illustration 2).[56] There on the upper portion the Augustus, Maximinus, and the Caesar, Constantius Chlorus, are shown, cheerfully, even if rigidly, receiving whole families from across the Rhine. One man is prostrate before the enthroned rulers. On the lower portion of the medallion a barbarian group of men, women, and children stride confidently over the bridge between Castellum (Mainz-Kastel) to Mogontiacum (Mainz). The lower scene can be understood to indicate the approval of the request for permission to enter Roman territory depicted in the upper field of the medallion.

The fact is that the settlement of another group of *laeti* hardly would have required the presence of even one imperial personage but rather could have been handled by a lower ranking imperial officer. The iconography, of course, is keyed to the source of policy and legislation—the emperor (seen here in the tetrarchic configuration). As the fourth century progressed numerous officers must have exercised authority over the routine task of receiving small groups of barbarians; the *laeti* were one result of "receiving" barbarians and figure prominently in the *Notitia dignitatum*, listed there under their Roman superior, the *praefectus*.[57] As long as the policy of *receptio* was followed the emperors need not have taken any direct action and everything worked without problems. However, if a fundamental change in the policy were to occur or a major influx of barbarians was anticipated, possibly one requiring transshipment far beyond the region of recruitment, only the emperor could have issued the necessary orders.[58] And that is one of the central problems of the last decades of the fourth century, when repeated crises gradually forced emperors to expand the *receptio* system.

Illustration 2. Tetrarchic medallion from Lyon

For defeated invaders of the Empire, there was rarely a formal treaty (*foedus*), for treaties were signed with some recognized authority, preferably a true king or at least a major ducal figure, typically elevated by the honor and Roman might to the kingship over a foreign people dwelling outside the Empire. On the other hand, *receptio* constituted a legal act in which the immigrant made a binding commitment or compact (also called a *foedus*) with the state, agreeing to serve in return for admission and employment. Romans entered into all sorts of personal agreements with other individuals, and any contract freely entered, including marriage, could be termed a *foedus*. The state, however, did not sign "treaties" with foreign powers serving inside the Empire, not, that is, until 418. By 418, moreover, the boundaries between an official diplomatic *foedus* and a personal contract with military recruits individually had blurred. Captives might be spared death or years of slavery in return for their enlistment, but for them there were no guarantees. Valens had shown mercy to the 3,000 Goths captured while attempting to cross the frontiers, but he had offered them no treaty as a group. Ariaricus and Aoricus, who concluded the first treaties with Constantine the Great in 332, were two *duces* among several living outside the Empire. So were the chiefs who, acting in concert, had dispatched the 3,000 warriors to Procopius.[59] Ariaricus and Aoricus had also apparently bet on the wrong side in a Roman civil war, fighting for Licinius.[60] The treaty (*foedus*) with Constantine had been dictated by the emperor and carefully and strictly regulated service and trade. The Goths had become just one of many clients of the Empire, receiving annual subsidies and permission to trade at designated locations.[61] Valens now prepared carefully for punitive action against the Gothic leaders who had supported his usurper.

Valens assembled forces at forts along the Danube and set up his headquarters at Marcianopolis. Auxonius, a new, younger, and more vigorous man, replaced the aged praetorian prefect Salutius, who was apparently retiring more and more into the study of history.[62] Valens effectively raised taxes without causing civil unrest and shipped supplies via the Black Sea and barges on the Danube to depots and troop concentrations.[63] Once the winter (366–367) had passed Valens attacked in force, throwing a bridge of pontoons across the Danube from Transmarisca to Daphne, a fortified landing area on the northern bank.[64] Such landing zones across the river frontiers were regular features of the fourth-century *limes*[65] and were not necessarily built for specific campaigns. The invasions required the improvement of the roadways over which the supplies and troops would pass. Nothing was left to chance. Needed armaments were forged and forts and watchtowers brought to combat readiness. Valens also increased the storage of provisions along the route from the harbors inland, and "soldiers were enrolled, garrisons brought up to true strength, not inflated [peacetime] figures."[66] Such preparations were hallmarks of the Roman army.

Arinthaeus, the *magister peditum*, showed no mercy, cutting down women and children alike.[67] He placed a bounty on barbarian heads.[68] The year 368 brought high water and made campaigning in *barbaricum* (barbarian territory) too risky and all the while strained Roman resources.[69] The Romans stayed in their camps throughout the year, but in 369 all the frustrations of a year at the ready were released in a devastating invasion. This time the Romans apparently launched their attack from Noviodunum in

Scythia.[70] Rome quickly succeeded in cutting the Gothic peoples in two, driving a wedge all the way to the Dniester.[71]

Sometime before this attack the Goths, probably actually their *duces*, had elected one of their leaders to unite their resistance. They thus recognized Athanaric as *thiudans*—the first in perhaps two decades. He was unable to stem the Romans, who were advancing so swiftly that he barely had time to rally his own followers. Ammianus Marcellinus recorded, "Because the barbarians, since commerce was cut off [at those points traditionally open to trade since 332], were so distressed by extreme scarcity of the necessities of life, they often sent suppliant deputations to beg for pardon and peace."[72] Athanaric, the supreme Gothic leader who had sworn never to set a foot on Roman soil, signed the *foedus* on a boat in midstream, thereby emphasizing his independence even in defeat.[73] The treaty remains only vaguely understood. In Zosimus's account of these events, both sides agreed to honor the Danube as the *de facto* frontier.[74] Some of the Goths, it seems, further sought *receptio* and recruitment into the Roman army.[75] Another possible interpretation of Zosimus's account would have the Danube closed to all barbarian contact, apparently to include trade, but that cannot be given much credence.

The fundamental point for the current problem is that Athanaric apparently struck a formal treaty for his whole people. Henceforth any Roman treaty with the Goths as a people would be concluded through the *thiudans*, the recognized preeminent chief. His authority, at least as perceived by Rome, could alone guarantee compliance over his diverse people. In point of fact, the Goths themselves doubtless did not see Athanaric as a permanent head of their people.[76] Indeed, Athanaric was much like the unfortunate Quadic ambassadors who confessed to Valentinian (thereby plunging him into a fatal rage), that no barbarian chief could so control his people as to prohibit traditional practices and personal relationships dependent upon occasional raiding.[77]

Valens seems to have intended that the Goths currently being recruited into the Roman army be assigned to Scythia, whence he launched his invasion and where he apparently strengthened the religious community to receive newcomers.[78] As an Arian his efforts had little appeal to the indigenous population in this largely Orthodox area; however, the episode again demonstrates the degree of preparation necessary for a successful *receptio* and the extraordinary religious influence that the reigning emperor could exert through the army. The memory of the establishment of Ulfilas and his followers, just a few years previously in Moesia, was probably still fresh. Paulinus of Nola, a contemporary, twice commented to fellow bishops on the conversion of certain Goths as an important step in securing peace.[79] Later, after Theodosius had subdued various groups of Goths following the Battle of Adrianople, another contemporary, Eunapius, commented that "they all claimed to be Christians and some of their number they disguised as their bishops and dressed them up in that respected garb. . . . " Some even went so far as to pretend to be "monks." According to Eunapius, this was as simple as changing clothes. He went on to report that they really worshipped their old gods, which was probably true even though they may well have included Christ in their prayers.[80] Perhaps not all Gothic monks were mere pretenders; events will reveal their fate too.

At the moment the technical and supply networks were needed for Valens's Persian campaigns on the eastern frontier. Thus it is not surprising that in 369 the emperor rejected the opportunity to gain more recruits and settlers, concluded the treaty with Athanaric, and discontinued operations. Valens may also have reflected that the Goths were more effective as clients buffering Rome's vital territories. Indeed, it is certainly conceivable that technically the *foedus* with the Goths in former Dacia placed them in a special relationship with Rome because the Roman imperial panoply continued, at a theoretical level only, to preserve all former territories as Roman.[81] Nor should Valens have been concerned that the Goths would violate the conditions of the *foedus*. In fact, Gothic loyalty to their treaties was well known. Writing of events prior to 363, Ammianus roundly praised their faithfulness.[82] Julian (360–63) apparently felt so secure that he taunted some Gothic representatives at court, suggesting that if they did not like the existing treaty they could go to war.[83] No war ensued. For Valens the current lull was not long in duration. The Persian war soon demanded all his efforts and dragged on and on, draining supplies and men. As a result of his losses against the Persians, when the Goths sought admission into the Empire in 376 he welcomed them, eager for the new recruits although ignorant as to just how many were encamped on the far bank of the Danube. So much for the actions of men and armies on the march; more attention must now be directed to the infrastructure hinted at in our recounting of Valens's logistical system and the historiographic problems that color our sources.

The victories and peace of 369–70 inspired unusual passion in Themistius (ca. 317–85),[84] an imperial panegyrist and eyewitness to some of the events of the three years of warfare. In his tenth oration he twisted events into a neat statement of rulership, one rooted in the imperial concepts of *clementia* and *pietas* but now forced onto a global stage. As he told it, the virtuous Valens spared the barbarians as mankind should have spared the already extinct Thessalian lions and Libyan elephants, almost as a breeding stock for the genetic pool of humankind.[85] A true emperor, as Valens might be cajoled into being, added Themistius, should spare "the rascally barbarians, not exterminate a part of humanity from its roots, but by restraining their violent habits, thus to save and protect them, for they are a part of the Human Race."[86] Such fondness for humanity was not apparent in the realities of the Gothic wars, as Themistius well knew. Nor was his use of the Goths as barbarous, irrational foils for Greco-Roman philosophic discourse either novel or near the truth.[87]

Although the Balkan provinces and the Empire as a whole were at peace at the opening of the fourth century's seventh decade, it was an anxious peace. Personal relationships figured prominently in imperial calculations, as did the strengths of fortifications. Exceedingly complex social and economic problems were clear to the imperial government, as witnessed in the laws, and to the literary figures of the age, even to the anonymous author of the *De rebus bellicis*. This work, offering advice on reforming the army and saving military manpower, at times by the use of ingenious machines, was very probably composed during the decade before the Gothic crossings of 376, if not more precisely in 368–69 and thus immediately following the revolt of Procopius.[88]

Most visibly dangerous was the oppression of imperial taxation, which inspired numerous appeals, flight, and vitriolic prose throughout the Empire. Taxes were decried directly and indirectly in Themistius, Ammianus, Zosimus (relying on Eunapius, a contemporary), and the *De rebus bellicis*. Thus when Auxonius, the praetorian prefect of the Orient, collected taxes without oppression in 366, it was worthy of note.[89] The motives of our sources for Auxonius and in general are often suspect and usually veiled. There is a constant need to ask: did the author have direct knowledge, and if so how, and to what purpose was he using it? In the case of Auxonius, Eunapius's likely goal was to reveal that philosophy produced better men, even better administrators. Themistius is particularly trying, rarely missing a chance to flatter the emperor Valens, and later Theodosius, into "proper action." Writing his seventh oration (dated 366–67) several months after the revolt of Procopius had been crushed but before the Gothic war, Themistius described Valens as humane in his generosity.[90]

Despite their ulterior motives the message of civil unrest and governmental oppression cannot be dismissed as empty rhetoric. For Themistius, Procopius had clearly stepped out of line by offering land and freedom from debt to his supporters. Ammianus too makes it clear that Procopius took some of his followers from among the lowest orders of society.[91] *Bacaudae*, sometimes rather well organized brigands, and other malcontents soon mounted a resurgence, particularly in the Western provinces. Themistius and the author of the *De rebus bellicis*, foreshadowing Patriarch St. John Chrysostom, urged fiscal restraint. They thereby hoped to lessen the burdens weighing upon an already desperate society. Much of the careers of Valens and Valentinian can, in fact, be viewed as an attempt to deal with increasing demands to ameliorate the effects of the expanding government upon those it governed. These pressures came at a time of heightened activity along the frontier and raised questions as to how to limit or cut defense costs in order to hold the line on taxes—an all too familiar modern dilemma. But the need for more troops, rather than fewer, was manifest. There would have to be new military programs ranging from improved fortifications throughout the Empire to new programs for the settlement of veterans. These undertakings were to have extraordinary importance later when Rome sought to adapt Valentinian's policies to even more trying circumstances following the death of Theodosius in 395.[92]

Although Valens was clearly unpopular among the literati, even he can be seen learning and respecting the limitations of the imperial system.[93] The task of restructuring the economy was beyond imperial capabilities, but these and other problems would become more pronounced after the death of Valentinian and Valens. One aspect of Roman society quite clear even before Valentinian took power was the widening rift between the civilian aristocracy and the leadership of the army. Valentinian and Valens also had little choice but to become involved in the explosive drive of Christianity to establish itself as the dominant religious force in the Empire, both psychologically and politically. Whereas quasi-pagans like Themistius carved out a special role for the emperor in humanizing the world, Christians sought to define his relationship to God and salvation. Some intellectuals tried to define the duties of the emperor with both Christian and pagan roles in mind. In the provinces the emperor was foremost a general and a lawgiver but his religious authority extended here too, particularly through his command of the army.

During the fourth century the Danubian provinces, which had been peaceful backwaters following Trajan's (98–117) successes against the Dacians, again became a major focus of Roman planning. These provinces gradually resumed their role as the frontier after Aurelian (270–75) withdrew most of the army from the transdanubian province of Dacia. Despite Constantine the Great's (307–37) reassertion of an active presence on the northern side of the river, the Danube was the real frontier. Military prominence brought men, money, and political power to the cities and garrisons along the southern bank of the river in the area comprising modern Bul-

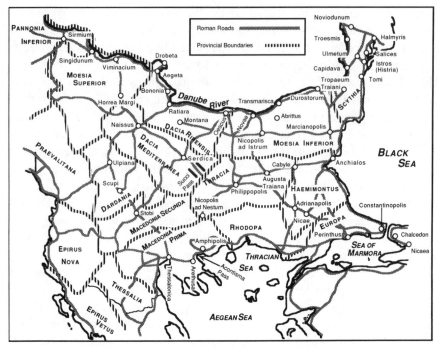

Map 2 Late Roman Balkan Roads and Provinces

garia and parts of Greece and Turkey. Towns along the *limes* grew rapidly during the first three-quarters of the fourth century (see map 2).

Novae, the headquarters of the First Italian Legion, controlled one of the easiest fords on the Danube. Here the fourth century witnessed extensive construction, including a new curtain wall replete with U-shaped towers, each carefully situated to provide an overlapping field of fire with its neighbors. So too Durostorum, Capidava, Tropaeum Traiani, Sucidava, and many other cities entered a new era of prosperity but also one in which their military role became paramount.[94] Iatrus, like neighboring Novae and other towns directly on the *limes*, expanded rapidly (see illustration 3). Imperial attention kindled renewed vigor at many towns of the interior as well; for example, Pautalia, Serdica, and Naissus in Dacia Mediterranea. Almost everywhere town size increased. The armaments industry flourished, as did mining and ceramic production. Large and frequent issues of coins were necessary and their circulation expanded. Trade with the Gothic peoples across the Danube thrived. These provinces also profited to a certain degree from the forced reliance on locally manufactured items. The changes in the economy were by no means uniform, but signs of prosperity abound.[95]

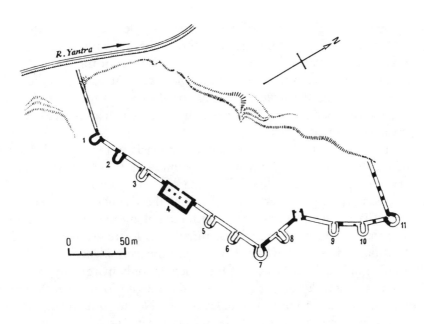

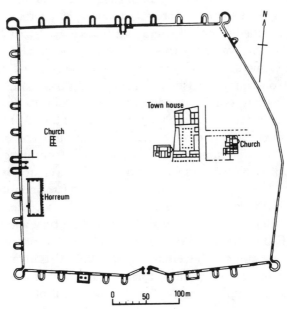

Illustration 3. Typical urban defenses in the Thracian area in late antiquity. Top, Iatrus, fortifications. Bottom, Abritus, city plan.

In the newly formed diocese of Thrace, for example, the diocesan structure provided uniform governmental control over the six provinces comprising it. Side by side with the civilian *vicarius* (the governor of the diocese) stood a *comes rei militaris* commanding the regional forces. At least from the era of Constantine's sons the *comes* routinely coordinated all military planning and operations for a diocese.[96] All along the Danube preparations for defense received constant attention.

The dioceses of Thrace, Macedonia, and Dacia were prepared to withstand much graver invasions than that mounted by a few thousand Gothic warriors in 367. The first line of defense was the chain of heavily walled towns along the right, or southern, bank of the Danube itself. Beginning at the estuary with Halmyris and continuing along the *limes* upstream to Durostorum, there were as many as thirty-four fortresses in the province of Scythia, nineteen of which have been positively identified, including Troesmis and Sucidava.[97] Many of these sites are only marginally excavated and published. The *limes* continued onward through Moesia II with important urban centers at Durostorum, Iatrus, and Novae, to name only a few. Dacia Ripensis, created on the southern bank when Aurelian withdrew from former Dacia, held Oescus, Ratiaria, Bononia, and Drobeta with at least eight other fortified towns of some significance. Each was linked by road to the next. Scythia was too narrow to have a true second line, but Tropaeum Traiani and Ulmetum could and did serve as staging and reserve areas as did Tomi (Constanta) and Istros (Histria) along the coast.[98] For all but a very few locations, our knowledge of precise troop dispositions remains incomplete. Nor does the *Notitia dignitatum* reveal the entire system. There were many fortifications, mostly small, that went unrecorded there.[99]

Behind the river frontier itself and typically commanding important supporting roads in Dacia Ripensis and Moesia II were towns such as Naissus, Montana, Melta, Nicopolis ad Istrum, and Marcianopolis. These were likewise linked to each other and to the Danubian centers.[100] This interior line of cities existed as early as the second century, and was ever more stoutly fortified in the course of the third and fourth centuries. To the south lay the Balkan mountains (Haemus range) with fortlets in or near key passes. Finally came the great fortified cities of Pautalia, Serdica, Philippopolis, Augusta Traiana, and Adrianople.[101] There were still other interior lines of strength deep into the Balkan peninsula. The work of fortification continued long after the Gothic problem in the Balkans had been "solved," particularly under Theodosius II. For example, the fortifications around Thermopylae and the Dhema Pass, once thought to have been built to confront Alaric and hence in keeping with the traditional view of Alaric the Plunderer of Greece, now seem to date to the reign of Theodosius II.[102] Thrace also had numerous *villae rusticae* (the standard farm in late antiquity), road houses, and fortified refuges similar to those in many Western provinces. The totality of the military, urban, and rural system must be kept in mind in order to appreciate the Gothic problem and Rome's responses from 376 onward. A basic familiarity with many of the physical features of the frontier provinces underlies the works of Ammianus and other authors. Although they took them for granted, we cannot.

The Goths Cross the Danube

The westward expansion of Hunnic groups a few years prior to 376 set up a movement of peoples that threw many Gothic families into headlong flight toward the Danube, which they knew they could not cross without Roman consent. Along with the Goths came a few bands of Alans and Huns, who were also on the move, perhaps taking advantage of the general collapse of political authority above the Danube. Caught by surprise, the Romans on the *limes* responded as best they could. There is little reason to describe the events of 376–78 from a tactical perspective in great detail.[103] Nonetheless, certain features of the strategic situation do illustrate the *limes* at work and need to be recalled.

Most of the Visigoths had rejected Athanaric and under their new leader, Alavivus, sought and obtained permission to cross the Danube under Roman supervision; i.e., the Romans activated the *receptio* system. Valens rejoiced at the thought of new recruits and the chances this would afford provincials to convert their service to cash payments now that substitutes were available.[104] High water initially delayed the crossings. The Goths loitered on the far bank in family groups, scouring the land for food.[105] The Roman command had no idea how many to expect. They had no way of knowing that over the next few weeks more barbarians would enter the Empire peacefully than on any previous occasion in Roman history. The figures in our sources are absurdly high; Eunapius recorded 200,000. For Ammianus they were a countless multitude.[106]

The primary entry point was probably Durostorum in Moesia II, chosen as in 367 because of its convenient road link to Marcianopolis, the operational headquarters of the Roman army. "Hostages," a term that included new recruits forcibly inducted, in fact the first to be processed, were dispatched to Julius in Asia Minor. By this time Julius had been promoted from *magister militum* in Thrace, where we encountered him during Procopius's revolt, to *comes et magister equitum et peditum per Orientem*.[107] With time running short the Roman command hurriedly began to disperse some Goths to wintering quarters while continuing to move others toward their more distant and permanent regular assignments. Some Goths were marched as far as Adrianople, some 600 km, where they were expected to winter before moving out the next spring. With families in tow the trek from Marcianopolis to Adrianople would have taken around a month, supplied from Roman stores along the way—a long walk, but it was better to walk and eat than sit and starve along the Danube. Just after the Goths settled in, the Roman command ordered them to pack up, march back to the north, and cross the Hellespont. They did not like it, but agreed providing money and provisions were made available and they could have two days to get ready.[108] The order sending them to Adrianople was one mistake of many.

On the Danube the Romans disarmed the Goths before allowing them to cross, just as they had done to the surrendering supporters of Procopius a decade before. Some weapons slipped through.[109] Later the Goths were able to loot more weapons from fallen Roman soldiers but still fought with clubs as well.[110] Weapons were very valuable and the victors in any battle took advantage of the chance for booty. Roman soldiers with instructions to confiscate them would only have disobeyed their officers in order to keep these precious trade items for themselves. Most Gothic horses were similarly confiscated. The tide of refugees backed up and grew restless. Lupicinus, *comes rei militaris* and in charge of the operation with the aid of Maximus, *dux Sythiae*, commander of the frontier defenses, ordered the pace quickened.[111] This deliberately stretched the processing mechanisms still further, but Lupicinus accepted the risk rather than have to face a revolt of the Goths at the crossing points. Ostrogothic (Greutungi), Alanic, and Hunnic refugees who joined the crossings later, when the *receptio* system was vastly overtaxed, did so armed and apparently with mounts.[112] A few weapons hidden here or there was not an issue. Numbers were.

This "countless multitude" was beyond Rome's ability to feed and process. The Goths resorted to eating dogs and selling children into slavery rather than watch starvation take its toll. These hardships struck even the families of the native leaders.[113] The Goths were victims of the nature of the Roman logistical system. Roman supplies were not concentrated in one great center but distributed for storage throughout the many camps, fortified road houses, monitored bridge crossings, and wherever else soldiers were billeted. The Romans surely used the time of high water to move as many supplies as could be spared to Scythia, but the Goths quickly consumed these. Lupicinus probably had received authorization to send only a limited number of refugees across the Hellespont, and no one had anticipated the magnitude of the influx. Seeing the mass of humanity at the river first hand, Lupicinus must have requested permission to transship additional people, all of whom had to be fed en route and escorted. While he waited for word, he had to hold as many as possible in his region, that is in the diocese of Thrace. The summer began to wane. After a time he received permission to send still more eastward. The process of *receptio* assumed the speedy redeployment of receptees to training areas, but not in the numbers now necessary. In the summer of 376 the Roman command had to adapt and make decisions on the fly. Under such pressure sometimes they erred.

There were no strategic forces (central field armies) assigned permanently to Thrace until Theodosius or slightly later, although temporary concentrations had been stationed there already under Constantius II (337–61).[114] The *Notitia dignitatum* attests to the office of *magister militum per Thracias*, but its origin cannot be dated precisely despite considerable scholarly effort. The heavy demand for field troops in Thrace and Illyricum under Theodosius was to create permanent needs for temporary measures.[115] Arcadius seems responsible for the creation of a permanent *magister militum per Thracias* as it existed in the fifth and sixth centuries, but its true origins were under Theodosius.[116] However, in 376 the local troops under the *dux* Maximus, further supplemented by and under the overall command of *comes* Lupicinus, had to make do.

The Gothic (Tervingi) leaders apparently had to accept Christianity, at least tacitly, as a precondition for *receptio*.[117] This might explain the rather confused accounts stating that Fritigern, by the Battle of Adrianople the paramount Gothic leader, offered to accept Christianity in return for Roman support of his position among his Goths both before crossing the Danube and again only moments before the onset of the Battle of Adrianople.[118] From Fritigern's perspective an offer to accept Christianity before crossing the frontier was a gamble to secure Roman military support against his Gothic rivals, particularly Athanaric, who just recently had carried out a persecution to purge his lands of Christians.[119] But if Fritigern made this offer again outside Adrianople just moments before the battle, the gesture could only have been interpreted by Valens as an effort to smooth the way for a *receptio* and secure Fritigern a higher place in the Roman army. On 9 August 378, however, its effect was to buy some needed time.

Once again in 376 the *receptio* system sought to split the Goths, which their chronic lack of cohesion should have made relatively easy, for ultimate recruitment and resettlement. Various groups, apparently under subtribal leaders (*reiks* in Gothic), were billeted in and around key urban centers often deep in the interior. There supplies were to be provided until the reassignments were completed. Marcianopolis was a major assembly point for re-distribution. Staging centers processed thousands of Goths and quickly dispersed them. Ultimately many went to Anatolia. Unfortunately, the size of the immigration exceeded the capacity of the supply depots and starvation ensued. When the Gothic leaders threatened resistance, Lupicinus attempted to annihilate them at a banquet, a practice used against the Quadi two years before. He summoned the Gothic leaders to his headquarters, probably at Marcianopolis. The time was probably autumn 376.[120] The new *thiudans* Alavivus himself fell, but Fritigern and a few others escaped and rose in revolt. The survivors fled back to their people and prepared for winter and battle.

Fritigern, whose personal followers must have been assigned to winter south of the Haemus Mountains, tried to round up as many Gothic immigrants there as he could find. Other than his own band, he had little real knowledge of where they might be. Some of them had probably lost their own leaders in Lupicinus's mass assassination attempt. He encountered those sent to Adrianople under their native leaders Colias and Sueridus. After agreeing to countermarch, they had made careful preparations before departing. These were misunderstood by the citizens of Adrianople, who thought the worst and panicked. In response, Colias and Sueridus revolted and attacked the city. They were futilely attacking the city walls in revenge for wrongs done them by its citizens when they learned that Fritigern was in the vicinity. By this time, although Colias and Sueridus did not yet know it, the Goths were in general revolt. Fritigern chose this opportunity to remind them that storming walls was not a Gothic specialty. Saying that he "kept peace with walls," he urged them to concentrate their attention on the undefended countryside. They stopped their attack and joined him in the wider rebellion.[121] They did not know it, but they were trapped south of the Haemus Mountains, isolated from the main body of their kinsmen in Scythia and Moesia II. Fortunately for them the Roman command did not know their whereabouts. None of Fritigern's force, including Colias and Sueridus, played any role in the conflict developing in the north.[122]

Lupicinus summoned help from Valens. The rebellion required far more forces than were on hand. The strategic situation was precarious. Valens was still at Antioch with the field armies, the one routinely stationed there and the units always under the emperor and typically billeted at or near Constantinople. Lupicinus was experienced, although brutal and shortsighted, and would not request aid if unneeded. Valens asked Gratian, who had some forces close at hand, to assist, and prepared himself to march. To move their main forces, however, took a great deal of preparation. There were treaties to be concluded on other frontiers and holding forces to be designated and stationed at strategic points. Troops everywhere were on the march. Valens's request for assistance from his nephew got prompt attention, despite the fact that Gratian was heavily engaged against the Lentienses (an Alamannic group).[123]

Both emperors ordered their ablest commanders into action and began to disengage their main units that were tied down in operations on the Rhine and against Persia respectively. Throughout this war imperial cooperation and that of their troops was exemplary, that is until the final battle. The first to arrive was Frigeridus, *comes rei militaris*, who commanded "some Pannonian and transalpine auxiliaries." He was probably stationed in the diocese of Pannonia, close to the theater of war.[124] Frigeridus continued the ongoing effort to contain the Goths and secure the passes in the Haemus Mountains. Goths were leaving their holding areas everywhere, forced to move or starve.[125] Richomeres, Gratian's *comes domesticorum equitum*, hurried eastward from Gaul with a few understrength units released from Gratian's palatine army. When he arrived Richomeres found Frigeridus ill with gout and ordered him home. But Frigeridus, apparently too sick to complete the journey, took up a temporary position near Beroea. There, perhaps as a part of Richomeres's effort to further strengthen key defenses, he supervised work on the walls while recovering enough to continue.[126]

Richomeres linked up with Valens's generals Profuturus and Trajanus in Scythia, who with their Armenian legions had left Valens and rushed ahead. By mutual consent Richomeres became the overall commander and probably took up residence at Marcianopolis. Profuturus and Traianus had arrived in Thrace during the summer of 377 and by fall were encamped near Ad Salices in Scythia. Profuturus was probably a *comes rei militaris*, and Traianus seems to have been raised to *magister peditum* for the campaign and as such was in charge of the Eastern force.[127] Profuturus and Traianus were in camp at Ad Salices for a purpose. A large concentration of Goths was nearby.[128] Fritigern was elsewhere, probably still south of the Haemus Mountains where he and various allied barbarians were running free. Despite the absence of Fritigern and many of their allies, the Goths in the north carried the day.

The Goths had drawn up their wagons in a protective circle which the Romans decided to assault. It was a standard German-Roman battle. The Romans relied upon discipline, the Goths upon impetus. As the Romans pressed the attack, the Goths charged out from their camp and hit the Roman line. The left side of the line broke. The Goths were about to administer the coup de grace when Roman reserves managed to strengthen the left side of the Roman line and thereby prevented a catastrophe. The Goths had fought on foot with swords (probably captured) and fire-hardened clubs; the Romans had met their charge standing shield to shield. Both sides had suffered heavy casualties. As darkness fell the Goths retreated to their wagons and the Romans left the field. The Goths, seemingly leaderless, remained "crowded together in their curving line of wagons" for a week, allowing the Romans to prepare.[129] *Receptio* was not working, but as events elsewhere had proved in the previous decades the Romans had no reason to abandon hope. Sooner or later they had always reestablished the mechanisms necessary to make *receptio* feasible. For the Goths there was now no choice but to continue the fight; they could not go home.

Rome temporarily lost the initiative as Richomeres returned to Gaul for reinforcements, but not before setting forth a plan of containment and starvation. Rome strengthened its pass defenses to prevent Gothic movements through the Haemus Mountains. These defenses effectively separated the main groups of Goths to the north of the range from those in the south, including Fritigern, and thereby prevented the full concentration of Gothic forces. Such measures already had reduced many Gothic bands to starvation and despair when a new Roman general arrived. Saturninus, apparently appointed *magister equitum* for this campaign, had come from Valens with a few reinforcements for Profuturus and Traianus. Perhaps not realizing that things were proceeding rather well under the circumstances, Saturninus decided that the garrisons in the passes had held as long as they could and withdrew them. With the garrisons gone the barbarians rapidly expanded their area of devastation and were able to link up with Fritigern and those in the south.[130] Perhaps only now did the Goths elect *reiks* Fritigern their *thiudans*.[131] Some groups approached Beroea and hastened Frigeridus's departure for Illyricum.[132] He quickly ordered his men to move out along the road to Serdica. Taifali under Farnobius attacked them. Frigeridus's Romans killed Farnobius and dispatched the survivors to towns in southern Italy to work in the fields.[133]

Shortly after his arrival in Constantinople on 30 May 378, Valens replaced Traianus as *magister peditum* with Sebastianus, who quickly proved himself a master of small force warfare. Sebastianus was assisted by Saturninus.[134] Traianus may have lost his command because of his Catholic sentiments or because of the defeat near Ad Salices. He was later recalled to assist, perhaps as a special *magister*, and fought at Adrianople. Until reinforcements arrived the Romans had little choice but to follow Richomeres's strategy of containment and staying on the defensive.[135] Now the tide changed. Valens immediately ordered some Saracen cavalry to ambush any

Goths in the vicinity of the capital. These horsemen made quite an impression in Constantinople when they returned with Gothic heads on their lances. Such attacks kept the Goths near their camps and thereby limited their range of plunder. Sooner or later, hunger would force them to move on. This happened around Constantinople. Their departure from the immediate area allowed Valens greater freedom to billet and organize his army.[136] Sebastianus, with a picked force, reinforced key garrisons and conducted a probe in depth, ambushing Goths from Roman strongholds and getting as far as Adrianople before turning back. No Goth could sleep peacefully with Sebastianus on the loose. While Sebastianus sliced through Gothic-held territory, Gratian's general Frigeridus fortified the pass at Succi to protect the provinces to the north and west.[137]

The presence of Valens and the Eastern army superseded the ordinary frontier commands and all recently assembled forces, which until then had conducted an almost classic exercise in control and containment under Richomeres and then Sebastianus. Most passes and all major towns were still in Roman hands. Just prior to leaving Constantinople Valens was reportedly distressed over the recent victory of Gratian over the Lentienses and concerned that if Sebastianus's constant claims were accurate there would not be any Gothic force left—in other words that his chances of equaling Gratian's exploits were narrowing.[138]

Near Nicae, just short of Adrianople and along the main highway, scouts (*procursatores*) reported seeing a force of only 10,000 Goths in the area.[139] Valens had marched from Constantinople expecting to engage the Gothic forces set in ambush at any time, hence the use of the defensive square deployment. However, he passed through Nicae and the potentially hostile territory without incident. At Adrianople he pitched camp to await Gratian.[140] Ammianus treats the report of the 10,000 as simply an error, but also notes that it was reported as only a part of the enemy, albeit a very large group.[141] Why then have so many modern historians found in this report either the explanation for Valens's rashness or an accurate figure for the Gothic and allied forces in Thrace? The second assumption follows the first. If Valens was still assuming that the report of 10,000 was an accurate summation of enemy strength at hand, then he must have received no further information about the Goths while on the march. That would not be surprising if, as seems likely, the Goths were rendezvousing to the north. If so, it was probably near Cabyle, due north of Adrianople and connected to it by a road running along the western bank of the Tonsos River. Water and forage were precious during the hot and dusty summer days, so conspicuously a part of Ammianus's account. In fact, only while at Adrianople did news arrive, but not news of the Goths. Richomeres reported that Gratian was approaching. Wait, he urged, at Adrianople.[142] Still no word about the Goths. Nevertheless, Valens prepared to strike, but whom and where?

To build statistical theories upon the report of 10,000 Goths mentioned by Ammianus is futile, especially since Ammianus immediately states that the report was false. Nonetheless, some have calculated 10,000 Tervingi (Visigoths) and 8,000 Greutungi (Ostrogoths) and their allies under *duces* Alatheus and Saphrax (cavalry for some analysts, despite the fact that so many horses would have starved even faster than the Goths).[143] This total of roughly 20,000 seems reasonable, though the method by which it was arrived at is suspect. If Valens aided Richomeres, who was somewhere to the northwest with Western reinforcements, by passing Adrianople to the north en route or, at least, dispatching a strong detachment to help him cut through to Adrianople from the vicinity of Gratian's forces, then these Goths blocking Richomeres would have constituted another group of Goths. Presumably these were women and children with baggage and a guard. The evidence for this hypothesis is marginal, but it would help reduce the necessary size of the Gothic encampments, first near Ad Salices and later at Adrianople, and would provide a better context for understanding many tactical decisions on both sides.[144]

Since the number given in our sources for the Goths crossing the Danube is meaningless, we are left to fashion our own estimates based on the circumstances of the Goths and of the campaign. An estimate of 15,000 Gothic males fighting near Adrianople, after their consolidation under Fritigern, seems reasonable. Then the total influx of Gothic population from beyond the Danube would lie between 60,000 and 75,000 heads, a number derived by multiplying the estimated troop strength by 4 or 5. The sum is consistent with calculations of other Germanic groups. The 15,000 might even include the contingents fighting with the *duces* Alatheus and Saphrax. These were generally the Greutungi (later labeled Ostrogoths in many sources and generally so identified in historiography) following Viderichus, the underaged son of Vithimir and successor to the great Ermanaric. Some Alans may have served with Saphrax, himself an Alan or a Hun by name.[145] The importance of the non-Tervingi Goths at Adrianople was one of surprise and timing rather than of crushing masses. Their mounts were probably among the few horses present among the Goths. Altogether, the Goths and their allies at Adrianople may have numbered 20,000 combatants plus dependents, still a very large number of people.

The magnitude of the Roman forces is equally perplexing despite much modern guessing. A. H. M. Jones, figuring from the "replacement" units raised in the decades following the battle, as he thought were indicated in the *Notitia dignitatum*, believed that the Romans had fielded an army of 60,000 men, two-thirds of whom Ammianus reports were lost. Unfortunately, Jones's calculations of unit size, particularly of legionary strength, were far too high, probably by as much as three times. Largely because there is no credible evidence of a major disproportion of forces, I believe that the Romans with the emperor actually numbered about the same as their Gothic opponents. My estimate, therefore, is that something like 15,000 to 20,000 Romans marched with Valens to meet their gods.[146]

Then suddenly came envoys from Fritigern. At the head of these men was a "presbyter of the Christians," obviously meant as a signal to Valens that Fritigern sought *receptio* and that his offer was genuine. They asked that the Goths "cast out" from above the Danube be conceded the right to settle in Thrace alone—not even it seems the whole diocese but perhaps only the province itself—and live there in *perpetuam pacem*. The Goths were hungry; the "flocks and crops of Thrace" were foremost on their minds. Richomeres's strategy of containment had indeed revived Rome's old ally, hunger.[147] In short, the Goths asked for *receptio* with one condition—that they be allowed to remain together. They were willing to accept Christianity, as was made clear by the dispatch of the Christian priest as their ambassador. Perhaps they had in mind something akin to the status of Ulfila's followers in Moesia. The envoys also brought "a personal letter from the same king [Fritigern]" asking that Valens assemble an imperial army and display its power "from time to time" to suppress the Gothic urge to war.[148] Although this was a calculated appeal to Roman pride, the episode of the Quadic ambassadors confessing to Valentinian that they alone could not prohibit the warlike actions of their people also attests to its truthfulness.

Ammianus states that Valens paid no mind to Fritigern's envoys, and they left empty-handed. Their presence had, however, betrayed the nearby presence of the Gothic king and his assembled army. Valens clearly did not hesitate to reject Fritigern's offer, perhaps because it had contained the condition that the Goths remain together in Thrace rather than offering themselves unconditionally for Roman service. After all, unlike Ulfila's religious converts, Fritigern's Goths comprised a very considerable hostile force, and the Roman command was not yet ready to cede whole areas of the frontier provinces to barbarians. Thrace was too central for an experiment with *laeti*, as Constantine (307–37) had done along the lower Rhine with some Franks. Transplanting numerous defeated barbarians of the same background to nearby lands, as Diocletian (284–305) had accomplished with some Carpi in the largely unpopulated Dobrudja, must have seemed equally unwise.[149]

Nor were the Goths a defeated and humbled foe from whom recruits could be extracted as Rome saw fit. Valens believed that in a few days he would not need to compromise. Roman policy toward invaders and rebels would be followed. Only after a Roman victory would he discuss the terms of "surrender," of *deditio*, before granting *receptio*.

The Roman army marched out at dawn. It seems highly unlikely that the emperor knew nothing about the hostile encampment. He must have known at least that it was to the north somewhere along the road to Cabyle, and reasonably close, for he ordered his army to march in column in order of battle rather than in the defensive square in which they had advanced from Constantinople to Adrianople. Whatever the Romans knew about the whereabouts of the Goths was obsolete. They unexpectedly came upon the Gothic camp with its wagons neatly circled, as had been those at Ad Salices. Surprise gripped both sides; obviously neither's intelligence system functioned well. Fritigern sent a messenger requesting hostages and Richomeres volunteered. The exchange never occurred, but the discussion may have bought a little time. The Romans attacked.[150]

There remains no way to ascertain just what the Romans expected or encountered other than a circular deployment of wagons in one or more concentrations, perhaps clustered. That Valens still held to a false report of 10,000, delivered a few days earlier while the army was advancing upon Adrianople, is possible, but Ammianus went out of his way to downplay the report.[151] If, however, the emperor based his calculations upon 10,000, this would help explain why he wanted to engage the enemy as quickly as possible. If he could strike a decisive blow quickly, the Goths would not be able to rally reinforcements. Alas, such military logic does not seem to have been present. It seems more likely that Valens's personal jealousy of Gratian took control, an antagonism clearly reflected on their coins as well as in Ammianus.[152] Thus it appears that it was a jealous senior emperor, Valens, who rejected all advice to await Gratian's army before attacking the Goths. Such advice had been given him by Richomeres and his own general Victor, *magister equitum* in the East, and perhaps by Sebastianus, whose harassing and containing tactics had worked quite well and whose own success may have troubled Valens's ego.[153] Still another possibility is that Valens, eager to bring the foe to heel without assistance, did act on the petition from Fritigern to "show the flag"—but had interpreted it as a request for immediate action. Valens died the next day and with him all real knowledge of his motivations.

On 9 August 378, under a scorching sun and in clouds of dust, at two o'clock in the afternoon and still without the noon meal, thousands of Roman soldiers rushed into formation a few kilometers outside Adrianople. Valens dismissed all advice to delay, and in great haste attacked. In assaulting the oval arrangement of Gothic wagons, the Romans weakened their rear ranks as their battle line bent to bring the leading units into contact with the Goths. Those Roman units on the far left virtually became detached from the main body in the rush to assemble and charge. Greutungi cavalry returning on the double from pasturing their horses in nearby streambeds sallied forth and caught the Roman line from behind. Attacking at a vital juncture of the left wing cavalry and the central infantry, the Gothic cavalry drastically aggravated the normal drift of ancient infantry to the right as each man sought to protect his sword arm behind his neighbor's shield. In the melee that followed, the compacted mass of Roman soldiers lost the integrity of their command. Gothic archers surrounded and cut them down. Many thousand lay dead or dying, including Valens. Both Traianus and Sebastianus died with their emperor. Richomeres and Saturninus survived. Lupicinus never surfaces in the historical record again, presumably dying on the field in 378.[154]

Ammianus reports that "barely a third of the army escaped."[155] Theodosius had to raise many units during his reign, some of which were to replace those who fell at Adrianople.[156] Many thousands died there, that is certain; yet the loss of so many field grade commanders—two *magistri*, 35 military tribunes, and numerous other officers—may have been more damaging than the losses of men.[157] The battles near Ad Salices and Adrianople appear to have been fought with the barbarians having a slight upper hand in manpower, but not by much. If only 15,000 Romans fought at Adrianople and 10,000 died, that still would have constituted a very grave disaster— despite the claims of Ammianus, probably not a Cannae or a Teutoburg Forest, but a stunning setback nonetheless. Seen against the loss of 10,000 men, primarily from the field armies (the garrisons seem to have remained at their posts throughout) and the presence of ca. 60,000 variously grouped and usually dispersed barbarians, including family members, the actions of Theodosius and Gratian, until his murder in 383, were indeed urgent yet not necessarily desperate and certainly not tainted by the shadows of the Apocalypse. For Ambrose and Jerome, however, these events inspired visions of the end of the world.[158]

Gratian was delayed, first by a tenacious Alamannic revolt, and then by sickness. As he approached Thrace from Dacia Ripensis, surprise attacks from groups of Alans, still only loosely associated with the Gothic forces in the Balkans, further slowed his progress. For most of the trek he allowed the Danube to carry the burden of his supply train, but once as far as

Bononia, probably around 9 June, he headed inland and quickly came upon
Alanic raiders. His last reported location in Ammianus was at Castra Martis
just inland from Bononia and near the Timacus River. Gratian had left most
of his heavy troops behind so that he could rush personally to Valens.[159]
Although such haste was surely necessary, his lightly armed men had to be
cautious in rugged country ideal for ambush.

Once established in Dacia Ripensis, Gratian was within the strategic
zone of the campaign and thus probably in contact with intelligence agents
of Valens's forces and the garrisons still holding the towns. After his encounter with the Alans (probably not those with Saphrax, who was at Adrianople
in August, but others only allied directly to Fritigern after the Battle of
Adrianople) Gratian apparently decided to await his main forces before
pushing on via Naissus and Philippopolis. He probably planned to rendezvous with Valens at Adrianople.[160] In hindsight, it seems clear that there were
no major Gothic forces in his path. Obviously Gratian's scouting and intelligence personnel let him down. Valens's death must have shocked the
Western emperor. Despite their rivalry Gratian seems to have done everything within his power to support his colleague and to personally join the
campaign. He did so swiftly and at considerable risk.

Events caught Gratian en route. Quick and perhaps even unauthorized
decisions were made at all levels of command. Julius, the *comes et magister
militum*, who had received the hostages and other Goths transshipped to
Asia Minor, arranged the murder of those in his custody, perhaps after con-
sulting with the Senate in Constantinople but clearly before the accession
of Theodosius in January of 379.[161] Ammianus's comment on Julius in-
structing his officers actually in charge of the new recruits is also instructive
in a broader context. In an offhand way Ammianus tells his readers that
most junior officers in the army were barbarian by birth: "When he [Julius]
learned of the disastrous events in Thrace, he gave orders by secret letters
to his commanders, who were all Roman (*a rarity these days*) to slay on one
day all the Goths who had been admitted and dispersed in various cities
and camps." He proposed that they be lured outside the defenses by telling
them to assemble there for pay.[162] Had they lived, the new recruits would
have found plenty of barbarian companionship in the ranks, and officers
whose backgrounds mirrored their own.

For their part, the victorious Goths did not linger near Adrianople but
moved on toward Constantinople, thus away from Gratian. They encamped
near Perinthus. Their efforts at storming Constantinople were as futile as
had been their earlier attempts at Adrianople. The frustrated Goths had to
settle for raiding and burning some armament factories beyond Constanti-

nople's walls before spreading out in search of supplies and booty.[163] Unlike the Goths of the third century, Fritigern and his people were barred from crossing the Hellespont into Asia where they may have expected to find their kinsmen sent ahead with Julius as well as rich new areas for plunder and/or settlement. In short, the Goths were still trapped in the diocese of Thrace. They could not remain there much longer. Gratian held fast, perhaps in the area of Naissus or at Sirmium, where he personally elevated Theodosius to the collegial throne on 19 January 379.[164] Constantinople remained impregnable; a Roman fleet patrolled the Danube and the Bosporus.

Parts of the Danubian fleet had escorted Gratian's baggage. Surely Roman naval forces had supervised many of the recent immigrations from their stations at Viminacium, Aegete, Ratiaria (where Gratian probably stopped), Transmarisca, and Noviodunum.[165] The fleet might have tried to block any effort to cross back into *barbaricum* or any further unauthorized movements southward of new barbarians. The fleet doubtless transported Athanaric and his followers onto Roman soil in 381. The only Goths to recross the Danube did so in 379–80 and with Roman blessing.[166]

Only after the Hunnic raids of the early fifth century did the fleet suffer. The *Notitia dignitatum* lists a *praefectus* in charge of the *classis Scythiae*.[167] In 412 Theodosius II ordered the repair of existing craft and building of new (reconnaissance and shallow-drafted patrol boats).[168] Writing ca. 435, Vegetius praised naval efficiency on the Danube in his last extant lines.[169] Therefore, the Goths after 378 could not have recrossed the Danube even had they wished to return to Athanaric's homeland and face the Huns, which they did not. In any case, Fritigern certainly would not have led them back to Athanaric. Although the prospects of destroying the military infrastructure of Thrace were hardly more promising, the Goths and their allies had little choice but to try. With the demise of *receptio*, the Goths were at a loss for solutions, particularly since their leadership structures and unity were only in the earliest phases of cohesion. Future political and diplomatic initiatives originated with the Romans. The Goths did not demand anything not traditionally a part of *receptio* for decades.

Ammianus speaks of the fixed or permanent garrisons at Beroea and Nicopolis ad Istrum as being withheld from the campaign while Valens neared Adrianople.[170] Ammianus, at least, recalled the horrors of the third century when "Scythians" besieged Thessalonica and Cyzicus and took Anchialos, Nicopolis, and Philippopolis.[171] But this time most cities held firm, their supplies safely in Roman hands. Up to and beyond the major Hunnic incursions of the 440s, the evidence, while certainly not overwhelming, is conclusive. The urban communities well behind the *limes* survived the struggles of the 370s and 380s and in several cases regained some of the prosperity lost during those years. They were islands of resistance and supply depots.

Philippopolis clearly weathered the era without serious disruption. Serdica too held its own until taken by Attila, although some sections of its early fourth century extensions of the defenses may have been breached or abandoned (the archaeological record is very slender). Marcianopolis, the principal imperial encampment in the struggles against Procopius and the Goths and a key transportation and communication center, ultimately fell in 447 to the Huns but, even then, later flowered anew.[172] At Adrianople a citizen militia was armed and at the order of their chief magistrate attacked some Goths late in 378. Although the citizens left many friends dead on the field, the Goths finally did depart after the regular garrison's slingers and archers struck down many during the Gothic siege of the city.[173] The major urban centers were at the hub of networks of *villae rusticae*, small towns and, often, military outposts in the area. Many, perhaps most, of these small outposts and communities fell, but once again the evidence is scanty and inconclusive.

Looking at the first series of towns directly south of the *limes* itself, Montana (Mihailovgrad)—Melta (Lovech)—Nicopolis ad Istrum (unoccupied in modern times, now the village of Nikyup), the conclusion that the last quarter of the fourth century were difficult years is manifest. So far excavation at Montana has uncovered very little: a single pylon from the second half of the fourth century within a U-shaped tower first laid down a century earlier, and bits and pieces of amphorae and small metal finds— not much, but perhaps enough to conclude that some level of occupation continued without interruption until the sixth-century movements of the Avars and Slavs.[174] Great walls seem to have effectively intimidated the Goths.

The lack of major reconstruction and new construction during the last quarter of the century at such sites as Montana probably reflects the lack of continuous contact with the central government, which alone could support such expenditures, rather than barbarian overlordship of the town itself. The same situation of very sparse activity but occupation nonetheless is typical for the cities within the area overrun by Gothic bands and foreshadows what will be equally true for many urban centers of the Western Empire during the fifth and sixth centuries. In the Balkans at this time often only private construction, particularly chapels and small churches, were repaired properly or built anew during the last quarter of the fourth and early fifth centuries. Small finds are generally unimpressive to look at, comprising the refuse and remains of domestic and routine municipal life. At Montana and elsewhere, however, these scraps of life are historically significant for the purpose of establishing continuity.

At Melta, next along the road east of Montana, what little has come to light suggests continued survival of the Roman population.[175] Further east the road passed through Nicopolis ad Istrum where the roads leading southward from Novae to Beroea and Arzos crossed.[176] Nicopolis ad Istrum received Ulfilas and his fellow Goths in 347–48. That town presents several difficulties in analysis, for it is impossible to determine whether the Nicopolis mentioned by Eunapius was Nicopolis ad Istrum or Nicopolis ad Nestum. According to Eunapius, the town looked to the Goths for its welfare during Theodosius's wars, perhaps thereby implying that its citizens had reached accommodations with the enemy.[177] Just prior to the Battle of Adrianople, the population of Nicopolis ad Istrum must have witnessed the Goths moving along the Nicopolis-Beroea road. There was little of importance outside the city. Villa life in the area of Nicopolis ad Istrum seems to have essentially ceased by the opening of the fourth century, probably because of the severe damage inflicted there during the third century invasions. A *castellum* was built there sometime in the first half of the fourth century, perhaps comprising all that remained of the town. Those Goths under Ulfilas were settled in the vicinity (347–48).[178] Sebastianus may well have stationed special troops there to ambush and generally harass the Goths as a part of his program to restrict their freedom and make foraging more difficult.

Jordanes reported that the Gothic followers of Ulfilas still lived near Nicopolis ad Istrum, peacefully farming and tending cattle in the area as late as the sixth century.[179] Did they play any role in the wars against the Goths ca. 378, and, if so, on whose behalf? Surely Theodosius would have exacted retribution and perhaps even relocated them had they opposed him, and so they must have kept to the sidelines. There are no definitive answers. At any rate, the city had passed its prime before the followers of Ulfilas were settled nearby. But there is no proof that the city fell or suffered extreme adversity in the last quarter of the century. Excavation remains incomplete. However, coin finds running to the middle of the fifth century and reference to the bishopric in 458 suggest that the city continued well beyond the era under discussion but clearly not as the major center it had been at the end of the second century.[180] Thus at Nicopolis ad Istrum the forces of reorientation and reduction were, at best, accelerated by the troubled events after Adrianople.

Marcianopolis (Reka Devnja) was the effective capital of the Balkans.

Despite the sparse documentation, both literary and epigraphic, there is no question that construction continued on the fortifications here as at most other cities in the diocese at a reduced level. Armaments industries in the area continued into the fifth century, according to the *Notitia dignitatum*, and at least one small, single-naved church was dedicated (ca. 375–425). The city fell to the Huns in 447.[181]

Thus all the cities lying directly behind the *limes* along the vital road link for Valens's campaigns survived well beyond 378, albeit in the case of Nicopolis ad Istrum in a diminished state. The examples could be readily expanded to include Philippopolis, Tropaeum Traiani in Scythia, Adrianople itself, and more. This is enough to prove that Ammianus and Eunapius were correct. For the most part the cities and their garrisons held on throughout the Gothic episode. Isolated from the central government and without much coordination, these centers of resistance remained refuges and potential supply points, whenever new crops could be harvested, for the campaigns that followed Theodosius's elevation.[182] Along the Danube itself much the same pattern is emerging.

The Goths, except for the Greutungi, had crossed under Roman supervision at fortifications where Roman garrisons monitored their arrival and processing. For Ammianus, the "frontiers were opened" and a river of armed men "like the glowing flows of mount Aetna" had run over the countryside far and wide.[183] However, unlike cities destroyed by a volcano (or a rhetorical flourish), the fortresses along the river retained their integrity during the initial crossings, indeed throughout the rest of the century and beyond.

The frontier defenses in Dacia Ripensis were systematically strengthened with additional towers and old ones repaired at least as recently as the summer of 364.[184] Other provinces along the Danube managed to maintain some taxable economic activity. For example, the provinces of Scythia and Moesia II were still being assessed clothing contributions for the army in August 377, and at the same rate as Egypt and most of the Orient, despite the hard times noted in the legislation. Thrace paid at a rate of two-thirds that of Moesia; specifically at one vestment (?) per 30 tax units rather than per 20 units.[185] But the presence of barbarians itself was reason to try to avoid taxation. As late as 386 the procurators of mines were still claiming barbarian unrest as an excuse for failing to collect the taxes in Dardania, Dacia (Mediterranea?) and Macedonia (Inferior?), but to no avail. The government forcefully rejected their claims to continued exception, calling their fears "pretended," and ordered them dragged back to their posts.[186]

In some places archaeology has yielded information only about the military camp, leaving us in the dark concerning civilian life. At Ratiaria, for example, the fortress and garrison remained, but of the civilian community nothing is known. The fort itself seems to have declined steadily in size until its capture by Attila.[187] But in and of itself the decline at Ratiaria signifies little. Troop reductions at many sites along the Danube began as early as the mid-fourth century and continued through the remainder of the century. These changes began as a part of the shifting dispositions necessary to achieve flexibility and mobility for the primarily offensive policies of Constantius II and Valens and continued, it seems, under Theodosius, perhaps as one aspect of his attempts to consolidate his forces to oppose the Goths and western usurpers. Thus even when archaeology can demonstrate a reduction in the size of fortifications, the diminished area of an individual fortification or even an entire fortification system, such scaling downward does not necessarily prove anything about overall military capacity.

Proceeding eastward along the Danubian river road, camps and fortified settlements were conveniently located for defense and communication all along the river. A selected survey of a few sites where rather extensive reports of excavation exist confirms the picture so far sketched for the last decade of the fourth century. Novae (Stuklen) was well protected by enhanced defenses throughout the fourth century. Characteristic U-shaped towers carefully protected the approaches with overlapping fields of fire. The survival of a substantial population and garrison cannot be doubted. However, someone, ca. 370, must at least have feared for his life and fled after burying 130 coins in tower No. 1 of the eastern wall.[188] Momentarily Novae assumed considerable importance as the seat of Ostrogothic power (ca. 487), thus apparently also surviving even the Hunnic destructions of the fifth century. However, Novae apparently did not escape the destruction of the Slavic/Bulgarian incursions and settlements of the seventh century.[189] Iatrus and most other Roman towns along and behind the Danube survived as small urban and military centers into the seventh century when they witnessed the Slavic incursions. Conclusions are premature. The "end of antiquity" in the general area of Bulgaria cannot yet be established. Nonetheless, it seems clear enough that the events surrounding the acceptance of new recruits at the end of the fourth century were of relatively little consequence to urban life.

The countryside, on the other hand, yields a sharply different pattern. In every sense and from every source comes the same picture. Very hungry Goths ravaged farms and *villae* with impunity and occasionally with help from indigenous peoples.[190] Denied the granaries of the cities and not overly successful even against small camps, they had no choice. Ammianus reported the distress of the *magistratus* (i.e., *duumvir*, one of the chief urban officers) at Adrianople, that his *villa suburbana* lay in ruins. Indeed, his was not the only villa in the area to suffer.[191] Near Ivajlovgrad (to the southwest of Adrianople) a lavishly appointed Roman villa built in the second century was destroyed and abandoned at about this time, the coin sequences stopping with Valentinian I.[192]

Humbler and more numerous *villae rusticae*, modest independent farmsteads, fared no better. For example, at Chatalka, Stara Zagora, lying just west of ancient Augusta Traiana, a *villa rustica* suffered destruction at about this time, although some occupation was present into the early fifth century.[193] Excavation of such modest farmsteads (ranging from ca. 25–75 *jugera* to as large as ca. 500 *jugera*) in the diocese of Thrace is far from complete, indeed has hardly begun. To the northeast, in the Dobrudja, excavations of *villae* support the pattern emerging near Adrianople.[194] In most cases the villa system had recovered from the crisis of the third century and enjoyed considerable prosperity during the first three quarters of the fourth. Their prosperity probably reflected indirectly the high levels of governmental expenditure on defense during the Constantinian dynasty and the return of the Danube as the frontier. The *villae rusticae* occupied the base of the supply system, their owners being prosperous farmers. The *villae suburbanae*, on the other hand, were fashionable dwellings typically near cities and were administered by overseers. These are the *villae* known to us elsewhere from the pens of their rich owners, men like Ausonius in Gaul. These estates could be made more defensible and thereby continue operation without the presence of the landlord, although the literary sources from such areas as Gaul and Italy make it clear that the owners' presence and attention did make a difference.

Clearly the case at Ivajlovgrad proves that some large *villae*, perhaps particularly in places like Ivajlovgrad, rather far distant from an urban center, ceased to operate. In some cases *villae*, although abandoned by their owners or, in the case of simple *villae rusticae*, perhaps allowed to remain in ruins so as not to attract further marauders, were in fact still worked agriculturally. Similar squatter-occupation generally characterized the collapse of midsized villas in many areas of the Empire, including even central Italy.[195] In a few instances excavation has revealed traces of small-scale building, squatter-type housing in or near the "abandoned" villas. Some of the refugees in the mountain and hilltop bastions returned to work the soil continuously throughout the late fourth, the fifth, and even into the sixth centuries.[196]

On the slim basis of a few field surveys, it would appear that refuges and subsistence farming survived the Goths without serious long-term disruption. Such farmers may have had to reach some accord with any Goths who controlled the countryside. Perhaps in this way the rural labor force felt freer than under the old regime of the great landowners. Theodosius may have had them in mind when he issued legislation binding the lower classes to the soil ever more tightly. Specifically, the edict drafted sometime after 393 addressed the problem of *coloni* in the diocese of Thrace, who by wandering about had adopted the airs of freedom. They were to be instructed that they remained attached to the land of their origin and that they were still under the care of their traditional patrons and could not move without consent.[197] *Coloni* here and elsewhere in the surviving legislation seem to have comprised the general agricultural population and were not necessarily limited to what we traditionally regard as a tightly defined and oppressed group at the very lowest level of "free" society.

Once again, the basic outline of resistance and destruction in Eunapius and Ammianus is both confirmed and refined in considerable detail. Nonetheless, there were many features of life and defense which went largely unrecorded and have yet to find secure archaeological verification. There were numerous refuges, temporary occupations during invasion, scattered throughout the frontier provinces from Raetia and Noricum to Moesia. In general, these were characterized by their small internal area and maximum use of natural topography. A few storage buildings and, in Moesia II, at least, churches were common features of refuges. Most were virtually inaccessible. They served the local agrarian workers as final bastions. The presence of churches has led one scholar to stress the possible role of the local clergy in defense. Extremely little is clear about these civilian refuges; they remain virtually unexcavated and unknown.[198] Yet the legislation referred to above concerning wandering *coloni* could easily have had them in mind as they took up new residences after danger passed. Some of these same people might well have been among the collaborators reported in Ammianus. Unfortunately, none of our sources allow us to explore the pathos of the men and women actually confronting these crises. For many these years must have assumed the appearance of an unbroken chain of tragedies. Stone monuments, broken pottery, and the carefully chosen phrases of even an Ammianus Marcellinus cannot truly reflect their lives.

In summation, the available data suggest that the Gothic crossings of the Danube were in keeping with Roman policies along the frontier. The mechanisms for *receptio* were implemented, but the demands for provisions were vastly more than anticipated and starvation led to rebellion. Even after the rebellion, the Roman command in the area pursued effective policies that relied upon the Romans holding most supply centers and forcing the invaders to either get bogged down in siege warfare or disperse to live off the land. The emperors decided to bring the struggle to conclusion with armed might, but failed in two ill-advised engagements. Nevertheless, until the Roman defeat at Adrianople in August 378, the initiative lay with Rome. Neither the losses of Roman troops in the Gothic campaigns, whatever their precise dimensions, nor the number of the Gothic and allied peoples to be contained after Adrianople were such that new programs were suddenly imperative. The urban infrastructure of those provinces immediately threatened by the Goths remained basically intact, although the rural communities and agricultural production were severely disrupted. Rome still retained the requisite military capacities to reduce the Gothic menace and ultimately implement *receptio*, providing it had patience and could find a capable leader.

Summary

By the ascension of Valentinian in 364, the Roman army had already profited greatly from barbarians serving within it. In particular Constantine the Great's implantation of barbarians as *laeti* in the provinces along the lower Rhine River had proven a great success. There Germanic and indigenous populations had made long strides in the formation of a cultural amalgam within the context of Roman military service. At times units of *laeti* served beyond their settlement areas. The frontier provinces under their *duces* handled normal frontier operations including small-scale and peaceful recruitment. In case of the rare general invasion the diocese was the effective unit of organization. Still rarer was a massive incursion that threatened areas beyond one diocese and required the coordination of an entire region. Recruits regardless of their origin or legal status upon entry served at the discretion of the Roman army. Many, perhaps most, junior officers were from barbarian stock. The primary goal in most but not all cases of recruitment was transshipment of the new enlistees for service in regular units at some distance from their homes, but this was not always followed. The emperors repeatedly demonstrated a high degree of cooperation when called upon to assist each other in times of crisis. The incredible depth of fortification enabled a high percentage of the infrastructure to survive attack, although rural areas suffered terribly.

THEODOSIUS IN ACTION

MANY SCHOLARS are currently studying the career of Theodosius the Great, a grand but daunting subject. It is extraordinarily difficult to determine even the emperor's movements, much less his reactions to the barbarian problem. Indeed, no less an authority than A. H. M. Jones regarded the years 379–82 as essentially undecipherable.[1] Nonetheless and despite the constraints of the sources, it is clear that Theodosius never regarded the Gothic problem as insoluble or, indeed, truly threatening to the ultimate security of the Empire. At the tactical level, as we shall explore, imperial troops contained, then divided, and finally began to absorb the barbarian presence. This was accomplished within the context of the traditional *limes* system and the policy of *receptio*. These steps took on an accustomed cadence and have left telltale marks in the evidence. If we know what contours to seek from the set of circumstances, then the sparse data clearly reflect traditional troop dispositions and logistical systems rather than innovation. Obviously, the first priority is to limit the data to trustworthy sources. *A priori*, this implies the temporary rejection of much of the anxiety in the Christian sources in which visions of the end of the world flowed into and over the realities of the battlefields.

Almost immediately Gratian recalled Theodosius from his retirement in Spain, made him *magister equitum*, and ordered him into battle against some "Sarmatians." Then on 19 January 379, after his brief trial period as a *magister*, Theodosius became emperor at Gratian's hands at Sirmium.[2] What happened next is subject to debate. Matters stood at a difficult juncture. The surviving garrisons within the stricken provinces were isolated and probably out of touch with the central command. The fleet on the Danube facilitated limited communication, for it was almost certainly still in operation and its harbors safe from surprise assaults. The Gothic forces were demonstrably unable to sustain siege warfare, numerically limited, and already hungry. Accordingly, the primary task at hand was to block all passages out of the Thracian area, adequately but without an extraordinary sacrifice of the available manpower, just as had Valentinian I in aiding his brother

Valens against the supporters of Procopius in 366–67. And, if this were not possible or already too late, the Empire had to contain the barbarians to the smallest area practical in terms of topography and troop commitments. Second, appropriate administrative measures had to be undertaken at once to coordinate supplies, levied from the areas neighboring the Thracian diocese as well as perhaps within those parts of Thrace itself still under Roman control, and to unite various jurisdictions (military and civilian) into a higher state of cohesion. These matters had to be accomplished immediately; the actual relief of the towns and garrisons could wait.

Temporarily abandoning the towns and fortifications to their own defenses was in keeping with the elaborate care expended upon their walls in late antiquity, and a well established part of Roman defensive strategy. Moreover, the sense of desperation typically imparted to these events by later commentators is difficult to corroborate with contemporary evidence without resort to the virtually apocalyptic literature of the Christian tradition.[3] A digression into the fifth century perhaps can illustrate the realities of life in cities thrown upon their own resources.

The situation in the Balkans during the decade after Adrianople parallels and foreshadows that of numerous other areas in the fifth century, after "law and order" had collapsed and communities were isolated for long periods. A few cases come to mind as offering a vision of life roughly comparable to the present crisis but which, because of the survival of literary texts, are better known. Chronologically the first instance is Emperor Honorius's casting the *civitates* (towns and their environs) of Britain adrift on their own defenses in 409. The documents for early fifth century Britain, however, are hardly able to provide a solid parallel, although the incident will occupy our attention in the final chapters. Better examples come from the continent during the last half of the century.

During the famous barbarian siege of Auvergne in Gaul, Bishop Sidonius Apollinaris could still report (ca. 470) a surprising fullness of life, spiritual and earthly, during the interval between actual attacks, which were themselves very modest affairs in terms of troop strengths. His son-in-law, Ecdicius, with hardly more than a handful of men, fought his way into the city during such a siege. In general, the populace went on about its business; messengers occasionally arrived and departed, linking the world of the aristocrats into a functioning and far-reaching social network.[4] Perhaps more instructive still are the reports from the *Vita Severini* (also ca. 470) of events in Noricum Ripense, a frontier province. Here, despite notorious brigandry from groups of barbarians often under no one's authority at all, a precarious life went on within the shadows of the town walls. Archaeology in and around Passau (ancient Batavis) and elsewhere offers strong confirmation of the survival of late Roman town life and supports the veracity of the *Vita* in an often startling detail.[5]

In the *Vita* farmers are depicted harvesting grain, with the true believers occasionally receiving better treatment from the Heavens, of course. Occasionally raiders took helpless tillers by surprise. Captives were redeemed, and the Roman and barbarian peoples mingled in various ways (hinted at in the archaeological record but still unclear in detail). Though sometimes interrupted, river traffic continued on the Danube. St. Severinus could even send a spy into a barbarian village without difficulty or detection.[6] Surely this would have been difficult but not impossible among the Goths in 379, for there were already Gothic speakers in the Roman army. Just such Roman soldiers successfully infiltrated Gothic bands across the Danube and discovered invasion plans only a few years later. There were in addition numerous prisoners and defectors to assist the regular Roman espionage system. What all this seems to imply is that there was often little hostility between common people based on perceived ethnicity. Examples of lower class tolerance even amid violent struggle can be found throughout the following centuries. So-called fifth-column movements that inevitably cropped up during invasions were not really movements but rather modestly orchestrated means of staying alive with change in one's pocket—a town, a villa, or an individual coming to terms with the invaders. Under these constraints life went on during invasions.

In 379, Rome for the first time in over a century had to contemplate sustained interaction with hostile barbarian peoples inside the Empire. However, since the basic fabric of the frontier provinces was so carefully geared for such an enterprise and had been for many generations, Theodosius could anticipate the survival of many, perhaps most, Roman strongholds for months, even years if necessary, while they alternately defended against and dealt with the barbarians in their vicinity. This had in fact begun at no less crucial a place than Adrianople itself, months before Theodosius ascended the throne.[7] But Theodosius and Gratian now had to stabilize the zone of conflict and isolate the invaders as soon as possible. After that Theodosius could proceed to reestablish links to the principal towns along the roads, thereby also further cleaving what little unity the Gothic groups possessed. First things first.

Zosimus, the only continuous "historical" account extant, relates that near the end of the Battle of Adrianople Victor, the *magister equitum*, escaped, rode westward through Macedonia, Thessaly, and Moesia to Pannonia without opposition, and informed Gratian.[8] If accurately reported, this was a most unusual route, and might imply Gothic control of the more direct roadways. Zosimus was unaware of or uninterested in Theodosius's Sarmatian campaign. According to him, Gratian immediately appointed Theodosius to rule "Thrace and the East" as his co-emperor, while he himself returned to settle affairs in western Gaul, specifically to address incursions there from across the Rhine.[9] Sozomenus alone records the transference of territorial jurisdiction that went along with Theodosius's elevation to the purple, a move which placed the prefecture of Illyricum (until then in the Western sphere) with its dioceses of Pannonia, Dacia, and Macedonia under the new Eastern emperor along with all the provinces that Valens had ruled.[10] As usual the prefecture was the unit of imperial military command, since the emperor was present. Traditionally in late antiquity the praetorian prefect of Illyricum resided at Serdica. It was standard late Roman practice not to appoint a lower official when the superior resided in the district,[11] and therefore Theodosius and Gratian may have felt in no hurry to rush into new civilian appointments as long as one of them was actively engaged in the area. Many parts of the Balkans were hard pressed. Thrace in particular was hardly a prize worth the having; as Zosimus notes, it was occupied by barbarians. Thrace had been the responsibility of the Eastern emperor since 364; therefore no special assignment was in order, and none is extant. By 379 Illyricum had already witnessed barbarian incursions westward from Thrace. It now needed a regionally coordinated defense. Whatever the state and structure of its civilian administrative apparatus, prosecuting the war took precedence. On the civil prefecture there are many opinions and insufficient facts to completely prove any.

Discussion has tended to focus on what happened and for how long to the diocese Pannonia and whether it was included in Gratian's transfer. I believe that the campaigns themselves will reveal that the entire prefecture was initially given to Theodosius and returned in two stages. Theodosius restored first Pannonia in September 380, when the emperors met at Sirmium, and then Dacia and Macedonia, probably sometime after September 381, but certainly by the summer of 383.[12] That the bishop of Thessalonica alone of Western clerics attended the Council of Constantinople in May 381 strongly suggests that the diocese of Macedonia was then still Theodosius's. E. Demougeot, long a leading voice on this problem, posited the creation of a new and temporary prefecture of Eastern Illyricum.[13] This was rejected in part by J.-R. Palanque and replaced by a regional partition within the one prefectural administrative unit as a part of Gratian's realignment of western prefectures and, for Palanque, this state of affairs (i.e., with Pannonia tied to Italy) held down to the death of Gratian in 383.[14]

V. Grumel suggested a similar but very short-lived regional division ending in September 380, when Valentinian II assumed the rule of the entire old prefecture under the regency of Gratian. Thus for Grumel any split of Illyricum lasted only from January 379 to September 380, fifteen months.[15] Grumel was probably correct on the timing but only of the return of the diocese of Pannonia. It appears rather that after September 380 Macedonia and Dacia alone constituted the administrative prefecture of Illyricum under Theodosius and remained so for one or two years, Demougeot's Eastern Illyricum. That Gratian was again in military control of Pannonia after September 380 was demonstrated when from his forces there he was able to dispatch powerful aid to Theodosius against rebelling barbarians in Macedonia and Thessaly in 381.[16] The state of the evidence for these troubled years will not produce certainty on the administrative sequence for Illyricum and its dioceses. Regardless how one reads the data, however, there can be little doubt that Theodosius was the principal military commander in the entire prefecture as of the winter of 379.

Scholars postulating that Illyricum was immediately split into two functioning prefectures typically have based their theories on one edict in the *Codex Theodosianus*—13.1.11 concerning taxes and addressed to Hesperius, praetorian prefect (dated 5 July 379). A few inscriptions although inconclusive are also pressed into service as is the coinage.[17] The edict of 5 July cannot bear such weight. Hesperius had been praetorian prefect of the Gauls since 378 with his father, the poet and imperial tutor Ausonius.[18] After the retirement of Antonius as praetorian prefect of Italy (that is after 18 August 378), Hesperius and his father apparently assumed prefectural duties in Italy and Africa as well.[19] At some point in 378, probably early in the year, Olybrius had succeeded Ausonius (not Hesperius's father) as praetorian prefect of Illyricum.[20] Ausonius and Olybrius had been the only independent prefects of Illyricum since Claudius Probus in early 364.[21] By the end of 378 Olybrius was praetorian prefect of the Orient. Illyricum too seems to have fallen to Hesperius, which in the fourth century, particularly under Valentinian I, was rather standard. So in July 379 Hesperius held the office of praetorian prefect virtually without territorial limits! As such he is addressed in the edict and accordingly he is ordered to attend to some fiscal matters in Italy, Illyricum, and Gaul. By May 380 he was praetorian prefect of Italy and Africa alone.[22] Throughout his long career the edict of 5 July is the only one specifically concerning Illyricum ever addressed to him.[23]

Theodosius appointed Eutropius his praetorian prefect of Illyricum not later than 6 January 380, and numerous matters concerning Illyricum were soon coming his way.[24] Theodosius did not meet with Gratian until September 380. Other than Eutropius, who served on until at least 28 September 381, no other praetorian prefect of Illyricum is known for these years.[25] Even if the edict of 5 July 379 to Hesperius is correctly dated, it was probably the result either of administrative convenience, since edicts were issued to the prefects and there was none other for Illyricum since late in 378, when he had probably assumed that post too, or of a decision made at Sirmium. If Theodosius had not yet made his appointment of Eutropius, Hesperius and his father were the only prefects except for that of the Orient. There were, after all, other things for Theodosius to do, probably including clearing a path to Serdica. A hypothesis is that at Sirmium Gratian, despite his age the senior Augustus, offered to channel laws through Hesperius for Illyricum until Theodosius could get his house in order. There are no restrictions as to dioceses in the law of 5 July addressed to Hesperius. As soon as possible, perhaps after connections with Serdica were again secure, Theodosius was able to name his own civil officers and did. That Theodosius could campaign in Pannonia without prefectural consolidation is militarily unlikely, but given the fact that there was no real prefectural presence there (Hesperius was almost certainly conducting affairs from Italy) perhaps Theodosius just took several months before setting up his own civilian administration. This would have been increasingly necessary as his health went into serious decline. This was a major crisis in which imperial trust and understanding were paramount.

Despite the extraordinary complexity of conceiving of dual Illyrican prefectural governments in 379–80, many scholars do accept that possiblity. This solution, however, would have been overly bureaucratic and what little evidence exists either points to one prefecture or is ambivalent. A great deal of complexity is avoided if we hypothesize that the grant of 379 was for the entire prefecture of Illyricum, so that it could function as the operational unit that it long had been, and that it took a few months of 379 for the law clerks and civil administration to work out the details and for Theodosius to set up an operating prefectural structure. Tax collecting could not wait, but in reality no one was likely to see the taxes from much of Illyricum for some time.[26] Gratian had the Rhine frontier to worry about. Circumstances improved in the Balkans more slowly than on the Rhine, and it appears that Gratian pressed for Illyricum's return, or even part of it, as quickly as possible. In that context new administrative arrangements became necessary. There is further evidence to suggest that in 379–80 Theodosius governed all of Illyricum including the diocese of Pannonia. At the very least, there is no denying that Theodosius was the emperor in charge of the campaign in the area and that his efforts repeatedly took him into Pannonia. Furthermore, as will be demonstrated, Gratian acknowledged him as such.

In 366–67 Valentinian had ordered his commander in Illyricum to hold open a path into the heart of Thrace and seal the diocese's western exits in anticipation of Valens's campaign in Thrace. Gratian knew that it was already too late to contain the incursion within Thrace. Theodosius would have to launch immediate counteractions in southern Thrace and had to have whatever support Illyricum could provide while trying to limit the spread of destruction there. Much of Dacia and Macedonia had to wait until the Empire stopped the barbarians from moving further westward. Everywhere Theodosius's primary mission was to confine the scope of the invasion. Gratian had many problems to confront in the West, including barbarian invasions along the frontiers, and so transferred Illyricum and all three of its dioceses to Theodosius. The mint at Thessalonica apparently struck coins for Theodosius at once. So too the mint at Sirmium briefly resumed activity with the presence of the imperial *comitatus*, but whose, Gratian's or Theodosius's, is debatable and a subject to which we shall soon return. Naissus cast gold ingots under Theodosius, thereby proving that the diocese of Dacia was under his control. His repeated use of Thessalonica as his headquarters, as well perhaps as the various issues from its mint, amply attest that Theodosius also controlled the diocese of Macedonia.[27] The province of Moesia I in Dacia was clearly in need of his assistance, and neighboring Pannonia II in the diocese of Pannonia was likewise disrupted by the barbarians there.[28]

Whatever the precise jurisdictional arrangement, Theodosius and Gratian both could take initiatives beyond their administrative spheres in the course of operations, just as Valentinian had moved forces into Thrace in 366–67. Theodosius was later in the year responsible for campaigns near Mursa in Pannonia II.[29] It seems highly likely therefore that he had received this province from Gratian in early 379, while they were both at Sirmium, as a part of the diocese of Pannonia. The best and most recent study of the gold ingots found in Transylvania lends support to earlier and detailed study of the reverse types on coins to place Sirmium in Theodosius's sphere of administration from early 379, despite the lack of coin legends specifically indicative of Theodosius himself. This in turn forces a more straightforward reading of an essential passage in the *Getica* of Jordanes.

J. Pearce writing in 1933 proposed that the mint at Sirmium, idle since its closing in 364–67, was briefly reactivated in 379, when the imperial *comitatus* was present. Pearce thought that the gold struck with the mint

mark of Sirmium and two seated emperors with the inscription VICTOR-
IAAVGG was best assigned to the year 379, when coin was needed to pay
troops for the ensuing campaigns against the barbarians. Since, however, the
same type was issued also at Aquileia, Milan, Trier, and Thessalonica, it cannot prove anything about which emperor officially administered Sirmium.
Emperors routinely minted coins with all emperors on the obverse. There
is nothing unusual in this issue, and unwarranted efforts to use these coins
to prove Gratian's control of the diocese cannot stand unchallenged. Theodosius was in Sirmium at least three times in 379, for his coronation and
to and fro while on campaign in July and August. The ingots add clarity to
the question of the status of Theodosius in Illyricum.

Nearly all the ingots in question were cast in Sirmium, Naissus, and
Thessalonica and are appropriately marked, and virtually all were found in
Transylvania, today central Romania, but not in one hoard. They have an
inherent unity therefore in location of discovery and general area of production. On those grounds it has also been presumed that these gold bars
were manufactured for a common purpose. This could not be established
more firmly, for, despite much effort, precise dating of these ingots was long
beyond reach. That has changed. One bar discovered at Feldioara on the
Oltul River just north of Brasov, Romania, was stamped COMIT, for *comitatus*, i.e., and *NAISI* (for Naissus) at the order of the emperor (see map 3
and illustration 4). This particular bar is now dated to early in the reign of
Theodosius, 379–80, from the inscribed name of Kalyopius. Kalyopius is
securely identified as a magistrate under the *comes sacrarum largitionum* in
charge of the *fabrica* supervising the casting of ingots at Thessalonica. Kalyopius was probably a member of the imperial *comitatus* and as such moved
with the emperor as did gold moneyers. His presence at Naissus and Thessalonica is crucial for the dating, for only during this brief interval when
Theodosius was campaigning along the Thessalonica-Naissus-Sirmium
road—July and August 379—could Kalyopius have been the responsible official at both places.[30] To have amassed such a quantity of gold all imperial
fabricae would have had to pool their resources, and we have ingots from
Thessalonica, Naissus, and Sirmium in the same context. No ingots have
yet appeared bearing the stamps of both Sirmium and Kalyopius, which
would clinch the argument as to whether Sirmium struck gold for Theodosius. But with the publication of the Feldioara ingot from Naissus, the
probability is now much stronger.[31]

Jordanes reports that Theodosius gave his official assent to Gratian's actions of 379–80, including his making an agreement with the barbarians—
to which we shall return. Everything was "as he himself wished."[32] And

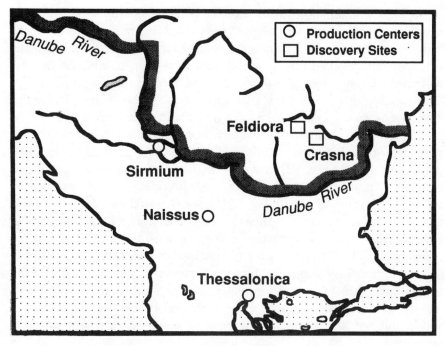

Map 3 Production and Discovery Sites of Gold Ingots

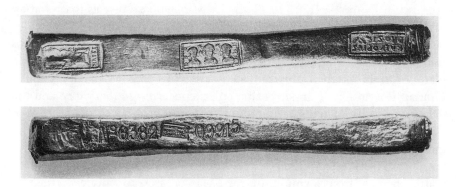

Illustration 4. Gold ingot from Feldioara, Romania

in the same vein, in 389 Pacatus praised Theodosius's military accomplishments in Pannonia ten years before.[33] Had the Pannonian diocese in Illyricum not been under Theodosius's control, Gratian, the senior Augustus, would not have asked for his junior's approval. Gratian did not seek his colleague's blessing for any other military action during his entire reign. The meaning of Jordanes's text now appears quite clear. Gratian knew that Theodosius was ill and moved a force into the Pannonian provinces. In order to establish a continuous linkage of the fortifications along the Danube, the campaign carried this force into Moesia I. There can be little question remaining that Pannonia II was part of the temporary arrangement that gave Theodosius administrative control over Illyricum. Without Pannonia II any lesser division of the diocese of Pannonia would have been administratively untenable and militarily irrelevant. Therefore, a simpler agreement between the emperors, one truly in keeping with the military situation, seems likely. This was not a time to confuse administrative planning and support for tactical operations. Since the entire prefecture was under assault and required direct imperial command, Gratian, I believe, agreed to transfer Illyricum to his colleague for the duration of these campaigns, but he also established that the arrangement would come up for review as events warranted.

Theodosius is next seen at Thessalonica administering to petitioners from across the Empire.[34] There is no difficulty in confirming these events, for the Codes contain two routine decrees of Theodosius issued from Thessalonica and dated 17 June 379. Thessalonica would have held important gold stocks as well, something not available at Sirmium, although some gold from taxes must have been present there. Another source was the traditional *aurum coronarium* or special tax for the new emperor collected in the cities in the provinces. Theodosius called for one on 10 August 379, while at Vicus Augusti in Pannonia II.[35] The *Codex Theodosianus* also reveals that Gratian was active in Sirmium at least through 24 February, hardly the abrupt departure reported by Zosimus.[36] Perhaps winter weather was a factor. Thus there was ample time for Gratian and Theodosius to confer, settle upon a plan of action, and then depart in late February or early March. By 5 April, Gratian was at Trier issuing routine edicts concerning inheritance and the delayed opening of wills; 2 July 379 found him back south of the Alps at Aquileia, the administrative center for northeastern Italy and, more importantly, for the series of defenses running through the Julian Alps. This defensive network effectively blocked any barbarians from trafficking westward. The road from Sirmium up the Sava via Siscia to Aquileia remained open. Gratian remained in northern Italy (edicts from Aquileia on 2 and

5 July, Milan on 31 July and 3 August) through the summer but was back in Trier by 14 September.[37]

Theodosius was in Scupi on 6 July addressing problems of the imperial fisc in Cappodocia. On 10 August 379 he was at Vicus Augusti on the road from Sirmium to Emona, that is, securely inside Pannonia.[38] His subsequent whereabouts are unknown until 17 November, when he celebrated a victory over the Goths, Alans, and Huns in Constantinople.[39] Gratian too celebrated a victory over the barbarians. Excavation has revealed something more about the general context of this area during the turmoil of Theodosius's reign.

There have been few excavations in Pannonia II except in ancient Sirmium (Sremska Mitrovica) and its environs and the frontier fortifications within the Iron Gates. At some point, perhaps in 379–80, many of the small Roman fortifications inside the Iron Gates sustained significant damage; some were burned.[40] The state of the published finds from these excavations suggests that a few of these fortlets and fortified towers were abandoned prior to the death of Valentinian II in 392. Of course, it is possible, perhaps likely, that some type of military occupation continued without payment in coin here as elsewhere into the fifth century. One site, Rtkovo-Glamija I, has provided a large number of coins distributed among the emperors from Valentinian I through Honorius, in other words at least until the latter's accession in 393.[41] The ceramic evidence establishes an even more imprecise terminus for most sites as sometime between 375 and the middle of the fifth century. In general many, perhaps most, of these small fortlets and towers suffered burning on two occasions toward the end of their Roman phase, and in many places the carefully fortified late fourth century structures were replaced in the course of the fifth century by simple walled enclosures.[42]

There can be no question, however, that by the last quarter of the fourth century it was not uncommon for garrisons at frontier posts in the Iron Gates, as throughout the area, to include soldiers of Germanic extraction, at least as judged by the presence of bone combs of characteristic Germanic shape and design.[43] The combination of a few Germanic items in what were still Roman contexts is, of course, typical of this era along the Danubian and Rhenish frontiers. It seems that in Valeria and the Pannonias primary fortresses fared similarly, but again the degree of chronological precision necessary to distinguish between the events of 379–80 and 392–94 is not to be had.[44] Sándor Soproni is surely correct in summarizing the data from Valeria and two Pannonian provinces by stressing that the events of ca. 380 were difficult indeed but not an unmitigated catastrophe. Rather, the armed conflicts beginning at that time led to a progressive but usually slow decline in the effectiveness of the fortification system and an apparent diminution in the level of troop strengths.

One certain sign of decline was the employment of small groups of barbarians under a Roman-appointed commander as garrisons in a few frontier outposts. The best documented example is the settlement of some Marcommani under a *tribunus gentis Marcomannorum* in Pannonia I not later than 395.[45] Theodosius had had to reduce troop strengths to a minimum in order to field an army against the usurper Magnus Maximus (388). Then in only five years he again had to raise an army to fight the usurpers Arbogastes and Eugenius (392–94). As a result, by his death he had abandoned some fortifications outright, while manning others with barbarian units under "Roman" command. The commanding officers of these barbarians held the rank of tribune. The smallest posts along the frontier were never again garrisoned. Some were burned, perhaps intentionally. The evacuation of fortified towers and fortlets followed logically once the complements of the larger fortifications fell to levels too low to spare troops to post there or to rescue them when attacked. The practice of abandoning the smaller towers was not confined to the area of northern Illyricum. Many of the towers built under Valentinian I met this fate, not necessarily because of any immediate threat.[46]

Within little more than a year following Adrianople, Theodosius had been able to stabilize the military situation, though fewer troops remained in garrison. Most important, he had made real strides toward containing the westward drift of what were probably some very hungry and frustrated barbarians. Certainly his presence at Scupi, between Thessalonica and Naissus, was because of his campaigns, which continued well into Pannonia II. In general, however, Theodosius, often ill, was content to remain in Thessalonica. In Thrace his general Modares, recently raised to *magister militum* and of "royal Scythian ancestry," perhaps meaning that he was a Hun or quite possibly a Goth of ducal rank before entering Roman service, was smashing Gothic resistance.[47]

> The whole of Thrace was now occupied by the above-mentioned peoples [the Goths] and the garrisons in the cities and forts there did not dare go even a short distance outside the walls, let alone engage the enemy in the open. Now Modares, without the barbarians seeing him, led his soldiers up a level, deep-soiled hill which was extensive itself and overlooked wide plains. There he learned from his scouts that the whole enemy force was lying drunk in the plains below the hill after having availed itself of the delicacies in the fields and the unwalled villages. . . .

Thus shortly before dawn the soldiers attacked the barbarians and slaughtered all of them, some not even knowing what was happening, others dying in various ways as soon as they found out. When none of the men was left alive, they plundered the bodies, before turning their attention to the women and children. They captured four thousand wagons and as many prisoners as could be carried in them, apart from those who accompanied them on foot and had a rest by changing places. . . . Thus . . . Thrace was quiet for a while, the barbarians there having been destroyed.[48]

Zosimus goes on to report that all this took place while Theodosius remained in Thessalonica, at which place and time Zosimus erroneously has him reorganize his top command.[49]

The chronology of these events is far from clear despite the relative simplicity of Zosimus's account. In fact, Zosimus either telescoped or omitted so much that there is virtually nothing beyond dispute except for the victory itself. Our other sources, also largely based upon Eunapius of Sardis, are no better. None mentions Modares in this context, although Gregorius Nazianzus later (ca. 382) addressed him as *strategos*.[50] Both Sozomenus's and Socrates's *Historia Ecclesiastica* add but little new information. Sozomenus has Gratian grant Theodosius the government of Illyricum and the East and then immediately turn westward to face the Alamanni, while Theodosius defeated the barbarians along the Danube and "compelled them to sue for peace, and, after accepting hostages from them, proceeded to Thessalonica."[51] Socrates recorded a further point: that before setting out from Sirmium, Gratian and Theodosius divided the "managing of the war against the barbarians."[52] Furthermore, Socrates noted that each emperor obtained a victory over the barbarians, after which Gratian departed for Gaul to confront the Alamanni, and Theodosius erected a trophy and departed for Constantinople. While in Thessalonica the emperor took so ill as to request Christian baptism.[53]

Orosius adds some of his own misunderstandings to what Socrates called the shared "management of the war." According to Orosius, Gratian "placed him [Theodosius] in command of the East and likewise of Thrace." The inclusion of Thrace must be Orosius's textual emendation substituting Thrace for Illyricum, which by the time that Orosius wrote (ca. 417) had in part returned to the West, but then Illyricum was only the diocese of Pannonia with its name changed to Illyricum.[54] In other words, it was sufficient for Orosius that the general Thracian area was placed under Theodosius as emperor.[55] Theodosius then "attacked and overcame the Alans, Huns, and Goths in many battles."[56] Then so as not to exhaust his "small band of Roman troops by constantly making war, he [Theodosius] struck a treaty with Athanaric, king of the Goths."[57]

Concerning these events, Zosimus inserts into his narrative on 381, almost as an aside, Gratian's actions of 380, when he sent assistance to the bedridden Theodosius. In that year Gratian's general Vitalianus, *comes rei militaris* (ca. 380), commanding a Western army, attacked barbarians in Illyricum.

> Meanwhile, the emperor Gratian sent out Vitalianus as Magister, a man totally inadequate to deal with the army's distressed condition. During his command, two *parts* of the trans-Rhenish Germans, one commanded by Fritigern, the other by Alatheus and Saphrax, so menaced the Celtic peoples that Gratian had to authorize them to cross the Danube and occupy Pannonia and Moesia I, providing they first quit Celtic lands. By such plans and efforts he hoped to gain freedom from their constant attacks.[58]

There are problems with this text: the barbarian leaders mentioned were already across the Danube, not the Rhine; and there was no such thing as Celtic lands. "Trans-Rhenish" and "Celtic" were standard literary expressions in the East, commonly used in discussing barbarians. These points aside, the offensive went poorly and Vitalianus ended up giving the barbarians a lot of gifts and recruiting some into the army.[59] It is noteworthy that Vitalianus acting for Gratian reportedly recruited barbarians into service in Moesia I, a province within the decidedly Theodosian diocese of Dacia, as well as in Pannonia. In the very next passage Zosimus reports that some Goths decided to recross the Danube and attack Athanaric.[60]

The "hope" in the passage from Zosimus quoted above was quickly dashed, as Zosimus immediately pointed out.[61] Zosimus here has compressed several different aspects of Vitalianus's campaign and other actions of 379–80 into a few lines, with considerable distortion resulting. Fritigern and many Goths had crossed the Danube three years before and hardly needed permission now. But Zosimus continues: "They crossed the Danube," as agreed, but "with the intention of going through Pannonia to Epirus [often a lure to barbarians over the next century] and thence across the Archelaus to attack the cities of Greece." "They decided first, however, to secure supplies and to topple Athanaric, leader of all the royal family of the Scythians, so as not to have a threat from the rear. Thus attacking him they easily drove him out of his territory, but he went to Theodosius, who was recovered from a grave disease [not before summer 380]."[62] During this same period, Zosimus tells us, Theodosius defeated some Sciri and Carpodaces with Huns among them and forced them to return home.[63] Just how many groups were in movement? Who were these peoples, such as the Carpodaces? Clearly the participants, chronology, and significance of the events presented in this short passage, just one chapter of 37 lines in the standard edition of Zosimus, are far from clear. Orosius condensed everything even further, into a simple statement that Theodosius fought many battles with only a small army.[64] Jordanes reports that Fritigern's Goths struck Epirus, Thessaly, and Achaia, while Saphrax and Alatheus plundered Pannonia.[65]

In late 380 the old Gothic king (*thiudans*) Athanaric was indeed forced from his stronghold probably somewhere in the Carpathian Mountains in central Romania (the former province of Dacia). Only the date of Athanaric's formal entry into Constantinople is known precisely, 11 January 381.[66] Despite having vowed never to set foot upon Roman territory, and thereby having forced the emperor Valens to sign a treaty on a ship in midstream back in 369, the old warrior now asked Theodosius to receive him and his followers into Roman service. In other words, Athanaric asked for *receptio*. It is possible that the ingots that ended up in Transylvania had belonged to some of the barbarians in Illyricum who recrossed the Danube because of Theodosius's campaigns along the Sirmium-Naissus-Stobi highway in 379 and died or were captured fighting Athanaric. It would help if we knew for sure where Athanaric had been before turning up in Constantinople. We do not. We know only that back in 376 walls had been built, perhaps the one stretching between Brahasesti on the Siretul to Stoicani on the Prutul, a distance of 85 km, and somewhere behind them Athanaric had retreated into the interior of the Carpathian Mountains to await the Huns.[67] Feldioara, the location of the ingot datable to 379–80, lies on the Oltul River just north of Brasov, Romania, high in the Carpathians. The Goths had no leader worthy of note still living, for Fritigern had almost certainly died sometime in 380.[68] With Athanaric in Roman service Theodosius might be able to bring about a general peace and end the turmoil in Thrace. We do not know what rank and command Theodosius had in mind for the fallen king when he granted *receptio* in 380.

A fragment of Eunapius, himself a contemporary, notes that about the time that Athanaric sought entry into the Empire the barbarians in Macedonia gave up large-scale operations and returned to hit-and-run tactics, striking from hiding places in the marshes.[69] Theodosius's actions are reported to have restored military morale and allowed the farmers to return to their occupations.[70]

A detailed picture of what actually occurred in 379–80 is beyond our grasp. Nevertheless, we can see the outline of the policies followed and clear evidence that they were generally successful. Rome was engaging many small groups of barbarians and offering them opportunities to enroll in the Roman army. Theodosius was drawing upon units of his best troops from as far away as Egypt to intersperse along the Danube. All of these reports make sense if we hypothesize that Eunapius learned of and recorded many small engagements. Had a much later Byzantine manual not preserved these highlights of minor engagements, many would have passed out of our view forever. Zosimus, Jordanes, and Orosius were at pains to demonstrate other "truths" and compressed greatly. Jordanes was primarily concerned to reveal the long line of Gothic victories and thereby greatness. Orosius sought to magnify the deeds of Theodosius, the establisher of a Christian monopoly of worship. The pagan Zosimus's task was just the reverse. Nonetheless, on the scene the problem confronting Gratian and Theodosius was singularly focused—restrict the area of invasion to roughly a triangle bounded by the Danube, the Rhodope Mountains, and the Julian Alpine defenses.

In 380 Gratian ordered Vitalianus to proceed down the Danubian *limes*, and his thrust took him even into Moesia I. Vitalianus had little need to coordinate with the civilian government as he cut through hostile territory relinking fortified centers. Some barbarians on the opposite bank, probably realizing that the door was closing, asked for and received permission to cross the Danube. They were lucky. Theodosius's generals fought against small clusters of barbarians all along the southern tier of the triangle and opened the Thessalonica-Stobi-Naissus-Sirmium road.

Not all of the defeated barbarians would accept the obligations of *receptio*—specifically enrollment and some degree of dispersal within the Roman army; these took the only other option given them, that of returning to their homes across the Danube. The Carpodaces, if we may trust the name, may well have been a remnant of the Carpi, some of whom had merged with Goths in the course of the third and fourth centuries while others were settled in the Empire. In fact, there had been an encampment of Carpi along the Danube near to where Valens spent the winter of 368, perhaps founded long before but still bearing the name *vicus Carpi*.[71] Other Carpi were still distinguishable as a group in Pannonia, having been established there by Diocletian (284–305). In fact, Maximinus, the praetorian prefect of the Gauls, 371–76, claimed a distant ancestry to the Carpi settled there.[72] In 380 the Carpodaces chose not to reside permanently in the Empire, and, with a few Sciri and Huns, recrossed the Danube. They could not have gone home without imperial consent, for the river was closed. So, passes in hand and probably gold to boot, these barbarians faced new opponents: either the Huns, who were rapidly consolidating their hold on the region, or those Goths under Athanaric who in early 380 still remained holed up somewhere in the Carpathian Mountains.

Those accepting enrollment in the Roman army might have found themselves in an encampment like the *vicus Carpi*, or they might have had to say good-bye to the Balkans forever and go where ordered. Some of these groups were split and their fragments enrolled in the army in new units perhaps bearing one of their accepted names. This seems the likely explanation for those units listed in the *Notitia dignitatum* with two names for the same people; for example Visi and Tervingi from some of the Goths recruited under Theodosius.[73] On at least one occasion newly enrolled barbarians and regular troops crossed paths while proceeding to their new duty stations. One group of barbarians was to replace men taken from Egypt and transferred to the Danube, and in the process of changing places they met in Lydia. Fistfights followed. The Egyptians came out of the scuffle on top. Both, however, continued to their destinations. These barbarians were commanded, at least henceforth, by Hormisdus, a Persian by birth but a seasoned veteran who had campaigned with Julian in the Persian wars. The Goths were outclassed by the well-trained "Egyptians," but obviously their new Roman commander would have ample time to instruct his new recruits along the Nile before they saw real action.[74] The incident recalls many inter-service rivalries in modern armies. More significantly, it illustrates another aspect of traditional *receptio*: the regular transfer and integration of new recruits under trustworthy Roman commanders. As Ammianus reminded his readers, many of these Roman officers had barbarians for parents.[75] That Hormisdus was of Persian ancestry was as irrelevant now as it had been when he fought against the Persians with Julian. Equally inconsequential was the fact that Vitalianus, the *comes rei militaris* leading Western Roman forces in Illyricum in 380, was from the Gothic-speaking Heruli, for both Hormisdus and Vitalianus had risen through the system since Julian's days.

The Egyptian elements arrived in the Balkans only to find, according to Zosimus, that all discipline had vanished among the Macedonian units, with the barbarian recruits freely loitering about and thereby confusing their legion's operations.[76] This seems to be an oblique reference to bottlenecks at the processing points. In such circumstances Theodosius himself was almost slain in a night ambush against his camp, when roving barbarians "crossed the river unopposed."[77] Logically, this passage must report a raid from Epirus Nova into Macedonia and later into Thessalia, where, we know from Zosimus, "they took over the unprotected area and let the cities be, in hope of gaining a reasonable tribute from them."[78] The raiders' aggressiveness alone could not take the towns and force access to supplies, so in a short time they had to disperse into the hills from which they had come. Theodosius left appropriate garrisons in "the forts [probably in the passes] and walled cities" before departing for Constantinople to greet Athanaric. All these events are usually assigned to 380. If we are correct, they may have followed the occupation of Epirus by those groups so authorized by Gratian earlier in 380. These actions help explain the fact that Gratian's plan to relieve pressure along the frontiers of the Danube had temporarily sacrificed the security of the diocese of Macedonia. It appears that the integrity of the Danubian *limes* itself was restored no later than early 381 and was further strengthened by the recruitment of Athanaric's followers. Gratian reached Viminacium in Moesia I without difficulty in 382.[79] Rather than explore strategy, Zosimus stressed Theodosius's weakening of the army through barbarianization, but this smacks of the standard literary devices used to castigate an emperor.

As if there were not already sufficient ambiguity, Jordanes, writing in the middle of the sixth century and drawing to an uncertain extent upon Cassiodorus's *Getica* (or *Gothic History*), adds several new dimensions. Jordanes is very late and wrote for a different audience, and so must be approached with extreme caution. Nevertheless, although much of his account is clearly slanted toward his own society's needs and aspirations and the visions of his mentor Cassiodorus, he adds what appear to be factual details for which there seems little editorial inspiration. While Theodosius was gravely ill, he says, the Goths, with renewed boldness, again rose to plunder. This time Fritigern struck "Thessaly, Epirus, and Achaia while Alatheus and Saphrax with the rest of the troops made for Pannonia." So far this is essentially the same account as recorded in Zosimus. Gratian was in Gaul fighting Vandals along the Rhine but nonetheless ordered troops pushed across the Alps and into action. Jordanes continues, now going beyond Zosimus or any other source: "He put no trust in arms, but sought to conquer them by kindness, giving them needed supplies and gifts. Thus he entered on a truce (*foedere fecit*) with them and made peace, giving them provisions." [80] This would have been in 380. Next Jordanes reports the standard account of Athanaric in Constantinople with certain rhetorical flourishes and some colorful details.[81]

There are several possible interpretations of the events of 379–80 and their relative chronology, primarily those offered by Várady, Demougeot, and Chrysos. Building upon Várady's contributions, Demougeot has argued that the "truce" of the *Getica* applied to the so-called Alatheus–Saphrax group and was technically the first instance of the creation of the new federates, i.e., independent, virtually autonomous allies under their own leadership and within the Empire. She suggests that Theodosius accepted these decisions as, in fact, Jordanes specifically states. According to Demougeot, Theodosius used this "truce" as the essential precedent for his own establishments of federates, first those of Athanaric and then the followers of Fritigern. This train of events culminated in 382 with the peace celebrated by Themistius in oration 16.[82] Demougeot's theory is, however, open to doubt.

First of all, the stress on Alatheus and Saphrax by Cassiodorus-Jordanes cannot simply be taken at face value to mean that they were the leaders of a group comparable to Fritigern's. Second, there is no reason to believe that the Romans regarded these various peoples as constituting a *gens* or *natio* for the purposes of group recognition and a higher level of diplomatic status. Besides, these people were *inside* the Empire where standard diplomatic niceties did not apply. The Roman aim was *receptio*, not the creation of barbarian enclaves inside the Empire. Alatheus and Saphrax were after all at best only the guardians of Videric, heir to Ermanaric, and, as such, representatives of the future continuity and greatness of Ostrogothic history in the eyes of sixth-century Jordanes. A major thesis of Jordanes's *Getica* is the flow of greatness in all rivulets of Gothic blood, but particularly that of its kings. That noble blood, and the noble deeds it inspired, together justified and legitimized the rule of Theodoric in the minds of his people. Thus achieved, Theodoric's ancestral legitimacy paralleled Roman dynastic consciousness for Jordanes and Cassiodorus, and provided another support to their vision of a restored imperial greatness shared between Goths and Romans. What is equally clear—but this time from the far more reliable contemporary sources, especially Ammianus Marcellinus—is that the so-called Alatheus-Saphrax group was not the major element of either the Greutungi or the alliance loosely fastened to Fritigern. Roman writers acknowledged Fritigern as being the preeminent leader of the Goths just prior to the Battle of Adrianople.[83] No Roman recognized his right to be king inside the Empire.

In fact, with the cities and garrisons still holding, supplying any large group for long was an impossibility for the native leaders. That fact was a basic premise behind the entire Roman system. Supplies were the key to military operations, and they remained under Roman control. To establish cohesive groups of barbarians would have entailed a major and permanent diversion of the supply network of the dioceses in question. This diversion in turn would have left some traces in the legal and administrative records.

None are evident; all seems to have been proceeding as usual. In fact, since the civilian government was entirely centered in the towns, it was quite safe from barbarian influence. Moreover, militarily there was as yet no need to contemplate so desperate an innovation as barbarian autonomy. Traditional *receptio* did require that the enemy be first defeated. The awkward fact was that this had not yet occurred. But hungry Goths could not live off the land in large groups, even if tacitly admitted that way, and had no alternative but to disperse. Even if Rome had so wished, there were very few places where the government could have supplied these barbarians en masse from existing stores. Only in small groups could they be dealt with by the surviving communities. And in such groups the Roman authorities could integrate them into existing garrisons or, if need be, the forces of the central authority could defeat them in battle.

There is likewise no archaeological evidence (such as an unusually large cluster of burials with peculiarly Gothic materials dating to this era) of the Alatheus-Saphrax group's independent existence. The great "first treasure of Szilágysomlyó" is not an exception as sometimes thought, for it seems to be an early fifth century cache and of decidedly unclear ownership. The slender physical evidence associated with the events of the last quarter of the fourth century found in this area, particularly materials from Regölyi and Csákár, suggest the continuation of the practice of routinely dispersing new recruits behind the frontier and their gradual integration into the existing military structure.[84] The integration of new troops—probably including the so-called Alatheus-Saphrax groups—into existing ones would naturally have created new challenges for the local commanders.[85] Once we accept that the forces following Alatheus and Saphrax were small and vulnerable, there is no mystery about their inconsistent behavior. As in the third century, some members of such units might have served for a time under their own leaders, now accorded Roman rank, while others ended up elsewhere.

According to the literary sources, some establishment of barbarians must have been accomplished along the Drau in the area of Iovia (modern Ludbreg) and Poetovio (modern Ptiys). Saint Jerome speaks of his birthplace Stridon as plundered.[86] The epitaph of Amantius, bishop of Iovia, refers to his success in the area (ca. 380–400) under the "two peoples and paired dukes." This is usually given as testifying to his efforts toward the Gothic-Alanic-Hunnic group here under discussion.[87] The relevant lines of the text read, "dign(u)s, ita geminis ducibus consortia sacra participare fidei, consilio regere, . . . bis denis binis populis presidit in annis."[88] The inscription derives from Aquileia, Amantius's place of burial. Várady suggests

Alatheus and Saphrax as the paired leaders and Alatheus's Ostrogoths and the Alanic-Hunnic group of Saphrax as the two peoples, and he further accepts the date of 379 as the effective one for the actions.[89] Mócsy believes that "the two peoples" cannot be determined, but asserts that Alatheus and Saphrax were certainly the *duces*.[90] Amantius's special holy relationship with the two *duces* apparently refers to some type of mission. A conversion (to Orthodoxy in this case) seems to have been an accepted aspect of *receptio* in the second half of the fourth century.

Mursa on the Drau near its confluence with the Danube may have been damaged in Theodosius's actions of 379.[91] The Roman commander was probably Maiorianus, *mag. mil.*, stationed at Aquincum and assigned to Theodosius at Sirmium in January 379.[92] Thus all that seems certain is that the towns in the Drau valley witnessed attacks and counterattacks and probably the recruitment of barbarians (including the Alatheus-Saphrax groups) during the years immediately following Adrianople. The attackers do not seem to have been numerous. Libanius, the famous sophist and teacher at Antioch (314–393), may have had Pannonia in mind when he drafted his 24th oration, obviously written before Theodosius's victory celebrated on 17 November 379, but after Adrianople (August 378). Libanius cast a sense of profound foreboding:

> These last disasters are obviously those of an ill-starred people. We have lost twenty-five provinces, and the natives who lived outside walled towns have been taken off as prisoners, while those inside eat up everything they have and then, when they die of starvation, they are not even buried, but their relatives drag them up to the top of the wall and throw the poor wretches down from there, naked. Such is the carnival that the Goths have held. Up to now they used to shiver every time they heard mention of the Romans' skill in warfare, but now they are victorious, and we die, nobly and as befits brave men, but perishing all the same. And now that those who have spent their lives in arms have gone, we resort to our peasantry. We can expect the worst and have no gleam of hope unless you take my advice, Sire, and do away with what I affirm to be the cause of our troubles.[93]

It is important to stress, however, that although the picture of undefended peasants being carried off as prisoners is moving and even may be correct, there is ample evidence elsewhere that imperial troops were fighting and winning. The state was not thrust into the hands of its peasantry, peasants themselves running, hiding, and dealing with the powers that be. What was the professed motive of this melancholy oration? The allegedly unavenged death of the emperor Julian! It was not until the invasion of Radagaisus in 405 that we have certain proof of refugees from Pannonia. These apparently included Amantius, who returned to his birthplace of Aquileia sometime prior to his death in 413.

What does all this imply about Gratian's peace of 380? He granted supplies to some barbarians, recruited as many as possible into the regular military units (significantly, for service in the vicinity), and probably supported missionary activity by Amantius and perhaps others.[94] Imperial actions and the lack of any demonstrable future group activity by these barbarians[95] suggest that Gratian, hard-pressed as he was, and despite the fact that his generals sometimes operated in territory at the time not technically his, did not depart radically from the mechanisms of *receptio*. The barbarians, moreover, still posed a serious threat. Could it be that they too had no other goals in mind than those originally articulated by Alavivus and later Fritigern, i.e., permission to participate in *receptio*? And this despite their apparent successes? The answer seems to be yes, *receptio* is what they were after. Supplies were probably the major issue, for doubtless the obstinacy of Roman towns and strongholds aggravated the logistical situation among the Goths and their allies.

The Romans, however, could not relocate these new barbarian recruits as had been customary prior to Adrianople. One reason was the large number of recruits, another the precariousness of transport on the roads. Instead, they dispersed them into existing units in the vicinity. Even this must have taken advanced preparations no longer apparent in our sources but necessarily included as a part of imperial instructions. The traditional mechanism used along the Rhine as early as 286 to create units of Germanic colonizers, *laeti*, could have guided Gratian's planning. However, *laeti*, farmer-soldiers with their families, were established from among recent immigrants, and were closely supervised by the Roman military prefects, as we can still observe in the *Notitia dignitatum*. They could upon occasion serve on campaign elsewhere. Such units cannot be shown to have existed in Pannonia, although occasionally one will turn up on a special assignment in the Balkans.[96] Indeed, if the barbarian groups in question were those of Alatheus and Saphrax, as seems possible, then the *laeti* precedents could not have been easily implemented. Ammianus was clear that the Goths with Fritigern were in family groups but that the Greutungi and others crossed later in secret with their mounts. In other words, the groups around Alatheus and Saphrax constituted mounted warbands of men only. As such they would have been recruited as a unit (*numerus*) or units into the Roman army. The case of Vitalianus, who became a *comes rei militaris*, shows how high such native barbarian leaders could rise in the late fourth century.[97]

Fritigern, Fravitta, Eruilf, Modares, Vitalianus, Colias, and many other "Gothic" leaders are known from contemporary sources to have agreed to serve Rome. Fravitta, Eruilf, Modares, and Vitalianus appear in the records only after they had risen high in imperial service. Many other Germanic soldiers reached the highest ranks under Theodosius, Richomeres and Hellebich to name but two. What is striking about the Gothic nobles at the time of Adrianople is their inability to cooperate among themselves and the willingness of most to serve Rome. Such Gothic independence was traditional. There were no Gothic organizational structures which could rival those of Rome for scope or cohesion. The Roman victories of Modares, recounted from Zosimus above, capture a sense of the Gothic presence in the area around Naissus, Ulpiana, and Scupi. Prudence demands that we reject the figures of 4,000 prisoners and wagons taken, but the remainder of the account could have described a raid under Valentinian I against barbarian villages across the Danube. What if for the sake of argument we momentarily assume that Alatheus and Saphrax commanded two such groups and that still other barbarian forces existed, including groups like those surprised by Modares? All known data are in harmony with this hypothesis.

The Romans and particularly Theodosius knew precisely how to deal with barbarians and so too did Gratian: with gifts according to rank, provisions, and employment in the Roman army. Theodosius often gave such presents as armbands, torques, and other special ornaments of personal attire. Earlier in the century Valentinian I carefully and ceremoniously presented gifts to Quadi and Alamanni.[98] The insignia of the *comes sacrarum largitionum* in the *Notitia dignitatum* for both the East and West portray fibulae, belt buckles, ingots, treasure chests, etc., in addition to coins as items characteristic of the emperor's largess (see illustration 5).[99] Probably the first treasure of Szilágysomlyó reflects such a gift-giving mentality; however, the predominance of late pieces, barbarous imitations, or reworked Roman heirlooms within this great collection of medallions suggest that the emperor's ability to provide had been compromised. These inferior pieces might best be explained as having been created by rather good but clearly unofficial Roman craftsmen. Nevertheless the neatly ordered items of varying size and weight make the hoard seem to have been destined for distribution among some great chief's followers by order of rank. Who among the great princes placed the order, to whom they were to be awarded, and when the different pieces were made, remain parts of a riddle.[100] Other near-contemporary hoards, e.g., Kertch, offer similar and perhaps less controversial examples of the pervasiveness of the practice, and of the Roman inspiration for many of the items making up the exchange.[101] The point

Illustration 5. The insignias of *Comites sacrarum largitionum* from the *Notitia dignitatum*

here is that this pattern of treatment was traditional, and so too was the granting of supplies and even temporary billets as a step in the eventual assignment and redistribution of barbarian recruits. We need search no further than the provisions made for the Goths themselves prior to the uprisings leading to Adrianople.

There is no doubt that the payments made under Theodosius were official and very substantial, demanding, in fact, the official issuance of gold ingots from the imperial government's *fabricae*. There is a possibility that the ingots we now possess were part of the booty taken by the barbarians, but that seems very unlikely. Such a cache would have required them to attack the emperor and his *comitatus* directly, an event unlikely to have escaped the notice of Eunapius and his derivative historians. The barbarians were not naive. They would only accept official gold.

If Theodosius's gold ingots were a continuation of the *tributa* once paid to allies beyond the Empire, then giving them to autonomous barbarians inside the Empire indeed represented a notable departure from precedent. Tribute payment was not necessarily their purpose, although possible. More likely, this gold was a payment to barbarian leaders about to be recruited into the Roman army, whose followers required provisions obtainable only in a very tight market. Alternatively, it might have been payment to induce them to quit the Empire entirely, buying supplies while crossing Roman territory. The repeatedly demonstrated fact was that food was difficult for the barbarians to find after their first raids. Emergency provisionment often took the form of payment in cash before and long after the events in question. Even as late as the 480s, when true *foederati* were commonplace in every respect, Zeno agreed to pay Theodoric the Great for his settlement near Pautalia "two hundred pounds of gold to buy the provisions necessary for survival."[102] Such a sum, if actually paid rather than advanced as vouchers for requisition, would have been paid in ingots.

In the fourth century as in the late fifth the presupposition was that the Roman communities still held the grains and other supplies in question and would sell them to the barbarians for cash if so authorized (and perhaps even if not) or would receive credit against their taxes. As early as Constantine, payment of taxes in bullion was urged by the imperial government. There are fairly numerous examples, in fact, of the Roman government between Constantine and Theodosius exploring possible use of bullion payments for large financial transactions.[103] The "provisioning" of various Gothic factions (ca. 379–80) was certainly a large and problematic operation, but the policies and concepts employed to handle them were traditional and remained so into the next century. These were not merely a set of legal niceties designed to preserve Rome's pride. The basic system of welcoming barbarians through *receptio* prevailed. There is no mention of exceptional tribute under Theodosius in the extant sources, not even in Zosimus, who would have relished the opportunity to so expose the emperor. Although Theodosius through his generals defeated various barbarian groups, taking many hostages, he personally spent much of 380 ill in Thessalonica.[104] So Gratian took the initiative in the northern part of the theater of operations for him, formally requesting that Theodosius ratify the measures he took. That was done, and Gratian's actions were indeed just as if Theodosius had ordered them himself.

With whom did Gratian then conclude the "truce" in 380? Even Jordanes does not say, and he surely would have had it been Alatheus or Saphrax. Nor does he claim that any lands whatsoever were awarded. Zosimus would have the barbarians occupy specific territories but without temporal qualifications. No wonder Theodosius "was very well pleased and gave his assent." Vitalianus, acting for Gratian, must have concluded *receptio* agreements with many minor leaders in the course of his campaigns. In every sense Gratian's actions were in accord with precedent and probably with the policies understood since his meeting with Theodosius in Sirmium. Furthermore, since some, perhaps most, of these events apparently took place in territory then officially under the ailing Theodosius, specifically Pannonia II, this would explain why Theodosius was asked to give his assent. Theodosius himself and his generals continued to "divide and conquer" throughout the next decade and more, but, after the restoration of the diocese of Pannonia to Gratian's control in September 380, Western commanders routinely dealt with incidents there.[105]

Some of the divisions that resulted from Theodosius's policies were not just statistical but quite personal. Late in his reign (ca. 393) a dispute arose between Fravitta and Eriulf at a banquet celebrating the former's wedding to a Roman woman.[106] After too much wine the two Gothic *duces*, now Roman commanders, squared off against one another over a point of honor. The issue was their duty to the emperor versus their oaths of eternal opposition to Rome, pledges apparently struck secretly at the time that they had entered Theodosius's service. Fravitta argued for the former, Eriulf the latter. Each man had his supporters, Eriulf more. Theodosius sent the revelers home, but once they were outside, Fravitta fatally wounded Eriulf. Both had, in fact, moved swiftly upward within Roman service, but that was hardly novel by this time.[107] "*Imitatio Romana*" was a very common theme, but Eriulf would have nothing to do with it.

Chronologically confused as these first years were, perhaps a few points are clear enough to arrange and build upon:

(1) In January 379, Theodosius and Gratian, while at Sirmium, decided upon a joint plan to contain and ultimately integrate the new barbarians. This plan demanded an overall control of the threatened areas and required that the immediate buffer zones be under unified command. The prefecture of Illyricum with its dioceses of Dacia, Macedonia, and Pannonia was to be temporarily administered by Theodosius along with the permanent assignment to him of all the lands formerly ruled by Valens. Thus the emperors planned for a unified command of the threatened areas of the Balkan peninsula.

(2) Next, Theodosius proceeded to Thessalonica, where he arrived no later than June 379. Gratian remained in support at Aquileia, the nexus of the Julian Alpine defenses. By late July he was at Milan. He did not recross the Alps until after 3 August, probably passing through Bolzano on 19 August en route to Trier.

(3) Later in 379, Theodosius launched an attack via the Scupi-Naissus highway and into Pannonia, successfully fragmenting barbarian forces, including certain Alans, Huns, and Goths. Gratian's forces too seem to have achieved some results against those bands further west earlier in the year, although most were technically within Theodosius's sphere. Both emperors celebrated victories. Perhaps they actually drove some barbarians back across the Danube or bribed them with "gifts" to return to the troubled lands still under Athanaric's rule. They recruited others, possibly including Alatheus and Saphrax, into Roman service.

(4) Theodosius's health failed and Gratian had to resume the direct supervision of events in the Pannonian area, although at that moment it was not officially his to control.

(5) The bands of barbarians driven out in 379 soon returned with others, some perhaps new to Roman soil. By 380 the imperial policy of restoring the *limes*'s integrity, especially along the Danube itself, was in jeopardy, but throughout this entire period the principal garrisons held firm. Theodosius was ill. Gratian, the senior Augustus, took action, but with only very limited manpower at his disposal, since the bulk of his army was tied down on the Rhine. Both emperors integrated new recruits into the existing units where and when possible throughout the East. Considerable success in this pol-

icy had already neutralized many barbarian groups. Others were scattered and in hiding by 380.

(6) On the other hand, some of those beyond the frontiers were more and more troublesome, the probable result of the return of various groups to the far bank of the Danube. As Theodosius recuperated, their attacks intensified. Thus in 380 Gratian admitted some in order to relieve pressure along the *limes*, especially in the area near the mouth of the Drau River. This action was in keeping with the policy already familiar under the tetrarchs, when for example Diocletian settled groups of Carpi on Roman soil in the Dobrudja. Of the post-Adrianople groups only those led by (a) Alatheus and Saphrax and (b) Fritigern, who certainly never returned to the lands north of the Danube, are mentioned by name. The emperors intended that these barbarians "occupy" parts of Pannonia and Moesia (areas under Theodosius and perhaps pacified in the previous campaigns of 379). Gratian sought and obtained Theodosius's assent and support for these actions taken in his stead. The barbarians, however, had other goals; they sought instead to enter the as yet undisturbed province of Epirus Nova and plunder Macedonia and Thessaly.

(7) Some of these groups, specifically those who had recrossed the Danube in 379, forced the only Gothic power north of the Danube to leave for Constantinople. Thus did Athanaric early in 381 break his oath made in 369 never to set foot on Roman soil. Some of the raiders attacking Athanaric perhaps planned to return eventually and permanently to their ancestral lands, free of Athanaric. They were given supplies, and perhaps the gold bars found in Transylvania, before leaving Roman soil and, if these hypotheses are valid, may have buried some of the ingots in Transylvania for safekeeping while they attacked Athanaric or renewed their attacks on Roman territory. If they lived long enough to return to the Empire, they never went back to reclaim their gold. This fact might serve as another reminder of the restoration of Rome's control of the river and its success at recruitment, or simply testify that the raiders were themselves but mortal—they died. There are, of course, other hypotheses (booty from raids, etc.) to explain the presence of gold bars in Transylvania. Throughout 380 the cities of Macedonia, Epirus Nova, and Thessaly held, but as usual the countryside suffered.

(8) Nonetheless, the autumn of 380 witnessed Gratian and Theodosius again both in Sirmium, most likely meeting in late August or early September. They probably met to restore traditional civil and mili-

tary government and thereby end Theodosius's temporary control of the diocese of Pannonia and to discuss the future conduct of the Balkan war now that the tide seemed in their favor. In essence, the emperors concluded the western Balkan campaigns, allowing Theodosius to concentrate his efforts closer to Constantinople—in Dacia, Macedonia, and especially Thrace proper. The diocese of Pannonia then would have returned to regular government under a *vicarius*, who reported to the praetorian prefect of Italy.[108] Gratian may have pressed Theodosius about when he anticipated returning the rest of Illyricum, but of that we know nothing. Eutropius, Theodosius's appointment for praetorian prefect of Illyricum, continued in office alone. This meant that for awhile the integrity of the prefecture of Illyricum was sacrificed to military necessity, but Pannonia no longer required military operations.

(9) None of the events of 378–80 shook Roman resolve. Theodosius's generals were active throughout this period. Theodosius continued his offensives personally whenever his health and circumstances permitted and was almost slain in a raid on his camp while on campaign in the autumn of 380 (probably in early November). But it was a raid and nothing more, and as usual the raiders could not long remain in the area without appropriating its supplies, which were by then safe behind city walls. Theodosius, scarcely unnerved by these actions, simply left garrisons there in Thessaly and Macedonia while he himself departed for the capital to prepare for the welcoming of Athanaric. During 381 he coordinated with Gratian further offensive action in the area where he had been ambushed. Gratian's actions to release pressure along the frontier, which the unjustly damned Vitalianus carried out earlier in 380, was one part of this year's campaigns to divide and conquer. Those actions, however, represented neither a permanent concession nor a fundamental modification of Roman policy. Vitalianus's placating measures were wildly misunderstood by those in Constantinople. Setting the entire Balkan peninsula straight would only take a little longer because of these emergencies. The balance of forces to guard the border defenses and to defeat and absorb the barbarians within was extremely delicate and had to respond to the ever-changing realities.

(10) The westward expansion was checked. The river line was secured. Constantinople held firm and no significant barbarian forces entered Greece. The Empire had sealed off most of the Balkans from further damaging incursion.

The year 380 ended in anticipation of Athanaric's arrival. Nothing could have been more auspicious than to recruit the great Athanaric into Roman service. He and his followers constituted a potentially precious resource for the army. No important positions were in hostile hands, and Roman forces were in overall control, although the system was still clearly fragmented with considerable isolation and deprivation, particularly perhaps in central Thrace. The great Athanaric could be expected to draw off most of the remaining Gothic groups to his own and therefore Roman service, just as so many other barbarian leaders of lesser note had done for generations. There was still much for Theodosius to do. Nevertheless, by the spring of 381 the crisis had passed, and passed within the context of the traditional responses to a breakthrough of barbarians. The situation continued to improve as one barbarian group after another was isolated and defeated. The costs, however, were high.

Summary

The problems posed by the defeat at Adrianople were met by traditional military responses at least up to 381. Imperial cooperation was manifest. The basic coping mechanism was still *receptio*, although presumably one far more complex than any heretofore seen in Roman history, especially in that previously Rome had driven the barbarians out before letting them in. This too was attempted when possible. However, let us not exaggerate. The similar solutions to barbarian invasion explored by Probus, Diocletian, Constantine, and others toward the end of the third century may have involved essentially the same choices. The need to break radically from Roman tradition and create new, large, and permanent forces, the *foederati* under their own leaders, within the Empire, did not arise in the aftermath of Adrianople. The military system employed throughout the campaigns of Theodosius, seen here for the first time, might be compared to a simple cellular animal in which foreign bodies from time to time cross the membrane into the heart of the organism, only to be gradually devoured by the host and their elements integrated into the cell itself. In the case of Roman vulnerability immediately after Adrianople, the greatest threat was posed in the western Balkans. Accordingly, it was precisely there that Gratian and Theodosius concentrated their efforts during the first two years of Theodosius's reign. Diplomatic, legal, and political precedents, or the lack of them, were problems subordinate to military necessities.

CONCLUDING THE
GOTHIC WARS

Libanius's twenty-fourth Oration, on avenging the death of Julian, should serve as a warning that even well placed contemporaries did not necessarily know the operational details of the imperial army in the field. Perhaps there are no completely reliable sources in antiquity, but credible sources are especially scarce for these years of intense military activity. Nevertheless, the situation at the end of 380 is tolerably clear. Two major problems of 379–80 had been solved: the area of incursion had been sealed on the western and southern flanks, and the threat of barbarian "reinforcements" arriving from beyond the Danube had been nullified. Theodosius with some important aid from his Western colleague had opened and maintained communications along the Emona-Sirmium road and thence via Naissus and Scupi to Thessalonica. Furthermore, it seems very likely that a drive southward from Aquincum under Maiorianus in 379 had restored the integrity of the *limes* in the area of Mursa and the confluence of the Drau River with the Danube. In 380, Theodosius lay gravely ill in Thessalonica where he remained from January until August. During his indisposition Gratian acted to relieve the pressure by concluding an agreement admitting groups of barbarians into the Empire. This concession was made on condition that the newcomers would be deployed to strengthen the garrisons along the Drau, not as front-line troops. In a manner that remains obscure, some of the barbarians decided to abandon Roman territory and return to their former lands beyond the Danube. There they proceeded to topple Athanaric, who had remained north of the Danube throughout.

Some of the barbarians concluding agreements with Gratian's general Vitalianus probably were those Greutungi, Alans, and Huns led by Alatheus and Saphrax and who had played a role at Adrianople all out of proportion to their limited numbers. Once the barbarians still seeking to cross into Roman territory had done so and, like those following Alatheus and Saphrax, had been assigned their positions and perhaps instructed in the basic tenets of the Orthodox Christian faith, the military situation eased. Gratian and Theodosius concluded that conditions along the western flank had stabilized and the emergency conditions that had necessitated transferring all of Illyricum to Theodosius were no longer compelling. Gratian arrived in Sirmium no later than 2 August 380, Theodosius by 8 September. There they agreed to restore the diocese of Pannonia to the original jurisdictional boundaries. By 20 September Theodosius was once again in Thessalonica and gravely ill, this time to the point of receiving baptism. With his health suddenly restored, he resumed campaigning that autumn. He arrived in Constantinople on 24 November to celebrate a victory and was on hand to welcome the fleeing Athanaric with great pomp on 11 January 381. Gratian too celebrated a victory.[1] The Roman plan must have been to use Athanaric to further weaken the unity of the Gothic forces still operating in Thrace. The Gothic king's untimely death on 25 January, only two weeks after his arrival, thwarted that idea. Nonetheless, his men eagerly swore allegiance to Rome and were integrated into the Roman units along the Danube, thereby strengthening the northern side of the box that now enclosed the remaining barbarian forces, primarily Goths. Here then was a traditional *receptio*. The followers of Athanaric, dwelling until then beyond the Danube, were not given special treatment upon entry into the Empire and clearly were integrated into the regular army units, where they continued to serve Rome with unquestioned loyalty for many years.[2]

Throughout the first half of 381, Theodosius remained in the capital tending ecclesiastical affairs that included the Council of Constantinople, which lasted until 6 July, and the election of Gregory of Nazianzus as Bishop of Constantinople. He then departed for Heraclea probably on 20 July, and was conducting business there by the next day. There is nothing in the legal codes to suggest that anything concerning the barbarian incursions was discussed, but, of course, the codes only reflect those matters addressed at law. Nonetheless, they do locate the emperor and the court in late July and August and leave no doubt that the emperor was not on campaign. The emperor's next known location was Adrianople, where on 5 September he took measures for recruitment. The edict gives sharp testimony to the times:

> If any person by the disgraceful amputation of his fingers should evade the use of arms, he shall not escape that service which he seeks to avoid, but he shall be branded with a stigma, and he shall perform military service imposed as a labor, since he has declined it as an honor. The option shall be unalterably decreed for the provincials, who because of such au-

dacity in those persons often suffer a shortage of the recruits whom they have to supply, that when recruits begin to be demanded from them in common at the time when the levy is being made, they may furnish two mutilated recruits for one whole one, by the direction of Your Eminence.[3]

By 28 September Theodosius was back in Constantinople, where he was to remain almost continuously until the summer of 384.[4] Significantly, there is no gap in the datable edicts issued from the capital of sufficient length for him to have mounted an unnoticed imperial campaign. The actions against the barbarians had passed into a mopping-up operation conducted by his generals and their lieutenants.

The demands of the imperial office were all but overwhelming by the late fourth century and anchored Theodosius to the capital. The office required so much of its holder because all major command decisions concerning diplomatic and military policy emanated from the emperor. Unlike other areas of policy where his chief advisers can be seen directly involved in the process,[5] we are left largely in the dark concerning the role of advisers in the formulation of military decisions. However, since the military was so central to the creation and support of the emperorship, and since Theodosius was a tested field commander himself, there can be little doubt that the emperor personally directed policy during these crucial years. The basic plan to suppress and absorb the barbarian incursions in the Balkans was still in place. Now that the area of penetration had been limited, the objective was to reduce, fragment, and eliminate pockets of resistance. It is not surprising that the first areas to attract attention were precisely those areas where the emperor had himself almost been killed in ambush, Thessaly and Macedonia, in November 380.

Gratian, none too pleased, according to Zosimus, dispatched his *magister militum* Bauto assisted by Arbogastes. This was probably rather early in 381.[6] Thessaly and Macedonia were administered from Constantinople, so Gratian, himself in need of all the troops he could get for campaigns against the Alamanni, cannot be blamed for a few hard feelings. What mattered was a quick and powerful response to the situation, and Gratian delivered. Bauto and Arbogastes were top-notch field commanders of proven loyalty and efficiency. The barbarians foraging in the hinterlands of Macedonia and Thessaly fled at the approach of the Western troops. Bauto's force had probably marched eastward along the via Egnatia, assisted by the garrisons and provisions provided by order of Theodosius before his departure for Constantinople. The fleeing barbarians crossed into Thrace but could find no sustenance left from their previous forays—the towns and granaries were safely fortified; the system worked—and therefore sent representatives to imperial authorities in Thrace pledging their loyalty and support in whatever the emperor should command. In short they requested and received *receptio*. When word of this spread, others entered "the gates of Rome" through imperial service.[7] Since they had fled into Eastern territory they would have pledged obedience to Theodosius first. Traces remain of a systematic relinking of the defensive system throughout the Thracian diocese during Theodosius's reign and, although difficult to date precisely, they best fit the circumstances of 381 to 386.

In order for the defensive system to function as designed each component ultimately had to be linked with other units by road until all parts were interconnected. Even along the Danube itself road transportation provided for the daily comings and goings associated with life in the walled cities and fortifications. Prior to his successful campaigns against the supporters of Procopius and then in preparation for the transdanubian operations against the Goths in 367–69, Valens had shown himself well aware of the necessity of adequate transportation and communications by paying careful attention to road and bridge repair as well as augmenting the garrisons in passes and strategic focal points. Fortunately his efforts are demonstrable in the literary record. Parallel information about Theodosius is scanty by comparison.

Only occasional milestones and building inscriptions still attest to the work done during Theodosius's reign in this regard, but their testimony is sufficient to prove that the plan was coherent and consistently followed. All date from the years after Arcadius was declared Augustus in 383 and before Honorius too shared the honor in 393. More precision is impossible. With such evidence it is safe to conclude that work was done on the section of road between Serdica and Philippopolis.[8] The road from Odessos and the Black Sea to Marcianopolis, a very important transportation nexus and sometimes imperial residence during Valens's campaigns, was also repaired.[9] Workers labored too on the road going north from Marcianopolis and joining the *limes* road at Sucidava and on to Noviodunum in northernmost Scythia.[10] The important road between Philippopolis and Nicopolis ad Nestum, which then followed the course of the Nestus River south to the via Egnatia on an as yet unestablished route, was repaired, thereby providing strategic access through the Rhodope Mountains. This route was always of vital importance throughout all late Roman Balkan campaigns.[11] If all the entries on these and other milestones were taken into account, not simply those dated to the reign of Theodosius, one fact is striking. The Romans typically undertook road projects in this area when planning and carrying out campaigns, not to tidy up. The defensive system responded easily to the crossing of Odotheus in 386, when Roman sailors and soldiers massacred the Goths on river and land.[12] The year 382 held genuine promise.

"On January 25, 381, Athanaric died; in the year 382 the entire Gothic people with its king delivered itself to the Roman world." So reads the *Consularia Constantinopolitana* for the years 381 and 382.[13] For some scholars, the year 382 "marks the end of the Roman Empire,"[14] for it began the penetration of the barbarian world into the Roman one and was the beginning of the process that led to the creation of the barbarian kingdoms in the next and following centuries. In this view, the Middle Ages had begun. However, before entering into the apocalypse of the ancient world order, let us examine all the evidence for the year 382 and this great event more closely.[15] Several questions are obvious. Who was the king of the Gothic people referred to in the chronicle? What role did Theodosius play in the event? And what is the context for the welcoming of the "entire Gothic people"?

Surely the king was not Athanaric, dead since January 381, as noted in the *Consularia* itself. Or was it? Perhaps Fritigern had thrown up his hands in surrender. Or perhaps a new and as yet unknown man had emerged at the head of the Goths. In all likelihood the answer is none of the above. The last historical reference to Fritigern concerns his actions in 380 in connection with his attacks on Epirus Nova, discussed previously. Fritigern probably died in that year and certainly by October 382, or, at the very least, he had nothing to do with the events recorded for that year in the *Consularia*.[16] The historical writers in antiquity themselves seem to have struggled with these issues, each in his own way reflecting a solution acceptable for the author and his age.

The major source for the following is Themistius's sixteenth oration; however, that speech is so troublesome because of its purpose and style that an independent context must be established first. Zosimus is totally silent concerning a great Gothic surrender, moving quickly to Gratian's defeat and death at the hands of Magnus Maximus, and then back to Theodosius's great victory over the Goths of Odotheus in 386. Pacatus delivered his panegyric to Theodosius in Rome between June and September 389, and thus is the nearest contemporary reference other than Themistius. The relevant passage in Pacatus usually used to support the discussion of 382 neglects to specify dates. It could just as easily be applied to the aftermath of Athanaric's death in 381, or to the reception of the barbarians who had fled the approaching army of Bauto and Arbogastes later in that same year, or, for that matter, to any of Theodosius's many small victories over the barbarians. Indeed the language is so vague that it merely alludes to the general practice of *receptio* and says nothing about a great treaty with "the Gothic king." Speaking at Rome, Pacatus extolled his emperor: "May I speak of the Goths received into the Empire in order to serve us, to furnish troops for your army and to cultivate our soil?"[17] But further on, Pacatus lets us know the real outcome of Theodosius's Gothic wars—service in the Roman army:

> Then you divided your forces into three, so that you might upset the confidence of the enemy by multiplying his terror, and cut off his retreat by surrounding him. Finally you granted the privileged status of fellow-soldiers to the barbarian peoples who promised to give you voluntary service, both to remove from the frontier troops of dubious loyalty, and to add reinforcements to your army. Attracted by your kindness, all the Scythian nations flocked to you in such great numbers that you seemed to have imposed a levy upon barbarians from which you exempted your subjects. O event worthy of memory! There marched under Roman leaders and banners the onetime enemies of Rome, and they followed standards which they had once opposed, and filled with soldiers the cities of Pannonia which they not long ago emptied by hostile plundering. The Goth, the Hun, and the Alan responded to their names, and stood watch in their turn, and were afraid of being marked down as absent without leave. There was no disorder, no confusion and no looting, as is usual among the barbarians. On the contrary, if at any time the supplying of provisions was rather difficult, they endured the shortage with patience, and they made their rations, which were reduced because of their number, last longer by using them frugally. They demanded as their sole reward and salary this one thing, that they should be spoken of as yours.[18]

The panegyrist has taken the usual chronological liberties with events in this marvelously rhetorical reflection on a decade of war. Dividing his "forces into three" is difficult to pin down to a specific historical event. It might apply to his wars with Magnus Maximus (388), but it seems more applicable to Theodosius's campaigns in Thrace. Pacatus does refer to the early years and the struggles with Alans, Huns, and Goths in Pannonia (with Gratian's important aid now submerged beneath that of Theodosius, the overall theater commander). Pannonia was certainly still of great interest to the Roman audience. There seems to be a clear statement of overall imperial policy to divide and starve the barbarians into submission while sealing off the theater of operations. Coming where it does in the oration, after an apparent reference to the Persian peace negotiations of 384–87, the thrust of the text is to commemorate Theodosius's victories of 386. Still, the reference to Pannonia makes it clear that this passage is a summary of his military accomplishments for Theodosius's *decennalia*, or tenth anniversary. The most important point for any discussion of Roman military policy regarding the barbarians is the unequivocal declaration that the defeated barbarians served under Roman command including some in regular garrisons in the fortified towns in the Balkans. The prominence of supplies in successful recruitment is also manifest. Throughout 389 Theodosius remained in Italy, not returning to Constantinople until July 390.[19]

Paulus Orosius, writing in 418, saw Theodosius as the model of the new Christian ruler leading man to God, and adopted a very favorable attitude toward his Gothic policies. Orosius uses language similar to that of the *Consularia* in his narrative on Theodosius's reception of Athanaric and the Gothic people, presumably in 381, but Orosius, unlike the chroniclers, is not concerned with an annual recording of events. He leaves no doubt concerning the character of the emperor and its significance with regard to Athanaric; however, he makes no reference at all to another and later event which also supposedly culminated in a formal agreement. On Theodosius in 381, he wrote:

> He entered the city of Constantinople as a victor, and made a treaty with Athanaric, the king of the Goths, so that he might not exhaust the small body of Roman troops by continual campaigning. Athanaric, however, died immediately after reaching Constantinople. Upon the death of their king, all the Gothic tribes, on seeing the bravery and kindness of Theodosius, submitted to Roman rule.

Orosius continues:

> At the same time [actually 384] the Persians voluntarily sent ambassadors to Theodosius at Constantinople and humbly begged for peace. These Persians previously had killed Julian and frequently defeated other emperors. Recently they had put Valens to flight and were now venting their satisfaction over this latest victory by offering foul insults. A treaty was then made, the fruits of which the entire East has enjoyed in great tranquility until the present day.

After this discussion of the Persian situation Orosius concludes his narrative of events before the revolt of Magnus Maximus (383–88) as follows: "In the meantime, by subjugating the barbarian tribes in the East, Theodosius finally freed the Thracian provinces from the enemy. He made his son Arcadius associate emperor."[20] An obvious conclusion is that Orosius, drawing upon Eunapius, compressed many incidents concerning Theodosius's complex military crises into one narrative. Hydatius (ca. 470) in his continuation of Jerome's chronicle is even more concise: "381. Athanaric, king of the Goths, died at Constantinople fifteen days from his welcoming by Theodosius." "382. The Goths concluded an insincere peace with the Romans."[21]

In his important and intriguing chronicle Marcellinus Comes offers this for 381: "Athanaric king of the Goths concluded a treaty with the emperor Theodosius. He arrived in Constantinople in the month of January and died of illness in the same month."[22] For 382: "In this year the entire Gothic people, whose king Athanaric had died, delivered themselves to the Roman Empire in the month of October."[23]

Cassiodorus Senator's *Chronica*, ca. 519 and written in Italy, relates the death of Athanaric tersely: "Athanaric king of the Goths came to Constantinople and there departed this life."[24] He mistakenly dates the death in 382, and adds nothing at all about a treaty or a special peace.

Jordanes (ca. 550), writing in Constantinople, with some undeterminable but significant influence from Cassiodorus, adds interesting details concerning the agreement. In so doing, he injects terminology more appropriate for his own age, notably *foederati*: "Now when Athanaric was dead, his whole army continued in the service of the emperor Theodosius and submitted to the Roman rule, forming as it were one body with the imperial soldiery. The former service of the allies under the emperor Constantine was now renewed and they were again called allies."[25]

Our last significant source is the *Historiae...* (ca. 625) of Isidore of Seville. After relating the story of Athanaric's death, Isidore concludes his entry for 381 as follows: "But the Goths, upon the death of their king and seeing the benevolence of the emperor Theodosius, reached an agreement and delivered themselves to Roman rule."[26] For 382: "The Goths, rejecting the protection of the Roman treaty, appointed Alaric as their king, since they considered it unbecoming for them to be subject to Roman authority and to follow those whose laws and rule they had long ago cast off and from whose partnership they had alienated themselves after triumphing in battle."[27] Isidore thus sees the Goths repudiating in 382 the submission they had made a year earlier.

The foregoing survey of the standard sources has not solved our interpretive problems. Where are the answers to our rather simple questions concerning the events of 381–82 as related in the *Consularia*? Who was the king of the Goths who led his people to submit to Rome? What role did Theodosius play? What does the phrase welcoming the "entire Gothic people" mean?

Several of the Latin sources are obviously related. For example, Isidore's debt to Orosius is clear here and elsewhere, e.g., in the description and characterization of Theodosius. In other places he reveals a knowledge of Hydatius. There was agreement between Orosius and Isidore that something having to do with the *universae Gothorum gentes* occurred during the years 381–82, and, furthermore, that the great Christian emperor Theodosius had something to do with it, since after all he was very much in charge of military affairs. In addition, Isidore identified the Gothic king as Alaric (over a decade too early), and placed him at the head of independent Goths who had just rejected the benefits of their treaty with Rome. Presumably he referred to the treaty of 381 he had mentioned in the preceding entry. Neither of these authors suggests a second treaty for the year 382, although both clearly wished to stress the importance of the imperial character in achieving success. Orosius does not mention any treaty with the Goths except that concluded with Athanaric, whose followers were perceived as constituting "all the Gothic peoples." He then goes on to note, but only in passing, that at about the time of Arcadius's elevation to Augustus (383), Theodosius had so subjugated the barbarians in Thrace that he could turn his attentions elsewhere. Theodosius's first such effort, according to Orosius, was a meeting with Persian ambassadors which resulted in a lasting treaty. This event is supported by numerous sources and is beyond doubt.

Though very much within the historiographic tradition of Orosius, Isidore conflated events and persons discussed by the earlier author. Moreover, he apparently decided that 382 was the proper year to clarify another problem, the origin of the kingship of Alaric. Marcellinus Comes first refers to Alaric as king in his entry for 395, but its declaration probably took place even later.[28] Neither Orosius nor Isidore explains the role of Theodosius in any event of 382, nor does either identify the leader of the Goths after the death of Athanaric. Instead, both use the events of 381–82 to demonstrate other "truths": for both, the greatness of the Christian reign of Theodosius, and, for Isidore, the beginning of the historical kingship of Alaric. The latter was important to Isidore because it also marked the origins of the independent and proud traditions of the Visigothic monarchy, which was so central to his world.[29]

Hydatius (ca. 470) stood between Orosius and Isidore, was well known to the latter, and provided him with much of his information for the era 379–469. Hydatius, however, can be read to suggest another alternative: one agreement with one group of Goths spread over two chronicle years. At least that is a possible explanation for his not referring to a Gothic king in his entry for 382. There can be no doubt that Hydatius knew the *Consularia*, since he continued it for the years from 395 to 468.[30] That his continuation of Jerome's chronicle simplifies the narrative and calls the Goths "faithless" may suggest that Hydatius was wrestling with our dilemma with the hindsight of the late fifth century. In this case Hydatius appears more faithful to the evidence before him than was Isidore. Certainly Isidore did not read Hydatius in the way just suggested but went about exploring his own priorities instead.

Marcellinus Comes (ca. 535) clearly offers another solution, the same one that had perhaps occurred to Hydatius, which because of his testimony cannot be ruled out. Specifically he stretches the time between the death of Athanaric and the formal reception of his followers, so that the former dies in January 381 and the welcoming of his Goths into Roman service takes place in October of the next year, 382. Thus what had appeared in the *Consularia* as two events involving two different groups becomes two stages in the reception of one group. This is vaguely reminiscent of the two scenes of the Lyon medallion from the tetrarchy in which first came the request and then the crossing.[31] Presumably during the interval the Goths had ample opportunity to experience the manliness and generosity of the emperor, which is virtually a *topos* in all the sources, including Zosimus, for explaining their coming over to the Romans. The usually troublesome Jordanes, writing in Constantinople (ca. 550), also seems content with one event and one group, Athanaric's. Jordanes avoids most of the problems by passing directly to the events surrounding Eugenius's rebellion at the end of Theodosius's reign.

Thus the best alternatives offered in the Latin sources for understanding the events of 381–82 revolve around the reception of Athanaric and his followers, in which action Theodosius played the essential role. From these sources one cannot identify any new Gothic leader, let alone a new "king" for the Goths, in the era after the passing of Athanaric and Fritigern. They contain nothing that connects Theodosius with a new great event in 382 not flowing directly from his reception of Athanaric in January 381. This silence notwithstanding, there probably was an event in 382 that did concern the Goths, an event in which the imperially focused Zosimus had no interest, but one which did give rise to the problems which later sources could not correctly resolve. This was the event celebrated by Themistius.

Themistius composed his sixteenth oration, "On the Peace," as a formal thanksgiving in celebration of the consulship of the general Saturninus in 383. Doubly honored by the consulship because it fell on the *quinquenalia* (fifth anniversary) of Theodosius's reign, Flavius Saturninus must have merited great recognition. His colleague in the consulship was an equally deserving Western general of Germanic blood, Flavius Merobaudes. Now *consul prior*, Merobaudes had been *consul posterior* in 377 with Gratian himself.

Both had risen through Roman service for at least two decades. The time was at hand to acknowledge the support of the general staff, without which the victories and policies of the past five years would never have occurred. Saturninus was the first of the great generals so honored, but by the end of the decade several others had gained similar recognition: Richomeres (384), Timasius (389), and Promotus (389). Like Saturninus, all had survived Adrianople.

Themistius was a true veteran of courtly scholarship. In 383 he was appointed to the office of urban prefect and was as well the tutor of the young Arcadius. The position of tutor to the future emperor was not something for others to take lightly, as the career of Themistius's contemporary Decimus Magnus Ausonius (tutor to Gratian and consul in 379) had amply and recently illustrated. Themistius's political and philosophical agendas were considerably more intellectually lofty than were those of Ausonius. Themistius managed to convey a complex and consistent view of the imperial office leading a recast Empire on a new and more far-reaching mission. The emperor would fulfill his appointed role through the exercise of the traditional imperial virtues—manliness, clemency, and piety—only slightly redefined by the growing Christian aspirations of the late Empire. He would extend an intellectual vision of Roman civilization throughout the world. The old philosopher had hammered out these concepts in over two decades of turbulence going back to the days of Constantius II. He did not have to invent new categories for Theodosius, for the reigning emperor could be fitted nicely into the theoretical structures used, for example, to discuss Valens and Athanaric a decade and a half earlier.[32]

The destiny of Rome cast so clearly by Vergil at the very dawn of the Empire was broadened and "humanized" in Themistius's vision. The haughty would still submit, but now Rome would triumph as a cultural force by virtue of its intellectual powers; its Reason would transform the barbarians into civilized men. The emperor's task was to create the conditions necessary for Reason's conquests. Be the emperor Julian, Valens, or Theodosius, Themistius always strove to enlist him in the challenge by praising his personal manifestations of imperial virtue and cajoling him to use the carefully prepared moment to plant the seeds of Reason and Roman culture among the barbarians. In so doing the emperor became not merely the acknowledged leader of a political force, the Empire, but truly the guardian, almost the "tutor," of Mankind. The barbarians would, of course, accept the abundant wisdom of their own submission to a higher purpose.

Many have seen in Themistius an important philosophical bridge between the purely pagan world of traditional Hellenistic philosophy in its Roman form and the Christian outlook rapidly taking over men's minds. However, there is little need to look to Christianity as an inspiration for "On the Peace." For the Christian side of Theodosius, Orosius and others are much more rewarding.[33] Rather, Themistius stands early in the process by which Hellenism found a safe niche in East Roman and later Byzantine Christian society.[34] The oration for Saturninus is a rather straightforward blend of traditional images of victory and the resulting reception of barbarians onto Roman soil, common for over a century in panegyric and coinage, combined with Themistius's own well developed concepts of the role of Reason and Roman culture. His weaving of Homeric heroes and lessons from Roman history, a style also characteristic of Libanius and others, constantly demands that the audience relate the events of the day to the greatness of the legendary past. Both Saturninus and Theodosius are thereby raised onto the highest pedestal of rhetorical fabrication.

Theodosius, "like Achilles," who sent out Patroclus to save the hard-pressed Greeks, sent Saturninus but with far happier results.[35] Instead of arming his Patroclus in splendid breastplate and shield, Theodosius bestowed upon him "patience, gentleness and clemency (or a sense of humanity)."[36] Saturninus, suitably armed for the battle of Reason over barbarism, thus triumphed as soon as he approached the enemy. His method was simple. By setting before them the fruits of friendship and service to the cause of Empire, their savagery "was tamed." "One might almost say that he led them bound with their hands behind their backs, so that one might wonder if they had indeed been persuaded or conquered." The humbled barbarians presented their swords in surrender and "clasped his knees" in token of submission.[37]

Elsewhere, Themistius says that he himself had seen the "bringing of the barbarians into peace."[38] Imperial clemency revealed itself in the granting of pardon to the barbarians for their wrongdoings.[39] The roads and mountain passes stood open, and villas and farmsteads smiled again amid the harvest.[40] The entire Empire, like some great organism, ceased to suffer from its many wounds and drew a collective sigh of deliverance. The great ship had safely returned to port; peace was restored.[41] Themistius not only asks his audience to accept the fact that the Goths had not been totally crushed and humbled in the traditional Roman sense but to applaud it. The Goths had not been led off in chains but had been transformed into something better: they were now productive members of a redefined Roman Empire, an Empire for all Humanity. Themistius suggests that the question of whether the Romans could have militarily crushed the Goths into obedience was debatable, but not worth debating. More important, the barbarians were better men. Still more important, the Romans were better men and the Empire was a better Empire.

> Which, then, is better: to fill Thrace with corpses or farmers? to make it full of graves or humans? to travel through wilderness or cultivated land? to count those who have perished or those who are plowing? to resettle the Phrygians and Bithynians, perhaps, or to make them live with those whom we have subdued? I hear from those who return from there [Thrace] that they are now remaking the iron from their swords and breastplates into hoes and sickles, and that they who previously were lovers of Ares are now worshiping Demeter and Dionysus.[42]

Beating weapons into plowshares and turning to the gods of agriculture are rhetorical exercises, canons in the art of panegyric, and as such impossible to evaluate as simple facts. Behind the rhetoric stands Saturninus, who probably had been assigned the task of continuing the policy of carving up the Gothic enclaves into smaller and smaller areas and then receiving the leaders and their followers into Roman service. Many Theodosian victories were commemorated on coins, and Saturninus had doubtless been in tactical command for some of them. Despite the problems of precise dating of the various issues, an *aes* piece issued from Constantinople (ca. 378–83) is generally relevant here. It featured the commonplace reverse legend *GLORIA RO-MANORVM* and the emperor standing facing left, holding a standard in his right hand and resting his left on a shield. To his left knelt a captive, head right.[43] The issue of the *GLORIA ROMANORVM* was a standard type of no particular significance. The *VICTORIA AVGVSTORVM* coin issues typically commemorated particular victories but were struck routinely during the period 367–88 in various denominations.[44] Thus no one specific victory stands out in the coinage above all others as we might expect if the victory of 382 had the vast importance often claimed for it. Of course the loyalty of the army had to be acknowledged throughout the era, and these issues also often portrayed a captive in submission to the emperor. For example, *VIRTVS E-XERCITI*—another *aes* issued from Constantinople (383–88)—revealed the emperor with his foot on a captive.[45]

Themistius, however, seems at pains to distinguish between this type of victory, the traditional military success (from which he obviously borrowed symbolism), and a new type. The latter was a greater victory that flowed from the voluntary submission of peoples to Roman leadership over civilization itself: it led to positive transformation and partnership, not subjugation and discord. Moreover, he never used the technical words for treaty, the legal action between two groups that guaranteed the mutual under-standing of the principles involved.[46] What Themistius said he saw with his own eyes was the "bringing into peace."[47] Peace (*eireine*) for Themistius and his age was a general concept that might conveniently be defined in Themistius's own phrases as the end of the suffering and bloodshed that had resulted from a preexisting state of war. Clearly the peace that he had in mind was one of a higher level than any Rome could have forced upon a defeated foe. A treaty was between two groups; the peace of Themistius's oration produced one people working together within one civilization. The peace negated the boundaries of groups and of geography and even tran-scended consuls and emperors.

Whether Themistius's savages about to participate in the creation of a new civilization entered it as *dediticii*, that is, formally humbled by defeat and forever stained at law, or as reluctant volunteers was a matter far beneath his lofty vision. But aside from him, their individual civil and testamentary rights were largely irrelevant to the Roman army. The army kept records on the legal status of its men, but it did not regard being a formally defeated foe as a factor in assigning a new recruit. Athanaric's men had volunteered and were placed in regular units along the Danube. Gratian had posted *dediticii* to various regular units on the Rhine.[48] The rebelling Goths had not so long ago beseeched Valens to accept them and had sworn oaths of loyalty to the emperor. To Saturninus and his fellow officers the question was whether they would be able to recruit these warriors and make them soldiers. Civilizing them was something that the Roman frontier had begun long ago. When those actually defeated were assigned to regular units, they would in all likelihood have carried the personal status of *dediticus*. Many of these recruits, however, eventually served in various barbarian *auxilia*, where it is hard to imagine that much attention was paid to legal techni-calities. The Goths opposing Saturninus had suffered through years of hun-ger and hardship as Roman armies had systematically isolated them. What-ever Rome regarded as their legal due, these recruits stood defeated.[49]

What Themistius saw in Thrace, perhaps in 382 and under the overall command of Saturninus, was the formal reception of some group of bar-barians by Roman officials. Most likely these were either some of the groups in the area of the Rhodope and/or the Haemus Mountains (the Thracian provinces of Rhodopa and/or Haemimontus) or those around Marcianopo-lis in the province of Moesia II. These were areas for which we have evi-dence of road building about this time and whose tactical and strategic importance demanded early pacification in order to restore the diocese to a sustainable level of productivity. Others were perhaps settled now or slightly later in Macedonia, or so it seems from another oration Themistius composed in 385 or late 384.[50] There is absolutely no evidence in Themistius that there was a great treaty signing in 382, which would certainly have involved the emperor and not his general, or that Saturninus did anything other than continue to execute the policies in operation since 379–80. Saturninus's reward of the consulship was the crowning moment of three decades of service during which he and his lieutenants oversaw many instances of *receptio* in the name of the emperor, precisely as Vitalianus had done for Gratian and Theodosius in 380.

In late Roman literature subtlety was often the only way to influence the listener, especially when the principal member of the audience was the emperor himself. Libanius delivered his thirteenth oration, "An Address to Julian," in Antioch before the emperor in July 362. Libanius then stretched some of the same images found in Themistius's oration, though not so far. His text reads:

> In sober truth, you often returned requiring your gear to be cleaned, covered as it was with the blood of the barbarian, and a table, no different from that of the rank and file, then received you. While demanding of yourself the performance of greater deeds than theirs, greater luxury you refused. So the fruits of all this are that the cities of Gaul have risen again, by the labors of the barbarian, as we look on. For just as the shackled Spartans worked for their conquerors the land they had tried to wrest from Tegea, so they too were compelled to rebuild the cities they had ruined, and their hands, schooled in devastation, were taught to engage in reconstruction.[51]

Libanius and Themistius worked within the conventional limits of panegyric, but what distinguished them both was their skill in manipulating the genre to a higher purpose. They aimed for the instruction of the listener, not simply his entertainment.

Gratian went east in 382 as far as Viminacium in Moesia I, which probably was still within Eastern jurisdiction, where he issued edicts on 5 July 382.[52] Why Gratian was in Viminacium in 382 is a bit of a mystery. His rapid pace (not longer than two weeks between Padua and Viminacium) seems to preclude any type of military movement. Since as late as 20 June 382 Gratian was still in Padua, he certainly had no trouble getting to Viminacium.[53] If indeed Theodosius joined him there, neither did he. No army could have moved so swiftly. It is possible that Gratian hoped to meet Theodosius, but something came up and he departed after receiving only a messenger from Constantinople. Gratian could not have played any major part in a Balkan campaign. He merely turned around and returned to Italy.[54] Illyricum was largely pacified.

Theodosius's itinerary is known even more precisely for the summer of 382. He could not have ventured out from Constantinople in July or August for longer than two weeks. He was in Constantinople on 16 July, 6 August, 28 August, 29 August, and 14 (20) September.[55] Most probably both emperors had agreed to meet in Viminacium in order to brief each other on their respective campaigns against the barbarians. Religious policy probably also figured in their plans, for that issue too forced itself onto both of their calendars during 381–82.[56] Another likely reason to meet at Viminacium would have been to decide if the time was ripe to return the dioceses of Dacia and Macedonia to the West. Gratian after all had sent forces into Macedonia in 381. If that was a question, then the answer was yes.

The transfer could actually have occurred at any time after the last reference to Eutropius acting as Theodosius's praetorian prefect of Illyricum, which was in late September 381. But Gratian made no use of his authority over the dioceses until the summer of 382, when he first visited them. His trip to Viminacium in June of 382 is the most likely occasion for the transfer to have taken place. After Gratian's death in August 383, Theodosius moved quickly to restore the prefecture of Illyricum to Eastern jurisdiction.[57] By the autumn of 384 he had begun to set up a separate sphere for Valentinian II, under the tutelage of his mother Justina, that included Illyricum and Italy and that lasted until 387.[58]

The year 382 thus marked the transition to the final phases of the Gothic operations that had begun in the wake of the Roman defeat at Adrianople in August 378. There was no great victory over the king of the Gothic people because there was no such king and the "Gothic people" were fragmented into isolated groups without unified direction. The survival of the defensive system prevented large groups from forming because of the limits of their supply. That only a part of the fortification system, not every town or fortress, had to survive to assure the workings of the whole was a feature of the system itself that had accrued over the years. The population demanded such protection wherever they lived. In other words, the Roman defense had a built-in degree of redundancy that increased the survivability of the essential mechanisms. There had been many close calls such as the near slaying of Theodosius himself, and there were still pockets of recalcitrant barbarians in Thrace who could and did threaten transportation and communication. Some of these may have occasioned the celebrations of imperial power seen on coinage in the period 383–92 and not otherwise assignable to specific events.[59] Many of the smaller groups would presumably have fallen to the local authorities to handle as if they were mere bands of brigands, which indeed many were. Of course, such cases would not appear in the records.

Gratian and Theodosius had saved the Empire. In the future when barbarians attempted to enter it without permission the defensive system was alert and ready for action. When Odotheus hurriedly crossed the Danube early in 386 he and his followers faced the combined land and naval power of the East. Gothic speakers in the Roman army served as capable spies and bribed the followers of Odotheus to betray his plans to Promotus, then *magister peditum* in Thrace. He was promoted to consul in 389 as a reward for this service.[60] With his characteristic color Zosimus relates: "Since the Magister Promotus was informed of everything in advance by those sent to arrange the 'betrayal,' he prepared himself against the barbarians' plans, and by arranging his ships ready for action three deep and at the same time extending them as far as possible, he secured the river bank for upwards of twenty stades."[61]

The Roman fleet slaughtered the hapless barbarians on their hastily built rafts in mid-stream. Those who swam ashore got a demonstration of Roman might. Only after many bodies littered the river and beach did the Roman commander call a halt and round up the survivors. Promotus enrolled them into the Roman army. Our sources even give the emperor credit for this clemency. Perhaps he was already planning for his war with Maximus almost two years hence.[62] Maximus was certainly on his mind. Theodosius could have been near the scene of the battle.

Theodosius was in Valentia in Gaul tending to problems with Magnus Maximus as late as 3 September and was in Constantinople to celebrate the victory with a triumph on 12 October 386. It is possible therefore that Theodosius was indeed in the vicinity of the battle and could have directed the actions to spare the survivors as military recruits, as Zosimus suggests and which would have been in keeping with policy.[63] That he was actually present on the battlefield, as Claudian claims, is doubtful.[64] The magnitude of the victory celebration that followed, however, virtually required the story of the personal involvement of the emperor displaying his *clementia*.

Unlike the shadowy events of 382, the victory in 386 was cause for a real triumph, complete with the dedication of an obelisk in the Constantinopolitan hippodrome. This monument depicted the fleet in action, the suitably humbled long-haired barbarians and the august imperial family, court, and general staff (see illustration 6).[65] The event was recorded in a wide variety of literary sources and probably also accounts for some of the coinage issues.[66] If one event marked the end of the Gothic problem, it was

Illustration 6. Obelisk base of Theodosius the Great (erected in the Hippodrome in Constantinople)

the demonstration of the restored integrity of the *limes* in 386. By the time the obelisk was erected in 390 no doubt remained.[67] Zosimus preferred not to stress Theodosius's clemency against Odotheus and his followers after the great victory on the Danube. Introducing his detailed account, Zosimus in one sentence of summary tells his readers what he wished upon all barbarian invaders: they were butchered at the gates, never allowed admission.[68] Rome slaughtered many, but received many others into imperial service.

The story of a certain Gerontius is suggestive as to what happened after Theodosius or Promotus stopped the massacre on the Danube for the sake of recruitment. Gerontius was the commander of the garrison at Tomi (Constanta) in the province of Scythia. Outside Tomi's walls were some barbarians specially recruited by Theodosius for their fighting abilities and therefore probably destined for the imperial guard, which was composed of carefully recruited barbarians throughout this era. The barbarians outside

Tomi held the regulars in contempt until Gerontius single-handedly faced them down and reinfused Roman pride into the garrison. Together they then gave the barbarians a taste of Roman mettle.[69] When confronted by an angry Theodosius, enraged over the loss of so many fine recruits, Gerontius pleaded that the loss had also meant a windfall (he had returned the gold torques given the barbarians to the treasury).[70] The story of Gerontius is rife with moral overtones. More prosaically, it illustrates the difficulties involved in utilizing so many new recruits within the traditional mechanisms of the army and the resultant modifications that were attempted after 383.[71] But even five years later sporadic fighting continued and on one occasion again nearly cost the emperor his life. While passing through Macedonia and Thessaly in late 391, Theodosius and his small escort were surprised by barbarians, whom Zosimus characterizes as brigands sprung from their hideaways in the swamps.[72] While Theodosius struggled with the Gothic crisis, Rome's influence beyond the Danube, in the past sometimes capable of dictating events, was disappearing, lost to the Huns.

Rome had resolved the problem of the Gothic incursions by 386. As the events of 410 reveal, however, something went terribly wrong in the course of the next two decades. When, why, and how are the subjects of much of the remainder of this book. Many of the answers lie in the civil wars.

Summary

Theodosius staged a gala celebration in Constantinople to welcome Athanaric into the Empire. The aged king had finally requested *receptio* for himself and his followers. Military concerns progressed predictably and allowed Theodosius to concentrate more upon various civil concerns. In furtherance of the war against the barbarians key defenses were relinked into a network, thereby further isolating bands of hungry barbarians. Little by little Rome pacified and generally recruited these barbarians into the frontier life based on farming and soldiering with traditional frontier recompense— land and supplies. The remainder of Illyricum was restored to the West but remained there only until Gratian's death. From 384 to 387, Illyricum formed a part of the governmental sphere allocated to Valentinian II. Some barbarians were assigned duty in special units, particularly in the imperial guard. The river line of fortifications proved itself fit against the attempted unauthorized crossing of a large group of Goths in flight from Hunnic dominion. Their defeat in 386 marked the end of the Gothic wars and occasioned the erection of a triumphal obelisk in Constantinople. Only a few recalcitrant barbarian bands remained at large.

BARBARIANS AND CIVIL WAR

THE FINAL phases of the restoration of the military integrity of Thrace and the rest of the Balkans coincided with the collapse of the political structure of the Empire itself. It was this complex pattern of military integration and political disintegration that gave rise to the later barbarian problems. The same period witnessed the restructuring of the military command system to provide for tighter control in the Thracian area, the outlines of which are visible in the *Notitia dignitatum*. This military reorganization was part of the political realignments necessitated by the death of Gratian (25 August 383) and then that of his younger brother Valentinian II (15 May 392), after which Illyricum was again transferred to the East. So also Theodosius used the period from 383 onward to reaffirm and renegotiate the eastern frontiers with the Persians, culminating in the partition of Armenia, which had effectively served as a buffer state for centuries. The traditional date of the partition is 387; however, the expiration of the 30-year peace signed in 363 and other factors, including the death of the reigning Armenian king sometime late in Theodosius's rule, suggest a later date, perhaps 394.[1] None of these actions was forced upon Theodosius by the presence of hostile barbarians in Thrace. Rather they attest to his self-assurance that the barbarian threat no longer existed.

Throughout the Gothic wars Theodosius had been content, doubtless gratefully so, to leave well enough alone on the Persian flank. The treaty of 363 remained in effect, though actions taken by Valens may have compromised it. Valens evidently agreed to a Persian demand for a division of Armenia in order to extricate his armies for the Gothic campaigns in 378, whereas before he had strongly opposed the division of Armenia and had been ready to go to war to prevent it. Beginning with the rise of Magnus Maximus in 383, in other words, the Empire shifted its attention away from the Balkans to other, equally traditional problems: the Persians and, belatedly, usurpation. The Persian frontier had the higher priority but required patience more than force. Contrary to what our sources suggest, the Persian

92

ambassadors to Constantinople in 384 were probably seeking only the routine acknowledgment of the agreement of 363 and the addenda agreed to by Valens.[2]

So far as we can tell, Theodosius was equally content to accept the new facts of life in the West. In 384 he accepted Maximus as his colleague provided that Gratian's nine-year-old brother Valentinian II was given his own independent sphere, specifically Italy, Africa, and Illyricum. This arrangement took two years before the details were established to everyone's liking. Valentinian II's territory reconstituted the Italian prefecture created under Constantius II (337–60). One indication of just how difficult and fragile Theodosius's negotiations with Maximus and Valentinian's court were lies in the extraordinary rarity of coins struck for Maximus in the East. The fact that an entire department (*officina*) of the mint of Constantinople was devoted to striking an *aes* of the *virtus exerciti* type with Maximus should have made this coin relatively common today, yet only two specimens survive. It appears then that the mint never released most such coins but held them in storage awaiting a final decision. When it came, it was to destroy them. Theodosius had changed his mind.[3] Theodosius probably extended full recognition only in 386, after he had settled matters with Maximus and had obtained Valentinian's mother Justina's consent. Also in 386 Evodius, Maximus's praetorian prefect of the Gauls, held the consulship with the youth Honorius, son of Theodosius. The East proclaimed Evodius consul along with Honorius throughout its dominions.[4] Eastern recognition even included the staging in Egypt of an elaborate celebration of Maximus for the eyes of his representative.[5] The western mints, of course, struck for Maximus and continued to strike for Theodosius, whose legitimacy was unquestioned.[6]

Valentinian II had little chance to exert his "independence" and immediately became the prize in a tug of war between Maximus and his supporters and Justina, the young Valentinian's mother. She was usually allied with the powerful Ambrose, bishop of Milan, the residence of the imperial family. Among other things, Ambrose decried the presence of some Goths in the imperial guard.[7] As interesting as this struggle is—it involved great men and high drama—it has little relevance to our central theme of military organization until Valentinian finally repudiated Maximus. The latter responded by invading Italy during the early summer of 387, whereupon Valentinian and Justina fled to Thessalonica and Theodosius.

This new crisis forever changed the role of the barbarians within the Roman Empire. The barbarians did not yet exist as distinct "peoples" under their own kings, but some were moving in that direction because of Rome's needs for organized troops and proven commanders. At the lower levels of the Roman officer corps the tradition, common since the third century, of offering individual barbarian leaders a military tribuneship over small groups of their own men continued to evolve throughout the fourth century. Some of these barbarians proved exceptionally capable and advanced in rank all the way to generalships.[8] At the same time that this recruitment of junior officers was occurring, ever greater numbers of ordinary barbarians were finding service in the Roman army.

Both Maximus and Theodosius are noted in the sources as leaders who liked to surround themselves with high-ranking barbarians, and this despite Maximus's supposed hostility to the Germans.[9] But these *ex post facto* allegations demand scrutiny. Sufficient examples have already been addressed to establish the fact that by the late fourth century numerous men of Germanic ancestry had risen to the highest levels in the Roman army. As the case of Gerontius has demonstrated, Theodosius had accorded certain barbarian recruits special rations and privileges. Gratian had apparently done likewise with certain groups of Alans, and according to our sources (Zosimus and the *Epitome de Caesaribus*) this was one of the causes of his undoing. The hindsight moralizing of these pagan sources is strikingly clear, but there is no reason to doubt that both emperors willingly employed certain barbarians in sensitive roles. Gratian's favoritism for the Alanic recruits supposedly undermined the loyalty of the regular army. Maximus seized upon this and led the regulars in revolt, first in Britain and then in Gaul.[10] At Paris Gratian's troops deserted, leaving him little choice but flight.[11] Some sort of employment in the Roman army for the Alans "received" in 380 must have ensued as a part of their agreement. Given the imperial penchant for barbarian bodyguards, that Gratian incorporated a few Alans among them is not surprising. Perhaps the regulars were jealous of their position, pay, and privileges. The selection of a few Alanic recruits for Gratian's personal guard derives more clearly from a traditional *receptio* than from a treaty giving them an independent role in Pannonia after 380.

The nature of the personal relationship between Theodosius and Maximus cannot be satisfactorily established, for the sources are simply too opinionated and partial to their own causes. Ambrose, the most eloquent and feisty of the witnesses to the age, presents a picture of Maximus as a ruthless soldier, ever ready to slay his opponents. In fact, other than Priscillianus and a handful of his followers, Maximus killed very few. Pacatus also criticized Maximus for brutality in his panegyric to Theodosius in 389, but that was a year after Maximus's fall. What is clear is that in official acts Theodosius was quite proper in according his Western colleague due recognition and acknowledgment of his prerogatives, such as the naming of consuls.

Perhaps Theodosius always harbored plans to settle affairs in Gaul and avenge Gratian, but such ideas only surface in the written sources as innuendoes, usually long after the fact. Still, Theodosius had other pressing concerns, and clearly was in no hurry to confront Maximus; on the contrary, he seems to have gone to considerable lengths to make him acceptable to Valentinian's court. The Persian ambassadors arrived in Constantinople in 384 seeking to renew the long-standing treaty struck with Valens. In that year Stilicho, the future commanding general of the Western army and guardian of Theodosius's son Honorius, was *tribunus praetorianus militaris* and as such probably went on the return mission to the Persians at Ctesiphon.[12]

At the same time Theodosius confronted vexing religious issues at home. Religious problems concerning the suppression of paganism, the clarification of Orthodox doctrine, and the resulting troubles with heresy certainly occupied much of the rest of his reign. These conflicts brought out some of the emperor's worst qualities. His vehemence culminated in 390, when he had turned the soldiers loose on the Thessalonicans for allowing a mob to kill his *magister militum*, the Gothic-born Butheric. His subsequent humbling before Ambrose in public penance became standard fare for those who sided with the church in medieval struggles of Church and State.[13] It is from this date that Theodosius became ever more committed to crushing paganism. Even before 390 he had promulgated laws against pagan sacrifice (381, 385) and sanctioned the use of troops to destroy pagan temples in the area of Apamea.[14] Riots accompanied zealous attempts to defile pagan cult objects in Alexandria to the point that the *dux* of Egypt was ordered to assist in the destruction of the temples.[15] To launch a major war against Maximus would have stretched his resources dangerously thin.

Nevertheless Theodosius prepared for war, meeting Valentinian at Thessalonica and moving westward in early 388.[16] Theodosius had recently reassured the Persians of Rome's peaceful intentions, and they remained quiet on his eastern frontier.[17] Supplies and soldiers required major funding and the regular issuance of gold coins, a task now exclusively in the hands of the *comitatus*. From his departure from Constantinople in September until his victorious return in July 391, no gold was minted at the eastern capital and western mints struck gold issues with eastern reverse types, doubtless as a result of Theodosius's presence in the West.[18] The campaign required all the forces that Theodosius could muster, good strategy and logistical support to break through the defenses in the Julian Alps, and luck. He dispatched Valentinian and Justina to Rome, while he marched with the army north and then westward, probably along the road to Naissus and then through Sirmium and up the Sava. Valentinian's party avoided interception in the Adriatic.[19]

Pacatus the panegyrist tells us that Theodosius routinely welcomed barbarians into his units and asserts that these recruits served loyally, demanding only their due wages and provisions.[20] Zosimus offers a contrary verdict. For him, the barbarians enrolled in the Roman army were mere opportunists enticed by Maximus's agents. Learning that their treachery was discovered, they hid in the swamps and heavy undergrowth in Macedonia. There most were hunted down and executed, allowing the emperor to proceed without concern for his rear areas.[21] Perhaps Zosimus emphasized this incident to stigmatize Theodosius's earlier decision to spare Odotheus's followers and enroll them in Roman service, for Zosimus alleges that Theodosius's act of clemency then had been made with an eye toward his troop needs against Maximus. Since Rome defeated Odotheus in 386, two years before Theodosius broke with Maximus, Zosimus reveals primarily his own anti-Theodosian bias rather than much about either the sparing of Odotheus's defeated followers or the war against Maximus.[22]

Where lies the truth? Two different stories? Two different sources? Two different groups of barbarian recruits, the old Goth-Hun-Alan group in the Pannonian area and the recently pacified Goths in Macedonia and Thessaly? Or just two more episodes serving the ulterior motives of two authors who were ideological enemies, the Christian courtier Pacatus and the pagan Zosimus? Pacatus emphasized the incredible leadership of Theodosius, who could inspire such loyalty to the cause of Rome that even the most rambunctious barbarians responded, while Zosimus relished an unflattering episode to prepare us for the detailed character-sketch of the unpredictable emperor at the end of his fourth book. Whatever the case, two points seem beyond dispute in all sources. First, the barbarians were enrolled in the Roman army and served there, loyally or not, during the struggle with Maximus. Second, these barbarians served as individuals in regular units, for no barbarian units are reported as engaged in battle during Theodosius's campaign. The second point must be stressed. These newly recruited soldiers never played an independent role in any of the ensuing battles of that war.[23] The highest ranking generals, the *magister peditum* Promotus and Arbogastes and *magister equitum* Timasius and Richomeres, accompanied the emperor.[24] All but Arbogastes, who committed suicide after his own rebellion failed six years later, were eventually rewarded for their service with the consulate.

Theodosius and his army proceeded from Thessalonica northward via Stobi and Scupi and then westward past Sirmium as far as Siscia, where he

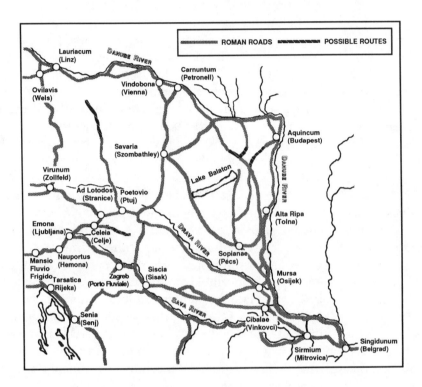

Map 4 Roman Frontier and Hinterland, Lauriacum to Singidunum

had considerable difficulty crossing the Sava (see map 4).[25] Rather than proceeding direct to Emona along the highway and through the passes (perhaps
manned by Maximus's troops who had briskly defended Siscia), Theodosius
again turned north. He marched through Andavtonia and up to the Iovia-
Poetovio road, following the Drava upstream. He fought another hard battle at Poetovio against troops under Marcellinus, brother of Maximus and
comes.[26] The survivors of Maximus's army, according to the panegyric, immediately and successfully sought service in Theodosius's army, where they
joined as one in the celebration of the emperor and his victory.[27] Perhaps
certain Frankish and Saxon recruits helped win the day for the emperor,
who continued on to Emona and then Aquileia.[28] Somewhere along the
route from Thessalonica, probably when stopped on the Sava, supplies seem
to have become an acute problem.[29] Little else is known about the campaign
itself. The legions deploying in square formation with the cavalry on the

wings and the cohorts breaking down into maniples, as in the panegyric, are too reminiscent of a bygone era to be believed. They fall into the same fanciful categories as many passages of Vegetius, another contemporary with a flair for the past days of glory.[30] Theodosius's forces caught up with Maximus on 28 August 388 near Aquileia, where loyalists beheaded the Western usurper.[31] Arbogastes,[32] *magister peditum* of Frankish origin and soon to be the dominant personage behind the newly reinstated Valentinian II in the Western Empire, summarily dispatched Maximus's son Victor, left behind to defend Gaul from barbarian attacks. Otherwise there were no reprisals, no purges. In fact, all the sources note the imperial clemency that welcomed the usurper's defeated followers into Roman service.[33]

Theodosius felt confident enough about the Balkan situation that he remained in Italy until 391. From Italy early in 389 he ordered Valentinian— that is to say his court and advisers, for the youth was still a minor—to Gaul to ward off attacks from across the Rhine. In June of that same year Theodosius introduced his youngest son Honorius to the Senate. While in Italy he also may have reorganized the senior command structure of the Eastern army. He was still at Milan to face the outraged Ambrose after slaughtering so many citizens of Thessalonica in 390. Of these actions only the possible reorganization of the Eastern army directly concerns the problem at hand. At long last Theodosius may have taken time to rationalize the command structure so hastily modified by repeated campaigns, recruitment and temporary depositions since 378. By finally taking pause Theodosius may have confirmed, if only to himself, that the decade of struggle since the death of Valens was over. Alas, the evidence for Theodosius's administrative reforms of the army is just as ambiguous as that for the rest of his military program. Since the nineteenth century there has been no shortage of hypotheses regarding the Theodosian reorganization of the *magistri*, but no convincing account.

The heart of the problem is the maddening vagueness of the literary sources, particularly Zosimus. Regardless of his intentions, Zosimus's Greek might sometimes have obscured Latin military terminology. Although he certainly could display considerable precision upon occasion, he was more often careless, as were many of his sources. As an example of precision, Zosimus correctly and clearly identified Promotus as *magister peditum* commanding in Thrace against Odotheus along the Danube in 386.[34] At the other end of the spectrum is the *Notitia dignitatum* with its apparent clarity, order, and symmetry, but without an established date or corroboration for many sections. The bureaucrats who amended it obviously had little personal concern for its technical precision or for making timely and thorough revisions. Moreover, the entire document suffers because of the modern historian's tendency—often unwarranted—to stretch its chronological limits. For the East, this often involves extension throughout the last quarter of the fourth century and even the first decade of the fifth.

The most troubling point regarding the Balkan policies of Theodosius concerns the establishment of the "territorialized" *magistri* as attested in the *Notitia*. Particularly relevant here are the *magister militum per Thracias* (master of soldiers for Thrace) and the *magister militum per Illyricum* (master of soldiers for Illyricum).[35] Outside the *Notitia* the first datable official notices of the so-called territorial *magistri* are found in the *Codex Theodosianus*, and were issued in 412.[36] Despite the logic of assuming that Theodosius I created the territorial *magister militum per Thracias* to respond to the recently stabilized events in Thrace, which so often demanded the presence of an officer of *magister* rank, the lack of supporting evidence demands caution. Claudian writing against Eutropius in 399 casts Alaric as the master of Illyricum. The Gothic leader, now "as a friend," freely enters walls which he once besieged and pronounces judgment over the wives and children of his former enemies.[37] This has been identified, probably correctly, as a reference to Alaric's exercise of the office of *magister militum per Illyricum*. 399 thus appears to be the earliest secure date for the creation of "territorialized" *magistri* in general. Others argue for an earlier date of origin (usually 388) and subsequent modification (ca. 392–94) even before the present entries in the *Notitia*.[38] The lack of inscriptional data and the absence of secure and detailed evidence of any type other than that in the *Notitia dignitatum* itself cannot resolve these issues, certainly not at the level of precision necessary to confirm the tactical deployments noted therein.

These problems notwithstanding, the circumstances before Theodosius in 388 were right for restructuring the Eastern command. There were clearly two areas which would need special attention for the foreseeable future: Thrace and the frontier with Persia. After the death of Valentinian II in 392 and the transfer of Illyricum to the East, that area too should have required special provisions similar to those for Thrace and the Orient.

The creation of the dual praesental command would ultimately have required the restructuring of the Eastern army throughout. This is reflected in the various sections of the *Notitia*, none of which can be precisely dated. It seems clear that circumstances did not allow for the immediate implementation of a grand plan, for sound redeployments and new assignments back to the East would surely have required a period of adjustment. Theodosius, like Constantine and his dynasty, always had to balance the military need for tightly coordinated command with the political threat posed by overly powerful military leaders. Furthermore, one must keep in mind that the *Notitia* reflects an entire generation of military reorganization in both the East and West, with the very important anomaly and link in the person and career of Stilicho. Having married into the imperial household, Stilicho rose rapidly in the eastern command system but found himself the supreme military officer in the West after the unexpected death of Theodosius, not yet fifty.

The eastern command system which ultimately emerged, as outlined in the *Notitia*, had five basically equal supreme commanders over both infantry and cavalry units. Two of these headed the praesental armies, while the other three commanded regional forces in the most sensitive areas: the eastern frontier, Thrace, and Illyricum. All five armies had approximately the same strength and composition, and thus no one general could challenge the authority of the emperor. Every one of the five regular Eastern *magistri* commanded all the units of his army, both cavalry and infantry, and hence each was also *magister utriusque militiae* (abbreviated *MVM*). In the East, future holders of the imperial office did not have to contend with rival generals often, but with imperious ministers advising the inexperienced successors of Theodosius. Had Theodosius lived to see both sons reach maturity, he probably would have brought the entire military system into line with the eastern reforms in order to achieve a consistent structure under three emperors: Honorius in the West, Arcadius in the East, and himself exercising senior supervision over the Empire as a whole. His death cut short such planning, if in fact he had so planned. In truth, what we may see as his plan may be no more than the goals of Stilicho cast backward onto the legend of Theodosius in Stilicho's search for validation of his claims for guardianship over both Honorius and Arcadius.

Military evolution in the West did not keep pace with that in the East. The West kept the older system of titles longer, although by the reign of Theodosius the Western *magister peditum* was already superior to his cavalry colleague as was denoted by the higher status of *patricius*. The original Constantinian divisions of infantry and cavalry, essentially established for political stability, during the fourth century gave way to the reality of combined operations. The Western *magistri*, although both commanded units of both types, did not have a place in the command structure as a *magister utriusque militiae*, though their Eastern peers did. Obviously this was more a matter of title than function. The various titles in our sources,[39] even including inscriptions, are ambiguous and cannot be pressed to relieve the distressed text of the *Notitia*. In other words, there is no sure way to identify specific commanders known from the literary sources and inscriptions with the commands listed in the *Notitia* for the period prior to 412. Frustrating as all this seems, perhaps the confused state of our knowledge accurately reflects the ambiguities inherent in this period of rapid flux.

At any rate, the sum of the evidence and the theories built upon it makes it clear that no later than 392, and probably as early as 388, Theodosius had begun the reorganization of his command. In all likelihood his plans could never have been fully implemented before he was forced to prepare for a major war against Arbogastes and Eugenius in 394. Nor are we likely to find inscriptional data to confirm the presence of the units listed in the *Notitia* for this early period, for even if the units existed, they would hardly have had the time for inscription-generating activities. The essential point may be that Theodosius did not provide for a true hierarchy of command under himself, but continued to strive for a non-threatening balance. He was the finest commander of his age, and in the 390s could look toward many years of personally vigorous leadership. Not even all of Thrace was stable enough for a return to "business as usual" routines, as Theodosius was to discover as soon as he left Italy for Constantinople in 391.

A question of fundamental importance may be: who was left tending to the defense of Thrace when Theodosius went west in 388? The answer might be the least effective elements of the army, units of the *limitanei*. These were composed of men and their families stationed on or near the frontiers, part-time farmers when possible. These forces probably now included barbarian recruits, such as the followers of Athanaric and others like those Pacatus tells us were guarding the cities in Pannonia.[40] On the other hand, perhaps the task was entrusted to newly raised recruits of barbarians serving on some sort of special assignment while undergoing training and integration, such as those who caused Gerontius trouble at Tomi in 386.[41] Gratian had apparently already used some Alans in special detachments directly associated with him through the imperial guard. All the sources agree that Theodosius took elaborate measures to raise an army to fight Maximus. And despite the claims of Socrates and the other ecclesiastical historians the victories over the Western troops had not come easily.[42] Throughout the Empire soldiers continued to abuse their power over civilians; some had become brigands and were to be treated as such according to the legislation issued from Aquileia in July of 391.[43] This edict seems most applicable to the areas recently denuded of their best troops and commanders for the western war.

The use of new or poorly prepared troops to safeguard the rear areas would hardly have been a radical idea. Pacatus states that one of the principal reasons for Theodosius's recruitment of barbarians was to replace frontier soldiers of "dubious loyalty."[44] Indeed, the regular transfer of recruits to safe areas, for example the documented use of Egypt as a training ground in the years immediately following Adrianople, was routine. But was Thrace an appropriate area for such trust? In retrospect, probably not. By 388, however, many of the barbarians recruited throughout the last decade had been in the Roman army for many years. Athanaric's followers, for example, were enrolled in 381, perhaps those with families into the *limitanei* and those without dependents into special units. Just how long did it take to integrate and train new recruits? Surely not longer than three years. That no barbarian forces played a role significant enough to be noted in the sources for 388 may simply indicate that most barbarians were serving in the regular units of *limitanei*. The *limitanei* typically stayed home, while the comital and palatine troops went on campaign. Whatever the case, there is no denying that groups of barbarians did remain in Thrace and that some were in rebellion when Theodosius returned East. Their "rebellion" was quite limited but almost caught the emperor off guard.

The story of Theodosius's narrow escape from the barbarians after returning as far as Thessalonica in 391 is embellished by another account of the emperor discovering things while among the ordinary people, this time in the humble home of an elderly woman. There, according to Zosimus, he and only five horsemen sought food and lodging while they made for Constantinople in secret. The old woman relayed her suspicions about another guest, whom she thought to be a spy. Sure enough, the barbarian spy spilled the whereabouts of the barbarians who were hiding in the swamps. As Zosimus tells it, the barbarian withstood torture and threats to his life and only divulged his secrets when tricked. The entire episode is clearly an *exemplum* of imperial conduct, reminiscent of Hadrian and the old woman on the road in Cassius Dio.[45] We might doubt the whole story as a didactic fabrication were it not at least partially corroborated by Claudian, who wrote of these same events from a different perspective.[46] The story continues as Theodosius personally returns to his army and leads it against the hiding barbarians. Only the advice of *magister militum* Timasius that the men needed food and rest stopped the emperor from annihilating the already routed foe. Alas, too much food and drink numbed the army into such slumber that the barbarians took heart and attacked, almost catching the emperor himself napping. Promotus urged Theodosius to flee and leave the barbarians to him. Theodosius, with only a small band of retainers, departed hastily for Constantinople, while Promotus successfully upheld Roman honor, according to Zosimus, slaughtering almost all the barbarians who were still engaged among the sleeping Roman soldiers.[47] The emperor, once safely inside his capital, then "renounced wars and battles" and resumed his decadent lifestyle of old.[48]

The reader of Zosimus could not miss the message that Theodosius had not merely fled the barbarians, but lacked the moral stature to give Rome the leadership demanded by the times. Disasters were surely in the making. As difficult as it is to escape from Zosimus and his morality play on the decline of Rome, there is at least one set of facts in all this. The same barbarians who had caused trouble before the campaign against Maximus and had deserted into the wilds of Macedonia were again to blame. What Theodosius faced then was not the collapse of his recruitment program, but the final suppression of a band of barbarian deserters turned brigands. This group was atypical, for it had never acquiesced to the Roman policy of *receptio*.

Theodosius entered Constantinople on 10 November 391. Whether there is any truth in Zosimus's claim that he forsook war and battle, Theodosius stayed in the capital tending to a wide range of civilian and clerical problems until late in the spring of 394, when he took up arms against Arbogastes and Eugenius.[49] Shortly after his return to Constantinople a clash arose between his most prominent advisers: Timasius and Promotus, on the one side, and Rufinus, *magister officiorum*, on the other. Perhaps justly enraged at the conduct and growing power of Rufinus, who it seems had only recently had the supervision of the armament factories added to the powers of his office, Promotus apparently returned a verbal insult with a blow to Rufinus's face delivered in full public view. According to Zosimus, again our only source for such spicy details, an outraged emperor then threatened to make Rufinus emperor if this type of conduct did not end. The story then has Rufinus conspire to have Promotus "reassigned" to training duty in Thrace, ordering a company of barbarians to ambush him there. In Claudian the assassins were Bastarnae.[50] Some of these people had been settled in Thrace as early as the reign of Probus (276–82), while others had perhaps entered much more recently.[51] However, the lack of specific references to the Bastarnae, one of the oldest of the various Scythian peoples (second century B.C.), other than in Claudian and a few still later sources, all written after the end of the third century, must give us pause. This long silence on the Bastarnae raises the possibility that their name had become a convenient poetic device; certainly it should not be pressed.[52]

The same contrast between the incorruptible and loyal Promotus and the deceitful and treacherous Rufinus appears in another of Zosimus's pointed character sketches. Theodosius's own failings and their consequences for the Empire are thereby brought into still sharper relief.[53] The important aspects of the story are the regularity of Promotus's assignment—to inspect the training of the army in a recently threatened diocese—and the possibility that another source confirms the presence of barbarians within his command. Writing in 404 Joannes Chrysostom, bishop of Constantinople, noted a Gothic monastery then existing on Promotus's former estate, perhaps thereby attesting to the ethnicity of some of Promotus's veterans.[54]

Activity in Theodosius's court was directed toward a variety of problems then confronting the Empire. It included bureaucratic restructuring, legislation against counterfeiting, and progressively more determined anti-pagan policies inspired by the Christians. Sometimes actual campaigning might have seemed less violent than the struggles at court for the emperor's ear. The only contemporary imperial legislation bearing directly upon the military was an edict of 29 April 394, which required that the children of soldiers having attained the minimum age for enrollment in the army begin their service at the lowest rank.[55] Valentinian's apparent suicide on 15 May 392 (he was said to have been driven to despair by his own helplessness) did not provoke Theodosius to immediate retaliation against his colleague's tormentors. Nor did Arbogastes's elevation of Eugenius to the purple on 22 August of that year. The immediate result of Valentinian's death was the transference of Illyricum to the East. Arbogastes's first actions were to continue the campaign against the Franks. He launched the last successful Roman sortie beyond the Rhine from Cologne and concluded a treaty that provided for the recruitment of Franks into the Roman army. These were remarkably traditional achievements by Arbogastes, himself Frankish-born, and some sources claim he went too far in promoting other Franks to high positions on his staff.[56]

All Arbogastes's efforts to secure Theodosius's blessing upon him and Eugenius went coolly unacknowledged until no doubt remained that the Eastern emperor was preparing for war. Eugenius and Arbogastes took the initiative by quickly gaining control of the defenses in the Julian Alps, where they planned to meet the inevitable approach of the Eastern army with a series of ambushes leading to encirclement.[57] The emperor departed Constantinople about the middle of May and was at Adrianople on 20 June 394.[58] Renewed efforts enrolled some additional barbarian recruits, probably filling out existing units.[59] Theodosius remained some time at Sirmium. His seemingly leisurely pace must have resulted from the need to assemble troops along the route. Theodosius long hesitated before attempting a breakthrough of the Alpine defenses. While the emperor lingered, Eugenius and his "supporter" Arbogastes decided that Theodosius intended to turn their flank by an amphibious assault behind the defenses on the Adriatic coast.

In response to the supposed threat to the south they weakened the center. Western military intelligence was wrong, their troop displacements fatal. Theodosius struck the center with his entire force. At some point prior to the battle the commander of Arbogastes's strike force, a certain Arbitio,[60] deserted and thereby took with him any chance of implementing the original plan of a series of ambushes. Arbogastes and Eugenius withdrew to the last line of defenses before the route from Emona descended to the plains leading to Aquileia.[61]

Theodosius was desperate for recruits and stripped those fortifications in the Julian Alps not controlled by his rivals for the final phase of his campaign against Eugenius. On 5 and 6 September 394, near the Frigidus (Wippach) River, Theodosius defeated the usurper on the second day of battle. Eugenius and Arbogastes attacked in force from ambush along the flanks as Theodosius descended the road through the narrow valley, attempting to stop his emergence into the plain below. Eugenius was captured and beheaded; Arbogastes took his own life.[62] The events of the battle in later accounts focused on the supposed clash of the gods there represented: Jupiter and Hercules versus the Christian God of Theodosius. Although the divine presence greatly interested Saint Augustine and the ecclesiastical historian Theodoretus, spiritual intervention is not the issue here.[63] Nor is the role of the Bora wind that rolled down from the mountains into the face of the rebels, which is so prominent in Christian accounts (replacing almost all other factors in Orosius). Even the solar eclipse credited by Zosimus for turning a daytime battle into a virtual night of bloodshed is impossible to confirm for these dates. What is, however, clear and relevant to our current discussion is the important role that barbarian troops played in this battle. Indeed, the Frigidus battle witnessed the first demonstrable large-scale use of barbarian recruits in the reign of Theodosius.

A very substantial number of barbarians seems to have fought and fallen in the opening phase of the battle. The only figures given in the sources are 10,000 deaths among Theodosius's barbarians in Orosius and Jordanes's report that twice that number participated with the emperor in the campaign, both of which seem to be wild guesses seized upon to strengthen the impact of their narratives.[64] Socrates, Zosimus, Rufinus, and Joannes Antiochenus, our most detailed sources, make it clear that a large number of barbarians took part, but give no estimates. At the top of the Eastern command stood Timasius and Stilicho, both with the rank of *magister militum*, Stilicho probably of Thrace. Theodosius's barbarian allies or auxiliaries (συμμαχοῦντας)[65] were commanded by Gaïnas, Saul, and Bacurius.[66] Gaïnas, a "Goth from beyond the Danube," had risen from the ranks and after this battle rose to the very highest levels of command in the Eastern army.[67] Saul was an Alan and withdrew his ravaged command to safety on the first day without disgrace, only to die eight years later fighting with Stilicho against Alaric at Pollentia.[68] Bacurius had been a king of the Iberians in Asia Minor at the time of his entry into the Roman army. He was *tribunus sagittariorum* at Adrianople in 378 and then *dux Palestinae* until 394, when he seems to have become *magister militum vacans* (a special command limited to a specific campaign). As such he probably died at the Frigidus.[69]

The highest levels of command over the barbarian units appear to have been quite traditional. Little is known about the more junior officers. There is no question about the availability of Roman officers of barbarian origins, however. For every Gaïnas at the top there were scores of junior officers. Tribigild was but one example. Roman recruiters had long used the rank of military tribune to interest barbarian elites in Roman service and continued doing so.[70] Military tribunes probably commanded the small units of barbarians on the Frigidus. Such young officers preferably were not closely related to their men, but sharing their mother tongue was probably helpful. Given the fact that Theodosius did not restore all garrisons to their former strength, perhaps these barbarian auxiliaries reflect his successful hoarding of manpower. He had no choice but to field every available unit against the usurpers, even barbarian auxiliaries whose planned role was probably in local frontier defense and reserve. Similar circumstances existed in the West. A key factor in creating barbarian units, and one to which we shall return with later and better evidence, was almost certainly the lower cost of their maintenance.

In addition to the regular barbarian units commanded by these three Roman generals, certain Huns from Thrace were especially summoned and fought under their own native leaders.[71] This was apparently not the case for the other barbarian units, and this even though Alaric fought in this battle. Alaric did not command either a large force of troops or his own Gothic followers, if he had any, but "only those barbarian troops given him by Theodosius." For his valor he received not an important command but a dignity, perhaps the title *comes;* only later did he actually gain a true command.[72] On the other side, Arbogastes fielded an army of Roman troops drawn perhaps primarily from the Gaulic provinces and barbarian auxiliaries (*auxiliis barbarorum*) apparently largely Frankish.[73] The barbarian units (βάρβαρα τάγματα) of the Eastern army under Gaïnas led the way, accompanied by the other leaders (ἄλλων ἡγεμόνων), who were in command of barbarian units of cavalry, mounted archers, and of infantry. They were soon in great difficulty, outnumbered by the West's barbarian auxiliaries under

Arbogastes.[74] Both sides clearly fielded very powerful forces of barbarian auxiliaries broken down into Roman tactical units and placed under Roman field commanders.

Contrary to Orosius, the loss of Theodosius's barbarian troops was not a blessing in disguise. Theodosius certainly did not think so, for he took aggressive action to shore up their ranks, dispatching Bacurius and his personal guard to assist. According to Socrates, Bacurius had to fight his way to the hard pressed barbarians under his command, but rallying his forces he turned the tables on the enemy.[75] Zosimus, having just stated that Theodosius deliberately chose to risk his barbarian units (τάγματα) first, is at a loss to account for the survival of all the generals except Bacurius, who apparently gave his life to rescue his forces. The barbarian troops, except possibly the Huns, were incorporated into traditional types of Roman units. Accordingly, they fought in the front ranks and bore the brunt of the first day's combat, suffering near annihilation according to Orosius. The Huns fought under their native leaders (φύλαρχοι) but the remainder fought under duly appointed Roman commanders, all of whom probably had had considerable experience with frontier troops. Many of these troops would, of course, have been entirely or partially of barbarian blood by this period because of long-standing recruitment practices. In recent years the majority of the recruits had spoken Gothic. That a commander such as Gaïnas, having risen through the ranks of the Roman army, happened to find himself leading a unit of men who spoke Gothic is categorically different from specifically recruiting native leaders to bring their own men to battle. This is what Theodosius did with certain Huns. Probably he did so only because there was no time to acculturate these rough outsiders into regular units, but it was an important though limited innovation. No account underestimates the severity of the barbarian casualties or calls them cowards. They fought well but were in no shape to participate in Theodosius's decisive attack just before dawn on the next day.[76]

Theodosius's victory restored unity to the empire, but ever so briefly. Four months later, on 17 January 395, Theodosius died.[77] Never again would the Alpine defenses be completely manned. When Alaric passed through the area in 401 on his march to Italy, these crucial northern defenses could offer him little resistance.[78] Aetius apparently garrisoned some cities against Attila, but the general instability of Noricum, Raetia, and Pannonia prevented any systematic attempt to reconstitute a physical defense for Italy. Theodosius's hesitation before attacking the defenses attests to their strength. Archaeology confirms the energy and care the Romans expended on these walls and fortresses. Moreover, the archaeological record supports an impression of a very fluid situation during the fifth century and on into the sixth.

Some sites in the Julian Alps, such as Gradisce, near Dolenju Lagatec, were permanently abandoned in the late fourth century.[79] Others, like Polhov Gradec, continued into the fifth century, as attested by coin finds.[80] After 490 the Ostrogoths under Theodoric apparently took over most of the northern sites in an attempt to block the routes leading from the Drava and Sava rivers. At Studeno a coin dates from the reign of Arcadius (491–518). Forum Julii was probably a regional command center for the northern defense even before Theodoric, but under the Ostrogoths it became the fulcrum of the system. The Tarsatica–Nauportus barrier was manned at least into the middle of the seventh century.[81] In other words, although there was no one date at which all the fortifications were evacuated, the coherence of the defensive system was never restored after the death of Theodosius. Routine, systematic maintenance was replaced by a long series of *ad hoc* and often temporary moves designed to secure a particular route or meet a particular emergency.

By the death of Theodosius in January 395 Rome had begun to shift to the use of new deployments of barbarian manpower, some with lasting effects for future military policy. Nevertheless, even at this late date no radical departure from fourth-century military practices had occurred. In the absence of any more data only a series of hypotheses seems warranted. Beginning in 379–80, Rome regained the initiative in the field by containing the barbarian incursion within Thrace and Illyricum. Already several groups of barbarians had accepted traditional *receptio* in the Empire and were dispersed among existing units or as small specialized units served under Roman appointees, rarely but sometimes from among their traditional leadership. This phase culminated with the reception of the aged Athanaric in Constantinople in 381, but *receptio* continued to be employed successfully throughout the next decade. Some barbarian groups, particularly in the more remote areas, were quite reluctant to remain in Roman service and had to be forced into submission on more than one occasion. The traditional method of mustering barbarians into Roman service was to transship recruits elsewhere for training and deployment within regular units. That approach was increasingly less practical as operational losses in the Balkans mounted, and as other troops were needed for various local disturbances throughout the East and so could not be spared for reassignment. In some cases, particularly before 384, the road system to transport military redeployment was unsafe or unserviceable. Numerous pieces of legislation regarding problems of recruitment document imperial concern, while the large number of new or restored units in the *Notitia dignitatum* reveals the ultimate success of the search for military manpower.

As a result of logistical pressures, some barbarians—for example Athanaric's followers—were enrolled in existing units of the frontier forces (*limitanei*) to defend the Danubian crossings from further violation. It had long been Roman practice to accord barbarian leaders special recognition and command in the specialized forces of the Roman army, a pattern so prevalent from at least the third century that it has even left traces in the archaeological record.[82] The special forces such as light cavalry were typically taken from peoples with a prior record of success in that aspect of warfare. The highly skilled slingers of the Balearic Islands, whose employment dated from Republican times and continued under the Principate, are the clearest example of this. More recently Alamannic chieftains had been brought into imperial service in the fourth century, and many became successful Roman commanders, usually far from home. Some lower level barbarian leaders and even a few ordinary warriors also rose to high command in the Roman army before and during Theodosius's reign.

The central problem, then, was not the recruitment of barbarians—neither the rank-and-file nor leaders—but rather their proper training during these difficult years. A few small groups of highly skilled barbarians apparently required little or no retraining and were immediately used as special detachments: for example, certain Alanic troops at the court of Gratian, and those haughty warriors who underestimated the Roman commander Gerontius at Tomi in 386. The sources also reveal examples of restless barbarian veterans awaiting newer Roman troops. The Romans thus seem to have paired new units with experienced units in their training process. This hypothesis may explain the assignment of barbarians to Tomi and elsewhere where Roman units were already present. It may also account for some of the paired units found in the *Notitia*, for example the peculiar auxiliary pair of the Iberi-Thraces.[83]

In the campaigns against Maximus in 388 barbarian forces did not figure prominently, indeed played no identifiable role. Possibly the newly formed special units were better suited to home defense at this date because of their incomplete training or questionable performance under combat conditions with other Roman troops. Nor was it likely, despite Ambrose's charges to the contrary, that either Maximus or Theodosius would depend too much on barbarian units. Hence, Theodosius may well have decided to leave them under properly trained and seasoned commanders at the garrison sites as a home guard. Even after the emperor's prolonged three-year stay in Italy, only a few barbarians in Macedonia, troublesome even before his departure, caused trouble. Most must have deserved his trust.

By the outbreak of war against Arbogastes and his creature Eugenius circumstances had again changed. Barbarian units figured to play a prominent role in any operation led by Arbogastes, as in fact they did, and Theodosius's own special forces were as well prepared for service as they would ever be. Large numbers of Eastern barbarians were appearing for duty at often distant posts, including, as we shall explore in the next chapter, some in the West. Theodosius's desperate need for troops is amply demonstrated by his stripping of the Julian Alpine defenses; he could not afford not to use his barbarian forces. At the Frigidus, Theodosius's army was drawn from all available units; his forces included men that Bacurius, recently *dux* of Palestine, had brought, perhaps from the Orient. For the most part the barbarians served in traditional units of Roman design: especially the cavalry, mounted archers, and infantry.

Only certain Huns can be proved to have served under their own native leaders. Perhaps they had a special shock effect. The Huns' very appearance, their peculiarly shaped features, etc., should have surprised a few westerners who may have heard stories like those told by Ammianus Marcellinus. Perhaps their language skills were still limited to Hunnic so that they were unintelligible to Roman command; even those Roman commanders who were of Gothic ancestry could not have led such men. And, if we may believe the old saga of the Goths and the Huns or later history, Goths and Huns were hardly friends.[84] Nor is there any reason to assume that the Hunnic forces in 394 were the same as those under Alatheus and Saphrax, who presumably had settled in Pannonia in ca. 380. In fact, the sources would hardly have overlooked such a fact. There were numerous groups of Huns, most still living beyond the Danube, without any central leader until Uldis emerged at their head around 400. Some were at Adrianople and others were with the "Carpodaces," defeated by Theodosius in 379–80.[85] Finally, after the battle at the Frigidus Theodosius rewarded bravery with Roman dignities: probably the honorific title *comes* to Alaric, and, one must suppose, other appropriate honors to less historically significant men.[86] Had Theodosius possessed a sorcerer's eye and seen into the future, he would have rewarded Alaric with a sword thrust to the heart.

Barbarian auxiliaries had proven loyal and courageous on the Frigidus. The next step in their use within the army was to place major barbarian units in more independent roles and allow them to be led by men of their own ethnic background, though not necessarily of the same precise origins.

This was a step Theodosius did not live to take. In essence, so far the experiment was not too different from the use of auxiliaries during the Principate. Theodosius's use of some newly recruited auxiliaries had been traditional; that is, he intended them to assist in major campaigns and hold areas of potential unrest and concern when other troops were unavailable. Other barbarians were deployed in specialized units, equally traditional. Still another traditional practice remained in effect under Theodosius: commanders were regularly transferred from unit to unit. A significant distance was thereby maintained between field commanders and their troops. In time this policy too gave way. But we are getting ahead of ourselves.

As is so often the case with the study of the Roman army, many of the most telling details on the employment of barbarians have come to light in modern Germany. Britain, the other traditional source of comparable data, is not as useful for the latter phases of life on the frontiers because of its peculiar development during the later fourth century, which focused attention on the defense of the coast. So let us turn instead to an excursus on the Raetian provinces. The relatively plentiful sources for this area illuminate otherwise obscure details of late fourth and early fifth century Roman military policies regarding the use of barbarians; moreover, probable presence there of recruits from Theodosius's Balkan victories and the vital role of Raetian troops in the campaigns of Stilicho gave it a central role in shaping those policies.

Summary

Barbarian soldiers played a minor role in the struggle between Theodosius and Magnus Maximus. But barbarians serving in new type units—the barbarian *auxilia*—fought and died in their thousands on the banks of the Frigidus. Both the Western army of Arbogastes and Eugenius and the Eastern forces of Theodosius fielded large numbers of barbarians serving in auxiliary units. These units were under traditional Roman general officers and probably commanded in battle by military tribunes recruited from among all sorts of barbarian peoples. In the battle of the Frigidus all units— regulars and auxiliaries—fought with distinction. One barbarian officer of junior rank believed his valor deserved a promotion—Alaric. His superiors disagreed.

STILICHO'S TRANSALPINE
RECRUITMENT AREAS

ALTHOUGH THE Roman armies survived Adrianople and adapted new techniques of deployment and supply, the period from 378 to 400 was nevertheless a time of steady retreat for Roman power and civilization. Limited economic and military resources confronted extraordinary demands. The campaigns of the usurpers Magnus Maximus and later Arbogastes-Eugenius against Theodosius cost the Western armies dearly. Arbogastes in particular relied heavily upon his Germanic auxiliaries. Raetia, in many ways a microcosm of frontier life, contributed its share to these armies and suffered in their losses.

Theodosius sought to strengthen the armies in the years following the defeat of Maximus by a process of upgrading and transferring existing units of the *limitanei* into the *comitatenses* and *pseudocomitatenses*. The *comitatenses* consisted of elements of cavalry and infantry stationed in the interior areas of the frontier provinces under the command of a *comes*. Service in them carried greater prestige and pay. By this time the distinction between the *comitatenses* and the *pseudocomitatenses* had blurred. Originally *pseudocomitatenses* was a temporary designation for units moved under the command of the *comes* from the *limitanei*. While on duty in the *pseudocomitatenses* soldiers received higher pay. By the late fourth century the temporary nature of the posting had lapsed. The technique of upgrading units was widely used in the East after the defeat at Adrianople. In the West this process established many "new units" of the *comitatenses* which bore the name Honorius.[1] The gaps created in the frontier defenses had to be manned somehow.[2] There were other possibilities along the Rhine and Danube, many as yet only poorly understood.

The building campaigns of Valentinian I (364–75) had brought a significant increase in general economic activity along the Rhine and Upper Danube, as elsewhere. One reflection of this is the number of coins found from his reign in these regions.[3] This chapter explores the nature and limits

Illustration 7. Depiction of *villa rustica* from the era of the Principate

of the Roman army here at the opening of the fifth century. By then the Raetian provinces and Noricum Ripense had declined considerably from the era of Valentinian. Even the energetic Valentinian should be regarded only as an aberration in the overall retreat of many aspects of Roman civilization, particularly villa agriculture, from the frontier provinces (see illustration 7). In Raetia this retreat began around midcentury, but elsewhere in the West the transformations begun during the crisis of the third century were never reversed.

This chapter will highlight some of the more recent archaeological discoveries in the Raetian provinces and Noricum Ripense, especially those of the last decade. Some of these have yet to be published except in local announcements.[4] These discoveries will enable us to understand more precisely what types of deployment and recruitment possibilities existed in the transalpine areas nearest to Italy. This region was of central importance to the contenders for military superiority in the era dominated by Stilicho, despite what was clearly a very small Roman military commitment. Among the Roman options being explored during the second half of the century was the establishment of regular ties with barbarian communities well beyond the frontiers, which would thereafter serve as buffers. Another was the increasing reliance upon recruits from the Germanic villages on the opposite side of the river from Roman installations.

The literary sources rarely distinguish the late Roman provinces of

Raetia Prima and Raetia Secunda. Rather, most authors were content with earlier governmental units and literary traditions. For example, the poet Claudian wrote of "Raetia" rather than Raetia Secunda. As a result, attention must be given to both Raetian provinces. Their frontier garrisons also were combined under the command of the *dux Raetiae primae et secundae*, through whom orders from Stilicho to withdraw elements from them would have passed.[5] In this way all the possibilities raised in the sources for recruitment from "Raetia" will be addressed, though the two late provinces are not of equal interest. Because of its close relationship with peoples beyond the frontier, Raetia Secunda is crucial for understanding Roman policies in the region. It therefore will receive the more careful treatment. Within this context, my primary goal is to go beyond surveying and integrating new data to offer a picture of life along and just behind the Danubian frontier. This area extended eastward from approximately modern Regensburg to Linz, westward from Regensburg to Ulm, and then south to Lake Constance and the Alpine Passes of Grisons during the fourth century.

The essential features of the transformation of the late ancient world in this area are similar in outline to developments elsewhere in the West, especially those along the middle Rhine and in northern Gaul. These common trends were so strong that even Britain seems to follow along at least until the first decades of the fifth century. Much of what follows is a review and reorientation of earlier discussions of the frontier environment on the lower Danube, but refocused on the upper Danube. This region provides better data for the era ca. 375–425 than are typically available elsewhere. It was an area of special interest to Stilicho and other contemporary military leaders, many of whom contended for support in Raetia and/or Noricum.

Until recently it was widely believed that a general breakdown of Roman control followed virtually everywhere upon the Roman defeat at Adrianople in 378 and (for the West) the death of Gratian in 383. Grounds for that belief eroded in further study. The initiative still lay with Rome, and, although the manner of Roman control had certainly changed from the early fourth century, substantial changes had begun before Adrianople. The last two decades of the fourth century appear to have witnessed an intensification of earlier Roman programs designed to exploit nearby sources of Germanic recruits. Roman ideological patterns and the material symbols used to convey them remained dominant, although in forms characteristic of the frontiers rather than the core provinces of the Mediterranean. This Roman legacy, military or provincial bureaucratic, outlasted effective Roman political control and stretched beyond it geographically. Barbarian officers took on the styles of dress indicative of their Roman commands, and some of them are now known to have recrossed the frontier at the completion of their service. Their remains occasionally come to light today. These Roman military traditions continued throughout the fifth century in the West, where barbarian kings built new societies upon the office of *magister militum*. As military command matured in stable kingdoms, the process of political definition often involved an eclectic borrowing of titles and iconography associated with the highest levels of Roman provincial government as well as the customary military traditions. The roots of these processes were in the military contexts of frontier life and can be seen in detail in several recent discoveries in Germany.

Along the lower Rhine, Rome continued to make use of *laeti* to defend the territory largely abandoned by the Roman army at the opening of the fourth century, when a quick release of pressures along the frontier there had been imperative.[6] Elsewhere, including Raetia, this was not the preferred or typical response. As Rome reasserted its military power in the fourth century—it had never lost its psychological and economic preeminence—Germanic peoples along the frontiers were routinely lured into the Empire, where the men found ready service in the army. *Receptio* in Raetia as elsewhere was a routine responsibility of local commanders, although, of course, officially decisions to admit barbarians flowed from the emperor himself. Many barbarians entered Roman service under Constantine's sons. Constans (337–50) and Constantine II (337–40) struck a numerous issue of "hut-type" coins to commemorate the process on the Rhine.[7]

Rome pursued a "carrot-and-stick" policy. If you were peaceful, cooperative neighbors—as most Germans were—you were welcome to trade and work with Rome. Often you could emigrate with your family and be trained to serve in the Roman army. If, on the other hand, you plotted against Rome or allied with potential enemies, the same Roman army that your brother or cousin had joined might descend upon your village unannounced! Threatening groups awoke to find themselves under attack, their villages burnt, their leaders captured or slain. Julian's raids across the Rhine and Valentinian's across both the Rhine and Danube are well documented.[8] Almost everywhere along the frontiers there was a local equilibrium. We are learning much more about its late phases in Germany because of recent excavations there. Moreover, there is scattered evidence elsewhere, particularly along the middle and lower Danube, which suggests that trans-frontier interaction had become routine. Behind the frontier, Roman rule remained secure, although progressively transformed to meet the needs of a militarized society with ever-increasing Germanic components.

One of the most interesting—and frustrating—characteristics of artifactual remains is their diversity. Nevertheless they reveal a clear preference for Roman goods, so long as they were available, among all segments of the population. This makes the judgment of "ethnicity" difficult, especially since the contemporary usage of terms for various Germanic "tribes" and even the identity "Roman" was not rigorous or consistent. New recruits did not ordinarily seek to preserve the material aspects of their previous lives—unless, that is, the old tradition had produced something technically superior or culturally venerable, a religious artifact, for example.[9] Other than personal items, particularly ornamentation for dress, recruits assigned to posts beyond the original area of their recruitment lost the ability to acquire traditional replacement products when the old ones gave out. Pottery, for example, would have been among the first items needing to be replaced by local wares. The fluidity of people and cultures along the frontier clouds discussion of the flow of ideas and loyalties. It also demonstrates the continuing power of the Roman army to assimilate and transform.

As numerous inscriptions attest, throughout the fourth century many of the recruits who had risen through the ranks, and therefore could afford to have their lives noted in stone, continued to recall their ethnic origins: Burgundian, Frankish, Gothic, or whatever. This included some who had served along the Rhine and Danube. Still, this was in keeping with the epigraphic tradition of Romans giving their place of birth. These successful soldiers had no Roman towns to provide the starting place for their Roman lives. Hence they substituted their "nation" of birth for this birthplace. That they note a "nationality" did not reflect a mixed loyalty after they entered Roman service, although the dispute between Fravitta and Eriulf under Theodosius makes it clear that serving Rome was not always easy for some Germanic chiefs at the end of the fourth century.[10] Earlier, when Julian attacked barbarian villages across the Rhine (ca. 360), a few of his recruits from those villages advised their relatives to flee. They did not advise waiting in ambush. By transferring recruits to new areas whenever possible, Rome always hoped to prevent conflicting loyalties to relatives still beyond the frontier. Theodosius was similarly concerned, though along much of the lower Danube the peoples living on the opposite shore were not relatives of the victors of Adrianople but rather were subjects of the Huns and their allies.

Like many earlier families to have entered the Empire, men of Germanic origins were proud of the successes of their forbears. Indeed, toward the end of the fourth century there are examples of men of distant Germanic origin noting their Roman places of birth, the Roman careers of their ancestors, but also the ethnic origins of the family at the time of its settlement in the Empire.[11] The examples here having to do with Germanic recruits into the army could easily find their early parallels among many other peoples conquered long before. Throughout the Roman era imperial iconography for dealing with foreigners, on coinage as well as in literature, was readily adapted to whichever group was then under discussion. But until the establishment of the first Germanic kingdoms in the fifth century there never existed a political context within the Empire to focus and re-invigorate previously foreign identities.[12]

The fourth century was relatively stable in the Danube region of Raetia despite the raids of the Iuthungi in 357 and various incursions of Alamanni, particularly during the reign of Valentinian. Beginning in the third century, the tenor of life had progressively moved away from the world of the Principate. Throughout most of the fourth century Rome was everywhere on the offensive against increasingly tenacious Germanic groups. The offensive extended along most sections of the northern frontiers and seems to have accelerated after the revolt of Magnentius (350–53). This rebellion illustrated once again the fragility of the late Roman peace, especially when the usurper's barbarian allies and rowdy soldiers continued to harass towns and villas long after their leaders' demise. Constans (337–50), Constantius II (337–61), Julian (360–63), and Valentinian I (364–75) systematically addressed sections of the frontiers and specific groups of barbarians: Constans was active on the Rhine, Constantius II concentrated on the Danube, Julian took over on the Rhine, while Valentinian I (364–75) built almost everywhere, particularly along the upper Rhine and the middle and upper Danube. The system of fortifications connecting the Danube to Lake Constance—the so-called Danube-Iller-Rhine *limes*—owes its origins to the end of the third century. Valentinian took personal interest in these defenses. He was near Basel supervising work on a fortification in 374 when word arrived of Quadi raids into Illyricum.[13] Roman sorties across the frontiers often took advantage of Roman control of the rivers and fortified landing areas on the barbarian shore to strike deep within *barbaricum*.[14]

The heart of *barbaricum*, a Roman territorial concept not likely shared by those living there, had gradually shifted to the *limes*. In fact, Ammianus Marcellinus writing ca. 395 stated that along the Rhenish frontier most barbarians lived within ten miles of the river. Numerous coin finds and their chronological spread reveal a continuous interaction across the frontier through the end of the first decade of the fifth century. At that point the numismatic evidence ends, although most probably not the relationships which its presence denotes.[15] Much the same could be said for the upper Danube.[16] This movement to the *limes* continued until its collapse or, in the case of Raetia, its gradual transformation and redefinition. Germanic peoples often moved first into the direct proximity of the Roman fortified camps and towns along the river, then crossed and entered into Roman military service. Behind and along the *limes* Romans in Raetia and Noricum Ripense lived in a complex environment dominated by the military and the atmosphere of impending crisis that it fostered. That foreboding can still be sensed by anyone who sees the extremely stout walls, often a meter or more thick in even the watchtowers, erected during this period. Soldiers built these massive defenses in the Raetias and Noricum Ripense as everywhere along Rome's frontiers in spite of the widely acknowledged barbarian inability to surmount any fortifications.

As it had for centuries, the Roman army continued to recruit heavily from among veterans, themselves often of Germanic origin, and barbarians beyond the frontier. The military culture of the camps introduced the recruits to concepts and lifestyles that were peculiar to the late Roman army. Since Roman urban and civilian populations dwindled more rapidly than the army units, the military culture of the soldiers was left without significant challenge from the civilian side. The army's dominance of the frontier setting reached a new high. It was still the Roman army, with its traditions of service to one's unit and commander and dependence on the original supply network. Loyalty to your fellows in arms was a commitment some Germanic warriors too knew well. The voices around the camps by now echoed in many dialects and languages, but most must have been Germanic. Latin remained the language of record.

The influence of Roman military rank and its display transcended the political demarcations of Roman territory, as well as any lingering civilian, or "Mediterranean," influences thereabout. In the long run, military culture assimilated Roman civilian culture on the frontier, along with whatever existed of Germanic culture. This process accelerated as centralized Roman political control waned and vanished in the course of the fifth and sixth centuries. But because the Raetian provinces were a part of the diocese of Italy, they remained under Italian-based government longer than many other areas in the West (see map 5). Everywhere, but particularly visibly in Raetia Secunda, the Roman military played a dual role. On the one hand, it acted as a vehicle of acculturation; on the other, as a machine that processed and redeployed peoples without regard to ethnic background and points of recruitment. Aspects of the later and perhaps the former characteristic could still be witnessed as late as 500. Raetia was able to resist uncontrolled immigration-invasion well into the sixth century, and therefore beyond the chronological boundaries of this study. In a sense, late Roman

Raetia reveals distinctive qualities of the earlier forms of Romanization through provincialization, but now without the civilian emphasis of the Antonine era.

In the Raetian provinces the urban orientation of Roman civilization gave way to an increasingly rural environment. Indeed, Augsburg (Augusta Vindelicum) alone came close to retaining an urban complexity, but only just into the early decades of the fifth century. Augsburg was not only the civilian capital of Raetia Secunda, but the residence of the *praepositus thesaurorum*. As such it served as a supply depot for the army and headquarters for the unit of *equites stablesiani seniores* that was doubtless assigned to guard it. One of the cavalrymen may have lost or discarded a typical Germanic style triangular bone comb, recently discovered in the Jesuitengasse. The exact role of the martyr sites of St. Urich and Afra during the later fifth century is unclear, as is the fate of the Romanized population.[17] From the mid-sixth century on, especially after 600, there is evidence of a small Germanic presence inside the city. At the distance from the ancient city of the modern suburbs, the dates for Germanic burials are considerably earlier, perhaps as early as ca. 500.[18]

Whatever Romanized populations survived in ancient Augusta Vindelicum after ca. 415 at first may have felt isolated, then gradually realized that their neighbors on all sides were even more Germanic than they themselves. Sidonius Apollinaris refers to Aetius's success "against" the Vindelicans in 429. This is usually interpreted to mean that he defeated Iuthungi in Raetia, as he did less ambiguously in Noricum.[19] These campaigns were part of his attempt to restore Roman control in the frontier provinces, but what level of control he strove for or achieved is unknowable. Perhaps the most compelling evidence of Rome's continuing involvement in Raetia under Honorius are two of his *solidi* struck in 422, one found at Bludenz and the other at Salez in Raetia Prima. Both are in proof condition and may have been the pay of officers in Aetius's campaigns.[20] There can be no doubt that at least in Batavis (Passau-Altstadt) some troops remained until around midcentury. But Batavis was isolated. Other units are reported to have disbanded when their pay no longer arrived.[21]

At Kempten-Lindenberg (Cambodunum), the only other truly urban site in Raetia Secunda before the crisis of the third century, and one with an especially noteworthy religious precinct, the situation is even less clear and certainly less impressive. There the evidence for occupation is sparse and sporadic from the third-century invasions through the fourth century. Although noted in the *Notitia* as the post of the commander of a detachment of the Third Italian Legion, the other two units of this command

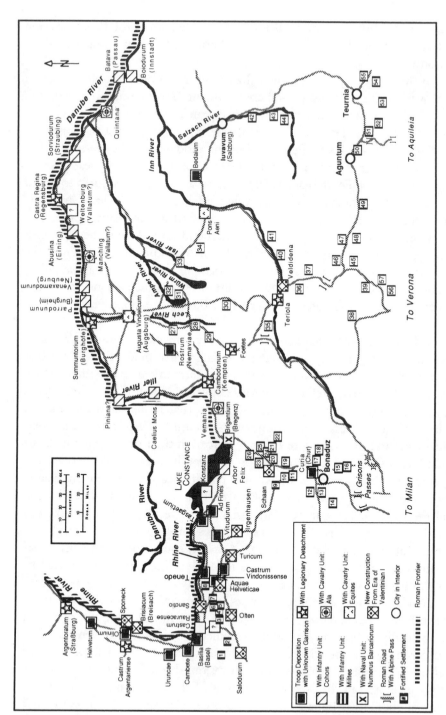

Map 5 The Late Roman Danube-Iller-Rhine Frontier and Hinterland

LIST OF FORTIFIED SETTLEMENTS

MAXIMA SEQVANORVM

1 Stürmenkopf/Wahlen
2 Portifluh/Erschwil
3 Renggen/Diegten
4 Frohburg/Trimbach

5 Groß Chastel/Lostorf
6 Wittnauer Horn/Wittnau
7 Frick
8 Mandacher Egg/Villigen

RAETIA I

9 Georgenberg ob Berschis
10 Castels/Mels
11 Burg/Vilters
12 Belmont/Flims
13 Schiedberg/Sagogn
14 Surcasti
15 Tiefencastel
16 Motta Vallac/Salouf
17 Castiel

18 Tummihügel/Maladers
19 Gutenberg/Balzers
20 Krüppel ob Schaan
21 Stellfeder/Nenzing
22 Montikel/Bludenz
23 Lutzengüetle/Gamprin
24 Heidenburg/Göfis
25 *Clunia(?)*—Liebfrauenberg/Rankweil
26 Neuburg/Koblach

RAETIA II

27 Stoffersberg/Igling
28 *Abodiacum*—Lorenzberg/Epfach
29 Altenstadt
30 *Coveliacae*—Moosberg/Murnau
31 Widdersberg/Herrsching
32 Weßling
33 Römerschanze/Grünwald

34 Valley
35 Kalvarienbergl/Imst
36 Sonnenburg/Natters
37 Vill
38 Zenoberg/Meran
39 *Sabiona*—Säben/Klausen

NORICVM RIPENSE

40 Himmelreich/Volders
41 Hochkapelle/Brixlegg
42 *Cucullae*—Georgenberg/Kuchl

43 Bachsfall/Bischofshofen
44 Götschenberg/Bischofshofen

NORICVM MEDITERRANEVM

45 Hinterbühel/Ehrenburg
46 Burgstall/Niedervintl
47 Sonnenburg/St. Lorenzen
48 Burgkofel/Lothen
49 Innichen
50 Kirchbichl/Lavant

51 Pittersberg/Laas
52 St. Helena/Wieserberg
53 Kappele/Jadersdorf
54 Duel/Feistritz
55 Heidenschloß/Weißenstein

ITALIA

56 Peterbühel/Völs

57 Katzenlocherbühel/Kastelruth

were far away at Vemania and Cassiliacum. Life at Kempten could hardly have been very "urban."[22] Elsewhere in the interior of the province other small garrisons watched over roadway junctions and bridges from hilltop redoubts such as Lorenzberg/Epfach (Abodiacum). Recent coin finds extend the chronology of that outpost back to at least the first decade of the fifth century.[23] Other such islands of defense offering security behind the frontier included Coveliacae, Stoffersberg, Grünwald, and Rostrum Nemaviae, where even Ostrogothic coins (ca. 500–550) have come to light in excavation. Foetes, like Kempten, housed a detachment of the Third Italian Legion.[24] A few men scattered about a decayed landscape that had once been a prosperous Roman countryside now constituted the province of Raetia Secunda.

To the south, Raetia Prima fared little better. Its capital, Chur, remained an important site throughout this period and during the Middle Ages, although then mainly as a small, heavily fortified center atop today's cathedral hill overlooking the Rhine valley.[25] Bregenz Oberstadt (Brigantium), on Lake Constance just east of where the Rhine enters the lake, like Chur, was an urban fortified retreat much smaller than in former times. From around 300 the high fortified area at Oberstadt dominated the lower and less defensible Oelrain settlement at Bregenz. The *Notitia* lists Brigantium as a base for the fleet patrolling Lake Constance. The latest coins date to ca. 388–408, while some *fibulae* are typologically very late fourth or early fifth century Roman military styles, one probably east Germanic.[26] Another unit of the fleet was stationed at Arbor Felix, on a narrow peninsula surrounded by swamps, 30 km westward along the coast from Bregenz.[27] Both units were under the command of the *praefectus classis barcariorum* stationed at Eburodunum (Yverdon-les-Bains).[28] Up the Rhine at Schaan the late Roman fortification, built after the raids of the middle of the fourth century, superseded an earlier refuge atop the hill at nearby Krüppel. In the late fourth century perhaps 50 men in the garrison took advantage of the stout fortification at Schaan to defend and monitor the road between Brigantium and Chur, thereby blocking the route to the Grisons Passes further south.[29]

A good example of late Roman hilltop fortifications in Raetia Prima is that at Balzers. This site was occupied from very early times until it was abandoned under the Principate, only to be resettled again in the fourth century; it remained so until at least the end of the sixth century.[30] Probably the best evidence of continuity and complex ethnic relationships at such sites ca. 400–600 is the grave field at Bonaduz, the burial site for an as yet unexcavated hilltop fortification. The artifacts there are highly diverse, with a wide assortment of items suggesting relationships with Roman, Alamannic, and later Frankish customs.[31]

Throughout the Raetian provinces the wealthiest families left their estates for the more secure provinces to the south in the course of the second half of the fourth century, if not earlier. With them departed a strong impetus for the preservation of the various ideological aspects of *romanitas*, as well as the physical symbols of Roman life and culture that accompanied it. The differences between Raetia and Noricum were marked in this regard. Raetia was highly exposed, bordered on two of three "sides" by *barbaricum* and rather easily fordable rivers. In Raetia Secunda we know of no examples where normal villa agriculture continued to the end of the century. Southeast in Noricum, however, most of the indigenous Roman population persisted, and with it, most traditional aspects of late Roman life and culture.

Late Roman *villae* offer only one, commonly cited, demonstration of these shifts and the distinctions between north and south.[32] In Noricum the fortified villas near Wimsbach (Wels) and Heilbrunn survived as agricultural centers with little interruption until the end of the fourth century. But even in the south not all farmers found refuge on the surviving villas. Temporary refuges, apparently numerous in naturally defensible terrain (though few are excavated or published), offered safety from hostile forces here as throughout the frontier provinces.[33] At least three fortified hilltop camps are known in Noricum Ripense; those at Gröbming, Kuchl, and Micheldorf.[34] Refuges and the gradual cessation of villa agriculture before 400 can be seen, for example, in the area around Salzburg.[35] Maxima Sequanorum, indeed Noricum Mediterraneum and even Italia had fortified settlements at this time. Life behind walls and towers typified existence, particularly in the frontier provinces where military activity was a commonplace.[36]

In the region beyond the Danube-Iller-Rhine *limes* there was a concurrent development of defensive settlements on promontories, with clear relationships in personal ornament to the Roman military and civilian styles a short distance away. The ethnic identification of the population at these sites is not readily apparent because of the complex intertwining of "Germanic" and "Roman" artifacts. Nor is it certain which Germanic influence was most prominent; identifiable inhabitants even included elements of east Germanic troops recruited into the Roman army far down the Danube. This complex settlement situation continued until ca. 500 at least.[37]

In Raetia Secunda an example of still another type of defensive enclave

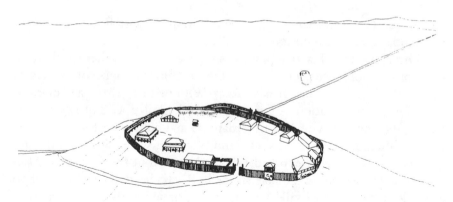

Illustration 8. Late Roman farmstead near Weßling, Germany, in the era of Valentinian I

is now fully excavated and soon will be completely published.[38] This was a very small fortified farming community, a permanent settlement, not a temporary refuge. It lies about 25 km southwest of Munich, near the small village of Weßling, so-called Weßling-Frauenwiese (see illustration 8). Here were discovered ten structures, of which a half dozen may have been occupied in the second half of the fourth century. They range from a small and rather primitive bath and a large dwelling with impressive stalls, presumably the residence of the headman of the community, to very humble accommodations for others and livestock. The site lies 3 km off the Roman road connecting Augsburg to Salzburg. It began in the second century as a *villa rustica* and reached its maximum fortified extent after the middle of the fourth century. It was definitely occupied into the early years of the fifth century, as is proven by many coins, including some of the very small bronze pieces characteristic of the last phase of Roman minting in the West, as well as small finds and stylistically datable fibulae (see illustration 9). Of the 319 coins so far reported, 298 date to the fourth century, with 24 struck between 383 and 400.[39]

The fortified farmstead of Weßling-Frauenwiese, together with its previously excavated grave field (1965, 25 interments), promises to provide an extraordinary glimpse of late Roman life far removed from both the waning *villae rusticae* and the dwindling urban centers like Augusta Vindelicum (Augsburg). Farmsteads like Weßling-Frauenwiese must have contributed their surplus to the towns and garrisons, hence the proximity to the Roman road; however, at the moment the presence of other Weßling-type sites in Raetia and elsewhere has yet to be proved definitively by excavation. It is safe to generalize only that the *villae rusticae* declined more rapidly in

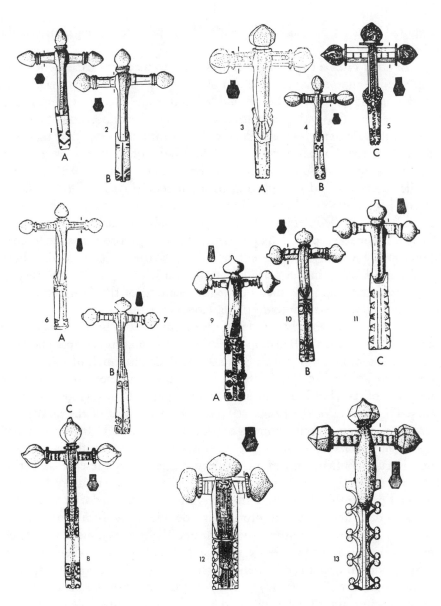

Illustration 9. Types of late Roman "onion-topped" fibulae

exposed areas, in part at least because of the permanent departure of the property owners.

In other cases the transition from Roman to medieval settlement seems to have had another pattern: the end of Roman settlements that had begun in the second century or before and lasted in some manner until ca. 400; next a period of no active habitation; finally the superimposition of an early medieval settlement, typically during the seventh century, upon the stone remains of the Roman occupations.[40] In other words, some sites ceased as centers of resident populations in the last decades of the fourth century, while others lingered a couple of generations longer as small fortified farmsteads. People who could not afford to risk flight had no choice but to remain behind walled defenses, be they farmsteads, fortlets, or hilltop settlements. The markets provided by the small military garrisons and the Roman bureaucracy were also still present in some of the towns. To generalize about settlement history in the period of transition is to slight the diversity of local resources and ingenuity, but at the opening of the fifth century all these events were still unfolding in a Roman context.

Until at least the early decades of the fourth century units of the reserve army were stationed at Bedaium (Seebruck) in Noricum Ripense and Pons Aeni (Pfaffenhofen) in Raetia Secunda. At Bedaium much of the civilian community seems to been destroyed in midcentury, perhaps during the invasions of 357, but life continued on a meager level throughout the century. The destiny of the troops at Pons Aeni—one unit of the *pseudocomitatenses* and, around midcentury, a cavalry unit of the field army, the *equites stablesiani juniores*—remains unclear.[41] Elsewhere, however, there is recent numismatic confirmation of a continued regular army presence at fortifications, and even at select river crossing sites in the interior, until at least the end of the fourth century. In a minimum of half a dozen cases such outposts definitely persisted into the first decade of the fifth century.

Two *siliquae* of the usurper Constantine III (407–11), minted at Trier, have turned up at the previously excavated sites of Bürgle (ancient Piniana, near Gundremmingen) and Lorenzberg near Epfach. These coins along with a few "small finds" of jewelry, pottery sherds, etc., push the occupation of these sites into the fifth century, perhaps even into the middle of the century. Constantine rose in Britain in 407, was captured at Arles in 411, and was soon summarily executed, so that his coins provide an unusually unambiguous date (see illustration 10). As usual with new issues, these coins were struck to gain the support of troops. Discovery of Constantine's coins at Bürgle and Lorenzberg probably reveals the presence of his veterans there, which suggests that the Raetian provinces sided with him briefly. Another

Stilicho's Transalpine Recruitment Areas

Illustration 10. Siliqua of Constantine III

of Constantine's *siliquae* was discovered at Gelbe Bürg, beyond the frontier in Unterfranken, perhaps the pay of a former Roman soldier who had returned home.[42] A Milanese *siliqua* of Arcadius was also recently found at Putzmühle, like Gelbe Bürg not a military site at all. At Burghöfe a *siliqua* of the usurper Magnus Maximus (383–88) and one of Arcadius reveal late fourth century continuity there; two coins of Constantine III carry it to ca. 411. The hoard of 43 coins (late third century to Arcadius) found near Grünwald, where the Roman road from Salzburg to Augsburg crossed the Isar, contains a *siliqua* struck at Constantinople under Arcadius, 392–95.[43]

A single coin on any one site hardly proves a theory; however, the appearance of rarities like the coins of Constantine III demands a hypothesis. I suggest that they represent a payment made by Constantine to the officers of the garrisons on this his eastern flank so as to secure their nonintervention against him in his struggle with Honorius's government in Ravenna. Rome essentially ceased striking bronze coins after the death of Theodosius in 395, relying upon existing supplies and non-monetary rewards. The latter, however, could be effective only when proffered by a commander the troops knew and respected. Constantine lacked such influence in Raetia: he was an upstart stranger desperate to win allegiance quickly and from afar. Accordingly, he had little choice but to "bribe" the local officers with precious metals. That he never called upon them for active support is clear enough. Instead, in his hour of need at Arles in 411, he turned (fruitlessly) to barbarians, particularly certain Frankish auxiliaries. Had the Raetian provinces actually rebelled, some literary source would surely have noted it. Virtually every coin of Constantine III so far unearthed in Raetia was discovered in or around a military encampment whose existence is confirmed by the *Notitia dignitatum*. None have turned up in the fortifications at Regensburg and Straubing (Sorviodurum), that is, in the frontier area unaccountably absent from the *Notitia*. Perhaps this is significant, but many fortifications that are listed have yet to yield coins of the usurper.

This distribution of coins of Constantine III in Raetia suggests a scenario somewhat as follows. At the death of Theodosius the small Roman military presence in the Raetian provinces was continued or restored following his defeat of Arbogastes and Eugenius. Stilicho was so certain that this was the case that he turned to Raetia at least twice for recruits between 395 and 401. Constantine III tried to secure his flank by "a few pieces of silver," and the troops did stay put. They were still there when Constantius restored military order on the frontiers shortly after 413 as appears to be implied in the Raetian sections of the *Notitia dignitatum*. If the minting of coins makes them reliable indicators of a *terminus a quo*, their great durability renders them problematic as indicators of a *terminus post quo*. Coins alone therefore cannot provide a credible date at which the Roman army in Raetia metamorphosed into mere bands of Roman barbarian auxiliaries. Small finds suggest a date not before the opening of the second quarter of the fifth century. The solitary coin of Arcadius found at Putzmühle could have been lost by anyone any time after it was minted, but the most common use of silver coins was to pay officers. Perhaps this one was lost during a routine and unreported trip into the countryside. Even if Constantine III's agents gave some coins to some barbarians serving in Raetia—which seems unlikely—that could not account for their distribution at Roman camps.

These various finds, especially the coins of Constantine III, reveal that some regular Roman garrisons were still serving in Raetia as late as 411 and probably a decade or two later. That seems clear even though another raider, Radagaisus and his bands (ca. 405), may have caused considerable damage in the Alpine foothills, and even though downstream in Noricum tax contributions had slipped so low that the emperor Honorius may have disdained their worth in 408.[44] In his *De civitate Dei* (written ca. 413–22) Saint Augustine comments about a man's dream that featured a horse carrying supplies to the soldiers in Raetia.[45] This may be read as implying that local provisions were inadequate for even the modest forces present there. More likely, Augustine's story points to the continued utilization of the requisition and supply system in which transportation costs to frontier provinces were state responsibilities. Such augmentation of the local resources had been routine for the regular units of the army for a long time. A continuing importation of certain foods and manufactured items into Raetia is what we would expect if even semi-regular troops, not merely farmer-soldiers, were still garrisoned there. The increasing use of barbarians established upon lands along the frontiers as their principal recompense diminished these transportation costs to regular forces.

In short, the traditional assumption of an abandonment of Raetia under Stilicho does not find support on the ground. There is absolutely no evidence that Rome abandoned these provinces in the first half of the fifth century, and much to the contrary. The references in Claudian to Stilicho's actions in Raetia, as we shall see in the next chapter, are not to an evacuation at all.[46] This is quite apparent at numerous sites along the river from Eining to Künzing. This stretch of the Danubian frontier centered on the legionary fortress of Regensburg (Castra Regina) and included the important archaeological sites in and near Straubing. At Straubing the late Roman camp was no longer occupied by the middle of the fifth century, when the earliest Alamannic (or "Bavarian") graves appear at Alburg near the small stream flowing from Oberharthausen. The Germanic presence was continuous there for the next two centuries and included a brief but significant Ostrogothic presence.[47] Eining, Straubing, and Regensburg will be revisited shortly.

With this background, the following themes within the context of Raetia Secunda can be explored in greater detail: (1) Rome's relationship to and involvement in the Germanic world along the Roman frontier, (2) the disparate evolution of various *limes* camps, and (3) evolution within the interior of the province, especially with regard to Augsburg and roads. Obviously this is a formidable task and cannot be accomplished completely; however, a few representative examples can provide some flesh for the skeletal outline above.

Around the middle of the fourth century, Rome seems to have encouraged or at least allowed the erection or continuation of numerous Germanic settlements well beyond the Rhine and Danube. Many of them were perched on fortified hilltops near Nürnberg and Würzburg in what presently appears to be a broad band stretching to the vicinity of Mainz on the Rhine and Regensburg on the Danube.[48] Some of these sites lay within the former Roman *limes* of the Principate, abandoned over a century before. Others were further north, where the *limes* of the Principate and concepts of Roman territory, had they somehow endured, played no role whatsoever in the establishment of Germanic settlements.[49] The apparent patterns reflect natural features of terrain. Many settlements overlook important rivers; others lie on ridges or hills that dominate valleys without major water routes but doubtless with well-trodden pathways; some are on the Main itself. All were strategically situated. This is not meant to imply Roman site selection, but only subsequent fortification of defensible locations along trade routes running to the Roman frontier camps.

Such sites, occupied by friendly people, could not but have served as intelligence posts or even as a buffer. Numerous historical precedents reveal how important such relationships could be to the Roman army.[50] Many such sites have already been found, and the discovery rate is quickening. These sites often were occupied into the sixth century, occasionally even into the seventh. Virtually all of them have demonstrable connections with Roman territory through manufactured items extending chronologically to the mid-fifth century and often into the early sixth century.[51] To the east of Regensburg there appears to have been a considerable migration toward the Roman Danube from Bohemia, although any actual movement of people is always extremely difficult to prove archaeologically. Obviously even these modest generalizations cannot stand much stretching, although a similar set of hilltop sites is available for investigation in southern Alamannic territory near Lake Constance.[52] The best approach is a few specific examples, site by site.

Berching-Pollanten lies 45 km north of Ingolstadt in the Oberpfalz, and, like most of these trans-*limes* sites, is more complex than the above generalizations would suggest. Possibly begun just after the collapse of the former *limes* and the withdrawal of Roman forces southward to the Danube, Berching-Pollanten has yielded four burials and several important finds scattered by erosion. The artifacts thus far recovered are not later than ca. 400. Included in the finds are: (1) From grave number 2, female, a cobalt beaded necklace such as found throughout the area of the so-called Elbgermans (a common and convenient category to group the people behind this fairly uniform archaeological assemblage of artifacts), but with a special concentration in that part of southwestern Germany under Alammanic control; the beads were of Roman manufacture. (2) Scattered finds including an armband, a late fourth century military fibula ("onion-topped fibulae" were probably official insignia of rank in the Roman army and changed regularly), bronze vessels, small metal pieces, late Roman coins, and belt-fittings. Also present is the handmade pottery characteristic of the "Elbgermanic" group, typically shallow, dark bowls often decorated with a band of double-apsidal indentations, stempeling, and incised lines.[53]

A Germanic settlement near Treuchtlingen-Schambach has revealed a small bronze coin ca. 335–340, a fragment of a bronze fibula from the fourth century, a triangular—that is to say Germanic style—bone comb of the late fourth century, and "Elbgermanic" pottery. The archaeologist suggests a tentative dating from mid-fourth to mid-fifth century.[54] Gelbe Bürg

Stilicho's Transalpine Recruitment Areas

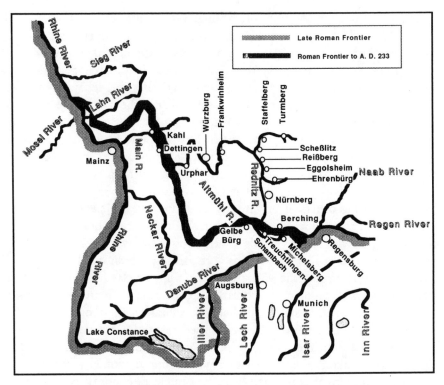

Map 6 Hilltop Fortifications beyond the Upper Rhine and Danube Rivers

near Dittenheim was the location of a Germanic hilltop settlement ca. late fourth century through early fifth century. A coin of Constantine III was discovered there quite recently.[55] The site has an extensive history of settlement from the Stone Age to the Middle Ages.[56]

Proceeding northward into Oberfranken there are several sites of the type here being surveyed, for example: (1) Reißberg near Forchheim, (2) Ehrenbürg near Forchheim, (3) Turmberg near Kasendorf, (4) Scheßlitz, (5) Eggolsheim, and (6) Staffelberg. These sites are far from the nearest point of contact with the Roman frontier, which in this case would have been at Regensburg ca. 125 km away (see map 6). Contact down the Main River to Mainz must have been easier to maintain. All have yielded Germanic and Roman military artifacts from the late fourth–early fifth century. The excavator suggests that the inhabitants were Germans, who had been or were in Roman service. Very recently an extremely rare fibula with polyhedron caps on the top and foot was unearthed. It is only the third known example of this type, and probably belonged to an officer. At Eggolsheim the channeled-style pottery may suggest a relationship to Thuringia ca. 500.[57]

Westward, down the Main from the sites in Oberfranken, several such sites lie near or directly on the river. The Germanic settlement at Frankenwinheim in Unterfranken has two phases: (1) first and second centuries, and (2) late fourth century, ca. Valentinian I. Only the later phase concerns our present inquiry, but one of its features is perhaps the most fascinating discovery in the area. Lying ca. 25 km SSE of Schweinfurt and approximately 140 km from Rome's frontier fortifications on either the Rhine or the Danube, one would hardly expect this site to be a late Roman villa estate, but that is precisely what it is. It was built in part with legionary bricks, as well as others of private manufacture. The archaeologist suggests that the owner was a former high-ranking Roman officer, doubtless of Germanic origin, who retired to his estate, constructed with technical advice and assistance from Roman artisans.[58] If this hypothesis can be confirmed and the chronology of the various building phases clarified, Frankenwinheim will attract considerable scholarly interest. Elsewhere in Unterfranken a grave of a Germanic soldier, probably a veteran of the Roman army, has come to light. The ceramic bowl is of the Prest'ovice-Friedenhain type.[59] A cache of late fourth–early fifth century metal items, bronze and iron, also from Unterfranken, must have had a wide range of domestic purposes. It suggests some sort of continued but as yet unclear economic activity with metal goods.[60]

The careers of very few Germanic recruits are as interesting as that of the Frank Mallobaudes. It is not hard to envision that his life bore striking similarities to that of the unknown landlord at Frankenwinheim. Mallobaudes entered Roman service as a youth, perhaps one of noble parents. In 354, while a military tribune in the emperor Gallus's imperial guard, he was one of three men charged with an important mission to Histria. A year later, still *tribunus scholae armaturarum*, Mallobaudes protested against the court's unfair treatment of Silvanus, a fellow Frank whose career had mirrored his own but had ended in usurpation. By 374 Mallobaudes had returned home and had become a Frankish king, but in 378 he was back in Roman service as *comes domesticorum (equitum)* holding joint command with Nannienus in a successful campaign against the Alamanni.[61]

On an oxbow on the Main near Urphar in Unterfranken lies another fortified hilltop settlement. Until recently this site and others like it were overlooked as possible late Roman settlements because of their simple construction technique (wood and earth with drywall fronts). Again, the small finds suggest a late fourth century origin with continuation until around

500. Personal ornaments and belt-fittings demonstrate continued contacts with Roman territory on the west bank of the Rhine. Certain belt-fittings appear to be east Germanic, stylistically originating along the lower Danube. Any ethnic linkage with a known Germanic group probably presses the evidence too much.[62] The presence of Roman and later east Germanic goods cannot yet assist in that regard. Exploration continues.

Among the finds at Urphar was a hoard of 137 bronze coins. The specimens are extremely small, perhaps half-centenionales. Difficult to date precisely, they must have been struck just before 400 or during the first decade of the fifth century. Some carry a legend: *salus reipublic(a)e* or *victoria auggg*. Some coins clearly identify the mint; examples exist from Trier, Lyon, Arles, and Rome. Despite their size, these coins from Urphar, like those at Eisenberg in the Pfalz and Weßling just outside Munich, are official products of a Roman minting. As such they represent the final step in the long history of the western mints. The investigation suggests that whether the coins were used as small change (however unlikely that seems), or intended to be melted down for reuse, or merely deposited as grave goods, the owner clearly had some prolonged relationship to neighboring Roman territory.[63] A settlement contemporaneous with that at Urphar existed not far away at Kahl, down in the flatlands in the valley of the Main. It contains the same types of artifacts as the hillforts.[64] Dettingen, also in Unterfranken, lies near the Main and 48 km from the Rhine. Again, pottery and glass can be dated by parallels within the Rhine-Main area to the late fourth century and the first decades of the fifth. The finds reveal regular and complex cultural exchanges with Roman centers.[65]

The foregoing evidence indicates that ca. 350–425 Rome supported a system of transfrontier fortifications at chokepoints between Mainz and the upper Danube at Regensburg. Dittenheim took advantage of neighboring Alamannic groups for recruitment, whereas the sites in Ober- and Unterfranken apparently drew upon more northerly peoples. Nonetheless, some sites may have been ethnically quite complex, reflecting perhaps retired soldiers bringing friends acquired in Roman service back home with them. That would explain why a few finds point hesitantly to east Germanic origins. The Main seems to have been a key to the northern defensive settlements. If so, then the Roman command at Mainz would have provided initiatives and whatever assistance or supervision was necessary. Ethnic identification is extremely hazardous and probably misguided. At present, principal investigators usually stress an Alamannic-Thuringian origin for the "recruits" or "settlers" in most of the sites so far discussed.[66] The composite nature of late Roman units is also reflected in several other sites not far to the south. The hilltop settlements in Alamannic territory—roughly the triangle formed by the upper Rhine, Lake Constance, and the Iller River—are quite similar, particularly in their ethnic complexity.[67]

In writing about the sites of Treuchtlingen-Schambach and Berching-Pollanten I introduced the "Elbgermanen," as archaeologists have labeled them. In Raetia some of these barbarian people seem to have moved from the headwaters of the Moldau River north of Prague. B. Svoboda postulated this group in 1963 to explain the relationships between archaeological finds in Bohemia and Bavaria.[68] The 1980s saw numerous new finds and publications confirming Svoboda's linking of the find-complex of Prest'ovice in Bohemia and that of Friedenhain opposite Straubing. H. Thomas Fischer has fashioned an elegant theory connecting the "Elbgermanen" to the "Land of Baio," Bohemia, and hence to the origin of the Bavarians.[69] Not all scholars accept the clarity and simplicity of Fischer's thesis. In particular, some question the important role that Fischer suggests that these peoples played in the post-Roman, internal development of "Bavaria" inside the former Roman frontiers.[70] The chronologies involved are, at least for now, too imprecise. "The Elbgermans" (or, for some, "the Elbgermani-Alamanni") is a purely hypothetical entity. It reflects archaeologists' succumbing to the almost irresistible desire to visualize people behind artifacts. These people are supposed to be "Germans" from the river Elbe, the main drainage system in the area. Perhaps so, but there is no historically demonstrable group called "Elbgermani" or anything that can be established as an equivalent name. If such a group did exist, it was surely not in the sense of a politically coordinated people—nothing like even the contemporary Alamanni.

"Elbgermans" is thus a heuristic label useful for the time being to denote the people(s) responsible for a coherent assemblage of characteristic artifacts. Their existence in southern Bohemia is attested from the third century, at which date they were using their characteristic pottery for cremation burials. The determinative core of this archaeological matrix is the finds from Prest'ovice in Czechoslovakia and Friedenhain in Bavaria, linked together by the Cham-Further-Senke region. This aggregate is most consistently characterized by a peculiar ceramic style, handmade bowls and pots, usually very dark with slanting sides prominent, often in a faceted design, typically taking the form of a double apsidal indentation with stempeling in bands. Cremation was characteristic beyond the Roman frontier, but usually was abandoned upon entry into Roman service in favor of inhumation—burial in graves.

Everywhere from about 360 the Romans turned to the direct and extensive recruitment of those people directly opposite the fortifications. In addition, the Romans must have welcomed the establishment of hillforts manned by allied or at least friendly groups as a sort of defensive shield and early warning system well forward of the *limes*. Thus Roman commanders were simultaneously using barbarians for defensive goals in two different ways. First, they were intensively recruiting their neighbors, whole families whose villages in many cases lay within sight of the Roman camps across the river frontiers. Second, barbarians outside Roman territory, some far beyond, also played a role in imperial defense, if only by checking movement through their own settlement areas en route to Roman soil. Sometimes soldiers chose to retire at considerable distances from the Roman camps in which they had served. Some probably returned to their original homes, or chose locales that had struck their fancy during their travels. Regardless of where they ended their lives, they carried with them aspects of their Roman experience.

There seems little doubt that beginning around the middle of the fourth century Rome recruited increasingly heavily from among these people. By that time the Elbgermans had shifted their population focus from Prest'ovice to settlements near or, in some cases, directly opposite the Roman forts on the Danube centered on Regensburg. Their sites extended upstream at least as far as Neuburg an der Donau (Venaxamodurum), and downstream below Straubing.[71] The Altmühl and Naab river valleys were particularly well settled. Given Rome's contemporary policy of surprise attacks on unwelcome barbarian villages beyond its frontiers—*magister militum* Arbogastes (388–94) led such a raid to destabilize native leadership, crossing the Rhine at Cologne[72]—this movement and settlement could only have occurred with Roman consent and assurances. The presence of Roman items at these sites, the known recruitment patterns of the Roman army, and the gradual disappearance by 500 of the characteristic items in the area of their origin, together suggest a plausible migration scenario: that those peoples now conveniently called Elbgermans were not pushed out of their homeland. Rather, they were pulled by opportunities to the vicinity of the Roman camps, particularly the main one at Regensburg.

From around the middle of the fourth century and at least into the early decades of the fifth, the characteristic grave goods of the Elbgermans appear on Roman soil in direct association with Roman camps. These fortifications extend from Neuburg an der Donau eastward, and included camps at Eining, Weltenburg, Regensburg, and two sites at Straubing. Finds

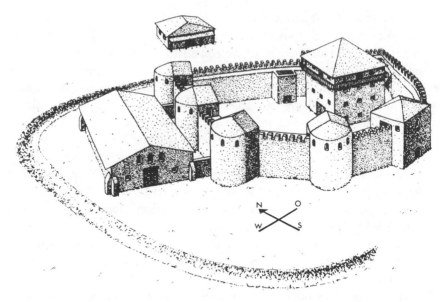

Illustration 11. Depiction of Goldberg near Türkheim in the era of Valentinian I

were also found at Goldberg near Türkheim, Passau, and elsewhere (see illustration 11).[73] The *numerus* encampment at Straubing is not listed in the *Notitia dignitatum* ca. 415. If deliberate, this omission suggests that Straubing may no longer have been regarded as Roman in the sense of the chain-of-command governing the relationships of regular units.[74]

It is time to confront the problems surrounding the *Notitia dignitatum* that so often have haunted our studies in the Balkans. The fact that the extant manuscript is Western but nevertheless includes older sections on the East is puzzling, to say the least. The Western sections alone are quite trying and in general must be approached region by region, for several different stages of revision are apparent. Several modern scholars have echoed earlier ones who contended that Stilicho made major changes in the Raetian forces in preparation for his campaigns against Alaric, ca. 400. They go on to argue that the Raetian section reflects events at this time.[75] Others have favored a general date of ca. 425 for all the Western sections, including that for Raetia.[76] More recently the summer of 408 (coinciding with Stilicho's preparations for his Balkan campaign against the East following the death of Arcadius) has again emerged as a promising alternative.[77] A date coinciding with Stilicho's preparations for his Balkan campaign is attractive, for it may well have been the last time anyone in the West would have wanted a copy of the Eastern sections, despite the fact that they did not reflect the Eastern army after 395 and probably not after 388. They would not have been of much help to Stilicho.

A date in 408, however, is unlikely. Even if we assume for a moment that Stilicho wanted a copy of the full *Notitia*, he would have ordered it well before the death of Arcadius on 1 May 408. Any useful revision of the Western section should have reflected those areas in the West which could have contributed troops to Stilicho's planned offensive in the Balkans, there being no other logical reason to bother. By May 408 plans for the "invasion" of the Balkans had been brewing for a long time and now had reached their final stages of preparation; Arcadius's death merely provided one more convenient excuse. If the revision of the *Notitia* was at all thoroughgoing, then it had to have been composed at least a year earlier and probably two.

Stilicho had learned of Constantine III's rebellion almost a year before the death of Arcadius.[78] If Stilicho was responsible for a revision of the *Notitia*, his version would have to have been drafted in 405–6—that is, immediately after the defeat of Radagaisus, when, with the aid of Alaric, he began to move troops into position for a new campaign against the East. Whatever parts of the extant *Notitia* date to Stilicho, the extant document reflects several later additions to ca. 420, most having to do with the deployment of troops.[79] For the present, only those sections of the *Notitia* having to do with the Raetian provinces and Noricum Ripense are under discussion.

The new archaeological information and especially the coin finds from the usurper Constantine III (407–11) cast a new light upon Raetia up to 411 and hence upon the Raetian portions of the *Notitia* itself. Raetia may well have been at least tacitly a part of Constantine's sphere by the time of Stilicho's planning for the campaign of 407–8. If so, its manpower would have been unavailable to Stilicho. Four circumstances—the withdrawal of the command of the Third Italian Legion from Regensburg, the clear presence of Germanic troops there nonetheless, Saint Augustine's reference to supplying the army in Raetia, and the presence of coins of Constantine III—suggest a later date for these sections of the *Notitia*. All indicate that the *Notitia* here reflects conditions after the defeat of Constantine, but not much later, probably just after his fall or that of Jovinus in 413. Thus I suggest ca. 415–17. At that time Constantius III was still in Gaul struggling to reorder the areas that had supported the usurpers in order to secure his rear, and to check the Visigoths, who were plundering Aquitaine and Spain.

He had yet to decide to settle them in Aquitaine, a decision which came in 418.[80]

Now that we have established a working date for the Raetian section of the *Notitia*, let us return to the exploration of Roman recruitment policies as manifested along the Danubian frontier. Neuburg an der Donau, home of the *cohors VI Valeria Raetorum*, is perhaps the most important site yet excavated and reported for understanding the processes at work. The grave field at Neuburg was divided east to west into three topographic zones corresponding to three approximate periods: Zone 1 (54 graves), ca. 330–60; Zone 2 (54 graves), ca. 360–90; and Zone 3 (25 graves), ca. 390–400+. In Zone 1 the first two phases witnessed burials that were Germanic, provincial Roman, or culturally mixed. The clearest examples yield the following totals: 5 purely Germanic, 6 purely Roman provincial, and 5 or 6 culturally mixed. Zone 2 corresponds in grave goods to the period of heavy Elbgermanic recruitment. However, Elbgermanic graves are interspersed with indigenous provincial Roman graves in the final stage of Zone 1 as well. Burials in Zone 2 are also characterized by the strong continuation of Roman military and provincial artifacts, particularly military belt-fittings, among the Elbgermanic settlers. Zone 3 contains the fewest burials and was in use for the shortest period. Again provincial Roman materials are present, but no longer in an Elbgermanic context. This final phase of the Neuburg grave field witnessed the burial of artifacts of east Germanic–Gothic types whose stylistic origins lie in the Cernjachov archaeological complex north of the lower Danube.

Similar late fourth–early fifth century east Germanic finds have turned up in Gaul, along the Danube-Iller, and along the Rhine as well. Together these finds leave little doubt as to an infusion of east German—that is, Goths—into Roman military service from at least as early as the last decade of the fourth century.[81] For Rome these Gothic-speaking barbarians were readily available and easily deployable. Their homeland was under Hunnic dominion and of no concern to these recruits. They and their families had every reason to welcome a new home far from the war-torn Balkan provinces. In general many of the finds thought to be east Germanic are small, often otherwise insignificant metal pieces, precisely what one would expect to see in the graves of men recruited into regular units of the Roman army and stationed far away from the mass of their kinsmen. These soldiers probably would not have wanted to stand out from the others and so perhaps had their larger pieces of traditional dress recast or traded them away. They kept only the little pieces that did not obviously announce their origins and some personal religious items which would have had only private uses. In the fifth century, after the establishment of barbarian kingdoms, there were reasons to show off items of traditional dress associated with being a member of the ruling group and to indicate your rank within it. At the end of the fourth century this situation did not exist.[82] Even within the so-called barbarian kingdoms of the fifth century, moreover, this was not always the case.

The presence in Raetia of artifacts stylistically characteristic of east Germans, that is to say Gothic speakers, appears to be the end product of Theodosius's successful recruitment and dispersal of many of the Gothic peoples defeated and/or won over in the Balkans, most probably settled here after Theodosius's defeat of Magnus Maximus in 388 and after his victory over Arbogastes and Eugenius at the close of 394.[83] In Raetia, at least, the fact that these recruits were integrated into various units, including those assigned to the *comitatenses*, cannot be doubted. There is also no doubt that at least some regular units (those stationed at sites with coins of Constantine III) occupied their duty stations throughout the first quarter of the fifth century.[84] The actual size of these units must have been quite small, perhaps not more than twenty to twenty-five men.[85] Theodosius had pretty well concluded his Gothic campaigns by the mid-380s. In 386 the lower Danubian frontier repulsed a major Gothic crossing. This occasion may have seen the largest single reception of defeated Gothic soldiers and their families under Theodosius, and doubtless provided many new recruits for imperial service. Contrary to accepted opinion, the sudden appearance of east Germanic–Gothic recruits in Raetia and elsewhere does not prove the admission of Gothic "federates" as new internal allies under their own leaders. Rather, it is the logical result of the traditional Roman policy of *receptio* as practiced since the third century.

Thus throughout the fourth century Rome defended Neuburg and similar sites with Germanic troops in a Romanizing environment. In these frontier outposts family ties between provincial Romans and Germans seem to have been common, at least as judged from the number of culturally mixed burials and repeated laws against intermarriage between Romans and barbarians. The fact that Germanic burials often contain specific late imperial necklaces with rings or disks and armbands with convex ends also reveals close personal and exchange networks in the fourth century. Especially numerous examples of these distinctive artifacts have been found in the Danube-Iller and Mainz-Main areas.[86] The most important circumstance underlying this pattern is obvious: trust. The Roman authorities clearly had learned to trust the defenses of territories threatened by German groups to Germanic troops, sometimes even from the same ethnic stock. What is even more remarkable is that the policy clearly worked. Despite the growing dominance of Germanic soldiers in the garrisons, Roman provincial elements continued throughout the century, although ever less prominently. By the middle of the fifth century the *castrum* at Neuburg was no longer garrisoned. The ethnically diverse garrison, including east Germanic–Gothic troops, may have been stationed elsewhere nearby in a small and as yet undiscovered camp from ca. 390. Around the same time that Neuburg ceased as an active fortification a new Germanic settlement arose on the opposite side of the Danube at Bittenbrunn.[87]

Downstream about 50 km from Neuburg lies Eining (Abusina). In the second and early third century it was an auxiliary fort anchoring the *limes* connecting the Danube and the Rhine. After the abandonment of the Agri Decumates to the Alamanni, Eining was refortified under Probus (276–82), if not slightly earlier. Only the southwest corner of the original fort was used, resulting in a smaller but stouter fortification typical of the late third and fourth centuries. The barracks rested against the inside of the defensive walls, and a well stood at the center. The civilian community here also took refuge inside what remained of the old camp. Restoration work and the addition of an artillery tower were accomplished under Valentinian I (364–75). Eining, like many other sites in this area, was home to a garrison of Germanic recruits in the second half of the fourth century. The site was clearly and increasingly Germanic from the opening of the fifth century. Recent excavations have revealed a pattern of fourth-century development consistent with Neuburg an der Donau, including the presence of ceramics characteristic of the Elbgermans.[88]

Just 8 km downstream from Eining and 37 km from Regensburg the Romans built a quite small fortification on the Frauenberg near Weltenburg (see illustrations 12 and 13). Here the Danube passes through an impressive and turbulent narrows, now identified hesitantly as the seat of the commander of the Third Italian Legion noted in the *Notitia dignitatum*. The modest size of the camp on the Frauenberg demonstrates once again the greatly reduced numbers in the garrisons. Erected as a part of the expanded network along the frontiers built under Valentinian I (364–75), Weltenburg too reveals the patterns of Germanic recruitment and settlement characteristic of Neuburg in the late fourth and early fifth centuries. The Germanic materials suggest a significant Germanic demographic component before the end of the fourth century.[89]

Regensburg was the fulcrum of the defenses on the upper Danube

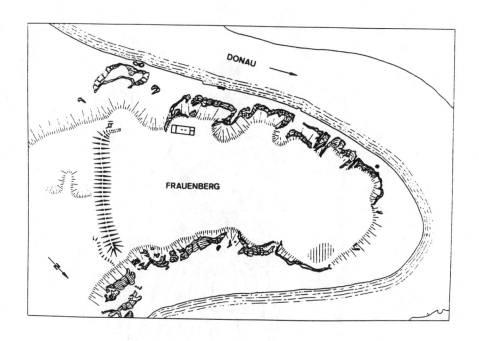

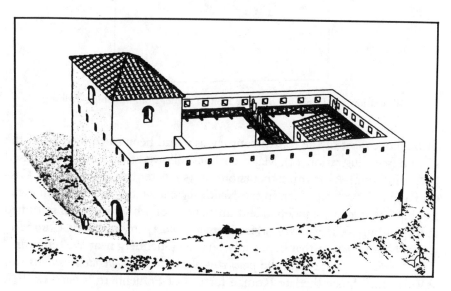

Illustrations 12–13. Frauenberg near Weltenburg

Illustration 14. Depiction of a late Roman soldier from Straubing-Azlburg

throughout most of the fourth century, as it had been since the end of the second (see illustration 14). Major changes followed the destruction caused by the Iuthungi-Alamannic incursions of 357. After this the picture at Castra Regina is far from clear. In the *Notitia dignitatum* the *Legio III Italica* exists, but has at least six independent units, none of which was then stationed at Regensburg. The *praefectus legionis tertiae Italicae partis superioris, Castra Regina* was *nunc Uallato*, that is, possibly on the Frauenberg near Weltenburg.[90] The *Notitia* also states that the *praefectus alae secundae Ualeriae singularis* was at Vallatum.[91] Since the late Roman fortress of Frauenberg is very small, it is difficult to see it as the seat of a legionary commander with his headquarters company and a unit of cavalry. Unless these two commanding officers resided there without the men of their commands, there was not enough room in the late Roman fort. No two units, even skeleton commands of 25 to 50 men each, could have been accommodated there. This difficulty would be eliminated, however, if the entire area within the so-called fourth-century wall was considered part of Vallatum. Most of this area remains unexcavated, and its dating is very insecure. The last word on Vallatum has yet to be heard. The traditional assignment of Vallatum to Manching may yet carry the field.[92]

Whatever the strength of the Roman garrison on the Frauenberg near Weltenburg, archaeology leaves no doubt that some sort of Roman military presence remained at Regensburg, specifically in and around the northeast corner of the great fortress. Late fortification, similar to that in the corner at Eining but as yet undiscovered, may have been located there.[93] The *Notitia* omits not only Regensburg as an encampment, but Straubing too. Attempts to fill the supposed Regensburg-Straubing gap in the Roman defenses with other units, as attested by brick and tile stamps, have not produced any secure solutions. One possibility is that Regensburg was often a temporary residence of construction battalions from other legions.[94] There was an undoubted Roman and Christian presence at Regensburg, but one in rapid decline as the fourth century rolled into the fifth. On the other hand, the evidence of Elbgermanic pottery and small finds increases simultaneously and substantially.

Two recent excavations in Regensburg have added greatly to our information and have produced several new hypotheses: the sites at Niedermünster and Grasgasse. Both have demonstrable continuity of settlement from the fourth into the early fifth century, primarily through stylistically datable finds: metal fibulae and belt-fittings as well as Elbgermanic ceramics.[95] The presence of a gilded bronze fibula of Roman military type ca. 400 at Grasgasse has raised the possibility that a Roman regular officer or a person trying to imitate one in dress was present. This person was probably himself of Germanic ancestry and in command of a troop of Germanic soldiers, whose presence is well attested in the ceramic remains. Was this "unit" thus linked to the Third Italian Legion now headquartered at Vallatum? If so, why was it not listed in the *Notitia dignitatum*? The *Notitia* did list similar units, such as the various *praefecti laetorum* for Tarraconensis in Spain and the *praefecti Sarmatarum* for Italia Mediterranea. Was the omission merely because the garrison at Regensburg (and as we shall see, that at Straubing) was a new creation, not corresponding to existing categories, perhaps a new type of auxiliary garrison? Could the area of the *limes* between Eining and Straubing—also not given in the *Notitia*—have ceased to be regarded as Roman? Was it instead conceived as a southward extension of the "system" of Germanic hilltop fortifications long acknowledged beyond the frontier of the Danube? Or had Rome accepted a "purely Germanic rule" upon its former territory under only the loosest supervision?[96]

These are questions without answers, although several possibilities seem less likely than others. There most probably was a terminological problem with the clerks in charge of updating the *Notitia* that prevented them from defining the nature of the troops assigned there.[97] The most compelling historical explanation for such a clerical difficulty is the creation of a new category of auxiliary composed of barbarians and operating without any regular affiliation with other units of the army. As a table of organization, the *Notitia* would have had a difficult time including such auxiliaries unless a regular Roman officer was appointed over them. That was the case with the *laeti*, but not with these auxiliaries. Reluctance to mention what had long been unthinkable—virtually autonomous barbarian auxiliaries—also would explain other similar omissions of barbarians whose services to Rome are documented in contemporary literary sources.[98] At Regensburg-Niedermünster there is a gap in reported settlement after the mid-fifth century of about a century. At Grasgasse the picture seems slightly different, with slender evidence for continued or renewed influence from Ostrogothic Italy ca. 500.

Straubing, the next late Roman camp downstream from Regensburg, is another site that has recently yielded important new information. Over half a dozen excavations in Straubing and its vicinity provide detailed evidence for the entire span of the crucial era of transition, i.e., from the mid-fourth century into the early seventh. The density and coherence of this data make Straubing pivotal to any reconstruction. The importance of the Elbgermanic settlement at Friedenhain, just across the Danube, has already been mentioned. Clarification of the chronological problems at this site is handicapped by the paucity of published data. The demographic pattern in the region again appears to be threefold: movement from the lands to the north drained by the Elbe River toward the Danubian frontier, settlement at times within sight of the late Roman camps as at Friedenhain, and finally gradual recruitment into the Roman army stationed on the opposite bank.

At Straubing the late Roman fortress ceased to hold a garrison at this time and a new settlement(s) was established some distance away in the agricultural zone—not next to the river, where the fortress lay. The Straubing-Azlburg (I and II) excavations are most relevant for the fourth-century phases, and Azlburg I for later phases as well. Azlburg II reveals the early period of recruitment into the Roman units and the resulting integration of the Germanic elements into the traditional culture of the Roman camp, still much in evidence. The site extends at least through the third quarter of the fourth century.[99] Azlburg I provides data on the transition to an even heavier reliance upon Germanic recruits from the opposite side of the Danube at the end of the fourth and early decades of the fifth centuries. For example, in grave number 79 were discovered bronze belt-fittings ca. 400, and number 60 contained a Friedenhain-type vessel of the same era. Early reports from the site suggest that the garrison at Straubing was reconstituted with Germanic recruits in the early fifth century. This might help explain the omission of Straubing from the *Notitia dignitatum.*[100]

Alamannic incursions into Raetia and adjoining areas increased, particularly between 380 and 383. Soon a crescendo of crises—the revolts of Magnus Maximus and Eugenius, the Vandalic immigrations, the invasions of Italy by Radagaisus in 405–6, and then Alaric's challenge—supposedly left Stilicho with no choice but to withdraw the remaining forces from Raetia and other areas in order to defend Italy. At least, that is the traditional explanation, based on a few rather cryptic allusions in the sources. The archaeological data amassed over the last decade, however, compel a reassessment of Stilicho's policies. There can be no doubt that the Romans had begun to use recruits drawn from the barbarian groups neighboring Raetia long before Stilicho, indeed long before the Theodosian dynasty. During the last decade of the fourth century the Romans began introducing some east Germanic–Gothic replacements into the area both as supplements to the border defenses and as recruits into the garrisons behind the *limes.* Some of these newcomers were thus incorporated into the so-called field army, the *comitatenses.*[101] There may even have been a flourish of activity circa 406 to midcentury, as Rome struggled to shore up the Danube-Iller defenses against the Vandal-Alanic invaders and then the Hunnic Empire. It responded by repositioning troops across Raetia and deploying new recruits from the Balkan area, including a few non–Germanic elements, perhaps including other Alans or Huns. Their remains are found in rare and isolated burials in the interior of the province, as if the interred had died en route.[102]

The gradual and controlled penetration of neighboring Germanic peoples into the area of eastern Raetia and to a lesser extent Noricum Ripense now seems to have begun around the middle of the fourth century and gained momentum thereafter. The process clearly remained under Roman control at least through the first quarter of the fifth century. Around 390–95 a significant influx of east Germanic recruits made its presence felt in some frontier camps. Few Germanic settlements of any type have been located in the interior of the province dating to the fifth century, and those few appear after the middle of the century. Altenerding near Munich[103] and München-Aubing are such places. Both reveal that by the late fifth century Germans were living side by side with surviving Roman elements, or at least among strong Roman influences. At the time of Stilicho, except along the frontier itself, there seem to have been very few inhabitants in the Raetian provinces at all. The modest Germanic settlements of the middle of the century, such as Altenerding, survived the hard times of the late fifth century to witness the ever-accelerating expansion of Germanic settlement in the sixth and seventh.

Even if ca. 400 Stilicho had commanded the loyal support and full strength of all the units stationed in the Raetian provinces, he could have transferred only a few thousand ethnically diverse men to meet the crises he faced elsewhere. Such drastic action was not contemplated, as we shall see. The addition of even a thousand men from Raetia and Noricum, however, need not have disappointed him. This was an era when a few thousand men made a big difference, that is, when they could be found. But getting a realistic sense of manpower availability is not the only lesson to be learned from this chapter. Our case study of Raetia suggests that we will not be able to call the armies of Alaric "Gothic" and those of Stilicho "Roman"— unless, that is, we wish to accept the anachronistic arrogance of most of our sources. In Alaric, Stilicho would face a tough and frustrated Roman soldier, and their armies were very much alike.

Summary

The survey of the transalpine areas that Stilicho drew upon for recruits reveals in detail many aspects of frontier life and recruitment alluded to in previous chapters in a general way. Raetia provides compelling evidence of Roman military occupation at least to the death of the usurper Constantine III in 411. Everywhere in these provinces urban civilization had virtually vanished by the death of Valentinian I. Few people of any sort lived here. The camps were small with often tiny garrisons. Roman *receptio* attracted numerous barbarians to the frontier in a long and peaceful process. Many of these so-called Elbgermans entered into the Roman army and served in this region. Roman influence as seen in material remains extended a considerable distance beyond the frontier, particularly up the Main and several rivers flowing into the upper Danube. It appears that barbarian settlements there were in contact with and probably linked diplomatically to the Roman army on the Rhine and Danube. Toward the end of the fourth century artifactual evidence suggests that Roman authorities were deploying east Germanic recruits into regular units stationed in these frontier provinces. Finally, Rome may have assigned the military defense of the area from roughly Regensburg past Straubing to barbarian auxiliaries, who like all other such forces were unlisted in the *Notitia dignitatum*. Stilicho did not strip these provinces of their defenders. Even if he had, he would have obtained only a precious few replacements.

FOUR GENERALS

THEODOSIUS, UNDISPUTED emperor of Rome, died on 19 January 395. Present at his side during his final hours was his kinsman Stilicho, whom he had named guardian over his younger son Honorius and probably over Arcadius, his elder son, as well. Perhaps some were shocked over the suddenness of the emperor's passing; he had rallied enough to attend the games only the day before. But most of those familiar with life at court were well aware of Theodosius's long struggle with fragile health, which had led him to take baptism at Thessalonica in 380. In recent months, he had expended tremendous energy and exposed himself to countless dangers while personally suppressing the rebellion of Arbogastes and Eugenius. The ordeal which led to the emperor's final victory at the Frigidus River may also have led to his death barely four months later. On 20 January, Stilicho stood alone at the apex of the Roman world.

Stilicho was preeminently a politician. He had risen rapidly to the highest levels of the officer corps with only limited command experience. Even his participation in 384 or 385 in an important diplomatic mission to the Persians was probably in only a minor capacity, magnified by the poet Claudian to suit his later eminence. But give Stilicho his due; he had married well. He was the logical guardian for the imperial family. At the Frigidus he had shared command of the Roman forces with Timasius, a true veteran, but there Theodosius himself had really directed operations. Stilicho does not appear to have distinguished himself in this battle—or any earlier one. The death of Theodosius forever changed his fate.

If Stilicho were to maintain his influence at court—or even survive— he would need more than Theodosius's blessing and his own political skills. He would need a loyal army, men willing to die for him. No one could transfer such a force to him; he would have to fashion it for himself. The first task of a late Roman commander, be he emperor or commanding general, was to raise and train an army equal to the challenges at hand. The second was to lead that army to victories which swept challengers away.

Since the time of Augustus no truly successful ruler, and that is what Stilicho now aspired to be, was devoid of military victories. Admittedly some had grossly inflated their exploits, and Caligula had made only martial gestures. Moreover, no late emperors (except child-emperors like Arcadius and Honorius) could afford to avoid spending long periods with their troops. All emperors from Constantine to Theodosius did so. Military triumphs were the bedrock of imperial political success.

The most dependable forces available to Stilicho in early 395 were the surviving units of the Eastern army brought west by Theodosius. These troops apparently did not return to the East until November 395. We need not see a sinister motive for this delay, or even a delay. Dating anything precisely in the *Notitia dignitatum* is notoriously difficult, though it does provide clues when it reports the naming of new or newly reformed units after the reigning emperor, or the withdrawal of troops from frontier armies to bolster the field armies. Whatever the details, certain facts about the general approach to recruitment under Theodosius and his sons are clear. In numerous cases Theodosius and later Stilicho raised new units for the *comitatenses* by transferring units of presumably lesser quality from the *limitanei*. These newly elevated units were sometimes given the dubious status of *pseudo-comitatenses*.[1] The label *Honoriani* distinguishes several such units raised under Honorius, many apparently from units of a lower status. In the last chapter we demonstrated from archaeological evidence that the old units which survived these troubled times received infusions of new recruits, both from neighboring barbarians and from among the Goths pacified and enlisted under Theodosius. Moreover, these recruits went both to the frontier forces and to the field armies. The essence of the process was to revitalize worn-out units by using their remnants as a core around which to cluster recent recruits, so that the latter might better learn combat, discipline in battle, and survival skills from the veterans. This had worked for generations, and for the most part continued to work. Thus Stilicho's problem was not so much methodological as temporal. He had to have time. Time, alas, was not his to be had.

Even if the remnants of the defeated Western armies had been forgiven and returned to their duty stations—as was common during these years and in the next two decades and probably done here—there was no easy solution to Stilicho's need for an army centered upon Italy, Honorius, and, of course, himself. The Western army's top officers had perished or were in disgrace. Stilicho had to find new commanders; some like Saul would come from the Eastern forces. On the Frigidus Stilicho had probably served as *magister militum per Thracias,* a regional command only created by Theodosius some-time after 388, perhaps in 392. Timasius then would have shared equal title and status, perhaps as *magister militum per Orientem* or as *magister* over one of the praesental armies, there being no demonstrable gradations among the Eastern *magistri.* The presence at the Frigidus of Bacurius, formerly king of the Iberians in Asia Minor and a survivor of Adrianople, is note-worthy. Bacurius was *dux Palestinae* until at least 394 (still *dux* on the Frigi-dus according to the ecclesiastical historian Rufinus), when he seems to have been designated *magister militum vacans.* This suggests that he may have brought auxiliaries from the eastern frontiers. Timasius and Bacurius may have occupied positions corresponding to those of Stilicho and Gaïnas. This parallel structure, however, may be more apparent than real. Eunapius clearly makes Stilicho greater than the others, equal in command to Theo-dosius himself, but Gaïnas was not a subordinate in the Eastern system of command.[2] There can be no question, however, that in the two years prior to launching his campaign Theodosius assembled all available troops from his domains. Of the five generals with Theodosius, Bacurius alone died on the field of battle.

Timasius returned to the East soon after the victory with some of his command, perhaps the "unfit and worthless" recorded as sent back at this time in Zosimus.[3] This left Stilicho to defend the imperial court in the West and restore control over the transalpine lands with an incongruous army. It included his Thracian command, presumably some units of the praesental army, that had been attached directly to Theodosius, and what was left of Saul's and Gaïnas's barbarian auxiliaries.[4] The hasty return of the soldiers once assigned to the Persian frontier makes sense in light of the handling of the unrest in Asia Minor in the ensuing years. The departure of Timasius and the death of the rebel Arbogastes left Stilicho the undisputed com-mander of the Western armies, or what was left of them. Gaïnas and Saul were in no position to challenge his authority and never did so. But how could Stilicho justify the retention of the Eastern troops of the Thracian army, when Thrace was not the Western emperor's to command, let alone his? Neighboring Illyricum did not belong to the Western emperor either. It had been transferred to the East upon the death of Valentinian II in 392 and had not yet been returned to the West.[5] Stilicho could gain the forces he needed only if he were recognized as acting on behalf of the entire Empire and both of its child-emperors. Only then could he order about what few troops remained in the Balkans, including those from Illyricum, and legally retain those soldiers under his own Thracian command and

Gaïnas's as well. In other words, whatever may have transpired between the dying Theodosius and Stilicho—and we will surely never know—by pushing his claims to complete guardianship over both sons, Stilicho was also addressing urgent military problems that had no other ready solutions.

Gaïnas, a Goth by birth and an Arian Christian, was a volunteer recruited as a youth and a career Roman soldier. He had commanded a major contingent of the barbarian auxiliaries on the Frigidus. His command probably included those barbarian units gradually recruited and trained in the wake of Theodosius's victories and assigned to strengthen the garrisons along the Danube, in some cases perhaps to replace units now elevated and removed to serve in the field armies. Gaïnas led his men in the vanguard on the opening day of the battle, evidently with staggering losses. One of his first acts upon returning to the East was to invite fellow Goths to enlist in the Roman army, explicitly promising that their leaders would be given the rank of military tribune and command over units.[6] That Gaïnas spoke Gothic must have smoothed his way as a recruiter, but he did not lead these Gothic-barbarian forces as some sort of "tribal" leader; he commanded them as a Roman general. Nor did Saul, who one source reports was an Alan, lead Alanic units. Nor would Bacurius, who died heroically leading his bodyguard to the aid of the surrounded barbarian units on the first day of battle, have commanded the barbarian auxiliaries from the East, because he was one of them. Each held command over auxiliaries because Theodosius knew that they could get the most out of their men. Furthermore, since Gaïnas commanded units of auxiliaries regularly assigned to Thrace, there is every reason to assume that he and Stilicho were allies in these undertakings. Before Gaïnas returned to the East, however, there was a virtually complete absence of Roman troops in the Balkans. Stilicho did not move to fill this dangerous military vacuum. Rather, Alaric did.

All the sources agree that Theodosius's barbarian forces had suffered heavy losses against Arbogastes. Even Gaïnas must have found it difficult to find replacements. Contrary to popular belief, then and now, there were no inexhaustible supplies of Goths clamoring to join the Roman army. The growth of Hunnic power was gradually putting a stop to the free implementation of *receptio*. This ultimately would have profound repercussions, not only upon the Roman army but upon those barbarians caught in the middle. Probably almost all of the victors at Adrianople had either been recruited or killed long before Theodosius's death. In fact, many must have already had their eyes riveted upon retirement. Their children were now the object of Roman attention. Alaric had fought with distinction on the

Frigidus and had received the honorable title of *comes*, but probably not a separate command.[7] After receiving what the emperor thought was his due recognition, Alaric left the Roman army. Who was this Alaric?

Since Alaric seems to have led the band that attacked Theodosius returning to Constantinople in 391, he must have been one of the last to accept Roman employment. Technically he could not have served long enough to be eligible for retirement, but he was probably about the same age as many who were. Following a recent suggestion, perhaps he and his men had signed on only for this one campaign against Arbogastes, and had now departed.[8] For whatever reasons—disappointment over not getting a separate command, end of enlistment, or forced retirement—Alaric now turned away from the regular but slow career path that had led Gaïnas and several other soldiers of barbarian origins to generalships. He emerged as the leader of an assortment of men, most of whom spoke Gothic, wandering about and available if the price were right. On the one hand, these men might serve as a nucleus around which new units might be raised for Rome. On the other, Alaric might become a challenger, vying with Stilicho and Gaïnas for recruits, or, even worse, directly opposing their efforts by military force. Stilicho was determined not to provoke such a confrontation until all efforts to undermine or enlist Alaric and his followers had failed.

The Eastern court had a different perspective. From Constantinople the vulnerability of the Balkan peninsula was painfully obvious. Although the city walls were stout, the great land walls that would turn Constantinople into an impregnable bastion were a half century away. Nor was it acceptable to allow this vital military theater, with its time-honored traditions, to fall to Stilicho. Until the return of the bulk of the Eastern troops, what was the East to do? The old generals had left the stage or remained in the West. Timasius had returned but had soon fallen from grace in a palace intrigue. He was in exile at an Egyptian oasis, never to return. There were no other experienced generals and the peace with Persia was cracking. Rufinus, *magister officiorum* under Theodosius, took command of the army and of Arcadius. Surprisingly, he showed true promise as a military successor to Theodosius before his career was brought to an abrupt end. To date, scholarly attention has focused almost exclusively upon the political struggles between Stilicho and Rufinus, and later on those between Stilicho and Rufinus's successor Eutropius. To focus on these struggles rather than the military situation that dominated everyone and everything is to miss the forest for the trees.

The evidence demands much effort before it surrenders its secrets, for most sources are decidedly biased. The Western court poet Claudian has justly received a great deal of attention, but his desire to laud his patron Stilicho precluded much historical data from leaving his pen even on political events, let alone on military matters. Our other sources are hardly sources at all, but rather fragmentary abstracts from their sources, selected for other purposes. Behind Zosimus and some of the ecclesiastical historians, particularly Sozomenus, lurk the works of Eunapius of Sardis and Olympiodorus of Thebes, two very different practitioners of the historical craft. Eunapius's work has already served our cause. On Stilicho and Alaric, these sources are often at loggerheads. R. Blockley's efforts allow us to better appreciate how the same passage in, say, Eunapius or Olympiodorus could be differently colored by later authors. There are some brief entries in later chronicles, but no surviving continuous historical narrative except that of Zosimus.

The year 395 was crucial, for so much was in flux in both East and West. While Stilicho maintained his force in northern Italy, Alaric, at the time a nobody, slipped out of the army and returned to the diocese of Thrace with some followers. He marched without opposition as far as Constantinople. There he burned the countryside outside the walls.[9] Clearly he did not want to return to some Gothic village from which he had been recruited, or where he had once stood watch for Rome. He and his followers at this stage were not settlers in any sense. They were malcontents, no longer under Roman command and without futures. Stilicho, ever the politician, used this time to solidify his hold over Honorius. But Stilicho claimed guardianship over Arcadius too. This included taking back Illyricum from the East, but he knew that he had no right to do so.[10] Rufinus took the only course open to him to fend off an expected invasion from Stilicho: he enlisted Alaric and his men, "barbarians and others." Rufinus first dispatched Alaric, then in Thrace, to march via Macedonia to Thessaly to check Stilicho's foray there.[11] Stilicho is said to have employed units from Gaul and Armenia; that is, troops from both Western and Eastern commands.

At the very moment of decision, Claudian relates, an order arrived from Arcadius to cease operations and send his eastern units home.[12] If this passage from Claudian is taken at face value, it suggests that the Eastern court believed that Stilicho was stalling on the return of all elements of the Eastern army, perhaps in order to use some of them against the courtiers in Constantinople. Arcadius's order had the effect intended. According to Claudian, daunted by the order of the emperor (even though forced by Rufinus), Stilicho, ever loyal to the family of Theodosius, sent some of his Eastern troops packing. This probably included the Armenian contingents so sorely needed on the Eastern frontiers. If true, Stilicho deliberately gave away any chance of intimidating Alaric. Since Stilicho almost certainly now lacked decisive advantage over Alaric in manpower, he also offered him a great opportunity.

Alan Cameron first noted the coincidence between this event and a similar staying of Stilicho's hand in 392 against the Bastarnae (by which Claudian meant "barbarians"), warning us not to take these passages too literally.[13] Loyalty to imperial orders and clemency to fallen enemies were virtues the poet had to twist to fit Stilicho. The battle in 395 in Thessaly as reported in Claudian is preposterous. The imperial order demanding the return of the Eastern forces must have been handed to Stilicho before any fighting took place. It is impossible to believe that Stilicho would have released a major part of his force in the face of the enemy unless he was already on the verge of a major defeat and this was a condition for his safe withdrawal. Never known for his ability to inspire men, Stilicho probably could scarcely restrain his Easterners, specifically the Armenian troops, from "going home." Probably he made an imperial virtue of necessary acquiescence, and so withdrew with what remained of his forces. His Western contingents were too few to take on Alaric's mixed forces, especially when they might be supplemented by his own former Eastern elements. There was no battle. The result of this confrontation, this stalemate, was that Rufinus had begun to solve his recruitment problems at the expense of Stilicho. There was now something of an army in the Balkans, the one under Alaric, and any further efforts by Stilicho to intervene in affairs in Constantinople would have to be based on stronger measures. The campaign of 395, which was to have been a quick strike against Rufinus, not a well planned invasion, failed. Fresh from his fabricated "victory" in Thessaly, Stilicho made haste back to Italy.[14] There he and Gaïnas plotted the overthrow of Rufinus. Stilicho decided that this was the time to return the remainder of the Eastern army, his since the death of Theodosius in January.

Gaïnas proved his loyalty to Rome when he led the Eastern forces then remaining under Stilicho back to Constantinople in November 395. Upon meeting Rufinus, who as praetorian prefect accompanied Arcadius outside the walls of the city, Gaïnas's men seized him and put him to death. Gaïnas did nothing to stop them. This occurred on the 28th of the month, 20 days after Constantinople had welcomed back the body of Theodosius, which Gaïnas's returning army had probably accompanied most of the way. One ceremony at a time was best, so as to make the most out of both occasions. Rufinus fell as the returning army hailed Arcadius. Those witnessing Rufinus's fall must have thought that Stilicho had triumphed and that Gaïnas would now become a surrogate guardian of Arcadius for Stilicho. Gaïnas, however, was unable or unwilling to install himself as Arcadius's protector. Rather the eunuch Eutropius outmaneuvered him and took control of Arcadius and his court. Upon filling the void left by the assassination of Rufinus, Eutropius immediately faced the grim realities of recruitment. Gaïnas remained loyal to Arcadius, but was not called upon to participate in the repelling of Stilicho from Greece in 396. Gaïnas may have found himself with title, probably *magister militum* for Thrace, but was without troops to serve in the command. Eutropius quickly provided an appropriate staff, but Gaïnas probably had to find recruits and see to their training himself.[15]

Gaïnas had come to Constantinople as a general of the Western army, that is, at least *comes rei militaris*[16] and perhaps *magister equitum*. The highest-ranking general in the West except for the special role of Stilicho as *comes et magister utriusque militiae*[17] was marooned in the East. Eunapius calls Gaïnas the personal guard of Arcadius, perhaps thereby indicating that Gaïnas had at that moment no official command in the East.[18] Moreover, Eutropius promptly dismantled still more of the old general staff of Theodosius's final campaigns. He sent Timasius[19] and Abundantius, his own early supporter,[20] into exile. This left Eutropius free of potential rivals, especially unbeholden generals, and able to appoint his own men to office. In an act of practical expediency, Eutropius restored Gaïnas to his old command in Thrace, *magister militum per Thracias*, perhaps initially only a paper army. It is from this base that we first see Gaïnas wielding power, now in court and now against it until the rebellion of Tribigild in 399.

The return to his old regional command may well have been regarded by Gaïnas as a demotion from his position in the West, and thus his recorded disappointment in the honors paid him.[21] A symmetry between the command structure of East and West no longer existed, probably because Theodosius had died before he could impose one. The type of central command under Stilicho and (before his departure) Gaïnas did not exist in the East. Gaïnas's old command needed his attention. Rufinus had placed Alaric in Illyricum; with the former's death, it was anybody's guess how the latter would react.[22] Unless Gaïnas could raise an army in Thrace the Eastern army units that he had returned would have to stay put. It turned out that Eutropius had other plans for them.

In 397–98 Eutropius took personal command of the troops and led them against some Huns in Asia Minor. These Huns had descended through the Caucasus and were then attacking Phrygia and Cappadocia. Several contemporaries charged that they had been invited onto Roman soil by Rufinus.[23] Perhaps these hostile accounts reflect Rufinus's attempts to use Theodosian recruiting techniques in the East to create a regional defense network. If so, Rufinus should have also recalled that Theodosius treated the Hunnic recruits differently from other barbarians: as short term levies under their own commanders. The ancient writers' treatment of Eutropius's success also provides an interesting glimpse of the difficulties then still present in reconciling manly virtues with a eunuch's physical deformity. Claudian taints Eutropius's triumph with the tensions between his effeminacy and tradition. Where custom placed soldiers in parade dress passing in review, Claudian has Eutropius enraptured by the defenders of Rome—units of eunuchs.[24] The fact is, however, that this was a victory over a foreign foe such as Stilicho could not boast of. Eutropius was the only eunuch in Roman history to hold the consulship, but he certainly was not the last to have a sense of military strategy and personal courage.

For Stilicho, restoring Gaïnas and the Eastern army to Constantinople after his confrontation with Alaric in Thessaly meant that he could waste no time raising a new force. He soon crossed the Alps with Honorius in tow, halting on the Rhine to greet a new group of barbarians. This was probably in 396 and was not a war; no weapons clashed.[25] Instead, it was a classic instance of *receptio*, commonplace along the frontiers since the third century. Let us compare Claudian's account with the tetrarchic medallion of Lyon (see again illustration 2):

> Chieftains whose names were once so well known, flaxen-haired warrior-kings whom neither gifts nor prayers could win over to obedience to Rome's emperors, hasten at his command and fear to offend by dull delay. Crossing the river in boats they meet him wheresoever he will. . . . Those dread tribes whose wont it was ever to set their price on peace and let us purchase repose by shameful tribute, offer their children as hostages and begged for peace.[26]

And Claudian goes on: "Nay more, devoted to their conqueror this people offers its arms in his defense. How oft has Germany begged to add her troops to thine and to join her forces with those of Rome!"

These two views of *receptio* are equally formulaic, and describe a special moment of a common process that required only local Roman permission. The men Stilicho would have received from his Rhineland excursion would have been green recruits, but perhaps they could have replaced others in the frontier garrisons and thereby released a few men—hundreds, not thousands—for duty elsewhere. The likelihood that he got many able replacements is low. He certainly did not get enough to better his fortunes of 395 by much, when he next took an army eastward in 396. While Stilicho was on the Rhine, Gaïnas led the remaining units of the Eastern army

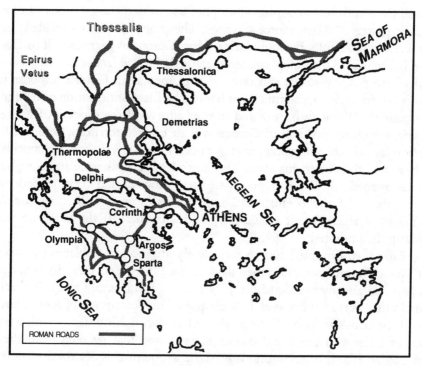

Map 7 Late Roman Greece

back and overthrew Rufinus. With the Eastern elements back in the East and Gaïnas there as well but unable to help and perhaps uninterested, Stilicho had only the newly formed armies he himself had raised when he landed in Greece. He was then, I believe, en route to Constantinople.[27]

We are better informed about the campaign of 396 than that of 395. It was a vastly more important campaign, for it marked the beginning of open warfare between the Western and Eastern empires. Eutropius seems to have used the intervening months to further reorder the Balkan defenses, virtually all of which had survived Adrianople and had been relinked into a system by Theodosius. Gerontius was ordered to command the garrisons guarding the chokepoints in Greece, Thermopylae, and the Isthmus (see map 7). (This was quite possibly the same Gerontius who as a junior officer had taught a newly recruited elite barbarian force at Tomi a lesson back in 386.) Antiochus, formerly perhaps prefect of the grain supply of Constantinople, was made proconsul of Achaea.[28] Alaric announced his pending arrival at Thermopylae to Antiochus and Gerontius, which must have enabled those officers to coordinate supplies and to alert the garrisons to allow Alaric passage.[29] Alaric's force traversed Thermopylae without incident and proceeded peacefully through Attica. Next, Gerontius permitted it to cross the Isthmus into the Peloponnese where Stilicho had landed.[30] These carefully directed maneuvers can only be explained as an Eastern response to Stilicho's invasion or, and much less likely, a brilliant anticipation of it. Since Valentinian II's death in 392 and forever afterward the diocese of Macedonia, which included all of Greece, was an Eastern territory. One justification for Stilicho's invasion may have been to add Illyricum to Honorius's sphere and thereby to his own. The East's legal claims were stronger, but more importantly the East possessed these dioceses and commanded the forces there.[31] Stilicho either had a spy in his camp or dallied in Greece thinking perhaps that it would rally to his banners. If the latter, he was greatly disappointed.

Eunapius, Zosimus's source, was clearly attempting to blame the woes of Greece upon Eutropius when he described the events there in 396. Eunapius had already branded Eutropius as being too friendly to the barbarians. In this section of his work he interspersed his description of Antiochus's and Gerontius's actions—Eutropius's men following his orders—with a litany of cities plundered and countrysides looted that resulted from their misguided efforts to accommodate Alaric. None of this destruction, however, can be confirmed archaeologically.[32] Zosimus by condensing Eunapius merged the two campaigns (395 and 396) into one. He gives the impression that Rufinus was still at the helm of the Eastern government during the campaign of 396, though he had been assassinated one year before. Without a fragment of Eunapius preserved in Joannes Antiochenus we would have no idea what transpired in Greece in 396. According to this fragment, later, after Stilicho and Alaric had worn each other down, it was Stilicho who, "having ravaged the barbarians by starvation, ceased his assault upon the inhabitants" of Greece. In other words, it was Stilicho who plundered Greece, not Alaric. We also learn that Alaric decided not to besiege Athens but rather negotiated the right for himself and his officers to bathe![33] Zosimus is only slightly less harsh on Stilicho, but considerably less clear.[34]

Obviously these barbarian bathers had been Roman soldiers too long. Do we not see in these several vignettes extracted from Eunapius an underlying simple, but desperate, Eastern strategy of recruiting barbarian auxiliaries to operate under only very loose Roman control? Should not Stilicho and his men, who were living off the land as they attempted to "starve out the barbarians,"[35] bear the primary responsibility for ravaging Greece—to the extent that it was indeed "ravaged"—rather than Alaric's "barbarians," who were in fact obviously supplied and garrisoned in the towns by the Eastern government? The answer to both questions is yes. Alaric's men surely walked into the towns of Greece, including Athens, without opposition. That is proof that they were there on orders from the Eastern command. These same soldiers in Liguria only a few years later proved themselves so inept at siege warfare that they, the besiegers, rather than the besieged were ravaged by hunger.[36] While Stilicho was devastating Greece, Eutropius defeated the Huns invading Asia Minor. In the relevant passages of Eunapius (and the derivative Zosimus) the central theme is the excoriation of both Rufinus and Eutropius, not the rational assessment of their policies. For the Roman elites there was no better way to condemn commanders than to brand them as barbarian sympathizers, a label that Claudian knew was being applied to his own patron by others. In truth, probably no emperor or field commander since the ascension of Valentinian I, most certainly not Theodosius, could have escaped similar vilification had his opposition dared to attack him. Once again there was no battle, merely another standoff.

Stilicho did not advance upon Constantinople but went back to Italy to raise more troops. Within a year of his return he must have learned of Eutropius's overtures to Gildo, *magister utriusque militiae per Africam* and son of King Nubel of Mauretania.[37] In the autumn of 397, Eutropius scored an important victory. Gildo declared himself for the East and stopped the grain ships destined for Rome. Eutropius moved quickly against Stilicho, declaring him a public enemy. For Stilicho, Eutropius would have to wait; the grain crisis superseded all others. In 398 Stilicho drained his reserves by dispatching perhaps 5,000 foot soldiers under Mascezel, Gildo's brother, to North Africa. Gildo had opened himself to charges of murder by ordering the execution of Mascezel's three children.[38] A few thousand men were sufficient. Mascezel killed his brother and confiscated his estates for the state. While all this was going on Stilicho moved his family even closer to the imperial throne by marrying his daughter Maria to Honorius (see illustration 15).[39] The marriage was almost predictable. Three years before, Arcadius had married Eudoxia, daughter of Bauto, *magister militum* and consul in 385. Bauto was a Frank by birth, Stilicho a Vandal. Stilicho simultaneously proceeded against Eutropius on the political front.

From June or July 397 through at least 12 November 399, a certain Anatolius was praetorian prefect of Illyricum. The laws issued to him in the name of both emperors were in fact rendered in Constantinople and somewhat peculiarly always note his regional command, Illyricum, as a part of his title.[40] At the same time in the West, Theodorus was praetorian prefect

Illustration 15. Two-layer sardonyx cameo showing Emperor Honorius and Empress Maria

(397–99) of Italy and Africa, and, at least at court, also of Illyricum.[41] The title had traditionally included the Illyricum with Italy and Africa, as recently as under Valentinian II, until Theodosius detached the Illyrican dioceses in 392. In other words, the title Claudian accorded Theodorus stated a Western claim to the prefecture of Illyricum with its three dioceses (Pannonia, Dacia, and Macedonia) and to Africa. It is important to note, however, that none of the actual recorded edicts addressed to Theodorus gives him a title more specific than praetorian prefect, and that all concern matters only of Italy, Rome, or "the provinces." There is no mention of any of the Illyrican dioceses in any of these laws.[42] Nor is there mention of his holding a prefectureship over Illyricum in any inscriptions bearing his name, including two commemorating him as *consul posterior* for 399.[43] From Gildo's defection to the East in 397 until his fall from power in 398, Theodorus had no authority in Africa either.

The best explanation of all this is that Theodorus's so-called praetorian prefectureship of Illyricum, Italy, and Africa were responses to Eutropius's provocative actions in 397 (that is, accepting Gildo, transferring Africa to the East, and declaring Stilicho a public enemy). Anatolius, always addressed as praetorian prefect of Illyricum, was actually in charge of affairs there, and reported only to the East. This means that Alaric as *magister militum* worked with Anatolius for the maintenance of his forces and the administration of justice for the whole of Illyricum. Theodorus's praetorian prefectureship of Illyricum was purely a political statement without substance. Theodorus, in fact, was praetorian prefect of Italy alone. Alaric's command was a part of Eutropius's defense against Stilicho, as it had been in 396 in Greece. The dark picture of Alaric in Illyricum in Claudian's *In Eutropium* was just another instance in which Claudian deliberately smudged everything Eutropius touched.[44] Claudian had someone of kindred spirit in Constantinople.

In early 398 Synesius of Cyrene wrote his speech *De regno*, "On Emperorship." He had just arrived back in Constantinople. Recent readings of the speech date it to 398 and relate it to Eutropius and indirectly to Alaric rather than Tribigild. These arguments are cogent. Nevertheless there is still great reluctance to see Alaric as Eutropius's ally. Rather he is seen in his customary role as a treacherous rebel.[45] This was not the case. Speaking of Alaric, clearly *magister militum per Illyricum*, Synesius says:

> But first let all be excluded from magistracies and kept away from the privileges of the council who are ashamed of all that has been sacred to the Romans from olden times, and has been so esteemed. Of a truth both

Barbarians within the Gates of Rome

Themis, herself sacred to the Senate, and the god of our battle-line must, I think, cover their faces when the man with leathern jerkin marches in command of those that wear the general's cloak, and whenever such an one divests himself of the sheepskin in which he was clad to assume the toga, and enters the council-chamber to deliberate on matters of State with the Roman magistrates, having a prominent seat perhaps next to the consul, while the lawful men sit behind him. Then again such as these, when they have gone a little way from the assembly, are again attired in their sheepskins, and once in the company of their followers, laugh the toga to scorn, and aver that they cannot even draw the sword in comfort with it.[46]

After reminding his audience that there are many Scythian slaves serving their Roman masters and recalling Spartacus and his slave revolt, Synesius recommends that the emperor purge the haughty foreigners from the army before they rebel and with the support of their servile kinsmen bring the Empire down:

Consider also that in addition to what forces they already possess, they may, whenever they will, have the slaves as soldiers, right reckless and courageous ones too, who will perform the unholiest deeds to glut themselves with independence. This fortress of theirs you must pull down; you must remove the foreign cause of the disease before the festering abscess actually declares itself, before the ill-will of these dwellers in our country is exposed. For evils may be overcome in their infancy, but when they progress they gain the upper hand. The army must be purified by the emperor, as is a heap of wheat from which we separate the coarse grain and what other elements sprout side by side with it, ruinous to the noble and legitimate seed. Now if I seem to you to give counsel that is no longer easy to follow, have you not considered to what sort of men and to what sort of race those belong of whom I am speaking to you who are their king [emperor]. It is a race whom the Romans conquered, and from such conquest their name has renowned amongst men.[47]

Through the De regno Synesius advises Arcadius to put aside his reclusive ways, sheltered from reality by his chamberlain, Eutropius. The first step of his self-assertion should be to remove Alaric, the skin-clad general's general (that is to say, *magister militum*) and his fellow Scythians from the army. After all, Rome had won fame in subduing these people. The task will demand all the energy Arcadius has, but he must—and here Synesius quotes Homer—"drive out these ill-omened dogs." Once these vermin are removed and replaced by native Roman troops, they will have no choice but to till Roman soil or flee.[48] And, it should be understood, their removal would deal a blow to Eutropius's power at court.

Synesius struck at what he saw as an alliance between Alaric and Eutropius, but his purpose was political and personal. He wanted imperial favoritism turned his way.[49] Just how genuine his anti-barbarian sentiments were is suspect, perhaps only a recent acquisition for the occasion.[50] By attacking Alaric and the Goths, he urged Arcadius to reflect upon the sad state of affairs existing under Eutropius. Eutropius was still very much in power when Synesius penned his speech, for otherwise there would have been no point in delivering it. The events described have not happened; they might. In reality none of them took place. Alaric had rebelled in 395 but was now *magister militum* and serving Eutropius loyally, as Synesius knew. The Scythians (Goths) had indeed been defeated. Some were slaves, others were tilling the soil, and many were serving throughout the army, not just with Alaric. Eutropius and Alaric are one problem here linked for rhetorical purposes to another, at least as perceived by the courtly rhetorician, that of the composition of the army. Scarcely beneath the surface of this oration is an attack on the army as a whole, not just those Goths within it. He also warned the emperor on the use of foreign mounted archers, surely meaning the Huns.[51] The Romans had not fielded the sort of "Roman army" he recommended for centuries. Synesius despised not only Eutropius, whose opposition blocked his career, but also Alaric and anyone else who supported him. He lamented the army as it currently existed. He knew, but did not want to admit, that purging Alaric and a few other officers of barbarian heritage was a totally unrealistic solution for the bigger problems.[52] What he really objected to was the power that Alaric and other generals exerted at court, his personal domain. His advice was nevertheless simplistic: Arcadius should rid himself of bad advisors and bad soldiers through an uncharacteristic assertion of manliness. It did not happen.

Alaric, perhaps feeling somewhat betrayed at the lack of support in repelling Stilicho from Greece—though his ally Gerontius may have died fighting in some skirmish there (never again surfacing in our sources)—withdrew to Epirus. Synesius's oration mattered to him not at all.[53] Epirus was probably one of the few areas relatively nearby still able to supply him, and there he took what he needed. Stilicho returned to Italy chastened. Arcadius's ministers had demonstrated their adamant refusal to come around to Stilicho's terms in battle. Once home he apparently redoubled his efforts at securing Illyricum for the West.[54] This was in 397. Apparently no provision had been made for Alaric's withdrawal, but Greece was barren of supplies and he had to move. There were very few Roman troops left anywhere in the Balkans and probably none in Epirus, a part of the diocese of Macedonia. There is no way to check the extent of Alaric's alleged plundering alluded to in the literary sources. Epirus was hardly an ideal location for Alaric's force, unless he were already *magister militum per Illyricum*, and thus could legally draw upon its stores.

The archaeological data make it manifest that the passes in the Julian Alps were never again systematically defended after their denudation in 394 and that defensible refuges increasingly replaced exposed civilian settlements.[55] The appointment of a capable *magister* was necessary to continue the development of the Macedonian area as well as the rest of Illyricum. Alaric was available with soldiers, probably the only mobile force between Constantinople and Italy. Several difficult problems now come to the fore. First, what commands did Alaric hold and when? Second, when did the East return Pannonia, the westernmost diocese of Illyricum, to the West?

Unguarded references to Illyricum during these years can easily lead to confusion. Whenever we speak of a "return," only the return of the diocese of Pannonia to the West is at issue. Theodosius had transferred the entire prefecture of Illyricum to the East in 392. At some later date Pannonia alone was again restored to the West, and that date is a part of our discussion. The return of Pannonia fixed the boundaries between Arcadius and Honorius, and the Roman East and West, forever. The military command of Illyricum, *magister militum per Illyricum*, was a regional command first established by Theodosius the Great not later than 392 (the probable date of the last major changes in the Eastern sections of the *Notitia*), probably in order to facilitate coordinated command in this war-torn area. This so-called regional magistership then became one of three such commands in the Eastern army, its *magister* being equal to the two magisters of the praesental armies. It thus was one of five supreme commands in the East at the time of Theodosius's death. These commands were obviously something new and were still not truly fixed to sharply defined areas. They did, however, at least in 392 (as witnessed in the *Notitia dignitatum*), have specific troop units assigned to them. Unfortunately the eastern section of the *Notitia* does not give specific locations for the units of the *magister militum per Illyricum*. In any case, after the campaigns against Arbogastes and Eugenius in 394, the extant Eastern sections were essentially obsolete. The East must have maintained an up-to-date version now lost.

Throughout most of its history the diocese of Pannonia was a Western jurisdiction and is so presented in the *Notitia*, whose relevant Western sections all date to after 400 and many are probably later than 405. However, the *Notitia* records the diocese with a new name, Illyricum.[56] Since this

Illyricum is in the Western section, it is often referred to as *Illyricum occidentale*.[57] Precisely when this transfer took place is unknown and demands a hypothesis. I will make a case for ca. 400 later in this chapter. From 392 until its transfer back to the West sometime after Theodosius's death, the diocese of Pannonia belonged to the East along with the rest of the prefecture. So long as Theodosius lived, until 395, there had been no urgency to straighten out jurisdictions. At his death the troops then under the *magister militum per Illyricum* probably were to have been distributed temporarily throughout the dioceses of Illyricum. This did not take place because of the eruption of conflicts involving Stilicho. The office of praetorian prefect of Illyricum without Pannonia had existed for a short time before (ca. 380–82), and this may have provided an important precedent when the time came to restore only the diocese of Pannonia to the West.[58]

There was no praetorian prefect of Thrace, although the region had a *magister militum per Thracias* at the head of its military forces. For purposes of civil government the diocese of Thrace, like all other dioceses in the East not under the praetorian prefect of Illyricum, fell under the praetorian prefect of the Orient. As of 392 Thrace and Illyricum shared some government agencies under the *magister officiorum*, such as a subofficer of the *schola agentum in rebus*.[59] Until the diocese of Pannonia was returned to the West, it must have militarily been under the *magister militum per Illyricum*. After the transfer of the diocese, its forces (probably never again regular garrisons) were commanded by a *comes rei militaris*. The civilian establishment of the diocese was in the hands of the standard vicars and provincial governors.[60] Alaric would figure prominently in the Eastern command of Illyricum, the transfer of its diocese of Pannonia, and ultimately the history of the Western diocese of Illyricum as well.

What command, if any, had Rufinus granted to Alaric, and when? Was this relationship continued or enhanced by Eutropius? We have no indication of any specific Roman command for Alaric prior to Synesius's somewhat obscure comments in *De regno* in early 398. Claudian in his second *In Eutropium*, written in early 399, is clearer: Alaric "the ravager of Achaea and recent devastator of defenseless Epirus is lord of Illyria [presides over]; he now enters as a friend within the walls to which he was laying siege, and administers justice to those whose wives he has seduced and whose children he has murdered."[61] Stripped of the charges of ravaging and murdering, Alaric's actions in Epirus, however decried by Claudian, only seem bad by association and, in fact, were just what Alaric ought to have been doing if *magister:* fighting and rendering justice. The reference to Illyria and its people must apply to the prefecture where the civil population lived.

Only soldiers fell under commands. *In Eutropium* was an attack upon the eastern court and policies of Eutropius, which in fact were creating an effective barrier between Stilicho and Constantinople, not an indictment focused on Alaric. But Alaric in Illyricum was more than just another affront to Rome offered by the regents at Constantinople. Unfortunately for Stilicho, Alaric was the one that endured.

The problem of when Alaric did become *magister militum per Illyricum* is sometimes tied in to the question of the return of Pannonia to Western jurisdiction. A standard theory is that the diocese was returned to the West in the context of the events of 395—either as a prelude to Stilicho's first "invasion" of Greece, or as a part of a *quid pro quo* for the return of the Eastern army to Constantinople.[62] The promotion of Alaric to the magistership of Illyricum is typically dated to the same year or to 397. In other words, for its proponents, for a few years (at least from 397 to 399) Alaric was *magister* over an Illyrican command without the diocese of Pannonia. No one denies that he was *magister* in 399. Technically this is possible but highly unlikely. The repercussions of one event upon the other have not attracted much notice. Nor do traditional hypotheses explain how Alaric came to be in the diocese in 399–401. To make headway we must at first address the issues of the military command and the return of the diocese separately. We will begin with Alaric's magistership of Illyricum, which is somewhat easier to deal with.

It appears that the most likely year for Alaric's promotion to *magister* is indeed 395, perhaps after briefly having been *comes rei militaris*. It seems highly probable that a military appointment, at least as high as *comes rei militaris*, would have been necessary to buy Alaric's departure from Constantinople early in 395. Then after Stilicho's withdrawal from Greece later that year, Rufinus rewarded Alaric, whose troops had thwarted Stilicho in Thessaly, with the magistership of Illyricum. Both were prior to the "return of the Eastern army" led back to Constantinople by Gaïnas on 28 November 395, which was accomplished without incident or opposition. If Gaïnas marched overland, as surely he did, he crossed through territory that Alaric controlled. Perhaps Alaric thought better than to confront Gaïnas, but more likely he had orders to let him pass. The year 395 also is the earliest, but hardly the most likely, date for Alaric to have styled himself king (or more likely "prince") to his followers, as the chronicler Marcellinus Comes, writing under Justinian, has him do.[63] As *magister*, he for the first time would have had the resources to reward and maintain his followers in a "regal manner." Perhaps his appointment to Roman command was part of the "secret understanding" that Rufinus reached with Alaric before sending him to Greece.[64] "Secret" perhaps, but it was only until after Alaric had proven his loyalty against Stilicho's invasion.[65] Following this line of reasoning, Alaric's promotions were acts of Rufinus, who, according to Marcellinus Comes, had urged Alaric to "attack Greece."[66] More likely, Rufinus urged Alaric to attack Stilicho in Greece.[67]

A decision to appoint Alaric to Roman command in 395 also fits nicely with efforts then to secure the Balkans. Alaric could provide some military control in Illyricum, and the arrival of Gaïnas in November with the Eastern army gave the East a modest force with which to maintain and reinforce Thrace, address concerns on the eastern frontier, and perhaps attend to other areas as well. Of course, much depended upon Alaric, Gaïnas, and the Eastern government working together. That could hardly be assumed. Moreover, both East and West had other problems demanding attention and troops. Although this sequence makes sense for Alaric's command, the hypothesis that Illyricum was returned to the West in 395 has yet to be validated. Rather, it seems clearly refuted.

Another possibility is that the magistership may have been a reward for Alaric's service against Stilicho in 396, the latter's second invasion of Greece, thus an action by Eutropius. The circumstances of that campaign suggest that Alaric already held a high command, which enabled him to pass through Roman defenses and garrison his men in the cities of Greece. In either case, 395 or 396–97, the grant of the command of Illyricum was prior to the earliest references in Synesius and Claudian by at least a year and perhaps four. At the opening of 399 Illyricum remained Eastern and under Alaric as *magister*. No transfers had occurred. Alaric was not out; he was in Arcadius's service.

Although the possibility is seldom raised that Pannonia was not returned to the West at all in either 395 or 396–97, this seems the case. Rejection of the two traditional dates raises a question about the actions of the Western emperor in 407–8. If Illyricum, by then a new Western diocese, was not then within his sphere, how could Honorius appoint Alaric to command the Roman troops there, as *comes rei militaris*, and name Iovius as praetorian prefect of Illyricum?[68] That he did makes it clear that by then the diocese was Western, renamed Illyricum, and that Alaric obeyed Honorius. So the issue of when these alignments changed is still unresolved. It is very difficult to see why Eutropius would have rewarded Stilicho's second failed invasion of Greece by giving him Pannonia, part of the command of Alaric, the general who had repelled the invader. It is equally hard to believe that after this transfer Eutropius proceeded immediately to welcome the African provinces and Gildo into the Eastern Empire and to declare Stilicho a public enemy. So late 397 and 398 are out. There is no circumstance after 397 under which Stilicho and Eutropius could have come to terms. We must look beyond the rule of Eutropius, beyond the summer of 399.[69] Something had happened shortly before these events that entirely changed the position of Gaïnas, Alaric and his men, and many others. A major rebellion occurred in Asia Minor.

Late in 398 or early in 399 a certain Tribigild was in Constantinople, probably to receive a new command as *comes rei militaris* to suppress some localized rebellions in Asia Minor. These disturbances were probably the result of Eutropius's recent levies there to support his successful campaign against some Huns. Tribigild had distinguished himself in this campaign as a military tribune in charge of a cavalry unit composed of barbarians and now stationed at Nacoleia in Phrygia.[70] Not all sources agree on the path of his career. Claudian places Tribigild at the head of an *ala* of Gothic cavalry during the rebellion, in other words still a tribune, but Claudian probably did not know of his appointment as *comes*.[71] The troops of his previous command were not just some bands of barbarians. Before turning to rebellion they had been "a Roman legion, conquered we gave them laws, fields and places to live."[72] Which also underscores the nature of what barbarian recruits might expect: service, land, and dwellings, typically in places far from home. There they would serve under a Roman commander. That the Roman officer might speak their language or something close may have made matters easier, but he was otherwise foreign to them. The barbarians at Nacoleia probably were Greutungi, but this says nothing about Tribigild.[73] Socrates called him a kinsman of Gaïnas, almost certainly not a Greutungi.

Perhaps he like Gaïnas had entered Roman service under Theodosius and had risen through the ranks.[74] Or more likely he owed his enlistment directly to Gaïnas himself. Gaïnas had used this rank to lure barbarian leaders across the frontier and into Roman service, being at pains to stipulate that officers who held it would have command of units of the army.[75] Philostorgius went to some length to distinguish Tribigild from the numerous other "Scythians"; he was specifically a "Goth."[76] Tribigild was just another Roman commander in charge of a unit raised from newly received barbarians. He was almost certainly not their kinsman. Once back in Nacoleia, he rebelled.[77]

If this reconstruction of his career is correct, then *comes* Tribigild left Constantinople assigned to command all the troops in the theater of the unrest, not just barbarians; but it was the barbarians at Nacoleia who formed the nucleus of his insurrection. As tribune he had been a regular Roman officer commanding a regular cavalry unit, and so too as *comes*. Once Arcadius learned of his rebellion, he would have stripped him of his command and those troops with him were legally free to desert. The brevity of his tenure as *comes* led some observers to believe that he remained only a military tribune. His being merely a tribune also worked to Claudian's advantage, since it made Eutropius appear even weaker by failing to quash the rebels. Whatever his rank and the motives held by Tribigild and his men, they plundered the province of Asia, gathering to their side many runaway slaves and dispossessed farmers. In Lydia refugees flocked to the seaports hoping to escape with their families to the safety of the islands.[78] The rebels returned to Phrygia, where they probably picked up their dependents and other members of their unit, and proceeded to plunder that province as well before moving on to Pisidia.[79]

To meet this crisis Eutropius raised Gaïnas to the command of a praesental army, including whatever barbarian auxiliaries he could muster. These were difficult times. Both East and West desperately needed men to replace the fallen. Gaïnas fielded whatever other troops were available. Many were barbarians, most raw recruits.[80] Gaïnas was a master recruiter. At the moment of Tribigild's rebellion or shortly before, he had served for at least a decade, probably more. In all that time he had not deserted, had not rebelled, had not pillaged Phrygia or anywhere else. He was just another capable Roman officer of Germanic birth about whom we would know nothing had he not turned a rebel. Gaïnas, whose own career since returning to the East may have suffered a setback or at least was now subject to the whims of a eunuch—doubtless an affront to a soldier from the ranks—seems to have chosen to exploit Tribigild's anger and disappointment to his own advantage.

This version of Gaïnas's motivation is all but ubiquitous in the sources. Only the ecclesiastical historian Theodoretus ignores it in favor of a religious motive: Patriarch John Chrysostom's denial of Gaïnas's request to have a church set aside for the Arians.[81] All other sources, most based in one way or another upon Eunapius of Sardis,[82] attribute collusion with the rebels to Gaïnas. Why else, they ask, did not Gaïnas press the issue and defeat Tribigild in the field? Obviously, to their minds anyway, the answer was that Gaïnas was in charge and Tribigild, a Goth too, took orders. There were clear and compelling reasons why Gaïnas could not press the issue against Tribigild. For one thing, Tribigild was a strong leader and held his forces together despite setbacks. For another, Eutropius had dispatched what men he had readily available with Gaïnas's colleague Leo to the province of Asia, where losses had been heavy.[83] With what few forces he had, probably centered around those that he himself had managed to raise from among the barbarians in Thrace, Gaïnas was to march to Thrace and secure the Hellespont.[84]

Fravitta *magister militum per Orientem* remained at his headquarters in Antioch until late in the year. The Persian frontier required constant attention despite the various treaties signed since 363.[85] Fravitta must have held this key post from 398.[86] At the outset of the rebellion Arcadius must have decided that like Illyricum the Persian frontier could not spare any troops to challenge Tribigild. The initial reports of the rebellion suggested that it was a relatively minor military revolt.

Eutropius's plans ran aground in Asia Minor. Leo, a man with no prior command experience, proved hesitant to take the offensive. Learning that Tribigild had evacuated the Hellespont area, Leo lingered there rather than pursuing him. By this time Gaïnas was Leo's superior.[87] He finally ordered Leo to leave the safety of the Hellespontine cities and march southward toward Phrygia. In order to facilitate Leo's move, Gaïnas dispatched some newly raised barbarian auxiliaries to his aid, thereby weakening his own reserves. Leo must have reported that Tribigild had acquired a much more sizable following than he had originally thought, and asked for reinforcements. It may have been Leo's only prudent move. Gaïnas then took the field himself, crossing the Hellespont and advancing southward at a careful pace, dispatching some troops to block Tribigild if he moved east. If Tribigild was thwarted in his efforts to escape, he would have had no choice but to stand and fight.[88] Tribigild, rather than face Leo and Gaïnas, left Phrygia for Pamphylia.

The terrain in Pamphylia favored the Roman defenders. Local forces organized by some retired veterans succeeded in holding key passes and river crossings against Tribigild's forces.[89] Gaïnas ordered Leo to advance to the aid of the Pamphylians.[90] Tribigild turned around to face Leo. The barbarians sent by Gaïnas to support Leo went over to Tribigild, and together they annihilated Leo and his army. Leo had apparently violated every axiom of Roman tactics to the point of not fortifying his camps and not even posting guards.[91] Gaïnas, now in Phrygia, stood alone against the rebellion. He too had underestimated his opponent and had committed the great military blunder of splitting his army in the face of the enemy. Gaïnas dispatched a message directly to Arcadius stating that he could not match forces with Tribigild. He demanded as a condition for his further service the dismissal of Eutropius, whom the emperor was to hand over to him for punishment. Gaïnas knew he had become indispensable. The date was sometime in late July 399.[92] He and Fravitta were the only seasoned field commanders from the days of Theodosius who remained in the East. Fravitta stayed in Antioch.

Gaïnas summoned Arcadius to Chalcedon and dictated his terms: the surrender of all his opponents. Arcadius complied at once. He exiled Saturninus (the ex-consul of 383 and judge in the case against Timasius in 396). Arcadius even had to cast out his favorite Joannes. Gaïnas was no longer inferior in rank to Stilicho; he was Stilicho's equal. As satisfying as that thought must have been, Gaïnas needed support in Constantinople and knew it. He found Caesarius unacceptable, probably because of his service to Eutropius. Instead he chose to pardon his brother Aurelianus and took him into his government.[93] Aurelianus must have been one of those whom Gaïnas "just touched with the sword." Events in the East had reached the boiling point and were about to involve Alaric and the West again. Eutropius fell, along with his praetorian prefect of the Orient, Eutychianus, sometime in early August. Eutropius went into exile on Cyprus, whence he was recalled to stand trial for treason and executed. This could not have occurred before 1 October and probably took place at least two months later.[94]

With Eutropius out of power, Gaïnas must have thought that his will alone held sway in Constantinople. He then struck a deal with Tribigild, something that had apparently been unacceptable to Eutropius. There was little in the way of an alternative. Both commanders set off for the Hellespont on separate paths, according to Zosimus, "granting permission to their barbarian armies to plunder at will."[95] In fact, there was no need for Gaïnas or Tribigild to "plunder" their way through the provinces, for Gaïnas was *magister militum praesentalis* and only had to requisition supplies. Their armies were heavily, not exclusively, barbarian, which had been true for decades. Gaïnas and Tribigild crossed into Europe independently. Tribigild died shortly thereafter.[96] Gaïnas recrossed the Hellespont, ordering Fravitta to proceed northward from Antioch and set straight any unrest in the provinces afflicted during the rebellion.[97] Gaïnas proceeded to Constantinople. Zosimus's distortion supports the view that Gaïnas was always the main rebel, now at last stripped of his disguise.

Aurelianus's pardon meant that he could assume power, and he at once replaced Eutychianus as praetorian prefect of the Orient.[98] Eutychianus was Eutropius's appointee as had been Caesarius. Therefore in all likelihood Eutychianus and Caesarius were factional colleagues. Caesarius held the consulship in 397, and Eutychianus in 398, while Eutropius made policy. Neither was exiled, although Caesarius may have become the butt of jokes to the point that he stayed out of sight and claimed to be sick.[99] Aurelianus sat on the "opposite side of the isle," and with Gaïnas's support now became the principal civilian at court from early August. He and Gaïnas must have gotten along, if they were not outright allies during these months.[100] At first Gaïnas needed his support in Constantinople to establish a new order among the civilian courtiers. Without Gaïnas Aurelianus had no office. Aurelianus presided over the trial and execution of Eutropius in Chalcedon, probably in the early autumn, perhaps as early as September.[101] Chalcedon was appropriately within the jurisdiction of the praetorian prefect of the Orient. Aurelianus served as consul posterior with Stilicho in 400, who refused to acknowledge him.[102] That Stilicho had not accepted Eutropius as consul in 399 is understandable, but why Aurelianus was not accepted in 400 is more difficult. In not doing so Stilicho revealed his continued hostility toward the East. At the opening of the year Aurelianus was still praetorian prefect, receiving the edict confiscating Eutropius's property and destroying all statues of him.[103]

Eutychianus is a key figure in all this. Anatolius is another, and although of lesser importance of no lesser mystery. Eutychianus's career flourished under Eutropius as praetorian prefect of Illyricum in 396–97 and consul in 398.[104] He was praetorian prefect of the Orient in 398–99 and fell with Eutropius. He rose from the ashes to again be praetorian prefect of the Orient in 404–5. Alaric was in Illyricum in 395–96, perhaps as *comes rei militaris* or more likely as *magister militum*. There, if, as seems almost certain, Eutychianus was praetorian prefect of Illyricum in 396, the two necessarily would have worked together. Anatolius succeeded Eutychianus in 397 and served on into November of 399.[105] Around the middle of April 400, Gaïnas returned to Constantinople, dismissed Aurelianus, and sent him into exile. The East may have had no consul for the remainder of 400.[106] Gaïnas was now the paramount figure in Constantinople and consul designate for 401. There was no civilian government in Constantinople. Gaïnas had seized all power. Apparently only the Senate and emperor remained. Aurelianus and his brother were master chameleons and soon bounced back.[107] Of Eutychianus we hear nothing until February 404, but he evidently lived in Constantinople throughout these turbulent years.[108]

On 12 July 400, the citizens of Constantinople rose. Led by members of the imperial guard and perhaps urged on by members of the Senate, the Constantinopolitans slaughtered Gothic civilians and many of Gaïnas's soldiers, nearly a fifth of his army according to Synesius of Cyrene. Being barbarian did not inhibit the imperial guard. Seven thousand of Gaïnas's followers are said to have sought asylum in a church near the palace. Arcadius himself ordered their deaths.[109] The Goths were virtually defenseless, armed with only a few weapons smuggled into the capital. Gaïnas himself had left the city only shortly before the killing began. No one in authority made any effort to stop the massacre. Patriarch Chrysostom never condemned it. Many of Gaïnas's men were not in Constantinople but billeted roundabout as was the norm. With them Gaïnas retreated to Thrace, where he found the gates of the cities locked and defended. Tribigild, who had crossed to Thrace, had died but some of his followers may still have been around.[110]

Gaïnas's vague political aspirations, not his military background and not his ancestry, led to the carnage. He did not lose control of himself because Chrysostom opposed his wish to have a church officially dedicated for Gothic use. After all, he was himself a supreme example of someone who had made it in the Roman world without much notice of his personal life and beliefs. There were churches open to them already, in one of which thousands sought refuge in vain. The consulship for 401 was insufficient, so was supreme command.[111] He coopted the nimble politician Aurelianus to further his aims and listened to his counsel until he had no more need of him. Aurelianus abetted those in power while keeping a side door open. Perhaps as a military commander of long standing, Gaïnas ran out of patience. Gaïnas was a man of decision. His followers' blood stained his hands. Arcadius, the Senate, and the people of Constantinople cast out a despot. This particular one was a Goth.

Arcadius named Fravitta *magister militum (praesentalis)* to prosecute the war against Gaïnas. This was the same Fravitta who had killed Eriulf in front of Theodosius years before—a tough, skillful commander, passionately loyal to the House of Theodosius.[112] He was already in Asia tidying up after Tribigild's rebellion, and with his fleet in readiness could move swiftly. As a Roman pagan, Eunapius and Zosimus treated him with exceptional kindness. Thrace could no longer provide Gaïnas with fresh troops; perhaps Asia Minor could. But Fravitta thwarted Gaïnas's attempt to cross back into Asia and on 23 December 400 destroyed his ships at sea.[113] On 3 January he paraded Gaïnas's head through the streets of the capital. Circulating and displaying the heads of usurpers and slaughtered foes on pikes was a Roman practice with a great future in the following decades.[114] The Huns had not yet adapted the sport to politics. There would have been no head displayed in his victory parade unless Fravitta, the victor and consul for 401, had wanted it so. The consulship was his reward; the pike, Gaïnas's.[115]

Within a year or two of Fravitta's victory Arcadius ordered the erection of a column to commemorate it. Some sixteenth-century artists took interest in the now lost column and made a series of sketches. Their drawings and a few later ones survive. The column had a spiral frieze running from a large rectangular pedestal to a statue of Arcadius, not placed there until 421.[116] The base, which scarcely survives, reminds one of the base of Theodosius's obelisk set up in the hippodrome to commemorate the conclusion of the Gothic wars. The frieze was in the manner of Trajan's famous column in Rome. Among the scenes are: departure from Constantinople under the aegis of Fortuna; marching through the countryside, with dwellings and civilians tending livestock; camps and weapons; heavily loaded pack animals; a stalemate along the Hellespont where Fravitta's fleet blocks Gaïnas's passage; Fravitta's soldiers disembarking; and three battles in which cavalry is clearly playing a part. Arcadius and Honorius, as if on a medallion, stand in the middle of the topmost scene on the column base flanked by their principal officers.

Fascinating as all this is, historians studying the column have found little to agree about. There is no reason to conclude from the lack of detail that the forces were ever portrayed as distinctively Gothic or Roman. If what seems to have been on the monument, as judged from the drawings, was there on the original, Arcadius's column would certainly be the most amazing artifact from the era, had it survived. The details in the drawings are generally taken from the traditional repertoire of triumphal iconography,[117] but with some inexplicable and otherwise unknown components such as the repeated use of standards bearing the Christogram as booty. The carefully sketched depictions of booty also include characteristic Roman parade helmets. It is surely inappropriate to hazard a Gothic identity to any aspect of the monument as seen in the drawings. This applies to the soldiers, the peasant huts, the booty, and so on. Perhaps the sculptors did not portray Gothic warriors at all since to distinguish the actual troops of the opposing armies was probably impossible. The extant materials support no conclusions and cannot bear the weight of many hypotheses either.[118]

Fravitta, another Roman general of barbarian paents and the fourth in this chapter, continued to serve Rome. His death in 404 came about because of his accusations against Joannes, the Empress Eudoxia's favorite, and charges raised by Hierax, a courtier and governor of Pamphylia. He accused Joannes of trying to foment hostility between Arcadius and Honorius.[119] Fravitta, in other words, died because of a power struggle at court, an arena from which he should have withdrawn but could not as *magister*. Stilicho had no difficulty recognizing his consulship, which seems to have inaugurated a relaxation of tension between East and West that was to endure for but a year or two.[120] Despite the fall of Gaïnas, the East's policies of recruiting and promoting Germanic barbarians in the army did not change. Caesarius seems to have survived in office until perhaps 403.[121] There were still many capable soldiers and officers of Germanic parentage in the military pipeline, but the East's supply of replacements was drying up.

The Huns put a stop to recruitment beyond the Danube unless with their consent. Thrace was played out and soon fell into chaos. Theodosius II recognized this when he ordered the great landwall built across the isthmus to protect Constantinople. He also strengthened interior defenses throughout the Balkan dioceses. Many Thracian towns, after having hosted so many Roman soldiers in the fourth century, gradually ceased. The East had to look elsewhere. In his last march Gaïnas had pointed the way: the recruitment trail led to Asia Minor. Contrary to long-held beliefs, the East did not impose a litmus test of ethnicity and reject Germans after the citizens of the capital rose and slaughtered thousands of Goths, mostly dependents. The policy remained constant: get the best recruits available, at the least overall cost, wherever they could be found. Then train them to fight as Romans or take advantage of their existing skills.

Concerning the diocese of Pannonia, there was no occasion after the massacre in July to worry about it. No one considered Alaric as an ally for or against Gaïnas. Therefore it is reasonable to conclude that by July 400, Alaric was out of the picture and the diocese of Pannonia with him. I therefore suggest that the most likely time for the transfer of Pannonia back to the West was near the end of 399, probably in December, or early in 400. It surely would have occurred after the trial of Eutropius as a part of the further effort to secure Aurelianus's and Gaïnas's power in Constantinople, and probably after the absorption, rather than suppression, of Tribigild, when the military situation appeared under control. There is no apparent reason why they would have waited from early October until 17 January to confiscate Eutropius's property and tear down his statues. It would have been utterly unbearable for Gaïnas and Aurelianus to endure passing by Eutropius's likenesses in stone for four months! The date for the trial should be moved much closer to the end of the year. This redating also provides for a much more realistic pace of travel for all participants during the last half of 399.[122] Another indicator that events surrounding Eutropius's fall culminated late in 399 and early in 400 is the crowning of Arcadius's wife Eudoxia as empress on 9 January, perhaps in return for her support during Eutropius's ouster.[123] If Anatolius was in fact considered a principal supporter of the fallen eunuch, Gaïnas and Aurelius may have replaced him too.

Anatolius received his last edict as praetorian prefect of Illyricum on 12 November 399 and disappears from historical record. Everything we know about Anatolius relates to his prefecture.[124] His disappearance after 12 November is odd. He was the only principal player never to return to politics. Could he have stayed with Alaric? Neither were felons. The Eastern government simply no longer wanted their services. Associating with each other was not a crime in December of 399.[125] Just after Eutropius's execution Gaïnas and Aurelianus were at the height of their cooperation and power. They needed to consolidate their positions quickly. Gaïnas had forces available to check Alaric if he invaded the East. The transfer of the diocese was, I believe, at the initiative of Aurelianus, perhaps as a gesture for the holding of the joint-consulship with Stilicho. This was inherently a civilian matter since it required the realignment of the responsibilities of the prefecture of Illyricum. Conversely, abandoning Alaric to his fate was a military decision and as such was Gaïnas's to make. That one decision invariably affected the other made cooperation between the civilian and military heads imperative. Aurelianus and Gaïnas each acted with the full knowledge and support of the other.

Their decision was primarily a part of the process of solidifying power in Constantinople.[126] There was another reason as well. By restoring Pannonia to the West they might forestall Stilicho's planned invasion. There could have been no doubt that something was brewing. In his diatribe against Eutropius, delivered in January 399, Claudian had noted the submission of some Germans to Honorius and Stilicho just after the goddess Roma asks rhetorically whether Eutropius is worthy of her anger.[127] Their deployment in a war to the East was obvious. Eutropius was gone; now was the time to extend an olive branch. A more distant consideration was Alaric, who was unpredictable, usually loyal but always restless. He and Gaïnas were probably already working the same turf searching for recruits. Alaric probably had few admirers at court but must have had some. For Synesius Alaric, the *magister militum*, had been a real power in court circles, one seated at the side of the consuls during Eutropius's rule.[128] A few former Eutropius supporters might have turned to him for help. They could do so no longer.

The dates assigned to the imperial edicts being what they are—indispensable but very insecure—it is impossible to have complete confidence in any hypothesis based solely upon them. But in this case there is strong corroborative evidence elsewhere. According to Jordanes, Alaric was first king in the consulship of Stilicho and Aurelianus, that is in 400—a consulship Stilicho chose to ignore. This is a very precise reference, especially for Jordanes. It would be nice to know which month! I think January or February are most likely. Just prior to this the customary payments to Alaric's force as Roman auxiliaries ceased.[129] This must mean that in 400 Alaric declared himself king. At last the problems of Alaric's tenure as *magister militum* and the return of the diocese of Pannonia come together. Out of the turmoil surrounding them, Alaric's kingship emerged. The *Notitia dignitatum* indirectly provides further assistance for dating the transfer.

The *Notitia* is the source that first notes Illyricum as a diocese in the West. We know apart from any discussion of Alaric and the return of Pannonia that a clerk incorrectly deleted the province of Valeria in Pannonia from the *index* of the *Notitia*, when he should have struck the Italian province by the same name. The last time a law mentions Italian Valeria was on 1 December 399.[130] Elsewhere in the *Notitia* Valeria is provided with a complement of troops only appropriate for the frontier province of Valeria in Pannonia.[131] The return of the diocese of Pannonia, which included the province of Valeria, would have been a powerful stimulus for simplifying the administration of Italy by dropping the duplication of the name Valeria. Whenever the clerk finally posted the change in the *Notitia*, probably around 405–6 in order to bring it up to date for Stilicho, he was careless. That the last date for Italian Valeria is so close to the dates arrived at from other sources for the transfer of Pannonia to the West is one more hint that something major involving Pannonia-Illyricum then took place. According to this line of evidence, the date for the change must have fallen after 1 December 399 but before Stilicho ordered a revision of the *Notitia*. The legislative silence on Italian Valeria joins the other evidence pointing to the earlier date, very late 399 or early 400. Renaming Pannonia, on the other hand, carried with it political overtones and need not have occurred simultaneously with the restoration of the diocese to Western authority.

There is no contemporary evidence other than the *Notitia* for the renaming and so no way to establish anything more than a tenuous hypothesis. Assigning a new name to the diocese could have saved face for Stilicho by giving him the legal control over "Illyricum" that he had long sought unsuccessfully—a diplomatic triumph for the Roman audience. There would have been no reason to delay such action as far as the West was concerned. Yet the East could easily have misinterpreted it at a time when Stilicho did not want to send any sign of softening to Aurelianus and Gaïnas. A better opportunity arose when the consulship of Fravitta in 401 ushered in a brief period of reconciliation. As a part of this healing process Pannonia may have become Illyricum, thereby proclaiming Stilicho's contentment.

Stilicho could not refuse the return of the diocese of Pannonia from Arcadius's government but had no cause for rejoicing. He manifestly did not accept, however, the East's obligations to Alaric. Aurelianus did not return Dacia and Macedonia but kept them under Eastern jurisdiction, and so obvious points of contention still existed. The posts of *magister militum* and praetorian prefect of Illyricum, for example, remained Eastern appointments. Since it is likely that Alaric had worked with Eutychianus in Illyricum in 395–96 and Anatolius in 397 until his dismissal, it was also sound policy for Aurelianus to drive a wedge between Alaric and his civilian colleagues. And it is no wonder that Stilicho refused to recognize Aurelianus as joint-consul with him in 400.[132] Aurelianus had bested him.

Gaïnas and Aurelianus must have conspired to produce a plan of such subtlety. In one stroke they had struck a blow at their political opponents and rid themselves of a difficult military problem. Alaric and his men were now Stilicho's concern. Aurelianus thus had strong political motives to strip Alaric of his command and transfer Pannonia to Stilicho. Gaïnas would have had good cause to applaud these moves. Alaric was a rising star in the Balkans and a rival in recruitment and command. Thus at the opening of 400, the Western court again administered Illyricum, but it was only a diocese renamed, or about to be. Aurelianus had deftly removed Alaric's base of support from beneath his feet by returning the diocese to Stilicho and the West and thereby removing Alaric from his office of *magister militum*. Alaric had no choice but kingship. Aurelianus and Gaïnas now only had to deal with the court. Stilicho had received only half a loaf, for Dacia and Macedonia were still beyond his reach.[133] Any possibility of his controlling Arcadius receded further into the distance. His military problems were fundamental and made worse by the return of a stricken diocese, garrisoned by an old adversary. His anger smothered. He must have hated Gaïnas almost as much as Aurelianus. Stilicho must have applauded Fravitta's triumph; at least he welcomed his consulship. But the events in Constantinople throughout the remainder of 400 could only have left Alaric increasingly worried and angry.

Alaric had always known that his position was precarious. But he had fared well under Rufinus and Eutropius. The collapse of Eutropius's regime, however, was disastrous for him. Rome had set him and his men adrift. As far as he was concerned the emperor had dismissed him without cause. The massacre of the Goths in Constantinople in July 400 must have led Alaric to ponder his own fate. He bided his time. Perhaps he thought that somehow the confrontation between Fravitta and Gaïnas might work to his advantage. If so, Gaïnas's demise in December proved his hope a dream. He apparently arose from this uncharacteristic exercise in reflection a new man. At any rate, he had a new direction. In 401, Alaric took advantage of Stilicho's presence in Raetia and invaded Italy. Not fearing an attack in midwinter 401, Stilicho had crossed the Alps, probably into Raetia, sometime in late summer or early autumn.[134] It was a hurried visit indeed; there was hardly enough time to unpack.[135]

Why Alaric destroyed the peace in 401 and risked all troubled Jordanes in the sixth century and virtually every commentator since. Look again at the circumstances from Alaric's perspective. He was dismissed from Roman service. He had been deprived of his command. He stood at the head of a body of armed men in a diocese that until recently he had defended against Stilicho but over which he now held no authority whatsoever. That he and his men were as far away as Pannonia had made it relatively safe for the Eastern court to renounce him, but he was well placed to invade Italy. This would explain why he was able to strike so quickly and at the most opportune moment in 401. No one other than he himself was providing for his men. Since he had no command, Alaric had no way to requisition supplies legally. He still had an army but no way to pay it. His claims to kingship were recent and dependent upon his ability to take care of his followers. He was in a tight spot. Rather than accept himself as nothing more than an outlaw, Alaric had fallen back upon Gothic concepts of leadership, knowing that in Roman eyes there could be no such thing as a "king" inside the Empire. Alaric took what circumstances allowed. To the Romans he may have been an outlaw leading armed men without legal right to do so, but to his Gothic followers he was a tribal leader. In Roman sources he was *rex* of the Goths, but to his followers probably *reiks*, not a king but a prince, *regulus* in Latin. Had he really wished to press his challenge to the emperors, he might have chosen to become *thiudans*. This title, once held by Athanaric, represented an authority beyond the various *reges*. Ammianus Marcellinus had called Athanaric *iudex* rather than *rex*, but such precision is not to be expected in sources on Alaric. The confederacy over which Athanaric held sway had long since been shattered.[136]

If Alaric did now claim to be a new *thiudans* (proof is lacking) he would have been declaring his intention to lead a major revolt, one that would destroy Theodosius's careful integration of Gothic recruits into the Roman army. It appears, however, that Alaric's plans were far less sweeping. He evidently was seeking a secure base from which to bargain his way back into Roman office, for that is exactly what he soon succeeded in doing. The bargaining chip he minted for this occasion may have been base, but it was more valuable to him than gold. It was to foment intolerable chaos in the Balkans at a time when neither East nor West possessed the forces or will to suppress him. One or the other, perhaps both, would have to buy him off. Alaric knew his opponents well. He was a good teacher too, for many barbarian leaders were to learn the game from him.

Stilicho's attitude toward the East was abundantly clear. Despite the fall of Gaïnas and the return of Pannonia, Stilicho was still contesting with the court in Constantinople. Illyricum was the only route over which a force large enough to challenge the Eastern army could approach the Eastern capital, so sooner or later Stilicho would truly have to control all of it, not just the Western diocese by that name and not just on paper. Stilicho wasted no time and set out to Raetia for more men. Most pressing from Alaric's point of view was the fact that he now stood alone, isolated from the East and on Western territory. His influence over his followers must have been precarious, for he had little to give them. Every time Stilicho had launched a major campaign against him, Stilicho had prepared for his attack by recruiting forces in the transalpine areas. Alaric must have learned of Stilicho's recent departure for Raetia,[137] reasoned that an attack on his own army was imminent, and that his own force could not be quickly augmented by new recruitment. The sources of Gothic manpower lay beyond Alaric's reach. There may or may not have been a few small Gothic groups living in the Pannonias and not yet tapped. There had not been any military force other than his own in the diocese since 394. Neither East nor West recognized him as a Roman commander. He decided to launch a preemptive strike, a good Roman tactic since at least the time of Constantine. On 18 November 401, probably just before the Julian Alpine passes themselves closed, Alaric crossed into Italy.[138] By the time this news reached him, Stilicho was snowed in, in Raetia.[139] Treacherous and perfidious in the eyes of the Western court, Alaric was not censured by the East. His attack force was small, but his timing was nearly perfect. Honorius transferred the court from Milan to the safety of Ravenna.

While Stilicho was in Raetia, Alaric attacked Italy from Pannonia (Illyricum). Stilicho marched south as soon as the passes cleared, doubtless at a quicker pace than on his northward trek. Even according to his poet Claudian, Stilicho returned to Italy with but a few men, for both men and provisions were very scarce. These were not raw barbarians but, at least for Claudian, Roman "legionaries," needed elsewhere for the border defense. With what troops he could muster, Stilicho met Alaric at Pollentia in the spring of 402.[140] Again no decision could be reached on the battlefield. Stilicho fared better at Verona a few months later, but not decisively so.[141] Claudian writing between the battles inadvertently captured Alaric's predicament after Pollentia. Alaric boasted to his men: "but now that I [Alaric] hold sway over Illyria, now that its people has made me their leader, I have forced the Thracians to forge me spears, swords, helmets with the sweat of their brows, and Roman towns (whose rightful overlord I now am) to contribute iron for my own uses."[142]

Alaric was independent of Rome because "the people of Illyria" had made him their leader. Tellingly Claudian does not have Alaric claim power through the illegality of being a *rex Gothorum* inside the Empire. No, Claudian's Alaric is still a Roman general, but in revolt. In a way Claudian mocks Alaric for pretending to be a Roman general when he is not. It is only his new independence which distinguishes him from Claudian's Alaric in Epirus three years before. Claudian cannot, despite himself, envision him otherwise. Alaric could not do so either. Alaric was a Roman soldier, a general, claiming to be legally able to requisition supplies from the grateful population in a blighted diocese. After Pollentia he retreated back toward that home, undefeated but knowing he could not win.[143] This was reaffirmed at Verona. At the time of the composition of the *De bello Gothico* Alaric was really not a Roman general. Until and unless Stilicho recognized him in command, Alaric had no legal claim to anything.

These two great protagonists had played to a draw. Neither could raise sufficient trained manpower to overcome the other. Neither of their principal areas of recruitment—Raetia and the German provinces, on the one hand, and the new Illyricum, on the other—could produce men sufficient for a decisive advantage. Cooperation began to seem more attractive than fruitless confrontation. Possibly at Pollentia but certainly after Verona, Stilicho accepted Alaric and recognized his command in the diocese of Illyricum.[144] Henceforth and until Stilicho's own death in 408, he treated Alaric as a subordinate commander, *comes rei militaris*. Their relationship must be analyzed accordingly.

Summary

Four men of barbarian blood emerged as Rome's senior generals: Stilicho, Gaïnas, Alaric, and Fravitta. Each found himself with no alternative to getting involved in court politics. In the case of the later three this was directly linked to their need to guarantee supplies and replacements for their armies. All personally identifiable barbarians in the Roman army held traditional Roman commands. They acted out their lives inside the Empire's military and political structures. Shortly after the death of Theodosius, Stilicho determined to take control of Arcadius as well as Honorius. Invasion and war followed in which Alaric, an Eastern general, thwarted Stilicho. Throughout this era Alaric was particularly vulnerable, since he commanded the only army, a ragtag force at that, in the disastrous western Balkans. Finding recruits was ever more difficult. The Balkan peninsula was exhausted. Gaïnas and Aurelianus decided to transfer the diocese of Pannonia to the West in late 399. They acted with full knowledge that their decision would cast

Alaric into limbo. Confronted with the loss of his command and its right to draw Roman supplies, Alaric fell back upon Gothic traditions of leadership. His followers declared him *rex Gothorum*, a completely illegal position in Roman eyes. There was no concept of a king within the Roman Empire in 400. Despite much civilian distrust and outright hatred of the army and the barbarians in it, there were no anti-barbarian or pro-barbarian parties at the courts. Barbarian sympathizing was a useful brush with which to tar and feather a political opponent, one with a long tradition.

ALARIC AND STILICHO
WORKING TOGETHER

Overview: The Empire at the Turn of the Century

THE SIX YEARS between the Battle at Verona and the death of Stilicho (402–8) tested the accord between Stilicho and Alaric to the limit. Since its inception in 402, the agreement had evolved in the wake of a series of virtually unprecedented military crises. Stilicho doubtless supposed that this pact would give him time to recruit new troops, tighten his grip on command, and restore ordered government to Italy. These were false hopes. The stability in the East brought about by the return of units of the Eastern army in 395 under Gaïnas and the rapid rise of Eutropius soon unraveled. Until late in 399, Alaric was *magister militum per Illyricum* and thus a key officer in the Eastern army. By early 400 he was forced to look out for himself once again. In July of that year the citizens of Constantinople rose up and slaughtered the Gothic troops and their families garrisoned in the city. Gaïnas met his end before the year was out. In 405 Radagaisus invaded Italy, and in 406 the Vandals and Sueves crossed the Rhine. In 407 Constantine III, a reluctant British usurper, landed in Gaul to pursue his fortunes there. On 1 May 408 Arcadius died in Constantinople. On 22 August 408 Stilicho offered himself to the executioner's axe. These events must now be positioned within their common context: Roman military policy and the role of the barbarians within it.

All parties, West and East, Stilicho and Alaric, Gaïnas and Tribigild, Fravitta, Eutropius, and Constantine III—each and every man who held high military command during these years—had to scramble for recruits and supplies. This is clear in the literary sources and runs through, or scarcely beneath, the imperial edicts preserved in the codes. Supplies (rations) had constituted a regular part of the pay of various types of *limitanei* since at least the reign of Valentinian I, whether individual soldiers liked it or not, and some did not.[1] To prevent spoilage, care was taken that issues of foodstuffs were regular and prompt. Soldiers were urged to collect them in a timely fashion or request that their accounts be credited.[2] The same system of payment in supplies was extended under succeeding emperors to include virtually all military personnel. Refinements and stipulations for eligibility and conversion of some kind payments into cash continued in both the East and West for many decades after the death of Theodosius.[3] With difficulty the Romans had restored the Danubian frontier in the early 380s, accomplishing this by recruiting Gothic soldiers in unprecedented numbers.

By 400, over two decades had elapsed since Adrianople and fourteen years since the last major Gothic crossing of the Danube. In the interim Roman recruitment efforts had had to focus on the task of attracting and utilizing the new Gothic-speaking peoples now permanently in the Balkans, as well as boosting enlistments within the Empire and along its other frontiers. The possibilities of further recruitment beyond the lower and middle Danube were rapidly decreasing. Any men recruited into existing units would have fallen under the existing payment system, but if Theodosius expanded upon the idea of an auxiliary force he need not have guaranteed them precisely the same benefits. Land was available for direct settlement and exploitation, and at least one account specifically states that he gave barbarians land along the frontiers for resettlement.[4]

The use of land was a cheaper and more efficient alternative to transporting supplies from considerable distances or squeezing them from frontier provinces where discouraged Roman landholders (*possessores* in the code) were pulling out. Off duty or off the record, many of the frontier troops in regular garrisons would have had good reason to engage in a little farming, especially if their families were not provided for in their rations. The question of whether the soldiers of the frontier garrisons, the *limitanei*, were so engaged in farming that they were ineffective as troops has concerned many investigators.[5] The possible role of Theodosius in this raises an antecedent question. Did Theodosius grant supplies and *land* (κτήματα and χώραν) to exploit (perhaps temporarily) a circumstance familiar to his *limitanei* in order to provide adequate maintenance for new recruits in regular units? Or did he intend to provide some barbarians special, and in the long run cheaper, arrangements to serve as auxiliary units? Or did he pursue both alternatives as opportunity arose? There were ample precedents for assigning lands to *laeti*, but *laeti* were not established in the Balkans. Zosimus leaves us no doubt that the men of Athanaric were integrated into the regular Roman defenses along the Danube after their king's death, not assigned lands apart.[6] The combination of supplies and land is precisely what actually supported the regular forces of the frontier guard, although nowhere in the legislation organizing their pay is there official notice of their landholding.

There is, of course, no way to overcome the absence of consistent records concerning so many of Theodosius's actions. Yet it is striking that none of our sources was upset about the offer of land on the frontiers to barbarians.

As Ammianus noted time and again, the Goths of 376 crossed onto Roman soil with their families, including the family dogs. Whereas Alaric and most of his men may have cared little for settled life in some Balkan village, this cannot be said of the majority of Goths recruited under Theodosius. Goths with family concerns might have been assigned to different kinds of units—garrison units or even regular forces of the *comitatenses*—from those assigned to men without families. Little by little, as Alaric and his Roman contemporaries sought to recruit other Goths (probably the children of the men and women who had sought *receptio* in 376), more permanent billeting arrangements such as those typical along the frontiers became increasingly practicable.

In the West, Theodosius's use of Gothic speakers to replace the losses suffered by Magnus Maximus in 388 seems established by the archaeological records from numerous sites along the Raetian frontier and elsewhere. Some of the Gothic recruits who made up a large segment of Theodosius's army on the Frigidus may similarly have ended up on the upper Danube to replace the losses incurred when Arbogastes led the Western armies into revolt, for after his victory Theodosius and then Stilicho had had to reman the West from their available manpower pool. There are occasional glimpses of other barbarian auxiliaries being assigned and reassigned in other areas of the frontiers as well. For example, some Marcomanni were employed on the middle Danube in Pannonia I during the last decade of the fourth century.[7] The fact is that Rome had reached the limit of its traditional sources of soldiers. The sons of veterans and the peoples bordering on the frontiers were no longer numerous enough to meet recruitment needs. To supplement and eventually replace them, Rome turned to the barbarians. Such recruits were much easier to obtain, cheaper, and far more flexible in their deployment. In some cases Rome seems to have created new *gentes* in the process. That is to say, they created small groups from disparate barbarian recruits by placing them under native or regular Roman officers, *tribuni* of the various *gentes*.[8]

An interesting situation seems to have arisen in the course of the late fourth and throughout the fifth centuries along some stretches of the frontiers where recruitment of at first individuals and then increasingly larger groups was pursued with vigor. The lure of Roman service depopulated some areas beyond the *limes*, sometimes far beyond it. An early phase of this is attested by Ammianus when he notes that along the Rhine almost all the

barbarians lived within ten miles of the river. This is confirmed archaeologically for the so-called Elbgermans. The results of the larger-scale re-
cruitments at the end of the fourth century and the first decades of the fifth
appear to resemble those following the successful establishment of *laeti* at
the end of the third century along the lower Rhine, where Rome gradually
withdrew its garrisons in favor of local defense. A similar set of circumstances may have interacted in the sixth and seventh centuries. By that time
so many of the former frontier peoples from beyond the Rhine had crossed
into the Empire, or what had once been the Empire, that we rarely learn
of further troubles with westward invasion. Indeed, under the Carolingians
the thrusts were eastward, back across the Rhine. The fifth-century developments were complicated by the creation of a Hunnic Empire and then
by its disintegration. In those areas where the need for frontier garrisons
decreased, Roman policies can be hailed as successful, if only in the limited
sense of having resolved the tensions along the frontiers and reduced the
need to maintain an offensive capability by relocating the problems into
the interior. To the extent that the Romans were able to settle barbarians
in the manner of frontier troops paid in rations and/or land, Rome also
might have expected to save money on the army.

Early fifth century imperial legislation reveals some of the forces that
rapidly transformed recruitment patterns to admit larger and more cohesive
groups of barbarians. In 400, Stilicho, doubtless at his own instigation, was
charged by an imperial edict to press into service any "laetus, Alamannus,
Sarmatian, vagrant, son of a veteran, or any person of any group" subject
to the draft and conduct them to the training centers. He was to be especially careful in checking documentation, presumably often in the hands
of young men of draft age, that either conveyed to them the status of veterans or gave them honorary rank. These types of cheating are denounced
as especially grievous because they took men out of service early or even
before their service had begun.[9] This interpretation of the edict might be
subject to discussion, but it seems clear enough that its intent was to
strengthen recruitment within the Empire from all the most likely sources
of manpower. In 400 these included: *laeti*, Alamanni (that is, those sons of
laeti and Alamanni already serving or having pledged to serve Rome), Sarmatians (by which designation is probably meant any barbarian group and
their offspring originally enrolled along the Danube, including Goths), and
unattached and unemployed men of the lowest social order. This edict goes
on to require similar screening among those young men claiming Christian
clerical exemption.

It is abundantly clear that word went out to the local commanders along the peaceful frontiers to encourage those across the rivers and walls of the *limes* to seek *receptio*. In Raetia, for example, this probably accounts for some of the late examples of Elbgermanic materials interred there. The actions spelled out in this imperial edict were not those of an administration that could be too particular about its recruits. Training and receiving centers must have been extremely hard-pressed, and the poor discipline in the ranks during these years reflects their inability to keep up. The new pressure upon the sons of veterans also reflects changing circumstance. These young men had been the principal source of manpower throughout late antiquity; they knew the lifestyle of Roman soldiers and its benefits. They had grown up sometimes literally inside the fortifications and traditionally did not have to be coerced into service. Had something basic changed? Or had the Empire finally reached the bottom of the recruitment pool? Almost certainly, the latter.

A common misconception is that Alaric's force somehow comprised a "tribe" that had a self-defined mission during these years.[10] It is even maintained that it is already proper to speak of a Gothic *patria* in the Balkans.[11] Yet what remained of "Gothic" self-identity after the reorientation and fragmentation of their political leadership in the course of recruitment is very difficult to discern. There also lingers a romantic sense that for some unstated reason Alaric and his followers possessed certain noble qualities. This myth was already current in the writings of Saint Augustine and Orosius. It is nothing more than the timeless twisting of the concept of the "noble savage" into a larger Christian vision of these events, the marking of a moment in the divine plan. The facts speak otherwise. The Gothic forces of the Roman army that ended up under Alaric were a military command only in the sense that they were recognized as such, first by the Eastern and then years later by the Western emperors. This had occurred primarily because Constantinople and Rome had no better solutions to the manpower crises in the Balkan realm or in Italy: that is, unless they were to abandon any hope of bringing stability to this entire region, throw up their hands in despair, and surrender the Balkan peninsula to chaos. The emperors faced staggering problems of all types throughout the Empire. Most of these problems, however, were geographically peripheral; the Balkan problem was central. To abandon the Balkans would have meant the abandonment of the reality of a unified Empire, for connecting Rome and Constantinople was vital. The Mediterranean was too unpredictable, especially in the winter, or when troops had to be moved from one part of the Empire to the other. Both East and West turned to Alaric simply because they had no other units available.

Barbarians within the Gates of Rome

The Goths of Alaric were the outcasts and refugees from the upheavals in the Balkans and within the Roman army; they were the recalcitrants who did not, or could not, accept the confines and rigors of Roman service; they were the dispossessed and their children. Most spoke Gothic tongues because they derived from those Gothic peoples splintered and recruited under Theodosius. Alaric wielded the powers both civil and military appropriate to his Roman command and its circumstances. So long as he held that command he probably exercised it more easily over Romans than over Goths, whose desertions were frequent and whose leaders he had to placate. His men had no common *patria;* they had few shared experiences beyond their military service. They followed Alaric and his council of elder men. Veterans with personal memories of the glories achieved at Adrianople must already have been senior in years and few in number. These various followers stood with Alaric because through him they were fed and housed; that is, they were fed Roman requisitions and housed in Roman towns. Unless one is prepared to deny them common sense, we must acknowledge that they recognized the importance of Alaric's Roman command to their own welfare. Alaric thereby secured their assignment to provinces in which the support base could provide for their needs.

Alaric was only *primus inter pares* before his war council.[12] His fame is mainly posthumous. It is inextricably linked to the capture of Rome in 410, an event of little military or policy-making consequence but one fraught with emotional, intellectual, and religious significance. In Illyricum and, prior to 400, the other dioceses under his command, he was not anathema to the Romans living there. He did not have to fight his way around but rather took advantage of the established roads and supply system.[13] He faced no organized opposition, unlike the local militia that effectively slowed Tribigild in Asia Minor or that which would confront Theodoric the Great later in the century. Alaric was equally, perhaps preeminently, a prisoner of the problems of military recruitment and supply. The further he strayed from the base of his command in Illyricum, the greater his problems became.

The great days of recruitment in Illyricum had long passed. Even after his accord with Stilicho in 402, Alaric's best hope to enlarge the territory under his command (and thereby his supply and recruitment base) was by "going through channels." His optimum solution was to have his entire command reassigned to a more promising area. His first success was in 402, when he convinced Stilicho and the Western court to accept him in parts of Illyricum, since that diocese was again Western and thus administered through Stilicho and Honorius. Later, however, he failed to persuade the same court to grant him other areas to tap. The relative strength of Alaric's force should not be exaggerated. His followers, whatever their precise ethnic stock, surely began to respect Alaric in the course of the decade following his acceptance of the kingship in 400, but the group was probably still quite modest in size and with very limited goals.

Stilicho managed to assemble an ill-coordinated force to oppose Alaric in the spring of 402 at Pollentia and then a few months later again at Verona. Claudian, writing shortly after the Roman "victory" at Pollentia, cast Alaric prior to the battle as a braggart before his veterans, clearly overstating his victories over Roman emperors. Yet none of these so-called victories took place after his appointment as *magister* for Illyricum (no later than 397).[14] Given the circumstances, Alaric had been effective in a limited and difficult command. There was, of course, no need for Claudian to stress that fact. The *magister militum per Illyricum* held a circumscribed command in the East. Until the return of the diocese of Pannonia (Illyricum) and his loss of his Roman magistership, he theoretically commanded all the Roman and auxiliary units in the Illyrican prefecture. In reality, these areas at this time supported very few troops, if any. The returning Eastern army in 395 almost certainly went to the Persian frontier immediately and did not even, as would logically have been the case, remain in Thrace under Gaïnas.[15]

Traditional sources of barbarian recruits had been dwindling for years. Theodosius had stripped most garrisons from the Julian Alps during his last campaign and had dispersed some of his Gothic recruits throughout the frontiers of the Empire. Saul, a hero at the Frigidus, died leading an Alanic cavalry contingent against Alaric at Pollentia.[16] Alaric, unlike Gaïnas, did not actively attempt to draw men to his side from beyond the Danubian frontier. Though in decline, the defenses there still functioned to monitor coming and going. It is unclear just how many of the old Greutungi, Alans, and Huns, some recruited under Alatheus and Saphrax following Adrianople, remained distinct "auxiliaries" in the Pannonias.[17] At least some enrolled in the old commands. The main point, however, is that—whether as Roman recruits integrated into the existing units on the frontiers or as allied forces settled by and under Roman administrators—these remaining so-called barbarian forces and their second-generation replacements would have been part of the command of any *magister militum per Illyricum*, not just Alaric. Because he was legally able to command them, Alaric was able to supply them. With provisions came respect for his leadership. Leadership aside, the few units of trained manpower that still existed in Illyricum in 397 would have fallen to Alaric from the beginning of his command. They did not constitute a reserve force as such. He had none. Thus it was that when Alaric lost the backing of the East and his right to his entire command and support base with the return of the diocese of Pannonia toward the end of 399, he assumed the kingship and pressed the West for recognition. To be acknowledged as an officer in the Roman imperial army was to be a part of the Roman provisioning system. Alaric's kingship seems to have been an act of desperation provoked by the abrupt end of imperial support. Nor is the question of "Gothic" loyalty relevant, since many soldiers along the Danubian frontier of Illyricum and elsewhere would have spoken Gothic in common speech. That few appear in the archaeological record in Illyricum is adequately explained by the fact that most were not there long enough to be represented in the grave fields. Elsewhere that is not the case.[18]

In fact, if supplies were as decisive as they seem to have been, Alaric had cause for concern even after the accord at Verona acknowledged him as *comes rei militaris* in Illyricum, now under the West. Illyricum could not stand alone economically. The garrisons along the Danube would have received supplies from government transport and the localities,[19] but those sources were beyond his reach. Alaric's men must have relied upon the requisition system which had long functioned to support the Roman army on the move. That is, they drew upon the credits advanced them by the government at granaries and supply depots in the towns until those credits were exhausted, or they paid in precious metal. Recourse to this system was made throughout the era and accounts for the itineraries of various barbarian leaders and some of the specific sums of money recorded as being given to them.

Even before the loss of his magistership Alaric was in no position to challenge either Gaïnas or Stilicho unless he could strike quickly and decisively. This he was long unable or unwilling to do. His passivity probably reflects his contentment with his position between 397 and 399. In this brief span he had secured himself as *magister* (at least so he believed), having fought Stilicho to a draw. Moreover, both Stilicho and Gaïnas, unlike Alaric, had been generals under Theodosius and had retained the recruitment networks that had long served the emperors. They also used their access to the emperors to shape legislation for the army and to make the special accommodations that successful recruitment of barbarian leaders often demanded. Gaïnas's successor Fravitta held the same advantages over Alaric. Alaric got only what the imperial courts wished to grant him, or what he could take. Plundering was apparently not Alaric's style in Illyricum, since it was probably seen as an unnecessary and counterproductive alternative to legal requisition. He invaded Italy very soon after being cast out of the Eastern command and perhaps in the short period of building up his supplies for invasion he had to resort to confiscation. He also lived off the land while in Italy. His need to reward his troops must have weighed heavily upon him even after 402, when he had only the diocese of Illyricum for support, and perhaps only a portion of that.

Pollentia, Verona, and Their Aftermath

It is impossible to estimate the size of Alaric's army after Verona, but it surely was much smaller than the 80,000–100,000 often claimed.[20] Many of his men must have had families in tow or back in Illyricum. This was a common military practice in this era, not one peculiar to Gothic recruits. A soldier's family often lived in a town nearby, and sometimes, especially along the frontiers, women and children actually moved into the barracks. Alaric's wife is mentioned by Claudian while praising the Roman "victory" at Pollentia. He blames her for having instigated her husband's conquests in order to secure for herself Roman jewels and Roman slaves; her fitting reward was to lose all.[21] Stilicho's family is well known, Gaïnas's much less so.[22] Claudian's rhetorical flourish about Alaric's wife proves only that Alaric had a wife, though it strongly suggests that he lost his baggage train to Stilicho. My reading of *De bello Gothico* and *VI cons. Hon.* is that she, like the wives of Gaïnas and Stilicho, did not accompany her husband. She was important to Claudian only as a character to be juxtaposed with the happy Roman captives liberated by Stilicho, whose victory is compared to that of Marius over the Cimbri half a millennium before. The stalemate at Pollentia was followed within months by that at Verona, which was closer to being a "Roman" victory. At Verona Alaric lost men to desertion and disease, and his store of supplies had yet to recover from the losses at Pollentia.[23] He stood his ground on a small hill cut off by Stilicho from further retreat toward Illyricum. Stilicho's forces throughout this campaign were small. According to Claudian, Stilicho had had to leave many legions and auxiliaries behind in the frozen north, that is, beyond the Alps, rather than order them to Italy.[24] He had not hesitated, however, to withdraw troops from elsewhere. Although these reinforcements may not have arrived in time for his confrontation at Pollentia, they might have been with him at Verona. Claudian then says he withdrew legions from as far away as Britain and left the Rhine defended only by the "dread" of Roman retaliation.[25] Still, Stilicho's hurried campaign suggests that his army included only the few units already in Italy, along with a few soldiers detached from the garrisons in Raetia. Orders went out to units further removed and set in train events far beyond what Stilicho had in mind, but had little or no effect on the battles at Pollentia and Verona. Given all these factors, surely neither side fielded more than 10,000 men in 402.

The units that came from Britain and perhaps the Rhine probably joined in reestablishing Stilicho's force in Italy, which had sustained some casualties fighting Alaric. The small army that Stilicho had managed to assemble in Italy in 402 became his only army-in-being to confront the many crises that were about to descend upon the Empire. There are some clues in the *Notitia* as to the identity of some of the troops involved. Perhaps he moved the Seguntienses, listed in the *Notitia dignitatum* (ca. 405–6) as a unit of the field army (*aux. pal.*) under the *comes* of Illyricum from Caernarvon in Britain and upgraded it from the *limitanei*.[26] In fact the entire listing in the *Notitia* for the *comes* of Illyricum suggests recent redeployments or new creations in order to build an army for Illyricum at some time during Honorius's reign. These were perhaps originally intended for Stilicho's campaigns against Alaric there in 402. They would likewise have figured in Stilicho's plan for a campaign against the East, a campaign aborted by his death in 408. Finally, perhaps they were actually deployed in Illyricum after Stilicho's death. Ultimately in 409 Generidus, who as Zosimus relates was a fine leader, restored Roman control to parts of the diocese at least. This discussion also brings into sharper relief the significance of Stilicho's dispatch of 5,000 men to fight Gildo in North Africa in 398, shortly after his foray of 396 into Greece.[27] In addition to the Seguntiensis, the *Notitia* mentions the Raeti and three units of Honoriani.[28] The Raeti may have been a unit created from those few men taken from Raetia by Stilicho to face Alaric in 402. Upgrading former units of the *limitanei* to a higher status and pay was doubtless necessary to get them to leave their long-time homes for duty elsewhere.

Stilicho did not transfer this force to Alaric when he appointed him *comes*. Alaric is never seen in command of such units, and Stilicho could never risk finding himself with fewer soldiers than his nearest subordinates. When he did, it cost him his life. The principal force that Alaric commanded in Illyricum was the army he had with him when the East cut him loose. Stilicho's plans for an Eastern expedition never materialized, mainly because new crises kept coming faster than he could raise troops to face them. No sooner had he and Alaric appeared to have worked out a durable relationship than another invader forced his way into Italy.

In 402 Stilicho had no desire to improve Alaric's status any more than necessary. Any new relationship had to make Stilicho's superiority abundantly clear. Since the return of Pannonia (Illyricum) relieved him of worry that Alaric could be launched against him with Constantinople's support,

Stilicho probably thought he had time to get his political house in order. There is no question that Stilicho and Alaric reached some sort of accord at Verona. The question is precisely what. The evidence is chronologically obscure but forces the conclusion that by no later than 407 and probably as a part of the agreement reached at Verona Alaric was *comes rei militaris* in Illyricum. There is no other reported incident involving the two leaders in the interim. In 407 Alaric was still king of his followers, a title that he did not press at this time, at least insofar as Roman sources reveal. He was also a *comes* of the Romans, and so he remained until he lost even that with the fall of Stilicho. He was not a *magister*.[29]

After Verona Stilicho, whose forces were drawn up to block eastward movement, allowed Alaric to cross into the diocese of Illyricum and establish his force in the provinces of Pannonia II and Dalmatia. There Alaric busied himself until ordered to Epirus in 407.[30] By making Alaric *comes rei militaris* in Illyricum and perhaps by restricting his requisitions and garrisoning to two provinces within the diocese, Stilicho solved his problem of how to anchor some sort of military force there. Alaric's comital office, even if only exercised in two provinces, would have given him the necessary minimum to maintain control over his troops. We hear of no mention of him styling himself a king of the Goths during these years. Strategically Dalmatia and Pannonia II blocked most approaches to Italy from the East. Thus tied down, Alaric was unlikely to get much stronger or press for a change of location or rank. Every soldier Alaric had lost while on campaign was a loss almost impossible to replace. This was not so with Stilicho to nearly the same degree. Until the threat of invasion from Gaul by Constantine III in 408, which also challenged Stilicho in his transalpine recruitment areas, Alaric needed Stilicho more than vice versa. Stilicho could abide the current situation indefinitely and indeed was probably quite content to do so. Alaric now stood between the East and the West effectively blocking an invasion or, with some assistance, poised to launch one to the East against those who had turned him away. Alaric's force was small, appropriate to its supply base.

There is no moment other than immediately after Verona when an arrangement giving Alaric a field command would have made sense to Stilicho. Alaric could not have just gone off to Dalmatia and Pannonia II without the legal right to draw requisitions, and he clearly had no interest in a permanent, frontier-type settlement in and around existing defenses. He could not even have reached Illyricum without passing through Stilicho's lines. Since Alaric's force at this time probably contained few men willing to establish themselves as farmer-soldiers, land was not yet an issue. Nor would Alaric, unable to defeat Stilicho, have been able to demand more than an appointment as *comes*. He got what he probably had long thought was his due reward for his conduct on the Frigidus: a military command as a *comes* of the first order. Making him *comes rei militaris* of Illyricum was the best compensation the West could offer Alaric for his lost Eastern command of *magister militum per Illyricum*. The East, of course, continued to appoint the *praefecti praetorio Illyrici*, the civilian parallel to the *magister*.[31] Alaric was after all familiar with the territory; he probably had left his wife and the wives of his men there while he sought a resolution of his fate in Italy. Moreover, given the fact that Illyricum had few, if any, regular units stationed there and had witnessed repeated war for much of three decades, it was not a plum.

The fact that Generidus, Alaric's successor as *comes Illyrici*, held a similarly restricted (but not identical) command after 409 is instructive. Several of the Illyrican provinces were in a state of near chaos. Alaric's base was centered upon Pannonia II. Both Alaric and Generidus sought to expand the areas of Roman control. They faced lawless bands preying upon whatever remained of the civil population clustered in towns and refuges.[32] Stilicho in 402 had good strategic reasons to circumscribe carefully Alaric's area of movement and supply within the most important areas of Illyricum. He had to pacify Illyricum piece by piece. At some point Stilicho decided he could use Alaric's force to expand the West's military control beyond the diocese of Illyricum.

The original agreement of 402 is the so-called secret pact that Stilicho reportedly made with Alaric sometime after Pollentia. According to Orosius, that pact assigned Alaric a place to billet his men, but restricted his freedom to engage his troops in making war or peace.[33] A second stage of the Stilicho-Alaric accord is recorded in Zosimus when he suggests that some sort of agreement (σύνθημα) or understanding was made sometime before the invasion of Radagaisus (405). Unfortunately, he clouds the chronology by linking this understanding with the cessation of pillaging Greece and the temporary settlement of Alaric in Epirus. Zosimus's word choice reflects the fact that this second agreement between Alaric and Stilicho was not a treaty, for no treaty could exist between the senior commander and a subordinate. The agreement of 405 was directed at coordinating an attack on the Eastern dioceses of Dacia and Macedonia, which constituted the remaining portions of the prefecture of Illyricum. Alaric's force was already well positioned in the diocese of Illyricum and additional forces under Stilicho, the overall commander, were to link up with it in Epirus. Whether Stilicho would have stopped short of Constantinople is unknown but seems unlikely. Alaric's phase of the invasion was actually launched against Epirus, but not until late 406 or 407. The passage has obtained critical historiographic importance.[34]

Renewed friction over Illyricum is already apparent in a curious letter from Honorius to Arcadius written in the summer of 404. In this letter, written in a carefully circumspect manner, Honorius clearly reprimands his elder brother for not keeping him informed "concerning the destruction of dying Illyricum" and "the losses to the State" there.[35] The West withheld recognition of Aristaenetus as Eastern consul for 404.[36] Also in 404, Fravitta's fall from power left the East without a proven commander. I suggest that after four years Stilicho thought that the time had come to reassert a claim to the remaining dioceses of the Eastern prefecture. The instrument he chose was this imperial letter subtly suggesting that these dioceses would be better off under their traditional Western guardians. When this diplomacy failed, his next step was to marshal troops, and for that he needed Alaric, whose support he received apparently in 405. In any case, Radagaisus's invasion detoured Stilicho from any immediate adventures in the East. Manpower to repel Radagaisus was so scarce that Honorius promulgated a law urging all Roman soldiers regardless of status (regulars, auxiliaries [federates], and *dediticii*) to allow their slaves to fight at their sides. Stilicho realized late in 405 that he could not attack the East and so needed to extend the olive branch, if ever so briefly. Therefore he apparently offered a belated recognition of Anthemius as his fellow consul for that year.[37] Stilicho had cause to look to Alaric. If the agreement reported by Zosimus was in fact made in 405, then it represents a second agreement made between Stilicho and Alaric, clearly different from the one alluded to in Orosius. The first would have been at Verona establishing Alaric as *comes* in Illyricum with considerable restrictions, and thus in 402. The second was an early stage of what would shortly become an invasion of the East.

Within a year Stilicho was able to start his invasion of the East and ordered Alaric to advance into Epirus. Once in Epirus, Alaric as *comes* for Illyricum had no legal rights at all. Epirus was in the diocese of Macedonia, an Eastern jurisdiction since 392 and not returned to the West along with Pannonia (Illyricum). Alaric was the spearhead of an invasion. If he prevailed, Alaric could gain his old office back—that is, *magister militum per Illyricum*.[38] This was the same policy long used to move *limitanei* away from their families to fight elsewhere by promoting them to the *comitatenses*, but now applied to an individual, Alaric. Thus when Alaric invaded Epirus and vainly awaited Stilicho in 407, he did so with a promise of a magistership over this province and all the others in his former command. Technically this would have also enabled him to requisition supplies there for his men; Stilicho named Jovius as *praefectus praetorio Illyrici* to assist.[39] Stilicho could only have made good on these appointments and promises after establishing control of the Eastern government or at least seizing the dioceses of Dacia and Macedonia. Of course, the East had no intention of going along with Stilicho's usurpation of the Balkans; it continued to appoint its own officers to these posts. Unaware of this second occupation of Epirus, Zosimus confused it with the "settlement" there in 397. Can there then be any question as to why Arcadius's court (led by Anthemius, praetorian prefect of the Orient and joint-consul with Stilicho in 405 and by April 406 *patricius*) was opposed to this annexation?[40]

Later, Generidus as *comes Illyrici* (ca. 409) in theory held command over much more area within Illyricum—at least the provinces of the Noricums, Upper Pannonia (Pannonia I), the Raetias, and just then additionally, Dalmatia—but apparently not the entire diocese.[41] If he commanded the units listed in the *Notitia dignitatum* for Illyricum, then he commanded a considerably stronger force than Alaric had after Verona.[42] Moreover, Generidus was roundly praised by Zosimus for training his men and paying them their full rations, even providing additional incentives from his own pay. They returned his care with loyalty, something Zosimus thought quite rare in this age, allowing Generidus to strike terror in the ranks of the nearby barbarians.[43] Since Generidus was himself of barbarian parents, we need not see in this reference any statement concerning the "ethnic purity" of his troops. Since it seems that Pannonia II had long been the home of Alaric's followers (402–7), and further that Generidus is specifically said to have commanded only Pannonia I (not II) and recently Dalmatia, it seems possible that Generidus's principal "barbarian" foes were the remnants of Alaric supporters still in Pannonia II and Dalmatia. Perhaps they are now combined in some sense with the *antiqui barbari*, against whom they very likely had previously fought.[44] Generidus had only recently reestablished Roman control in Dalmatia and had yet to move into Pannonia II, as he apparently did later.[45] He may also have been occupied in the northern part of the diocese suppressing the surviving followers of Radagaisus, to whose raids of 405–6 we must soon turn our attention. The diocese had lost its cohesion since 395; it was a lawless and dangerous place, but still Roman.

The archaeological records for the Illyrican diocese, still rather incomplete and inadequately published, reveal continuity of urban settlement in most places through at least the mid-fifth century. We know extremely little about rural society, though it is clear that for some time people had been leaving for more defensible terrain, either to walled towns or fortified refuges in the central mountains. The general urban continuity is manifest in religious foundations and in the various distributions of typologically arranged archaeological materials. At least up to the second half of the fifth century mixed Germanic-Roman grave assemblages remain clearly visible. It is best to associate them with the ongoing changes in the frontier provinces rather than any new ethnic group settled there. The general pattern is similar to what is emerging from excavations elsewhere along the upper Danube.[46]

Alaric never tried to destroy his Roman base of operations either as an Eastern *magister* or as a Western *comes*. He continued to live—to thrive—within its parameters. Alaric "behaved himself," kept to the sidelines, and did not participate in the campaign against Radagaisus. Indeed, he may actually have regarded Radagaisus as a competitor for leadership over any still restless barbarians on Roman soil, perhaps including some of his own supporters. When Radagaisus crossed the Danube in 405 several sources portray him as aspiring to be another *rex Gothorum*.[47] But in Roman eyes any *rex* inside the Empire was outside the law, and by definition not entitled to Roman supplies and support. There could be no king over a distinct people within Roman territory unless the Romans acknowledged him with an office of their own, such as *magister militum*. That would render his kingship superfluous in Roman eyes, a mere honorific among his own people, and therefore tolerable.

Athanaric would have provided an interesting case in point had he not died within two weeks of setting foot on Roman soil. Were our sources more adequate, perhaps we could discover what Roman command Theodosius had planned for Athanaric when he greeted him in Constantinople. We know only that in 381 the emperor planned to use Athanaric and his men to defend the Danubian frontier. Alaric's "kingship" was not a preexisting fact like Athanaric's but rather an unauthorized creation within the Empire. The best Alaric could hope for was that, once back in the Roman command, Stilicho would ignore this awkward pretension. He apparently did just that. Stilicho had no choice, on the other hand, but to challenge Radagaisus.

Reports on the size of Radagaisus's force vary wildly even by the standards of the ancients. Orosius says 200,000, adding that this was the lowest estimate he could find.[48] The report in Zosimus leaves food for thought: Radagaisus "assembled 400,000 Celts and Germans from beyond the Danube and the Rhine and began his invasion of Italy."[49] These incredible numbers, if they were current at the time, must have precipitated the panic that ensued. Stilicho took his army stationed at Pavia, comprised of 30 *numeri* and as many auxiliaries from the Huns and Alans as he could get (these too must have been billeted in northern Italy), and met Radagaisus at Fiesole. By all reports Radagaisus had divided his force into thirds, doubtless for reasons of supply, and failed to consolidate them before Stilicho attacked and surrounded him and the principal body on a ridge. Starvation, an old and proven Roman weapon, led to the capitulation of Radagaisus. He was captured trying to escape, and executed on 23 August 406.[50] Casualties must have been quite light if we believe our sources, particularly Orosius, who credits the lack of bloodshed to the power of God on Rome's side.[51] Some 12,000 prisoners were reportedly recruited into the Roman army.[52] Given the nature of the final battle, or lack thereof, this was probably the entire force. Olympiodorus recorded the number of prisoners but turned them all into leaders, thus endorsing the grossly inflated size of the force then in circulation and also reported by him (and accepted by Zosimus) of 400,000. Olympiodorus probably had two accounts of the Radagaisus campaign, one based on wild rumors, the other upon an official account of recruitment figures. He recognized the discrepancy and reconciled it by identifying the prisoner-enlistees as the warrior elite of Gothic society.

Stilicho's force as reported, then, would have consisted of something less than 15,000 men.[53] Given the swiftness of Radagaisus's penetration as far as Liguria and the lack of any evidence of his passing through the Julian Alps, he probably entered Italy through the Brenner Pass.[54] Alaric was too far away to assist Stilicho in time. Radagaisus must have recruited men from beyond the Danube in eastern Noricum or western Pannonia and passed quickly through the defenses there. So little is known about the motives for his "invasion" that it is possible to think of it as at least partially inspired by Stilicho's demands for recruits along the river. Thus it may have begun as an uprising rather than an invasion. Radagaisus and his mixed force of followers clearly fit the pattern of Roman garrisons along the middle and upper Danube since the time of Theodosius. Zosimus's "Celts and Germans" under Radagaisus were perhaps Alamanni or others recruited along the frontiers. In fact, they could have been almost any warriors living beyond the frontiers within hearing distance of Radagaisus's call.[55] Perhaps because of the lack of soldiers in Noricum (some having joined Radagaisus) and therefore competitors for supplies and billets, Alaric the following year chose to base his own force there. He argued that Noricum was now in desperate need of defenders and currently paid little in taxes to the treasury. In other words, he would restore the defenses, thereby reviving normal activities and the flow of provincial taxes.[56] The relationship between a shrunken corps of defenders and a shrunken contribution to the treasury was a major policy question for Roman leaders at this time, and included considerations far beyond the issue of Alaric and Noricum.

In 406 no decisions had been reached on these issues, but they would have to be made very soon. At some point a diocese or province could become simultaneously indefensible and an intolerable fiscal burden. Many parts of the Western Empire were shifting away from taxable resources, particularly those activities centered upon towns, toward more diffuse forms of agriculture and social organization. As these trends continued, the mutually sustaining interrelationships between taxing, marketing, and military-political support were undermined. One approach to this dilemma was to lessen the cost of the military in that area by recourse to ever more extensive use of non-monetary rewards for military service. Theodosius had developed this approach, and it was still being pursued under Emperor Maurice (ca. 600).[57] The Roman military leaders had two obvious resources to exploit: land along the frontiers, and a wide variety of material benefits for servicemen and, especially, veterans. Land on Rome's side of the frontier was more valuable because much of it had been cleared to produce wheat for Roman markets and fuel for Roman fires. In addition, Rome could offer a host of intangible incentives to would-be enlisters who were from among the leadership of the peoples beyond the frontiers, most especially rank in the Roman army. The privilege of wearing the soldier's cloak in the community was an attraction to countless young men without prospects. These were not inconsequential lures to recruits used to believing that things Roman were superior.

Some of the best or most notorious barbarian Roman soldiers, the *buccellarii,* were ridiculed by giving them a nickname derived from their hard, dry bread (similar to the hardtack common on the American frontiers), in Latin called *buccellatum.* This usage was common by ca. 425–50, when Olympiodorus noted it.[58] The reality, of course, is that a durable food ration for mobile troops was important to them and to Rome. This innovation may indeed have distinguished those who received such rations from the ordinary soldiery, adding to the former's prestige rather than detracting. The word was not barbarian in origin or usage, but well known to Romans of the upper classes. Paulinus of Nola used it to describe how a Roman soldier might take Holy Communion.[59] What may have singled out the *buccellarii* was that they liked their dry fare and were proud of its effectiveness in the field that lay behind the ridicule!

By accomplishing a major reduction in the cost of the military, the state lessened the need for increased taxation with its detrimental effect upon loyalty and participation in the imperial system. The laments of the taxpayers reach us from the law codes, which imposed ever-escalating penalties for delinquency, and from the vitriolic pen of Salvian in the fifth century. Since the primary purpose of minting coins was to pay the troops, we might expect to see a major reduction in the amount of coinage being minted, as indeed we do. We would still expect some issuance of prestige coinage in silver and especially in gold whenever a special reason existed to distribute coin that was beyond the capacity of the local stocks, and we see that too. Such examples are very rare and include the gold and silver issues of the usurper Constantine III and the legitimate but tenuous co-emperor of Honorius, Constantius III.[60] With a lowering of the requirements for taxes paid in gold because of the success in recruiting soldiers on a non-monetary basis, the need and the opportunity for citizens to go to their local *numerarii* to exchange their bronze for silver or gold diminished and in the frontier provinces disappeared. Now only the officers were paid in coin—silver and gold—while the lower ranks were paid in kind. But the broad exchange revealed by the use of bronze coins and the presence of bureaucrats was a major determinant of the local urban market economies to which people still came to be taxed. The three factors—military pay, taxable resources, and the general economy—were deeply intertwined. None was the basis of the other two. By disconnecting one aspect the entire system was put at risk.

It is doubtful that any Roman actually understood the stimulative effect of taxation and the redistribution of tax revenues on the local and regional economies. If any did, his insight went unrecorded in the sources. So far as we can tell, Roman policy makers looked at only two sides of the triangle: taxes and defense costs. Alaric mentioned only these two in his appeal to Stilicho for the Norican provinces. Looked at from this cramped perspective, solving the problem is simply a matter of bringing these two factors into balance. Lower defense costs to match anticipated revenues on hand, and the result should be a new and maintainable equilibrium. Of course, the reality is that the third side of the triangle, the local market, is immediately weakened and the process of economic reallocation to the agrarian countryside is strengthened. The result of the movement away from urban resources and values reduces the taxable resources still further. At some point the central government can no longer justify economic and military intervention, and all components are reduced to local values and support networks. What military forces exist must either cease entirely as a "paid" army (whether in benefits or coin is now irrelevant), and find support at the local level. One sign of such disintegration of taxable resources is that the striking of copper coinage ceased. Simultaneously, the relative prosperity of the towns in which resources had been concentrated went into steep decline and often collapsed. The challenges that such a system had posed to those outside it—whether rural producers catering to the towns or barbarians wanting but not affording their riches—disappeared as well. The interlocking relationship between the army and the local economy is apparent everywhere but nowhere so clear as in the frontier provinces.[61]

Rural producers now eliminated marginal lands and labor-intensive crops in favor of concentrating upon the richest fields and the hardiest crops and animals. The barbarians no longer had a frontier system to assault or to trade with. In the case of Noricum, the decision not to allow Alaric in had to take into account the strategic importance of Noricum—the link between Italy, the Balkans and the northern provinces on the upper Danube and the Rhine—and perhaps its mineral wealth, especially iron. When finally the linkage with the north became itself irrelevant from an Italian perspective, Noricum Ripense was allowed to drift out of the system after Odovacar decided to withdraw his military commitments (ca. 480). Noricum Mediterranean never ceased to be worth the costs of inclusion in the Roman military and political system centered upon Italy. Britain, on the other hand, apparently did.

The cost containment policies of Theodosius and his dynasty can be seen throughout the frontier areas of the Western Empire, as items other than coins, often exceedingly difficult to date precisely, apparently replaced coin for pay. Many such materials continued to be deposited in late Roman archaeological horizons. Their presence is strong evidence of continuity for Roman military occupation, albeit on a minimal level, without pay in coin for decades after the death of Theodosius. For example, North African glazed pottery and late terra sigillata tableware from outside the district are well documented at many very late fourth and early fifth century sites. Such goods often would have accompanied military supplies. Because the state absorbed the transportation costs for military provisions and indirectly any items illegally shipped with them, products produced at great distances were available at bargain prices around military installations.[62] The gradual collapse of the military supply system delivered a fatal blow to many aspects of long distance trade. Less durable items such as foodstuffs and intangible benefits such as status will never be adequately documented. But in the long run cost containment, however necessary (and to the Roman administrators it was imperative), obviously led to shrinkage of the tax base because of the influence of the tax cycle upon the general economy. This in turn led to new rounds of cost reduction. If we are to understand Stilicho and Alaric in a broader context of imperial policy, we must look beyond them to the Empire itself and far beyond the literary stereotypes of Roman and Barbarian. To the extent that the leaders of Roman society understood their world and its interrelationships, they acted rationally upon them. The fundamental fact of political life for Stilicho was a paucity of resources for an infinity of problems. Alaric's alleged statement concerning the situation in Noricum at the very least proves that Olympiodorus recognized two sides of the triangle that was forcing Rome to recruit more and more barbarians for its defense. Even had Roman leaders fully understood the economic forces they were contending with, it is not clear that they could have identified better policy options. There was no large-scale dissipation of troops, even in Stilicho's struggles with the East.

The processes of agrarian evolution to less labor-intensive crops to supply the towns and garrisons had begun in many areas of the West long before. With it came ever greater difficulties in tax collection, decried repeatedly in the law Codes. Nor was the problem essentially demographic or a sociological response to military service whereby men avoided or refused service through a variety of means. The legendary citizen-soldiers of the Republic who fought without pay for family and friends were dust in their graves. Not even Vegetius could conjure up their shades as he longed for a return to the army of Julius Caesar. The *limitanei* and barbarian auxiliaries were about as close to those old soldiers as the times could provide; they at least were willing to spend their time and their efforts where they were needed. The Republican amateur warrior, had he existed beyond the world of myth, would never have left Italy to live permanently on the frontiers and relish a soldier's diet of hardtack and cabbage. Nor was the problem one of generalship. Even when competent commanders rose to the top—shrewd and tough men like Constantine III or Constantius III—their victories over their opponents, barbarian or rebel, mattered little. The armies of the day were small and incapable of grand operations. Even their annihilation, which never occurred, would not have drastically changed the situation. Stilicho feverishly manipulated the military and political structures to balance and control the rapidly deteriorating imperial system. Alaric was but one part of the problem.

With Radagaisus dead and the army mustered to defeat him still intact, Stilicho returned to his conflict with Constantinople. He ordered Alaric to take Epirus and hold it open until he could arrive with his army from Italy and settle the Eastern situation once and for all. As a part of this new thrust he must have promised Alaric to restore his old command, that is, to install him as *magister militum per Illyricum*.[63] Jovius was appointed praetorian prefect of Illyricum for 407. Recall that this office traditionally administered the dioceses of Dacia and Macedonia as well as the new Illyricum and that the *magister militum* held corresponding military powers. This was an attempt to reconstitute the prefecture of Illyricum. Had the assault been launched as planned, there can be little doubt as to its success. There was perhaps neither a *magister militum per Thracias* nor a *magister militum per Illyricum* to offer organized opposition and even the lesser commands may have been in disarray.[64] Alaric waited as did Jovius. In fact, they struck a mutual chord of trust that ultimately made Jovius a mediator between Honorius's court and Alaric.

Waiting in Epirus could not have been easy. It certainly was costly. The province was after all under Eastern supervision. Constantinople had appointed Clearchus a prefect of Illyricum, and Epirus fell under his jurisdiction.[65] Some walled enclaves that may have put up resistance were dismantled.[66] Jovius's job was to supply Alaric with provisions and make ready for the arrival of Stilicho. Alaric had marched his troops in accordance with orders, and even if Jovius provided all their supplies, Alaric himself was responsible for paying and feeding his troops on the march. Sozomenus clearly relates that Stilicho, who held the greatest power of Honorius's generals and commanded the best men available, Roman and barbarian, had appointed Alaric, leader of the Goths, to the command of the Roman soldiers and ordered them along with Jovius to Epirus.[67] Stilicho, again according to Sozomenus, was about to join Alaric and set things straight with Arcadius's court, when letters arrived from Honorius that put a stop to the enterprise.[68] This could only have been news from the court that his army was needed elsewhere. Indeed it was. Vandals and others had crossed the frozen Rhine on the last day of 406.[69]

As is typical, our principal source, in this case Jerome, records that "countless numbers" of the most ferocious barbarian nations entered the Empire and overran its defenses. He identifies these mindless assailants as Quadi, Vandals, Sarmatians, Alans, Gepids, Herulians, Saxones, Burgundians, Alamanni, and "even the Pannonians."[70] Jerome indicates that the crossings took place in the vicinities of Mainz and Worms, both of which fell. He relates that the invaders proceeded to take Rheims, Amiens, and Arras and continued on to overrun Tournai, Nemetae, and Strasbourg. Whole provinces, according to Jerome, were devastated, including most of their towns. So went Aquitania (Aquitanica), Novemque Populorum (Novem Populi), Lugdunensis, and Narbonensis. Toulouse escaped only because of the actions of its bishop, Exsuperius. Even Hispania was on the brink of disaster when

Jerome penned the epistle.[71] There are difficulties with Jerome's account, but the date of the crossing is secure enough: 31 December 406.[72]

Jerome is also clear about who deserved the blame: not the most religious emperors but the "semibarbarian who has betrayed Rome by arming our enemies against us with our own riches," Stilicho.[73] Jerome wrote of things reported to him by others, sometimes second or third hand, while he sat in Bethlehem. Contrary to Gibbon and others, this is not a passage that necessarily refers to Stilicho's acceptance of Alaric. Rather, it condemns the basic recruitment strategy of Theodosius and his dynasty led then by Stilicho. Indeed, Jerome ridicules the entire policy of appeasing barbarians during the last thirty years (per annos triginta), that is, since the defeat at Adrianople. That policy, he charged, had brought Rome to the point that even a victory over the barbarians now would not restore its greatness. The best that could now be hoped for was to recapture the booty taken from it.[74] Contrary to many historians, Jerome did not say that this policy has stripped the frontiers. He explicitly declared that several of the towns taken had withstood long sieges, for example Worms. Clearly garrisons were fighting even by Saint Jerome's account, a man who otherwise preferred to emphasize the role of God's bishops. At Toulouse there was no garrison, so the bishop was the logical spokesperson for Roman interests. Nor should we assume the Roman army and auxiliaries did not offer any other resistance. For the moment, however, the question is one of timing. When did news of the crossings and their consequences reach Stilicho at Ravenna?

Once again precise chronology is crucial but unobtainable. Sozomenus's paraphrase of Olympiodorus indicates that the imperial order countermanding Stilicho's invasion of the East was inspired by the death of Arcadius and Honorius's determination to go personally to Constantinople to set up a government for his young nephew Theodosius II.[75] Sozomenus's account of Alaric's departure from Epirus, having accomplished nothing, is followed by his comment that Honorius himself planned to go to Constantinople to install his nephew on the throne, without so much as a clause between.[76] Arcadius in fact died on 1 May 408, a year and four months after the Rhine crossings.[77] Therefore the death of Arcadius is irrelevant to the reassignment of Stilicho's force. The only military explanation for Honorius's action was the threat in Gaul. According to Zosimus, the emperor was most worried about the usurpation of Constantine III in Britain and his crossing of the Channel. Zosimus's explanation is quite reasonable. Constantine's name and those he gave his sons staked a claim to the whole Empire, but when would Honorius have acted? On 22 March 407, Honorius then in Rome signed an edict expressing to Stilicho his concern with maintaining an exemption for those who had risen in the army to the rank of tribune or provost from liability for supplying military recruits.[78] This may indicate that Stilicho was pressing every landowner for men, but it surely does not suggest official panic. Probably it was signed before the bad news arrived from Gaul, and so concerned the impressment of recruits for the Illyrican campaigns. When news of the new threats in the north did arrive, shortly afterward, Honorius was forced to reorder his priorities.

Many sources provide bits and pieces of information about the invaders of 406–7. Procopius, like Jordanes, wrote in Constantinople ca. 550 (and, like Jordanes, is not particularly reliable). Procopius relates that the Vandals, one of many groups represented in Jerome's account of the exodus, were forced to leave their eastern homes because of famine. They sought refuge in the lands of the Germans, specifically those called the Franks, along the Rhine. From there they moved against Roman territory under the leadership of Gunderic.[79] Gunderic, who is often mentioned in the sources, led the Vandals for twenty-two years.[80] Jordanes relates another vignette about these invaders. He states that sometime in the early fourth century a remnant of the Vandals, in flight from the victorious Goths who had just had the better of them in the lands of the middle Danube near the Marisia River, was granted *receptio* by Constantine I somewhere in Pannonia. Much later Stilicho ordered them to depart Pannonia for Gaul. There, having no place to stay, they fell to plundering.[81]

Some Vandals were definitely recruited under Theodosius or before, which gives some credence to Jordanes here. The *Notitia dignitatum* (ca. 392) lists a group of Vandals serving in Egypt as an *ala* under the *comes limitis Aegypti*, the eighth such unit raised, *ala octaua Uandilorum*. No other Vandal units are listed in the *Notitia* in either section.[82] Probably Stilicho did order Vandalic cavalry stationed in Pannonia to cross the Alps to confront the invasion in 406–7, but the Roman garrisons there must have been too afraid to open their gates to any Vandals. These Roman-Vandals, distinct from those with Godigisclus and later with Gunderic, were the "Pannonians" of Jerome's account. What ultimately happened to the seven Vandalic cavalry units not stationed in Egypt remains a mystery. One scenario for some of them would be that, having crossed the Alps as Stilicho ordered, they were rejected and forced to plunder just as Jordanes states. Others may have died fighting as reinforcements for the Gallic army. These units ceased to exist in 407 and so were not recorded in subsequent updates of the Western sections of the *Notitia*. It is important to note what Jordanes does not say. He does not say that the Vandalic units of the Roman army went over to the invaders. Jerome kept them separate as "Pannonians."[83]

Procopius tells another interesting but unverifiable story about the ancestors of some of the Vandals who forced their way into Gaul in 406. Not all Vandals gave up on their homelands during the famine of 406; some had stayed behind. Some of those who had come to the Rhine had followed Godigisclus, who died in the initial engagements. He too is known from other sources.[84] Godigisclus was the father by a concubine of Geiseric, king of the Vandals (428–77) and one of the men most feared by the Romans.[85] Those Vandals who had stayed home in 406–7 sent an embassy to King Geiseric asking him to renounce any claims that he and his people, then in North Africa, might have upon their ancestral lands. Those lands were said to be somewhere "near the Maeotic Sea," meaning "beyond the Danube." Prudent second thoughts prevailed over an initially rash acceptance of this idea, but Geiseric's decision not to abandon ancient claims made no difference. Procopius's general Belisarius cut off those in North Africa before they had a chance to escape.[86] Those who had refused to migrate believed that their kinsmen in North Africa were so wealthy they could afford to go along with this. The Vandals still on the ancestral lands were worried because they were weak and could no longer defend their lands against any returning Vandals whose fortunes had turned.

All this was perhaps just a story to illustrate the rapidity of Belisarius's reconquest of Roman North Africa, but it may reflect at least a lingering sense of the hard times that beset the barbarians in the winter of 406 and the bitterness which lingered over the decision to leave. Not even families had held together. The Rhine normally did not freeze enough to support heavy traffic. The winter of 406–7 must have been unusually severe. The Vandals went where they knew food would be: to the Roman frontier outposts. The Roman garrisons, secure in winter quarters, would not have had the authority or resources to grant so many barbarians admission (*receptio*). Evidently they did not even venture out to hinder the Vandals' passage; normally only the bridge would have demanded defense. Hungry barbarians would have plundered whatever foodstuffs they found and would not have taken time to storm many towns, since that would have required the concentration of supplies over snow-clogged roads. The barbarians, who according to Jerome came from many groups, would have had to split and resplit for subsistence.[87] There would have been no engagements against them until the spring, for winter was the best ally the Roman defenders had.

The court of Honorius may not have learned of the crossings until spring and by then the Roman units and auxiliaries, particularly the Frankish forces, would have been in action. What failed to materialize as ordered was the redeployment of forces from other theaters. Stilicho perhaps had some luck in transferring units from Pannonia. Redeployment from beyond the region affected was standard imperial procedure in cases of major incursion, and would have occurred prior to the clarification of Constantine III's usurpation. The time had long since passed when Rome hesitated to dispatch units of related barbarian groups against their cousins. Usually the worst that had happened, as during the reign of the emperor Julian (361–63), were some modest breaches of security and pressures for a quick peace. There were several different groups of "Vandals" and other barbarians moving about in 406–7; some were under Roman command, others not.

Orosius passes along the preposterous charge that Stilicho urged the barbarian invaders of 406 to take up arms so that he could use their invasion to strip Honorius of his crown and place it on his own son's head.[88] This piece of slander probably goes back to Stilicho's well-known half-Vandalic parentage. It is just one more indication of the contemporary make-believe that consistently blamed "barbarians" for all of Rome's troubles, in the same vein as the maudlin laments of Orosius's spiritual adviser Jerome. But one fact goes unstated. Rome stood to profit immensely if the new barbarian raiders could be brought to heel and recruited into existing garrisons or the growing corps of auxiliaries.

Hunger gave the barbarians no chance to await *receptio* along the Rhine, where it seems they had stopped under Godigisclus before crossing into Roman territory. After Godigisclus's death his son Gunderic took command and led the assault on Roman territory until his death in 428. There is no validity to the old belief, current since the days of Edward Gibbon, that both the Vandals and Radagaisus before them had been forced to invade because of the Huns.[89] The Huns did not directly push anyone into Noricum or Raetia at this time.[90] No other groups of barbarians had to push the Vandals to seek Roman aid; their stomachs did the job. The Roman garrisons, very modest, numbering perhaps as few as a hundred men in most cases, did not have the supplies to feed such a mass.[91] Only the *comes* and the comital armies could have helped, but the roads would never have allowed for that in the winter. The fact is that so many starving people could not be fed and processed by the Roman system. The will to do so may have been there, which would explain why the barbarians sought out the garrisons and the Frankish auxiliaries in the first place. The warehouses were simply too small and the need too great.

From Stilicho's perspective, even the news that so many people were pressing for admission would not have been cause for great alarm. He did not react in haste. He needed more men and supplies on the scene and methodically went about providing them. The reinforcements he dispatched were largely barbarian units that included Franks and some Burgundians. He ordered some cavalry reinforcements to hasten to the Rhine from as far away as Pannonia. Many small units, heavily Germanic in origin but Roman nonetheless, had been established in northern Gaul—primarily, it appears, in areas of very sparse population.[92] All these Roman forces combined to achieve significant initial successes, killing many barbarians including their leader and newly made "king," Godigisclus.[93]

In other words, Stilicho at first had no more reason to panic than had Valens in 376. Valens had sought to capitalize on a similar threat by granting *receptio* to the Goths. Militarily things seemed to be going well enough. The second round of news from the Rhine that reached Stilicho was different. The barbarians had been reinforced and could no longer be contained and brought into line by local and regional forces. Word must also have reached him that earlier the army in Britain had rebelled and thrown up a series of claimants to the imperial throne. The last of these was a certain Constantine who seemed to have achieved some staying power. Stilicho, as commander of the Western armies, was responsible for dealing with both military emergencies. Accordingly, he probably considered cancellation of his foray against the East even before he received orders to do so from Honorius. Surely he knew about the previous British usurpers Marcus and Gratian and the crossings of the Rhine. But it was the receipt of Honorius's order that redirected Stilicho. Something very distressing, not some new resolve on the part of the weak-kneed Honorius to take matters in hand, lay behind Stilicho's response. Word had come that Constantine, whose name alone indicated a claim to rule the whole Empire as a descendant of the house of Constantine, had dared to usurp the emperorship and thereby threaten the line of Theodosius over which Stilicho himself struggled to rule. Now political considerations had to enter any calculation. Constantine's crossing into Gaul in the spring of 407 could only be seen from the imperial court as a march on Rome, and so it was portrayed. He had taken "the provinces beyond the Alps." Was Italy safe? Was Honorius in danger?

The precise sequence of events at the end of 406 and the spring of 407 in Britain and Gaul is critical to interpretation of the collapse of Stilicho's regime, and ultimately the fragmentation of the Western Empire. Despite prolonged investigation and discussion, all is not yet clear.[94] Marcus is the first candidate raised to the purple in Zosimus (6.3.1), Sozomenus (9.11.2), and their source, Olympiodorus (frag. 13, from Photius, 80) but is not mentioned in Gregory (2.9 from Renatus) nor in Orosius (7.40.4), both of whom begin with Gratian's usurpation followed by that of Constantine. Bede too omits Marcus entirely, thereby attesting to the further absence of Marcus in the Western traditions. According to Olympiodorus, four months elapsed between the ascension of Gratian and the proclamation of Constantine.[95] Olympiodorus is very explicit that even before Honorius assumed his seventh consulship in 407, the British army had elevated Marcus to the purple.[96] Despite the criticisms of N. Baynes and his redating of the revolt, part of his argument still rings true. He is most persuasive about the date for the usurpation of Marcus: 406, perhaps early in the year.[97] There is no reason to doubt the explicit date of 406 provided by Olympiodorus. Let us continue then with the fact that Gratian was proclaimed four months before Constantine. Gratian was a civilian, *municeps eiusdem insulae,* to quote Orosius. In other words, he was a townsman, probably a *curialis* (a town councilor), and because of his usurpation a tyrant.

The Greek sources are in agreement that Gratian was proclaimed and later removed by the army in Britain. A civilian would be a very strange choice for these troops to make if they were restless about the Vandals in Gaul and wanted to go to Boulogne as Stevens suggests.[98] There can be no doubt that, whatever the original purpose of their rebellion, the soldiers replaced Marcus with Gratian in 406. Perhaps they made the change because something had come up which a *curialis* might handle better. Possible such issues include pay, some local military problem between factions, perhaps even a disagreement among the *dux* commanding the *limitanei*, the *comes litoris Saxonici* and the *comes Britanniarum* (created ca. 395).[99] All of these officers fell under the *magister peditum praesentalis,* but that was Stilicho whose principal concerns were elsewhere.[100] Since their commander could not resolve such a dispute promptly, if at all, perhaps a resident civilian could mediate it. The *limitanei* were highly sedentary compared to the favored *comitatenses,* much of which Stilicho had perhaps sent over to Britain from Gaul for his wars against the Picts and Scots. Later he weakened their force by redeploying a legion from Britain for service in Italy in 401–2.[101] There were also some Germanic troops being stationed in Britain, serving, it would seem, under Roman officers at least in some locations. Such units here as elsewhere were not noted in the *Notitia.*[102] There was no threat of a major invasion of the Empire anywhere near Britain until early 407.

But even then, what possible invasion could have so concerned Britain? Only the Vandals and their allies could have remotely threatened the isle, and then only after the failure of the Frankish *laeti* and other Roman garrisons and allies to contain the situation. But even then it seems farfetched that the British army would risk civil war by "invading Gaul." They would not have gone unbidden, and there was no need for them until the invaders had bested the Gallic army, which did rather well initially. Perhaps in March, news of the demise of the Gallic army arrived in Britain. Until then that army would have treated Constantine's force as rebels. Now, despite their initial successes, the frontier troops on the Rhine needed reinforcement. In Gaul Rome could not have launched any campaigns until the roads were clear of the snows of a very harsh winter. Only then would Roman forces have tried to defeat the invaders. If successful, they doubtless would have proceeded to recruit the survivors. In the first encounters Roman forces more than held their own. Then reinforced barbarians overwhelmed the defenders. If we offer 1 March as a likely time for the Roman forces in Gaul to have been defeated in their sorties against the invaders, then the elevation of Constantine followed very soon thereafter. It follows that Gratian was acclaimed around mid-November 406, and Marcus sometime earlier in that year.

The point is that news of the usurpation of Marcus must have reached Italy while Stilicho was either preparing to confront Radagaisus (died 23 August 406) or immediately thereafter when arranging for his Illyrican adventure with Alaric. Word of Gratian surely arrived while he was organizing for Illyricum. He abandoned neither. Why? The reason must have to do with the perceived ability of the Gallic army to take care of these disturbances in due course. What changed during the first months of 407 was the destruction of much of the Gallic army and the loss of several key centers along the Rhine. Stilicho now faced a very difficult dilemma. On the one hand, he did not have the troops to cross the Alps without risking a rebellion from Alaric. There was no telling what this Gothic upstart would do if he did not receive his new (or rather old) office of *magister militum per Illyricum*. Alaric had yet to receive that or an appropriate reward for his service in Epirus. On the other hand, Stilicho could not ignore an imperial entreaty to do something. He was about to receive several of those from Honorious, each one more pathetic. Perhaps he held his breath for awhile, hoping that the situation reports would change for the better. They did not.

Gratian had his own anxieties. Foremost must have been his awareness that he was totally unprepared for emperorship. News had probably arrived in Britain that the Vandals had broken the defenses and that one group was proceeding in the general direction of Boulogne, the primary embarkation point for supplies and men bound for Britain (see map 8). The threat to their lifeline may have provoked the army in Britain to race the Vandals to Boulogne. This perceived need for immediate action also may have led units of the *comitatenses* to reject Gratian in favor of the old soldier, Constantine.[103]

Alaric and Stilicho

Map 8 The Rhine and Late Roman Gaul

Or perhaps these units acted because of a message, direct or indirect, from Stilicho. What if he had suggested that if they came to the rescue of the Roman army in Gaul, there was indeed hope that their new emperor, the Empire's tyrant, might be recognized in some high capacity, perhaps even as Honorius's colleague? This might well have combined with their own yearning to return to Gaul, if that in fact was where some of them had been stationed just a few years before.[104] It would indeed have been a sound and predictable move had there been no rebellion and no usurpation, the very type of redeployment for which Stilicho was himself famous.[105] The commander of those units of the Roman forces then in Britain was probably the only Roman commander able to move his troops. But this commander had to be a man of some military experience, not a *municeps*, not Gratian. The troops again forced a new man to wear the purple, Constantine. It is quite possible that Stilicho chose to ignore this usurpation, as had Constantius II that of Vetranio.[106] If an understanding had been reached between Constantine and Stilicho, Constantine, unlike Vetranio, did not accept a subordinate and temporary role. He was more directly following the path marked out by Magnus Maximus, to the point of appointing two *magistri militum per Gallias* before even departing for Gaul.[107]

Neither Magnus Maximus (383–88) nor Constantine III (407–11) was directly responsible for the increasing use of barbarians in all ranks and as auxiliaries, but each created a crisis that furthered the need for trained manpower and took advantage of that need. The coinage of Constantine III minted in Gaul suggests an eagerness to proclaim himself as a colleague of the House of Theodosius but, nevertheless, emperor (see illustration 10). In his earliest issues, those from Lyon, in both silver and gold Constantine takes up the Theodosian practice of expressing the recognition of all legitimate emperors by adding an appropriate "G" to AUG on the reverse. Thus, for example, *siliquae* issued at Lyon (407–8) have the obverse D N CONSTANTINUS P F AUG and on the reverse VICTORI-A AAAUGGGG (on *solidi* as well). After the death of Arcadius in 408, the reverses drop one "A" and one "G."[108] By splitting the A from Victoria on some issues, the mint master created an especially neat symmetry to the four "G"s, perhaps catching a nuance of two pairs of co-emperors: Honorius and Constantine III in the West, Arcadius and Theodosius II in the East. However, only after the death of Stilicho was Constantine briefly accepted, but never acknowledged on Honorius's coinage or other official notifications as legitimate.[109] Honorius's first response was quick and hostile. Up to the point of recognition, the pattern follows the career of Magnus Maximus, who also was rejected, used, briefly given recognition, and then discarded by Theodosius I. The earlier British usurpers Marcus and Gratian had no access to a mint and so issued no coins, another reason for the soldiers to overthrow them. On the continent, however, even the very short reign of Maximus in Spain found numismatic commemoration.[110] Constantine III is well represented in Britain as well as Gaul, where his coins were all struck.[111] His claims were clear to all who held his coins.

How many men did Constantine take to Gaul? If we adopted the traditional (and incorrect) figures of A. H. M. Jones of 3,000 for the legions of the *limitanei* and 1,000 for each smaller unit, and then the better but still traditional figure of 1,000 each for the legions of the *comitatenses* and 500 for each other unit of the field army, and applied these estimates to the units listed in the *Notitia dignitatum*, then the total number of troops in Britain stood at 33,500.[112] A more realistic figure that takes into account the archaeological picture of life inside the last phases of Roman fortresses is 12,000, not including probable but undocumented *laeti* (also not taken into the traditional figure). Of this number 5,500 still stands as the figure for the elite forces of the field army under the *comes rei militaris Britanniarum*, an office apparently created by Stilicho. The *limitanei* would have stood at 6,400, of whom 1,200 were in garrisons in the forts of the Saxon Shore.[113]

The new figures are based on the common practice among the late fourth century *limitanei* of occupying "chalets," one-family dwellings, inside the walls. The result was that a fort which had once held several hundred could now serve only a much smaller garrison. Presumably, but not certainly, the units of the *comitatenses* would have remained at strength and may not have had their dependents in tow. If some of their dependents were still in northern Gaul even after a decade, the ca. 5,000 men of the *comitatenses* had strong reasons to return when news arrived of the collapse of the Gallic field army in the early spring of 407. They surely still had friends there. Little likelihood exists that the *limitanei* departed, which explains some of the last vestiges of Roman military presence in Britain. Only the *comitatenses* was prepared for and worthy of transporting. Constantine, however, had a compelling reason to move his command to Gaul and aid the embattled remnants of the Roman army there. His life hung in the balance.

Constantine may have been an unknown soldier who was without merit other than his name,[114] but more likely was a man of some importance chosen with the hope that his name would help.[115] Why most scholars have preferred Orosius and the Latin tradition, demonstrably less informed than the Greek tradition derived from Olympiodorus (as reported in Procopius), is baffling. It is especially puzzling since Sozomenus (9.11.3–5) and Photius (*Bib. Cod.* 80.12), both also derive from Olympiodorus, and all other sources are neutral, giving no information about his origins or prior rank. Had he been truly a man from nowhere, some Greek author would have picked up on it.[116] There is nonetheless no doubt that Constantine possessed considerable military and diplomatic skill. A humble man may be competent and even wise, but it usually takes an experienced man to rally defeated men. Constantine accomplished that by quickly taking ship to Boulogne and drawing the surviving remnants of the Gallic forces around him.[117]

Before departing Constantine assumed the title Flavius, as befitted the highest members of the imperial aristocracy, and renamed his sons Constans and Julian, presumably to exploit the legends still associated with those emperors in Gaul. Had he wished to build directly upon the previous usurpations in Gaul, he could have chosen Magnus, Flavius Victor, or Eugenius. He ignored those names, for he hoped that his usurpation would be different—that is, successful. He was to be the successor of the great Constantine, who had been acclaimed emperor in York.

News of Constantine III's crossing the Channel and declaring himself emperor as well as a false report of the death of Alaric reached Honorius at Rome. Doubtless the *agentes in rebus* had reported all this through the *comes domesticorum*, a member of the imperial *comitatus*. Honorius issued orders for Stilicho to place his invasion of the East on hold and wheel about to strike against Constantine. The rumor about Alaric was quickly dispelled, but Constantine's usurpation brought all preparations for the Illyrican adventure to an end.[118] Exactly when Stilicho learned that Alaric was still alive is unknown, but Zosimus indicates that this was in short order.[119] The time was probably April or May 407. In a year the emperor Arcadius would be dead. Events were fast outrunning reactions.

The distribution of Constantine's coins in northern Gaul reflects his success in recruiting Roman federates and indicates his general route into Germania I. This thrust culminated with his recapture of Trier.[120] He struck his first coins at Trier and Lyon in 407. Stilicho dispatched Sarus, perhaps elevated to *magister militum* for the campaign, to confront Constantine before he could reach Arles. Recent discoveries of his coin issues in Raetia point persuasively to Constantine's influence in that area as well.[121] Constantine had appointed two *magistri* before crossing to Gaul. He now ordered their forces against Sarus. *Magister* Justinianus died in battle. The other *magister*, Nebiogastes, tried to conclude terms with Sarus, but after exchanging oaths Sarus had him murdered.[122] Sarus next besieged Constantine at Valentia but was driven off by the new Constantinian *magistri*, Edobinchus, a Frank, and Gerontius, a Briton. Sarus barely escaped over the Alps, leaving his baggage to the Bacaudae as the price of his passage.[123] In late spring 408, Constantine established his court at Arles and minted coins demonstrating again his willingness to participate in a co-rulership with Honorius and Theodosius II (Arcadius having died on May 1). About this time Stilicho renewed his family's claim to the imperial household by marrying his second daughter, Aemilia Materna Thermantia, to Honorius. Thermantia's sister, Honorius's first wife, Maria, had died late in 407 or early in 408.[124]

While Constantine marched southward without opposition, Alaric withdrew from Epirus for Noricum. He crossed the Sava at Emona, potentially cutting off traffic to Aquileia, and poised if necessary for moving into Italy himself.[125] Taking advantage of the facilities along the main road through Celeia to Ad Lotodos, he proceeded to Virunum, perhaps posting troops en route.[126] Alaric's march to Noricum was a logical tactical move, and very Roman. The two Norican provinces were within the diocese of Illyricum and thereby within the technical jurisdiction of the *comes rei militaris per Illyricum*, Alaric. His redeployment into the Noricums was a defensive move to thwart Constantine if he attempted to move through Raetia and descend into Italy by way of the Norican passes, or at least to hold the provinces from going over. Contrary to Olympiodorus and the derivative accounts in Sozomenus and Zosimus, Italy was not invaded.[127] If a potential invader lurked in the north, it was not Alaric but Constantine. Alaric, however, had a grievance. He dispatched a formal request to Stilicho in Ravenna for reimbursement for his expenses in Epirus.

Stilicho hastened to Rome and pressed Honorius to pay Alaric's claim for 4,000 pounds of gold. He argued that Alaric had stayed in Epirus a very long time, perhaps almost a year, on the emperor's behalf. Stilicho overcame those in the Senate and court who claimed they preferred war. Alaric got his pay. Of course, bellicose rhetorical exercises are safe whenever a peaceful conclusion is not in doubt. In the course of these debates, a certain nobleman, Lampadius, declared as an aside: "This is not peace but a pact of servitude." It was a pronouncement so poignant to the Roman elites, East and West, that Zosimus quoted it in Latin but then translated it.[128] Honorius decided to return with Stilicho to Ravenna, ostensibly to review and congratulate the troops. Stilicho's supporters are said to have believed that he also aimed to remove their chief, which seems doubtful at best. Other rumors were afoot that Serena feared for the emperor's life if Alaric invaded and besieged Rome. Italy was safe; no invasion occurred. Perhaps Honorius and the court wanted to deal directly with the agents of Alaric still waiting in Ravenna. This was something that Stilicho surely dreaded. He may even have ordered Sarus to stage a mock mutiny of some troops near Ravenna, but Honorius was determined.[129]

They may have set out together, but Stilicho proceeded more swiftly and arrived while Honorius was still at Bononia, 70 miles distant. The Senate, the emperor, and Stilicho had only begun to spar over Alaric's claim when word came (probably while Honorius was at Bononia) confirming earlier rumors of Arcadius's death. At least the government did not act upon unofficial reports. The date must have been at least mid-May, probably early June, 408. Honorius summoned Stilicho to Bononia, perhaps to calm quarreling troops but certainly also to discuss the death of Arcadius.[130] Honorius at first responded to the news of his brother's death by proposing that he himself go to Constantinople and see that his nephew Theodosius II got off to a good start with trustworthy ministers around him. Stilicho demurred, arguing that he could do the job himself, and at much less cost. He also reminded Honorius that Constantine had recently established his tyranny at Arles and that the emperor's presence at the helm in Italy was essential. There Honorius could coordinate setting up a new command for Alaric, to be charged now with removing Constantine.[131] Honorius backed down. Stilicho, not the emperor, would go to Constantinople armed with imperial letters, four legions, and a *labarum*, a standard carrying the sign of Christ and closely associated with the emperor on coins and in processions.[132] This was not a delegation of authority that a suspicious emperor would have given, even if pressured. Clearly Stilicho was still *the* imperial adviser. Many of the troops so carefully garnered previously for Stilicho's projected campaign with Alaric against the East were now committed elsewhere. Some of them had probably been sent with Sarus against Constantine, and had been lost.

Honorius provided the appropriate letters for Theodosius II and Alaric.[133] If, as seems to be the case, Sarus had been made *magister militum* for his campaign in Gaul against Constantine in 407, his defeat created a potential vacancy for Alaric. Thus Honorius's letter to Alaric was probably an order of appointment as *magister*. He was clearly to command barbarian and Roman soldiers, i.e., the regulars and the auxiliaries. Sarus had lost his command when he came back in defeat. He was perhaps succeeded by Chariobaudes, who received a regular appointment as *magister militum per Gallias*. Chariobaudes too was soon forced back over the Alps in retreat.[134] If Raetia had not yet come under Constantine's influence, it certainly did at this time. Honorius departed for Ravenna, but Stilicho remained at Bononia. Zosimus relates that Stilicho waited, making no preparations for departing for Constantinople, because he did not want troops from Ticinum or elsewhere encountering Honorius en route and then being aroused against Stilicho by the emperor. This makes little sense. But as late as August he was still at Bononia and Honorius was by then at Ticinum with some of the army intended for Gaul. Why then did Stilicho suddenly become immobilized?[135] In part, he had to wait for his escorting legions to assemble, but there may be more to it.

Alaric must have been expected to march south from Noricum to link up with Roman armies in Italy before moving against Constantine. Presumably the rendezvous would be at or near Ticinum after a slight detour to Bononia to get Stilicho's briefing before the latter's departure for the East. After Honorius departed, Bononia was a convenient place for Stilicho to wait to parley with his old rival alone. If the emperor were to decide to leave for Ticinum first, as seems to have been the case, Stilicho would then have forces ready to move between them if necessary. If Honorius had left Bononia and continued on to Ravenna, he would have had another and unreported encounter with Stilicho. We do not know the whereabouts of Honorius until he arrived at Ticinum; he could have proceeded at a leisurely pace up the Po.[136]

Alaric's agents had departed Ravenna about the same time that Stilicho moved his headquarters to Bononia. Perhaps he had already told them of his plans for Alaric and set a rendezvous at Bononia. Surely Stilicho did not invent his complex plan to go to Constantinople on the spur of the moment. He had already heard rumors of Arcadius's death, he knew that Constantine III had usurped the crown, and he had no reason to doubt that Honorius would again see things his way. If Alaric was indeed expected at Bononia, Stilicho must have wanted to remind him that now at last he was about to achieve his goal of a magistership—and that he had Stilicho to thank. Nothing ever came of Alaric's taking up arms against Constantine nor of his possible appointment as *magister*. Alaric had not yet marched when news of great importance arrived in Noricum that changed him and history. A coup d'état had taken place.

Olympius, the master of the imperial secretaries, a man who owed his career to Stilicho, had turned on his patron while en route to Ticinum with Honorius.[137] He declared that Stilicho's journey to the East was nothing more than a plot to overthrow Honorius's nephew and replace him with his own son Eucherius.[138] Honorius apparently was not impressed by these accusations and proceeded to Ticinum. There, on 13 August 408, four days after his arrival, he assembled the troops to inspire them for their coming battle with Constantine. Olympius signaled his co-conspirators (mainly soldiers, it seems) with a nod of his head while they listened to their emperor.[139] In their outrage over Stilicho's alleged plot, the soldiers slew all of his principal supporters at court as well as many bystanders. No one mentioned barbarians.

Among those slain were Limenius and Chariobaudes, praetorian prefect and *magister militum* for Gaul respectively, who had fled from Constantine III. The *magister equitum* (*magister praesentalis* II) Vincentius, second in rank in the Western army only to Stilicho, *magister peditum* (*magister praesentalis* I), died. Honorius was unharmed.[140] Olympius and his backers had staged a very successful palace coup. Only Stilicho and his brother-in-law, Bathanarius, then *comes Africae*, remained alive. The heads of all the important civilian agencies rolled beside those of two of the Empire's ranking generals. No charge had been levied against Stilicho for his recruitment of barbarians or what some called his "pro-barbarian policies." The events of

13 August constituted a "conservative revolution," one ostensibly undertaken to protect the State and its emperor from a vast plot to change the ruling order.[141]

Stilicho's response to the upheaval at Ticinum was to convene the commanders present with him in Bononia, where he was probably awaiting Alaric, and plan a counter-revolution. Quite logically they decided that if Honorius were still alive, and therefore able to rally the troops to his side, only the conspirators themselves need be eliminated. If the emperor were dead, everything became much more complicated. A new emperor would have been proclaimed by the army in Ticinum as a matter of course. That would mean that another usurper, perhaps even Constantine III, and his army would have to be dealt with. Moreover, a legitimate successor would have to be installed at once. One likely candidate was Stilicho's son Eucherius. He certainly would have been the choice of the troops had Honorius actually died in the bloodbath at court, as a rumor suggested. Indeed, perhaps this certainty that Eucherius would be the army's choice to succeed Honorius is the origin of the tradition that Stilicho had schemed to place his son on the throne.

Stilicho had yet to assemble his troops for the Eastern expedition. Certainly they were not at Bononia. These were the four legions he had been given as a guard to protect him on his mission to Constantinople. Therefore the only troops likely to be with him were the barbarians under Sarus, his personal bodyguard (buccellarii, primarily Huns), and probably some units of auxilia that he would have transferred to Alaric for use in Gaul. The rest of the army was either en route to Ticinum, in Ravenna, or aboard ship to Dalmatia. There was at least one garrison in Ravenna, and it later arrested him.[142] Knowing that he was outnumbered, Stilicho was not sure how to handle Honorius, presumably a captive in all but name. When he learned that Honorius had avoided all harm, Stilicho moved his headquarters to Ravenna to consider his next move. He was doubtless relieved that he might not have to pit his meager forces against the slightly larger but decidedly superior Roman units assembled at Ticinum.[143]

Sarus then rebelled. His men killed the Hunnic guards in their sleep. Most of the other barbarians withdrew to await events. Many must have decided to return to their families in nearby towns, billeted there according to recently clarified procedures.[144] Stilicho promptly issued orders that those barbarians returning to their wives and children not be admitted into the cities in which their kin were housed.[145] These are not the actions of a unified barbarian force or of a barbarian Roman commander conspiring with them to overthrow the State. On 22 August 408, orders came from

Olympius to place Stilicho under house arrest, but word of this reached Stilicho in time for him to seek asylum in a church. To no avail, however, for when the first body of soldiers had succeeded in removing him by declaring that they had no orders to kill him, a second unit awaited him outside to do just that. His followers tried to organize a hasty defense, but Stilicho would have none of it and surrendered himself to the sword. He died bravely. Eucherius fled to his mother in Rome, not to Alaric. This is a peculiar route for the son of one allegedly in league with Alaric to replace the son of Theodosius with his own![146]

Stilicho, so often hailed as a savior, had proven unable to save himself. Why had he fallen? Did it really have anything to do with his relationship to Alaric or his barbarian policies in general? Perhaps, though no such connection appears in Zosimus, our most extensive source. What about Olympius's charge that Stilicho plotted the overthrow of Theodosius II in favor of his own son? Olympiodorus, as preserved in Zosimus, alone suggests any reservations about Olympius's charges. In his epitaph on Stilicho, Olympiodorus notes that Stilicho never promoted his only son beyond the so-called rank of *notarius et tribunus,* and declares that he had planned no leading position for him. He gives the precise date of Stilicho's death almost as if he were copying from Stilicho's gravestone.[147] Except for possibly Olympiodorus, however, all of our sources, both Greek and Latin, opine that the "true" intention of Stilicho in these last days was to place his son Eucherius on an imperial throne. Which throne depends on the source. Sozomenus and Zosimus are unequivocal, the throne of Theodosius II.[148] Orosius is equally positive, but for that of Honorius.[149] Philostorgius and Marcellinus Comes agree with Orosius.[150]

There may have been some Eastern involvement in Stilicho's death based on his supposed designs upon Theodosius II's throne. Varanes, a man of good eastern stock, quickly replaced Stilicho as *magister peditum* (*praesentalis* I). In 409 Varanes was back in Constantinople probably as *magister militum praesentalis II* and in 410 stood in Constantinople as sole consul, none having been nominated from an occupied Rome. Varanes's sudden appearance in 408 and his meteoric rise, over Stilicho's dead body, after an absence of fifteen years from our records, are very suspicious. He must have been among the conspirators, possibly one of their leaders. He had apparently gone west with Theodosius to fight against Eugenius, stayed, but kept in touch with friends in Constantinople. Of all the conspirators, he alone found lasting profit in Olympius's palace revolution.[151] Unfortunately, about Varanes and his eastern connections we know next to nothing. At the very least Varanes's appointment as *magister peditum,* Honorius's general-in-chief, must have sent a reassuring message to Constantinople that Western meddling in Eastern affairs had come to an end. Varanes will reappear in our discussion on one more occasion, and perhaps then some of the mist surrounding his career will lift.

Orosius was convinced that Stilicho deserved the contempt of Honorius and all true Romans. Stilicho had plotted the replacement of Honorius himself with Eucherius and had plotted in secret with Alaric and other barbarians to crush the Roman army on the Rhine and settle the barbarians inside the frontiers. Indeed, by his writing the Goths were already in southern Gaul. For Orosius, Stilicho and his son Eucherius were steadfast pagans, determined to restore the temples and destroy the churches of Christ. As a direct result of their conniving, Rome itself was besieged and looted.[152] This father and son personified the evil that God sought to purge from the Earth. Alaric may have been a heretic, but he was at least a Christian who had spared the holy places and holy virgins in Rome. Jerome is similarly harsh, blaming Stilicho (a half-barbarian traitor) for using Roman money to arm its enemies against it. Jerome roundly condemns the entire Roman approach to the barbarians since Adrianople, but in a context of providing an even greater challenge for true Christians to live virtuous lives.[153]

Jerome and Orosius combined discordant historical themes, but failed to reconcile them fully. Like Ambrose, Jerome was almost obsessed with the end of the world. At times he thought that the Huns descending through Armenia into Asia Minor were heralds of the apocalypse.[154] At other moments, the Goths assumed that role in the guise of the biblical Gog and Magog.[155] Yet the Goths were fellow Christians, even if Arians. Jerome and his disciple Orosius could not blame Theodosius, who had made Christianity the state religion, for the destruction of their homelands in Illyricum and Spain respectively. Orosius was generally favorable to Theodosius's barbarian policy, but (apparently unaware of his inconsistency) damns Stilicho for continuing it. His bitterest charge was that Stilicho's relationship with Alaric had led directly to Goths ravaging his beloved Hispania. The real Stilicho lies somewhere between Olympiodorus and Orosius, between a worthy servant of the State and a devilish pagan.

We can safely ignore the charges of paganism against Stilicho since they are totally without support, being indeed just one more *typos* like being a "barbarian." Stilicho was often praised for his support of the Church in better times, and Theodosius would never have allowed a pagan into the imperial family. The charge of conspiring secretly with Alaric was at least partly true, but not in any significant or sinister way so far as the West was concerned. Even from our limited sources it is quite clear that Stilicho forthrightly supported Alaric's claims to reimbursement for the Epirus adventure, and even nominated him to be a principal commander in Honorius's war against Constantine III. What went unrecorded (probably because it was conducted in secret) was Stilicho's acceptance of Alaric's desire to achieve high military command including *magister militum*. That circumstances prevented Alaric from ever taking up the Illyrican or Gallic posts was chance. Had either gone further toward completion, there can be little doubt that the sources would have recorded Alaric as a *magister*. As offensive to the Roman literary aristocracy as it was, the barbarian presence in the Roman army had a very long history by 408. Theodosius and Stilicho had had to depend upon barbarian auxiliaries in ever increasing ratios as the recruitment and training of non-barbarians broke down under ever mounting pressure from events. As of Stilicho's death, no barbarians had been accorded "kingdoms" within the Empire. Those with regal titles were either dead or held Roman commands that made their kingships superfluous. Stilicho was not, however, the pure and humble servant of Zosimus's epitaph.

As the iconography of the famous diptych of Stilicho, Serena, and Eucherius manifests, Eucherius was, contrary to Zosimus, destined by his father for greatness (see illustration 16). There probably was truth in the charges Olympius made against Stilicho, for he was in a position to know whereof he spoke. Olympius had been a close associate of Stilicho in his early years and later was a highly placed official in Stilicho's government.[156] Olympius and his compatriots were not innocent children; they profited immensely from the demise of Stilicho and his lieutenants. Nor were they the first traitors in Roman history. Although he misidentified the emperor Stilicho aimed to replace with his son Eucherius, Orosius is the most interesting of the ancient authors writing on Stilicho's fall. In his peculiar late-Roman Christian manner, Orosius tells us that Stilicho died because he wanted to go down in history as the father of an emperor, but that he deserved to die because as the man on watch he had allowed Alaric, symbolizing all barbarians, to enter forever the gates of Rome. The emperor Stilicho sought to supplant was Theodosius II, not as Orosius writes, Honorius. Writing of events of 408, Orosius knew well where they led during the next decade, because it was his past.

Charges of the "barbarization" of the army were not decisive or even effective in removing Stilicho. It took the army at Ticinum and at Ravenna to do that. Anti-barbarian slogans were rallying cries for some members of the aristocracy, Christian and pagan, mostly outside Stilicho's circle. In that

Illustration 16. Both panels of an ivory diptych with Stilicho, Serena, and Eucherius

respect they were very real. In some cases, an anti-barbarian ideology replaced the traditional aristocratic antagonisms toward the military. This was
easy enough since barbarian recruits filled its ranks from top to bottom. As
Roman soldiers, regulars or auxiliaries, barbarians were proving their loyalty at precisely the same time that Stilicho's detractors found in his barbarian origins a standard Roman explanation. To them, Stilicho's prior loyalties meant that his failures were really betrayals—not just of them but of
the Empire. Roman authors cast stereotypical barbarians in the role of un-
derminers of the very Empire that in fact real barbarians were dying to
defend against other, equally real barbarians and Roman usurpers. If "barbarian" may have been as potent a political term as ever, it had ceased to

be a useful descriptive term. Nevertheless, one Roman general of barbarian origins was poised to march into Italy, meet Stilicho for a briefing at Bononia, and take charge of the Roman army assembling to challenge Constantine III in Gaul. Alaric was the only battleworthy general left.

Summary

Stilicho allowed Alaric's dismissal from his Eastern post of *magister militum per Illyricum* to stand and prepared for war. Alaric invaded in November 401 in a preemptive strike while Stilicho was raising men in Raetia. Stilicho's battles with Alaric in 402 and with Radagaisus in 406 reveal an acute manpower shortage. After Stilicho had fought Alaric to a draw, he offered him a command in the diocese of Illyricum. Actually he agreed to recognize Alaric's de facto army and made Alaric *comes rei militaris*. Initially this plan was to establish some order in the diocese. But shortly Stilicho was again planning an invasion of the East. Events intervened. Thousands of starving barbarians crossed the frozen Rhine near Mainz on the last day of 406. Their invasion struck just as Britain, the nearest source of reserves for the Gallic army, had fallen into a political crisis with a series of usurpers coming to power. Constantine III, a veteran, emerged triumphant in Britain and crossed the Channel with an army in 407.

By 408 Honorius's government had to concentrate all its resources on quashing Constantine's rebellion, which by then encompassed Gaul and probably most of the transalpine provinces. The demise of the Gallic army and Constantine's rebellion left Honorius with no source of manpower to complement Stilicho's modest force except Alaric. Alaric was to be given command as *magister militum* and with Honorius stop Constantine, while Stilicho went to Constantinople to establish the late Arcadius's son on the throne. On 22 August 408, Stilicho fell to a palace coup. Like all Stilichoians Alaric lost everything and once again fell back upon being *rex Gothorum*, a title that he had allowed to lapse since becoming *comes*. Great religious fervor cast its shadow across these events.

{ 8 }

THE SACK OF ROME

THE NEW REGIME moved swiftly to replace Stilicho's men at court. Varanes had been appointed *magister peditum* (*magister praesentalis* I). Turpilio took over from Vincentius as *magister equitum* (*magister praesentalis* II). When Varanes returned to the East in 409, Turpilio succeeded him as *magister peditum* (*magister praesentalis* I).[1] Vigilantius was made *comes domesticorum equitum* and moved up to *magister peditum* in 409, replacing Turpilio.[2] Olympius, content to allow others the military commands, now became *magister officiorum*. The first round of appointments must have taken place immediately at Ticinum while all were still present, for the army was assembled there for campaign and new generals had to be named at once.[3] The purge of Stilicho's appointees quickly gathered steam. Heliocrates, appointed *comes rerum privatarum* at Olympius's request, received an imperial decree ordering that all property of Stilicho's supporters be confiscated.[4] Stilicho's chief household officer and his head secretary were tortured and then killed when they refused to supply names to their tormentors.[5] Honorius ordered the eunuchs Terentius and Arsachius to return Stilicho's daughter Thermantia to her mother, Serena, in Rome and to execute her brother, Eucherius.[6] Serena moved quickly to protect her son, however, and Honorius's assassins found Eucherius in asylum in a church in Rome, having been rushed to safety by some of Stilicho's barbarian troops. These men were hungry and took what they needed in Rome but did not then seek to join Alaric.[7]

Until this point the tide of revolution had not lapped over into the realm of barbarian problems. A great effort had rid the highest echelons of the Western Empire of Stilicho's supporters, including his immediate family, as far even as his daughter the young empress. The issue of what to do with the barbarian auxiliaries recruited by Stilicho, and presumably loyal to his memory, had yet to be resolved. One of Stilicho's last acts had been to order those towns providing billets for his barbarian troops to shut their gates against them. These men, supposedly his "supporters," had drifted home in confusion after Sarus rebelled and killed Stilicho's Hunnic bodyguard. When the towns barred their gates they made it impossible for these barbarian soldiers to be reunited with their wives and families. Their help-less dependents now bore the weight of Olympius's wrath. The regular Roman garrison troops slaughtered them and seized their property throughout all the towns in which they were resident, "as if on one command, when told of Stilicho's death."[8] There can be little question that the garrisons proceeded according to the orders of their superiors and the edict authorizing the seizure of Stilicho's supporters' property as drafted by Heliocrates.

In other words, with many of Stilicho's Roman supporters having been eliminated, the barbarian supporters were now to take their turn. Such focused cruelty clearly rallied these barbarians to a new standard of mutual interest, though they could have disputed the charge that they were Stilichoian sympathizers. After all, they were at that very moment still suffering at Stilicho's hands. Unless we assume extreme stupidity for Olympius and Varanes, they probably had not known about Stilicho's order closing the gates and thereby locking the barbarians out. They had hoped to achieve the same devastating results as had the Constantinopolitans in 400, when they had locked the barbarians in. The new rulers in the West knew little of military realities or of Rome's true relationship to so-called barbarian recruits. This time, moreover, the barbarian soldiers still lived.

What would these barbarian auxiliaries have thought beyond their justifiable outrage? Unspeakable betrayal. In their passion for vengeance, they decided to flee to Alaric and join forces with him.[9] Alaric had yet to march on Italy, but remained in Noricum where he received the barbarian refugees. His new volunteers could have numbered nowhere near the 30,000 reported in Zosimus, for Stilicho had had very few troops at Bononia in the first place (see map 9).[10] These recruits to Alaric's army were perhaps only those troops usually stationed near Ravenna. At any rate, Alaric did not jump to attack Italy. Instead, he reportedly offered to exchange a few hostages, specifically Gaudentius's son Aetius and Jovius's son Jason, sought a modest sum of money, and requested permission to move his troops to Pannonia.[11] If true, this means that Alaric had offered to return to his status as a mere *comes* in Illyricum provided that the state pay his relocation expenses. Given the circumstances, this gesture to relieve tensions still tests one's credulity. An exchange of hostages was not something that necessarily indicated a relationship between foreigners or enemies. Romans had long exchanged hostages among themselves, sometimes even among friends, as a demonstration of trust. Constantius Chlorus, for example, had sent his son Constantine, later emperor, to his colleague in the tetrarchy, Galerius, to be reared at his court. Naturally a hostage exchange offered a greater *securitas* to the relationship and underscored the *gravitas* of the moment. The

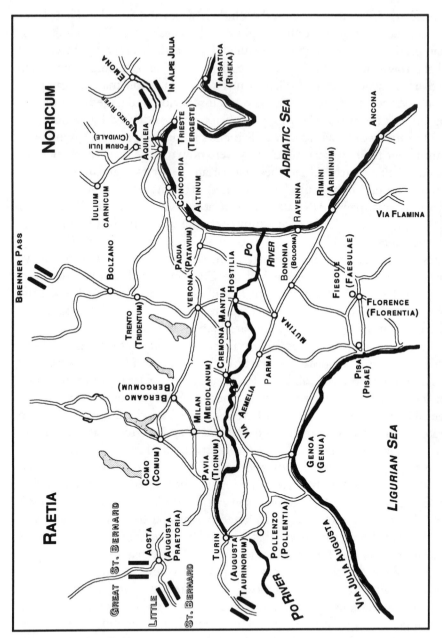

Map 9 Northern Italy and the Late Roman Alpine Passes

ancient hostage was a far cry from the ancient prisoner—a distinction that modern events make it difficult to recall. Aetius, for one, never regretted his several occasions as a hostage to Alaric and later with the Huns.

Nevertheless, Zosimus reports that Honorius rejected Alaric's proposal. As a former supporter of Stilicho, Alaric was evidently beyond forgiveness. By seeking noble Roman hostages Alaric merely noted his awareness that all was not normal. When this overture was rebuffed, only war could follow. Alaric, typically concerned with troop strength, ordered his brother-in-law Athaulf[12] to bring up his army of Huns and Goths from Pannonia I. This force too was Roman but was made up exclusively of auxiliaries, there being no regular units worthy of mention in the area. Perhaps sensing from the barbarian refugees the true vulnerability of Honorius and his army, which had only just begun to make preparations against his advance, Alaric attacked at once, not awaiting reinforcements.[13]

The proof of the hypothesis that Stilicho was waiting in Bononia for Alaric when word of Olympius's palace revolution arrived may lie in Alaric's route of invasion in the autumn after he had learned of Stilicho's death and Honorius's court had made it clear that he would find no employment with them. Alaric went via Aquileia, Concordia, Altium, apparently to Cremona, then southward across the Po to a small military post of Oecubaria near Bononia before marching on Aemilia and Ariminum.[14] Except for the detour to Cremona (we would have expected him to turn south at Verona, cross the Po at Hostilia, and pick up the via Aemilia at Mutina), Alaric's route makes perfect sense for anyone seeking to take advantage of the supply network along the principal highways. Had he approached Ticinum as far as Cremona to be doubly sure that the army of Honorius was no longer there? There was no opposition.[15] Or is this a manuscript problem or a mere reflection of Zosimus's ignorance of Italian geography? Perhaps he confused Cremona with Verona. Let us assume, however, that the text as we have it is correct and that Zosimus made no mistake. If for some reason Alaric felt unable to cross the Po at Hostilia, his next opportunity came at Cremona. Alaric's decision to bypass Ravenna and Honorius proved a mistake.[16] At the time he betrayed no sign that he worried about it. Could he have followed a route fixed in advance by Stilicho with prepositioned supplies and appropriate requisitions in hand? That is possible, even probable. Only six weeks or so had elapsed between the death of Stilicho on 22 August and Alaric's drive into Italy in October. Furthermore, the towns and garrisons opened their gates in welcome, just as they should have done to a Roman general marching along a planned route. Zosimus says that Alaric proceeded as if it were a festival.

What happened to the army bound for Gaul, whose mutiny had led to the fall of Stilicho? It seems to have disintegrated and disappeared, leaving Honorius's government in a desperate situation. Except for Alaric's men it may have had no significant body of troops to send against Constantine. There seem to have been only enough to shadow Alaric as he labored to bring the government around to his demands. Only a few defended the approaches to Ravenna. Until the death of Stilicho and Honorius's rejection of him in favor of Olympius's men, Alaric was a commander in the Roman army, legitimate, a Roman. Olympius's palace coup had removed those whom Alaric regarded as also legitimate. Still convinced of his own legitimacy, Alaric was determined not to share their fate.

Insofar as our sources permit clarity, it seems that the court had decided not to compromise with Alaric, period. Why it showed such obstinacy baffled Zosimus, and baffled his source, Olympiodorus. Had Alaric sought from the outset to depose Honorius in favor of his own hireling, the refusal to negotiate with him would make sense. Alaric had no such plan in October 408. Perhaps it was because he was a barbarian commander, commanding a force largely composed of barbarian auxiliaries. But this was true of many, including Gaïnas and Fravitta in the East, and Arbogastes and later Allobichus and Generidus, promoted under Honorius in Italy itself. Unlike some, particularly Generidus, Alaric was Christian, albeit an Arian, so that even allegations of paganism were inappropriate.[17]

There was no way to drive out men of "barbarian ancestry" from the army or its command. Roman society had long ago abandoned that as an anachronism. Rome had by now a well established pattern of favoring Christianity, and Christianity had lent its strong support to dynastic succession. In this one respect, at least, blood mattered. Alaric was beyond redemption for one reason only: his late role as a key lieutenant of Stilicho. He was the last important Stilicho supporter left capable of realigning military and political power by his personal affiliations, and that is why he could not remain alive.

The laws against Stilicho's supporters remained on the books and were enforced until the fall of Olympius. To his enemies Stilicho had sought to overturn the basic principles of right rule. He had done so in two very clear ways, both of which involved playing Alaric as a trump card in the Balkans. Stilicho had undermined relations between East and West to the point of invasion and had consistently tried to insinuate his blood into the dynastic confraternity of the Theodosian house, marrying two daughters in succession to Honorius and having greater plans for his son. Thus within a decade Orosius saw him as a pagan, virtually an Antichrist at the head of pagan armies seeking to plunder Christian churches and bring down the pious emperor.[18] He had offended man and God. Jerome saw Stilicho as a semi-barbarian traitor, who deliberately armed the enemies of Rome against it. His crimes put good Christians to the test.[19]

Pagans too regarded Stilicho as a betrayer of Rome and its gods. Zosimus reports his condemnation among pagans for ordering the doors of the Capitol (the temple of Jupiter Capitolinus) stripped of their gold. The men hired to do the job reportedly found an inscription hidden beneath the gold: "These are reserved for a terrible tyrant." After Stilicho's death the inscription was understood to have prophesied it.[20] For Rutilius Namatianus, Stilicho's treason included letting the barbarians into the heart of the Empire, there to learn its true weakness. And "nor was it only through Gothic arms that the traitor made his attack: ere this he burned the fateful books which brought the Sibyl's aid." Stilicho replaced Nero in Tartarus, for "Stilicho's victim was immortal, Nero's mortal; the one destroyed the world's mother, the other his own."[21] The burning of the Sibylline Books is mentioned only in Rutilius, not in any of the accounts derived from Olympiodorus, not even the pagan Zosimus. As has been suggested, Olympiodorus probably drew upon sources favorable to Stilicho for this portion of his history.[22] Rutilius was an embittered contemporary and eyewitness writing in 417, as he journeyed northward in Italy past scenes of war and suffering on his way back to Gaul. He blamed Stilicho. Alaric was merely the executor of Stilicho's diabolical plot to destroy Rome and raise his line upon its ashes.[23] Thus the nearest contemporary sources, written very shortly after these events, had damned Stilicho for his betrayal of the divinities. Orosius seems to have forgotten that none other than Augustine had once praised Stilicho for his Christian zeal.[24] Orosius and Rutilius blend his dynastic goals, his admission of the barbarian destroyers, and his religious transgressions into one sinister plot. Not even Eunapius of Sardis, Zosimus's principal source for the first part of his *Historia nova*, who is often viciously anti-Stilicho, had directly attacked his religious character.[25]

Just as the Sack of Rome would reverberate throughout the Empire with profound religious tones, so too did the reaction to Stilicho's bid for the purple for his family. In the eyes of many people, they became inseparable. For his part, Alaric seems to have appreciated the religious energy of his age and acted to accommodate or even exploit it. For example, he was apparently the first to use bishops as envoys[26] and to observe holy asylum for the Christian women when he sacked Rome.[27] Unless the sources have overlooked a very important aspect of Alaric's early career, he was not known for his religious principles but rather for being a man of iron determination and great political savvy. His new religious sensitivity was in keeping with his political foresight. It worked to his advantage in our sources in that they often exonerated him from primary responsibility, which they reserved for Stilicho.

Bypassing Ravenna, Alaric marched on Rome from Picenum along the via Flaminia. It was autumn 408, and the "first siege" was about to begin. Eucherius secretly left the safety of the Church and attempted to link up with Alaric, en route to Rome, but imperial troops caught up with him and took him back to Rome, where he was executed.[28] His barbarian guards only now left for Alaric's camp.[29] Here, as near Ravenna, Stilicho's former soldiers did not want to join Alaric until they had no choice. Heraclianus, the murderer of Stilicho, was honored as *comes Africae*, replacing Stilicho's recently executed brother Bathanarius.[30] Meanwhile, Thermantia had been returned to her mother, Serena, in Rome. The pair had only weeks together before Serena was herself executed as if a clandestine agent of Alaric, though, as Zosimus pointedly notes, she certainly was not. Rumors of paganism tainted even her.[31]

Assertions that Stilicho and his elite circle were worshipers of the ancient gods cannot be dismissed as a quirk of Zosimus's later pagan longings. The family of Stilicho was eradicated with the ardor of Christian zealotry that was a hallmark of the dynasty. Stilicho had indeed been guilty of something, apparently not pride, and not necessarily or even probably his military use of auxiliaries (on that score, it was obvious to all that he had no alternatives). Surely his son had no policies at all. Serena had raised a few eyebrows back in 394, when she had entered the temple of Magna Mater and walked out with the divinity's necklace around her own neck. Some, according to Zosimus, regarded her execution during Alaric's siege of Rome in 408 as justice for her impiety. Those offering this explanation were obviously pagans.[32] She had absolutely no role in military affairs but was known to have had a keen interest in the succession, and for this she died. Thermantia would never have produced a legitimate heir, so it seems, through no fault of her own. Stilicho and all who depended upon him paid for Stilicho's relentless efforts to dominate the house of Theodosius, East and West, and ultimately to supplant it. In the age of Theodosian Christianity, austere and punishing, false accusations that he had favored the ancient gods were sufficient grounds for the extinction of his line. For others he was later condemned as a traitor for opening the Empire to barbarians. Among pagans, he and his wife were denounced for slandering the ancient gods. Rumors were not facts or even consistent.

The old hostility that occasionally surfaced between the civilian and military aristocracies and the standard paradigm of civilized and barbarian—so long a central and creative concept for social criticism—after 410 were incorporated into a comprehensive Christian indictment of late imperial politics. Barbarian soldiers abetted God to chasten Christian sinners. The sack of Rome in 410 brought these and other discontents to the fore and, because of Saint Augustine in particular, into all discussions of Christian destiny and the meaning of history. In the hands of a brilliant person like Augustine they came together, but for most such unity of vision was unattainable. The fruit of these attempts to reconcile conflicting ideas, events, and personalities was bittersweet. Late fourth and fifth-century attempts to fit barbarians, particularly Goths, into the Christian historical vision as precursors of the Apocalypse addressed only a part of the centrality of barbarians in the Late Roman World; they could no longer successfully be regarded simply as pagans and wanton destroyers.[33]

The barbarians of the late fourth century practiced various mixtures of paganism and Arian Christianity. The former was often Greco-Roman, at least among the elites, while the latter was especially influential among the Gothic speakers. They were truly not Gog and Magog but could still be seen as uncouth heralds of the Coming. Alaric is an example for Augustine and Orosius of what a little Christianity, even with heretical central beliefs, can do to pure barbarism.[34] For Orosius, the friend and admirer of both Jerome and Augustine, the Goths had been charged by God with the punishment of the impure Christians. Since they hesitated to carry out God's instructions to the letter, God personally wielded the lightning bolts that destroyed the most sacred of Rome's monuments. Galla Placidia's long captivity under Alaric and Athaulf had done much good for her fellow Christians, just as God knew it would.[35] Jerome saw the Goths only as a pestilence devouring the heart of the Empire; the very best that could be hoped for was the restoration of the body, for growth and material progress had ceased forever.[36] Of course, Jerome's Bethlehem and Augustine's Hippo in North Africa were both far distant from the realities with which this book deals. In the case of Hippo, Augustine died as the Vandals took over.

Socrates portrays Alaric as a reluctant instrument of the Christian God, responding to an inner voice saying, "Go to Rome and destroy that city."[37] So too Sozomenus has him tell a monk while en route to Rome that although he himself had no desire to besiege Rome, he was responding to an irresistible force.[38] Nevertheless, the Alaric of Socrates and Sozomenus, of Jerome and Orosius, and of Augustine perhaps most of all, represents an important aspect of the way the real Alaric was seen by the contemporary literary elites and the civilians who listened to them. Stilicho's fall isolated

Alaric in an intellectual spotlight. His actions cast illusions like those on a Wayang theater screen, where real figures serve only to produce their shadows. The imaginary Alaric ultimately was much more important than Alaric the general. Alaric surely knew how he and his command were perceived by many, and he may well have acted in a fashion calculated to calm their worst religious fears. There is, of course, a danger that this impression of Alaric is itself the result of the religious cast of our sources. Still, there are facts, such as his use of Orthodox bishops and his upholding the right of Christian asylum, which attest to his religious sensitivity.

The anti-Stilichoian policies of Olympius thrust Alaric ever more into the role of *rex Gothorum*, a title he had probably first donned in 400 but had apparently held "in reserve." He had used it, if at all, only among his closest advisers, who were Goths and could relate to the need for a supreme leader, reminiscent of a *thiudans*, in times of great danger.[39] The purge of barbarian soldiers previously under Stilicho's command solidified his position as the highest Gothic leader. Theodosius the Great's policies of divide and recruit, the traditional and effective policies of the Roman Empire, were now turned against Rome. Olympius and his fellow conspirators, by branding Alaric an enemy of Rome once again, provided him with recruits and left him no choice but to strengthen his position as *rex* by denying him access to comparable Roman command, the magistership. There was no way to harmonize a king within the Imperium Romanum in either barbarian or Roman tradition. Alaric was determined to achieve the only acceptable status imaginable, *magister militum*, whereas Honorius was equally determined to crush him as a barbarian chieftain gone astray. The equipoise created a new beast: part *rex Gothorum*, part *thiudans*, and part general of the Roman auxiliaries.

There is no reason to elucidate the various tactical aspects of the struggle between Alaric and Honorius's court, for many others have put their stamp on these events, notably J. B. Bury, E. Demougeot, S. Oost, and F. Paschoud. Militarily Orosius was right; it wasn't much of a contest.[40] The struggle for Italy was fought in much the same way as any frontier campaign: the Romans were secure behind their fortifications, the barbarians had to live off the land and carry the initiative until Roman reinforcements arrived. For two years the available manpower on either side was unable to defeat the other. The same conditions prevailed as in the days of confrontation between Stilicho and Alaric but without the possibility of recourse to transalpine sources of manpower. Constantine III was largely responsible for that. Moreover, Alaric and his brother-in-law Athaulf retained control over the roads and passes leading to Italy from Pannonia and Noricum, thereby blocking any reinforcements coming to Honorius from that quarter—that is, until the spring of 409, when Athaulf crossed into Italy.[41]

The Romans refused battle. Alaric could not spare men to besiege and garrison even the principal towns and so concentrated his efforts upon Rome. He knew that it was the only focus of political power outside the court, which was protected by the swamps of the Po surrounding Ravenna, and hoped that the great families residing there might press a compromise upon Honorius. As Gildo had demonstrated in 398, the key to Rome was its belly. Accordingly, Portus rather than Rome itself became the focus of most military operations. The events of 408–10 underscore the point that even during this famous clash the terms barbarian and Roman were largely rhetorical. Barbarians and Romans, to the extent that such terms still had any clear meaning, served on both sides during the struggles. The overriding circumstance was the fact that the arrival of a very modest force could decide a battle, because neither side could count upon reinforcements. Even runaway slaves, not all of whom were reported as barbarians, were welcomed into the ranks of the Gothic force.[42]

Just prior to his siege of Rome in 408 the citizens of Rome mistook Alaric for "someone else, one of Stilicho's friends, who was commanding the army besieging them," for rumors persisted that Alaric was elsewhere or had died.[43] When Roman ambassadors saw Alaric in the flesh and heard him boast of his power, they shed their illusions. After learning that he planned to besiege Rome unless all the gold and silver and movable property, including barbarian slaves, in the city be handed over, they returned.[44] At this point Zosimus injects a comment that the Romans thought about their turning away from the ancestral gods. Indeed, all our sources, pagan and Christian, henceforth are at pains to attribute religious significance to these events through caressing a common set of vignettes derived in part at least from Olympiodorus into manifestations of their god's will. As they tell it, no principal actor and only a rare bit-player enters onto the stage without manifesting a key virtue at a critical moment. But because Zosimus, the main pagan interpreter, is so lackadaisical and inconsistent, the Christian version of events, primarily as preserved in Sozomenus, although briefer and less detailed, appears smoother and often more convincing. Only occasionally can we catch a glimpse of Olympiodorus himself, and then only as epitomized by Photius. The sources of Olympiodorus himself are the subject of controversy.[45] Olympiodorus must have said that during the siege some people turned to cannibalism, but Zosimus, perhaps dubious or more likely wanting to deflect this, the most savage allegation against paganism, says merely that they came close.[46] By all accounts these were dreadful days in Rome.

The first crisis passed once the senators, after much discussion, finally agreed upon a payment to be given to Alaric: "5,000 pounds of gold, 30,000 pounds of silver, 4,000 silk tunics, 3,000 scarlet-colored skins, and 3,000 pounds of pepper." Each senator was to contribute according to his means, which left much to chance and corruption. The total could only be met by melting down the gold and silver from the pagan shrines, a point Zosimus delights in stressing. With so much gold at issue, Alaric must have demanded official payment in ingots. The melting down of public treasures was his idea and a good one too, since it produced pure and readily convertible wealth. Virtus, the goddess of manliness and courage, thus stripped, deserted Rome and took Roman strength and bravery with her, so says Zosimus.[47] Alaric again demanded and received noble youths as hostages. Honorius concurred, as well he should have since the Senate had taken a special census to assess and levy the ransom. Food now entered the starving city. Alaric used these days to recruit slaves into his army, said now to number 40,000.[48]

Forty thousand, including allegedly "virtually all the slaves in Rome," seems a reasonable estimate of Alaric's force. Surely this is the largest acceptable figure for total troop strength, and not all of these troops were truly effective. The month was December 408. To appreciate the sums involved, Zosimus reports that in the next year Marinianus redeemed his son Maximillianus for 30,000 solidi, that is, slightly over 400 pounds of gold.[49] Maximillianus was rich, perhaps *vicarius urbis Romae* at this time or slightly later, but not super-rich, not like Symmachus, for example.[50] The ransom payment did not bankrupt his family. The amount agreed upon by the senators to buy off Alaric was well within their reach even without recourse to the pagan temples.

Did Alaric intend to distribute the 7,000 garments, a form of portable wealth as well as prestige, to his troops? Is 7,000 then a realistic number for the total force of "regular" barbarian soldiers in his command? Perhaps. At the height of the siege Pompeianus, urban prefect, seriously considered trying a few pagan incantations to bring on thunder and lightning, reportedly effective elsewhere against Alaric's men. He even convinced Pope Innocent I to go along. Innocent, however, agreed only on the condition that the sacrifices be conducted in private. Nothing came of this after visiting Tuscan priests declared that the Senate had to perform the rites in the Forum.[51] The essential point is that everyone, including ordinary Roman townsmen and barbarian soldiers, was caught up in the spiritual struggle going on around them. Money rather than gods resolved the impasse. Alaric made peace and pledged to fight alongside the emperor against any foe. No treaty was signed. There was no public display of Rome coming to terms with a foreign people, as might have happened with a new group of barbarians recruited to serve as auxiliaries. Alaric saw himself as still a general in the Roman army and simply pledged his personal loyalty as a soldier to fight for the emperor.[52] He withdrew his forces from Rome to regroup and allowed supplies to enter the city without harassment. While Alaric remained in Tuscany, slaves flocked to his standards.[53]

The year 409 opened with unexpected good news for Honorius from an unlikely source, Constantine III. The usurper sent an embassy of eunuchs (note, in contrast, Alaric's use of bishops) to seek pardon for his "unanticipated" elevation at the hands of his soldiers. This must have been a rather standard pose by this point in Roman history—its truth or falsity mattered little—but in this case Honorius chose to accept it and pit his new "colleague" Constantine against Alaric.[54] Honorius sent the eunuchs back to Constantine carrying an imperial cloak symbolizing his acceptance or at least his willingness to move in that direction. Constantine apparently thought that he was thereby made Honorius's consular colleague and proclaimed himself as such throughout his domains, as an inscription at Trier recording the death of a young woman in the year of his consulship attests. He was wrong. Honorius and Theodosius II were consuls for 409, and neither stepped down for him.[55] The peace Honorius had just concluded with Alaric, the sum having been paid, now became but a truce to buy time. Honorius also apparently believed that his relatives Didymus and Verenianus were being held at Constantine's court.[56] Constantine had, in fact, ordered their deaths.[57] Honorius delayed sending the agreed-upon hostages to Alaric.

The Senate, realizing that something had delayed the hostages and therefore the final conclusion of the peace, dispatched an urgent mission to Honorius in Ravenna. The three senatorial envoys were Caecilianus, Attalus, and Maximillianus. Caecilianus in particular was a man to be listened to at court. He had been *praefectus annonae* (in charge of the grain supplies from Africa), then vicar and proconsul of Africa, and had previously served as a senatorial legate in 400. He therefore knew firsthand about the needs of the city and how best to present the Senate's concerns to the emperor.[58] Attalus too had served before as a legate; in 398 he had succeeded in winning some respite for senators ordered to provide recruits to Stilicho. He had also probably been a vicar or proconsul by this time. Ultimately he became Alaric's choice for emperor.[59] Together they made a very capable delegation.

Honorius ordered Valens, a *comes rei militaris* in Dalmatia, to march with five legions comprising 6,000 men, reportedly the best in the Roman army, to Rome to man the defenses.[60] This would have been equal to the task of guarding Rome against Alaric's force, which included perhaps as few as 7,000 first-line troops. Only Valens and Attalus made it to Rome. No relieving troops appeared. Caecilianus remained in Ravenna as praetorian prefect. Alaric's men captured Maximillianus and held him for ransom. The Senate sent a second embassy to Ravenna led by Pope Innocent I and escorted by a barbarian guard. Perhaps the Senate hoped that Alaric would show greater respect for the pontiff and his barbarian guardsmen than he had accorded the first senatorial ambassadors. Just then Athaulf crossed the Julian Alps into Italy. Honorius ordered out all the troops at Ravenna and nearby towns to defeat him before he could link up with Alaric. Olympius, then still *magister officiorum* and still chasing down Stilichoians,[61] was given command of the Huns of the imperial guard, some 300 men. Whoever was placed in command of the entire force, if not Olympius, went unrecorded. Zosimus seems to say that only the 300 Huns actually took part, slaying some 1,100 Goths with losses of seventeen to the attackers before the rest of Athaulf's command could rally and drive them back to Ravenna.[62] These numbers seem preposterous, but it is clear that Honorius's efforts to assemble an effective blocking force were fruitless. Perhaps a bold raid was all they could pull off.

According to Zosimus, Olympius fell to a court cabal led by some palace eunuchs who persuaded Honorius to withdraw his support from his minister. Events just outside the palace may have been even more persuasive. In the absence of any coherent policy during Olympius's rule except chasing down Stilichoians, desertions and subterfuge from one faction to another were commonplace. Olympius's pitiful policy of persecution, little more than a political vendetta, held opposing factions at bay until about the middle of 409, when the emperor turned against him. Olympius, the former bounty-hunter, fled to Dalmatia.[63]

The confiscation of Stilichoian property had offered its own rewards to the state and its supporters, but this could not continue forever. Soon a mutiny of the garrison in Ravenna, engineered by Jovius and Allobichus, praetorian prefect and *comes domesticorum equitum* respectively, brought another set of office-holders to power. This new ruling clique seems to have had no clear policy except to find personal ways to survive the growing confrontation between Alaric and Honorius. From time to time the emperor, autocrat of the Roman world, actually seems to have made his own decisions. Most, though not all, were bad. After the collapse of Olympius's government, Honorius showed uncharacteristic resolve by continuing to refuse Alaric a magistership. Perhaps Allobichus was at work behind this decision, since later Honorius had him executed for conspiracy with Constantine. For whatever reason, Honorius would rather accept a usurper, Constantine III, than give in to Alaric despite the fact that it was abundantly clear to everyone that Alaric's demands were negotiable and, ultimately, reasonable. That this dramatic farce took almost two years to resolve is a testament to the military paralysis of both the Empire and its auxiliaries commanded by Alaric. Attalus, newly appointed *praefectus urbis Romae*, and a certain Demetrius, who now succeeded Attalus as *comes sacrarum largitionum*, hastened to Rome to see how much the confiscations from Stilicho's supporters had netted the treasury.[64] The state needed every *siliqua*. The garrison at Ravenna had mutinied, perhaps at the urging of Jovius, now praetorian prefect of Italy and previously praetorian prefect of Illyricum for Stilicho's aborted campaign. During his stay in Illyricum and Epirus, Jovius and Alaric had become close.[65] The *comes domesticorum equitum*, Allobichus, also seems to have been involved.[66] Both Jovius and Allobichus must previously have been able to convince Olympius and his supporters that whatever relationship they or their families had had with Stilicho was over. Otherwise their property would have appeared on the registers of confiscation that they now set about examining. Allobichus is another example of the numerous officers of Germanic descent who had little or nothing to do with Stilicho or some supposed pro-barbarian faction in the government. Jovius was a political chameleon of the first rank.

At this point in his narrative Zosimus inserts a timely vignette about Generidus, a barbarian by birth, a Greco-Roman pagan in his faith. Generidus endeared himself to Zosimus because here was a real Roman commander of the old school: a tough disciplinarian, a scourge to the barbarians on the field of valor. Yet here was also a true believer in the pagan gods, ready to lay down his command rather than accept an exemption from a recent law that barred pagans from the officer corps. In order to gain his services, Honorius rescinded the law. An edict, perhaps the one in question, against pagans holding office is preserved in the *Codex Theodosianus* (16.5.42). Applying to the palace and the troops of the *comes domesticorum equitum*, this edict was issued at Ravenna on 14 November 408 and was addressed to Olympius, *magister officiorum*, and Valens, *comes domesticorum equitum*.[67] The law, although one of a series of laws restricting pagans, also perfectly fit the current efforts to purge Stilicho's supporters. Like their late leader, they might conveniently be branded as pagans. The repeal of this law for Generidus and others like him reflects a temporary relaxation of the manhunt for Stilichoians and the desperate straits that the Roman army in Italy found itself in against Alaric. It did not betoken a reversal of the overall trend of repression directed at pagans. This easing of anti-pagan legislation ended no later than 25 August 410, when another imperial edict restored the full effect of previous laws circumscribing the practice of pagan rites.[68] Generidus's appointment may have hastened Athaulf's departure for Italy.[69]

Jovius and Allobichus, who is not known to us prior to becoming *comes domesticorum equitum* but perhaps was a *comes rei militaris*, brought in a new council of officers. Jovius remained praetorian prefect of Italy. Valens, previously *comes domesticorum peditum*, took over Turpilio's post of *magister peditum (magister praesentalis I)*, Turpilio himself having replaced Varanes in that position. This Valens, now *magister peditum*, is not the same as the Valens who had attempted to garrison Rome and would soon also become *magister equitum* under Attalus. Allobichus took over from Vigilantius, who had taken his office when Turpilio moved up to *peditum*, as *magister equitum (magister praesentalis II)*. Turpilio and Vigilantius met violent ends on their way into exile.[70] Allobichus and Jovius wanted a clean sweep. They also exiled the chief palace eunuchs, Terentius and Arsacius, who had executed Eucherius and returned Thermantia to Serena. Eusebius replaced Terentius as *praepositus sacri cubiculi*, but soon Allobichus had his head smashed in front of Honorius.[71] These replacements were part of a political housecleaning having nothing to do with barbarian policy, despite the fact that one of the principal players was of Germanic descent. For a moment it seemed that the army and the new government were strongly behind Honorius, but if so this unanimity was fleeting.

Jovius immediately sought to bring the struggle with Alaric to a peaceful conclusion. He urged Alaric and Athaulf to come as far as Ariminum (Rimini) to negotiate the terms of peace. Jovius himself, Alaric's old friend from Epirus days, met them in Rimini and set down Alaric's demands: an annual payment of gold and grain, the amount to be fixed through negotiations, and permission to settle with "all those with him" in the combined province of Venetia and Histria, the Norican provinces, and the province of Dalmatia. Jovius wrote this down and added a suggestion that Honorius make Alaric *magister utriusque militiae*, in return for which Alaric would probably soften his other demands considerably.[72] This was obviously only the opening round of discussion.

Several of Alaric's demands were clearly unacceptable to Honorius, or were unacceptably vague. "All those with him" included numerous slaves whose masters might seek compensation from the state. More importantly, the number of people, especially "soldiers," had yet to be fixed. Alaric probably did not know it himself. This might explain why no specific weight of gold and amount of grain was included, for if this sum was in any way calculated upon the military ration system, knowledge of the number of soldiers was essential. Of course, this assumption rests, perhaps unwarrantedly, upon the idea that our sources did not just create these numbers from whole cloth. Since in this case we are dealing with matters of official discussion potentially leading up to a formal legal agreement, there seems reason to have more than the usual confidence in the sums listed.

Perhaps a major stumbling point in Alaric's initial demands was permission to establish himself in Venetia and Histria. To accede to this demand would have put Alaric in Italy with no possible line of defense against him until he reached the Po. Usually the final defense of Italy took place at the Isonzo river, the boundary between Venetia and Noricum, between Italia and Illyricum.[73] Although we may be sure that Alaric would have welcomed supreme command of both forces in the West, *magister utriusque militiae*, Stilicho's old position, he would have accepted the purely military command of *magister peditum (magister praesentalis I)*. Alaric later did accept the latter command from Attalus, from whom Alaric got anything he wanted. If Olympiodorus was correct in stating that Jovius recommended *magister utriusque militiae*—and clearly Olympiodorus gave this precise title since it is in Zosimus and Sozomenus—then Jovius had again inflated Alaric's real demands, and again with unfortunate consequences.[74]

It is conceivable that Jovius, a civilian administrator throughout his public career, did not realize the impossibility of his idea and had merely heard Alaric use the title in Epirus as either a leftover from the old days or as a hope for the future. There were no such positions in the Western army, and under the circumstances Honorius and his advisers could easily have thought that this was a move to take over supreme command. Stilicho had carried his title of *magister utriusque militiae* with him in 395, and Honorius was not ready for another Stilicho. Alaric was himself obviously much better informed about the command structure in the West than was Jovius. Honorius, however, must have thought that Jovius's suggestion was Alaric's idea. He responded accordingly, and in words that apparently slandered Alaric and his family. Jovius further demonstrated his stupidity by reading the emperor's response, intended for him personally, to Alaric and those with him.[75] Honorius may also have decided to hold firm until he was better able to gauge the extent of the aid he would receive from Constantine III.[76]

Alaric broke off negotiations at once over the insults hurled at his family and vowed to march on Rome. Back in Ravenna, Jovius sought to cleanse himself of any stains attached to his role in the negotiations by contriving to have himself and other dignitaries at court swear an oath upon the welfare of the emperor never to make peace with Alaric, an oath Rome would regret.[77] Honorius prepared for war. He summoned Hunnic auxiliaries—Zosimus records their number as 10,000, unacceptably high—probably from Pannonia and Valeria. They were now able to march because the passage of Athaulf into Italy had cleared the defenses on the roads leading westward into Italy. Honorius also ordered that provisions of sheep, oxen, and grain be shipped from Dalmatia and that scouts report Alaric's whereabouts.[78] Somebody was clearly in charge in Ravenna, most probably Allobichus.

Rather than take Rome, Alaric decided to give diplomacy another chance, and sent Orthodox bishops from all the towns under his control to Ravenna with a new set of conditions. He backed away from Jovius's suggestion that he be made *magister utriusque militum*, which had never been his idea anyway, and gave up on occupying Venetia and Histria. He further stipulated that he would settle for an annual subsidy of grain to be determined by the emperor, no gold, and permission to settle in the two Norican provinces, pointing out that they were not contributing much to the treasury in their current state. These conditions when met would secure his friendship and an alliance with the Romans to defend the Empire against anyone who took up arms against it.[79] Such an agreement would almost certainly have led Alaric to return to Noricum, especially since he probably knew that Honorius had just summoned the Huns living in the area of Valeria and Pannonia—traditionally no friends of the Goths. If these terms are reported accurately, conditions in Italy must have become very difficult. Alaric yielded much, even the gold. Grain had emerged as his overwhelming need. Thanks to Dalmatia and his policy of not offering battle but holding onto the towns, Honorius had more food than anyone else. Alaric must have chosen not to attack Rome again because he did not believe that its capture would better his lot. Little grain had entered Portus and perhaps none from the principal supply centers in North Africa, where Heraclianus still maintained control for Honorius. Alaric may also have realized that Constantine III was preparing to march against him.

Honorius refused even Alaric's new conditions forthwith. Zosimus claims that he did so because Jovius pleaded this peace would violate the oath taken on the fortunes of the emperor and therefore would be an offense sure to bring down God's wrath.[80] A more likely reason for the swift rejection is that Ravenna sensed Alaric's weakness; the policy of choking off his supply of African grain was tilting the balance in their favor. They could await Constantine. Alaric marched again on Rome, took Portus, and quickly forced the Senate to yield with a threat of withholding grain. So, without a siege, Alaric concluded his "second siege" of Rome. This time Alaric abandoned working with Honorius's government and in late 409 set up Priscus Attalus, then urban prefect, as emperor.[81] Attalus, a pagan, accepted Arian Christian baptism.[82] As if to dramatize his complete break with Honorius, Alaric took Honorius's half-sister Galla Placidia hostage. With the return of Honorius's second wife, Thermantia, all hope for continuity of succession had fallen upon her.[83] Alaric took for himself the office of *magister peditum (magister praesentalis I)* with Valens, the same commander who had attempted to relieve Rome earlier, as his junior colleague, *magister equitum (magister praesentalis II).*[84] Athaulf became *comes domesticorum equitum.*[85] Although Attalus named Alaric and Athaulf to "Roman commands," he could never deliver on the means needed for maintaining their troops. Regular provisions were unobtainable with or without a usurper's order. An embassy arrived in Ravenna from Constantine to confirm the peace. Jovius asked Honorius to put aside the deaths of his relatives Didymus and Verenianus, whose murders in Gaul had just been announced at court, and to dispatch him personally to negotiate the bringing of all of Constantine's force against Alaric as soon as possible. Honorius agreed, and Jovius departed toward Gaul.[86]

The purple blinded Attalus to the realities of his situation almost from the moment he accepted the imperial mantle. Despite the recent failures of Alaric to besiege Ravenna, Attalus decided to concentrate his forces for another try. As a result, he did not go along with Alaric's advice to send a modest force under Drumas to enforce the eviction of Heraclianus and his command from Africa. Nor did he listen any better to his *magister officiorum* Joannes, who advised a bit of chicanery. His advice was to send Constans to replace Heraclianus with an imperial decree removing him in the name of Honorius since no news of Attalus's usurpation could have reached Africa.[87] Attalus dreamed of restoring the Senate to its rightful place and bringing Egypt and the East under Rome once again. Convinced that he was the legitimate ruler, Attalus rejected Joannes's ploy, but issued a similar decree in his own name. Unfortunately for Constans, it turned out to be his death warrant. The army Attalus and his commanders Alaric and Valens led against Ravenna was composed of Romans and barbarian troops. This distinction probably reflected their units rather than their ethnic identity. Perhaps "regulars and auxiliaries" would have been more accurate. The former were very few in number, for Valens's force from Dalmatia had been annihilated earlier and no replacements had arrived.[88]

The plan worked! When Attalus and his army reached Rimini early in the new year (410), Jovius, Valens (Honorius's *magister peditum*), Potamius, *quaestor sacri palatini*, and Julian, *primicerius notariarum*, delivered a statement from Honorius accepting Attalus as his colleague, doubtless only until Constantine arrived from Gaul.[89] Attalus, perhaps knowing of the impending invasion from Gaul, rejected the proposal of co-rule (κοινωνία). His counteroffer was stingy: only that Honorius could choose a place to which to retire, if he wished to preserve even the trappings of being an Augustus. When Jovius delivered this counterproposal before Honorius, he added his own unauthorized embellishment, which had been sharply rejected by Attalus, specifically that Honorius would also be maimed before going into exile. In other words, deformed and disgraced, Honorius could have a pension. Jovius did everything he could to get the emperor to flee Ravenna and clear the way for Attalus. He almost succeeded.

Jovius's handling of this embassy suggests that he was already far along in his defection to Attalus and Alaric. Perhaps he thought that if Honorius fled now, Constantine could be stopped or a new regime established in which Attalus and Constantine shared power. This also meant that there was an increasing rift between Jovius and Allobichus, who was emerging as the strongest backer of Constantine at Ravenna. Whatever Jovius's motives, Honorius assembled ships to carry him to safety with his nephew Theodosius in Constantinople. Suddenly, as if from nowhere, a force of 4,000 men arrived during the night, providing a strong garrison and a renewed willingness to await the outcome of Attalus's attempts to replace Heraclianus in Africa. If Heraclianus could hold, the spreading famine in Italy would force Alaric and Attalus to offer better terms. That the population of Rome, with the government's largest concentration of supporters, might starve did not appear to concern Honorius. The towns of the Po valley still held out for Honorius, making their grain unavailable to Alaric. Honorius stayed.[90] Ravenna received supplies and reinforcements by sea. Relief came.

The text of Sozomenus reads literally: "an army of 4,000 soldiers arrived in Ravenna unexpectedly at night from the East (ἀνατολῆς)."[91] Zosimus says that just when Honorius had decided to quit Ravenna "a force of six units, which had been expected since the time of Stilicho, arrived by sea, deriving from an alliance with the East (ἐκ τῆς ἑῴας). This force totaled 4,000 men, and with these men from the East Honorius garrisoned the walls."[92] The relevant fragment of Olympiodorus from Photius contains no reference to these troops, nor does Socrates. Where these troops came from seems clear—the Eastern Empire—but not why. Whose diplomatic effort produced them?

Only Zosimus reported a vague Stilichoian connection. Stilicho himself surely made no such gesture to the East, against which he spent his last years planning an invasion. Zosimus must mean shortly after Stilicho's death which had reopened avenues of cooperation. At that moment Olympius and Varanes, *magister peditum (magister praesentalis I)*, were desperate for troops for the inevitable struggle about to begin with Alaric. In 409 Varanes resigned his post and returned to Constantinople. Honorius's salvation must derive from the diplomacy that Varanes had undertaken.[93] Honorius took heart and held on in Ravenna.

Honorius again sent Jovius to Rome, where he allowed himself to come under the influence of agents of his old colleague Alaric. Jovius defected to Alaric, and Attalus soon rewarded him with the title *patricius*.[94] Jovius announced his defection in a speech to the Senate in which he asked it to relieve him from his place on Honorius's embassy to them. Jovius urged the Senate to send some of Alaric's force to Africa to crush Heraclianus. These were harrowing times for senators, for they were trying to walk an indistinct line between the two camps, keeping one foot in each. An embassy from Attalus or Honorius was welcome, but to neither side would they give their unqualified support. No army was resident in the city to force their obedience.

Attalus, who was with Alaric and not in Rome, sensed that Jovius was effectively using the issue of Africa to come between himself and Alaric. He ordered that more men and money be sent there forthwith, but still refused to send Drumas's force of barbarians against Heraclianus. Since it must have been clear to everyone that Heraclianus's control of the grain fleet had to end or the city and much of Italy would starve, Attalus's reluctance makes little sense. Perhaps Attalus believed that they should not deplete the forces Alaric was using to besiege Ravenna. That excuse soon evaporated when Alaric abandoned the siege, perhaps to give diplomacy another chance.[95] He then concentrated on subduing Honorius's supporters in the towns of Aemilia, but could not take Bononia. Ravenna was now stoutly defended, and Constantine may have already crossed into Italy.[96] Attalus's new mission to Africa met defeat, and Jovius, sensing a weakness in Attalus's relationship with Alaric, insinuated himself between them.[97] Alaric may have defeated Constantine in Liguria, but that was probably not the main reason that Constantine abandoned his invasion. It seems clear that Constantine was more influenced by the fact that Honorius had ordered the death of his principal military supporter at the court in Ravenna, Allobichus, *magister equitum*, on suspicion of conspiring to overthrow the emperor.[98]

The importance of Heraclianus's victory in Africa was soon demonstrated: famine, more frightful than ever before, struck Rome. The circus crowds are said to have cried out, "Set a price on human flesh," thereby protesting the inflated cost of food.[99] At this juncture Attalus returned to Rome and convened the Senate. In the debate that followed, he and his dwindling number of supporters were resoundingly voted down on the issue of sending a barbarian force to deal with Heraclianus and open the grain routes to the city. Attalus's opposition to this plan cost him the emperorship. Alaric deposed Attalus and took him and his son, Ampelius, to Rimini. There he again encamped and attempted to reopen negotiations with Ravenna, probably believing that by deposing Attalus he had removed an obstacle to peace.[100] Alaric also had Honorius's half-sister Galla Placidia with him as a hostage. She had probably been his hostage since late 409, when Alaric had negotiated with the Senate and placed Attalus on the throne. He did not turn Attalus and his son over, but kept them with him—ostensibly until he could arrange a pardon.[101] It was midsummer 410, probably July. Characteristic of the near anarchy current in Italy, Sarus, Alaric's old rival, recently forced to withdraw from Gaul with his tail between his legs by Constantine, was at large in Picenum, accountable to no one for his 300 men. He now threw in his lot with Honorius and harassed Athaulf's force with no significant result.[102]

Perhaps because of Sarus's raid but more likely because by now he knew that Ravenna was beyond his reach, Alaric struck camp and marched on Rome once again. This time he was determined to force the Senate to its knees. There was no need for a prolonged siege, for Heraclianus's stranglehold had created a continuous famine. Some of our sources duly offer treachery as an explanation for the sudden collapse of Rome's defense, but the facts are otherwise. Rome opened its gates in desperation. There was no need for a "third siege." Alaric gave orders to respect those who had sought asylum in holy places, especially the basilicas of Saints Peter and Paul, then turned his men loose. And so on 24 August 410 began a three-day-long Sack of Rome.[103] Orosius, like other Christian writers, recorded vignettes of the occasion celebrating the power of God to shine through any catastrophe. One such involved a dialogue between a virgin and a Christian Goth arguing over whether the Goth should take the sacred vessels of the church. In that instance right prevailed. There could not have been many like that. After three days the Goths left with Attalus, their loot, and Galla Placidia, still in tow as a hostage.[104] There was nothing more to accomplish there. Honorius had stubbornly refused to give in to Alaric's demands; in truth, he made no effort even to discover them.

Alaric called his forces together and marched southward through Campania and Lucania to Rhegium in Bruttium.[105] There he sought to cross to Sicily and then to Africa, but storms smashed his ships. The plan was logical and sound. The only way to bring Honorius around was to replace Heraclianus and seize the African grain trade. Attalus was still available for the emperorship, as time clearly revealed. Alaric need not have ordered all his men to Africa; Stilicho had managed with 5,000 against Gildo in 398.

Alaric, the sole surviving general from the days of Stilicho, King of the Goths, Sacker of Rome, died of sickness at Consentia in Bruttium. He had apparently given up, at least for awhile, on taking ship to Africa. His resolve to force Honorius to yield went unrewarded. His followers diverted the course of the Busentius River and there committed the body of their leader, Alaricus *rex Gothorum* but not *magister militum*, to the afterlife. The captives who dug the graves were slain and the river returned to its channel.[106] Despite recent bogus announcements to the contrary, Alaric and his share of the spoils of Rome still lie there undiscovered. The "Sack of Rome" in 410 was not the victory of barbarism any more than had been Constantine the Great's "Sack of Rome" after his victory at the Mulvian Bridge in 312. From the perspective of the Roman Army both were the predictable consequences of civil war. Alaric passed swiftly from the field of battle into the realm of legend. He had not lived long enough to solve the riddle of how a barbarian could be acknowledged as a king within the Roman Empire. He had, however, established a core of myth and people around which the Visigoths coalesced into a new society. Rome had given him and them no choice.

Summary

With Stilicho gone and his supporters, including Alaric, purged, a power vacuum existed at court. There was no army left to defend Italy. Honorius's government lured Constantine III with talk of recognition into marching his army to Italy's rescue, but he soon departed without accomplishing his mission. Alaric seized Rome three times (408, 409, and 410) with little resistance. Only on the first occasion did he even have to pause. Starvation was the weapon of choice for all participants. Honorius's government controlled the supplies of imported grain and left Rome and the towns of Italy to fend for themselves. Stilicho's troops, mostly barbarians, eventually joined Alaric as did many fugitive slaves. Alaric steadfastly demanded a Roman generalship and thereby recognition of his followers as Roman soldiers, but Honorius always refused. Alaric took Honorius's half-sister Galla Placidia hostage in 409 in Rome and so she remained. When nothing softened Honorius, Alaric raised Priscus Attalus as his puppet emperor in 409. Attalus gave him his generalship but could do nothing about guaranteeing his army provisions. When Honorius was at the point of abandoning Ravenna for Constantinople, aid arrived from the East. Stilicho's death had allowed the restoration of imperial cooperation between East and West. On 24 August 410 a very frustrated Alaric seized Rome a final time and gave his troops free rein. By sparing some Christians seeking asylum, he secured for himself a special place in history. After three days he marched his army, becoming a people since they had no choice, southward. Alaric died in southern Italy after an unsuccessful attempt to get to Sicily and Africa, where he hoped to control Italy's grain supply.

THE SETTLEMENT OF 418
CONSTANTINE, CONSTANTIUS, ATHAULF,
WALLIA, AND ROME

WITH ALARIC BURIED, the Goths turned to his brother-in-law, Athaulf, and accepted him as king. Athaulf had held some lower-level Roman command as early as 408. Perhaps he was a *tribunus gentis* or *praepositus limitis*,[1] for his command was a mixed force of Hunnic and Gothic auxiliaries and a frontier force.[2] But in 409, when Alaric summoned him to reinforce his own army in Italy, Olympius reportedly pressed him hard with a force of only 300 Huns, who supposedly killed 1,100 of Athaulf's men near Pisa. Olympius, even though he held not a military post but the office of *magister officiorum*, led a hastily assembled force of the garrisons of towns, a few additional cavalry units, and these Huns, who had been stationed at Ravenna.[3] Once again the forces involved were very modest, and that is the essential point. Despite Olympius's effort to prevent it, Athaulf had joined up with Alaric, whereupon Attalus quickly appointed Athaulf *comes domesticorum equitum*, a grooming post for a magistership. The arrival of this new command near Ravenna pushed the reluctant Sarus into imperial service.[4] Athaulf still technically held the post of *comes* in 410, when he succeeded Alaric. Since there can be no doubt that Athaulf's composite force, at least those surviving the raid by Olympius's Huns upon their camp, merged with those men in Alaric's army, it is clear that "Alaric's Goths" included many non-Goths. Several thousand other barbarians, locked out of their garrisons in cities in northern Italy shortly after Olympius seized power, had joined Alaric. So had runaway slaves. Over all these men and women, Athaulf now ruled as *rex Gothorum*.[5]

Athaulf, though he had been promoted by Attalus, was the ranking Goth in Roman terms as *comes domesticorum equitum*. He was also the closest surviving relative of Alaric. Which of these two relationships mattered more to those following him is not so obvious. Claims to some sort of Balthi family relationship through marriage probably did not convince anybody

a   b   c

Illustration 17. Solidi of a) Honorius (393–423), Obv: DN HONORI VSPFAUG,
Rev: VICTORI AAVGGG, Spurning Captive (ca. 404); b) Galla
Placidia (421–450), Obv: DNGALLAPLA CIDIAPFAUG, Rev:
SALVS REI PUBLICAE, Victory seated right on cuirass, inscribing
shield with Christogram (421–22); c) Priscus Attalus (409–16), Obv:
PRISCVSATTA LVSPFAVG, Rev: INVICTARO
MAAETERNA (409–10)

to fight and die, although Jordanes writing ca. 550 thought it did.[6] Alaric
had himself risen to the top of Gothic leadership through the ranks of the
Roman army, and he had set his brother-in-law on precisely the same climb.[7]
Like Alaric before him, Athaulf found himself barred from Roman command and its guarantees of supplies and rewards for his followers. Athaulf
apparently thought that he possessed two important bargaining chips: the
deposed emperor Attalus and Honorius's half-sister, Galla Placidia (see illustration 17).[8] But in practice his custody of these imperial personages,
far from inducing Honorius to negotiate a permanent solution, presumably
a magistership, acted as an impenetrable obstacle to any imperial recognition
of Athaulf's position. Attalus's presence in his camp made Athaulf a com-
rade in usurpation, just as it had Alaric, and before them Arbogastes with
Eugenius.

Athaulf reigned for over four years. Despite numerous attempts to satisfy his needs for supplies, only short-term grants came from Ravenna. He
never achieved effective Roman command, though he did make Attalus his

stooge-emperor. Athaulf had to define himself as a king, which, in Roman eyes, made him an outlaw. He was ready to surrender his throne in exchange for Roman recognition, but Honorius and his advisers always stood mute and defiant.

Rome consistently treated Athaulf as a usurper. Since the Roman experience shared by all was now politically out of reach, Athaulf and his followers had little choice but to build a *new* identity upon the Gothic traditions shared by most of them. They, of course, did not give up the many Roman ideas and practices that already had influenced them profoundly through their contacts with and service in the Roman army. They could not have shed the strong Roman component of their culture even had they wanted to. Only against this background do Athaulf's career and actions make sense. He continued the process of redefining Gothic society hesitantly begun under Alaric, but in circumstances even more unsettled than those Alaric faced in Illyricum.

Athaulf led his followers northward up the via Aurelia into Gaul, arriving in 412.[9] He discovered in Gaul a battle-scarred land of refugees now in the grip of a new usurper, Jovinus, a Gallo-Roman, who owed his throne to barbarian auxiliaries. Alaric and Athaulf had not faced stiffer opposition while in Italy, partly because Constantine's rebellion in Gaul prevented Honorius from redeploying troops from beyond the Alps. Until his defeat in the summer of 411, Constantine—not Alaric or Athaulf—was the principal threat to Honorius and his family. One of Stilicho's last acts was to convince Honorius not to go to Constantinople but to stay in Italy and accompany Alaric, appointed as *magister militum* for the campaign, against Constantine. Meanwhile, Stilicho would secure conditions in the East for Honorius's nephew, Theodosius II. This plan evaporated with Stilicho's death.

In 409 Honorius even gave Constantine partial recognition (a robe but no notice on coinage), for with Stilicho dead he had no alternative manpower in his struggle with Alaric.[10] Olympius fell in a palace intrigue shortly after his successful raid on Athaulf's camp in early 409, then fled to Dalmatia, but was briefly restored to office late in 409 or in 410. His career and life ended simultaneously, probably in 410, when thugs cut off his ears and beat him to death at the order of the emperor. The instigator of this assassination was probably Constantius, perhaps then already *magister peditum*, senior commander of the Western armies (see illustration 18).[11] The new government headed by Jovius and Allobichus succeeded that of Olympius but proved itself equally ineffectual and ephemeral in the confrontation with Alaric. Jovius defected and Allobichus fell in clouded circumstances but probably in a military coup led by Constantius. If the rumors of Allo-

Illustration 18. Solidus of Constantius III (421), Obv: DNCONSTAN TIUSPFAUG, Rev: VICTORI AAVCCC, emperor standing, looking right, holding labarum and globe surmounted by Victory.

bichus's pro-Constantinian sympathies are correct, he was caught playing off Constantine against the emperor, probably with assurances from Constantine that he would become *magister peditum* in the new regime. Allobichus's plotting brought him into direct confrontation with Constantius. Constantius emerged the victor. There is no doubt that Constantius held the supreme command of the Roman army by 411.[12] He was a native of Naissus in Dacia Ripensis and a veteran, enrolled under Theodosius. An inscription testifies that he was *comes et magister utriusque militiae*, an imprecise title but one denoting political power. Constantius took overall command of all Roman forces and personally led the "infantry" against Constantine at Arles, while Ulfilas, a Goth by birth and *magister equitum*, directed Honorius's "cavalry" in the field.[13] The titular distinctions of leading the cavalry or infantry had long ago lost their significance in the field, where mixed forces held sway. Constantine did not just sit on his hands. He ordered Edobich, his *magister utriusque militiae*, to the Rhine to recruit from among the Franks and Alamanni. Successful in this mission, Edobich returned to Arles too late to relieve his besieged emperor. Defeated himself, Edobich fled to his friend Ecdicius's estate nearby. Ecdicius did not welcome Edobich; instead he murdered him. With his last hope for rescue gone, Constantine III surrendered.[14]

In Constantius Rome had a proven commander of great talent and severity. He concentrated his efforts first upon the principal foe, Constantine, and then upon Athaulf. Until Constantius had restored the legitimate government to Arles in 411, Gaul was the principal focus of Rome's military attention. Generidus and Illyricum aside, lasting military solutions to invasion and usurpation had to be found in Gaul or the Western Empire would cease to exist. There was no alternative source of revenue. The frontier provinces were in economic collapse and their small garrisons, moreover, still needed support. Athaulf faced hunger, supplies safe behind locked gates, but few Roman troops. Britain, which had opened the fourth century with unparalleled prosperity, now charted its own course, cut loose sometime in 409.[15] Britain had given birth to Constantine III's rebellion and now Honorius had no choice but to acknowledge that Britain was outside his jurisdiction, for Constantine controlled the island and much of what lay between it and Ravenna. Honorius's letter, if it had any effect at all, could have only encouraged British independence against the usurper and anyone else until the central government was able to restore itself beyond the Alps. Following such instructions would have carried even greater risks than it in fact already did had not Constantine stripped the island of its effective military manpower. The units of the *comitatenses* had gone with him to Gaul, leaving only a policing force along the coast and the northern frontier. The interior was without any significant military presence. To explain Honorius's letter we must assume that somehow somebody in Britain had requested direction from Ravenna, perhaps asking when Britain might expect the return of imperial troops. Perhaps some towns had already revolted against the military government left behind by Constantine. That would explain why the imperial reply was addressed to the *civitates*. Whatever lay behind Honorius's letter to Britain, Constantius had to concentrate his efforts in Gaul. He did not abandon Britain, nor did the British revolt against him, at least not in the extant historical records.[16] Constantius through Honorius's letter just told them to do what they could without him for awhile. During 411 the torn threads of Roman military policy based on economic and human resources were patched together in Gaul and, to a lesser extent, Spain. Let us catch up on events.

Southern Gaul and Spain, 409–18

From 407 on Roman authorities in the West confronted a two-headed monster: barbarian invasion and usurpation—the Vandals and their allies, on the one hand, and Constantine III, on the other. The death of Constantine in 411[17] did not change the script, only the cast. Undefeated Goths moved northward into Gaul, Vandals of questionable status occupied Spain, and a new usurper replaced Constantine. This was Jovinus, who assumed the purple in Germania Secunda in 411 with the support of barbarian auxiliaries, particularly some Alans and Burgundians led by Goar and Guntarius respectively.[18] Rome had no choice but to deal with these crises serially and within the military constraints imposed by the creeping anarchy. One approach worked well. Let Constantine deal with the Vandals and their allies.

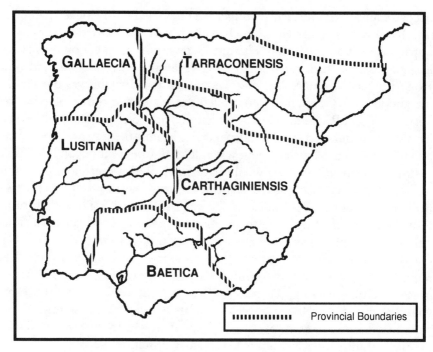

GALLAECIA   TARRACONENSIS

LUSITANIA

CARTHAGINIENSIS

BAETICA

▮▮▮▮▮▮▮▮▮▮▮▮   Provincial Boundaries

Map 10 Provinces of Late Roman Iberia

Ravenna's first priority had to be Constantine himself, for his usurpation threatened the imperial dynasty. There was no way that Honorius could have given direct assistance to local efforts to stem the Vandalic incursion into Aquitaine anyway, since Constantine's presence at Arles blocked any relief force coming from Italy to its rescue.

In chapter 7 we took leave of Constantine III shortly after he had arrived at Arles in 408 with his sons, renamed Constans and Julian. The Vandals had suffered through a terrible winter and punishing skirmishes with the Roman-Frankish forces along the Rhine. Whatever Honorius's government thought about Constantine's usurpation, there was no denying his military success. By moving from the Channel to Trier, to Lyon, to Arles, Constantine interposed his armies between the Rhine and the Vandals pushing southwestward into Aquitaine. He thereby cut off their retreat and blocked any further invaders from joining forces with them. Meanwhile some of Honorius's relatives in Spain raised a private army, technically illegal but not hard to do from the estates of the very rich with their close ties to the local

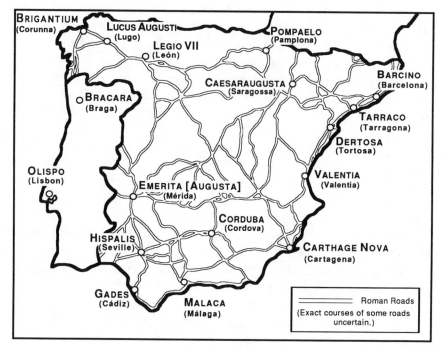

Map 11 Late Roman Iberia

officer corps. With this modest force they set about checking the advance of the Vandals through the passes to Spain (see maps 10 and 11).

They were successful in blocking the Vandals, Sueves, and Alans from crossing the Pyrenees, but their victories were short-lived. Their success was a challenge to Constantine, for they still adhered to the government in Ravenna. Constantine elevated his son Constans to a share of the purple and dispatched him along with his *magister militum (peditum?)* Gerontius to deal with Honorius's supporters in Spain. Despite their use of the few regular troops stationed in Lusitania and finally some slaves and coloni, the forces loyal to Honorius were easily overpowered somewhere near the passes of the Pyrenees. Constans left Gerontius and much of the army to guard Spain. The regular Roman troops stationed in Spain, except for those from Lusitania, had remained on the sidelines in the struggle against Constans. Gerontius nonetheless did not trust them and refused their offer to guard the passes for him, an offer they doubtless made hoping to ingratiate themselves with the most recent victors.

Constans took Honorius's cousins Verenianus and Didymus, the ring-leaders of the opposition, as captives to Arles. There Constantine ordered their execution.[19] The Vandals and their fellow raiders were still in Aquitaine, becoming more dangerous as they ran out of easy provisionment. In the process of coming to terms with these barbarians, Gerontius concluded some sort of peace with them. Shortly afterward he rose in revolt against Constans and Constantine, who had appointed him to his command. Brazenly, he appointed the head of his own household staff, the *domesticus* Maximus, as emperor.[20] These are perhaps the only incontrovertible facts surrounding these chaotic events.[21] These sparse but intriguing bits of information hint at a greater significance for Gerontius's actions. Perhaps there is a coherent link between these events that can reveal something more about the acceptance of barbarians upon Roman soil.

My hypothesis is that Gerontius's peace was the "settlement" recorded by the chroniclers that established the Asding Vandals and Sueves in northwest Spain and thereby induced them to stop their plundering. Earlier Gerontius, charged with the defense of the Pyrenees by Constans, had replaced Honorius's supporters and whatever remained of their defensive deployments in the passes with "the *Honoriaci*" and other troops he and Constans had brought from Gaul. The new Roman forces could not hold the passes. The *Honoriaci* reportedly turned instead to plunder.[22] A reasonable possibility is that the *Honoriaci* in Orosius were, in fact, a Taifalian cavalry unit of the Gallic army called "Honoriani" (like many new formations created under Honorius[23]) and that this unit was reassigned back to Gaul shortly after 418. That was the date of Orosius and the year that may also have witnessed the restoration of regular Roman troops in Spain. Since the Roman troops available to him were unable to accomplish their mission—to stop the Vandals from moving southward into Spain—Gerontius himself had failed, and with him Constans. Constans returned to his father at Arles.

The Vandals and their allies crossed into Spain in 409 without resistance.[24] Constantine, angered by this new threat to recently conquered Spain, ordered Constans to return there. Constans was to replace Gerontius, whom Constantine now regarded as ineffectual, with a certain Justus. Gerontius, rather than accepting his disgrace, rebelled and quickly came to terms with the barbarians. A further hypothesis is that Gerontius concluded his agreement with the barbarians in order to replace or supplement the Roman troops in the north and to help pacify the other provinces still resisting Constans's original assumption of power in Spain. This would have allowed him to remove substantial portions of the modest regular Roman garrison in Spain to serve alongside the Gallic forces still under his command. He could thereby create an army sufficient to challenge Constans and Constantine. This "civil war" within *the* civil war ended at Arles in 411, first with the desertion of Gerontius's army to Constantius and then with the capture of Constantine. Gerontius fled to Spain only to die at his own hand rather than submit to a mutiny of the few soldiers who until then had remained loyal to him.[25] Gerontius's candidate to the purple, Maximus, found refuge with some of the barbarian troops, whom Gerontius had left behind to hold Spain. Maximus escaped his executioners until 418.[26]

The theory that Gerontius used the Vandals and their allies to free troops for his campaigns in Gaul is even more compelling if we accept some of the reconstructions and interpretations of an *epistula* (ca. 416–18) of Honorius. Here the emperor clarifies some technical issues of military pay and reminds his soldiers to thank those who had provided them with billets.[27] Dating this document to at least May 416, when Honorius made his last visit to Rome,[28] or (rejecting the first four lines as a sixth-century addition) to the general return of peace in 418[29] suggests the following sequence of earlier events. The usurper Gerontius concluded an agreement with the Vandals whereby they replaced the traditional Roman garrisons in order that Gerontius might have an army to field against Constantine. These forces were unsuccessful, going over to Constantius, the legitimate authority for those garrison units from Spain, without struggle. The victorious Constantius, rather than trying to expel the Vandals from their positions in Spain, positions not necessarily poorly and disloyally held, decided to leave well enough alone and return to Italy. He would temporarily accept the status of the Vandals and their allies in Hispania, just as he had accepted a temporary solution in Britain. After all he needed as many troops as possible to stabilize Italy. He thus would not have been in Arles when Athaulf passed through in 412, having already returned to Ravenna.[30] Once Roman control was reestablished in Spain, probably as a result of Gothic campaigns against the Vandals and the settlement of the Goths in Aquitaine (416–18), Constantius shifted Roman garrison units from temporary to permanent billets. The *epistula*, to which we shall return for further analysis of the events of 416–18, was composed in the context of these repeated dislocations and addressed issues of concern to all Roman soldiers affected by them.

Roman recruitment problems had become even more acute since the death of Stilicho, many of whose barbarian auxiliaries had gone over to Alaric sooner or later.[31] In a sense, the only way to reenlist the services of Stilicho's former troops was to shift Athaulf's force, which now included them, into some sort of Roman service. In whatever manner Ravenna tried to manipulate Athaulf's force it would have to entail extending to it access to Roman supplies. Efforts in that regard bore immediate fruit when in 413 Athaulf attacked and crushed the usurper Jovinus in Gaul. His victorious army was basically the same as that Constantius was to send against the deceased Gerontius's barbarian troops in Spain in 416 under Athaulf's successor. Some of Jovinus's Alanic supporters may have gone over to Athaulf at this time, but they stayed with him only for a few months.[32]

The use of Athaulf in 413 is also interesting in its own right. Athaulf's first thought upon entering Gaul in 412 had been to join forces with Jovinus, but he and Jovinus soon had a falling out, perhaps over the relative status of the various barbarians in camp. Athaulf then decided to see what the other side had to offer, and found Constantius more forthcoming. Perhaps because of Constantius's eagerness to recruit Athaulf, Alaric's kin and successor, Alaric's old foe Sarus determined to cast his fate with Jovinus. Unfortunately for Sarus, his path brought him first into contact with Athaulf's entire force on its way to engage Jovinus and his brother and co-emperor Sebastianus. Sarus and a few retainers were captured after a struggle. Athaulf later had Sarus executed, but may have recruited the others, perhaps including even Sarus's brother. Olympiodorus gives us a figure of precisely 10,000 for the army of Athaulf and 18 to 20 men for the number of Sarus's retainers. He goes on to attribute such a lopsided confrontation to Athaulf's conscious decision to send such a large force against his old opponent, apparently just to be sure that old scores were settled. Olympiodorus's interpretation is but another example of the insertion of colorful personal tidbits by the ancient historians even when unnecessary.[33]

Athaulf first defeated, captured, and later beheaded Sebastianus. He then commenced a siege against Jovinus, whom he took alive. Then at Narbo, Claudius Dardanus, praetorian prefect of Gaul since its restoration, ordered Jovinus's death—another Roman usurper brought to justice.[34] Scrupulous attention was paid to legal propriety. Athaulf had acted completely within the law, handing Jovinus over to Dardanus for execution. The heads of Sebastianus and Jovinus arrived in Ravenna on 30 August, perhaps after a tour that included Carthage and Rome, and were displayed as reminders of the price of rebellion. Constantius, never known for his *clementia*, was the teacher in this gruesome classroom.[35] The Romans recruited Jovinus's Burgundians to guard a section of the Rhine, thus allowing them to remain inside the Empire.

Sending the usurpers' heads on tour apparently backfired, at least in Carthage. There Heraclianus, the slayer of Stilicho and since then *comes Africae*, rose in revolt in 413, shortly after Honorius had announced him as consul elect.[36] Perhaps even before this Heraclianus had feared that his career too would end on a pike, for Constantius must have been a favorite of Stilicho to have advanced so far in the army.[37] In fact, one probable reason that Constantius had decided to remain in Italy in 413 and instead employ Athaulf against Jovinus was the continuing dilemma of what to do about Heraclianus and the African grain shipments. Heraclianus set sail with a small force to Italy, but met with defeat and fled back to Africa, only to be murdered upon his arrival.[38] His assassin was probably Marinus, *comes rei militaris* and perhaps the intended replacement for Heraclianus as *comes Africae*.[39] Marinus's purge of Heraclianus's supporters, however, cut too deeply into the aristocracy and Honorius recalled and dismissed him from service. The fact that Heraclianus thought that he had a chance of success in invading Italy is proof of the pitiful state of Roman defenses there.

Athaulf had proven his worth in combat against Constantius's foes, but he still had no regular command, perhaps because Galla Placidia and Attalus were still in his camp. Whatever Constantius's reason for not making Athaulf a regular Roman general, he did not hesitate to employ him as a seasonal ally.[40] Under this arrangement Athaulf drew supplies for each campaign or for its anticipated duration, not to exceed one year—the standard fiscal unit for the calculation of requisitions. Each year the authorizations had to be renegotiated and renewed. From his victory over Jovinus until his death in 415, Athaulf fought both for and against Rome, but most notably for Rome against the Vandals left behind in Spain by Gerontius. When fighting for Rome his primary condition of service was Roman subsidies, and his overwhelming desire was to secure legal recognition of his possession of a Roman command that would carry with it the right to regular requisitions and maintenance for his followers. When Honorius could not or did not provide the necessary supplies promised Athaulf,[41] the latter rebelled.

The traditions concerning Athaulf's career between his defeat of Jovinus and his death in Spain in 415 are confused. To the Gothic historian Jordanes he "liberated Gaul and Spain" and "grieved for the people in Spain" from the moment of his entry into Gaul, that is from 412.[42] He was, of course, always *rex Gothorum* for Jordanes. What is certain is that late in 413 Athaulf suffered wounds in battle at Marseilles,[43] took Toulouse and Bordeaux but failed to take Bazas, whence one of our sources, the aristocrat Paulinus Pellaeus, had fled the barbarians. More important, he failed to round up the gangs of slaves then looting the countryside.[44] Thanks to Paulinus, the situation around Bazas was saved when he persuaded certain Alans to break from the Goths, enter Roman service, and defend the otherwise defenseless city.[45] Saint Augustine, writing in 417, penned a letter to Bonafatius, who had almost killed Athaulf at Marseilles. At this time Bonafatius was an officer serving against the Moors in North Africa, a *tribunus cum paucis foederatis*. That is to say, he was a junior officer, perhaps a *tribunus gentis*, commanding a few barbarian recruits. He went on to achieve great military renown, *comes Africae* and *magister utriusque militiae*.[46] In 413 Bonafatius must have been a very young soldier near the beginning of his career, but the point here is the use of the term *foederatis* by Augustine in 417. This small unit of barbarians was not on temporary assignment nor did its members constitute a large unified group. They were just barbarians recruited into the Roman army who had recently achieved some success on the frontier. Athaulf's followers had forsaken that status.

Athaulf withdrew his force to Narbo, where he married Galla Placidia in January 414. The wedding took place "with the advice and encouragement" of a Roman, Candidianus, in a grand and carefully choreographed ceremony. The bride, dressed in royal attire, was seated next to Athaulf, cloaked in the garb of a Roman general. Lavish gifts were presented to Galla: fifty attractive young men dressed in silk, two large platters filled with gold and precious jewels that had once belonged to the great families of Rome. Finally the "emperor" Attalus sang a wedding song composed by the poets Rusticius and Phoebadius, who themselves joined in. Evidently Attalus sang better than he schemed, for this was his last recorded act. All present, Roman and barbarian, joined together in celebration.[47]

Word of this wedding and a speech that Athaulf apparently made in his cups traveled far and fast. Jerome in Bethlehem heard it from a noble pilgrim from Narbo, who claimed to be a close friend of Athaulf. Orosius himself heard the story from Jerome while the former was also in Palestine. Athaulf's alleged speech is certainly the most discussed utterance ever made by a Goth:

> At first he ardently desired to blot out the Roman name and to make all the Roman territory a Gothic empire in fact as well as in name, so that, to use the popular expressions, *Gothia* should take place of *Romania*, and he, Athaulf, should become all that Caesar Augustus once had been. Having discovered from long experience that the Goths, because of their unbridled barbarism, were utterly incapable of obeying laws, and yet believing that the state ought not to be deprived of laws without which a state is not a state, he chose to seek for himself at least the glory of restoring and increasing the renown of the Roman name by the power of the Goths, wishing to be looked upon by posterity as the restorer of the Roman Empire, since he could not be its transformer. On this account he strove to refrain from war and to promote peace.[48]

Whatever significance this passage may have for the secret beliefs and longings of Athaulf and the Gothic and Roman nobilities assembled for the wedding, the circumstances must not be forgotten. Athaulf was desperate. He had to achieve an agreement, peace, for the Romans had placed Narbo under blockade. Athaulf could have expressed his fondest wish, a Roman command, much more succinctly. Attalus must have appointed Athaulf *magister utriusque militiae*, which uniform Athaulf wore for his own wedding. Indeed, there was no better reason for Athaulf to resurrect Attalus's emperorship than to legitimize his office. Athaulf expected that he would soon be, like Stilicho and Constantius before him, *parens* of the Augustus. He was not thinking about Honorius, but having his own son by Galla. He would be disappointed. Attalus's appointment of Athaulf to command carried with it nothing more than a uniform, a suit of clothes for a wedding.

Constantius forced Athaulf out of Narbo sometime in 415. This was largely due to his naval blockade, which cut off such quantities of supplies that the Goths had to quit Gaul entirely and were forced southward into Spain. Spain was still occupied, if not "defended," by the Vandals and their allies established there by Gerontius, who still had their own emperor, Maximus.[49] If Athaulf indeed entered Spain on Rome's behalf, as Orosius and Jordanes both would have us believe, then Constantius had brought him to heel at Narbo and concluded another campaign agreement with him. If so, it probably included the proviso that he must abandon Attalus.[50] Pregnant Galla remained with her husband. For Athaulf their child offered a final hope of forcing a recognition from Ravenna, since Honorius remained childless and needed an heir. Galla gave birth to Theodosius, but the child soon died.[51]

In June 416 Attalus, abandoned to his own fate by the Goths, was led in triumph through Rome. Constantius and Honorius looked on as he lost his hand, or at least two fingers of it, as punishment.[52] Whatever transpired between Constantius and Athaulf near Narbo in 415, the summer of that year found Athaulf in Barcelona, where his infant son was buried.[53] Leaving his baggage and the wounded with a small guard in Barcelona, he fought successfully against some Vandals. Apparently these were the Asding Vandals, later settled in Gallaecia, where Jordanes reports that Athaulf drove "the Vandals." While in Spain, one of his household retainers killed Athaulf with a sword thrust to the groin. Olympiodorus provides us one motive and assassin, Jordanes another. For Olympiodorus the assassin was a certain Dubius, who had formerly served with Sarus. Dubius had finally found an opportunity to avenge his former master in the stable where Athaulf was tending his horses.[54] Some scholars, relying upon the account in Olympiodorus, have developed a conspiracy theory surrounding Athaulf's fall and the subsequent struggle for succession. These scholars see in these events a reflection of basic divisions within Gothic society into pro-Roman and anti-Roman, that is to say "traditional," factions, perhaps even a split between the Gothic nobility and the lesser followers.[55] Conclusive evidence for the existence of internal Gothic factionalism between the elite and their followers is lacking. There are better explanations of those incidents when Goths came to blows with other Goths.[56]

Jordanes gives us a different version of Athaulf's death, saying only that the assassin, named Euervulf, was outraged at being constantly taunted for his short stature![57] Jordanes's version probably reflects Gothic oral history, though stripped of unwanted complications over the founding of the Visigothic royal house that ruled southern Gaul for the rest of the fifth century.[58] Although the factional or conspiratorial theories are overblown, there were violent personal animosities within Gothic society. Affronts to honor led to feuding and death. So too the bond of a retainer to his lord was potent. Rivalry was at the heart of these warrior societies, and Athaulf had failed to provide for his followers. Athaulf did not die immediately but lingered long enough to urge his brother to return Galla Placidia to the Romans and thereby ensure their friendship. By turning to his otherwise unknown brother at this moment, Athaulf revealed his hope that he would succeed him, but this was not to be. Singeric, Sarus's brother, seized power instead.[59] Until the end Athaulf remained committed to gaining Roman acceptance. Whatever agreement Constantius had had with Athaulf lapsed at his death or the end of the year.

Singeric unleashed terrible vengeance upon Athaulf's family. He ordered the execution of Athaulf's children by his first wife and commanded Galla Placidia to walk before his horse, sharing this disgrace with the rest of his prisoners. Galla Placidia owed her humiliation to her marriage, not to her Roman birth. Singeric's reign lasted but seven days before a certain Wallia overthrew him. Olympiodorus called Wallia a φύλαρχος, a leader of a group usually related by blood. As such, Wallia may have been superior in rank to a man like Sarus, who commanded only a small warband.[60] Ultimately only the Roman fleet prevented Wallia from taking ship with his followers and crossing to Africa. The Goths, once again without Roman supplies, either directly as payment or through their king because of a regular Roman command, turned to plundering Spain for provisions. They were on the edge of starvation and were blocked from returning to Gaul,[61] in part perhaps by the Alanic garrisons recently established nearby.[62] They were also hard pressed by the Vandals and other barbarian troops formerly established in Spain by Gerontius and still in place.[63] In early 416 Constantius and Wallia concluded an agreement to employ the Goths as Rome wished in exchange for the return of Galla Placidia to Honorius. The treaty of 416 with Wallia was mainly designed to bring about another seasonal redeployment of Roman troops within the context of Roman fiscal realities. Possibly more important, it also eliminated one of the remaining obstacles to a more permanent solution, namely Galla Placidia, who was handed over to Constantius.

The Goths received 600,000 *modii* of grain in order to supply them while on campaign. Following the return of Galla Placidia, Constantius sent Wallia and his followers, possibly as many as 15,000, against the Sueves and Asding Vandals. Perhaps Constantius strengthened Gothic forces with the addition of the regular Roman troops destined to stay in Spain and addressed in the *epistula*, for the same Goths who had had great difficulty just months before against the barbarian forces in Spain suddenly had no problem routing them. If so the figure 15,000, calculated from the amount of grain accorded to them, accurately reflects an increase over the force of 10,000 that Olympiodorus gives for Athaulf's command earlier.[64] Whatever the exact figure, assembling so much grain was very difficult. Roman supplies were dispersed throughout the provinces. Even though coastal transport would have eased the burden, it would have taken a real effort to collect and ship 600,000 *modii* of grain. The Roman command had only kept armies this large in the field during major crises and then for the shortest periods possible.

Rome must have simultaneously suspended its support of the Silings and those Alans allied to them. Roman subsidies apparently continued for the Asdings and Sueves, who this time did not come to the aid of their former allies. Just months before, the Asdings, Silings, Sueves, and Alans had together informed Honorius's government that their campaigns against the Goths were going well, and told the government to expect Gothic peace overtures soon. It was apparently the report of troops loyal, in their own eyes at least, to the emperor.[65] Now it would appear that the Romans had successfully divided barbarian forces in Spain for reconquest. The support that these barbarians had given Gerontius had not been forgotten. Maximus was still at large somewhere under their protection. That they had crossed the Rhine and plundered Roman territory was a matter routinely overlooked for recruitment's sake once the invaders were brought to submission. Constantius allowed the Goths to annihilate the Silings, but only to cripple the Asdings and Sueves before recalling the Goths to Gaul. Constantius must have intended to enlist the remaining Asdings and Sueves, now properly humbled, into Roman service. Wallia died before leaving Spain.[66] Perhaps it was no coincidence that sometime in 418 Maximus, the sole surviving usurper in the West, also died somewhere in Spain.

The troops mentioned in Honorius's *epistula* correspond loosely with those listed in the notorious *Notitia dignitatum*,[67] which contains some units doubtless no longer stationed in Spain and for these entries is most probably a later document (ca. 425) than the *epistula* (ca. 416–18).[68] Whereas the *Notitia* reflects bureaucratic accretion and carelessness and is rent with chronological complexity, the troubled text of the *epistula* is vague but chronologically narrow. Accordingly, the *epistula* cannot support any detailed reconstructions except for the period 416–18 and the events surrounding the reintegration and pacification of Spain and southern Gaul after Constantius's reconquests. At this time Constantius must have reestablished some degree of regular Roman military presence. Doubtless it was more than a paper army, but, like the one in Raetia, a very modest one. The sparse and incomplete archaeological data only hint at the continued presence of *limitanei* in a few areas.[69] This force cannot have numbered more than a few thousand, and perhaps significantly less.[70] It was nevertheless now seen as an extension of the Gallic army and hence assured comparable pay.[71] The Goths had dislodged and defeated the Siling Vandals and Alans sufficiently for them to be replaced by regular forces, perhaps those which had just fought alongside the Goths under unknown command.[72] The reestablishment of regular forces in northwestern Spain required also the renegotiation of the agreement with the Goths, and probably the placing of the Goths and Roman garrisons in near proximity. This would have been risky in many ways and certainly would have placed a great strain on the local communities. By returning Roman troops to such key areas as Pamplona, where the manuscript of the *epistula* was discovered, the passes could be secured. Almost as helpful, the Sueves and Goths could be kept isolated from each other with their hatreds simmering for Rome's use.

The Goths returning to Gaul under Wallia's successor, Theodoric I (418–51), would hardly have found the opulence that so excited the wrath of Salvian, the bishop of Marseilles and an important source for contemporary interpretation.[73] There can be little doubt that the Vandalic raids and Gothic sieges had raised havoc in Aquitanica II. The cities from Toulouse to the Atlantic at Bordeaux had had virtually no regular Roman units, and like Bazas were essentially defenseless. The small naval garrison near Bordeaux might have been useful in Constantius's naval blockade but could not have assisted much in the defense of the towns. These populations had suffered accordingly despite the possible efforts of a few great landlords and bishops.[74] Refugees were showing up in Italy and even in the Holy Land. Moreover, to this point the Goths had not been offered anything other than annual supplies. One point must be forcefully stressed. Aquitanica II had no previous Roman troops, and the share of its taxes directed toward the military went to support troops nearer the Gallic frontier on the Rhine.

A major condition that had changed between the death of Theodosius in 395 and the settlement of 418 was the level of unity among the Goths and their allies. This made a traditional frontier solution based upon recruitment and dispersal impossible. Alaric had established the foundations of Gothic kingship anew over a disparate soldiery. Athaulf had had no choice but to continue to base his rule upon kingship, but it was still in the formative stages as late as 418. Roman recruitment and training practices continued in the early fifth century and ran counter to the enhancement of Gothic kingship. Those Goths following Alaric and Athaulf in Italy, Gaul, and Spain, however, had rediscovered an identity. Honorius had given them no choice. The settlement of 418 allowed this identity to evolve along with other new identities that were emerging during the transformation of the Christian-Roman world. Like those Romans searching for alternatives to total reliance upon the Empire, the Goths, Franks, and other barbarian groups had to find historic justifications for their existence.[75]

The Mechanisms of Settlement in Transition

In 418, the Roman aristocracy in Aquitanica II surely had no right to complain about the establishment of the Goths in their province, regardless of the mechanisms used to establish them.[76] For Constantius the main issue was the resolution of various military problems in Gaul. There were very good reasons to enlarge the Roman military presence there, above all to finally assure some local defense of this region. Since the losses suffered against the Vandals and Constantine III, Gaul had had virtually no reserve forces to rush to threatened areas of the frontier. The Frankish *laeti* and auxiliaries had lost heavily fighting the Vandals in 407. The Gallic reserve forces had fared no better. Heightened civil unrest may have been an additional motive for establishing a military presence. Bacaudae and the continuing flow of refugees southward required additional security forces.[77] The unsettled conditions in the countryside had after all forced Paulinus Pelleus and others to abandon their estates. Many slaves had run away. Seaborne raids also may have been increasing.[78] Constantius also needed to break out of the logistical bind of providing annual grain subsidies to the

Goths. But surely the most pressing need was to station support troops nearby in a cost-effective manner in order to assist Rome, if needed, against the still undefeated Asding Vandals. This is precisely what the Goths did in 422.

Aquitaine's tax base must have been in shambles. Whatever mechanisms were used to install the Goths, the Roman government could not significantly alter the flow of tax revenues to the highly militarized provinces nearer to the frontier, where most of the remaining Roman army was still stationed. The traditional assumption that these units had for all practical circumstances ceased to exist, except on paper, cannot be allowed to stand unchallenged. They were small and composed of Germanic recruits and other Germanized local populations, but they were Roman nonetheless.[79] By this time Rome had lowered some of its costs by employing newly recruited barbarians, making land a standard incentive for service, and even granting some sections of the frontier to barbarian auxiliaries. The barbarian auxiliaries in particular may have served along the frontiers primarily in return for readily available land and Roman military benefits, perhaps including those conferred upon retirement.[80] Most would do so without a second thought in Aquitaine, if given the chance.

The sources for the settlement of 418 unfortunately do not immediately support or reject any theory about the meaning of its terms. There are two current explanations of how this settlement was supposed to have worked: the traditional and quite complex understanding of *hospitalitas* as in some way a direct sharing of lands and/or their revenues, or the recent suggestion that stresses the direct reassignment of local tax revenues.[81] Most of the evidence and, therefore, the debate concerns events after 418. The latter theory's greatest strength is its beguiling simplicity of application. If existing units were drawing upon local resources through the tax cycle, the simple redirection of paper credit would have provided a ready solution. The barbarian holder of credit would be able to collect at the source. The taxpayer would welcome not having to transport the product to the state. Nobody loses; everybody wins. Indeed, there would have been no technical problems to be solved. The "guest," living elsewhere, would be told where and to whom to present himself for drawing his ration. The state is the only loser, since it can no longer freely dispose of a high percentage of its local revenues. But, the theory claims, the state would have not lost much either, since this revenue would have gone to support the army anyway.

There are several difficulties with the new theory. The most trying technically is its requirement that we read all texts concerning the settlement as if written in the vocabulary of tax law, not that this vocabulary itself is beyond dispute, although a simple translation as "land" seems better. A major conceptual problem is its assumption that Rome would have voluntarily assumed the incredible commitment of fiscal resources that it would have permanently entailed, since the grant involved something very specific (rations) rather than the land itself with all the uncertainty that went with its cultivation. In other words, the new theory suggests that the Romans freely redirected the most valuable commodity they had, food, rather than land, much of which was almost certainly unusable to its owners. The Roman government would have locked itself into supplies without regard to market conditions. The barbarians are all housed in the cities and are completely supplied with provisions. By such a decision, if made in 418, Rome would have also had to decrease very significantly its commitment to the northern frontier defenses which some of the tax resources of the interior provinces still maintained. If barbarian soldiers could have tapped the tax system at its source, this would have been an administrative revolution that would have generated the type of explicit imperial legislation which is lacking. Taxpayers would have dreaded the sight of armed soldiers arriving at their farms and presenting credit receipts (documents the barbarians could not have read). Abuse of military prerogatives was an age-old problem, and much specialized legal attention had been paid it. The direct collection of taxes by barbarian soldiers would have led to a torrent of claims and arguments. Disputes over barbarian settlements were rare, and for the Gothic settlement in Aquitaine nonexistent.

The logic of looking for the least painful and most efficient mechanism has compelled a very careful reexamination of the texts and circumstances supporting the traditional land-based explanations. The proponents of the tax-based thesis believe that no Roman landowner worth his salt would have shared land unless looking at the point of a sword. This assumption is unwarranted. A much stronger case has been created for land division than ever before.[82] I find the supporters of tradition convincing and will try to suggest how their findings may relate to 418. Between 418 and the last barbarian settlements in the second half of the sixth century, there were evolutions in procedure and practice. Exploring the mechanisms for barbarian settlements after 418 would require another book rather than a section of the final chapter of this one, and shall not be attempted here. In 417–18 Constantius had two systems in place, but neither of them could accommodate the settlement in Aquitaine that he had in mind. From these two mechanisms would come the procedure for settling barbarians in the Empire's interior.

One manner of providing for troops addressed the problem of what to do with troops moving about the primarily civilian parts of the Empire. Honorius and Stilicho outlined this procedure in a series of laws issued which culminated in 398 in *Codex Theodosianus* 7.8.5. This much-discussed piece of legislation guaranteed to the quartered soldier the use of a third of the house in which he was billeted. The owner got to choose the first third and took the last third as well. Workshops were excluded unless the soldier had no other place to stable his horse. If the soldier was a senior officer of Illustrious rank (for example, a *comes*) then he was guaranteed the use of half of the house. These were onerous procedures. Similar ones contributed to the American colonists' decision to declare their independence and throw out their king.

There would have been no need to demand such quartering among civilians in Rome's frontier provinces, for there were very few civilians near the frontiers by 400. The frontier provinces were highly militarized and soldiers could take advantage of the numerous military installations along their routes. Those civilians living in the frontier provinces were dependent upon the camps for selling their surpluses and buying otherwise unobtainable commodities. The sight of soldiers milling about was routine. Honorius's concern was how to handle the rapidly expanding need to move troops around the civilian provinces in the interior such as Aquitaine and those in Italy. Whenever the Romans were moving troops from one theater to another his legislation provided the legal justification for the army to billet its men upon the civilians temporarily.

A second plan provided for long-term garrisoning but was based upon conditions near the frontiers where the army was still concentrated. There land was plentiful and virtually all ordinary soldiers and their families needed a plot. The interior space of most fortifications was very restricted. Every soldier, barbarian or not, recruited into the imperial armies would have expected land if assigned duty defending the frontiers. Land granted to the soldiers produced supplements to regular rations, provided perishable items, and lowered the transportation costs being borne by the state. The Romans also offered barbarian recruits land because they knew that this was a strong inducement for them to serve Rome faithfully. The policy had a long and impressive record of success.

Limitanei were virtually unmovable, and as the emperor Julian learned many units of the *comitatenses* were none too eager to pack their gear either. Elite units such as the imperial guard received higher pay and status. Quartered near the emperor, they had no need for land and little opportunity to exploit it. Probably this was also the case with the palatine armies, the top of the line fighting units closely attached to the emperor himself. In 376

Gratian had been able to dispatch some units of his palantine army very quickly to the aid of his colleague. Yet even the palatine troops were not all billeted all the time in the capital cities of the Empire. Most of Gaïnas's army had been billeted outside Constantinople and so had survived the massacre in 400. Except for the imperial guard, very few troops were regularly garrisoned in Constantinople. Soldiers could have profited from land even when they themselves never plowed a furrow. Others could do the labor. The Goths confronting Constantius were not candidates for the imperial guard or, for that matter, the palatine army. They were barbarian auxiliaries; or at best, as individuals they might be enlisted for units of the *limitanei* or *comitatenses*. There is no point in denying that along the frontiers the recruitment and establishment of barbarians included the actual occupation and cultivation of the soil. The Goths expected Rome to offer land.

Land once given, regardless of the complexity of the giving, was administratively finite. In the frontier provinces it was certainly cost-effective and probably was in Aquitaine under the current circumstances. The army depended upon land to support its soldiers. Taxing, despite providing for the army, was a civilian matter. The government preferred cash and, for large sums, bullion. Coins collected, particularly gold, were quickly melded down into ingots for convenience. When Stilicho posted Alaric to Epirus, he assigned Jovius as his praetorian prefect to collect taxes and supply his army. Except in the provinces directly along the frontier, where a *dux* headed all aspects of government, late Roman emperors since the days of Constantine the Great had kept the military and the civilian spheres distinct. Honorius's quartering legislation was designed to provide imperial approval and direction to their cooperation in a very restricted setting, but one with great potential for adaptation. The emperor stood alone at the apex of both the military and civilian administration. While failing to convince, the proponents of the tax-based theory of barbarian settlement engendered a fruitful discussion of the way the Roman army did business. The army did not collect civilian taxes. Tax collecting fell entirely under the praetorian prefects and beneath them the vicars and governors. If taxpayers needed encouragement, *compulsores* were specialists in coercion. This division of financial affairs remained unchanged into the sixth century.[83]

Constantius apparently took the principles of *hospitalitas*—until then restricted to temporary quartering—and applied them to the division of lands in Aquitaine. Shares of estates for quartering became shares of lands divided.[84] Thereby he got around the problem of dividing up civilian property without recourse to new and potentially slow-in-coming imperial legislation. Constantius did not pause to reflect upon his action. Had he not moved swiftly the alternatives for barbarians and taxpayers alike were grim. Given the choice of a permanent houseguest or a new neighbor carving up a farm out of one's un- or underutilized land, no one would hesitate to chose the latter. Aquitaine now had a strong military presence for the first time. Let us examine the texts for 418 more closely.

The legislation that provided the distribution arrangement for the *hospitalitas* system (*CTh*. 7.8.5) provided for troops in transit and can be seen in operation in the *epistula*, which strongly urges appropriate thanks to be given to the host when departing.[85] It was not obsolete so long as Rome moved troops from place to place in the interior of the Empire. The *epistula* also provides a refutation of the theory of tax-credit quartering. Why require adieux for the mere redirection of taxes? Between 398 and 411 all the so-called settlement acts of the emperors had to do with the establishment of *laeti* (as in 399), or clarifying the status of land granted previously to defenders of the frontier (as in 409), or the establishment of captured Sciri in various areas as active farmers or slaves.[86] Only with the establishment of the Vandals in 409–11 is there a possible application of these procedures to the settlement of barbarians.

The case of the "establishment" of barbarians in Spain as reported by Hydatius is the first instance in which the language of our sources hint at some sort of settlement procedure relating to barbarians after the enactment of the quartering legislation of 398. Hydatius reports that the Vandals and their allies, having arrived in a Spain weakened by pestilence and war and now looking to establish peace, "divided up the regions of the provinces among themselves and drew lots to determine who would live where."[87] The date here is crucial: the year was 411. By 411 they had been in Spain for two years but had not yet carved independent spheres from the Iberian provinces. In 411 their supporter Gerontius died outside Arles; the agreements he had made with them were null and void. Without a Roman general providing for them the Vandals and their allies had no right to provisions and so took what they wanted. Later they tried to justify their seizures through an alliance with Constantius against the Goths. The settlement of the Vandals was not a settlement at all; it was confiscation and so is irrelevant to the discussion of settlement procedures. We are left in the dark as to what Gerontius had arranged for them originally. It was not parts of provinces for their own use, or they would not have waited for him to die to move to their new homes. Quite likely he had billeted them on the local populations near the passes which they were to guard. He put off making any permanent decisions until he had secured his rebellion in battle. This he failed to do.

The passage in Hydatius then narrates the lands taken by the Asding Vandals—Gallaecia, the Sueves—lands in the extreme west. The Alans took as their share (*sortiuntur*) Lusitania and Carthaginiensis, and the Siling Vandals seized Baetica. Gallaecia was already in great turmoil before the Vandals established themselves there. So too must have been Lusitania, which had provided loyalist troops against Constantine and Constans, ultimately including farmers and slaves.[88] That the Goths later were recalled before engaging the Asding Vandals confirms that the Asdings were not in the same area as the Silings. In fact, the Asdings were doubtless still in Gallaecia, the province whose lot they had drawn and from which they may have emerged to attack Athaulf not far from Barcelona. He drove them back. Only later did the Asdings move southward into Baetica, old Siling territory, perhaps as a response to the reestablishment of Roman forces in the north. Roman forces under Castinus, employing Gothic auxiliaries, attacked them in Baetica in 422.[89] The Silings and Alans were in place for only a very brief time before they were virtually annihilated. Regular troops returned to Spain by Honorius reclaimed the areas they had previously dominated. The Asdings ultimately crossed to north Africa. The Sueves alone remained, but in the most remote area of the peninsula. The settlement of the Goths in 418, not that of the Vandals, offers the first opportunity to explore settlement procedures and Roman use of auxiliary service more fully.

For the year 413 Prosper of Tiro reports that the Burgundians *partem Galliae propinquam Rheno optinuerunt* (took control of a part of Gaul along the Rhine). This was a case of frontier-type settlement not involving the billeting of troops upon existing or former Roman estates and, although not directly relevant to the discussion of *hospitalitas*, is instructive nonetheless.[90] Concerning their *receptio* on the Rhine in 413, Prosper never mentions the only known Burgundian leader, Guntarius, who died fighting alongside Aetius against the Huns in 436. That Prosper knew of no Burgundian leader for the events of 413 is in keeping with the practice of *receptio*, in which the recruits often served under new leaders. Recall here tribune Bonafatius, Saint Augustine's correspondent, and his barbarians fighting the Moors in North Africa. The Burgundians along the Rhine are not mentioned in the *Notitia dignitatum*, although it was updated while they were there defending the frontier. This may be another example, like the barbarian auxiliaries guarding the upper Danube near Regensburg, of the *Notitia* deliberately omitting this new category of soldiers.

Frigeridus, a contemporary to these events, quoted by Gregory of Tours, recalls the roles played by Goar and Respendial, leaders of the Alans. What we know of them, although only marginally helpful for understanding the mechanisms of settlement, surely throws light upon the continuing success of Roman recruitment efforts. Goar first entered into Roman service as early as 406, when he and his followers split off from the Vandals and the main body of Alans under Respendial, early in the struggles of that terrible winter.[91] Obviously a survivor, Goar must have found service with Constantine. After Constantine's surrender, Goar helped raise Jovinus to the purple, and, after the defeat of Jovinus, he probably served with Constantius in some capacity. Later he fought alongside Aetius. In 440 Aetius settled some Alans on deserted lands near Valence. Two years later, almost thirty years after the defeat of Jovinus, Aetius settled "king" Goar and some of his Alans near Orleans in Armorica, ordering the current owners to share their lands. Other Alans had been in Roman service since 413, when they broke out of their alliance with the Goths at Bazas.[92] For the Alans Rome appropriated whatever types of lands were available, vacant as well as underutilized but occupied land.

Later fifth-century evidence is more compelling that settlements were based upon some sort of landed transaction, not less. There are two reasons for this. For example, in 446 it appears that Aetius urged some of Rome's newly recruited Hunnic auxiliaries to force the Burgundians, originally established upon Roman soil through *receptio* back in 413, from their homes along the Rhine. Aetius resettled these Burgundians in 443 in Savoy under quite favorable terms. They took possession of the soil from Roman landowners.[93]

Still later in the century, the Ostrogoths took possession of lands in Italy. In every case in which land was at issue, the nature of the soil—its arability, its water and timber—had to figure in. Characteristics of the units of production and of the slaves working them also mattered a great deal. There was probably considerable revenue-sharing from productive estates. Barbarian societies were never egalitarian. Barbarian nobles received preferred treatment regardless of the procedures employed. By midcentury the Roman aristocracy, at least legally, was expected to carry the burden of redistributing the land and some estate owners took legal action to redress wrongs done.[94] Each case of settlement was a unique event to which the Roman government had to respond as best it could given its means and the desires of all parties concerned.

Most of the basic texts of the settlement in 418 are extremely ambiguous and defy detailed analysis in terms of the theories of settlement procedures. Prosper reports that Constantius concluded a peace with Wallia giving him places to inhabit in Aquitanica II and neighboring provinces.[95] Hydatius relates that the Goths were recalled from Spain by Constantius and took up settlement in Aquitaine between Toulouse and the ocean.[96] Philostorgius writing in Greek is more explicit in terms of what the Goths received by their treaty with Honorius. Philostorgius states that as a condition for the surrender of Attalus and Galla Placidia, the Goths concluded a treaty "having received a supply of grain and having been allotted a part of the land of the Gauls for farming."[97] But which treaty is Philostorgius discussing? Galla Placidia was returned as a condition of the treaty of 416 and Attalus was abandoned to the Romans earlier, although his fall was celebrated in Constantinople in June 416.[98]

Philostorgius must have conflated the events of 416 and 418 into one incident—the return of Roman hostages and Gothic supporters, on the one hand, and the establishment of the Goths in Gaul, on the other. A. H. M. Jones, while accepting Philostorgius, apparently did not see the conflation of two agreements, probably originally in Olympiodorus, and suggested that this was a one-time-only grant of *annonae* to see the Goths through to the next harvest.[99] If, however, Philostorgius is correct, the Goths under Wallia asked for and received precisely the same grant that Theodosius had accorded the followers of Athanaric in 381, when settled along the *limes*, that is, *annonae* and land.[100] In the agreement of 416 the Goths had received only supplies. The source there was Olympiodorus, who would hardly have overlooked a land-based settlement. Unless we simply and incorrectly reject, as some have done,[101] the entire testimony of Philostorgius, there can be little doubt that the Goths as military colonists received both grain and lands for farming in a section of Gaul. There is some uncertainty in the Latin sources. They are not absolutely clear as to what the Goths did with the land. According to them, the Goths may have received land to live upon or from (*inhabitandum*). As a result these sources can also be read to support a tax-credit arrangement. In short, the Latin sources remain ambiguous.

The language of Philostorgius, however, is definitive. The purpose of the grant of land was for farming (γεωργίαν) and, just as Roman frontier soldiers would have, they were also to receive supplies (*annonae*, or σιτήσεσί). In this case, grain supplies were a one-time grant. In the future they could feed themselves. Nonagricultural items of Roman supply may have continued, which would help account for the remarkable disappearance of these settlers archaeologically. The lands were simply "a part of the land of the Gauls," probably by then *agri deserti* but still owned. With this clarification, "land" is also a better reading of the Latin sources, including later references in the Code of Euric to keeping to the early "boundaries."[102]

If regarded as deserted and in need of improvement, and surely Roman authorities would have granted this, then the Roman land tax would have been suspended legally for several years, depending on the land's condition, for anyone bringing it into production. Special provisions also existed for foreign soldiers serving Rome and for veterans. *Agri deserti* was an official category of land in need of reclamation.[103] Routine procedures existed to access and survey such "deserted properties" within existing estates in order to determine which lands were subject to which specific tax obligations. In the late fourth century the shift of population southward and the retreat from villa-type agriculture left other lands "deserted" in the eyes of the government. Squatters did not pay taxes and would have faced real difficulties when a new and active landholder moved in. These conditions were ubiquitous to a greater or lesser degree throughout the Western Empire. In other words, the government had abundant fiscal reasons to see that lands were exploited legally. Property owners had their own reasons to support the settlement of 418. Some, like Paulinus now absentees anyway, could shed the duty of having such properties periodically reassessed and simultaneously gain new local defense, now needed more than ever. With the urging of the army and the government, specifically Constantius, accommodations were made. Laborers had fled. Many Roman landowners, even if not possessing officially deserted parcels, needed to concentrate their remaining workers. For the barbarians, finding land was not difficult. Some barbarian auxiliaries had slaves, not just those who had recently deserted their Roman masters to fight at their sides. Slaves could till the fields.[104] Particularly if the barbarian newcomers paid taxes, as seems likely, there was reason for Romans to turn the other cheek to whatever insult they may have felt over having "barbarians" as neighbors.[105]

Although the sources are spare with details, the permanence of the division of land in 418 is clear enough.[106] The settlement was a success and became a model for generations of barbarian kings and imperial administrators. It was a departure from the temporary billeting arrangements set forth in imperial legislation. It belies theories of unchanging settlement practices as Rome moved away from concern with billeting soldiers on the move to securing hitherto unprotected interior regions of the empire. As usual the Romans saw no need to legislate anew. Instead, they merely transformed the existing legal precedents for maintaining troops. These barbarians were now "Roman soldiers" as far as Constantius was concerned. Since Constantius felt no need for new enabling legislation, there was none. This flexibility had long characterized Rome's approach to employing barbarians in the army as well as settling them upon Roman soil. In a modern army the "needs of the army"—a caveat known to every soldier—always take precedence, and Rome's large army required many types of service from its recruits. Many scholars have indulged in minute legal technicalities of *hospitalitas* to explain fifth-century settlement policy, as if the wording of fourth century laws truly reflected fifth-century practice. Perhaps we should look at our own legal proceeding, for example *habeas corpus*, to remind ourselves of how far organic societies can move within legal traditions without changing traditional formulae.

The frontier-based arrangement, which I believe was employed in a more structured way in Aquitaine, would have more easily facilitated the establishment of farmer-soldiers, which some of the Goths clearly were in the Balkans and which some of those with Wallia were again ready to become.[107] On the other hand, many of Wallia's followers had not held a plow for over a decade, and for them farming was clearly no longer their calling. Those who could not adapt turned up in Roman armies or as bands of raiders within a few years. For all but the poorest farmers and tenants, slaves did the heavy work. Knowledge of the land and its crop-potential was available. Farmers and those who owned land usually had something to eat at times when others did not.

There is still no way to be positive of the interpretation of all the texts relevant to the general problem of barbarian settlements spanning centuries. Yet, if the text of Philostorgius is accepted and compared to other texts relating to the establishment of barbarians along the frontiers, a plausible overall view emerges. The essence of the settlement in 418 appears to have been merely the transfer to an interior province, Aquitanica II, of the frontier program used for many generations to garrison and maintain the fortifications and agricultural systems along the *limes*. The laws concerning quartering provided mutual protection and direction for all the participants in the transaction—there would be no confiscations. The Latin texts do not contradict this conclusion. The Romans still dictated the terms and demonstrated considerable flexibility in the application of what looks outwardly like two simple principles for maintaining troops: one involved a short-term billeting procedure and the other the use of land on an extended basis.

In 418, for the first time, Rome had a "regular" force in a central area and did not have to divert revenues away from other priorities. In the Goths Rome had a standing military force sustained by local resources and available for a wide variety of missions. The Goths in Aquitaine almost certainly did not pay taxes on their holdings immediately, for the laws of reclamation alone would have provided a lengthy exemption. Perhaps they never paid taxes on those original grants. But, if so, why then toward the end of the century did Euric (466–84) bother to legislate the removal of their tax obligation? Other than those settled upon vacant land, the barbarians may not have received any exemption at all. Wallia's force would have had to have been much more robust than the one portrayed above to have expected and demanded preferred treatment. Paying their taxes under the terms of the laws applying to foreign soldiers and veterans should not have offended the new settlers in Aquitaine. To be sure, however, local Roman authorities would have had difficulty forcing the issue. But they had a powerful ally who stood to profit himself, the *rex Gothorum*. The restoration of the tax base by returning land to cultivation would help explain the success of the Gothic kingdom in southwestern Gaul. If, when their period of exemption for improvements had lapsed, these Goths paid too, it would help further explain the success of the Gothic government.[108] By the reign of Theodoric II (453–66), Romans paid a tax to the Visigothic court, but this was 30 years after the settlement.[109] People could travel freely in and out of Gothic territory and at least the archaeological data suggest that there was no measurable economic decline or distortion of trade patterns resulting from the settlement—perhaps even some improvement.[110] There are some indications that many Goths, particularly the nobility, quickly assimilated with their Roman peers.[111] Contemporary accounts like that of Paulinus Pelleus make it clear that some rich barbarians, in Paulinus's case one of the Goths in Aquitaine, once established immediately sought to invest in land through purchase as well, probably to round out their shares from the settlement. Other than such hints at conditions, knowledge of specific aspects of the years just after 418 is very limited.

After 418

The evidence for their use of the Goths in the years immediately after 418 tends to support the thesis that the Roman command regarded them as frontier troops available for specific duties in small units. The Roman *magister militum* Castinus supplemented his army in 422 with Gothic auxiliaries *(et auxiliis Gothorum)* in his campaign against the Asding Vandals in Baetica.[112] There is no mention of the Gothic king Theodoric I as participating in any way in Castinus's battles. Eight years later, Aetius destroyed a body of Goths and captured their leader, the optimate Anaolsus. Again Theodoric was not mentioned.[113] Castinus's Gothic auxiliaries in his war with the Vandals must surely have come from the Goths in southern Gaul. The case of Anaolsus's band reveals that the settlement had not altered the positions of the Gothic nobility at the head of their followers. The relationship between the Roman command and the Goths after 422 slowly began to disintegrate. Aetius was always on guard to limit Gothic independence and block their attempts to coordinate action with other barbarians in the area.[114] The use of the Goths by Castinus and the obvious independent action of Anaolsus, both clearly without a "royal" presence, suggest that the Romans were still able to recruit auxiliaries from among the Goths settled in Aquitaine. They probably did so by negotiating directly with the Gothic nobility. In 433 some Goths were again serving as auxiliaries.[115] Under Aetius in particular Rome expanded its use of barbarian auxiliary units but without the ability to enforce purpose and discipline.

The growth of Gothic power demanded a further evolution of the settlement procedures as Rome lost the initiative. In fact, the peace of 439, if not merely an annual renewal of an earlier agreement (none is mentioned in any source), may have come to grips with the reality of twenty years of permanent occupation for the first time.[116] These arrangements were troublesome, but Rome could no longer do without them. By ca. 440 the Goths had consolidated their control of the original settlement areas and had apparently expanded as well. By then the Roman authorities faced very stern challenges elsewhere, for example the Huns in Pannonia and Aetius's need for troops, that were not present in 418. There were no legions to spare for Spain.

As early as 439, Theodoric I used *legati* and expanded his territory at his own volition while technically honoring the commitments to Rome. He continued in this mode until his death in 451, while fighting alongside Aetius against the Huns on the Catalaunian Fields.[117] Litorius's ill-fated campaign against the Goths in 439 ended with his capture and death. The resulting treaty must have reflected the new realities of power manifest everywhere under Theodoric I, and made it more difficult for Rome to utilize Goths for regional operations or to recruit them piecemeal into whatever regular units remained. The Roman control of events, still clear in 418 and for a short time thereafter, had slipped. After 439 the Goths operated much more like a Roman field army in their own right, fighting under a central command. The redistribution of taxes to the frontier areas, increasingly irrelevant, had probably become impossible. Nonetheless, even up to the death of Theodoric I the Goths cooperated as dependable, if troublesome, allies. They did so with increasing royal involvement, confirming the importance of the settlement in the evolution of Germanic kingship.

Unlike the situation in areas such as Armorica, where civil strife led to a total breakdown of government and law, the establishment of the Goths in 418 did not lead to collapse. Rather it seems to have led to a modest recovery. Curiously, Honorius also decided to encourage provincial assemblies in 418. For some time Romans from all areas attended Gallic assemblies as if there had been no change.[118] Orthodox ecclesiastics likewise went about their business much as usual at least until midcentury, after which they seem to have kept to Gaul without traveling to Italy and beyond. Initially some, like Paulinus, were refugees and never returned.[119] However, Paulinus makes it clear that, to his surprise, the Goths had maintained the rule of law—Roman law—including that governing the sale of land. Little by little, more swiftly with the reign of Euric, Gothic modifications and overt direction replaced the regular functioning of Roman institutions. These were evolutions brought about by complex developments having to do with the attenuation of Roman power and the rise of the Franks to challenge the Goths for the control of southern Gaul. In 418 no one held a crystal ball revealing the decades to come. Romans continued to predicate policies upon tradition and their view of contemporary realities.

As Roman military power declined we might expect that the realities of settlement changed to favor the barbarians. Indeed, we can perhaps see this with the Burgundians, who were established in Savoy in 443 by dividing up the lands and inhabitants in a settlement apparently similar to that of the Goths in Aquitaine. By 456–57 the Burgundians, this time in alliance with the Goths, were truly a dominant force in southern Gaul and could demand senatorial property.[120] In this case there is no question that frontier policies that rested on vacant lands had been superseded. The legislation of 398 had been interpreted to implement the regular and permanent maintenance of barbarian forces by drawing upon the lands of the local elites.

The Goths were thus the Roman military presence in southwestern Gaul from 418, maintained initially through the standard mechanisms of the frontier system. When Aetius was hard pressed to stop Attila in 451, the Goths proved their worth. From their base in Aquitaine they expanded their power. They constituted part of still another new type of auxiliary force. The Visigoths preserved a great deal of Roman administrative procedure.[121] They were now a large and fairly unified group living under their own king and legally accepted within the Empire. Let me stress: Wallia and Theodoric were accepted as *kings within the Roman Empire*. They held no traditional Roman military command; they were not Roman generals as Alaric had been from time to time and as Athaulf had always aspired to be. Constantius had acknowledged their right to perpetual sustenance within Aquitaine as kings, not military commanders.

Since Wallia died so soon, Theodoric I was really the first of a new breed of *reges Gothorum*. Theodoric's problem was no longer Roman supplies but civil administration. He had to define the Goths, his rule over them, and—a new thing under the sun—his rule over the Romans in Aquitaine. Moreover, like other new barbarian *auxilia* recruited earlier, Theodoric's Goths were ignored in the *Notitia dignitatum*. Under certain monitored conditions the Romans believed that they could trust all these forces just as much as regular units, themselves decidedly "barbarian" in the sense of Germanic. The Roman command had removed the problem of pay for its forces stationed in Aquitaine, but probably not while they participated in a Roman campaign outside of it. For Rome 418 was a very good year. The settlement of 418 was a stage, temporarily successful, in the evolution of Roman policy concerning the barbarians. It manifested continued military flexibility and had relatively little effect upon the civilian community.

Such barbarian establishments as that of Wallia's followers in Aquitaine became equated with "federates," *foederati*. This was not the only or even the common meaning of the term in the years surrounding the settlement of the Visigoths, witness *Codex Theodosianus* 7.13.6, published in 406, Augustine, writing in 417, and Olympiodorus, ca. 425. The term clearly antedates their settlement. Federates were any barbarian group or individual serving in barbarian auxiliary units recruited through *receptio* at the end of the fourth century and early fifth. After 418 and particularly after the settlement of the Burgundians in 443, federates in the West became typically those barbarians settled with permanent claims upon the land in the interior provinces and legally governed by their own kings. Before 418 the Roman command had experimented for at least four decades with using barbarian recruits in many ways: as individuals and small groups recruited directly into existing army units, as special units of barbarian cavalry within the army (the Vesi of the *Notitia dignitatum*, for example), as auxiliary units taking charge of sections of the frontier (those near Regensburg or the Burgundians on the Rhine), either under native or Roman command. As auxiliaries they were not like the regular units of *limitanei* and *comitatenses*, who remained distinct with their own peculiar privileges and status.[122] They were not *laeti* like the Franks in the north. But they were Roman soldiers.

Finally Constantius, when he had few other choices, accepted the risk of deploying *auxilia* on a large scale in Aquitaine. He did so as cheaply and efficiently as possible. There would have been complex issues to confront even if he had been able to establish units of the *comitatenses* there. Constantius was a decisive leader and chose settlement over war. Any confrontation was almost certainly doomed to end without a victor. Hydatius, writing ca. 470 of events before 439, refers to the Goths as *auxilia* or as units or a body of soldiers (*manus*), a pattern reflected and in some cases amplified in Isidore of Seville's (ca. 625) partly derivative *Historia Gothorum*. Hydatius first used the term *foederatos* in the context of a struggle in 449 in Tarazona in which Bacaudi killed these federate troops.[123] For Hydatius the early fifth century Goths were essentially soldiers, often fighting alongside the Romans. The archaeological record suggests that these two populations had become virtually indistinguishable.[124] The term *foederati* was equally well known in the East at this time but was evolving in a peculiar direction.[125]

Kingship now came to be accepted as a regular feature of many barbarian groups admitted to the Empire, a regular office with a regular recompense. In this way, Wallia succeeded where Alaric and Athaulf had failed, in part because they had clung to their creature, the emperor Attalus, and shared with him his usurpation. Beginning with Wallia the Gothic king was not only their native leader but a *magister* without the title, an all-purpose officer whose rule Rome recognized over barbarians and eventually over Romans as well. The regular Roman provincial government continued for many decades.[126] Praetorian prefects for the Gauls held office throughout the fifth century. Romans adapted politically and psychologically to barbarian dominance.[127]

These barbarian kings resided permanently inside the Empire. As the other types of auxiliaries in the Western armies disappeared with the collapse of the regular army and the frontier system, federates like those in Aquitaine alone remained as examples. Not all problems had been magically solved by the settlement in Aquitaine. Roman civilians had many difficulties living in proximity to any soldiers, not just *auxilia*. The old order was cracking. The Goths were just one of many groups searching for a new identity in the fifth century, and their solution was the Gothic Kingdom. The later Visigothic laws may address some of them living in villages like so many Romans.[128] The Goths had much in common with the other searchers, most especially their long experience with Roman civilization, particularly the Roman army of which they may still have felt themselves a part. Nonetheless, for the first time since the Huns had destroyed Athanaric's kingdom, the Goths had a true king. They could now become a new people.

Summary

In 410 Constantius rose to power in Ravenna and began the restoration of order to the Western Empire. His most serious challenger remained Constantine III, now weakened by rebellion within his camp. In 411 Constantius crushed all of Constantine's forces near Arles. Almost immediately Jovinus usurped the throne with the backing of auxiliaries on the Rhine. In Italy Athaulf and his followers were in a bind. They had little to eat and no way to assure that this circumstance would change. Roman towns barred their gates and watched as he turned the countryside upside down. Athaulf quit Italy for Gaul in 412. His arrival there allowed Constantius to offer him a mission in return for provisions—attack Jovinus. This began a series of annual missions and grants of supplies, punctuated by brief flurries of siege warfare and blockade in which neither could best the other.

Nobody much liked the continued uncertainty, but so long as Athaulf kept Attalus and Galla Placidia there would be no solution. Athaulf declared Attalus emperor again, but apparently only to preside over his wedding to Galla. Their son and potential heir to the Western Empire died in infancy. Athaulf cast Attalus aside in return for a new deal that pitted his force against the Vandals in Spain. Athaulf died in Barcelona in 415. After a short interval Wallia succeeded him as *rex Gothorum* and returned Galla Placidia. Now the conditions were right for a permanent solution to many problems. Constantius settled Wallia's people—the Goths—in Aquitaine. By so doing he found a way to reestablish security there, defend against the Asding Vandals in Spain, and obtain the reserve force that Gaul had lacked since 407. The Goths received a permanent home and Roman acceptance of their king. There was for the first time a barbarian people under their own government inside the Roman Empire.

CONCLUSION

THIS STUDY HAS maintained that Roman might and Roman policy toward the Germanic barbarians remained effective for at least four decades after the Battle of Adrianople, although it was gradually modified. When Valentinian I (364–75) took his place on the imperial throne, the Roman army already had enrolled numerous soldiers recruited from the barbarians. They were serving at all levels in the army, including the officer corps. The disastrous Roman defeat outside Adrianople in 378 quickened the pace of experimentation with barbarian recruits. But until the civil wars, particularly that against Eugenius and Arbogastes, Roman commanders preferred to use barbarians within the traditional categories of service—placing them in units of *limitanei, comitatenses,* and so on. There were a great many traditional options available. The imperial guard and some specialized units were composed primarily of barbarian recruits. Frontier troops needed, expected, and received land near their posts. Military supplies gave them access to products from distant areas at reduced costs. There were many intangible benefits in being a soldier or veteran as well. By the death of Theodosius in 395, both East and West had created and employed units of barbarian auxiliaries commanded by Roman officers. Such units were constituted without apparent regard for the origins, ethnic or otherwise, of their soldiers.

The major innovation of the era was to organize so-called federate peoples operating inside the Empire into more independent commands under their own native leaders. The use of barbarians was primarily an extension of the traditional *receptio* program by which barbarians were welcomed or "received" into imperial service. Whatever ethnic self-consciousness existed prior to being "received" did not easily survive the recruitment efforts of the Roman army. The barbarian groups that supplied such recruits are conventionally called "tribes," now mainly for lack of agreement or a better term. ("Bands," a more ambiguous term, might better reflect the inchoate reality.) The groups that first entered the Empire during the period under discussion were not structurally the same as those whose names are associated with the barbarian successor states established in France, Spain, and elsewhere. Around 400 the Roman army still did not recruit and deploy barbarians by "tribes" or any other ethnic grouping, although "tribal" names were often associated with certain small groups serving in the Roman army. This changed after the settlement of the Goths in Aquitaine in 418 as Rome employed the same solution to other areas.

Rome settled barbarians under their own kings upon Roman soil because imperial leaders believed that this would solve more problems than it would create. There were no untapped sources of manpower to be had inside or beyond the frontiers. The Huns controlled much of the far bank of the Danube, and settlements along the Rhine had suffered greatly during the first quarter of the fifth century. The nature of the enemies of the state was changing—fewer invasions and more brigands. As land became the only means of compensating soldiers, they sank their roots ever more deeply into the soil. For that reason, the settlement of barbarian farmer-soldiers within the Empire, once begun, was nearly impossible to reverse. Constantius probably knew this better than we. The frontier provinces had demonstrated these truths over and over again. He accepted it, and moved ahead.

In the Latin sources the barbarians serving in the Roman army in units were usually called auxiliaries (*auxilia*). Some were *dediticii*, technically people who had surrendered to Rome and pledged their personal loyalty to the emperor. Many others volunteered to serve without coercion. Everyone entering the Roman army made a personal compact with imperial authority, which could also be called a *foedus*. But that in itself did not destine them for any particular lifestyle—farmer or soldier or both—and certainly did not allow them to retain their prior political bonds. That Roman policy changed at all was because those in authority changed it, not because someone else "forced" them to. Sometimes changes were so gradual as to escape notice by contemporaries. What decreased rapidly after 418 was the range of options available to the Roman command.

In many respects the use of those who became late Roman auxiliaries parallels much earlier establishments of *laeti* (barbarian farmer-soldiers accountable to Roman officers) upon Roman soil under Constantine the Great (307–37). Some of his predecessors had done the same on a smaller scale, and there were earlier auxiliary units under the Principate. This is not to say there were no significant differences between the early fifth century usage of barbarian troops and the usually restricted functions of the *laeti* who continued to exist, for there were. The *laeti* were only one branch on a complex evolutionary tree. Roman policy toward the barbarians included them but went beyond them as well. The employment of barbarians in the Roman army as of 418 was the result of a long and rich Roman-barbarian relationship, within which *laeti* were a single aspect. Rome recruited bar-barians into all types of military service. Their use in auxiliary units was only one manner of deployment in the late Roman army, one that gradually became more and more common in the era of Theodosius the Great and grew rapidly under his successors.

The new type of auxiliary unit grew out of the increasingly com-mon practice of placing barbarian recruits under Roman officers, who were themselves often of Germanic-barbarian background. Such composite units reflected the mingling of military elites within the officer corps and the diverse backgrounds of the masses serving in the Roman army. Another important factor was economic decline, which imposed ever tighter re-straints on the pay and benefits of soldiers. Still another was the profound difficulty of finding recruits. Finally, the Romans, who were traditionally sensitive to having barbarians serving in the army under the command of leaders from their own groups (something done nonetheless with specialized units at least as early as the third century), bowed to the unwelcome realities of their day. Reluctantly but inexorably they began to permit barbarians in Roman service to live and soldier under their own leaders. Even if a bar-barian unit's leader happened to be one of its own, he led and supplied it through the Roman system. Rome did not support barbarians drawing upon non-Roman customs or brute force to inflict their wishes upon the Roman provincials. Such actions were illegal, the deeds of an outlaw or renegade. Roman authority, conveyed in Roman military rank, sanctioned and made possible the exercise of military command among all units within the Empire. These considerations produced a new military system based in part upon utilizing barbarian troops, those "received" into the Empire for service in the army.

Because Alaric and Athaulf were unable to gain recognition of their commands inside the Empire, the decade 408 to 418 witnessed the forced birth of a new Gothic self-awareness as they and their followers were re-peatedly forced back upon their own resources and traditions. Alaric was too deeply associated with Stilicho ever to be accepted by Honorius. Rome manipulated Athaulf and his men for its own purposes but, because of Ro-man political concerns, refused to make him a Roman general. Roman strength kept the Goths at bay; Roman weakness allowed them to remain together. From this limbo state arose a new Gothic identity that was more newly created than remembered.

Prior to 418 the Roman army had accepted a pattern of command, even for large units of auxiliaries, that made use of the available leaders and manpower regardless of backgrounds. Leading examples of non-Roman leaders were Athanaric, Alaric, and Gaïnas, all Goths. But these commanders were dealt with as members of the traditional Roman command system. Gaïnas had risen through the ranks without incident, but Alaric had not. Athanaric died in Constantinople and Roman plans for him can be glimpsed only in the deployment of his men afterward. The career of the Frank Arbogastes is entirely comparable. The Roman careers of many lesser men followed the same path, if not as far. Those under them, with the possible exception of those under Athanaric before his death, did not constitute a united force of barbarian peoples except as integrated by the Roman system itself. They had marginal ethnic cohesion, and what did exist was important only when Roman support was withdrawn. In part at least this transformation in the recruitment and leadership policies was facilitated by the fact that the principal source of recruits under Theodosius was those Goths "received" in the Balkans. The Goths' primary enemies, the Huns, were also enemies of Rome. Most Huns remained beyond the Danube. Some Gothic recruits also served far away, in Raetia for example. For those who did serve in the Balkans, defending Rome's Danubian frontier was rather natural, regardless of who led them. Along the Rhine and upper Danube events took a less dramatic but parallel course.

The settlement of 418 was the culmination of this process of military development and a step beyond it. Rome now embraced native leaders—kings, not Roman appointees—as commanders of "army-size" units in legally specified territories within the Empire. These units were allowed to develop their own political leadership, which provided for them without recourse to the Roman command system, and usually without drawing upon the Roman supply network. In the case of the "Visigoths" their territory was within the province, or the two provinces, of Aquitaine. (This was actually a smaller command sphere than that sought by Alaric or gained by Gaïnas, both of whom had held legally recognized Roman commands over much larger territories.) Probably the most important aspect of the settlement of 418 was, however, nonmilitary.

By establishing the Goths in Aquitaine under their own king, the Roman authorities for the first time recognized and supported "kingship" within the Empire. King Wallia (415–18) never held a Roman command, nor did his successor Theodoric I (418–51). They were kings of those Goths under them, *rex Gothorum*. They were now acknowledged and supported by Roman authority as the rulers, both civilian and military, over their peoples. From this base Theodoric and Euric solidified their rule to levels undreamed of by Athanaric and Fritigern. After 395 in the West the *magistri* decided important matters, and the settlement of 418 was one. As long as Roman generals possessed forces to balance the barbarian auxiliaries, they called the tune. Stilicho, Constantius, and finally Aetius did so. After Aetius's death in 454 primarily barbarian kings commanded armies. In the East the reign of Theodosius II was much more balanced between military and civilian leadership. The barbarian settlements in the West provided a degree of military coherency ultimately unrivaled by anything emanating from Ravenna. While the West drifted into the era of barbarian kingdoms and warlords, the East held to the course set by Constantine the Great.

There was no clear crisis or event which marked a decisive change in military policy during these years. Economic and recruitment factors combined to limit Rome's choices in this regard and to force broader and more flexible deployments of barbarians between 378 and 418. If one concept can characterize Roman policy during this era, it was flexibility within the limits of fiscal reality and earned trust. Rome's barbarian soldiers were products of its own frontiers. It knew them well.

EMPERORS AND PRINCIPAL USURPERS, 284–455

Diocletianus, 284–305: Marcus Aurelius Valerius Diocletianus

Maximianus Herculius, 286–305 (306–7, together with his son Maxentius): Marcus Aurelius Valerius Maximianus

Constantius I Chlorus (Caesar from 293), 305–6: Caius Flavius Valerius Constantius

Galerius Maximianus (Caesar from 293), 305–11: Caius Galerius Valerius Maximianus

Severus (Caesar from 305), 306–7: Flavius Valerius Severus

Maximinus II Daia (Caesar from 305), 310–13: Valerius Maximinus

Maxentius (son of Maximianus Herculius, usurper in Italy), 306–12 (Augustus from 307): Marcus Aurelius Valerius Maxentius

Constantinus I (son of Constantius I Chlorus, Caesar from 306), 307–37: Flavius Valerius Constantinus

Licinius I, 308–24: Valerius Licinianus Licinius

Crispus (son of Constantinus I, only Caesar), 317–26: Flavius Julius Crispus

Constantinus II (son of Constantinus I, Caesar from 317), 337–40: Flavius Claudius Constantinus

Constans (son of Constantinus I, Caesar from 333), 337–50: Flavius Julius Constans

Constantius II (son of Constantinus I, Caesar from 324), 337–61: Flavius Julius Constantius

Magnentius (usurper in the West), 350–53: Flavius Magnus Magnentius

Vetranio (usurper in Illyricum), March–December 350

Julianus II (Caesar under Constantius II from 355), 360–63: Flavius Claudius Julianus

Jovianus, 363–64: Flavius Jovianus

Valentinianus I, 364–75: Flavius Valentinianus

Valens, 364–78 (brother of Valentinianus I): Flavius Valens

Gratianus (son of Valentinianus I), 367–83: Flavius Gratianus

Valentinianus II (son of Valentinianus I), 375–92: Flavius Valentinianus Junior

Maximus (usurper in the West), 383–88: Magnus Maximus

Flavius Victor (son of Maximus, usurper in the West), 384–88

Eugenius (usurper in the West), 392–94: Flavius Eugenius

Theodosius I, 379–95: Flavius Theodosius

Honorius (son of Theodosius I, emperor of the West, 393), 395–423: Flavius Honorius

Constantinus III (usurper in Gaul), 407–11: Flavius Claudius Constantinus

Constans II (son of Constantinus III, usurper in Gaul, Caesar 408–9), 409/10–11
Maximus (usurper in Spain), 409–11
Arcadius (son of Theodosius I, emperor of the East, 383), 395–408: Flavius Arcadius
Theodosius II (son of Arcadius, emperor of the East, 402), 408–50
Constantius III (co-emperor in the West), 421: Flavius Constantius
Valentinianus III (son of Constantius, emperor of the West), 425–55

CHRONOLOGICAL OUTLINE

364   Valentinian I becomes emperor (26 February) and names his brother Valens (28 March) co-emperor.

365   Procopius usurps the throne in Constantinople and moves against Valens.

366   Valentinian defeats some Alamanni in Gaul. Valens executes Procopius.

367–69   Valens conducts war against the Goths beyond the Danube.

367   Valentinian elevates his elder son, Gratian, to share the purple. Peoples beyond Hadrian's Wall invade Britannia.

368–69   The Roman *comes* Theodosius, father of the future emperor, reestablishes Roman control in Britain. Valentinian is active on the Rhine against the Alamanni. Valens forces Gothic king Athanaric to accept peace. Late in 369, Valentinian promotes Theodosius to *magister equitum* and orders him back to the continent.

370   Theodosius commands against the Alamanni in Raetia.

371–72   Valentinian formally receives some defeated Alamanni into the Empire but cannot bring about a total victory. Late in 372, Theodosius, probably accompanied by his son, engages some Sarmatians in battle along the Danube. Firmus, son of Nubel, king of Mauretania, leads a rebellion because of Roman exactions (372–73).

373   *Comes* Traianus and Vadomarius, formerly an Alamannic king, campaign with some success against the Persians. Theodosius, son of the *magister*, is *dux Moesiae Primae*.

373–75   *Magister* Theodosius suppresses Firmus's rebellion. Firmus commits suicide. Theodosius falls from favor and is executed (375 or 376) at Carthage. His son Theodosius retires to Spain.

375   Valentinian dies at Brigetio (17 November) while addressing some Quadic ambassadors just as he is about to launch a major campaign against them. Five days later the army raises his younger son, Valentinian II, to the purple at Aquincum (Budapest), but the eldest son, Gratian, takes over the government of the West as senior colleague until his brother comes of age.

376   Goths and fragments of other groups of barbarians cross the Danube seeking refuge from the Huns. The paramount Gothic king, Athanaric, remains behind to continue the struggle.

377   A major battle takes place near Salices in which a large group of Goths nearly destroy a Roman army.

378   Alamanni invade Raetia early in the year and occupy Gratian, delaying his march eastward to join his uncle Valens against the Goths in Thrace. The Goths celebrate a great victory over the Romans near Adrianople (9 August), killing Valens and thousands of Roman soldiers. Gratian recalls Theodosius from his self-imposed exile in Spain to take command against some barbarians as *magister equitum.*

379   Gratian raises Theodosius to the purple at Sirmium (19 January) and transfers to him the prefecture of Illyricum (the dioceses of Pannonia, Dacia, and Macedonia) as well as all the Eastern Empire which had been under Valens since 364. Theodosius takes over command of the entire Balkan theater of operations, while Gratian turns west to confront the invasions on the Rhine and upper Danube.

380   Gratian sends aid to assist Theodosius against barbarians in Pannonia and Dacia. Both emperors celebrate victories. Gratian and Theodosius meet late in the year at Sirmium. The diocese of Pannonia is again a Western diocese, but Dacia and Macedonia remain under Theodosius.

381   Efforts continue against remaining pockets of Gothic resistance, supported when necessary by Western troops.

382   Theodosius's generals subdue one of the last major areas in Thrace still under barbarian control and accept the resisters into imperial service. Gratian resumes control of the rest of Illyricum.

383   Theodosius raises his first-born son, Arcadius, to share the imperial throne (19 January). In the West, Magnus Maximus revolts against Gratian, who is killed on 25 August. Stilicho as *tribunus praetorianus militaris* probably accompanies a Roman embassy to the Persians. Theodosius takes back Illyricum for the East.

384   In an act of accommodation, Theodosius begins to create an independent imperial sphere for Valentinian II comprised of Italy, Africa, and Illyricum. Theodosius allows Magnus to retain the remainder of the Western dioceses. Stilicho marries Theodosius's niece, Serena, and is promoted to *comes domesticorum*. A Persian embassy arrives in Constantinople.

385   A year marked by routine imperial business. Saint Augustine delivers the formal speech in praise of the new consul, Bauto, in Milan.

386   *Magister militum* Promotus defeats some Greutungi led by Odotheus while they attempt to cross the Danube (probably in September). On 12 October Theodosius holds a victory celebration in Constantinople. Theodosius finalizes arrangements between Valentinian II and Magnus Maximus, whom he now formally recognizes.

387   Magnus Maximus invades Italy, forcing Justina and Valentinian II to flee to Thessalonica, where they meet with Theodosius in September. Theo-

dosius concludes a new peace with Persia in which Armenia is divided. This stabilizes his eastern frontiers.

388   Theodosius moves against Magnus Maximus. Their armies clash in Pannonia, but Magnus escapes to Aquileia, where he is executed in August. *Magister peditum* Arbogastes hunts down and eliminates Victor, son of Magnus, in Gaul and becomes the principal military figure in the West. Franks invade near Cologne. Valentinian II is now the Western emperor.

389   Arbogastes brings the Frankish invaders in Gaul to heel, accepting many into Roman service.

390   Theodosius orders the punishment of the citizens of Thessalonica for their murder of his *magister* Butherich. Many die. Ambrose, bishop of Milan, is outraged and excommunicates the emperor, who submits to public penance.

391   A few Goths, perhaps led by Alaric, ambush Theodosius while he returns to Constantinople, but he escapes.

392   Valentinian II dies, an apparent suicide. Illyricum is again shifted to Eastern administration—Dacia and Macedonia forever. Arbogastes raises Eugenius as a usurper to the Western throne on 22 August.

393   Theodosius elevates Honorius, his younger son, to the emperorship. Thereby Honorius joins his father and elder brother, Arcadius, at the head of the Empire.

394   Theodosius defeats Arbogastes and Eugenius in a two-day battle (5–6 September) along the Frigidus River in Pannonia.

395   Theodosius dies on 17 January in Milan, leaving Stilicho as guardian over his family. Rufinus takes power in Constantinople, thereby negating whatever guardianship Stilicho may have held over Arcadius. Stilicho invades Thessaly, but Rufinus orders Alaric there to counter him. The standoff forces Stilicho to withdraw. Gaïnas leads the remnants of the Eastern army back to Constantinople. The returning army topples Rufinus. Eutropius, the chief palace eunuch, seizes power over the Eastern court.

396   Stilicho goes to the German provinces to recruit more men. Stilicho invades Greece but again the Eastern government successfully deploys Alaric, by now probably *magister militum per Illyricum*, to counter him.

397   Alaric establishes his army temporarily in Epirus. If not before, he is now *magister militum per Illyricum*. Gildo, *comes et magister utriusque militiae per Africam* (386–98), revolts from the West, withholds grain from Rome, and places himself under Eastern command. Eutropius has Stilicho declared a public enemy. Eutropius takes personal command against some Huns invading across his eastern frontiers (397–98).

398   Mascezel, an African chief, brother of Gildo, and a former Roman commander, returns to Africa with an army provided him by Stilicho and defeats Gildo (July).

399   Eutropius holds the consulship and is made *patricius*. Stilicho refuses to recognize his consulship. Tribigild revolts in Asia Minor, and Gaïnas takes the field against him. Eutropius falls. Aurelianus takes over the civilian government as praetorian prefect with Gaïnas's support. Late in this year the East transfers the diocese of Pannonia to Western jurisdiction, where it remains for the rest of Roman history. Alaric is left unemployed.

400   On 12 July the citizens of Constantinople bar their gates and slaughter many of Gaïnas's Gothic soldiers trapped inside the city. Gaïnas flees, but Fravitta, *magister militum praesentalis* (?), destroys the rest of his army while it attempts to cross the Hellespont. Gaïnas flees and is killed (23 December).

401   The beginning of a period of reconciliation between East and West. The diocese of Pannonia is renamed Illyricum. Stilicho goes to Raetia to recruit troops. Alaric invades Italy in November.

402   Stilicho and Alaric fight two successive battles of limited military consequence (Pollentia in the spring and Verona in the summer), but Stilicho ends up recruiting Alaric by making him *comes rei militaris* in the recently restored and renamed diocese of Illyricum, to parts of which Alaric now returns.

403–404 Years of intense religious activity and court intrigue in the East. In 404 a civil insurrection breaks out in Spain, but otherwise there are no significant military crises. Clear indications of renewed friction between East and West.

405   Radagaisus invades Italy late in 405.

406   In August near Fiesole, Stilicho defeats Radagaisus with but few casualties on either side and accepts the survivors into Roman service. Stilicho orders Alaric to await him in Epirus for a combined march on Constantinople. On 31 December Vandals and others cross the Rhine in force.

407   The army in Britain raises Constantine III to the throne. Constantine takes most of his army to Gaul and engages the Vandals and their allies. Stilicho appoints Jovius as praetorian prefect of Illyricum and orders him to join Alaric in Epirus. Stilicho recalls Alaric and Jovius from Epirus. Alaric returns to Illyricum.

408   Arcadius dies on 1 May, and his son Theodosius II succeeds to the imperial throne. Stilicho falls in a palace revolution led by Olympius (22 August). Alaric invades Italy (October). Alaric conducts the first and only real siege of Rome. Constantine III orders his son and Caesar Constans to Spain

with Gerontius as his *magister militum* in order to put down a rebellion and prevent the Vandals from moving south.

409 Constantine summons Constans to Arles, probably elevates him to be his co-emperor, and sends him back to Spain with orders to replace Gerontius. Gerontius rebels against everyone, places Maximus on an imperial throne, and reaches an accord with the Vandals. Late in the year Alaric takes Rome a second time, proclaims Priscus Attalus emperor, and takes Honorius's half-sister, Galla Placidia, hostage.

410 Alaric deposes Attalus. On 24 August Alaric takes Rome and allows his men to sack most of the city for three days. By October Constantius III has taken charge of the imperial court in Ravenna; he probably is already *comes et magister utriusque militiae*, and as such Stilicho's successor. Alaric dies in southern Italy. Athaulf succeeds to the kingship of Alaric's followers.

411 Gerontius invades Gaul against his former masters Constantine III and Constans. Constantius defeats Constantine III, Constans II, and Gerontius at Arles. Troops at Muntzen in Germania Secunda with the support of some Germanic auxiliaries hail Jovinus as emperor.

412 Athaulf leads his followers into southern Gaul.

413 Athaulf's force defeats Jovinus and his brother and co-emperor Sebastianus. Heraclianus, *comes Africae*, revolts unsuccessfully but manages to cross to Italy with an army before being defeated (June).

414 Athaulf restores Attalus to the emperorship and marries Galla Placidia (January), his captive and the half-sister of Honorius. Their son, Theodosius, dies late in the year or early in the next.

415 Athaulf abandons his support of Priscus Attalus. Constantius III orders Athaulf to take his followers to Spain and fight some Vandals there on Rome's behalf. Athaulf dies in Barcelona.

416 Singeric succeeds Athaulf but holds the throne for only one week before he falls to Wallia. Galla Placidia returns to Rome. Wallia continues to fight Vandals for Rome in accordance with instructions from Constantius III.

417 Constantius III marries Galla Placidia in Ravenna (1 January).

418 Constantius establishes Wallia and his followers in Aquitaine. Wallia dies. Theodoric I (418–51) succeeds Wallia on the throne and concludes the settlement of the Goths in Aquitaine.

421 Constantius becomes co-emperor as Constantius III (8 February) but dies within the year (2 September).

423 Galla Placidia quarrels with her brother Honorius and flees with her son Valentinian to Constantinople. Honorius dies. Joannes, head of the palace

bureaucracy, seizes power in Ravenna. In Constantinople, Theodosius II supports the claims of Valentinian.

424   Theodosius makes Valentinian Caesar in Thessalonica on their way westward to assert his claim to the Western throne.

425   Valentinian deposes Joannes and ascends the imperial throne in Rome on 23 October as Valentinian III, a position from which he will reign but not rule for thirty years (425–55).

NOTES

Introduction

1. Those wishing to have modern American equivalents to the various senior ranks in the Roman army might think of a *comes* as the ancient equivalent of a major general, a divisional commander in today's American army. Above the *comes* came the various *magistri*, which in a way correspond to lieutenant generals, our corps commanders. By the death of Theodosius, the East had five permanent superior *magistri*, which were of equal rank, similar to today's full generals. In the West Theodosius's restructuring of the general officers did not take place, leaving the *magister peditum* as the supreme commander by virtue of his historical immanence. Those holding this position from Stilicho (395–408) onward typically carried the title of commander-in-chief for both branches of the army (infantry and cavalry), *magister utriusque militiae*, abbreviated *MVM*, a title that all five Eastern *magistri* also held and that clarified the tactical unity of their commands. If Eastern terminology is applied for parallelism, then the Western *magister peditum* is virtually the same as the Eastern *magister praesentalis I*, in status usually considered higher than his true equals. The United States has no equivalent rank, but came close to having one during WWII when President Roosevelt created a general of the army, or "five-star general," to have a rank equal to that of the British field marshall. Thinking in terms of modern generalships, however, cannot assist the reader in anything more than a superficial way, since the nature of warfare and troop deployment today is so vastly different.

2. There are a great many works devoted to Ammianus Marcellinus; most recently see J. Matthews 1989, 279–303, who correctly notes that sometimes the problem is that Ammianus knew so much about a specific episode he lost sight of the larger issues.

3. E. Gibbon (1776–88), 1897–1902, covers these events in chapters 26–27 (vol. 3, pp. 69–187, and includes the career of Theodosius); p. 112, "The event of the battle of Hadrianople, so fatal to Valens and to the empire. . . . " However, Gibbon's views on the Goths and Romans are still worth reading as he struggles with the rhetorical splendor and distortions of the sources. There is more than a glimmer of the essential dichotomy or historical contradiction in Gibbon's account that is absent from lesser followers until recently. Gibbon suggested but could not really prove that the Goths and Romans were in fact symbiotic antagonists.

4. Olympiodorus of Thebes, frag. 7: "the name *foederati* was given to a diverse and mixed body of men," trans. R. Blockley, p. 159. St. Augustine used the term while writing a letter to a military commander in Africa in 417, *Epistula* 220.7. The term again occurs in the *Codex Iustinianus*, 12.38.19 (henceforth abbreviated *CJ*); *Novellae*, 117.11, by which time in the East it clearly meant a soldier in a special detachment or a mercenary recruited for a specific campaign. By the end of the sixth century these recruits in the East were reorganized into a single command with different goals in deployment and recruitment. See further on the Eastern evolution J. Haldon 1984, 100–

18. The question that concerns us here is the contemporary meaning in the West during the reign of Honorius.

5. For example, B. Isaac 1990, particularly pp. 372–418.

6. The publication of J. Matthews's (1989) work on Ammianus has engendered a lively discussion. The issue of Ammianus's place of birth (traditionally thought to be Antioch), his method of composition (one continuous narrative or two, one through bk. 26 and then a later addition), the date or dates of composition (usually regarded as 392–95), and especially his virtual silence on Christian issues are again subject to debate; see particularly T. Barnes 1993 and C. Fornara 1992. These queries leave the credibility of Ammianus on the military untarnished. In fact, all scholars would probably agree that an understanding of what Ammianus does not say makes what he does say even more interesting. G. Crump 1975 also remains helpful on the military narratives. Like any author, Ammianus demands our careful attention at all times to his motives and the sources of his information.

I. Valentinian, Valens, and the Battle of Adrianople

1. A mistake which I myself have made; see T. Burns 1973, 344.

2. Ammianus's is the most detailed and dependable account, although not without problems; see especially bk. 31 in its entirety. Still fundamental is J. Straub 1943, 255–86.

3. For example, in 371–72 Valentinian is reported to have burned every Alamannic village within 50 Roman miles of Trier (Ammianus, 29.4.5).

4. For Constantine's policy of neutralizing the enemy before they had time to organize an invasion of Roman soil see W. Kaegi 1981a, 209–13. For Constantius II and Julian see T. Burns 1981, 390–404. The impact of Valentinian on the entire fabric of the Empire has yet to be addressed, but small hints of his effectiveness at reversing the generally waning confidence in the army and imperial defense are emerging. A case in point is the late Roman refuge at Krüppel in Liechtenstein, near the road running northward to Bregenz (Brigantium). Here a nearby Valentinianic castellum at Schaan appears to have made the refuge superfluous after almost a century of use; see H. Kellner 1978, 187–201.

5. J. Martindale et al., 1971, 1980, *Prosopography of the Later Roman Empire*, 1.935 (henceforth abbreviated *PLRE*).

6. Jovianus's treaty, Ammianus, 25.9–12.

7. *Codex Theodosianus* 7.22.7 (henceforth *CTh*), Ammianus, 26.6.7. Petronius (*PLRE*, 1.690).

8. Ammianus, 26.6.11.

9. Ammianus, 26.7.5.

10. See H. Böhme 1974, 200–7, and K. Böhner 1963.

11. *PLRE*, 1.352. K. Shelton 1981/83, 218, 232–35, demonstrates by careful numismatic analysis that from January to August 350 Magnentius extended his hand to Constantius II in hopes of recognition. He then ceased to strike coins in both names and settled on portraying only himself as the protector and benefactor of Rome and its citizens. Mursa was in the province of Pannonia II and had witnessed another battle against a usurper in 260 when Gallienus defeated Ingenuus there.

12. Gomoarius's reputation as a traitor may have resulted from his acting as a go-between for Vetranio while the latter held as much of Illyricum as possible until Constantius II arrived. Julian regarded Gomoarius as untrustworthy because of his proven loyalty to Constantius and so branded him a traitor. Ammianus, himself a loyal officer under Julian, agreed; Ammianus, 21.8.1.

13. Ammianus, 21.8.1. He was then only a military tribune in charge of a unit of archers, *tribunus scholae scutariorum*. Julian's father was Iulius Constantius, half-brother of Constantius II's paternal grandfather; *PLRE*, 1.226.

14. Ammianus, 21.13.16. The fortification at the Succi Pass was Soneium (modern Trajanovi vrata); *Tabula Imperii Romani*, K34, p. 117, coordinates XII-d; it barred passage between Serdica and Philippopolis on the Naissus-Serdica-Philippopolis-Constantinople road and was the scene of many engagements in late antiquity. *Laeti* first appear in the records at the opening of the fourth century, when Constantine the Great settled large numbers of defeated Franks on Roman lands along the lower Rhine, where they served as farmer-soldiers. They were supervised by Roman prefects, under whose command they fought. The settlement of *laeti* was not pursued in the East. The prefects of the *laeti* were specifically charged with this task. They and their *laeti* still existed within this system as of ca. 400 and are accordingly noted in the Western part of the *Notitia dignitatum*, on which see n. 37.

15. Ammianus, 26.7.4; 26.9.2; also *PLRE*, 1.397.

16. Socrates, *Historia Ecclesiastica*, 4.5.3; Sozomenus, *Historia Ecclesiastica*, 6.8.2.

17. Ammianus, 26.9.9; Zosimus, *Historia nova*, 4.8–10.

18. Ammianus, 26.10.6; 27.2.10.

19. Ammianus, 26.8.2; *PLRE*, 1.928; Vadomarius went on to become *dux Phoenices* (361–66), while his son briefly led the Alamanni as a king before his assassination.

20. Ammianus, 25.10.9.

21. Ammianus, 26.7.17.

22. In order to avoid unnecessary confusion, henceforth *praefectus praetorio Orientis* will appear in the text as the praetorian prefect of the Orient, and Oriens will be reserved for the diocese of the same name.

23. *PLRE*, 1.481. He played a major role after the Battle of Adrianople, while serving as *comes et magister equitum et peditum per orientem*. For Nebridius see *PLRE*, 1.619.

24. Ammianus, 26.7.5.

25. Ammianus, 26.10.4.

26. *Praefectus praetorio* is abbreviated PPO to distinguish him from a provincial governor, a *praeses provinciae*, which is abbreviated p.p. A *vicarius* is straightforward, *vic.*

27. Ammianus, 26.5.5. Under Valentinian, Illyricum, which had had its own praetorian prefect off and on since the death of Constantine, was combined with the prefecture of Italy and Africa (*PLRE*, 1.1050). This remained the case even during the revolt of Procopius.

28. Examples abound in Ammianus: e.g., 16.10.20; 17.13.24; 20.1.1; 21.10.3; 21.13.13; 26.5.11; and 26.10.3. Only under Theodosius, and not for some time after his elevation, did the Empire create regular senior military commanders generally corresponding to the civilian praetorian prefectures.

29. Ammianus, 29.6.3; Maximinus, PPO of the Gauls, and Aequitius, then, per Illyricum eo tempore magistrum armorum (dated 373).

30. Ammianus, 26.7.12; Acontisma is also noted in 27.4.8. It must lie east of Are-thusa, which is at the eastern tip of Lake Bolbe on the via Egnatia. Perhaps Ammianus is referring here to the extraordinarily defensible pass of Rendina, just east of Arethusa. See also N. Hammond 1972, 180, 196. The diocese of Pannonia was renamed Illyricum ca. 400 for complex reasons, explored in subsequent chapters.

31. Ammianus, 26.10.3.

32. Zosimus, 4.10.1.

33. Valentinian ordered his *magister militum* Aequitius to secure a line of commu-nication to provide aid if needed, but Philippopolis refused to yield to his siege until the head of Procopius made its way past them on its way to Valentinian. Ammianus, 26.10.4. On the name of the diocese of Thrace see n. 115.

34. For a reassessment downward, especially in regards to the construction and repair of fortifications and towns; see S. Johnson 1980, 94–98, who notes that in many cases work traditionally attributed to Theodosius can now be dated to the 350s and 60s.

35. Ammianus, 26.5.13. J. Matthews 1989, 206, regards Valentinian's orders to Aequitius concerning Procopius as a reaffirmation of the administrative division of the Empire which had grown up in the course of the fourth century. But the plan was to go beyond Illyricum and secure the road to Constantinople (Ammianus, 26.10.4). The reluctance of Valentinian to do more probably reflected all that he could do given the situation on the Rhine, which he was always convinced was the most important frontier (Ammianus, 30.5.17, on the day before his death). Aequitius (Equitius) is incorrectly given the office of *comes et magister militum per Illyricum* in *PLRE*, 1.282. The office of *magister militum per Illyricum* did not yet exist. Aequitius must have only held the rank of *comes rei militaris* until promoted to *magister* after reporting the news of Procopius's rebellion to Valentinian in order to command all military forces in Illyricum (Am-mianus, 26.5.11) and with this new rank he accompanied the emperor there. At least from ca. 370 inscriptions record him as *comes et magister utriusque militiae* and as such responsible for building projects at several Danubian fortresses in Norican and Pan-nonian provinces (ca. 370–72). That none of his recorded activities took place outside the diocese of Pannonia except his movement into Thrace underscores the care which must be taken not to leap too quickly into accepting later meanings for military titles under Valentinian, such as reading *MVM* as if it meant supreme commander of all troops in the West. Aequitius held a very special command, which in Valentinian's opinion was needed to counter Procopius's supporters. If Aequitius's defensive improvements later attested on inscriptions were directed against a specific threat rather than just routine repairs, the enemy would have been the Quadi, who replaced the Alamanni as Valen-tinian's principal opponents after 374. Aequitius's career culminated with the consulship of 374, held with Gratian, emperor and son of Valentinian himself. After this, he dis-appeared into honorable retirement.

36. Little is known about the *comes domesticorum* under Valentinian, especially his military duties; see A. Jones 1964, 143, 333, 372. In the early fifth century one such *comes* commanded an important unit of infantry and another of cavalry, and the post was a testing ground for the next step, that of *magister*. Even in the fifth century, however, the elite troops at his command were few in number. Severus became *magister peditum* in 367 and held the post until 372; *PLRE*, 1.833.

37. *Nd. oc.* 28; *PLRE*, 1.621. In Ammianus, 27.8.1, he is *comes maritimi tractus*. The *Notitia dignitatum* is the most controversial and difficult document relating to

the late Empire. Basically, it is a table of organization of the Roman army kept for an unknown purpose. Only one manuscript copy exists, and that one is Western and incomplete. The sections having to do with the Eastern army (*Nd. or.*) are less detailed than those for the West (*Nd. oc.*), and apparently no major changes were posted in the document for the Eastern sections after ca. 385–93. There is a possibility that minor changes in the administrative-political structure were made to the Eastern sections concerning the provinces of Moesia II and Scythia sometime between 401 and 409. At least in these two provinces Valens and Theodosius combined only added two cavalry units and one infantry. See further M. Zahariade 1988, 191–92. The Western sections are considerably more detailed as to unit postings but are extremely inconsistent. There can be no way to be certain when any section was last brought up to date, but it is safe to say that the various regions and commands were not handled systematically and that there is no one date at which all aspects were uniformly and finally corrected. The extant version suggests that the bureau responsible for it was sloppy and did not bother to cross-check entries even when updating. For most sections it is safe to conclude that the data reflect deployments and the command structure not earlier than the death of Theodosius the Great in 395, and in several Western sections it is very probable that the last corrections were made a decade or two later. Further discussion of this controversial document follows in several chapters.

38. *PLRE*, 1.375; Ammianus, 27.8.1.

39. O. Seeck 1919, 228–30.

40. Ammianus, 27.8.2, an incomplete passage in the text; and *PLRE*, 1.462–63 (Jovinus), 833 (Severus); O. Seeck 1919, 228.

41. Ammianus, 27.8.7, names the Batavi, Heruli, Jovii, and Victores. The later *Notitia dignitatum* has all four as units of the *auxilia palatina*, but by that time anyway most are listed as both *seniores* and *iuniores* units and not assigned to the same palatine force; see O. Seeck, *Notitia dignitatum*, pp. 321 (Batavi, perhaps the iuniores assigned to the *auxilia palatina* in Gaul), 323 (Heruli seniores of the *auxilia palatina* in Italy), 323 (Jovii, seniores part of the *auxilia palatina* in Italy, or the iuniores Galliani, by then part of the *auxilia palatina* in Gaul), and 327 (Victores, perhaps the *victores iuniores Britanniciani*, then listed as in Britain). There are no precise figures to indicate the size of these units. My estimate of 350 each is based upon Ammianus, 18.7.2, in which two units of horsemen, totaling 700 men, were transferred from Illyricum to the Persian frontier in 359.

42. Ammianus, 28.3.9. He replaced Jovinus (*PLRE*, 1.462–63). There is much difficulty surrounding the exact chronology of Theodosius's British campaigns and the Alamannic Wars; see J. Matthews 1989, 207 and 510, n. 7, for support of 367–68. In books 27 and 28, Ammianus condenses the Alamannic campaigns and much else into one narrative with an assortment of elucidations, particularly about Theodosius the Elder, and occasional reflections back to now lost books of his History.

43. Ammianus, 27.8.5.

44. Paulus Orosius, *Historiarum adversum paganos libri vii*, 7.33.6–7.

45. Ammianus, 28.3.2, in integrum restituit civitates et castra, multiplicibus quidem damnis afflicta, sed ad quietem temporis longi fundata.

46. Ammianus, 28.3.7, castra, limitesque vigiliis (watchmen) tuebatur et praetenturis (frontier garrisons).

47. *PLRE*, 1.935.

48. Ammianus, 27.8.5, 28.3.4–6, 30.7.10.

49. Ammianus, 27.8.10, nomine recturum Britannias pro praefectis.

50. Specifically, J. Pearce 1933, 298.1 (6), dtd. between 25 February 364 and 24 August 367. Similar mintings were numerous and widespread, so much so, in fact, that it is usually impossible to identify the coins with particular campaigns. For the most part the iconography of victory over the barbarians was already well established. Were it not for Ammianus's detailed account of Valentinian's successful campaigns one might doubt the sincerity of the reverses, as one should under other emperors such as Honorius, whose long career held few moments to celebrate. Compare the *centenionalis* of Valentinian I (*RIC* 10 [9]) and his recently discovered medallion (V. Kondić 1973, 48–49) and the silver medallion of Honorius (W. Kubitschek 1909, 375) for the consistent imagery. It is tempting to relate this particular Valentinianic medallion to the victories of Valens over the Goths here discussed but, clothing styles notwithstanding, the strongest evidence for such an identification remains its provenience near Veliko Gradište (Pincum) on the Danube in Moesia I, an area of known fighting against the Goths.

51. For a too narrow and misleading interpretation of this type based on a single coin see W. Weiser 1987, 161–74, who sees "handcuffs" on one example alone. The general approach to the type as illustrating *receptio* is best employed by K. Kraft 1978, 87–132.

52. Valentinian recruited from among the Alamanni in 372 (Ammianus, 29.4.7, near Mainz), giving important leaders Roman commands. One such officer was immediately posted to Britain. Valentinian also recruited among the Quadi just before his death in 375 (Ammianus, 30.6.1), as he had in 370 among the Saxons (Ammianus, 28.5.4, ex condicione proposita iuvenibus multis, habilibus ad militiam).

53. Ammianus, 17.13.3, on Constantius in 358 forcing the Limigantes to provide recruits which he then established in defense of the Iron Gates. Only in the case of the Limigantes (a curious name seeming to suggest those living on the borders), whom some Sarmatians had enslaved, do we know what was done with the general mass of recruits obtained forcibly through a treaty with Rome prior to the Goths. The Limigantes perhaps like many who saw their sons leave for Roman service threatened to rebel if their children were sent too far away. Constantius needed them relatively close by but did not make any promises.

54. *CTh* 7.13.16 dated 17 April 406, relating to the Western Empire, attests to their slaveholding. *Dediticii* were legally restricted in regard to citizenship and testimentary rights. The term *dediticii* had been in use since Republican times, when it applied to manumitted slaves who as slaves had been convicted of a crime. Despite their manumission they could never hold Roman citizenship, make a will, or inherit under one (A. Berger 1953, 427). These restrictions probably remained. In 212 Caracalla extended citizenship to virtually everyone else (C. Sacce 1958, who discusses the problem of the *dediticii* at length).

55. Ammianus, 31.10.17; Gratian recruited some young men from among the defeated Lentienses (a group of Alamanni) in 378 along the Rhine. He needed them to shore up the defenses there as he took a great many men to link up with Valens against the Goths. There was certainly an element of risk in integrating them along the Rhine, but Gratian took the chance and succeeded. After their *deditio*, that is their formal submission, supplication, and oaths of loyalty, they were received into Roman service and dispersed among other new recruits (iuventute valida nostris tirociniis permiscenda). The practice of distributing recruits in the general area of their recruitment was very

common, at least on the upper Danube and Rhine rivers from the middle of the fourth century, as is attested dramatically in the archaeological record to be discussed in chapter 5. Some scholars tend to forget that a great number of barbarian soldiers, almost certainly a decided majority, were volunteers. Chapter 5 explores the full impact of these many enlistments upon the army in Raetia; see particularly the discussion there of the "Elbgermans."

56. T. Burns and B. Overbeck 1987, no. 159, 66–67, with citations to the literature; see especially P. Bastien 1972–76, 157–76. That so much confusion has surrounded the medallion's date, almost a century in difference, offers indirect testimony to the remarkable consistency of Roman policy and its iconography.

57. Nd. oc. 42.33–44.

58. Julian apparently had to break a recruitment promise to the Batavians when Constantius ordered him to bring them east in 360 (Ammianus, 20.4.4). In fact, they raised Julian to the purple rather than abandon their families (Ammianus, 20.8.8), but he was taking them very far away indeed. Conditions placed upon service by recruits are otherwise unknown. The Batavians were not new recruits, either, and their claims seem false in light of subsequent events. Whatever the Batavians wanted, Julian soon violated these conditions without protest from them. This recorded incident is perhaps nothing more than a way for Ammianus to contrast the leadership styles of Constantius II and Julian.

59. On the duces Ariaricus and Aoricus, see Jordanes, Getica, 79.

60. Anonymous Valesianus, I.5.27; the principal Gothic leader under Licinius was Alica (PLRE, 1.45), who must have perished in the battle with Constantine at Chrysopolis.

61. T. Burns 1984, 35; P. Heather 1991, 115.

62. PLRE, 1.814, Secundus 3 (Saturninius Secundus Salutius).

63. Zosimus, 4.10.

64. Zosimus, 4.11. On the theory that this passage in Zosimus and the one in Ammianus, 27.5.2, both relate to the same campaign, specifically in 367, and not, in the case of Zosimus, to the 369 season, see M. Zahariade 1983, 57–70. But F. Paschoud 1971–89 (v. 2, pt. 2), 352–53, unaware of Zahariade, discusses both 367 and 369 and comes down in favor of 369 for Zosimus here.

65. Limes is the Latin term used here to describe the frontier fortifications system of the Empire. The term itself was rarely used in a military context in antiquity, but, when it was, it generally conveyed the meaning of the fortified frontier protecting the Roman provinces. Today it is increasingly common to see authors using the term limes when discussing the frontier zone that included but was not exclusively comprised of the fortifications on the boundaries of the Empire.

66. Themistius, Orationes 10, 138b; Corpus inscriptionum latinarum 3.12518 and 13755 (hereinafter CIL). On Themistius as a source for these events as well as the events themselves see also V. Velkov (1955) 1980, especially 172–75; however, the footnotes in the English version are not always faithful to the original.

67. Ammianus, 27.5.4. Arinthaeus apparently became mag. ped. after the suppression of Procopius, PLRE, 1.103.

68. Zosimus, 4.11.3.

69. Themistius, Or. 8, 114b–115d, pointing out that only the army profits from plunder but everyone benefits from cost-effective government; in other words, Them-

istius (March 368) advised Valens to settle for something short of total victory to save resources and to get on with other business. P. Heather 1991, 117, sees Themistius here and in general as an imperial mouthpiece, reflecting imperial wishes throughout his long career as court orator. If true, then in this case Valens would have been testing the waters for less than a complete victory while growing increasingly despondent at the weather. It would be nice to think that successive emperors could have appreciated the subtlety of Themistius; I doubt they inspired it.

70. *CTh* 10.16.2; 10.21.1. Again the roads were repaired; V. Velkov (1955) 1980, 177, with references.

71. Ammianus, 27.5.6.

72. Ibid., 27.5.7.

73. Ibid., 27.5.6–10. *Thiudans* is the correct Gothic term; Ammianus used *iudex*. For further discussion see T. Burns 1980, 36–41, and H. Wolfram 1979, 68f. The essential point here is the specifics of the terminology for the formal process of concluding a peace itself rather than the use of *iudex: recte noscentibus placuit navibus remigio directis in medium flumen, quae vehebant cum armigeris principem, gentisque iudicem inde cum suis, foederari, ut statutum est, pacem* (27.5.9). Athanaric was the recognized leader of his people (*gentisque iudicem*) and he himself met the emperor Valens and struck a formal treaty that brought peace. The verb *foederari* means to become allies through a treaty. One should keep this specific terminology in mind for the discussion of 382.

74. Zosimus, 4.11.

75. Sozomenus, *HE*, 37.5.

76. I cannot agree with P. Heather 1991, 103, 107, against all others, that the *thiudans* was a permanent office even before Athanaric, but he was unquestionably the last. For my reasons for impermanence see T. Burns 1984, 37f. All other traditionalists are cited in Heather's discussion.

77. Ammianus, 30.6.1–3.

78. Sozomenus, *HE*, 6.21, refers to Valens's activities in the context of discussing the Christian communities in Scythia Minor sometime prior to the Gothic crossing of the Danube in 376. I believe that the emperor ordered an increase in the Christian clergy to convert the barbarians being received into the Empire. The epigraphic evidence for the buildup in the late fourth century is discussed by E. Popescu 1973, 69–77, who suggests that it may have been a prelude to a missionary action. I doubt that Valens or any other emperor at this time thought of an official imperial Christian missionary program addressed to the barbarians, but they did expect newly received barbarians to accept Christianity once inside the Empire and this policy of conversion continued.

79. Paulinus of Nola, *Carmina* 17 and *Epis.* 18. On the importance of Arianism to Valens see H. Brennecke 1988, 181–242; on the Goths and Thrace in particular, p. 189.

80. Eunapius, frag. 2 (*Exc. de Sent.* 53). Eunapius is hardly to be trusted, especially in regard to strength estimates when he succumbs to one of his frequent rhetorical flourishes, but nevertheless cannot be dispensed with either. Whether Gothic monks existed so early is questionable, but there can be no doubt that there were Gothic monks by the first decade of the fifth century; see Chrysostomus, *Epis.* 207. Discussed briefly in chapter 4. On Eunapius see further A. Baldini 1984, F. Paschoud 1985b, and R. Penella 1990.

81. That these territories were militarily evacuated totally or in part is beyond debate; however, that does not mean legally surrendered as was the case of Jovian's infamous actions of 363 which Ammianus (25.9.9) reports as totally unprecedented, for this treaty gave up forever the goal of recovering any of the five provinces here ceded to Persia. Obviously Ammianus was aware of third-century withdrawals from the Agri Decumates and Dacia. The records are insufficient to prove just how deeply committed Rome was to "recovery" of the evacuated but not surrendered territories. Nonetheless, it is clear that Roman power, political and economic, still held importance in what was once transdanubian Roman Dacia throughout the era stretching at least up to the crisis of the seventh century. "Honorary patriciates" were accorded by Byzantium, and specific Roman symbols of power such as fibulae and finger rings attest to the constant lure of Rome in these lands into the seventh century. See further L. Bârzu 1980, 46–70, and J. Werner 1984, 38–43. The language used by Ammianus is itself important (25.7.13): Quo ignobili decreto firmato, nequid committeretur per indutias contrarium pactis.

In earlier imperial Latin *pactum* conveyed a clear sense of giving, e.g., the betrothed woman (in the feminine) or man (in the masculine) and came to mean (in the neuter) "tribute" or "levy," see J. Niermeyer 1976, 750; in other words the term conveyed a sense of concession not found in *foedus*. On these problems of the terminology of treaties of peace see E. Chrysos 1976, 1–48. On the ideological structure of *imperium* within and beyond the frontiers see J. Haldon 1984, 82–83, 362–63. The question of the terminology of peace occupies a considerable amount of discussion in chapter 3 as well.

82. Ammianus, 27.5.1.

83. So at least according to the rhetorician Libanius, *Or.* 12.78.

84. *PLRE*, 1.889–94. On Themistius in general but especially as a court philosopher see G. Dagron 1968 and the recent work of J. Vanderspoel 1989.

85. Themistius, *Or.* 10, 139d–140a.

86. Ibid., 10, 131d.

87. Ibid., 10, 131b.

88. A dating suggested by A. Cameron 1979, 1–10.

89. Zosimus, 4.10; Eunapius, *V. Soph.*, 7.5.9.

90. Themistius, *Or.* 7, 87–88. Themistius the moral philosopher trying to influence state policy and not merely applaud it is clearly brought out by L. Daly 1972, 351–79.

91. Ammianus, 26.7.1–7.

92. *CTh* 7.20.8 and 11 (dtd. 364 and 365 or 368), extensions of legislation enacted under Constantine I concerning the settlement of veterans. The importance of the forthcoming legislation for veterans is correctly stressed by H. Sivan 1987, 759–72.

93. Valens's career is appraised by K. Klein 1956, 53–69.

94. In addition to the works by V. Velkov cited, see as an introduction with site gazetteer up to mid-1970s R. Hoddinott 1975. More detailed references follow.

95. V. Velkov (1958) 1977, 135–90.

96. A. Jones 1964, 47, on the *vicarius* (a deputy of the praetorian prefect established under Diocletian), p. 105 (*comes rei militaris*, first recorded shortly after the death of Constantine the Great). In some areas the *comes* was a provincial level commander even after the establishment of the various *magistri militiae*.

97. C. Scorpan 1980, 117–41.

98. Phase C of the walls at Histria seems to have been begun toward the end of

the fourth century and witnessed repeated modification, especially in the early sixth century under Anastasius; see C. Domaneantu and A. Sion 1982, 393.

99. We do not know the true purpose of the *Notitia*, which, at least for Moesia II and Scythia, may have reflected only a "skeleton of the riparian defensive system"; so concludes M. Zahariade 1988, 189, on the basis of his comparison of the archaeology and all other references to these sites.

100. For a careful study of the road system with full reference to the literature see U. Wanke 1990, 15–65. Wanke's reconstruction of the campaigns is intelligently based upon the road network. Although I disagree with some of his interpretations, usually because he places insufficient stress upon the Roman need to disperse the immigrants quickly, I regard this as an important and useful synthesis. In what follows I have not tried to go into similar detail concerning the possible movements prior to the battle except when our interpretations differ markedly.

101. M. Biernacka-Lubańska 1982, 214–25, with gazetteer of sites, pp. 226–64.

102. W. Cherf 1983, 43. At Dhema earlier C-14 dating of lime mortar seemed to confirm that the work was done in the second half of the fourth century, probably near the end. So too Cherf 1984, 594–98. Cherf, however, has now recalibrated these studies because of samples run in 1988 against a better standard and concludes otherwise, suggesting instead that most of the work here was done under Theodosius II or later, Cherf 1992, 261–64.

103. U. Wanke 1990 offers a reconstruction based on Ammianus and the road system not terribly unlike my own and often in greater detail for the period from the crossing up to the battle. Nothing has led me to alter substantially the actual battle sequence and the overall problems of the campaign as set out in T. Burns 1973, 336–45, and the account that follows reflects that study and Wanke, recent suggestions of brooding antagonisms propelling Goths and Romans ever farther apart notwithstanding (e.g., P. Heather 1991, 128, 142).

104. Ammianus, 31.4.4. There is no reason to doubt Ammianus here when he states that Valens was genuinely pleased with the thought of new recruits (nevertheless, see P. Heather 1991, 133).

105. Ammianus, 31.4.2.

106. Eunapius, frag. 42; Ammianus, 31.4.8. For the incredible mathematical gymnastics that the figure 200,000 has produced among historians see U. Wanke 1990, 126.

107. Ammianus, 31.16.8; *PLRE*, 1.481. Zosimus, 4.26, provides essentially the same account. In English, Julius's title would be "count and master of the cavalry and infantry for the Orient."

108. U. Wanke 1990, 128–32. I doubt that the Goths were concentrated and long held in Marcianopolis (contrary to Wanke, 133, 224). His interpretation depends upon an unnecessary textual emendation of Ammianus, 31.6.1, from "apud Hadrianopolim" to "apud Marcianopolim" solely to lessen the difficulty, for Wanke, of the Romans shifting two Gothic groups (those under Colias and Sueridus, and those under Fritigern) ca. 600 km to the south. Wanke assumes that the Roman command knew beforehand how many immigrants were arriving and where to ship them. They knew neither. Ammianus goes to some length to explain Gothic actions and the fears of the citizens of Adrianople. Since Adrianople was near the site of the final battle, Ammianus and any copiers of his manuscript are unlikely to have erred. Ammianus probably talked to the

duumvir (town manager as head of the city council) of Adrianople himself after the battle. The idea was to winter these people in Adrianople and then see what to do with them. It was not clear when the order was issued that in fact these newcomers would go to Asia Minor (contrary to Wanke); they could have gone almost anywhere.

109. Zosimus, 4.20; perhaps a few Romans were not careful as Zosimus suggests. Every soldier knew that any weapon missed might be the one shoved into his belly someday in battle.

110. Ammianus, 31.5.9, states specifically that at the opening of the rebellion the Goths put on Roman arms: Post quae hostes armis induti Romanis. For use of clubs, 31.7.12.

111. Ammianus, 31.4.9; 31.5.1. *PLRE*, 1.585 (Maximus 24), *dux Moesiae* or probably *Scythiae*. *PLRE*, 1.519–20 (Lupicinus 3).

112. I can find no support for the thesis that the Romans sought to admit Tervingi and not Greutungi (contra P. Heather 1991, 131). The Greutungi simply arrived later, having had much farther to travel than the others, originating as they did east of the Dniester River.

113. Ammianus, 31.4.11.

114. A. Jones 1964, 124f.

115. Absolute precision is typically beyond reach whenever the *Notitia dignitatum* is under discussion. There is no agreement upon the dates of Theodosius's reform of the *magistri*. D. Hoffmann 1970 argues for a date of 387 or 388. On the question of *Thracias*, Hoffmann (2.180 [IX.59]) suggests that probably Ammianus, 31.9.1, and *Nd. or.* 1.7, used the plural *Thracias* either to distinguish the diocese in the plural from the province of *Thracia* in the singular, or because the real name of the diocese was *Thraciae*. That its vicars were *vicarii Thraciarum* is strong support for the idea that *Thraciae* may be the name of the diocese (*PLRE*, 1.1081). Like so much of the *Notitia*, however, this too is problematic (see A. Jones 1964, 1451f.). Whatever the significance of *Thracias* in the *Notitia* that the magisters commanded at the diocesan level or higher is demonstrable from their actions.

116. A. Jones 1964, 178 and n. 10, suggests that these divisions in the *Notitia dignitatum* reflect the hand of Eutropius and that the hasty creation of Thrace and Illyricum is reflected in the lack in the *Notitia* of regular civil officials (*officium cardinale*) under them unlike the *magister militum per Orientem*. Jones is convincing that Eutropius had to reconstitute these commands and provide them with staffs, but that does not contradict Hoffmann's dating of their origin to Theodosius ca. 388, D. Hoffmann 1970, 490–507. This is discussed more fully in chapter 4. When the final elements of the Eastern army returned in 395, much had to be done anew and quickly.

117. There is much discussion as to the relationship of various names associated with the Gothic peoples at the end of the fourth and early fifth centuries; for a recent view, see P. Heather 1991, 331–33. I cannot accept, however, his suggestion (p. 162) that "Visi" was used to designate a group that formed once the Goths were inside the Empire. Rather, I believe, it was one of several names in use among the Goths, perhaps second only to "Tervingi," and so was chosen by the Romans as a name for a unit of the *auxilia palatina* probably raised under Theodosius and stationed in the East at the date of the Eastern sections of the *Notitia, Nd. or.* 5.20 and 61 (that is, ca. 390). Once inside the Empire, the usage of "Tervingi" rapidly waned for unknown reasons, probably because

the old political structures that may have given it support were gone. Further discussion follows in several chapters in the context of military recruitment.

118. Socrates, *HE*, 4.33.1–4; Sozomenus, *HE*, 6.37.6; and probably one of "the necessary things" (et necessaria) he had to do, if he was to be accepted into Roman service, Ammianus, 31.12.14, and Fritigern's use of a Christian priest as an envoy to the emperor, 31.12.8.

119. Discussed in some detail in T. Burns 1984, 146–49.

120. Ammianus, 29.6.5 (Quadi); 31.5.5–7 (Goths and Lupicinus).

121. Ammianus, 31.6.4. Wanke by changing the text of Ammianus has Colias and Sueridus attack Marcianopolis. This would have been incredibly foolhardy: a few hundred warriors in a suicidal attack upon the main headquarters city of the imperial army in Thrace! Adrianople conversely had only the typical small garrison.

122. There were always some Roman troops guarding the passes. By this time word would have arrived for them to be on alert and not allow any Gothic refugees to pass. Since Fritigern and the others left Lupicinus's banquet and hurried back, they had been able to pass through the checkpoints unmolested. They still would have carried orders to report to Marcianopolis and return. A determined man on horseback with proper authorization, like Fritigern now, could travel very swiftly. By making his textual emendation U. Wanke 1990, 157–60, creates a different scenario. For Wanke, Fritigern plays a much more important role in the early phases of the rebellion including the struggle against Profuturus and Traianus (despite no mention of him in Ammianus's discussion of the battle near Ad Salices in Scythia). Under his leadership, according to Wanke, the Goths quickly created a complex federation (pp. 161–69) and relentlessly pushed the Romans back into their defensive enclaves. For Wanke, Fritigern's success at creating a working confederacy of many peoples, Tervingi and non-Tervingi, is the origin of those called the Visigoths (p. 224). My view, elaborated in the remainder of this book, is decidedly different, preferring to defer awarding the honor of forming a new people until Alaric and Athaulf.

123. Ammianus, 31.10 and 31.12. U. Wanke 1990, 175–78.

124. Ammianus, 31.7.3–4. Until now he probably was *dux Valeriae* (*PLRE*, 1.373), as such in command of frontier forces there. His forces would therefore have comprised some *limitanei* and any units of the *comitatenses* available in Illyricum. On his possible building activities in Valeria (? *dux* of Valeria), see further S. Soproni 1978. U. Wanke 1990, 151, thinks that this comital command was special personal *comitiva*. Valentinian I and later Theodosius created comital commands for specific campaigns rather frequently.

125. U. Wanke 1990, 151–52, 169–74. Wanke, believing that Fritigern-Colias-Sueridus had attacked Marcianopolis (rather than Adrianople), understands Richomeres's operations as blocking those Goths from moving westward from Marcianopolis on the road through Nicopolis ad Istrum. Richomeres certainly did use some of his forces to strengthen defenses in the Haemus, but this is not recorded as happening until after the defeat at Ad Salices (Ammianus, 31.8.1). The garrisons in the mountains had engaged the Goths before even Frigeridus arrived, but he gave them support and leadership (Ammianus, 31.7.3). Richomeres must have continued to support their efforts. Frigeridus's work on defenses in the area of Beroea may, as Wanke suggests, have been to further the earlier efforts in the Haemus Mountains at Richomeres's direction. Since Beroea lies south of the Haemus, however, work there is better understood as increasing

protection against barbarians already in that area, not along the road through Nicopolis ad Istrum, the trunk road in the plain north of the mountains.

126. Ammianus, 31.7.4 (and later at 31.12.4), notes Richomeres as *comes domesticorum*, but his entire career was in the military (*PLRE*, 1.766). He therefore must have been *comes domesticorum equitum*, arguably the second highest officer in the Western army.

127. *PLRE*, 1.749. *PLRE*, 1.922.

128. *PLRE*, 1.765; Ammianus, 31.7.4–5.

129. Ammianus, 31.7.5–16; 31.8.1. Perhaps had Fritigern been there, they would have followed up their success more swiftly and decisively.

130. Ammianus, 31.8.1–5.

131. Ammianus does not refer to Fritigern as king (*rex*) until 31.12.9, the day of the Battle of Adrianople, although he had plenty of opportunities before this, particularly in his discussion of the banquet. Either Fritigern was declared king by the survivors of Lupicinus's treachery, unrecorded in Ammianus despite his details on that event, or after the Goths were reassembled following Saturninus's abandonment of the pass defenses. The former would have been a hasty decision made by only a handful of leaders; the latter could have involved the entire barbarian population and all their leaders. I prefer the second possibility. See also T. Burns 1980, 44–47.

132. Ammianus, 31.9.2.

133. Ammianus, 31.9.3. Farnobius and his men were part of the mass that crossed as the system of *receptio* was breaking down. So did the Greutungi (Ammianus, 31.4.12). They kept their weapons and perhaps even their mounts.

134. Ammianus, 31.11.2–5. Sebastianus (*PLRE*, 1.812) took a picked force of 300 from each legion and harassed Gothic bands wherever he encountered them along the roads to Adrianople and back. This had a major effect upon Fritigern, who decided to move his men from near Cabyle on the Tonsus River to north of Adrianople in the plain between the Haemus and Rhodope Mountains. Saturninus (*PLRE*, 1.807) and Sebastianus despite their titles commanded units of both cavalry and infantry. In both East and West by this time the *magister peditum* was superior in rank. Sebastianus was ideally suited for this command, for he had participated in one of Valentinian's raids against the Quadi in 374 (Ammianus, 30.5.13). At Adrianople he had to convince the garrison that he was not a defector to the barbarians trying to trick them into opening their gate. Obviously some defections from the Roman army took place. That Sebastianus proceeded as far as Adrianople is further testimony that Rome had transshipped Goths there.

135. T. Burns 1973, 339, but with new insights from U. Wanke 1990, 157–60.

136. Zosimus, 4.22.2–4, but disregarding the story of how he unexpectedly arrived in Constantinople of his own accord.

137. Ammianus, 31.10.21 (Frigeridus) and 31.11.1–4; Zosimus, 4.23 (Sebastianus). Gratian replaced Frigeridus shortly after this with Maurus, probably for reasons of health. Zosimus's claim that Sebastianus retook walled cities is surely incorrect, contradicted by Ammianus and all other evidence.

138. On Lentiensian Alamanni, Ammianus, 31.10.1–10, according to which they chose this opportunity to break their treaty (of 354?), violato foedere dudum concepto (Ammianus, 31.10.2), and raided across the upper Rhine frontier. Gratian had to divert troops en route to the East then in Pannonia in order to strengthen his reserve forces still in Gaul (the *comitatus*). Nannienus, *comes rei militaris* (perhaps *comes utriusque Ger-*

maniae), led the Roman forces to victory, *PLRE*, 1.616. The decision to go it alone, Ammianus, 31.12.6–7; his envy of Gratian, 31.12.1.

139. Ammianus, 31.12.3, in numero decem milium. U. Wanke 1990, 198–217, also recounts these events of the summer of 378 and the fateful day in August. He stops short of offering a tactical reconstruction of the battle itself, declaring that impossible (p. 229). By this stage Wanke and I are in basic agreement on the tactical development; his account is considerably more detailed, with careful attention to the probable line of march based on his analysis of the road system.

140. Ibid., 31.12.4.

141. Ibid., 31.12.3, incertum quo errore procursatoribus omnem illam multitudinis partem, quam viderant, in numero decem milium esse firmantibus.

142. Ibid., 31.12.4.

143. H. Delbrück (1921) 1980, 292, suggests 18,000 warriors including all detachments. L. Schmidt 1941, 403, proposes 10,000 with Fritigern, 8,000 Ostrogoths and Alans with Alatheus and Saphrax, and at least 30,000 Romans. N. Austin 1979, 78, accepts Schmidt. K. Klein 1951, 189–92, avoids the problem while emphasizing the question of Roman tribute payments and the importance of the emergence of the Huns.

144. W. Judeich 1891, 1–17.

145. Ammianus, 31.3.3.

146. A. Jones 1964, 1434, calculated that Theodosius had to raise 30 units for the Eastern army after 379, which would be about 60,000 by his unit strengths; cf. pp. 154, 679, and 1425. P. Heather 1991, 147, following D. Hoffmann 1969, 450–58, who argued that the imbalance of 16 units of eastern *iuniores* was the result of Adrianople, also comes up with 15,000–20,000 Romans opposing ca. 20,000 barbarians.

147. Ibid., 31.12.8, habitanda Thracia sola cum pecore omni concederetur et frugibus: hoc impetrato, spondentis perpetuam pacem. The reference to "flocks and crops" is important to later discussion of the goal of the barbarians during the "settlements" that ultimately followed.

148. Ibid., 31.12.9.

149. On the *laeti* in Gaul under Constantine see E. James 1988, 38–44; on the Carpi see G. Bichir 1976, 143, who demonstrates that contrary to the views based upon Sextus Aurelius Victor, *Liber de Caesaribus*, 39, 43, and the *Consularia Constantinopolitana* (hereinafter *Cons. Const.*), 295, not all Carpi were transferred into the Empire at one time under Diocletian 295–97, but they still demanded Roman attention for at least another 25 years.

150. Ibid., 31.12.11–16.

151. Ammianus, 31.12.3.

152. For a discussion of their rivalry as seen on coinage see J. Pearce 1933, xv–xxii.

153. Zosimus, 4.23, over Ammianus, 31.12.6, for the advice of Sebastianus to wait for reinforcements. This is about the only time that Zosimus (drawing upon Eunapius) is preferable to Ammianus on details of the battle.

154. This is a summary of my earlier reconstruction; see T. Burns 1973, 340–44, for details and sources. An alternative version also reported to Ammianus placed Valens's death in a nearby farmhouse, which became his funeral pyre when Gothic forces set it ablaze. The cracking of the rear ranks is a familiar problem to anyone who has tried to bend a pipe around a curved mold; it results from the fact that circumference increases

with the radius. If the number of soldiers standing shoulder to shoulder is not increased, the space between them must. Richomeres served as *magister militum per Orientem* under Theodosius, became a friend of the rhetorician Libanius, and was *consul prior* in 384 (*PLRE*, 1.765–66). Saturninus played a major role in Theodosius's Gothic wars and was *consul posterior* in 383.

155. Ammianus, 31.13.18.

156. Many units including 11 *aux. pal.* had to be raised to replace the losses at Adrianople. The *Notitia dignitatum* gives 5 *vex. pal.*, 1 *vex. com.*, 11 *aux. pal.*, 1 *leg. com.*, 12 *pseudocom.* Dating the entry of these units into Roman service is beyond the state of the current evidence. See further A. Jones 1964, 1425, who estimates that up to one-seventh of the comitatus was lost at Adrianople or in the ensuing campaigns. Jones's estimates of the size of the Roman army and various unit types within it should no longer be taken at face value. This calculation of the units raised under Theodosius includes replacements for losses and troop buildups for war against two major usurpers, Maximus and Eugenius, as well as replacement for the dead at Adrianople.

157. Ammianus, 31.13.18.

158. Ambrose (Ambrosius Mediolanensis), *Expositio evangelii secundum Lucam*, 14, finem mundi videmus. They saw the Goths as Gog, the biblical Gog and Magog, "Gog et Gothi." Ambrose, 10, ll. 108f. and 156f.; *De Fide libri V (ad Gratianum Augustum)*, 2.16, ll. 14f., Gog iste Gothus est, quem iam uidemus exisse. Jerome (Hieronymus), *Liber quaestionum hebraicarum in Genesim* (ed. Lagarde), p. 14, ll. 18f., scio quendam gog et magog tam de praesenti loco quam de ezechiel ad gothorum nuper in terra nostra uagantium historiam rettulisse, and again, ll. 21f.; also his *Commentarii in Ezechielem*, 11, praef., l. 14. Jerome was followed much later by Rodericus Ximenius de Rada in his *Historia de rebus Hispanie siue Historia Gothica*, 1.9, ll. 39f.

159. Ammianus, 31.11.6.

160. Ammianus, 31.16.3. Perhaps he took advantage of the imperial villa at Gamzigrad, recently absolutely identified from a building inscription as ancient Felix Romuliana. This grand and stoutly fortified palace was built under the tetrarch Galerius and was still available for use in the second half of the fourth century; see for the crucial inscription and a brief survey of the site D. Srejović 1985, 51–67.

161. Zosimus, 4.26.5; Ammianus, 31.16.8. For Ammianus, late in 378, over Zosimus after accession of Theodosius in 379, see F. Paschoud 1971–89 (v. 2, pt. 2), 389.

162. The italics are mine; Ammianus, 31.16.8. Zosimus, 4.26.7, adds to Ammianus that Julius deceived them by offering them gifts, money, and land (ἀλλὰ καὶ γῆν). As we shall see over and over, this is precisely what new recruits expected and received in the frontier areas.

163. Ammianus, 31.16.3–7.

164. *Cons. Const.* 379; *Consularia Italica* 379.

165. For the fleet up to the end of the fourth century see D. Kienast 1966, 149, 156. As late as 443 units were at Viminacium, etc., *Nov. Theod.* 24.5.

166. Zosimus, 5.21–22, reports that Gaïnas and some of his followers recrossed the Danube in 400, but this probably never occurred. The recrossings of 379–80 and the events of 400 are discussed in subsequent chapters.

167. *Nd. or.* 39.20, 35.

168. *CTh* 7.17. These ships were to be equipped with weapons and supplies by

the respective *duces* for Moesia and Scythia. The order was transmitted to the *mag. militum p. Thr.*

169. Vegetius, *Epitoma rei militaris*, 4.46.

170. Ammianus, 31.11.2; they had held the cities safe and greeted Valens and his army.

171. Ibid., 31.5.16–17; Zosimus 1.24.

172. On the major sites see R. Hoddinott 1975 and references there to excavations, and more recently A. Poulter 1983a.

173. Ammianus, 31.6.3.

174. J. Rankov 1983, 40–73, especially 61.

175. In addition to R. Hoddinott 1975, see V. Velkov 1977.

176. A. Poulter 1983a, pt. 2, 74–118.

177. Eunapius, frag. 47.1; for V. Velkov, Eunapius meant ad Nestum; for A. Poulter, ad Istrum (1977, 114, n. 102). The reference is interpreted by E. Thompson 1966, 103, as implying the surrender of the city to the Goths. If so, it was unique among major cities; but, as Eunapius clearly states, it had no garrison and could expect none. Thompson's conjecture seems likely despite the lack of conclusive evidence.

178. Ammianus, 31.11.2; Zosimus, 4.23. See further A. Poulter 1988, 69–89. The building of the *castellum* may have been directly linked to the establishment of the Gothic settlers at midcentury upon what was apparently vacant land.

179. Jordanes, *Getica*, 51 (267). The fourth-century road may still have been in use even then; A. Poulter 1988, 88, n. 10. Throughout the following chapters Jordanes and his *Getica* come up for repeated use and discussion. The *Getica* is an extraordinarily complex document recently given a very insightful exploration; see P. Heather 1991, pt. 1.

180. A. Poulter 1983b, 94; coin-deposit patterns run through 425, 1988, 76.

181. In addition to the general works cited above (R. Hoddinott 1975, 268) see M. Biernacka-Lubańska 1982, especially 27–40, 214–25, with references to each site. The importance of the mid-fifth century crisis does not concern our question but it was then and during the seventh century that the towns experienced devastation and the dispersal of their inhabitants.

182. Fortified towns played the same role in the frontier provinces along the Persian frontier, where the regular frontier forces were only able to repel small-scale raids. There too the towns and their populations had to fend for themselves in the event of a major invasion; see B. Isaac 1990, 372.

183. Ammianus, 31.4.5; 31.5.3; 31.4.9, Per id tempus nostri limitis reseratis obicibus, atque (ut Aetnaeas favillas armatorum agmina diffundente barbaria). . . .

184. *CTh* 15.1.13, issued in the name of Valentinian and Valens. The emperors saw fit in this edict to threaten the *dux* of Dacia Ripensis with personal liability for the construction if he chose not to order it done by the soldiers with public funds.

185. *CTh* 7.6.3.

186. *CTh* 1.32.5.

187. D. Giorgetti 1983, pt. 2, 19–39, esp. 32.

188. M. Chichikova 1983, 15.

189. R. Hoddinott 1975, 128–33; V. Velkov 1980, 294.

190. Ammianus, 31.6.5–6. However, not a single city can be proven to have capitulated, although the countryside was pillaged. Cf. Eunapius, frag. 42, 75–77.

191. Ammianus, 31.5.2; *Passio S. Philippi*, 2.28, 2.17.

192. Y. Mladenova 1969, 527–534.
193. D. Nikolov 1976, 70.
194. V. Bauman 1983, 229–30.
195. A. Kahane, L. Threipland, J. Ward-Perkins 1968, 153–159. Evidence for Illyricum and other regions will be adduced later.
196. D. Nikolov 1976, 70–71; A. Poulter 1983b, 99, with examples of villas near Nicopolis ad Istrum. That these squatters survived hard times in the contemporary local refuges makes a great deal of sense but remains only a hypothesis.
197. *CJ* 11.52.
198. A. Poulter 1983b, 100.

II. Theodosius in Action

1. A. Jones 1964, 156.
2. For the most part, the careful chronology suggested by O. Seeck 1919 is based upon the dates and places of imperial subscription in the legal codes. These are usually unconfirmed otherwise. In several cases where inscriptions or papyri are available, changes are necessary. Despite its limitations, Seeck's work remains indispensable. Seeck's suggestion (1922, reprint 1966), v. 5, p. 479 (note to p. 124, l. 33) that Gratian made Theodosius *magister equitum* is probable (based upon Themistius, *Or.* 15, 198a, ἱππάρχων). Seeck's citations in his *Regesten* to the literary sources are still useful. For the elevation of Theodosius, *Regesten*, p. 250. See also J. Matthews 1975, 91–92, based upon Pacatus, *Latini Pacati Drepanii Panegyricus Theodosio Avgvsto Dictus*, 10.2; and C. Nixon 1987, 63, n. 38. The text reads that he defeated some Sarmatians, but "Sarmatians" was another of the favorite literary terms for any barbarians. Theodosius had retired to Spain after his father's execution in 375. *PLRE*, 1.904, suggests that his post immediately upon recall was that of *mag. militum*. Whatever the case, his experience as *dux Moesiae Primae* (ca. 373–74, commander of the frontier forces there) certainly made him an ideal choice regardless of whether his appointment was urged upon Gratian by members of Theodosius's family and supporters still in the government.
3. In addition to St. Ambrose, who was the most alarmed, St. Jerome and others held their breath to await the outcome. They too saw in the initial struggles a test of the Empire; cf. J.-R. Palanque 1952, 173–99. In general, J. Straub 1943, 255–86.
4. C. Stevens 1933, 130–60; more recently see R. Mathisen 1981, 95–109, and 1979, 597–627. See also *PLRE*, 2.383.
5. On the archaeological support for the Eugippius *Vita Severini*, see R. Christlein 1982a, 217–53, and J. Haberl 1976. The present controversies surrounding Severinus's identity and "purpose" also accept the central narrative as valid. Recent archaeology is summarized by H. Fischer 1987, 89–104, and clearly plotted in the *Archäologischer Plan von Passau in römischer Zeit* (Passau, 1991).
6. *Vita Severini*, 9.
7. Ammianus, 31.15.10–15, when the Goths, fresh from victory, unsuccessfully tried to capture Adrianople and the imperial baggage.
8. Zosimus, 4.24.3. Zosimus drew upon Eunapius of Sardis extensively, paraphrasing entire passages, page after page. Later he followed Olympiodorus of Thebes. Both men were contemporaries to the events described, but to what extent Zosimus

used other accounts remains in dispute as do the sources of Eunapius and Olympiodorus themselves.

9. Zosimus, 4.24.4. Thrace had in fact been Eastern since 364. Zosimus was careless.

10. Sozomenus, *HE*, 7.4.1; returning westward, Gratian turned over to Theodosius the government of "Illyricum and the eastern parts of the Empire": Ἰλλυριοὺς καὶ τὰ πρὸς ἥλιον ἀνίσχοντα τῆς ἀρχῆς Θεοδοσίῳ ἐπιτρέψας. Sozomenus writing ca. 440 followed the literary fashion going back at least to Thucydides of referring to governmental units by the people governed, thus Illyricum is literally here the Illyrians. So too the Eastern Empire becomes for Sozomenus "the parts of the Empire toward the rising sun." Prior to the work of E. Demougeot (1947, 1948) the passage was typically understood quite simply as giving Theodosius Illyricum and the Eastern provinces, that is those formerly ruled by Valens (for example, E. Walford 1855, 315, and C. Hartranft 1890, 378). That reading is still not only possible but correct. In any case, that Gratian turned over the whole of Illyricum is difficult to refute from Sozomenus.

11. Jones 1964, 373. See below on Hesperius, who probably held the post of PPO of Illyricum along with that of Italy and Gaul in 379. If so, he was certainly an absentee PPO of Illyricum and of no consequence in this crisis.

12. *CTh* 11.13.1, probably dated after May 383.

13. E. Demougeot 1947, 16–31, and 1948, 87–92.

14. J.-R. Palanque 1951, 5–14, with corrections to the notes of E. Demougeot 1947.

15. V. Grumel 1951, 5–46.

16. Zosimus, 4.33.2–3. This was probably rather early in 381; see chapter 3, n. 10.

17. For example, E. Demougeot 1947 and 1948, whose work remains fundamental despite my disagreements with some details.

18. *PLRE*, 1.427.

19. *PLRE*, 1.77.

20. *PLRE*, 1.641 (Olybrius); *PLRE*, 1.139 (Ausonius).

21. *PLRE*, 1.737, Sex. Claudius Petronius Probus.

22. *CTh* 10.20.10, perhaps issued in March.

23. Over fifteen laws are addressed to him in his various capacities (*PLRE*, 1.428).

24. *CJ* 1.54.4; *PLRE*, 1.317.

25. *CJ* 5.34.12. This and *CTh* 7.13.10, dated 5 September 381, make it very difficult to accept as conclusive the argument for July 381 for the return of Dacia and Macedonia to Gratian as advanced by P. Hill, J. Kent, and R. Carson 1960, 43, and based upon the absence of the bishop of Thessalonica on an edict issued 31 July 381 promulgating the results of the Council of Constantinople.

26. Thus so-called Eastern Illyricum (Dacia and Macedonia) came about only after the return of Pannonia in September 380, not as a result of the meeting in 379. Western Illyricum (first noted in the *Notitia dignitatum*) was created much later. That Gratian and Theodosius could have agreed to a temporary civilian expedient to preserve legal continuity for a short interval should not seem so far-fetched if we recall the regular use of temporary generalships throughout the period as various men of comital rank were elevated to *magister* for a specific campaign.

27. Zosimus, 4.24.3. Specific diocesan transfers within Illyricum are not attested in the sources. Sozomenus (*HE*, 7.4.1) only reports that the entire prefecture was given

over. For those doubting that the entire prefecture of Illyricum was transferred, the lack of specific confirmation has set off many searches to show the degree and timing of Theodosius's control over each. This level of precision is really beyond our grasp. The minting activity at Thessalonica confirms his control of Macedonia, although more ambiguously than J. Pearce 1933 believed. P. Hill, J. Kent, and R. Carson 1960, 43, challenge Pearce's belief that the mint was striking for Theodosius as of 379. They suggest not before 381, but this seems to misconstrue the events of 379 and a great deal of nonnumismatic data. There was, as Hill, Kent, and others before them suggest, a short period before his death in August 383 (not, I think, as of July 381 but rather after July 382) during which Gratian as Western emperor again administered the entire former prefecture of Illyricum. In fact Hill's and Kent's argument about the completeness of the Western series struck at the Thessalonica mint is strong confirmation of this. Hill and Kent note that the mintings at Siscia and Thessalonica at some point after the death of Gratian demonstrate that the entire prefecture of Illyricum had again returned to Theodosius. By August or September 384, Macedonia (and apparently all of Illyricum) was certainly again administered from Constantinople (*CTh* 6.2.14). By July 386 Illyricum including Dacia and Macedonia was back under Rome, apparently as a part of the sphere carved out for Valentinian II (*CTh* 1.32.5; A. Jones 1964, 159, n. 51). Siscia struck for all emperors including Theodosius, perhaps immediately (J. Pearce 1933, 149–52). Pearce (pp. 156–60) proposed that Sirmium came to life, so to speak, in ca. 379 to explain the mint mark SM at this time. M. Hendy 1972, 126–27, accepted this but believed that the *comitatus* at Sirmium was Gratian's not Theodosius's. That doubt exists concerning this affiliation follows from recent work on ingots and a closer look at the military campaigns. On the importance of the ingots see below. On the primary importance of the *comitatus* from the era of Valentinian I onward, see J. Kent 1956, 190–204.

28. Jordanes, *Getica*, 138; Zosimus, 4.24–25. On his campaigns in these areas see below. There has been a great deal of debate on the precise nature of the transfers; see in addition to the citations in note 10 especially E. Stein as edited by J.-R. Palanque (1941) 1968, v. 2, 193 (and p. 520, n. 5). That mints in new areas of his command struck coins in Theodosius's name, contrary to earlier opinion, really proves little, since mints always struck coins for all legitimate emperors, not just those in administrative charge of their area. On the other hand the complete run of Western types that took place at Thessalonica sometime prior to August 383 (Gratian's death) strongly argue that the mint there was Western again, even though only briefly (P. Hill 1960, 42–43). Because of their inherent chronological imprecision the coin issues really do not provide the absolute clarity needed to resolve the issue of Illyricum as many have thought.

29. L. Várady 1969, 37, n. 86.

30. B. Overbeck and M. Overbeck 1985, 199–210, at pp. 209f. Earlier dating without out the piece from Feldioara had placed the ingots ca. 367–75, under Valens/Valentinian; see G. Elmer 1935, 3–21. On Kalyopius's office see Overbeck and Overbeck, pp. 206–8; he supervised the production. The *Nd. or.* 11.37, places the *fabrica* at Naissus under the office of the *magister officiorum* within the prefecture of Illyricum. Kalyopius could only have held office under Theodosius at Thessalonica and Naissus while the dioceses of Dacia and Macedonia were Eastern, that is between 379 and 385 with some interruptions. During these six years Theodosius can only be located at Naissus in 379.

31. Still further discussion of these ingots follows later in the chapter. B. and M.

Overbeck 1985, 199–210, have made the traditional assignment of these ingots to Gratian impossible to maintain (see Pearce 1933, 156) and thereby have added substantial evidence that Theodosius's temporary sphere of governance included at least the province of Pannonia II within the diocese of Pannonia. On the technical developments of the mints, especially of the late fourth century monopoly of gold by the *comitatus*, see M. Hendy 1972, 117–39, who points out that Sirmium at this time (ca. 379) was purely a mint of the *comitatus* and minted only gold (pp. 126–30). Siscia was the location of the regular mint. The transferring of the staffs of regional mints to the *comitatus* had begun under Valentinian I. The regional mints struck gold only when the emperor and his *comitatus* were nearby. The casting of ingots need not have been connected to any "mint" at all and was an independent procedure. Ingots were distinct in the sequence of tax paying, whereas gold coins were used to pay the expenses of the imperial court and army. The arguments in the secondary literature up to 1972 are adequately summarized by Hendy.

32. Jordanes, *Getica*, 142, Vbi vero post haec Theodosius convaluit imperator repperitque cum Gothis et Romanis Gratiano imperatore pepigisse quod ipse optaverat, admodum grato animo ferens et ipse in hac pace consensit.

33. Pacatus, 32.3–5. Mention of Gratian's contributions were inappropriate to a panegyric such as this, but Pacatus could claim every right to extol Theodosius for the victories there. The interpretation and dating of this passage are discussed more critically in chapter 3, n. 19.

34. Zosimus, 4.25.1.

35. *CTh* 12.13.4 (O. Seeck 1919, 253). That Vicus Augusti is the same as Mansio Augusti in Pannonia see L. Várady 1969, 377–78.

36. O. Seeck 1919, 251.

37. Ibid., pp. 250, 252.

38. *CTh* 12.13.4. L. Várady, pp. 377–78.

39. O. Seeck 1919, 253. The edict is dated 19 August. Bauxare cannot be located precisely but must lie on the route to Milan. Bozen (Bolzano) in South Tirol is usually suggested as the site of the pronouncement of *CTh* 6.30.3. At any rate, the edict was issued by Gratian (and not Theodosius as in Seeck 1919, 253); for the victory of November, *Cons. Const.*, p. 243.

40. For example, Usce Slatinske Reke with coins from Constantius II through Valentinian II but not Theodosius (so far), A. Jovanović, M. Korać, and Đ. Janković 1986, 380. For a summary of the excavations see M. Tomović 1987, 91–100.

41. M. Gabričević 1986, 72. Of the small sites published this is the only one with a substantial number of coins (50) from Valentinian I through Theodosius I. A few coins of Theodosius have appeared at other locations such as Ljubičevac-Glamija, V. Kondić 1984, 131f., and M. Parović-Peškan 1984, 141.

42. Tomović's summary is, although accurate, very brief; for that matter so are many of the reports to which he refers for the evidence. See Tomović 1987, 99, on the humble fortified sites of the fifth century. The standard cutoff date in all the publications is taken to be 443 and the Hunnic invasions, which is believed to correspond in most sites to a level of burned remains. A first destruction in many sites seems to have occurred during the last quarter of the fourth century. Some sites were refortified in the sixth century.

43. For example, the triangular combs found at Borđej; see A. Cermanović-Kuzmanović and S. Stanković 1984, 219–20, comb (fig. 211.4). Contrasted with the comb of Roman type from the late fourth century level at Mihajlovac-'Blato', M. To-mović 1986, 401–31, fig. 23.4 (discussed p. 406) and dated to the last quarter of the fourth century according to decorative style by analogy to the work of E. Keller 1971, 46f., or early fifth century for this area (based on analogies to the materials discussed by I. Kovrig 1959, 209–25, esp. p. 217).

44. There is at Diana, for example, as at several of the fortified towers discussed above, ample evidence of two destruction levels, one around the turn of the century and another later, probably midcentury. But to assume as most writers have that all the former is because of Gothic attacks ca. 379–80 is to succumb to the temptation of pressing archaeological data to fit handy historical incidents, when in truth, of course, there is no way to assign such precision and causation to burn-levels. Nonetheless, so concludes J. Rankov 1987, 16–36, at pp. 21–24.

45. S. Soproni 1985, 95–106. For Soproni the decline continued until the reorganization of the *limes* in 409 under the direction of Generidus (Zosimus, 5.46), which gave the system another 15 years of life. The final collapse came with the Hunnic incursions of 425. Concerning the period between 378 and 409, this publication includes a detailed gazetteer of sites in Valeria, Pannonia I, and Pannonia II, the latter not yielding much data to survey, from which to draw important conclusions. This despite the fact that in most cases the data from any one site are inconclusive and that naturally arguments from the *Notitia dignitatum* will not stand up to rigorous chronological testing. Nevertheless, it is clear that in general the size of enclosures decreased significantly during these years. Furthermore, a reduction in the level of economic life in comparison with the era of Valentinian I is reflected in the paucity of datable materials such as ceramics. There are, however, sufficient late fourth–early fifth century ceramic types and sometimes coin finds to anchor the data within the period under discussion and thereby confirm some type of continuity. No one shock dissolved the frontier system in this area, but the garrisons faced very difficult choices.

46. For example, the Valentinianic watchtower at Passau-Haibach in Noricum, where coin finds end with Valentinian. See T. Burns and H. Bender 1982, 55f. On Passau (Batavis, Boiotro, and immediate area), see H. Fischer 1987, 89–104, who argues that the watchtower at Haibach may have been abandoned along with the removal of the garrison from Boiotro, ca. 375, when the redundancy of a double fortification on the boundary between Raetia and Noricum could no longer be justified. As yet unpublished ceramic finds, however, might carry some sort of meager occupation to ca. 400 at Haibach.

47. *PLRE*, 1.605, still probably *mag. mil.* in Thrace in 382, when Gregorius Nazianzus requested his support as a good Christian.

48. Zosimus, 4.25.2.-3. Contrary to F. Paschoud 1971–89 (v. 2, pt. 2), 387, that Modares was probably of Gothic ancestry does not demonstrate that he here commanded Gothic allies for Theodosius.

49. Zosimus, 4.27.1–2. The increase of the *magistri* and the structural reforms of Theodosius will occupy us in later chapters. Of course, Zosimus saw this as a needless waste of tax money. I agree with R. Ridley 1982, 191–92, n. 77, that Zosimus cannot be taken at face value. Ridley suggests that the change in the number of *magistri* was

not 2 to 5, as Zosimus states, but "from 3 to about 4," and not in 380 as Zosimus seems to suggest here, but ca. 386–88 as a gradual changeover. F. Paschoud too notes (1971–89 [v. 2, pt. 2], 392) that Zosimus is anachronistic here. This was a result of changed circumstances as Theodosius got control of the Balkans and elsewhere and could respond to the need for high-level general commanders in the various regions including Thrace as *mag. eq. et ped.* or elsewhere *utriusque mil.* So that he busied himself in 380 at Thessalonica with civil and military reforms seems less likely than during his visit there in the spring of 388. The barbarian crossing of the Danube in 386 may have served as a catalyst, but, of course, there is no way to be positive.

50. Gregorius Nazianzus, *Epis.* 136, to Modares then at Constantinople; see *PLRE*, 1.605.

51. Sozomenus, *HE*, 7.4.

52. Socrates, *HE*, 5.2. On both Socrates and Sozomenus see G. Downey 1965, 57–70, who emphasizes that they took "as heroes the emperors and the holy men," p. 67. Both authors were translated into Latin in the sixth century by Epiphanius Scholasticus and through this translation were used by Cassiodorus in his *Historia Ecclesiastica Tripartita.*

53. Socrates, *HE*, 5.6.

54. Orosius, 7.34. The special position of Theodosius as a Christian hero as seen in the early ecclesiastical writers was even more pronounced in Orosius, who saw him as the model Christian ruler and did much to pass this image on to the medieval West. This image of Theodosius affected all historiography concerning him until modern times. For the diocese of Illyricum and the exceedingly complex problems concerning its creation ca. 400, see chapter 6.

55. This should not be confused with Theodosius's action in 392 transferring Illyricum to Eastern control or the actions ca. 400 returning the western half to the Western Empire. On these events more later, but see the discussion by D. Hoffmann 1970, v. 2, 208–15.

56. Orosius, 7.34.5–6. This might refer to the victories over some of the same people believed later settled in Pannonia by Gratian (ca. 380). This would also explain why Theodosius was apparently on the Sirmium-Emona road in August 379. There seems to be every likelihood of at least two campaigns in this area, one by Gratian and a later finishing blow delivered by Theodosius. These groups were probably disunited and scattered. Nonetheless, the defeat of some of them would have allowed Gratian a parallel victory, as reported. The treaty would have come later when Gratian returned to Illyricum, perhaps in these same areas relatively pacified by the earlier victories. But, in truth, Gratian never produced the archetypal treaty attributed to him by E. Demougeot 1974b, 143–60, who assumes that Gratian gave a *foedus* to a group of Alans-Huns-Goths led by Alatheus and Saphrax and that this treaty then formed *the* precedent for Theodosius to create a new federate policy. The nature of this treaty according to Demougeot was a unified settlement and service agreement under their own tribal leaders, i.e., the first classic "federates."

57. Orosius, 7.34.6, et ne paruam ipsam Romani exercitus manum adsidue bellando detereret, foedus cum Athanarico Gothorum rege percussit.

58. Zosimus, 4.34.1–2. This is the same Vitalianus who had begun his career as a soldier in an Erulian *numerus* ca. 363.

59. Jordanes, *Getica*, 140, adds that at this time the Gothic forces split, with the army of Fritigern attacking Thrace, Epiros and Achaia, and Alatheus and Saphrax with the remainder striking Pannonia. According to *Getica*, 141, because of Theodosius's ill health and Gratian's troubles on the Rhine with Vandals, Gratian (actually accomplished through his general Vitalianus) decided to enter into a peace agreement with them. He succeeded thanks to his munificent gifts and provisions (*victualia*) after they had crossed into Roman territory and were becoming aggressive.

60. Zosimus, 4.34.3–5.

61. Note the aorist used throughout the passage.

62. Zosimus, 4.34.4 (F. Paschoud 1971–89 [v. 2, pt. 2], 408–10, discussing events of 381–83); Ammianus, 27.5.10.

63. Zosimus, 4.34.6.

64. Orosius, 7.34.5–6.

65. Jordanes, *Getica*, 140.

66. Seeck 1919, 257, from *Consularia Constantinopolitana*, p. 243.

67. Ammianus, 31.2.5–7; on the walls in this area see R. Vulpe 1957.

68. So I conclude from Jordanes, *Getica*, 142, that Athanaric had succeeded Fritigern: Aithanaricoque rege, qui tunc Fritigerno successerat.

69. Eunapius, frag. 55 (*Exc. de Sent.* 56), and not mentioned in Zosimus.

70. Zosimus, 4.34.6.

71. Ammianus, 27.5.5; see further G. Bichir 1976, 171. *Vicus carpi* is here a specific place but could be translated as "a village of the Carpi."

72. Ammianus, 28.1.5; *PLRE*, 1.577.

73. *Nd. or.* 5.20 (Visi, a unit of the *auxilia palatina praes.*), 6.20 (Tervingi also in the *auxilia palatina praes.*). D. Hoffmann 1970, who would assign a date to the Eastern section of post-386, has raised many questions about the pairing of units (the so-called double-troops) in the *Notitia* including the Visi-Tervingi. Rather than pairing, I suggest that some of these instances must represent the enrollment of people after a Roman victory and their subsequent division within the army. The Visi and Tervingi, both names given in the *Historia Augusta* (written ca. 395 and anachronistically discussing groups in the third century) for the Goths, are only referred to as Tervingi by Ammianus. I believe that the Romans made two such groups from one in the course of *receptio* by according each a name associated with the whole. The origins and meanings of these Gothic terms are controversial, but the Tervingi probably preceded Visi[gothi?], the later representing the larger level of confederation which occurred just prior to the crossing of 376. Perhaps these terms originally had something to do with the topographic setting in which their political cohesion took place—Greutungi relating to the steppes and Tervingi to the forest; so R. Vulpe 1957, 25 (accepted by U. Wanke 1990, 71, and T. Burns 1980, 34). I no longer believe that the topographic clustering led to the political structure; rather it seems the reverse happened. Political processes were primary in defining territory.

74. Zosimus, 4.30.

75. Ammianus, 31.16.8.

76. Ibid., 4.31.

77. Ibid., 4.31.3.

78. Ibid., 4.31.5.

79. *CTh* 12.1.89, 5 July 382. Zosimus, 4.35, that Gratian fled to Sigidunum (*sic* Singidunum ?) after his defeat at the hands of Maximus is simply in error. Gratian was slain at Lyon, 25 August 383, far from Moesia.

80. *Getica*, 140–41, sed gratia eos muneribusque victurus, pacemque, victualia illis concedens, cum ipsis inito foedere fecit.

81. Ibid., 142–45.

82. E. Demougeot 1974b, 143–60. L. Várady 1969, especially pp. 22–41; E. Chrysos 1973, 52–64, and E. Chrysos 1972, 138–45.

83. T. Burns 1980, 45.

84. J. Šašel 1979 must be correct (pp. 127–28) in his suggestion that these Goths and other small groups of barbarians served as a type of border guard. A few sites seem related to Gratian's "federates," e.g., Á. Salamon and L. Barkóczi 1970, 35–80. L. Barkóczi 1980, 118, summarizes current research that "the Hunnish-Gothic-Alanic *foederati* were first settled in southern Pannonia" but stresses the ethnic diversity of the populations, especially those of defensive centers near or on the frontier.

85. Zosimus, 4.40, where Gerontius, garrison commander at Tomi in the province of Scythia (ca. 386), had to confront severe discipline problems among the barbarians assigned there. This will be discussed in the next chapter in its chronological place.

86. Hieronymus, *Epis.* 66.14, ad Pammachium. Cf. L. Várady 1969, 422, n. 87, and Šašel 1979, 126). But A. Mócsy 1974b, 341, denies the possibility of identifying specific locations within Pannonia. The location of Stridon is unknown as is Jerome's date of birth. He died in 419 or 420.

87. See H. Wolfram 1979, 311, with references; L. Várady 1969, 168–69.

88. *CIL* 5.1623.

89. L. Várady is then the basis of L. Barkóczi 1980, 117.

90. A. Mócsy 1974b, 341.

91. Várady 1969, 37, n. 86, suggests this as an interpretation of Mursa's suffering because of the Arian presence in *Epistola Maximi Tyranni ad Valentinianum aug. iuniorem* in *Epistulae Imperatorum Pontificum Aliorum*.

92. These and Maiorianus's future exploits were praised in the next century by Sidonius Apollinaris in his panegyric to our magister's grandson, Emperor Maiorianus (*Carmen* 5.107–25). The presence of Maiorianus alone does not prove that Valeria was necessarily transferred to Theodosius, but it certainly does demonstrate the high degree of military cooperation between the emperors.

93. Libanius, *Or.* 24.15–16.

94. Jerome, *Epis.* 66.14, may be read in this light, although specifically only mentioning the half-destroyed countryside of the land of his parents.

95. The problem of *antiqui barbari* is dealt with by Šašel 1979.

96. Recall from chapter 1 the *laeti* ordered to hold the Succi Pass under Gomoarius, recently a general in the West who may have brought them to the East, against Julian in 363, Ammianus, 21.13.16.

97. Ammianus, 25.10.9, Vitalianus domesticorum consortio iungitur, Erulorum e numero miles, qui multo postea auctus comitis dignitate, male rem per Illyricum gessit. . . .

98. Olympiodorus, frags. 3 and 59; Zosimus, 4.56.2 (Theodosius); Jordanes, *Getica*, 141 (Gratian); earlier examples, Ammianus, 17.12.21 (Quadi), and 16.12.26 (Alamanni).

99. *Nd. or.* 13.1; *oc.* 11.1. Flavius Eucherius held the post of *comes sac. larg.* from spring 377 to spring 379 and went on to the consulship in 381 (*PLRE*, 1.288).

100. J. Hampel 1905, vol. 2, 15–26; the dating of the finds remains conjectural and disputed.

101. On the silver dish with Constantius II in triumph from Kertch, see J. Kent and K. Painter 1977, 28, and references to the full treasure.

102. Malchus, frag. 15.

103. B. Overbeck and M. Overbeck 1985, 206, with citations to the law codes. The use of ingots to determine the value of payment in coin from the era of Constantine also accounts for the virtual absence of worn gold coins in the fourth and early fifth centuries. New coins or other items issued by the *comes sacrarum largitionum* were issued from the gold, in essence, recycled through taxes.

104. Sozomenus, *HE*, 7.4.2; Jordanes, *Getica*, 140. Just how sick and for how long is a matter of dispute.

105. O. Seeck 1919, 254–55, places Theodosius at Sirmium on 8 September 380 (*CTh* 7.22.11, *CJ* 12.47.2) and Gratian there on 2 August after attending the church council at Aquileia. It is conceivable that they never met and only exchanged correspondence; see P. Heather 1991, 153.

106. P. Heather 1991, 186, dates the fight to late 392 or early 393 and suggests that the real motive for the struggle was contrary opinions over whether to serve in Theodosius's coming campaign against the usurpers Arbogastes and Eugenius (392–94). This is probably correct.

107. Eunapius, frag. 59 (R. Blockley, p. 87, from *exc. de Leg. Gent.* 7); Zosimus, 4.56.2–3.

108. That we have no record of the *vicarius* is standard for this diocese and many others. Syagrius (*PLRE*, 1.862) was the prefect of Italy by 18 June 380, serving until spring 382.

III. Concluding the Gothic Wars

1. O. Seeck 1919, 253–55.

2. Their integration into existing units is confirmed explicitly by Jordanes, *Getica*, 145; the passage is significant in that it employs the later terminology of *foederati* and suggests a return to their earlier status under Constantine as allies: cum milite velut unum corpus effecit militiaque illa dudum sub Constantino principe foederatorum renovata et ipsi dicti sunt foederati. That they continued to defend Rome against attacks for a long time, Zosimus, 4.34.5. Jordanes, *Getica*, 28 (145), notes that they merged smoothly into the army so as to make one body (unum corpus) and were always faithful to Theodosius. His estimate as to their number is pure fantasy—more than 20,000. This sum somehow derives from his thoughts on the number of barbarians Theodosius fielded against Eugenius in 394. F. Paschoud 1971–89 (v. 2, pt. 2), 409–10, addresses the difficulties in trying to clarify Theodosius's activities in 381–82.

3. *CTh* 7.13.10, addressed to Eutropius, praetorian prefect, and probably at his initiation, trans. C. Pharr 1952, 172.

4. O. Seeck 1919, 261–65. Selymbria, 27 July 383, was an exception but hardly a great distance.

5. A. Jones 1964, 347–57.

6. When in 381 this mission of assistance took place is impossible to ascertain with complete certainty, like virtually everything else that rests solely upon Zosimus. Zosimus reports this mission immediately after Theodosius entered Constantinople in triumph on 24 November (Socrates, *HE*, 5.6.6; *Cons. Const.*, 380) en route to which he was attacked passing through this same area (Zosimus, 4.31.5). As late as 28 September 381 Eutropius, Theodosius's PPO of Illyricum, was still in office (*CJ* 5.34.12), so Macedonia was Eastern at that date. Dacia and Macedonia were probably returned before or while Gratian visited Viminacium in July 382. The placement of the mission at the opening of the passage, the fact that Theodosius had just recently encountered rebellious Goths there, and that Zosimus stresses that Gratian was very upset that he had to come to Theodosius's rescue point to a response early in 381. Some Western forces were probably securing the diocese of Pannonia and were positioned to move relatively swiftly.

7. Zosimus, 4.33.2–3. The pagan Zosimus here plays out his themes of moral corruption, luxury, and decadence in this Christian empire. That the barbarians tricked the emperor by sending their worst men, etc., is all part of his unflattering portrait of Theodosius. In essence he twisted the *topos* already familiar to moneyers of the tetrarchy who struck the medallion of Lyon—humble barbarians beseeching the emperor for entry. In fact, of course, such small-scale activities were handled by lower-level officials. The emperor would handle only great leaders and events such as the entry of Athanaric.

8. V. Besevliev 1964, 23, no. 33b, Stambolovo (prior to 392). As in many cases the same milestone records the earlier maintenance projects as well; in this case under Valentinian I, Valens, and Gratian, and again under Constantinus I and Licinius.

9. Ibid., p. 54, no. 80.

10. Ibid., p. 100, no. 149.

11. Ibid., pp. 166–67, no. 232b.

12. So even Zosimus concludes, 4.35, who otherwise was critical of Theodosius.

13. *Cons. Const.*, 381. Eodem mense diem functus idem Aithanaricus VIII kal. Feb. 382. Ipso anno universa gens Gothorum cum rege suo in Romaniam se tradiderunt die V non. Oct.

14. A. Piganiol 1972, 235.

15. P. Heather 1991, 158–81, offers a considerably different and more traditional interpretation of the "Peace of 382" than the one that follows below. For Heather, as for several earlier scholars, the Goths received land in Thrace. Where Heather differs is that he correctly stresses that they were first defeated. I have no problem with the traditional belief that recruits on the frontiers received lands for themselves and their families, since some sort of landed establishment was quite common on the frontiers for Roman soldiers regardless of origins at this time. In short, there was neither something new nor extraordinarily important in the fact that new soldiers entering the Empire with families were given lands in the frontier areas in which they were to serve.

16. Perhaps Jordanes was troubled by these same questions when he stated that Theodosius offered gifts to Athanaric, "who had succeeded Fritigern," and concluded an agreement with him. *Getica*, 142. Before the crossings of the Danube in 376, Athanaric had been Fritigern's predecessor and rival. On the other hand, Jordanes is correct in one sense. Theodosius may have hoped that Athanaric really would succeed Fritigern inside the Empire, in peace rather than in rebellion. If one were looking for a "Gothic

leader," as Jordanes always did, with Fritigern's death and Athanaric's reception into the Empire, there was no other Gothic leader of stature available to Jordanes or more importantly to Theodosius.

17. Pacatus, 22.3, in *Panégyriques Latins*, v. 3, Dicamne ego receptos seruitum Gothos castris tuis militem, terris sufficere cultorem? The same accolades were heaped on Constantius I in panegyric, even including the barbarians cultivating Roman soil, in 297. See *Incerti Panegyricus Constantio Caesari Dictus*, 21.1, in *Panégyriques Latins*, v. 1. Pacatus surely would have devoted more to the formal conclusion of the Gothic wars than the stock phrases of the genre; he spared no effort when it came to the revolt of Magnus Maximus.

18. Pacatus, 32.3–5, trans. C. Nixon 1987, 41–42.

19. C. Nixon 1987, following the text chronologically (pp. 92–93, nn. 109, 110), places the passage entirely in the context of 386, whereas P. Heather 1991, 161, reads it as applying only to the events of 382, when he believes that the Alans and Huns were finally brought under control and participated in the Treaty of 382. On Theodosius's whereabouts see O. Seeck 1919, 75–79.

20. Orosius, 7.34.6–7. Urbem Constantinopolim uictor intrauit et ne paruam ipsam Romani exercitus manum adsidue bellando detereret, foedus cum Athanarico Gothorum rege percussit. Athanaricus autem continuo ut Constantinopolim uenit, diem obiit. Uniuersae Gothorum gentes rege defuncto aspicientes uirtutem benignitatemque Theodosii Romano sese imperio dediderunt. In isdem etiam diebus Persae, qui Iuliano interfecto aliisque imperatoribus saepe uictis, nunc etiam Valente in fugam acto recentissimae uictoriae satietatem cruda insultatione ructabant, ultro Constantinopolim ad Theodosium misere legatos pacemque supplices poposcerunt; ictumque tunc foedus est, quo uniuersus Oriens usque ad nunc tranquillissime fruitur. Interea cum Theodosius in Oriente subactis barbarorum gentibus Thracias tandem ab hoste liberas reddidisset et Arcadium filium suum consortem fecisset imperii. Trans. I. Raymond 1936, 376.

21. Hydatius, *Continuatio chronicorum Hieronymianorum*, 6 (a.381): Athanaricus, rex Gothorum, apud Constantinopolim XV die, ex quo a Theodosio fuerat susceptus, interiit. And 7 (a.382): Gothi infida Romanis pace se tradunt.

22. Marcellinus Comes, *Chronicon*, 381.2. Athanaricus rex Gothorum, cum quo Theodosius imperator foedus pepigerat, Constantinopolim 'mense Ianuario' venit 'eodemque mense' morbo periit.

23. Ibid., 382.2, Eodem anno universa gens Gothorum Athanarico rege suo defuncto Romano sese imperio dedit 'mense Octobrio.'

24. Cassiodorus Senator, *Chronica*, 382. Athanaricus rex Gothorum Constantinopolim venit ibique vitam exegit.

25. Jordanes, *Getica*, 145. Defuncto ergo Aithanarico cunctus eius exercitus in servitio Theodosii imperatoris perdurans Romano se imperio subdens cum milite velut unum corpus effecit militiaque illa dudum sub Constantino principe foederatorum renovata et ipsi dicti sunt foederati. Jordanes goes on to note that Theodosius recruited more than 20,000 of these trusted allies to fight against the usurper Eugenius; that, however, is not at issue at this point in the discussion and clearly dates to much later in the reign.

26. Isidorus, *Historia Gothorum Wandalorum Sueborum*, 11. Gothi autem proprio rege defuncto adspicientes benignitatem Theodosi imperatoris inito foedere Romano se imperio tradiderunt. Trans. G. Donini and G. Ford 1970, 7.

27. Ibid., 12. Gothi patrocinium Romani foederis recusantes Alaricum regem sibi constituunt, indiguum iudicantes Romanae esse subitos potestati eosque sequi, quorum iam pridem leges imperiumque respuerant et de quorum se societate proelio triumphantes auerterant. Trans. G. Donini and G. Ford 1970, 8.

28. Marcellinus Comes, 395; the subject and date of Alaric's "kingship" will occupy discussion in chapter 6.

29. On the evolving portrayal of Theodosius and the Gothic monarchy, see S. Teillet 1984, 83–160, 441–55, but not necessarily as integrated into her theme of nationalism.

30. His additions to the *Consularia* consist of brief listings, primarily the consuls and little else. The entire era covered by the addendum comprises only two pages in the *Monumenta*. On the connections between the East and Hispania in late antiquity and the evidence of Hydatius see J. Fontaine 1983, 832.

31. On the Lyon medallion see especially P. Bastien 1972–76, 157–76.

32. Themistius, *Or.* 10, 134d, where Valens deals with Athanaric using rhetorical persuasion combined with vigorous leadership. The classical Roman virtues of leadership were taken over and made imperial virtues when Augustus established the Empire and are present on his *clupeus virtutis*. They were *virtus, clementia,* and *pietas*.

33. Orosius, 7.35, where the emperor with God on his side defeats the "tyrants" Maximus and then Eugenius. The application of the term *princeps religiosus* by Rufinus and others to Theodosius is developed in S. Teillet 1984, 94–96.

34. On Themistius in general see foremost G. Dagron 1968, 1–242, whose basic thesis is that in his works Themistius found a separate and noncompetitive place for Hellenic philosophy within Christian society and that for Themistius traditional frontiers had no role, for different cultures could and would be assimilated into the Roman world. Thus the Empire was for Themistius a universal system without geographic and ethnic boundaries. In this vision obviously the emperor was the central figure of example and dissemination. There are several important studies of particular aspects of Themistius's thought, including L. Daly 1972, 351–79. Concerning Valens and the peace with Athanaric, see I. Barnea 1967, 563–76. On Themistius's view of emperorship, see S. Stertz 1976, 349–58. For a new viewpoint of Themistius at court see J. Vanderspoel 1989.

35. Themistius, *Or.* 16, 208c.

36. Ibid., 208d, p. 299.

37. Ibid., 209a–b., pp. 299, 210c, 301.

38. Ibid., 199c, p. 288.

39. Ibid., 208b, p. 298.

40. Ibid., 212a–b, p. 303.

41. Ibid., 212a–c, pp. 302–3.

42. Ibid., 211a–b, trans. L. Daly 1972, 373.

43. *RIC* 9, p. 226, no. 53a.

44. *RIC* 9, from Constantinopolis, no. 50, p. 225, no. 73, p. 231, no. 75, p. 232, and from the period 367–75, no. 26, no. 30, p. 217, no. 31, 32, p. 218. From Thessalonica, period 378–83, no. 34, 35, 41, pp. 180–82; period 383–88, no. 57, p. 185, and no. 63, p. 187.

45. Ibid., no. 83, p. 233.

46. That he never said "treaty" or "agreement" when he surely had the occasion to do so may have been another way of distinguishing between the new "peace by

choice" and the traditional "peace by compulsion." The appropriate terms then in use for the formal conclusion of a treaty were σπονδαί, σύμβασις, or σύνθακαι, none of which occur in this oration, although he used them frequently elsewhere in his literary corpus. See further on the vocabulary of Themistius the *Index Graecus* of the edition by W. Dindorf, *Themistii Orationes*.

47. Themistius, *Or.* 16, 199c, ed. Downey p. 288, ll. 6–7. On Themistius's unusual personal knowledge of Thrace see V. Velkov 1980, 171–98.

48. See Ammianus, 31.10.17, and the discussion of *dediticii* in chapter 1. On the fact that the Roman command knew its individual soldiers' legal status, *CTh* 7.13.16.

49. Roman propaganda typically portrayed defeated barbarians, but the bulk of recruitment was accomplished without war (see chapter 5, particularly the example of the "Elbgermans").

50. Themistius, *Or.* 34, 24.3–5, an oration occasioned by his resignation from the office of urban prefect accorded him in 384. This speech takes the form of a justification and recapitulation of his public career, during which he had personally witnessed many important events having to do with the Thracian area. Curiously, Themistius uses much more specific terminology in this brief passage than in the entire episode in *Or.* 16. Here the Scythians in Macedonia are housed (ὁμωροφίους), bound by treaty (ὁμοσπόνς δους), and share in the festivals (συνεορτάζοντας) celebrating victory over them. He did not choose to employ any of these terms in *Or.* 16. The barbarians in Macedonia were in fact hardly pacified or assimilated, and in 391 some group there again surprised and almost killed Theodosius himself. Besides proving that he knew the technical vocabulary associated with treaties, and that we could have assumed regardless, since they were common terms, *Or.* 34, 24 also stresses the merging of barbarian and Roman.

51. Libanius, *Or.* 13, 29–30.

52. Seeck 1919, 258, from *CTh* 1.10.1 and 12.1.89. The dating of the relevant edicts in the Theodosian Code is not straightforward. It might have been a year earlier, that is in 381, or there might be two dates reflecting separate meetings on the same day in different years. I believe there was one meeting, in 382. For two edicts to have been issued on exactly the same day at the same place in two successive years and in Viminacium is too much to accept; so too is the reference in 12.1.89 to "the year after" the consulship of Syagrius and Eugenius. This is simply not the accepted manner of dating. Both edicts were issued in the consulship of Syagrius and Eugenius, 382. The dating question is clearly discussed but without recommendation in relationship to the praetorian prefects of the Orient, Flavius Afranius Syagrius 2 and Flavius Syagrius 3, in *PLRE*, 1.862.

53. On 20 June Gratian was still in Padua (*CTh* 14.18). On 5 July he was in Viminacium (*CTh* 12.1.89: O. Seeck 1919, 258). No army could move so fast, and no emperor would move with only a small escort through hostile territory.

54. P. Heather 1991, 171, believes that Gratian was at Viminacium as a part of a great pincers movement that reduced the Goths and their allies once and for all and led directly to the Peace of 382. Under the circumstances this theory must remain a dubious hypothesis. Surely at least Zosimus, who loved to diminish Theodosius's accomplishments, would have noted Gratian's crucial role in any such great campaign. He did not. But the telling evidence is the rapidity of known imperial movement for both Gratian and Theodosius. Soon after his visit to Viminacium, Gratian's edicts were read at Capua (on 30 August, *CTh* 11.16.14) and posted at Rome (on 14 October, *CTh* 4.20.1), which

suggests that he had returned to Italy quickly. Another edict was issued on 1 August (*CTh* 8.9.2) but is given without a location in the manuscript. He issued an edict from Milan of 22 November (*CTh* 1.6.8), leaving little doubt that he was himself there (O. Seeck 1919, 258).

55. Seeck 1919, 261, from the edicts as preserved.

56. A. Mócsy 1974, 341, goes so far as to say that Viminacium became the "meeting place" of emperors. Gratian attended the Church Council at Aquileia that opened in September 381 and continued into early 382. The emperor celebrated Christmas there (O. Seeck 1919, 258). Theodosius faced questions of what to do with the properties of pagan temples and various issues of heresy.

57. Which accounts for the Roman coin types struck at Thessalonica and Siscia (P. Hill, J. Kent, and R. Carson 1960, 43).

58. Gratian was killed on 25 August 383 (*Cons. Const.* 383). On setting up the sphere for Valentinian II: *CTh* 6.2.14 (14 August or 13 September 384, probably the former) from Constantinople; *CTh* 1.32.5 (July 386) by Valentinian at Milan. Both addressed issues in Illyricum. The establishment must have occurred sometime in between the issuances of these edicts. Theodosius made a quick visit to Italy in August 384 (*CTh* 12.1.107, dated 31 August at Verona) but had returned to Constantinople by 16 September (*CTh* 7.8.3). Therefore I believe that the last Eastern edict concerning these dioceses (*CTh* 6.2.14) dates to 14 August, after which the emperor must have hurried to Italy, where he decided to transfer the dioceses to Valentinian. That his visit to Italy was to get Justina to agree to an accommodation with Magnus Maximus in Gaul see A. Jones 1964, 159.

59. For example, *RIC* 9, no. 73 and 75, pp. 231–32.

60. *PLRE*, 2.750. By 388 Promotus was *magister equitum*, in which capacity he served until he was ambushed by barbarians in Thrace, apparently at the connivance of Rufinus at court. Zosimus, 4.39.2, offers rare proof of the use of Gothic speaking Roman soldiers as spies among those Goths not yet enrolled in Roman service.

61. Zosimus, 4.39.1, trans. R. Ridley 1982, 88; see also *Cons. Const.*, 386, and Claudianus, *IV cons. Hon.*, 623ff.

62. Zosimus, 4.39.5, but Zosimus notes that Promotus's actions, which ultimately brought Gothic recruits against Maximus, were conducted in secret. Whether these very Goths were deployed against Maximus later is unknowable. So also concludes F. Paschoud 1971–89 (v. 2, pt. 2), 429. There can be little doubt that Theodosius did not long share the emperorship with the usurper, officially only briefly in 386–87 (see chapter 4), but Zosimus may be reading the future too clearly in this passage. The facts were separated by two years: first, in 386, another recruitment of some Goths, this time of a large group of able-bodied men, and secondly two years later (388) a war against Maximus in which Gothic and other barbarians played a role but not a very important one.

63. Seeck 1919, 271, *Cons. Const.*, 386, which succinctly tells the same story without color; in this year the Romans defeated the Greutungi and led them into *Romania*. The victory and triumph then were celebrated on 12 October of the same year. On Theodosius's efforts at recruitment, Zosimus, 4.39.5, and Pacatus, 32.3–5, quoted above.

64. Claudianus, *IV cons. Hon.*, 625–37.

65. On the obelisk see G. Bruns 1935 and, most especially on the depictions of the naval engagement found only recently through excavations, see further the discus-

sion by V. Velkov (1961) 1980, 49–62, reprinted in his *Roman Cities in Bulgaria* (Amsterdam, 1980) and also H. Kähler 1975, 45–55.

66. This might account for the *GLORIA—ROMANORVM* with Contantinopolis seated left on throne, holding victory on globe and reversed spear, her right foot resting on the prow of a ship, *RIC* 9, no. 65, and assigned to the period 383–88. There are, however, many problems with this suggestion, not the least of which is the existence of other prow-types assigned to earlier periods in the *RIC* e.g., no. 43, a *CONCORDIA AVGGG*, assigned to 375–78, with a similar scene of Constantinopolis foot on prow. The entire sequence of dating Theodosian issues is fraught with problems. For another suggestion for the prow-coinage of Theodosius see H.-R. Baldus 1984, 175–92, who, as the title suggests, stresses the relationship to the revolt of Magnus Maximus (383–88). The obelisk set up in 390 in the hippodrome leaves no doubt that the emperor wished to acknowledge this specific naval victory to the public at large, and other occasions remain speculative.

67. The setting up of the obelisk is securely dated by Marcellinus Comes to 390.

68. Zosimus, 4.35.1.

69. Zosimus, 4.40.1–5. Such special units were probably a source for the members of the imperial guard. Perhaps such special units also formed one of the types of soldiers later called *foederati*; see the conjectures in this regard by J. Liebeschuetz 1986, 463–74. Zosimus concludes this chapter with the barb that the emperor had given the eunuchs everything he had. This has nothing to do with Gerontius and the barbarians. F. Paschoud 1971–89 (v. 2, pt. 2), 431, notes this as another anti-Theodosian barb in keeping with Eunapius.

70. Zosimus, 4.40.6–8.

71. Such modifications were hastened still more by the demands of the civil wars and consequently are addressed in chapter 4.

72. Zosimus, 4.48–49, in this vignette set sometime in the autumn of 391 (so too F. Paschoud 1971–89 [v. 2, pt. 2], 445–46), Theodosius must seek refuge with an old woman, etc., hardly "the stuff of history."

IV. Barbarians and Civil War

1. On the later date see E. Chrysos 1976, 1–48, specifically pp. 37–44.

2. Ibid., 41, n. 1, with citations to all sources, among them Marcellinus Comes, 384, Orosius, 7.34.8, *Cons. Const.*, 384.

3. J. Pearce 1933, pp. xxii–xxiii, 233: P. Hill, J. Kent, and R. Carson 1960, 43. Pearce's suggestion that they were recalled is unlikely in the case of bronze coinage. Better is Kent's suggestion that they were stored at the mint. No other Eastern mints struck for Maximus.

4. R. Bagnall 1987, 307.

5. Zosimus, 4.37; F. Paschoud 1971–89 (v. 2, pt. 2), 423–25, notes all the literary sources. But the full recognition probably did not come until all the problems arising from Justina and Valentinian appeared settled in 386. Harmony lasted less than a year. See also *Cons. Const.*, 388, which places the Egyptian tour by Cynegius, PPO of the Orient, immediately prior to the entry noting the death of Maximus the *tyrannus* at Aquileia; further, Theodoretus, *Historia Ecclesiastica* (henceforth *HE*), 5.21, and Sozomenus, *HE*, 7.15. He also assisted Bishop Marcellus in destroying the temples at

Apamea (*PLRE*, 2, Cynegius 3, p. 236). On Maximus and Gratian see further Paschoud 1975, 80–93.

6. J. Pearce 1933, 204. It was standard practice that all mints struck for all recognized emperors regardless of the mint's location.

7. Ambrosius, *Epis.* 20; Ambrose was outraged that Arians could openly serve the emperor.

8. Tribigild, a rebel in 399, was "chiliarch of the soldiers stationed in Phrygia." The chiliarch is usually given in its military Latin equivalent as military tribune. Socrates, *HE*, 6.6. Gaïnas, who rose to general under Theodosius after a long career, apparently all the way from the rank-and-file, used the tribuneship as a recruitment tool in 399; Sozomenus, *HE*, 8.4. On the archaeological reflections of the practice as far back as the third century, see J. Werner 1980, 1–49.

9. On his supposed anti-German stance see J.-R. Palanque 1929, 33–36. But he was quite ready to use them in his army (Ambrosius, *Epis.* 24.8). Maximus was probably justifiably suspicious of *comes* Bauto whose loyalty to the House of Theodosius would be well rewarded. Although Magnus accused Bauto of inciting barbarians to invade his territory (Ambrosius, *Epis.* 24.4.6–8), his concern was Bauto, not the barbarians. Bauto went on to become *magister militum* and in 385 *consul posterior* with Arcadius (*PLRE*, 1.159). After his death his daughter Eudoxia married Arcadius.

10. Zosimus, 4.35.2–5, *Epitome de Caesaribus*, 47. On this passage in the *Epitome* see J. Schlumberger 1974, 220–21.

11. Perhaps led by their *mag. ped.* Merobaudes, consul in 382, and perhaps nominated by Maximus for 387 but slain just before the outbreak of war with Theodosius; see further for these suggestions B. Rodgers 1981, 82–105, conclusions, pp. 104–5. This article also provides a useful outline of the secondary arguments concerning these men.

12. Claudianus, *De cons. Stil.* 1.51–68, written to celebrate his consulship in 400. The date of his mission to the Persian capital is insecure; see Chrysos 1976, 41.

13. Ambrosius, *Epis.* 51.

14. *CTh* 16.10.7 and 16.10.9; on Apamea, Libanius, *Or.* 30.8; see further A. Jones 1964, 164–67.

15. Probably in 389, Marcellinus Comes gives 389 but elsewhere 391; see *Chronica Gallica*.

16. He met the imperial refugees in September 387 and departed for campaign in April. O. Seeck 1919, 275.

17. Socrates, *HE*, 5.12; this mission is usually dated to 387.

18. Hendy 1972, 127–29.

19. Zosimus, 4.45.4 and 4.46. But contrary to Zosimus this did not induce Maximus to weaken the Julian Alpine defenses and thereby allow Theodosius easy passage to Aquileia.

20. Pacatus, 32.3.–5.

21. Zosimus, 4.45.3. This passage seems drawn from Eunapius, frag. 58.

22. Zosimus, 4.39.5.

23. P. Heather 1991, 160, concludes differently, stating that the "Goths served *en masse*" against Maximus and later against Eugenius/Arbogastes. On their very important role against Eugenius I can agree.

24. Philostorgius, *Historia Ecclesiastica* (henceforth *HE*), 10.8.

25. Pacatus, 12.34. Edicts emanated from Stobi on 14 and 16 June and from Scupi on 21 June 388 (Seeck 1919, 275).

26. *PLRE*, 1. Marcellinus 12.

27. Pacatus, 12.36.

28. Ibid., 12. 36–38. On the possible importance of the Franks and Saxons, see Ambrosius, *Epis.* 40.23: Ille igitur statim a Francis, a Saxonum gente, in Sicilia, Sisciae, Petavione [Poetovio, modern Ptuj], ubique denique terrarum victus est. Pacatus speaks only of the valor of the troops who lived up to the Roman name and traditions.

29. Ambrose speaks of the army running out of food, when God threw open the granaries through enemy hands. Pacatus records only the hard and trying times. Ambrosius, *Epis.* 40.22, dtd. Dec. 388, perhaps in connection with the battle at Siscia; Pacatus, 12.32.

30. Pacatus, 12.35.

31. Philostorgius, *HE*, 10.8.

32. Zosimus, 4.47, on Arbogastes see further *PLRE*, 1.95–97.

33. Zosimus, 4.47.2, makes a point of stressing that Theodosius chose only the best for his army; Ambrosius, *Epis.* 40.32; Pacatus, 12.45.

34. Zosimus, 4.35.1.

35. *Nd. or.* 8 and 9, ed. O. Seeck.

36. *CTh* 7.17.1 dated 28 January 412 to the *mag. mil. per Thracias*, and for the *mag. mil. per Orientem* (not especially important here except as indicating the existence of other territorialized *magistri*) 12.1.175, dated 18 May 412, both by Honorius and Theodosius II.

37. Claudianus, *In Eutropium*, 2.215–20.

38. *PLRE*, 2.44 (Alaricus 1). Virtually every modern authority has offered an opinion on these problems, among them: E. Nischer 1923, 1–55, who at pp. 44–45 assigns the *mag. mil. per Thracias* to Theodosius; A. Hoepffner 1936, 483–98, who suggests that Theodosius made earlier temporary regional assignments permanent; J. Doise 1949, 183–94, who sets forth an evolutionary system in which the territorialization did not occur until Arcadius and Honorius; A. Jones 1964, who believes that Arcadius is probably responsible for the command system outlined in the *Notitia* including the regional *magistri*; D. Hoffmann 1970, 458–522. Hoffmann sets forth a complex evolution built upon the consistent use of paired legions under Theodosius and postulates that the establishment of paired-praesental armies in the East occurred in 388 or shortly thereafter, with the regional commands in the Orient and Thrace fashioned as a part of the concomitant restructuring, which required shifting troop assignments, including the dissolution of old pairs, in order to create the central armies themselves (pp. 507–9). According to Hoffmann the *Nd* lists for Thrace and the Orient commands do not correspond precisely to the changes of 388 but rather reflect the situation existing just prior to the launching of the campaign against Eugenius and Arbogastes in the summer of 394 (p. 516). Therefore, Hoffmann suggests that these two lists (as well as that for the eastern *magister officiorum*) must date from July 392 to May 394 and represent, for him, a slight modification of the structures established for the praesental armies in 388. Furthermore, he proposes that the Illyrican sections were altered to reflect changes sometime between 396 and 410 (pp. 518–19). With the creation of the new *magistri* in the East, all of which were combined commands over both cavalry and infantry, the old terms *equitum* and

peditum ceased to have military significance. Therefore *magister utriusque militiae* could have been used to denote any of them and so is rare. Literary sources seem to use it more frequently when discussing the most pwerful generals. In the West the term *magister utriusque militiae* sometimes continued to indicate specific commands, some special, others such as for Africa increasingly routine. At the highest level, *MVM* evolved from Stilicho's rule onward into the office of supreme commander and chief "advisor" to the emperor.

39. W. Ensslin 1930, 306–25; 1931, 102–47, 467–502, pt. 1, gives all the forms of the title, date, person, and source; for his discussion for the late fourth century see pt. 2, pp. 132–47; more recently, the brief survey of the problem in J. M. O'Flynn 1983, 4–15.

40. Zosimus, 4.34.5; Pacatus, 32.4.

41. Ibid., 4.40.

42. Socrates, *HE*, 5.14.

43. *CTh* 9.14.2, 1 July 391.

44. Pacatus, 32.3. P. Heather 1991, 191, following Zosimus, 4.38, suggests that all along Theodosius was recruiting barbarians for combat in the civil wars. The use of barbarian recruits was on a much vaster scale, for tactically and strategically Theodosius fitted them into many aspects of imperial policy.

45. Cassius Dio, *Historia Romana*, 69.6.3. The incident is that in which Hadrian, nearing the end of a long day of travel and inspection, was beset by a woman wishing him to hear her petition. At first Hadrian ignored her plea, but then she reminded him that to do so was his duty and, if he did not wish to honor it, then he should be emperor no longer. Hadrian stopped and listened.

46. Zosimus, 4.48; and Claudianus recalls an attack on Theodosius but without the stalwart barbarian, *De bello Gothico* (henceforth *BG*), 524, *VI cons Hon.*, 107–8, probably in reference to these same events of 391 as in Zosimus.

47. Zosimus, 4.49.3.

48. Ibid., 4.50.

49. O. Seeck 1919, 279, from Socrates, *HE*, 5.18.14.

50. In speaking of the death of Promotus, Claudianus (*De cons. Stil.*, 1.94–103) remarks: quis enim Visos in plaustra feroces reppulit aut saeva Promoti caede tumentes Basternas una potuit delere ruina? And Stilicho "like Aeneas avenging the slaughter of Pallas with the death of Turnus" offered at his friend Promotus's tomb turmas equitum peditumque catervas hostilesque. And to Zosimus, 4.51.3, the fact that this is specifically a unit of barbarians (λόχον αὐτῷ βαρβάρων) rather than merely "barbarians" may be significant that tactical units of men are stressed.

51. Zosimus, 1.71.1 (and the *Historia Augusta, v. Prob.* 18.1) for those under Probus.

52. For literary references to the Bastarnae see *R-E*, 3.110–14.

53. Zosimus, 4.51.3.

54. Chrysostomus, *Epis.* 207. Bishop Chrysostom seems to have played the issue of Gothic Christians as just one more piece in his complex web of political maneuvering in Constantinople. He was rather ambivalent on the issue insofar as the Goths themselves were concerned. His actions have no relationship to military policy, however, and therefore this very interesting aspect of the eastern court does not figure into our discussion. See J. Liebeschuetz 1990, on the career of Chrysostom, and A. Cameron and

J. Long 1993. There is nothing particularly surprising in the fact that Promotus, a general who had both defeated Goths and recruited them, might have set up a religious foundation for them that survived his own demise.

55. Seeck 1919, 283, *CTh* 7.1.14.

56. Gregorius Turonensis, *Historiae Francorum*, 2.9, and Poalino di Milano 30. The events surrounding Valentinian's demise are ably discussed and the primary sources analyzed by E. Demougeot 1951, 96–110, 201–5; by J. M. O'Flynn 1983, 6–13; and by J. Matthews 1975, 239–47. His activities at Cologne are confirmed in a building inscription testifying to restoration work (*ILS*, 790).

57. In general the account of the battle offered by O. Seeck and G. Veith 1913, 451–67, is widely accepted. Their topographic details have not fared as well; see J. Šašel 1971, 34.

58. Seeck 1919, 284.

59. Socrates, *HE*, 5.25.

60. *PLRE*, 1.94.

61. On the route see the *Tabula Imperii Romani, L-33, Trieste*. The texts have been collected by J. Šašel 1971. On Theodosius and Eugenius see P. Hitzinger 1855, 81–85, and O. Seeck and G. Veith 1913, 451–67. For Magnentius and Constantius II, Zosimus, 2.45.

62. Orosius, 7.35.13, Sanctus Ambrosius, *De obitu Theodosii*, in *Patrologia Latina* 16, 1386ff., along with all the other relevant texts can be found in Šašel 1971, 28–40. B. Overbeck 1982, v. 1, 219, on its effects on the Alpine regions. On location see further T. Ulbert 1981, 47, Wippach (Vipava) very near Castra-Ajdovscina.

63. Theodoretus, *HE*, 5.24, relishes the story of Theodosius spurning the statue of Hercules after his victory.

64. Orosius, 7.35.19; Jordanes, *Getica*, 28 (145), who has them selected from among the former followers of Athanaric, all noted for their loyalty. What is not so apparent is that 13 years transpires from the opening of this paragraph to its close!

65. Zosimus, 4.57.2. Perhaps the precise wording here is significant. Συμμαχοῦντας can mean auxiliaries attached to the army or those barbarians allied to him. The clause reads: τοὺς δὲ συμμαχοῦντας αὐτῷ βαρβάρους ὑπο Γαΐνῃ ἔταξε καὶ Σαούλ. Socrates states only that a very large number of barbarians from beyond the Danube volunteered for the expedition; nonetheless the voluntary aspect tends to support the translation of Zosimus's συμμαχοῦντας as allies. Moreover, further on in this passage (Socrates, *HE*, 5.25), Socrates states: οἱ συμμαχοῦντες τῷ βασιλεῖ Θεοδοσίῳ βάρβαροι (those barbarians allied to, or fighting alongside, the emperor Theodosius) and thereby more firmly supports a translation as allies over the more militarily specific term of auxiliary. Joannes Antiochenus, frag. 187, prefers to give three ethnic labels—Scythians, Alans, and Huns—without specifying a relationship to the Romans.

66. Zosimus, 4.57.2–3.

67. *PLRE*, 1.379–80.

68. *PLRE*, 1.809; and Orosius, 7.37.2. Only J. Antiochenus, frag. 187, makes him an Alan. That he may have led an Alanic contingent on the Frigidus, as is suggested by the *PLRE*, while possible, is not supported by this passage.

69. *PLRE*, 1.144. Rufinus, *Historia Ecclesiastica*, 2.33, still has him as *dux* at the Frigidus, whereas Socrates, *HE*, 5.25.13, gives him the title σταρτηλάτης. According to

Zosimus he died rallying his troops, but this is not the case in Rufinus. On the fifth- and sixth-century evolution of *vacans* as a quartermaster general, see R. Scharf 1991, who reconstructs its responsibilities and officeholders from 440.

70. Gaïnas is reported doing so in the 390s in Thrace; see chapter 6. Some archae-ological data help confirm this employment pattern, for example in Regensburg (see chapter 5).

71. This is only reported in J. Antiochenus, frag. 187, drawn from Eunapius, frag. 60, also a favorite source for Zosimus but not cited in full by the latter in his passage on the battle. The Greek reads: πολλούς τε τῶν Θρακίων Οὕννων σὺν τοῖς παρε-πομένοις φυλάρχοις διαναστήσας εἴχετο τῆς πρὸς τὴν Ἰταλίαν πορείας.

72. Socrates, *HE*, 7.10, Alaric a ὑπόσπονδος ὤν Ῥωμαίοις (one secured by treaty to the Romans), who had served the emperor Theodosius against the tyrant Eugenius as a συμμαχήσας. Zosimus, 5.4, a passage critical to this and future discussion, notes that Alaric had received command of barbarian troops only to counter Eugenius. Both Socrates and Zosimus are here discussing events occurring after the death of Theo-dosius.

73. Orosius, 7.35.11–12, apparently drawing at least in part upon Rufinus 11.33, although with considerable abridgement, and, like Rufinus, using the term *auxilia* to describe the barbarian units. Rufinus was contemporary to these events and was actually living in the vicinity at the time; see Šašel 1971, 34.

74. Zosimus, 4.58.2. οἰηθεὶς δὲ ἄμεινον εἶναι τὸ βάρβαρα τάγματα [barbarian units] τοῖς ἐναντίοις καθεῖναι καὶ τούτοις πρότερον διακινδυνεύειν, Γαΐνην ἔταξε σὺν τοῖς ὑπ᾽ αὐτὸν ἔθνεσιν ἐπελθεῖν, ἐπομένων αὐτῷ καὶ τῶν ἄλλων ἡγεμόνων [other leaders], ὅσοι τῶν βαρβαρικῶν ἔλαχον ἐξηγεῖσθαι ταγμάτων [who commanded other barbarian units], ἱππέων τε ὁμοῦ καὶ ἱπποτοξοτῶν καὶ πεζῶν. Socrates, *HE*, 5.25, alone records that the two groups of barbarian auxiliaries fought head to head with the West-ern forces superior in numbers. The constant use of "units" (τάγματα, the plural) in all accounts is significant.

75. Orosius, 7.35.19; but Socrates, *HE* 5.25, reports that Theodosius threw himself on the ground and in agony prayed for divine help. Then Bacurius was suddenly inspired to new levels of bravery. More than likely Theodosius simply dispatched Bacurius to rally the troops.

76. Zosimus, 4.58.2–5. Zosimus 4.58.2 (τάγματα); J. Antiochenus, frag. 187 (Huns under φύλαρχοι).

77. Ambrosius, loc. cit.

78. Texts of Turranius Rufinus, Zosimus, and others in Šašel 1971, 33–39.

79. Šašel 1971, 90–91.

80. Ibid., pp. 81.

81. Ibid., pp. 86–88, 97.

82. J. Werner 1980, 1–49, surveys the development archaeologically.

83. As noted in D. Hoffmann 1970, 467, but this is my suggestion.

84. C. Tolkin 1953–57, 141–63, concludes that the "kernel" may date to the late fourth or early fifth century.

85. During the early years of his reign Theodosius celebrated victories over several bands of Huns; see chapter 2. The Carpodaces and certain Huns were among these; see Zosimus, 4.34.6.

86. *PLRE*, 2.44.

V. Stilicho's Transalpine Recruitment Areas

1. See for example Jones 1964, 1425–28, D. Hoffmann 1970, 440–58. Units of the *equites*, Honoraci (Honoriani), seniores and iuniores are given by Seeck in *Notitia dignitatum*, p. 318.

2. Jones 1964, 1426, suggested that this was probably accomplished by the use of federates for cavalry units.

3. K. Stribrny 1989, 351–506, at p. 439, tab. 1. Stribrny has assembled much useful data, particularly on current coin holdings; however, his basic thesis is highly questionable. I cannot accept a continuous Roman presence at so many places beyond the frontier as having existed without historical note, particularly from Ammianus writing on Julian. Julian's many raids into *barbaricum* along the Rhine are reported in detail. Julian would have also exploited any chance to have appeared as a "savior of the Roman people" there, had they been there, in his own extant speeches. Ammianus never mentions a single Roman living beyond the Rhine but rather stresses that most Germans lived within ten Roman miles of the river. The evidence that Stribrny adduces can best be explained by employing a different historical model, one in harmony with Ammianus, such as proposed by H. Steuer 1990, 140–205, for the upper Rhine; see further discussion below. The coin evidence adduced by Stribrny clearly demonstrates that throughout the last half of the third century and throughout the fourth, there were people living on the right side of the Rhine who were well aware of the value and uses of Roman money. The ceramics as well as coins suggest a strong economic interconnection. It seems to me that, as Steuer develops for a somewhat later period, we have on the right side of the Rhine strong archaeological proof of the validity of Ammianus.

4. There are several regular venues for updates on the frontier provinces, most clearly the meetings of the International Congresses of Roman Frontier Studies. For the Raetian and Norican provinces there is a useful survey by H. Castritius 1985, 17–28, on aspects of these developments. An introductory survey of the archaeology is now also available, W. Menghin 1990, 26–65. Reference to sites below will include reference to the site numbers on the map in Menghin, when applicable, for scholarly convenience. At the next level, J. Garbsch and P. Kos 1988 have appended an extraordinarily helpful site gazetteer for the Danube-Iller-Rhine *limes* surveying watchtowers, various types of fortifications, and fortified settlements (pp. 105–27). Their list also will be referred to repeatedly below. Another survey with select site plans is available for Raetia II and Noricum Ripensis, S. Ciglenečki 1987, 14–30. The picture, of course, continues to sharpen its focus as materials come to light. Raetia Prima is surveyed in detail by B. Overbeck 1982, and more recently but succinctly by W. Drack and R. Fellmann 1988.

5. *Nd. oc.* 35 and 1.43; 5.139.

6. *Nd. oc.* 42.33–44; the listing of *praefecti laetorum* contains no reference to one for Raetia. There is a break at the end of 42.44, but no reason to assume that Raetia was there listed.

7. See on *receptio* at the time of Diocletian and Constantine P. Bastien 1989, 21–36; the tetrarchic medallion is the very best portrayal of this process, in which whole families were brought into the Empire under the technical auspices of the emperor. On the mid-fourth century, see K. Kraft 1978, 87–132, with special emphasis upon the

"hut-type" issues celebrating *receptio* on the Rhine. A contrary view based on a single example is that of W. Weiser 1987, 161–74.

8. T. Burns 1981, 390–404. For an example from the Rhine see the grave inscription for Hariulfus, a young member of the imperial guard, son of Hanhavaldus, a prince of the Burgundians (regalis Burgundionum), who died aged 20 years, 9 months, and 9 days. The inscription was set up by his uncle, Reutilo, and dates from the second half of the fourth century or early fifth; H. Heinen 1985, 325.

9. The ceremonial ax blades in some East Germanic burials come to mind since they have been discovered along much of the Danube as well as in Gothic lands above the river in former Dacia.

10. Eunapius, frag. 59; Zosimus, 4.56.2–3.

11. The case of Maximinus, praetorian prefect of the Gauls, 371–76, is a case in point; Ammianus, 28.1.5.

12. This is a central theme of T. Burns and B. Overbeck 1987.

13. Ammianus, 30.3.1; and 28.2.1 at Alta Ripa (Altrip). See on this frontier system J. Garbsch 1970 and the updates to excavations in J. Garbsch and P. Kos 1988, 115, Robur-Basel.

14. T. Burns 1981, 390–404, and on the revolt of Magnentius see J. Šašel 1971, 205–16. For similar landing zones on the Rhine, see H. Castritius 1988, 57–78 and 63, n. 19, but who essentially avoids the non-Roman developments beyond the frontiers. On the control of the rivers in late antiquity, still useful is O. Höckmann 1896, 369–416, listing early finds on both banks for middle and upper Rhine, p. 382, and concluding that the system remained essentially operative and as under Julian and Valentinian I as late as the Vandal crossings of 406, pp. 413–16.

15. Ammianus, 17.1.8; archaeological examples are numerous; see M. Martin 1979, 411–46. The distribution of Roman coins in *barbaricum* along the Rhine upstream from the confluence of the Lahn and Rhine rivers, and especially in the area of Mainz, reveals just how accurate Ammianus was in this regard. Exceptions occurred when river valleys or transportation routes penetrated deeper, for example on the Main or Neckar. See the statistical computations of K. Stribrny 1989. In several cases the series at the sites in Roman territory end with examples ca. 408; in almost all others the series end with the death of Theodosius. Coins could remain in use for many decades.

16. Note the coin distribution at Regensburg, for example; Stribrny 1989, 470.

17. Augsburg continued to manifest signs of economic life, specifically coins and small finds, into the first decades of the fifth century, but later developments are unknown, L. Bakker 1984, 82–84, comb, p. 4, Abb.4. *Nd. oc.* 35.14, equites stablesiani seniores, Augustanis.

18. V. Bierbauer 1984, 87–99.

19. Sidonius Apollinaris, *Carm.*, 7.233, nam post Iuthungos et Norica bella subacto victor Vindelico Belgam, Burgundio quem trux presserat, absolvit iunctus tibi. All other references mention only his actions in Noricum, *Chronica Gallica*, 106, only to Juthungi, and Hydatius, *Chronicon*, 93, he defeated Juthungi and Norici.

20. So suggests Overbeck 1982, v. 1, p. 220 (Bludenz, v. 2, p. 20; Salez, v. 2, p. 125).

21. Eugippius records that 40 were expected to be able to defend the fort at Batavis (*Vita Severini*, 22.4). The disbandment of other units: per idem tempus, quo Romanum constabat imperium, multorum milites oppidorum pro custodia limitis publicis stipen-

diis alebantur; qua consuetudine desinente simul militares turmae sunt deletae cum limite, Batavino utcumque numero perdurante (*vita*, 20.1). Thus for Eugippius, writing the *vita* ca. 480 but recalling events at least a decade earlier, the rest of the system had already disappeared long ago.

22. *Nd. oc.* 35.19 praefectus legionis tertiae Italicae pro parte media praetendentis a Uimania Cassiliacum usque, Cambidano. G. Weber 1989, 56–62, and G. Gottlieb 1989, 63–64, both in *Geschichte der Stadt Kempten*, ed. V. Dotterweich (Kempten, 1989). J. Garbsch and P. Kos 1988, 119, Cambodunum (Kempten), Vemania (Isny, Kr. Ravensburg).

23. J. Werner 1969. Epfach was virtually an island surrounded, except for a narrow spine of land, by the Lech River.

24. See J. Garbsch and P. Kos 1988, 124–26, for publications and notices. Abodiacum (Lorenzberg near Epfach, Gde. Denklingen, Lkr. Landsberg); Coveliacae (Moosberg near Murnau, Lkr. Garmisch-Partenkirchen); Stoffersberg (near Igling, Lkr. Landsberg); Römerschanze (near Grünwald, Lkr. München); Rostrum Nemaviae (Goldberg near Türkheim, Lkr. Unterallgäu); Foetes (Füssen, Lkr. Ostallgäu; Schlossberg).

25. G. Schneider-Schnekenburger 1980, 115–18; T. Burns 1984, 196–97; Overbeck 1982, 34–49. There was some but dwindling settlement in the old central urban area, Welschdörfli, at least into the reign of Arcadius, but the late Roman fortification atop the cathedral hill was the center for clerical and secular administration. Although there is no question of continuity at Chur (Graubünden) most details of the fifth and sixth century remain unknown, including those years when the Ostrogoths administered from here. On all sites in Switzerland, see H. Lieb and R. Wüthrich 1967, and W. Drack and R. Fellmann 1988, the latter with more recent archaeological data, although incorrect on Stilicho's alleged withdrawal of the garrisons, p. 296 (on Chur, pp. 380–84).

26. Overbeck 1982, 23–24, fibulae #167, Keller type 5, #168 in a style characteristic of east Germanic ornaments found near the lower Danube. *Nd. oc.* 35.32, numerus barcariorum. Bregenz (Vorarlberg). Further discussion of the problems raised by the appearance of apparently east Germanic materials on the upper Danube follows below.

27. *Nd. oc.* 40.22, numerus barcariorum Tigriesiensium. Coins end with those of Arcadius as is typical and which, of course, says nothing as to the end of the military establishment here. On coins, Overbeck 1973, 93–94, Arbon (Bez. Arbon).

28. *Nd. oc.* 52.15, Yverdon-les-Bains (Vaud); see W. Drack and R. Fellmann 1988, 562–65, with clear ceramic evidence for the late fourth and early fifth century and C-14 dating for the *horreum* to ca. 470. See also R. Kasser 1975, 62–64.

29. Overbeck 1982, 106–12; Schneider-Schnekenburger 1980, 117; W. Drack and R. Fellmann 1988, 499–500, all with reference to earlier publications. North African sigillata to the end of the fourth and a small church or baptistry in the fifth century attest to continuity here. Perhaps it is worthy of note that the burials around the church are entirely without grave goods. Remains of the late Roman fortification at Schaan (Fürstentum Liechtenstein) lie under the church of St. Peter as does the small fifth-century church.

30. Overbeck 1982, 95–100, Balzers (Fürstentum Liechtenstein), and map 71, p. 247, for the distribution of known hilltop fortifications in Raetia Prima.

31. Bonaduz (Kr. Rhäzüns, Bez. Imboden). Overbeck 1982, 122–27; Schneider-Schnekenburger 1980, 17–54; Drack and Fellmann 1988, 370.

32. The general problem of the decline of the villa system has been dealt with by scholars for several decades; K. Stroheker 1948 remains fundamental. Despite this there remain few fully excavated sites, and therefore too little attention is often paid to the latest phases with the poorest remains, so that conclusions concerning rural developments are even more dangerous to draw than at military sites.

33. On villas near Wels (Ovilava) and also for Heilbrunn where coins continue through Valentinian II, see G. Alföldy 1974, 205. Despite the large number of late refuges that have been identified through field surveys and chance finds, very few have been actually excavated and fewer still published.

34. S. Ciglenečki 1987, 28–30.

35. N. Heger 1988, 14–22.

36. J. Garbsch and P. Kos 1988, 125–27. Fortified hilltop-camps, refuges, and settlements of various dimensions certainly characterized life in the Alpine areas in general; see S. Ciglenečki 1987, 109–27.

37. H. Steuer 1990, 140–205, particularly pp. 144–45, 197–202. The picture here is very similar to that farther north in the area of the Main and the upper Danube west of Regensburg, to be discussed below in some detail.

38. H. Bender 1981a, 21, 146–47. J. Garbsch and P. Kos 1988, 126; for the fortified settlements as of date of publication see the province-by-province breakdown (pp. 125–27).

39. H. Bender 1988, 377 (now in prep.).

40. An example of this type is Sontheim-Brenz; see H. Nuber 1988, 3–24, at 14–18.

41. W. Czysz and E. Keller 1981, Seebruck, Gde. Seeon-Seebruck, Lkr. Traunstein. Pons Aeni (Pfaffenhofen, Gde. Schechen, Lkr. Rosenheim), J. Garbsch and P. Kos 1988, 124, and J. Garbsch 1975, 87–91.

42. B. Overbeck 1991b. W. Menghin 1990, map (Abb.43) p. 51, #93.

43. H. Bender 1986, 122–24; B. Overbeck 1990, 147–48; B. Overbeck 1991a, 135–36. See further B. Overbeck 1982, 208–28, for a survey of this important valley linking Raetia and Italy. Bürgle (near Gundremmingen, Lkr. Günzburg); Summuntorium (Burghöfe, Gde. Mertingen, Lkr. Donau-Ries); Putzmühle lies about 16 km southeast of Augsburg (Gde. Steindorf, Lkr. Aichach-Friedberg). Römerschanze near Grünwald, J. Garbsch 1988, 126, n. 33, for references.

44. Zosimus, 5.50.3; to be sure, one can find isolated examples of gold coin here until Odovacar; however, at some point, I believe after the death of Constantius III (421), there was very little economic or military relationship to Italy. On the vague relationship extending to Odovacar see H. Castritius 1983, 31–39.

45. Augustinus, De civitate Dei, 37.18.10, as discussed in B. Overbeck 1982, 223, n. 388. St. Augustine thus provides literary proof that no withdrawal of units took place under Stilicho.

46. Nor can I agree with Castritius that Stilicho's actions somehow weaken the Roman command structure in Raetia, H. Castritius 1988, 63–64.

47. See R. Christlein 1981, 154–55, and 1982b, 168–69. These excavations at Alburg are from the same large grave field explored later and known as the excavation at Straubing-Bajuwarenstraße; see H. Geisler 1987, 608–22. To date, a thorough publication of this site has not appeared, although aspects have appeared in article form. The site

manifests an extraordinary diversity of artifacts and people. On the significance of the Ostrogothic involvement see Burns 1994.

48. Most conveniently listed in W. Menghin 1990, map (Abb. 43) p. 51, three hilltop settlements lie northwest of Regensburg (Menghin 1990, #93 Gelbe Bürg, 98 Michelsberg, 101 Sulzbürg). Menghin notes 14 such fortified hilltop settlements.

49. I see no importance to the former *limes* of the Principate. For a radically different opinion, see K. Sribrny 1989, for whom the old *limes* is very important in understanding what he sees as Roman survivals.

50. A contemporary example would have been Theodosius the Elder, whose alliances beyond the Wall enabled him to withdraw forward troops and may have ultimately provided enough security for the Roman command to shift its focus to the coast; see S. Frere 1987, 340–42.

51. W. Menghin 1990, 59–60, postulates by way of an explanation for the abandonment of nearly all sites in the early sixth century that the Franks ordered the inhabitants down from their fortified hilltops for better control.

52. H. Steuer 1990, 139–205.

53. H. Fischer 1984, 123–28. The use of military fibulae as a dating system relies on the work of E. Keller 1971, here particularly types 5 (ca. 370–400) and 6 (ca. 400–450), who worked out a sequence of fibulae based upon datable contexts, typically by numismatic evidence. This pioneering work has now been elucidated by P. Pröttel 1988, 347–72, placing Keller type 5 at A.D. 350–415 and type 6 at A.D. 390–465 and merging and subdividing Keller types 3 and 4 into four variants with an overall chronology of 330–415, thus over 80 years, and a type 7 for the last third of the fifth century. For the discussion above, type 6 is especially crucial. For a discussion in a specific Elbgermanic context, see H. Böhme 1991, 291–304. For the area of the Oberpfalz north of the Danube a survey of the coins and archaeological finds also supports unbroken Roman influence into the early decades of the fifth century, H. Fischer 1981, 349–89, esp. 355–56. (W. Menghin 1990, map p. 51, site #4).

54. E. Weinlich 1985, 126–27 (W. Menghin 1990, map p. 51, site #26).

55. B. Overbeck 1991b.

56. H. Koschik 1983, 57–59. Koschik believes that the site was Alamannic (W. Menghin 1990, map p. 51, site #93).

57. B.-U. Abels 1983, 98–99 (W. Menghin 1990, map p. 51, site #45), and 1984, 129–30 (Menghin 1990, site #99), and 1987, 103–4. B.-U. Abels 1986, 88–90 (Menghin 1990, site #92). Staffelberg (Lkr. Lichtenfels) (Menghin 1990, site #100); Turmberg near Kasendorf, Lkr. Kulmbach-Oberfranken (Menghin 1990, site #102).

58. D. Rosenstock 1984, 120–22 (Menghin 1990, site #47).

59. E. Weinlich 1991, 136 and S. Gerlach, 1991, 136–37.

60. S. Gerlach 1991, 137–40, dated primarily by the chip-carved fittings characteristic of the frontier to ca. 400.

61. *PLRE*, 1.539.

62. L. Wamser 1982, 156–57 (near Menghin 1990, site #96). Wamser's extending the terminus to ca. 500 was conveyed to me by B. Overbeck and awaits publication of new finds. Wamser theorizes a basically Burgundian relationship for the site.

63. B. Overbeck and L. Wamser 1983, 96–97.

64. F. Teichner 1990, 149–51 (Menghin 1990, site #10).

65. D. Rosenstock 1985, 128–30 (Menghin 1990, site #6).

66. The problem of assigning ethnic labels to these and similar items is extremely vexing. For the Alamannic-Thuringian connection see E. Keller 1986, 575–92, at 590–92.

67. See the maps with such sites plotted in H. Steuer 1990, 144–45 and discussion.

68. B. Svoboda 1963, 97–116.

69. H. Fischer 1981, 349f., and more recently 1988b, 39–45.

70. See the discussion in E. Keller 1986, 583–87.

71. See for example the discussion by H. Böhme 1991, on Limetz-Villey, Yvelines, France; W. Menghin 1990, map (Abb.43) p. 46, reveals the distribution of Prest'ovice-Friedenhain materials in relationship to the late Roman fortifications on the Danube and Iller from Passau to Goldberg near Türkheim.

72. Gregorius Turonensis, *Historiae Francorum*, 2.9 quoting Sulpicius Alexander, Bk. 4. Arbogastes, *PLRE*, 1.95.

73. Rostrum Nemaviae (Goldberg near Türkheim, Lkr. Unterallgäu); Batava (Passau, excavations at Niedernburg, site of the *cohors IX Batavorum; Nd. oc.* 35.24). References as in J. Garbsch and P. Kos 1988, 122, 124.

74. K. Dietz 1985, 274f. Not all accept Dietz's theory, but I find it in keeping with Roman practice ca. 400–410. W. Menghin 1990, 47, accepts Dietz's line of reasoning but assumes that the Raetian section of the *Notitia* dates to ca. 430, much later than the ca. 415 that I propose below. It is difficult to imagine what Aetius would have gained from revising the *Notitia*, since by then large areas had been ceded to barbarian federates (not listed in the *Nd*), who played a crucial role in his planning, and not just for a few stretches of the frontier.

75. In particular see G. Clemente 1968, 208.

76. A. Jones 1964, 1423, but who believed that the last general revision probably occurred ca. 408 (p. 1451); and D. Hoffmann 1970, 9. Hoffmann also sees a military vacuum in the Gallic provinces because of Stilicho's withdrawal to fight Alaric and Radagaisus, thereby allowing the Vandals to cross the Rhine in 406, but surely this is a considerable overstatement of conditions; see Hoffmann 1973, 1–18, at p. 14.

77. W. Seibt 1982, 339–46.

78. See the detailed discussion of Stilicho and Constantine III in chapter 7 below.

79. See the comment by J. Mann 1991, 215–19, supporting Seibt's theory of an edition in the summer of 408. Both Seibt and Mann leave Constantine III out of the discussion. The entire theory of a Stilichoian revision also assumes that Stilicho anticipated needing every available soldier for his campaign, which need not have been so. Those aspects of the *Notitia*, which for Mann (p. 217) date the basic revision under Stilicho to between 399 and 408 are: (1) *CTh* 9.30.5 giving Valeria as an Italian province (thus from the return to the West of the diocese of Pannonia renamed Illyricum; see chapter 6); (2) that the Index of the *Notitia* properly places the *mag. eq. p. Gallias* after the *mag. eq. praes.*; (3) that after 408 (the disgrace of Chariobaudes) the *mag. eq. p. Gallias* remained vacant for at least 20 years. Mann perhaps overlooked Gaudentius who was *mag. eq. p. Gallias* sometime prior to Cassius (429), whom Mann considers next after Chariobaudes, *PLRE*, 2.494.

80. Constantine III's prowess as a general was widely recognized, *PLRE*, 2.321–25. All efforts to find the original provenance of the lost *codex Spirensis*, the oldest known manuscript of the *Notitia dignitatum*, have led to dead ends; see L. Maier 1968, 96–141, at p. 97, n. 3, and Maier 1969, 960–1035. The issue of the Raetian section, as alluded to here and as will be discussed later, is complicated by the lack of units of the *equites*

designated Honoraci (Honoriani) and the topographic gap including Regensburg and Straubing. Constantius III is a dimly understood figure whose relationship and marriage to Galla Placidia led to his taking on a co-emperorship with her brother Honorius for a few months in 421 before his death. More on Regensburg follows below. On 1 March 416 Honorius addressed an edict to Constantius III (*CTh* 15.14.14) on the subject of restoring order to those areas affected by recent invasions and the resulting lawlessness. Updating the section of the *Notitia* for these same areas would have made sense militarily and would have fitted in nicely with the general restoration of Roman administration after a tumultuous decade.

81. *Nd. oc.* 35.27. E. Keller 1979, and subsequently commented on several times by Keller 1985, 252–55. See also Keller 1977, 63–73, at pp. 65, 68–69. Some of the dating originally suggested by Keller may have to be modified because of recent work on datable fibulae styles (see P. Pröttel 1988, 347–72; however, the Type 6 start dates are the same as Keller's, only now the end dates are more secure and pushed to ca. 460). I have hesitated to offer a redating here, and have only added a "+" to the last phase.

82. On the use of potentially ethnographically distinctive dress styles, the circumstances which support their use, and the great difficulty in using archaeological artifacts in the context of politically identifiable groups see S. Shennan 1989, particularly 17–21, as well as many other contributions in this volume.

83. The important issue for Neuburg other than the Elbgermans is the identification of certain of the artifacts as east Germanic in style, and this is not in dispute, although Keller's dating of their arrival to ca. 390 is. W. Menghin 1990, 44, argues that the east Germanic materials should be dated to the early fifth century on traditional historical grounds (die historisch überlieferte Anwesenheit), but this is a circular line of reasoning from a false premise that literary sources can prove that the east Germans came to Raetia at the beginning of the fifth century, presumably because of something to do with Stilicho's actions ca. 400. Rather than focusing upon Stilicho's withdrawal of some troops, we should be asking when there might have been a significant influx of new recruits. The most likely time to have shifted some east Germanic troops recruited in the Balkans to the upper Danube and elsewhere in the West was after the fall of Magnus Maximus in 388, when Theodosius had to support Valentinian II, or when Theodosius and/or Stilicho had to redeploy troops in 394–95 after the defeat of Arbogastes/Eugenius. Either of these possibilities would accord well with Keller's dating even as revised. It is difficult to see any other time when Gothic recruits could have arrived in significant numbers on the upper Danube. On the distribution of Elbgermanic and east Germanic–styled artifacts on the Rhine and elsewhere see H. Böhme 1988, 23–37, and E. Keller 1986, 575–92, now also perhaps needing some chronological refinement because of the work of P. Pröttel, cited above.

84. H. Bender 1986, 122–24 (Bürgle, Lorenzberg near Epfach, and a *siliqua* of Arcadius from Putzmühle); B. Overbeck 1990, 147–48; B. Overbeck 1991, 135–36. All of Constantine III except as noted at Putzmühle.

85. The entire problem of the type and size of the last units garrisoning the frontier fortifications at the opening of the fifth century is especially vexing, since so few sites have provided us with indisputable statistical data, for example, of the number of military burials over the specific time frame of 375–425. The site of Vireux-Molhain, although outside our area of discussion, suggests that there at least the garrison between ca. 370–450 A.D. averaged 20–25 men with a gradual turnover in personnel; see

H. Böhme 1985a, 76–88, and Böhme 1985b, 131–33. Many of those fortifications excavated in Raetia certainly had garrisons of less than 100, probably less than 50, note again E. Keller's contributions beginning with his excavations at Neuburg an der Donau in which the burials in zone three were notably fewer in number than the two other zones (perhaps only a part of the burials of the last phase, however, lie there). Rather than suspect the presence of more graves elsewhere, perhaps the solution is simpler—a much reduced garrison. Often the burials and phases of fortification cannot be directly connected because of incomplete excavation or the unknown location of the other component or components. The reduction in garrison size during the last half of the fourth and early fifth centuries must be seen as a step beyond the creation of small late Roman fortifications, some inside the earlier constructions of the principate (for example at Eining, discussed below), since these dramatically reduced forts had been an ongoing development since the end of the third century.

86. E. Keller 1977, 67.

87. R. Christlein 1967–68, 87–103, at 102.

88. H. Fischer and K. Spindler 1984, 31, 95–99, with many clear indications of Elbgermanic items and a possible presence of east Germanic (Gothic) material as at Neuburg (p. 96). J. Garbsch and P. Kos 1988, 121, Abusina.

89. K. Spindler 1981b, 148–49; Spindler 1981a; Spindler 1985b, 235f.; Spindler 1985a, 179f. H. Fischer 1988, 24.

90. Nd. oc. 35, dux Raetiae 17 (p. 200). H. Fischer and S. Rieckhoff-Pauli 1982, 66. On late Roman Weltenberg see K. Spindler 1981a, 131–39.

91. Nd. oc. 35.26.

92. Unless a solution to the space problem is found, many scholars will continue to support the more traditional location of Manching, Lkr. Pfaffenhofen an der Ilm, as the site of Vallatum, but that site too is scarcely explored; see J. Garbsch and P. Kos 1988, 121.

93. K. Dietz 1979, 140–45; E. Keller 1986, 586–587.

94. K. Dietz 1979, 144–45.

95. On Niedermünster see K. Schwarz 1972–73, 20f. On the Grasgasse see H. Fischer and S. Rieckhoff-Pauli 1982, 52–63.

96. So hypothesize H. Fischer and S. Rieckhoff-Pauli 1982, 52–63, 66–68. The possibility of clerical error always exists with the Notitia.

97. Problems with the Notitia continue to come to light for virtually every part of the Western section. For example, in Noricum Ripensis the site of Boiotro (Vita Severini, 22.1, in loco nomine Boiotro trans Aenum fluuium constitutae) perhaps is given in the Nd as Boiodurum (oc. 34.44 Tribunus cohortis, Boiodoro) and on the Tabula Peutingeriana (Graz, 1976) sect. 3.4, as Castellum Bolodurum but located in Raetia Secunda (that is in modern Passau Altstadt). But the late Roman camp now customarily identified as Boiotro, just downstream from the Church of St. Severinus did not produce finds securely dated beyond Valentinian I, whereas further downstream a Valentinianic watchtower in Passau-Haibach (H. Bender and T. Burns 1982, 55–82) has, as have the excavations in Passau Altstadt at Niedernburg. At least as recently as 1982, all this seemed resolved (see, for example, R. Christlein 1982a, 230–36). T. Fischer 1987, 93, offers as an explanation of the lack of coins after 375 at Boiotro that it remained a purely civilian community in a greatly reduced area. Difficulties obviously remain.

98. Examples such as the Burgundians will be explored in subsequent chap-

ters. Neither part of the *Notitia* makes reference to Gothic auxiliaries, not even for the Balkans.

99. Azlburg II, see J. Prammer 1986, 117–19. See further Prammer 1987, 133–42.

100. J. Prammer 1982, 154–55. On the omission from the *Notitia dignitatum* see K. Dietz 1985. For a brief overview of the various materials from Straubing, see H. Fischer and H. Geisler 1988, 61–68. Prammer, like Menghin, favors the very late date of ca. 430 for the relevant sections of the *Notitia*.

101. H. Böhme 1988, 23–37, provides a very clear summation of these trends. See pp. 26–29 for his general assessment of Raetia.

102. On the possible explanation of the isolated early fifth century burials found in the interior see E. Keller 1986, 578–80.

103. W. Sage 1984b.

VI. Four Generals

1. See A. Jones 1964, Appendix II, tables 1, 5–7.

2. Eunapius, frag. 60. Eunapius, of course, may have been reading Stilicho's later preeminence to an earlier period.

3. Zosimus, 5.4.2.

4. Contrary to Zosimus, 5.4.2, Stilicho did not retain "virtually all of the army": with R. Ridley 1982, 207, n. 12; contrary to F. Paschoud 1971–89 (v. 3, pt. 1), 82.

5. As V. Grumel 1951 demonstrates, after 392 for as long as Theodosius lived, the East controlled the Illyrican prefecture. As will be revealed, however, I doubt his theory that the prefecture was divided in late 395 or early 396 and prefer a later date.

6. Sozomenus, *HE*, 8.4.1.

7. Socrates, *HE*, 7.10.

8. For the limited-contract theory of recruitment see J. Liebeschuetz 1990, 21. This theory cannot be lightly dismissed and would certainly have lessened some of the costs to the military. However, the primary uses of barbarians, as attested in the sources, were two: enrollment as recruits in the regular army, and establishment of groups at or near specific frontier fortifications, or possibly near fortified imperial *villae* in areas of their settlement, where their activities could be monitored. That they were cheaper is an imperative assumption, given the financial and recruitment realities. However, that they were then recruited still further for specific campaigns is an unnecessarily complex and unprovable corollary. Temporary duty for special pay or whatever had long been a feature of the Roman army; indeed in the earlier centuries *vexillationes* were at work everywhere. Temporary duty for those in the earlier *vexillationes* and perhaps barbarian auxiliaries was an accepted and anticipated aspect of their careers. Moving troops for permanent reassignment was very difficult; witness the episode of Julian and the Batavians who revolted at the prospect of transferral from the Rhine to the East. Newly raised barbarian contingents were always more easily reassigned, including obviously those listed in the *Notitia dignitatum* and the Marcomanni stationed in Cyrene, Synesius, *Epis.* 110, who were not a new unit but were recruited into an existing unit (J. Liebeschuetz 1990, 230, nn. 18, 19). At some point barbarian recruits and auxiliaries too would have resisted permanent transferral as an intrusion, yet the Burgundians were still being reassigned as a group near the middle of the fifth century. Alaric, as a recently

recruited barbarian leader, need not have held any command above that of military tribune.

9. Claudianus, *In Ruf.*, 2.36–85. See also *PLRE*, 2.44.

10. Claudianus, *In Ruf.*, 2.201. Despite Claudianus's statement here that Stilicho longed to be the savior of Illyricum, Rufinus surely never regarded him that way. But E. Stein (1941), 1968, 540, n. 53, J.-R. Palanque, and others have accepted him as such.

11. Zosimus, 5.4 and 5.5. Zosimus opens a discussion of 395 with the confrontation in Thessaly but quickly breaks away to the campaign of 396, which took place in Greece. Eunapius, frags. 63 and 64, as preserved elsewhere than in Zosimus, with typical disregard for chronological precision made no mention of Thessaly. Zosimus, drawing upon the complete Eunapius or other data, carelessly threw together both years. I believe that he thereby combined the movement to Thessaly via Macedonia from Thrace in 395 and the preparations for the struggles in the Peloponnese in 396. Only Claudianus makes it clear that there were two campaigns, stating that if the battle in 395 in Thessaly had been conclusive, the Peloponnese would have been spared the plundering of 396, *In Ruf.*, 2.185–87.

12. Claudianus, *In Ruf.*, 1.174, and the final disclosure of the imperial communique, 196–217. Perhaps it was these easterners who were sent back early in 395, Zosimus, 5.4.2.

13. A. Cameron 1970, 159, from *Stil. I*, 112–13.

14. The commemoration of nonexistent victories was also traditional and is reflected on numerous coins struck in late antiquity. Stilicho had good company in this regard, probably even Theodosius.

15. So I explain what appeared to A. Jones as the hasty establishment of civil staffs under the permanent *magistri*, 1964, p. 178.

16. And so in Marcellinus Comes, 395, *cum Gaina comite Arcadio*, but the precision of Marcellinus in this regard is lessened by the fact that he still accords Gaïnas this rank in 399 after his promotion.

17. A. Jones 1964, 175, an office foreshadowed by the special command given to Gildo in Africa by Theodosius, *comes et magister utriusque per Africam*. Stilicho held his peculiar title no later than 398, *PLRE*, Stilicho, 2.855. Stilicho always stood at the top of the Western command in the field as *magister peditum*, despite his more robust and descriptive public title. Two Western *magistri equitum* who held the office after the death of Gaïnas are known: Jacobus in 401–2 (*PLRE*, 2.581) and Vincentius in 408 (*PLRE*, 2.1168). There must have been others before them, and I believe that the first likely candidate would be Gaïnas. With or without this title Gaïnas was clearly the most important general in the West after Stilicho at this time, and his command of the barbarian auxiliaries on the Frigidus would have made him an ideal commander of the Western cavalry, especially since Arbogastes had fallen.

18. Eunapius, frag. 64 from J. Antiochenus, 190, his ἐφρούρει.

19. Eunapius, frag. 65.

20. Ibid., frag. 65.8; *PLRE*, 1.154; Zosimus, 5.10.4–5.

21. Zosimus, 5.13.1, records that he was disgruntled at the honors given him at court although a *magister*. I read that as meaning his position as *magister militum per Thracias*. Gaïnas did not hold a truly major command until 399, against the rebel Tribigild.

22. Recall that in 384 Theodosius had returned these dioceses to the West in or-

der to create a separate administrative sphere for Valentinian II. After the death of Valentinian II in 392, Theodosius took Illyricum back under Eastern jurisdiction. Dacia and Macedonia were never restored to the West, remaining Eastern for the remainder of Roman history. The diocese of Pannonia alone was returned, as we shall see, sometime between 395 and 400. Valentinian apparently took his own life.

23. Claudianus, *In Eutrop.*, 1.234–86; raids by Huns from the east had earlier shocked those with Jerome in Bethlehem. On Rufinus, Socrates, *HE*, 6.1; or Sozomenus, *HE*, 8.1.

24. Claudianus, *In Eutrop.*, 1.257–58. Obvius ire cliens defensoremque reversum complecti.

25. I cannot agree with A. Cameron 1970, 168, that Stilicho's recruiting trip in 396 means that he was "on good terms" with Eutropius at this time. On the contrary, his actions were a prelude to invasion.

26. Claudianus, *De cons. Stil.* 1, 188–217, especially 200–7. A. Cameron points out (1970, 96–97) that Claudianus lifted his information on the tribes directly from Tacitus (*Ann.* 1.59.4, 2.22.1, 2.41.2).

27. P. Heather 1991, 201f., provides a new version of the traditional, Claudianus-based, account which portrays Stilicho as the rescuer of Greece against Alaric.

28. Zosimus, 5.5, R. Ridley 1982, 207, n. 15.

29. Zosimus, 5.6.3–4. Much work has been done recently on the fortifications in the pass at Thermopylae. As recently as 1984 these fortifications were thought to have been refortified to counter Alaric (W. Cherf 1984, 594–98). However, the new analyses using the Stuiver-Becker method for C-14 dating now date all these repairs to after the first quarter of the fifth century, Cherf 1992, 261–64.

30. Zosimus, 5.6.3–4.

31. So too suggests A. Jones 1964, 183. However, because of the scanty source materials available, other than the court poet Claudian, there is no absolute proof. Claudian wanted his readers to believe that Macedonia was Honorius's, hence Stilicho's, and therefore Alaric and the East were the invaders. Legality was on the side of the East. Stilicho also probably found it very difficult to publicly take apart Theodosius's own handiwork.

32. This is not to say that there have not been attempts, but dating raids and sieges is one of the most difficult of archaeological tasks. It is not then surprising that what surely was an essentially small scale affair, regardless of who is deemed fighting for the government, is beyond validation.

33. Eunapius, frag. 64.1 (J. Antiochenus, frag. 190). Roman baths were perhaps just as popular among some of the barbarians as among the so-called regulars. That barbarians may have loved them enough to rebuild them while leaving so much else in decay, see J. Eadie 1982, 37. F. Paschoud 1971–89 (v. 3, pt. 1) cites H. Thompsen 1959, 61–72, that any sack of Athens in 396 left no trace in the agora and then explains this by suggesting that Alaric's devastation was confined to the suburbs. I doubt whether the agora would produce evidence of a sack even if one occurred, which I believe is not the case, since the bath in which Alaric bathed dominated the late Roman Athenian agora. There simply is no evidence for a sack because there was none.

34. Zosimus, 5.7.3.

35. Zosimus, 5.7.1, notes that Alaric's forces ultimately were cornered in Pholoe.

36. Claudianus, *VI cons. Hon.*, 242–45.

37. *PLRE*, 1.395–96.

38. Claudianus, *De bello Gildonico* (henceforth *Gild.*), 415–23; the figure 5,000 is Cameron's (p. 117) calculated from the full strength of the specific units listed. But the text suggests that he drew men from these units and therefore 5,000 is too high a figure.

39. *PLRE*, 2.720. When she died, probably in 407, her sister Thermantia followed her as Honorius's wife (married in 408, *PLRE*, 2.1111).

40. *PLRE*, 2.83, *CTh* 11.14.3, 7 June 397 from Constantinople; *CTh* 16.8.12, 17 June 397, from Constantinople; *CTh* 4.12.7, 7 March 398, from Constantinople; *CTh* 6.28.6, 12 November 399, no location given but in the sole consulship of Theodorus, that is after the fall of Eutropius, consul for 399. There is no doubt that he was PPO of Illyricum since every edict addresses him as such.

41. *PLRE*, 1.900. Theodorus was addressed by Claudianus for his consulship of 399 in the *De cons. Fl. Mallii Theodori v.c. panegyris*. Lines 200–5 assert that the sway of his justice extended to prima Padum Thybrimque ligat crebisque micantem urbibus Italiam; Numidas Poenosque secunda temperat; Illyrico se tertia porrigit orbi; ultima Sardiniam, Cyrnum trifidamque retentat Sicaniam et quidquid Tyrrhena tunditur unda vel gemit Ionia. The evolution of the office of PPO is disputed and complex; see A. Jones 1964, 370.

42. *CTh* 11.16.21 and 22, 31 January 397, at Milan; 7.13.13, 24 September 397, Milan; 14.15.4, 12 April 398, Milan; 14.19.1, 12 April 398, Milan; 2.1.11, 24 May 398, Milan; 12.1.157, 13 February 398, Milan; 6.27.12, 25 October 398 (ms. 399), Milan; 15.1.37, 21 December 398, Milan; 11.30.58, 7 January 399 in the same year as his consulship, Milan; 12.1.140, 20 January 399 (but date in dispute; this might be addressed to him as PPO Galliarum in 395), no place noted.

43. *CIL* 6.1717 (the most inclusive); 10.4493a. He carried on as sole consul after the fall around the middle of 399 of his consular colleague Eutropius, who was, of course, never recognized in the West.

44. A. Cameron 1970, 143, and elsewhere for other examples.

45. A. Cameron and J. Long 1993, 112–20, with a full historiographic discussion. This is in part because Cameron and Long believe that Alaric was a part of the Goths settled in 382 "in their own units and under their own commanders" (p. 113). Such was not the case on several scores. Otherwise I agree almost completely with their skillful reconstruction of the circumstances and dating of the speech. The passage in the speech "admitting the senseless and stripping in front of them" (Synesius, *De regno* 14, ed. A. Garzya, p. 419), trans. Cameron and Long 1993, 107 (to Synesius 15A-B numbered according to J. Migne, *PG*) can indeed only apply to Eutropius, who as chamberlain alone would have seen the emperor naked.

46. Synesius, *De regno* 20 (ed. A. Garzya, p. 430), trans. A. Fitzgerald 1930, 135–36.

47. Ibid., 137.

48. Ibid., pp. 432–36. Quoting from the *Iliad*, 8.527.

49. Tax relief, which he got (*Epis.* 34, Cameron and Long 1993, 190).

50. In his *De dono* presented earlier in the year he expressed no such animosity; Cameron and Long 1993, 136.

51. Synesius, *De regno* 20 (ed. A. Garzya, p. 434): καί τινες ἐκφοιτῶσιν ἱπποτοξόται ξένοι.

52. Synesius betrays his knowledge in the *De providentia* 108D (ed. J. Migne, *PG*),

written a few months later. There Osiris (that is Aurelianus) is reported to be solving the Scythian problem by infiltrating real Romans into units of the army. Synesius must have had regular units in mind. What lay behind this remark was the predominance of Germanic soldiers everywhere. Typhos's wife's passionate desire to eliminate them is also not unique. This does not make her views the focal point of party politics, however. In point of fact, had anybody in command or in the ranks cared about the supposed ethnic origins of their fellow soldiers, "infiltrating" would have been unthinkable.

53. Had such an anti-barbarian, anti-military view been shared by Arcadius's key advisors, Alaric might have had concern. This was not, however, the case. None of them shared Synesius's apparent hatreds; so too conclude Cameron and Long 1993, 121.

54. Zosimus 5.26.1–2. Scholars have expended much ink interpreting these passages. See the discussion in chapter 7, n. 34.

55. J. Šašel 1971, 81–97. See also T. Burns 1979, 51–68, at p. 52. The level of excavation in Pannonia II, for example, is as yet insufficient to press any conclusions, work on refuges in the mountains to the south of Sirmium has just begun, and only a few other sites are available to reveal the shrinking of the permanent rural population at traditional sites. See, for example, the site of "Jerinin Grad," a hill fort 25 km southwest of Svetozarevo, where a late Roman (4th-6th c.) refuge seems to have attracted a stable population at this time, " 'Jerinin Grad'—Belica (Explorations in 1987)," Glasnik 5 (1989), 82–86. This should not and increasingly does not, however, lead to the conclusion that organized agriculture necessarily ended entirely in Pannonia II; see T. Cvjeticanin 1988, 121–30. Equally certain from the literary sources is the fact that urban centers continued, albeit with probably fewer inhabitants; see the survey of the archaeological and literary sources, particularly ecclesiastical, by V. Popović 1987, 95–139, who concludes that much of the archaeological material also demonstrates the continuity of urban settlement.

56. Praetorian prefect, Nd. or. 3; on Illyricum as a diocese in the West, see Notitia, ed. Seeck, index, p. 289; on the dating of the basic revision of the western section, probably carried out under Stilicho, see chapters 2 and 4.

57. For example, N. Vulić 1916, 1087.

58. The importance of the administrative division of Illyricum under Theodosius as a precedent for that under Arcadius is a consistent theme in the work of E. Demougeot (1947, 1948, 1951, and 1974b).

59. Nd. or. 11.49.

60. The administrative structure of Illyricum as a Western diocese remained throughout Ostrogothic rule; see T. Burns 1984, 193f.

61. Claudianus, In Eutrop., 2.214–18, written sometime in 399 (see A. Cameron 1970, 134), after Eutropius's failures to deal with Tribigild's revolt but before his fall ca. 1 August. Text in Loeb edition, trans. M. Platnauer: vastator Achivae gentis et Epirum nuper populatus inultam praesidet Illyrico; iam, quos obsedit, amicos ingreditur muros illis responsa daturus, quorum coniugibus potitur natosque peremit.

62. E. Stein (J.-R. Palanque) (1941) 1968, 541, n. 54. Palanque (p. 230) thought that when Pannonia was returned it was smaller than it had been by the loss of Valeria. A. Jones (1964, 1421) argued conclusively that this was a misunderstanding based upon a clerical error made in updating the Notitia on the province of Valeria. The Western diocese of Illyricum was identical to what it had been as the Eastern diocese of Pannonia.

63. Marcellinus Comes, 395.4; Marcellinus was chancellor to Justinian and died in Constantinople ca. 534. His chronicle reads: Rufinus patricius Arcadio principi insidias tendens Alaricum Gothorum regem missis clam pecuniis infestum rei publicae fecit et in Graeciam misit. All other accounts that place Alaric's kingship to 395 are equally late and suspect. There has been much discussion of Gothic kingship by me and others, especially H. Wolfram, and this has clarified several levels of rule traditional to Gothic society in the later fourth century. (Burns 1980, 36–45, and Burns 1984, 164–69. Wolfram 1988, 91–103.)

64. Zosimus, 5.5.4. F. Paschoud 1971–89 (v. 3, pt. 1), 91–92, rejects any possibility of Gerontius and Antiochus voluntarily opening the defenses. Clearly I am of another opinion. I would even go beyond those who think them in collusion with Alaric. They were under orders to assist him, which alone explains the advanced preparations.

65. The question of secrecy is itself interesting. If truly a secret then how did it become common knowledge to Eunapius and Zosimus? It seems preferable to regard this allegation of secrecy as merely another rhetorical twist to demonstrate the betrayal of Rome to the Barbarians.

66. In Ruf. 1.308–22, whose comments, if they can be taken literally, clearly reflect the multi-ethnic forces assembled by Rufinus and led specifically in Marcellinus Comes, an. 395.4, by Alaric.

67. This is contrary to Cameron 1970, 168, who follows the traditional interpretation of these events in which Stilicho comes to Greece to rescue it from Alaric.

68. Sozomenus, HE, 8.25.3–4. On Iovius, see PLRE, 2.623.

69. The date of CTh 9.40.17, ordering the praetorian prefect (as successor to Eutropius) to confiscate all Eutropius's property. This act would have followed shortly upon Eutropius's exile.

70. The career of Tribigild is very difficult to reconstruct. Philostorgius and Socrates, who both may have been resident in Constantinople in 399, are probably more reliable than Zosimus in this regard. For Philostorgius, HE 11.8, Tribigild is *comes* prior to arriving back in Nacoleia and rebelling (Τριγίβιλδος, ἀνὴρ Σκύθης μὲν γένος τῶν νῦν ἐπικαλουμένων Γότθων (πλεῖστα γὰρ καὶ διάθορα τούτων ἐστὶν τῶν Σκυθῶν γένη), οὗτος δὴ δύναμιν βαρβαρικὴν ἔχων καὶ τῆς Φρυγίας ἐν τῇ Νακωλείᾳ καθεζόμενος καὶ κόμητος ἔχων τιμήν, ἐκ φιλίας εἰς ἔχθραν Ῥωμαίων ἀπορραγείς, ἀπ' αὐτῆς Νακωλείας ἀρξάμενος, πλείστας τε πόλεις τῆς Φρυγίας εἷλεν καὶ πολὺν φόνον ἀνθρώπων εἰργάσατο. For Socrates, HE, 6.6.5, he was one of Gaïnas's kinsmen who had commanded soldiers in Phrygia: Τριβιγίλδου δὲ ἑνὸς τῶν αὐτοῦ συγγενῶν χιλιαρχοῦντος τῶν ἱδρυμένων ἐν τῇ Φρυγίᾳ στρατιωτῶν. Socrates is followed by Sozomenus, HE, 8.4.2, and Joannes Antiochenus, frag. 190. Only Zosimus, 5.13.2, makes the statement that he was commander "not of the Roman, but the barbarian, troops in Phrygia." The chiliarch is usually given in its military Latin equivalent as military tribune. Gaïnas had used this rank to lure barbarian leaders across the frontier and into Roman service, being at pains to stipulate that officers who held it would have command of units of the army.

71. Claudianus has him *dux* of an *ala* of Getae (read Goths): Tarbigilum (Getae dux improbus alae hic erat) . . . In Eutrop., 2.176–77, which if taken at face value again makes him a commander of little importance, leader of a barbarian cavalry force of at most a few hundred men. Further on Claudianus again stresses that Tribigild's rebels had been Roman soldiers.

72. These men were a part of the Roman army before their rebellion. "A Roman legion, conquered we gave them laws, fields and places to live" (*In Eutrop.*, 2.576–77). As Cameron and Long 1993, 115, also point out, these "cannot have been federates."

73. The only reference to them as Greutungi is Claudianus, *In Eutrop.*, 2.153–54, 196–97, who notes that Ostrogoths and Greutungi both lived in Phrygia and together they rebelled. Perhaps like the *Notitia dignitatum* Claudianus is referring to two (?) units raised from among Odotheus's defeated followers in 386. Or he does not realize that they are the same people by two different names and hence only one unit, that at Nacoleia.

74. Sozomenus, *HE*, 8.4.8, in which John, Patriarch of Constantinople, reminded Gaïnas that he owed everything to Arcadius's father, Theodosius, including even his life, and to whom he had pledged his loyalty.

75. Sozomenus, *HE*, 8.4.1. ταῦτα δὲ βουλευόμενος τοὺς ὁμοφύλους αὐτῷ Γότθους ἐκ τῶν ἰδίων νομῶν εἰς Ῥωμαίους μετεπέμψατο καί τοὺς ἐπιτηδείους συνταγματάρχας καὶ χιλιάρχους κατέστησε. If Tribigild was recruited at the same time as Gaïnas, his career had suffered markedly in comparison.

76. Socrates, *HE*, 6.6.5; Philostorgius, *HE*, 11.8, noting that Scythian included many various people and that Tribigild was a Goth.

77. On this point there is general agreement: Zosimus, 5.13.3; and Philostorgius, *HE*, 11.8.

78. Zosimus, 5.13.4.

79. Zosimus, 5.14.5.

80. Socrates reports that Gaïnas, the commander of the Roman cavalry and infantry, proceeded against Tribigild with a very large force of Gothic barbarians. These were barbarians recently recruited into the Roman army, not "federates" but scarcely trained nonetheless. Socrates, *HE*, 6.6.1, στρατηλάτης Ῥωμαίων ἱππικῆς τε καὶ πεζῆς ικῆς ἀναδείκνυται. See also Sozomenus, *HE*, 8.4.5, πεζῶν καὶ ἱππέων τὴν ἡγεμονίαν ἐκ βασιλέως ἔχων. That is, he was a *magister militum praesentalis* with the titular dignity of *magister utriusque militiae*.

81. Theodoretus, *HE*, 5.32.

82. Eunapius, frag. 67.11 from *Exc. de Sent.*, 71, puts it succinctly—Gaïnas led, Tribigild followed. Sozomenus and Socrates stress his support of his kinsman Tribigild, and use this fact to understand the campaigns. That Eunapius was from Sardis probably explains what appears to be an unwarranted prominence for the city in these sources.

83. Zosimus, 5.14.1; 5.16.5; somewhat later Leo was subordinate to Gaïnas, but initially they were both just called generals (5.14.1). I agree with Cameron and Long 1993, 204–6 (against J. Liebeschuetz 1990, 102) that both Leo and Gaïnas commanded mixed troops. Furthermore, Cameron and Long are convincing that Zosimus's view of Leo and Gaïnas, one commanding Romans and the other barbarians (the basis of Liebeschuetz's argument), is tainted by his view of the sack of Rome in 410 and should not stand unchallenged. The distinction between barbarians and Romans was irrelevant in their commands. Each commanded whatever troops were assigned to him. Each was apparently *praesentalis*. No such general command separated troops by the ethnicity of the recruits or even by the nature of their service, infantry or cavalry. Gaïnas probably did have more barbarians than Leo but only because of his recent recruitment drive in Thrace. Even Zosimus (5.21.6) credits Gaïnas with having Roman troops later on, when he reportedly feared that they might desert and so had them killed.

84. Zosimus, 5.14.1–2; Sozomenus, *HE*, 8.4.1–3, there is no way to determine a precise chronology for Gaïnas's recruiting efforts in Sozomenus's account, only that it preceded Tribigild's rebellion. It is possible that Gaïnas was sent to Thrace to raise some recruits with whom to guard the Hellespont or that he turned to recruiting years before and now returned to Thrace. Giving the chiefs the rank of military tribune indicates, however, a regular enlistment, not one limited to only this campaign. Cameron and Long 1993, 227, also doubt that any collusion existed between Gaïnas and Tribigild. Their suspicions are aroused by Synesius's consistent avoidance of pinning the Tribigild revolt on anyone other than Eutropius. My conclusions flow from the campaign itself.

85. Isaac 1990, 33, and for Antioch as the headquarters, 436–38.

86. *PLRE*, 1.372; Eunapius, frag. 69.2 (Suda Φ 681) gives some important biographical information, particularly that he was general of the East (*magister militum per Orientem*) Φράβιθος. οὗτος στρατηγὸς ἦν τῆς ἀνατολῆς. Simplicius held the post from 396 to at least March 398 (*PLRE*, 2.1013).

87. Zosimus, 5.16.5, clearly places Leo under Gaïnas; on Gaïnas's rank cf. n. 80.

88. 5.15.3; Zosimus says that Gaïnas expected him, presumably Tribigild, to move east and so secretly sent troops "to assist him." My interpretation assumes that Gaïnas was still acting as commander of the Roman army, as Zosimus clearly states that he was, and that he was positioning troops to block escape routes so that he and Leo could smash the rebels between them. Philostorgius records also that Tribigild "ran away from Gaïnas" (*HE*, 11.8, p. 138, ll. 22–23). ἐκεῖθεν ὁ Τριγίβιλδος, ὡς δῆθεν τὸν Γαϊνᾶν διαφυγών, τήν τε Πισιδίαν καὶ Παμφυλίαν ἐπιών κατελυμήνατο. For Philostorgius Gaïnas delayed his attack on Tribigild while he himself contemplated rebellion. Running into the inhospitable countryside of Pamphylia is not the action of Gaïnas's ally, but that of his enemy.

89. Zosimus, 5.15.5; 5.16.4–5.

90. Zosimus, 5.15.5 (Tribigild to Pamphylia); 5.16.5, reports that Gaïnas ordered Leo to advance and "aid the Pamphylians."

91. Zosimus, 5.17.2. Claudianus, *In Eutrop.*, 2.417–22, but this is in the context of a vicious attack upon Eutropius.

92. Zosimus, 5.17.5–5.18.1. Certainly Gaïnas knew Fravitta after their many years in service. They were not friends.

93. Zosimus, 5.18.7–8. Although Aurelianus had not held office under Eutropius, he must have been involved with his government to have merited exile. He was not, however, a principal supporter or he would not have been pardoned so quickly. Even Caesarius, who held the PPO of the Orient and the consulship under Eutropius, was not exiled according to Zosimus. For the career of Caesarius, *PLRE*, 1.171 (PPO Orientis 395–97, cos. 397). That Caesarius and Aurelianus were often at opposite ends of factional struggles to gain the emperor's favor, much of the time outside the focus of this book, see Cameron and Long 1993, particularly 301–30. Neither was pro- or anti-barbarian, but each could use any weapon available at court. In Synesius's piece of historical fiction *De providentia* Caesarius is Typhos (contrary to *PLRE*, 1.171, which favors Eutychianus) and Aurelianus is Osiris. Contrary to R. Ridley 1982, 21, n. 52 (and other proponents of the Seeck thesis), Caesarius and his party were not pro-Stilicho, nor were Aurelianus and his party anti-barbarian. Aurelianus (*PLRE*, 2.128) and Caesarius had political careers extending back to the reign of Theodosius. Caesarius was probably the elder. They proved that they could at least tolerate each other when Caesarius allowed

Aurelianus to return from exile (perhaps toward the end of 400); on Aurelianus's date of return see Cameron and Long 1993, 233–36.

94. The date of "around 1 October" for Eutropius's trial and execution is that of J. Liebeschuetz (1990, 108). Cameron and Long 1993, 163, accept 1 October but only as an arguing point and would prefer a still later date. I will make a case below that the execution took place between 12 November 399 and 17 January 400. Gaïnas did not exile Aurelianus until April 400, when he decided to take a more direct hand in the government (Zosimus, 5.18; for delaying Aurelian's exile until April 400, Cameron and Long 1993, 161–70).

95. Zosimus, 5.18.6; moving two armies along two different routes now made good sense logistically, since there was no longer an enemy for either to face. There was no reason to "plunder" as reported, for Gaïnas was after all MVM.

96. Philostorgius, HE, 11.8.

97. Zosimus, 5.20.1–3; and probably based on Eunapius, 69.2, which praises him as the general of the East who so effectively suppressed the brigands that they ceased to exist. See also Fravitta as mag. mil. p. Or. in Cameron and Long 1993, 225–26. Fravitta's eliminating brigands (Zosimus, 5.20.1) from "all of Asia, from Cilicia to Phoenica and Palestine" only explains his fame, established in "many previous commands" (πολλαῖς διαπρέψαντι στρατηγίαις), in which he had suppressed brigands. Perhaps Eunapius (hence Zosimus) thought that this detail was relevant here because Fravitta was now being asked to do the same thing. Phoenica and Palestine were unaffected by Tribigild. Much more important than what Fravitta was doing in Asia before Arcadius and the Senate gave him the command against Gaïnas is the fact that he was there when called, ready with troops and a fleet (5.20.3). He could only have been in Asia then because of a command received from Gaïnas to go there and mop up. Zosimus does not report Fravitta suppressing bandits in any specific province on this occasion. Cameron and Long make a good case that Fravitta was active in Pamphylia at some time before 403 on the basis of Eunapius, frags. 71.3, 72.1. Pamphylia is linked to Asia by Caria and, depending upon the route, perhaps Lycia. These are the areas Tribigild plundered.

98. PLRE, 1.320. On Eutychianus see also Cameron and Long 1993, 151–61, who doubt, as do I, that he returned to PPO Orientis in December 399. They carefully reject the date given in the manuscript of CTh 12.1.163. Eutychianus's last secure notice as PPO Orientis is 25 July (CTh 9.40.18); Aurelianus's first is 27 August (CTh 2.8.23). So Aurelianus was named PPO Orientis earlier than 27, perhaps as early as the beginning of the month. See also Cameron and Long 1993, 160, 176–77, who date Aurelianus's PPO Orientis to not later than 27 August.

99. Caesarius may have been "ill" for much of Aurelianus's prefectureship as Synesius, De prov. 1078 (ed. J. Migne, PG), but his illness was extraordinarily convenient. In the De prov. it is Typhos who takes to his bed. This is a comment about Caesarius, not Eutychianus as suggested in PLRE, 1.320.

100. J. Liebeschuetz 1990, 108–10, believes to the contrary that they must have been rivals, basing his claim upon the conviction that Aurelianus encouraged Synesius of Cyrene to pen De providentia and that he agreed with its attack on the barbarians. This need not have been the case. Perhaps Aurelianus was entertained by Synesius, but his actions make it clear that he did not press any policy at all that centered on barbarians, pro or con. In this I agree with the interpretation of De prov. offered in Cameron and Long 1993, 122–24, 200–7.

101. Philostorgius, *HE*, 11.6. Philostorgius was a contemporary to the event.

102. Cameron and Long 1993, 166: R. Bagnall 1987, 335.

103. *CTh* 9.40.17, the act of confiscation (*confiscatio*) for the fisc followed the conviction of a person for a crime. The property became public and so was *publicatio bonorum*, A. Berger 1953, 661. The standard date of the edict is 17 August 399, but since this action clearly followed Eutropius's trial an August date must be rejected in favor of the variant date of 17 January 400.

104. *CTh* 3.30.6, 24 February 396, Constantinople; that Eutychianus (*PLRE*, 1.320) was the man behind Synesius's character Typhos and had succeeded Caesarius (*PLRE*, 1.171) as PPO Orientis in 397 and was deposed in the autumn of 399 is carefully argued by Liebeschuetz as before by A. Jones; see J. Liebeschuetz 1990, 261–67.

105. *PLRE*, 2.83.

106. For dating his fall to April, see Cameron and Long 1993, 161–75. Aurelianus did not hold the PPO Orientis again until 414, *PLRE*, 1.129. He may have returned to Constantinople as early as the autumn of 400, Cameron and Long 1993, 235–36. If so, then he could have resumed his consulship.

107. Cameron and Long 1993, 191–97, make a strong case for Caesarius becoming PPO Orientis no later than December 400 and remaining there until replaced by Eutychianus ca. 404. Aurelianus returned from exile soon afterward, probably invited back by his brother before the year was out. For Cameron and Long, these political transpositions demonstrate that the real issue at stake was the relationship and balance of power between the civilian aristocracy and the military. By supporting Fravitta and getting rid of Gaïnas, Caesarius won the confidence of the court and kept his job. Fravitta although extremely powerful never challenged Caesarius. For Gaïnas's designation as consul, Theodoretus (*HE*, 5.32.6). So also understood by Cameron and Long 1993, 203, 337.

108. *CTh* 16.8.15 dated 3 February 404; *PLRE*, 1.320. For a different opinion see J. Liebeschuetz 1990, 260–72. The issue of whether Eutychianus briefly returned as PPO very late in 399, while seeming to be a minor detail, is crucial. By rejecting it, as Cameron and Long (and now I) have, one is forced to realign virtually the entire sequence of events leading up to Alaric's dismissal. The other keystone of any argument is the consulship of Aurelian. The essentials of this discussion were fiercely debated at the turn of our century, when J. Bury and O. Seeck squared off. In many ways, but with substantial and necessary refinement, Liebeschuetz and Cameron carry on the tradition. I find Cameron and Long generally convincing, in part because they hold a very similar view to mine on barbarians in the army, but also because they have relative simplicity on their side, particularly in the case of Eutychianus. Also in many cases they have supported their theory with new evidence.

109. Zosimus, 5.19.4, for the report of 7,000. Synesius, *De prov.* bk. 2 (*PG*, 116B–21A, in which Gaïnas is the general-in-chief, the στρατοπεδάρχος, *PG*, 108B), notes that most were encamped beyond the walls but "they left behind about a fifth of the army" and these were trapped when the guards shut the gates and slaughtered them. The church was probably the same as the one permitted to them by Patriarch John Chrysostom in order to convert them (Theodoretus, *HE*, 5.30). The 7,000 (unconfirmed) would have included dependents. Synesius's "account" is hardly historical but nonetheless must yield as much history as possible. Perhaps no piece of surviving literature from this period

can rival it in ambiguity and in the weight and density of the resulting and conflicting historiography. J. Liebeschuetz 1990, Heather 1991, and Cameron and Long 1993 address *De prov.* differently. For a vivid recreation of the scene see Cameron and Long 1993, particularly 208–24. I believe that everyone could agree, however, that the massacre was an uprising and did not reflect or deflect military policy.

110. Zosimus, 5.19.6; Philostorgius, *HE*, 11.8 (p. 138, ll. 14f.) alone records his death.

111. Theodoretus, a younger contemporary of Gaïnas, wrote differently about Gaïnas's desire for a Gothic church (*HE*, 5.32.6). For him this was the issue that ate away at Gaïnas and led him to usurpation. Perhaps, but in his voluminous writings Chrysostom does not confirm this view. We know almost nothing of his private life. Cast as the supreme general in *De prov.* (ed. *PG* 108B), there at least he is married to a barbarian woman and has a family.

112. Zosimus, 5.20.1; *PLRE*, 1.372.

113. Zosimus 5.21 provides some details. Concerning the technical aspects of the Roman ship type "Liburnians," see F. Paschoud 1971–89 (v. 3, pt. 1), 162–65.

114. In this context, one should recall the bounty placed on barbarian heads (which turned out to look too much like Roman ones) under Valentinian I (Zosimus, 4.11.3). Or as recently as 378, when for a time Valens's Saracen cavalry daily brought back barbarian heads to the capital (Zosimus, 4.22.2).

115. Zosimus, 5.21.6–22.3 [there is a lost page here in the manuscript for 401–2, therefore ch. 22 ends abruptly], but not Sozomenus, *HE*, 8.4.20 (also Eunapius-based). They report Gaïnas's end differently. In Zosimus Gaïnas escapes and recrosses the Danube only to be captured by the Huns. Their leader Uldin then makes a gift of Gaïnas's head to Arcadius. There is no mention of Huns in Sozomenus's account, only that Gaïnas personally escaped but was soon rounded up by a Roman detachment. No one connects the incident of the head to Uldin except Zosimus. The *Chronicon Paschale*, 401 (the consulship of Vincentius and Flavitus [Fravitta]) is precise as to the dates. Zosimus somehow conflated two different accounts: one concerned the death of Gaïnas and the parade, the other an embassy from Uldin to Constantinople, probably concerning peace and military service. Soon after this some Huns appear in Roman service. What remains significant in Zosimus's passage is the appearance of a known Hunnic leader and the beginning of centralized direction among them. In support of this reconstruction see Cameron and Long 1993, 330–33; many others, including *PLRE*, 1.380, accept Zosimus at face value. F. Paschoud 1971–89 (v. 3, pt. 2), 166, 169, discounts the story of Uldin and the head, but stops short of connecting it to Fravitta.

116. Marcellinus Comes, 421, records the dedication. The discussion which follows is entirely based upon the Freshfield drawings. The 52-foot scroll from 1702 (Bibliothèque Nationale Invent. 4951, published by C. Menestrier), although delightfully detailed and generally consistent, is fanciful in too many of its details. For example, the Freshfield drawings have no dromedaries, yet dromedaries were prominent in the lowest portion of the frieze according to Menestrier. Menestrier's edition has remarkable detail for uniforms, almost certainly more than the original. I have examined only those drawings published in G. Becatti 1960.

117. On the theme of victory see M. McCormick 1986.

118. See G. Becatti 1960 for discussion and plates. Becatti is unconcerned with the

inherent impossibilities such as the Christograms among the booty. J. Liebeschuetz 1990, 120–21, and critical reconstruction, pp. 272–78, which gives a band-by-band discussion of the campaign and its battles as possibly appearing on the column; see also Cameron and Long 1993, 247, who see Caesarius standing next to Arcadius and Stilicho next to Honorius. Liebeschuetz notes (p. 276) that "the drawings do not show enough detail to distinguish Romans from barbarians by dress and equipment," but he believes them nonetheless ample to support a discussion of alleged "Gothic huts." The important fact was that victory was traditionally celebrated over foreign enemies. The column was part of Arcadius's effort to live up to the legends of his father. Arcadius had no real victories over foreign enemies to celebrate.

119. *PLRE*, 2.556 (Hierax). Dating to 404, see Cameron and Long 1993, 242–46.

120. R. Bagnall 1987, 336. There is no reason to believe that Fravitta was not still *magister* at his death. The next *magister militum praesentalis* known by name is probably Simplicius in 405, or certainly Varanes; see Fastes (*PLRE*, 2.1290). Stilicho's recognition of Fravitta's consulship in 401 suggests a softening on Stilicho's part (Cameron and Long 1993, 333). Moreover, I believe, Stilicho's recognition of Fravitta's consulship and especially that of Honorius and Arcadius in 402, which could not have happened without Stilicho's consent, should both be seen as a thaw in East-West relations. Perhaps Fravitta's victory over Gaïnas, whom Stilicho might have regarded as a traitor over the Alaric affair, precipitated this warming and may also have occasioned the renaming of the diocese of Pannonia to Illyricum. By the end of 403 events had resumed their accustomed frigidity. See further chapter 7.

121. Cameron and Long 1993, 191–97.

122. Estimates of travel time vary. Liebeschuetz's tight calculations yielded a date of 1 October, but see Cameron and Long 1993, 162–63.

123. *Chronicon Paschale*, 400. Cameron and Long 1993, 171–73, reject seeing in this any alliance between Gaïnas and Eudoxia (Cameron and Long 1993, 171). Nevertheless, the timing suggests that she had something to do with Eutropius's demise, perhaps restricted to prodding Arcadius to act. She may also have played an active role in getting the support of the imperial guard. The crowning still aroused Honorius to protest to his brother about not being consulted four years later (*Epis. imperaborum pontificum aliorum*, 38, dated after 20 June 404). The coronation of the empress had assumed a special significance and did not follow necessarily from being the emperor's wife. They had been married five years before. The fact that Arcadius had not discussed the event beforehand with his brother probably indicates that the occasion for the honor was quite recent and there was something of a rush involved. Eudoxia (*PLRE*, 2.410) bore Arcadius his son and successor, Theodosius II, on 10 April 401, after her coronation and thus this too was not its cause.

124. *PLRE*, 2.83.

125. Although not illegal, such a relationship may have struck a painful nerve in the government and as a result in our sources. Since both were outside imperial concern, perhaps imperial officials simply ignored Anatolius. We have no edicts after 12 November concerning him; especially not one confiscating his property for treason.

126. This is not a reaffirmation of O. Seeck's position of 1913 ([1920] 1966, v. 5, 318). The title of this chapter in Seeck's work speaks for itself, "Der Sieg des Antigermanismus"—the Victory of Anti-Germanism. For Seeck Aurelianus was a rabid anti-

German and the center of a party at court devoted to their elimination. The time was not the summer of 399, but the winter. The cause was Aurelianus's and Gaïnas's political concerns in Constantinople, not some fictitious anti-German policy. If one person must be held responsible for dismissing Alaric, it is Gaïnas, not Aurelianus. There were strong feelings about the Germanic elements in the army, most lastingly those of Synesius.

127. Claudianus, *In Eutrop.*, 1.377–82. The tribes noted there are as usual anachronisms borrowed from Tacitus.

128. Synesius, *De regno* 20 (ed. A. Garzya, p. 430), given in full above.

129. Jordanes, *Getica*, 146–47, adnihilare auxiliariisque suis, id est Gothis, consueta dona subtrahere, mox Gothis fastidium eorum increvit, verentesque, ne longa pace resolvere fortitudo, ordinato super se rege Halarico. Writing in Constantinople ca. 550, Jordanes would not have known that Stilicho had refused to recognize the consulship.

130. The discussion of the Valerias and the *Notitia* follows A. Jones 1964, 1417–21; *CTh* 9.30.5.

131. For example, *Nd. oc.* 1.95; see A. Jones 1964 for details.

132. Bagnall 1987, 400, concludes from the lack of inscriptional affirmation that Stilicho refused to recognize Aurelianus as consul in 400. The chronicler tradition consistently notes the year as the consulship of Stilicho and Aurelianus, probably because the East recognized both. I agree also with Cameron and Long 1993, 164–68, that Aurelianus was inaugurated consul, not just "designated." Whether one calls this act sending Alaric "to be a thorn in Stilicho's side" (quoted from Cameron and Long 1993, 333, but rejected by them) or something else, the East solved many problems and the West gained a major one when Pannonia again became Western.

133. The claims Claudianus made in 397 for Theodorus as praetorian prefect of Illyricum, Italy, and Africa (*PLRE*, 1.901) had again attested to Stilicho's goals in regard to the East and could not have gone unnoticed in Constantinople.

134. Claudianus, *BG*, 330–63. Some would doubt that this entire passage is directed to Raetia at all but merely sings of its virtues as a poetic device; see K. Dietz 1979, pp. 155f. But this doubt seems to be centered upon the now undeniable fact that Raetia was clearly not denuded of troops. Those who would still point to the absence of normal bronze coinage in Raetia and elsewhere after the issues of Theodosius should note that the absence of bronze coins, rather than saying something about troops, who were not paid in bronze coin anyway, much more clearly indicates that the economy no longer accepted bronze, preferring barter, presumably because the weakened state of the government meant that the exchange of bronze was no longer guaranteed. If we accept that Stilicho took very few soldiers with him back to Italy, as here indicated, then the poem and the facts along the frontiers are drawn closer to agreement. Nonetheless there is no denying the constant obscurity and anachronisms of the poet. There is also no question that in most cases the units guarding the frontiers continued on station.

135. Claudianus, *BG*, 330–63.

136. My own opinions as to the terms describing Gothic leadership and their development are set forth in detail in *The Ostrogoths: Kingship and Society* 1980, 35–40.

137. Claudianus, *BG*, 330–363.

138. *Chronica Minora*, I, 299.

139. Claudianus, *BG*, 330–63.

140. In general the account of the political events of these years in J. Matthews

1975, 274f., is adequate. On the military side, Matthews notes that Symmachus while on journey to Milan in early spring 402 was forced to detour through Pavia because of the war.

141. Cameron 1970, 180–81, dates Pollentia to April and Verona to July–August, which despite recent attempts to the contrary still seems appropriate. For recent attempts to redate the battles of Verona and then Pollentia see J. Hall 1988, 245–57, and the review and follow-up by M. Cesa and H. Sivan 1990, 361–74. The traditional datings are used here although the revisions would not alter the sequence of events as developed regardless.

142. Claudianus, BG, 535–39: at nunc Illyrici postquam mihi tradita iura meque suum fecere ducem, tot tela, tot enses, tot galeas multo Thracum sudore paravi inque meos usus vectigal vertere ferri oppida legitimo iussu Romana coëgi. Cameron 1970, 170, dates this piece to 402 after the Roman "victory" at Pollentia. The reference to Thracians is no more precise than Claudianus's reference to Spartan maids three years before (In Eutrop., 2.201, written early in 399).

143. On the other hand, the reference to Roman towns contributing iron should not be construed to mean that imperial armament factories now provided Alaric with weapons. The Notitia (Nd. or. xi.35–39) lists four fabricae in the prefecture of Illyricum, but none of them were in the diocese of Pannonia. On problems with the listing of fabricae in this section see A. Jones 1964, 1417. The praetorian prefect of Illyricum (by September 401 Clearchus, PLRE, 1.213, for this more precise date, Cameron and Long 1993, 222) no longer worked with Alaric. Imperial fabricae were under the prefects not the magisters. But the court poet had no need of such accuracy. His goal was to praise Stilicho after the battle at Pollentia and rally support against Alaric for the next confrontation. The civilian Claudianus's clear reference to the people of Illyricum must refer to the inhabitants of the new Western diocese of Illyricum alone, for the general population did not belong to a military command.

144. To be discussed in the next chapter, but a changed relationship was clear to A. Cameron 1970, 180–87. Alaric's whereabouts are unknown until 404, but he certainly returned to the new Illyricum with some form of recognition from the West.

VII. Alaric and Stilicho: Working Together

1. CTh 7.4.14, dtd. October 365 (or September 364) stipulated that those soldiers guarding the rivers shall receive their pay in kind for nine months of the year and in the remaining three months cash equal to the supplies due for that soldier. CTh 7.4.15 (3 May 369) orders that for omnes limites, all soldiers of the frontier commands, supplies species annonarias shall be assembled at the camps by the provincials living nearby. In 393 an edict addresses the problem of soldiers wishing to be paid in cash when supplies were in abundance and in kind when crops were meager. The solution was to calculate pay on the local market value at time of issuance (CTh 7.4.20).

2. CTh 7.4.16–17.

3. The system of annonae, payments in kind, is still present in Italy under the Ostrogoths in the sixth century. For the period under discussion see CTh 7.4.17–36; the last such edict in the CTh for the West is 414, in the East, 424. The system eventually included even the lowly ministeria of the palace. The existence of such a fundamental aspect of reimbursement challenges any historical interpretation based upon numis-

matic data even before the death of Theodosius and the cessation of Western bronze
coinage, especially as relating to the military; see, for example, the discussion of the
Siscia mint, appropriately reserved because of this problem, by C. Nixon 1983, 45–55,
particularly p. 54. Nixon makes a good case for quarterly payments at this time. *CTh*
7.4.17 (dtd. 377, Gratian, Valens, and Valentinian II); 7.4.28 (dtd. 406, Arcadius, Honorius,
Theodosius II); and 7.4.31 (dtd. 409, Theodosius II at Constantinople) may have provided allowances for families (*familiae*) and certainly included mounts and pack animals.
As C. Pharr 1952, 162, n. 68, suggests, *familiae* is not easily rendered into a precise translation; possibilities include household (nuclear family and slaves) or a military unit such
as a company of recent recruits. Pharr suggests the latter meaning as most likely in these
contexts; however, "household" seems quite possible, especially in *CTh* 7.4.28, ut tam
numeris quam familiis nec non et inpedimentis praeter eas annonas, where family and
military seem to be separately included.

4. Eunapius, frag. 45.3 (from Suda Π 2351). ὁ δὲ βασιλεὺς τούτους
δεξάμενος· κτήματά τε αὐτοῖς καὶ χώραν ἀπένειμε, καὶ προβόλους τε ὑπελάμβανε
γενναίους καὶ ἀδαμαντίνους ἔχειν πρὸς τὰς ἐκείνῃ τῶν Οὔννων ἐμβολάς. As will be
made clear in the later discussion of the settlement of the Goths in Aquitaine, the Greek
texts consistently leave no doubt when land was assigned rather than rations.

5. See in particular R. MacMullen 1963, who argues against A. Jones. Surely Mac-
Mullen is correct that some farming was a basic fact of life for most frontier soldiers;
however, that this circumstance somehow gave an advantage to the barbarians does not
necessarily follow, since the latter were hardly different but were rather a part of the
general pattern of self-sufficiency along the frontiers. As MacMullen clearly demonstrates, soldiers were called upon routinely from at least the era of Septimius to do and
make-do in a host of strictly speaking nonmilitary functions.

6. Zosimus, 4.34.5. R. Blockley suggests that the passage in Eunapius cited above
(frag. 45.3, Suda, Π2351) should be understood in the context of Zosimus 4.24.3–26.9.
Zosimus 4.26.7 does state ὡς ὁ βασιλεὺς ἁδραῖς σφόδρα δωρεαῖς αὐτοὺς ἀμείψασθαι
βούλοιτο καὶ διαδοῦναι πᾶσιν οὐ χρήματα μόνον ἀλλὰ καὶ γῆν..., that the emperor
offered them all money (χρήματα) and land (γῆν), but this was just a trick to lure them
into an ambush in which the credulous barbarians were utterly destroyed. Zosimus
(4.26.1) in a brief flashback to Valens says that before crossing the Danube the Scythians
(that is, the Goths) beseeched Valens to receive them into Thrace, promising that they
would be faithful συμμάχων τε καὶ ὑπηκόως (companions-in-arms and subjects), and
vowed to serve loyally however he wished. But by this they clearly indicated their willingness to serve as recruits in the army. They did not expect to be a separate force and
did not object at all to being split up for transshipment throughout the Empire when
Valens so instructed his command. They rebelled because of starvation and mistreat-
ment, not because of dispersal in the army, which they must have anticipated would
happen. The clearly restricted meaning of συμμαχοί (here best translated as "companions-in-arms" rather than "allies" as R. Ridley, p. 82) to mean simply barbarians vol-
unteering as recruits in this passage in Zosimus is important for understanding the
limited and traditional Roman goals in *receptio* at the time, for Valens and afterwards.
The passage in the Suda does not fit Zosimus 4.26 very smoothly. Rather, the Suda
states that the emperor actually gave the supplies and land, not money and land, which
would have been more than he offered his own soldiers and therefore highly unusual.
The only case in Zosimus that clearly resulted in an establishment of barbarians along

the Danube and facing the Huns was that of Athanaric's men. Perhaps then Eunapius frag. 45.3 relates to the settlement of Athanaric's men in 382 or to some totally other and undocumented case. If we trust the details of Zosimus's story of imperial trickery (4.26), it is no wonder that the barbarians flocked to their deaths. Land and often supplies were standard aspects of *receptio*, but money was not.

7. B. Lörincz 1989, 649.

8. For example, *Nd. oc.* 35.31 Tribunus gentis per Raetias deputatae; or, for Marcomanni, *Nd. or.* 34.24.

9. *CTh* 7.20.12, issued to Stilicho, at Milan, 30 January 400.

10. So H. Wolfram 1988, 150–53, e.g., "although he may have been able to once again preserve the core of his tribe," p. 152, after Verona; also P. Heather 1991, 193–99. The inappropriateness of this conception to Alaric, as I see it, is shared by J. Liebeschuetz 1990, 48–85, but with differences in what this meant in the field.

11. Wolfram 1988, 150.

12. Claudianus, *BG*, 480–517, has a scarred elder, a veteran since Adrianople, speak of the losses and suffering, not all of which should be regarded as mere poetic hyperbole, although doubtless all pure Claudianus.

13. Ibid., 537–43. In addition to the study of urban areas by Popović, there is some indication in pottery traditions, specifically stylistic types, that even in the countryside we have overestimated the extent of disruption during this era; see for example T. Cvjeticanin 1988, 121–30, who suggests that the strong evidence of survival of ceramic traditions here should be interpreted as indicating the continuity of rural populations far from the principal urban centers.

14. Claudianus, *BG*, 519–49, probably written shortly after Pollentia. All of the old man's speech (ll. 490–517) preceding Alaric's and angering him similarly concerned only events before Alaric became *magister*.

15. Zosimus, 5.14.1; 5.17.1; 5.19.6; 5.21.4.

16. Claudianus, *BG*, 581–93.

17. The supposition of a distinct presence of these groups forms a basic kernel of much of L. Várady 1969.

18. In addition to the east Germanic graves in Raetia and elsewhere discussed in chapter 5, see the discussion of the various theories of barbarian deployment in the light of recent archaeological data in Gabler 1989, esp. B. Lörincz 1989, 648–53, and the establishment of Marcomanni ca. 396–98 and who may have replaced an earlier group of barbarian auxiliaries. The *tribunus gentis Marcomannorum* (*Oc.*34.24) may have been stationed at Ad Statuas, a site not listed in the *Notitia*. The establishment of a unit recruited from among the Marcomanni discussed for Ács-Vaspuszta appears quite traditional in that the barbarians were under a Roman *tribunus* and therefore were expected to deploy according to orders from some higher authority. This was in keeping with the policies of Theodosius I.

19. The fleet continued at least as late as 443 (*Nov. Theod.*, 24.5) and was stressed in 412 (*CTh* 7.17.1) by Theodosius II.

20. For example, H. Wolfram 1988, 153, and the other authorities given there.

21. Claudianus, *BG*, 625–28.

22. Gaïnas, *PLRE*, 1.380, from Synesius, *De prov.* 108.

23. Claudianus, *VI cons. Hon.*, 251–53, entire units, sed cunei totaeque palam dis-

cedere turmae, the loss of women, children and supplies at Pollentia alluded to in Alaric's speech here, ll. 297–300.

24. Claudianus, *VI cons. Hon.*, 456–62.

25. Claudianus, *BG*, 414–22, Adcurrit vicina manus, quam Raetia nuper Vandalicis auctam spoliis defensa probavit; venit et extremis legio praetenta Britannis, quae Scotto dat frena truci ferroque notatas perlegit exanimes Picto moriente figuras; agmina quin etiam flavis obiecta Sygambris quaeque domant Chattos inmansuetosque Cheruscos, huc omnes vertere minas tutumque remotis excubiis Rhenum solo terrore relinquunt.

26. *Nd. oc.* 7.49; see further S. Frere 1987, 356. This unit would, if in fact stationed at Caernarvon prior to Stilicho's summons, have had to march ca. 400 miles to Dover via London, cross the Channel, then head southward across the Alps, and much of this in the winter, to have arrived in time for Pollentia. At a speed of 20 miles (30 km) per diem it would have taken 20 days just to make Dover! Even Verona is questionable. It never returned to Britain but served in Illyricum.

27. See Claudianus, *Gild.*, 390–414; the figure 5,000 is from Orosius, 7,36.6. In this same passage Orosius notes that Gildo's regular troops (*militum*) deserted first, followed some time later by the barbarian auxiliaries fighting with him (Orosius, 7.36.10–11).

28. The Raeti (7.44), the *Honoriani victores* (7.48), the *Mauri Honoriani seniores* (7.51) and the *Mattaiarii Honoriani Gallicani*. All were under the general command of the *magister peditum praesentalis* and would have served best as garrisons at key passes and cities.

29. Orosius, 2.3, Alaricho rege eorum, comite autem suo.

30. Sozomenus, *HE*, 8.25.4, a barbarous land, παραλαβὼν δὲ ' Ἀλάριχος τοὺς ὑπ' αὐτὸν ἐκ τῆς πρὸς τῇ Δαλματίᾳ καὶ Παννονίᾳ βαρβάρου γῆς, οὗ διῆγεν, ἧκεν εἰς τὰς 'Ηπείρους· καὶ συχνὸν ἐνταῦθα προσμείνας χρόνον ἐπανῆλθεν εἰς 'Ιταλίαν, staying there some months before going back toward Italy, in fact to Noricum via Emona. The fact that he was assigned to that part of Pannonia contiguous to Dalmatia demands that this must be Pannonia II since Pannonia I shared no border with Dalmatia.

31. There is an unbroken series of edicts addressed to various PPO of Illyricum by the emperors in Constantinople through the decades covered in this book, since that office, as the magister, remained Eastern even after the diocese of Pannonia was returned to the West. See the Fasti in *PLRE*, 2.1249, but Clearchus was probably in office since at least September 401 (cf. *CJ* 12.57.9–10).

32. On these survivals see V. Popović 1987, 95–139.

33. Orosius, 7.38.2 quamobrem Alaricum cunctamque Gothorum gentem, pro pace optima et quibuscumque sedibus suppliciter ac simpliciter orantem, occulto foedere fouens, publice autem et belli et pacis copia negata, ad terendam terrendamque rempublicam reseruauit. This passage follows the discussion of Radagaisus in 7.37, which begins with a discouraging note on Saul, a barbarian and pagan, commanding at Pollentia, then breaks away abruptly to Radagaisus. The lack of a transition suggests the insertion of Radagaisus's story, heavily laced with God's wrath and Justice, into a narrative about Stilicho and Alaric, which was itself crafted to amplify the effects of Christianity upon leaders and their successes and failures. Thus 7.37–38f. is a thematic whole from the Christian perspective but not from the historical. If the chronological sequence is therefore compressed and distorted with the inclusion, out of order, of Radagaisus temporally to strengthen the contrast spiritually, then the "secret accord" would have related

to removing Alaric from Italy sometime after Pollentia. The battle of Verona is not mentioned in Orosius.

34. Zosimus, 5.26.2. Τὰ ἐν Ἰλλυριοῖς ἔθνη πάντα, literally "everything among the Illyrians," but more correctly, all of Illyricum, is preceded by a vexing chronological compression which combines events ca. 397 and this reference to all of Illyricum into one passage. Most scholars (following Demougeot) regard the reference to Illyricum as indicating Stilicho's wish to add the remainder of Illyricum to the West and therefore as a preparation for war. I concur, but this was not the first time, for Stilicho had already invaded in 395 and 396. This was clearly a renewal of his active aggression abated since 401. According to Zosimus 5.26.1, Stilicho had decided upon this plan in 397, after his ignominious return from Greece where he had learned first hand that Arcadius's ministers were solidly against him. At some point Stilicho made an agreement with Alaric, that much is certain from 5.26.1, but when is the subject of profound disagreement. The chronological condensation represented in Zosimus (perhaps confused by the double appearance of Epirus in his sources) makes it appear to take place in 396–97, while or shortly after the two adversaries met in Greece, but that is highly improbable. Few scholars have succumbed to a literal reading of this distressed passage. R. Ridley 1982, 215, n. 84, succinctly lists the various academic views on the date of this particular agreement between Stilicho and Alaric: T. Mommsen (402); O. Seeck, E. Stein, L. Schmidt, and S. Mazzarino (405); and E. Demougeot's who suggests 406 and relates it to Stilicho's effort to recapture eastern Illyricum. F. Paschoud 1971–89 (v. 3, pt. 1), 196–200, follows Demougeot (1947 and 1948). I agree with Demougeot on the purpose of the agreement but date it to 405, prior to Radagaisus's invasion, when Stilicho still thought he had troops and time. The sequence of events in Zosimus supports a date prior to Radagaisus. Sozomus, 8.25.4, places Alaric in Pannonia II and Dalmatia prior to the invasion of Epirus, probably in 402, which was the result of an earlier accord, the one of 402 known from Latin sources.

35. Contrary to Cameron and Long 1993, 250, this letter does not relate to Alaric. For one thing, Alaric is never mentioned. Perhaps more telling, however, is the fact that in 404, the Illyricum where Alaric resided was a Western diocese and so Honorius's concern in this letter was Arcadius's inability to control his own Illyricum (that is what was left of the prefecture—the dioceses of Dacia and Macedonia) where unrest was apparently adding to the woes of "dying Illyricum." Honorius's criticism is tactful. He was careful not to tell Arcadius what to do, but by asking to be kept fully apprised he recalled his rights there. Illyricum was hardly the main subject of the letter, however. Honorius also deplored not being informed about the coronation of Arcadius's wife Eudoxia four years before, and about which no one could do anything. The letter hardly dwells on Illyricum at all—part of one sentence. Unrest there and Arcadius's decision to crown his wife Eudoxia empress were actually both minor points in a lengthy letter chastising his older brother on his treatment of Patriarch John Chrysostom. This is a letter Arcadius perhaps thought best left unanswered. At any rate, no reply is preserved.

36. Bagnall 1987, 343.

37. CTh 7.13.16 dated 17 April 406, relating to the Western Empire. Dediticii were legally restricted in regard to citizenship and testimentary rights but served in all types of units in the army. On Western recognition of Anthemius, see Bagnall 1987, 345.

38. He was made a general for these campaigns, Sozomenus, HE, 8.25.3 καὶ

στρατηγοῦ Ῥωμαίων ἀξίωμα παρὰ ᾿Ονωρίου προξενήσας ᾿Αλαρίχῳ τῷ ἡγουμένῳ τῶν Γότθων ᾿Ιλλυριοῖς ἐπανέστησεν. He was already a *comes rei militaris* so this new command could only have been as a magister.

39. *PLRE*, 2.623 (Iovius); for Alaric in Epirus, Sozomenus, *HE*, 7.25.3. Jovius and Alaric became friends there, Zosimus, 5.48.2.

40. Zosimus, 5.26.2, who states merely that the court had turned against Stilicho. R. Ridley, 215, n. 85, correctly stresses Anthemius (*PLRE*, 2.94–95).

41. Zosimus, 5.46.2. Upper Pannonia is clearly specified as are the Noricums and Raetias, ὄντα στρατηγόν καὶ τῶν ἄλλων ὅσοι Παιονίαν τε τὴν ἄνω καὶ Νωρικοὺς καὶ Ῥαιτοὺς ἐφύλαττον. The areas which Alaric and Generidus, both Western *comites* for Illyricum, commanded were not identical. Generidus had to repacify a diocese that had apparently slipped beyond any governmental control. Although the entire diocese was in theory administered from Ravenna, no one could rule much of it until Generidus began to reestablish Roman might. Contrary to F. Paschoud 1971–89 (v. 3, pt. 1), 303–4, there is no chance that Generidus was ever *magister militum per Illyricum*. See also *PLRE*, 2.500–1.

42. On the possible troop strengths for Generidus see Soproni 1985, 95–106.

43. Zosimus, 5.46.5.

44. On the *antiqui barbari* but not this interpretation see J. Šašel 1979, 125–39. There were clearly still some Goths around in 420. See B. Croke 1977, 347–67, from Theophanes, a.m. 5931; 94.19–23. Croke argues for the movement of Goths, said by Theophanes to have been originally from Pannonia, to Thrace at the order of Theodosius II in 422 (pp. 359–61). These were probably remnants of Theodosius's and Gratian's policies but could also have been somehow attached to Alaric by 409.

45. S. Soproni 1985, 95–106, sees the efforts of Generidus as providing an effective, if only partial, restoration of military organization to the Pannonian provinces of Illyricum and that this helps explain some of the archaeological materials.

46. See especially the summary by V. Popović 1987, 95–139; perhaps especially interesting is the clear relationship to personal Roman military ornaments in a context very similar to those late fourth-early fifth century sites in Raetia Secunda and the Elbgerman–east Germanic grave fields, both contexts linked to typologically similar personal items among the Sintana de Mures–Cherniakhov Culture. This is especially clear with Popović's discussion of the Gothic female grave from Vajuga, pp. 131–32, which he dates before 443 and probably nearer to 400. See also the distribution and discussion of comb-types at sites along the Danube, pp. 129f.

47. *Chronica Gallica ad CCCCLII*, 50 (XI), Radagaisus rex Gothorum Italiae limitem vastaturus transgreditur, an Arian here, a zealous pagan in Orosius, 7.37.5, who offered the blood of the entire Roman Empire to his gods. Prosper Tiro hopelessly conflates events, in 400, Gothi Italiam Alarico et Radagaiso ducibus ingressi. Marcellinus Comes dates the invasion to 406 and calls Radagaisus a pagan and a Scythian. For other references see *PLRE*, 2.934.

48. Orosius, 7.37.13.

49. Zosimus, 5.26.3; this section draws from Olympiodorus, frag. 1, but not as in Sozomenus, *HE*, 9.4.2–4, and therefore not collaborated in its condensation of Olympiodorus or perhaps of its expansion upon the lost text. O. Seeck (1920–22) 1966, v. 5, 375–78, thought that these Celts, of whom of course there were no more at this time,

were Alamanni. He may be correct, but so too might they have been the so-called Elbgermans who make their appearance in the archaeological records.

50. Addit. ad Prosper Haun. ad. a. 405., *PLRE*, 2.934.

51. Orosius, 7.37.14.

52. Olympiodorus, frag. 9, who calls these 12,000 the elite leaders, οἱ κεφαλαιῶται ὀπτίματοι, of Radagaisus's men. P. Heather 1991, 213, also reasons that this is the total force available to Radagaisus, but thinks that they soon went over to Alaric as a distinct element.

53. 30 x 250 = 7,500 men plus a few thousand auxiliaries. Even this is admittedly a generous calculation for the size of a *numerus*, but by the end of the fourth century this term could include almost any type of unit from a small garrison to an important unit with the emperor. There is sufficient archaeological information to seriously question A. Jones 1964, 682, that there were no units in the *Notitia* that would have possessed fewer than 500 men; the later surely the fewer. For the sake of argument, however, even if Jones is taken as the standard, the number produced is 15,000 in regular troops and some unknown number of auxiliaries. Sarus is later reduced by desertions and deaths to as few as 200 to 300 followers (Olympiodorus, frag. 7). Of course, there is no way of knowing how many Huns had been allowed to cross over to Roman employment. The source of many of these "statistics" is Olympiodorus, whose reliability is hotly debated at both ends of the spectrum; see for a positive appraisal of his accuracy E. Thompson 1944, 43–52; for a negative appraisal, see J. Maenchen-Heflen 1973, 459–61. As compared to his contemporaries Olympiodorus does seem unusually reasonable in the cases here cited.

54. See the discussion leading, however, to a contrary conclusion by Maenchen-Heflen 1973, 60. He incorrectly rejects the earlier theories of Seeck and Demougeot, both of whom argued for the Brenner because of an incorrect hypothesis about the destruction levels at Flavia Solvia.

55. Zosimus, 5.26.3, Ῥοδογάϊσος ἐκ τῶν ὑπερ τὸν Ἴστρον καὶ τὸν Ῥῆνον Κελτικῶν τε καὶ Γερμανικῶν ἐθνῶν, but ethnic labels along particularly this section of the frontier meant little as we see in the archaeological record. There certainly were no "Celts" as we now understand that term. "Germans" is hardly more descriptive, it too having no precise meaning at this time. Zosimus is merely passing along in a traditional literary fashion the fact that Radagaisus recruited people whom he regarded as non-Romans along the frontiers and with them invaded.

56. Zosimus, 5.48–50; this was his final negotiating point.

57. Theophylactus Simocatta, *Historiarum libri octo* 3.1.2; 7.1.2.

58. Olympiodorus, frag. 12, from Photius, *Bib. Cod.* 80.

59. Paulinus of Nola, *Epis.* 7.3.

60. For examples see P. Grierson and M. Mays 1992, 225–26. Also see Illustration 18 in chapter 9. Constantius was emperor only from 8 February to 2 September 421.

61. On the army's economic importance to the Late Empire and its localities see J.-M. Carrié 1986, who employs the *Notitia*, imperial legislation, and literary references to assess the overall impact of the army upon the economy. The archaeological record supports and deepens the discussion of this topic, particularly in the frontier provinces.

62. The abuse of military transport was an old problem. Diocletian (284–305) had addressed it by fixing the weight limits for military pack animals in his Edict of Maximum prices. What is important here is the datable contexts that these late items provide.

63. Sozomenus, *HE*, 9.4.4–8, based on the same passage of Olympiodorus as 8.25.3–4, is clear that promises had been made to Alaric to get him to leave Illyricum for Epirus, κατὰ τὰ συντεθειμένα (according to his agreements), and that he was made commander of both Roman troops and his own auxiliaries. Of course, the Roman troops at his command must have numbered but few if any. The title and level of support that went with it surely did matter to Alaric.

64. *PLRE*, 2.1297, Fasti can only suggest one possible commander near this time, a Fortunius who was probably *dux* in Moesia (*PLRE*, 1.371). After the deaths of Gaïnas and Fravitta, no other magister is known to have operated in Thrace until the appointment of Constans in 412 (*PLRE*, 2.311). No magister for Illyricum other than possibly Alaric, whose claim to the office in 407 he had yet to secure in battle, is securely known until Agintheus (*PLRE*, 2.34) in 449, although Macedonius held either the magistership for Illyricum or Thrace in 423 (*PLRE*, 2.697). Arsacius (*PLRE*, 2.152) *magister militum praesentalis* was present in Constantinople in 409 but is not known to have set foot west of the city walls.

65. *CJ* 12.57.9–10 the latter dated April 407 from Constantinople but probably in office since at least September 401. For this more precise date, Cameron and Long 1993, 222.

66. *CTh* 11.17.4, attesting to wall repairs and construction as of 11 April 408.

67. Sozomenus, *HE*, 8.25.3–4.

68. Sozomenus, *HE*, 8.25.4, μέλλων γὰρ ἐκδημεῖν ὡς ὡμολόγησε Στελίχων Ὀνωρίου γράμμασιν ἐπεσχέθη. καὶ τὰ μὲν ἐν τούτοις ἦν, from Olympiodorus, frag. 2, a much-condensed passage that in a mere 21 lines covers the events from the abortive mission to join with Alaric and march eastward to the death of Stilicho and his son Eucherius in 408. Apparently these letters contained a rumor, quickly dispelled, that Alaric had died and the fact that Constantine III had claimed the emperorship and was in Gaul (Zosimus, 5.27.3).

69. *Consularia Italica* reports that on 31 December 406 (Arcadio et Probo pridie kl. Ianuarii. ab urbe condita anni MCLXXII) Gunderic, king of the Vandals, led his people across the Rhine and cruelly laid waste all of Gaul in conjunction with the Alans. All sources are given by C. Courtois 1955, 38, n. 3, with a brief discussion of the dating.

70. Jerome, *Epis.* 123.15. The Pannonians perhaps but not necessarily were from a biblical allusion (Ps. 83.8) to Assur, so suggests his editor J. Labourt. Jerome states "hostes Pannonii uastarunt. Etenim Assur uenit cum illis." That the reference is in fact genuine, although confused, see below.

71. Ibid.

72. Prosper, *Epitoma Chronicon* 1230.

73. Jerome, *Epis.* 123.16.6–7.

74. Ibid., 123.16.24–27.

75. Sozomenus, *HE*, 8.25.

76. Ibid., 9.4.

77. Socrates, *HE*, 6.23.7, 1 May in the consulate of Bassus and Philip, Theodosius was eight.

78. *CTh* 7.13.18; and probably 7.20.13 (either 409 or 407).

79. Procopius, *BV*, 1.3.1–3, incorrectly has Godigisclus leading the invasion but he died near the Rhine fighting in the first round of engagements and was succeeded

by his legitimate son, Gunderic (Gregorius Turonensis, 2.9); see also for Gunderic *PLRE*, 2.522, and for his bastard son Godigisclus *PLRE*, 2.516.

80. *PLRE*, 2.522.

81. Jordanes, *Getica*, xxii (115).

82. *Nd. or.* 28.25.

83. I cannot accept L. Schmidt 1941, 12–16, that Godigisclus led the Vandals from Pannonia to the Rhine as does *PLRE*, 2.516 (Godigisclus 1).

84. *PLRE*, 2.516.

85. *PLRE*, 2.496.

86. Procopius, *BV*, 1.22.1–15, who notes that all trace of these people had vanished, their small numbers overwhelmed by other barbarians.

87. Jerome, *Epis.*, 123.15.

88. Orosius, 7.38.

89. For this old belief see J. Bury (1923) 1958, 186, who also blames the Ostrogoths.

90. This misconception was adequately exploded by Vercauteren and Courtois. Vercauteren also noted how little damage was actually done to towns because of these raids; Courtois showed that the source of this misinformation, Ambrose, was in fact reworking a passage written ca. 378 into an exposition ca. 390, which in turn has been extrapolated into the first decade of the fifth century. F. Vercauteren 1934, 955–63; C. Courtois 1955, 40.

91. On the assessment of the Rhenish and other garrisons see the comments of S. James 1984, 166, from unpublished assessments of M. Hassell and published ones of R. Duncan-Jones 1978, 541–60. Some were considerably smaller, probably in the 20 to 25 range; see H. Böhme 1985a.

92. For a summary of the data on these small camps see P. Périn 1987, 90f., including Rhenen, Haillot and Furfooz, Cortrat, and Vert-la-Gravelle.

93. Zosimus, 6.3.2; but especially Renatus Profuturus Frigeridus, as preserved in Gregory of Tours, 2.9, which gives 20,000 Vandals killed including their king, Godigisclus [Godigyselo rege absumpto]. Had it not been for the timely arrival of Alans, which saved the Vandals from annihilation, the problem would have been solved. See also Orosius, 7.40.4, and Sozomenus, *HE*, 9.11.2.

94. Surely the most significant arguments concerning the chronology of the events of 406–8 remain those advanced by C. Stevens 1957, 316–47. On Constantine III and his movements in Gaul see E. Demougeot 1974a, 83–125. Recently resurveyed by E. Chrysos 1991, 247–76.

95. Olympiodorus, frag. 13, from Photius, *Bib. Cod.* 80, and repeated in Sozomenus as well (*HE*, 9.11.2–12.3) with the added feature that the troops chose Constantine because with such a name at their head they were confident that they could conquer the whole Empire.

96. From Photius, *Bib. Cod.* 80, only.

97. N. Baynes 1922a, 217–19. Baynes's note is plagued by his own misreading of texts and sloppiness. Orosius does not say anything about Marcus nor does any other Latin source, nor does he make Marcus a townsman *municeps* but rather Gratian, and that appellation is carried forward by Bede. His argument about Radagaisus is correct only in that there was but one invasion. More problems are also apparent but need no comment after 70 years. However, Baynes suggested that the elevation of Marcus had

absolutely nothing to do with the Vandals on the continent but was entirely inspired by British fears of their own vulnerability to Saxon and Scottish raids (from Claudianus, *In Eutrop.*, 1.393 and St. Patrick on the Saxon raids on the Channel ports). Unfortunately neither Claudianus nor Patrick can hold up to tight chronology either. Nevertheless, even the most effective of his critics, Stevens, agrees that the usurpation of Marcus should be dated to 406 and perhaps early in that year; C. Stevens 1957, 321, n. 31.

98. C. Stevens 1957, 321, n. 31, does acknowledge the possibility that Gratian too was raised up early in 406 but rejects the conclusions that would follow from this in his arguments in the paper itself. That this Marcus may have taken his name from Marcus Aurelius Mausaeus Carausius (286–93) (Stevens, p. 321) seems but an interesting possibility. In fact, of course, Marcus had long been a common name in the military districts following the great emperor Marcus Aurelius.

99. The absence of post-Theodosian coinage in almost all sites has been noted by all investigators. For *dux Britanniae, Nd. oc.* 1.48; 5.142; 40. For the *comes litoris Saxonici per Britannias, Nd. oc.* 1.36; 5.132; 28. For *comes Britanniarum, Nd. oc.* 1.35; 5.131; 7.153, 199. Magnus Maximus probably had also been the equivalent of *comes Britanniarum* under Theodosius the elder (Zosimus, 4.35.3). Gratian had held the post (S. Frere 1987, 225). Basing himself on M. Miller 1975, 141–45, J. Mann 1991, 217, n. 45, suggests that Stilicho continued the work of creating regional commands beyond the provincial level that Theodosius had accomplished in the West. Mann's suggestion is that Stilicho's changes in Britain came about during 395 and included the creation of the post of *comes Britanniae*. At about the same time Stilicho created similar posts for Italy (*Nd. oc.* 1.31; 5.127; 5.24) and the *tractus Argentoratensis* (*Nd. oc.* 1.34; 5.130; 5.27). The *comes Italiae* would have been second only to Stilicho himself in Italy and would have confronted Alaric's first raids from Illyricum in the winter of 401–2. I have no problem with Miller's dating of Stilicho's Pictish war, or his suggestion that troops in Britain received "their marching orders" for the campaign against Alaric in 401. However, this was in preparation for Stilicho's pending invasion against Alaric, not a response to Alaric's invasion of Italy. It just so happened that those actually transferred arrived in time to take part at Verona, although I doubt that they played much of a role at Pollentia.

100. *Nd. oc.* 5.131.

101. The theory that Stilicho, and before him Magnus Maximus, dispatched only units of the Gallic *comitatensis* is an attractive hypothesis put forward by several scholars, especially S. James 1984, 161–86, at p. 170. This theory maintains that the existing British sections of the *Notitia* date to after 402 and that therefore the *comes* for Britain and some of his command returned to Britain following Stilicho's victory over Alaric. While agreeing with the idea that Roman emperors moved units rather than whole armies whenever possible, I cannot see any reason to date anything in the British sections after 400, including the *comes rei militaris Britanniarum*.

102. The example of Germanic soldiers of this type serving under officers buried with Roman army–related dress at Mucking, Essex, is in a great many respects like that found at contemporary Regensburg. On Mucking see H. Hamerow 1987, 245.

103. So suggests C. Stevens 1957, 322, on the basis of Zosimus, 6.3.1; however, this passage has the British troops elect Marcus, Gratian, and Constantine all for the same reason—fear of attack from the Vandals—and that cannot be. Nor should we accept that because of their concern for Britain they threw up Constantine and seized Boulogne from this same passage in Zosimus.

104. S. James 1984, 170–71. The debate has been focused on providing a date of establishment for the *comes rei militaris Britanniarum* and his command listed in the *Notitia* (*oc.* 1.35, 7.153f., 7.199f.).

105. Earlier his withdrawal of a legion was roundly praised in Claudianus, *BG*, 416–18.

106. Vetranio too minted coins but without his own name on them, only that of Constantius II, for example, *RIC* 8.272 variant (mint mark); see also T. Burns and B. Overbeck 1987, 32, no. 59. He died of old age while drawing a pension in Bithynia, Zosimus 2.44.4.

107. Nanninus and Quintinus, Gregorius Turonensis, *Historiae Francorum*, 2.9.5 (Buchner, p. 82). The parallels to Maximus are indeed close; note the approach to co-emperorship revealed in their coinage, for example. That Gregory chose to discuss them both in the same chapter heightens the comparison. Zosimus, 6.2.2 for Constantine's appointments.

108. J. Lafaurie 1953, 37–65; C. King 1987, 286–89. On the issues in general see R. Carson 1981, 79, and Constantine III in A. Robertson 1982, 445–46.

109. R. Bagnall 1987, 352–53. Constantine's alleged consulship in 409 was proclaimed only in Gaul.

110. C. King 1987, 291.

111. J. Kent 1979, 21.

112. Figures are those of A. Jones but given and criticized by S. James 1984, 162–63.

113. S. James 1984, 166–72. The question of *laeti* and other "barbarian" troops in Britain is taken up by D. Welsby 1982, 158–64, with great equivocation. Certainly there was no large presence. James and others have now demonstrated that the decline of the British army from the strengths of the principate began in the third century when Britain was at peace and the continent in flames. Along the wall the *limitanei* had turned into a police force only by ca. 400; see N. Hodgson 1991, 84–92, who refrains from offering a date for the British section but instead wisely settles for ca. 400, at which time, he believes, most units listed in *Notitia* were still present.

114. Orosius, 7.40.4, ex infima militia propter solam spem nominis sine merito uirtutis eligitur.

115. Procopius, *BV*, 3.2.31, "a not obscure man," βασιλέα σφίσι Κωνσταντῖνον εἵλοντο, οὐκ ἀφανῆ ἄνδρα. Sozomenus also notes the importance of his name (*HE*, 9.11.4–5).

116. C. Stevens 1957, 318, n. 12, and others follow Orosius and conclude that he was an obscure common soldier.

117. For this theory of his continental success see P. Salway 1981, 481. It fits nicely with all the known evidence, particularly the fact that at Arles in 411 Constantine sought and received, too late however, aid from the Gallic army in the north and the Franks and others previously seen fighting the Vandals in the opening round of hostilities (Gregorius Turonensis, *Historiae Francorum*, 2.9.32–34). His taking ship is reported in Procopius, *BV*, 3.2.31.

118. Zosimus, 5.27.

119. C. Stevens 1957, 319, n. 22, from S. Mazzarino 1942, 283, n. 2, on the assessment of *CTh* 11.17.4, dated to 9 April 407, states that Alaric's existence could not have been doubted after this edict. However, the edict probably dates not to 9 April 407 but to 11 April 408; it emanated from Constantinople in the names of Honorius and Theo-

dosius II, was addressed to Herculius (PPO Illyrici 408–10), and concerned the need to construct walls in Illyricum, that is to say in the dioceses of Macedonia and Dacia administered by the East. As such it is a good testament to the fact that the invasion by Alaric had caused considerable damage and that the threat from the West was not regarded as over. About Stilicho's knowledge or interpretations of events in the spring of 407 it says nothing.

120. E. Demougeot 1974, 101. This is far and away the most significant piece on Constantine III in Gaul and contains the texts for all relevant discussion, also the numismatic data available as to the date of publication. There is no reason to recapitulate her arguments and hypotheses in detail.

121. H. Bender 1986, 122–24, and B. Overbeck 1988, 143–44, with references to earlier finds. See chapter 5.

122. Zosimus, 6.2.2–3 (and discussion of literature in F. Paschoud 1971–89 [v. 3, pt. 2], 24–25). PLRE, 2.644, Justinianus was perhaps *praepositus* in Britain. Nebiogastes was a German, PLRE, 2.773. Sarus probably was named *magister militum* for this one campaign and as such would technically have been *magister militum vacans*, a type of extraordinary but active command increasingly common at the end of the fourth century and integrated into the system of ranks by Theodosius II (A. Jones 1964, 535).

123. Zosimus, 6.2.4. On his route see F. Paschoud 1971–89 (v. 3, pt. 2), 25.

124. Thermantia (PLRE, 2.1111); Maria (PLRE, 2.720).

125. Zosimus, 5.29.1; see also E. Demougeot 1951, 404, n. 265.

126. Tabula Imperii Romani, L-33, Trieste (Rome, 1961).

127. As R. Ridley 1982 notes (p. 216, n. 100), Olympiodorus must have confused the Apennines with the Carnican Alps. So Zosimus and Sozomenus, HE, 8.25.4, have Alaric invade Italy.

128. Zosimus, 5.29.2–9, non est ista pax sed pactio servitutis.

129. Zosimus, 5.30. The entire picture of what happened during these weeks and months is consistently colored by the end result: the death of Stilicho, the overthrow of his followers, and the fall of Rome. The first act of the uprising took place in Ticinum (Pavia) with the aid of troops assembled there for the campaign against Constantine III (5.32.3–7). Therefore I have disregarded 5.30.4 and its reference to Honorius going to Ravenna by way of Ticinum to pick up troops to suppress Stilicho, who was at this point to accompany the emperor himself (5.30.1). Unless Olympius did so with Honorius en route to Ticinum without declaring his plans for them (F. Paschoud 1971–89 [v. 3, pt. 1], 222–23). So too the entire passage smacks of the historian setting the stage for some great event. Zosimus was always most conscious of the fall of Rome in 410 and the decisive moments leading up to it. The later "rumors" that Honorius was already plotting the overthrow of Stilicho cannot be confirmed, but it would seem that only the mutiny of the troops later at Ticinum so moved the emperor. Others than the emperor were deep into their own schemes. Alaric received his gold sometime before Stilicho's death (Olympiodorus, frag. 7.2, from Photius).

130. Zosimus, 5.31.1–2. R. Ridley (1982, 217, n. 110) and others (but not received with enthusiasm by all, F. Paschoud 1971–89 [v. 3, pt. 1], 225–26) see this as "an early unsuccessful attempt by the anti-Stilichonians at what they managed successfully at Ticinum." Zosimus merely states that there was a lack of discipline in the ranks needing the hand of the *magister* Stilicho himself, whose threat to decimate their ranks was softened by the imperial pardon. I concur in Paschoud's coolness toward the conspiracy

theory. Discipline problems were hardly uncommon in these years as we have seen repeatedly. Like the earlier reference to the soldiers at Ticinum in the context of the motives for Honorius to insist upon going to Ravenna, the mutiny at Bononia is suspicious, given that the obvious reason for summoning Stilicho to Bononia was deciding what to do after the death of Arcadius. It was an event with potentially colossal repercussions. Stilicho had already paid Alaric's agents or had given them receipts to draw upon in Noricum and so had no reason to delay answering the summons. If 4,000 lbs. of gold was actually transferred, it is no wonder that neither Alaric nor Stilicho had yet moved in August. Such precious metal would have required elaborate security. See Paschoud as here cited for various reconstructions of the emperor's itinerary.

131. Sozomenus, HE, 9.4.6; Zosimus, 5.31.4–6. I dismiss as anachronistic the third reason for staying given by Zosimus, specifically that Alaric, "a feckless barbarian," would invade if Italy was left undefended, for the very same sentence goes on to suggest that Alaric be given command against Constantine.

132. Sozomenus, HE, 9.4.6 Θάτερον δὲ τῶν σκήπτρων, ὅ λάβωρον Ῥωμαῖοι καλοῦσι, καὶ γράμματα βασιλέως λαβὼν ἐπιτρέποντα αὐτῷ τὴν εἰς τὴν ἀνατολὴν ἄφιξιν, ἔμελλεν ἐκδημεῖν τέσσαρας ἀριθμοὺς στρατιωτῶν παραλαβών.

133. Zosimus, 5.31.6.

134. Zosimus, 5.31.5 σὺν αὐτῷ βαρβάρων ἄγοντα μέρος καὶ τέλη Ῥωμαϊκὰ καὶ ἡγεμόνας. Like Sarus's command Alaric's would necessarily have been for the duration of a campaign. It does not seem that he was to replace Chariobaudes, then *magi. mil. p. Gallias*, even though the latter was defeated and in refuge with the court.

135. Zosimus, 5.31.6. F. Paschoud 1971–89 (v. 3, pt. 1), 228–29, suggests that he waited there for his troops, assigned to accompany him to Constantinople, to assemble. Perhaps, but this still does not completely clarify why he waited where he did.

136. The references in O. Seeck 1919, 314, are irrelevant since they are ascribed neither as to issuance nor location.

137. Olympius 2 (PLRE, 2.801), entire career spent in the West.

138. Zosimus, 5.32.1.

139. Zosimus, 5.32.2–3, on the date see *Consularia Italica* p. 300, et Ticeno multi maiores occisi sunt id. Aug.

140. Zosimus, 5.32.4–7. Limenius, praetorian prefect of the Gauls; Chariobaudes, *magister* for Gaul; Vincentius, *magister equitum* (*magister praesentalis* II) (PLRE, 2.1288) [J. Bury and those following his incorrect reconstruction of Stilicho as *mag. utr. mil.* have equally confused the career of Vincentius]; Salvius a friend of Stilicho's who was then *comes domesticorum;* Naemorius, *magister officiorum;* Patroinus, *comes sacrarum largitionum;* the *comes rerum privatarum*, perhaps Ursicinus (R. Ridley 1982, 218, n. 121); Salvius, *quaestor;* and Longinus, praetorian praefect of Italy. Chariobaudes was a general of Germanic descent (PLRE, 2.283). Of these men most were within the literary network of Symmachus, specifically Limenius (PLRE, 2.684); Patroinus (PLRE, 2.843); Salvius (PLRE, 2.974); and Longinus (PLRE, 2.686).

141. Zosimus, 5.34.7.

142. Since Ravenna had a mint at this time, there had to be at least a garrison to guard it as well as whatever other troops happened to be there as palace guards, etc.

143. Zosimus, 5.33.

144. CTh 7.8.5. The meaning of this seemingly straightforward edict is hotly disputed (begun anew by the publication of W. Goffart 1980). This edict will be taken

up in the discussion of the settlement of the Goths in Aquitaine in 418. Certainly in 407, the date of issuance, there must have been a basic understanding of the procedure outlined and the need to clarify billeting arrangements because of recent events that witnessed a marked increase in troop movement at the very time when the economy was turning sour. There is no reason to assume, however, that the interpretation of 407, whatever it was, remained constant for centuries thereafter.

145. Zosimus, 5.34.1–2.

146. Zosimus, 5.34.3–5. On the death of Stilicho, Orosius records only that this wretched man got his just deserts from the army that properly rose up and killed him, who to adorn his son with the purple had risked the human race (7.38). Eucherius found temporary refuge in a church in Rome (5.35.4). Serena was strangled to death in Rome during Alaric's siege in 408.

147. Zosimus, 5.34.7, 22 August.

148. Sozomenus, HE, 9.4.1. So too concludes Zosimus, 5.32.1, despite what his source Olympiodorus said about Stilicho's limited favoritism toward his son and given by Zosimus only two chapters later.

149. Orosius, 7.38.

150. Philostorgius, HE, 11.3, as preserved in the epitome of his work; Marcellinus Comes, 408, parallels Orosius. Philostorgius is the sole Greek source for Honorius, a misreading of Olympiodorus on his part?

151. PLRE, 2.1149.

152. Orosius, 7.38.

153. Epis. 123.16, written ca. 408 but making no mention of Stilicho's death.

154. Epis. 77.8 (dtd. ca. 400); J.-R. Palanque 1952, 180–82.

155. See chapter 1, note 158, for full citations.

156. PLRE, 2.801.

VIII. The Sack of Rome

1. PLRE, 2.1133.
2. PLRE, 2.1165.
3. Zosimus, 5.35–36.
4. Zosimus, 5.35.4, 5.45.3.
5. Zosimus, 5.35.2.
6. Zosimus, 5.35.3.
7. Zosimus, 5.35.4; Philostorgius, HE, 12.3.
8. Zosimus, 5.35.5.
9. Zosimus, 5.35.6.
10. Zosimus, 5.35.6.
11. Zosimus, 5.36.1. Gaudentius was born into a very important family in the province of Scythia, had married a rich and noble lady from Italy, and along with Jovius (probably this same Jovius) had destroyed pagan shrines in Africa in 399 as comes Africae. He had perhaps already been named magister equitum per Gallias, which he held at his death in 425, but because of Constantine III had yet to take up his command (PLRE, 2.494). Jason, son of Jovius, is probably the son of the Jovius who had become Alaric's friend in Epirus (Zosimus, 5.48.2) and would soon become a key player in Alaric's dealings with Honorius and Attalus, Alaric's nominee for emperor (PLRE, 2.623–24).

In other words, these fathers were old colleagues of proven effectiveness, at least one of whom was personally known to Alaric and liked.

12. That Athaulf was Alaric's brother-in-law, see P. Heather 1991, 31, n. 49.

13. Zosimus, 5.37.1–2. Honorius's army had indeed made some preliminary moves, Zosimus, 5.36.3.

14. Zosimus, 5.37.2–3, from Ariminum (Rimini) he continued southward to Picenum and crossed the Apennines to Rome. Oecubaria has yet to be identified.

15. Zosimus, 5.37.2. *Tabula Imperii Romani*, L-32, Mediolanum (Rome, 1966).

16. Honorius was in Milan by 13 September (*CTh* 11.28.4) and in Ravenna by 14 November (*CTh* 16.5.42).

17. Augustinus, *De civ. Dei*, 1.2; *Sermo*, 105.10.13; Orosius, 7.37.2; *PLRE*, 2.248. On the attempt of *CTh* 16.5.42, dtd. 14 November 408, to prohibit pagans from holding military command and other anti-pagan legislation under Honorius, see below.

18. Orosius, 7.38, that he had secretly harbored a plan to persecute Christians from his boyhood. This was why Stilicho, according to Orosius, was so supportive of the Goths after he came to power and was part of the truth revealed to Honorius that led to Stilicho's downfall. His death freed the churches of Christ and the pious emperor from his attempted persecution.

19. Jerome, *Epis.* 123.15–17, especially 16, ll. 6–8 (p. 93), sed scelere semibarbari accidit proditoris, qui nostris contra nos opibus armauit inimicos.

20. Zosimus, 5.38.5. F. Paschoud 1971–89 (v. 3, pt. 1), 266–67, offers the opinion that this incident took place in early 408, when Stilicho was in Rome to confer with the Senate. Stilicho needed money throughout his rule. The coming campaign against Constantine III in 408 was but one.

21. Rutilius Namatianus, *De reditu suo*, 2.50–53; 55–60.

22. J. Matthews 1970, 79–97, 90–91.

23. So I understand Rutilius, 2.43, Romano generi dum nititur esse superstes, contrary to the Duffs, who suggest that he literally "counted on outliving the devastation of Italy," p. 826, n.b.

24. Augustinus, *Epis.* 97, praising the anti-pagan legislation inspired by him.

25. Eunapius, frag. 2 (Photius, *Bib. Cod.* 98) declaring Eunapius as a vicious attacker of Stilicho. In the other extant fragments there is plenty of proof to support Photius's judgment of Eunapius, but no attacks on his religion.

26. Zosimus, 5.50.2

27. Orosius, 7.39.1.

28. Zosimus, 5.37.4–5, so I interpret the reentry of Eucherius into Zosimus's account. See F. Paschoud 1971–89 (v. 3, pt. 1), 255–56, for all other sources on Eucherius's flight and death as well as scholarly discussions.

29. Philostorgius, *HE*, 12.3.

30. *PLRE*, 2.221.

31. Zosimus, 5.35.2.

32. Zosimus, 5.38.2–4; Zosimus is precise in dating this to 394, when Theodosius arrived in Rome after defeating Arbogastes and Eugenius. He places the remembrance in the context of senatorial fears that Alaric's march into Italy in the autumn of 408. But scholars have disputed these dates (see F. Paschoud 1971–89 [v. 3, pt. 1], 263–65, for a summary of their criticism). Paschoud thinks it possible that the incident at the temple took place as early as 389.

33. Commodianus is now usually dated to the third century, and it is his testimony more than any other's that casts the Goths and barbarians in apocalyptic tones and sets the stage for later uses of this paradigm in an altered state. Commodianus, *Carmen apologeticum*, 810–19. Older arguments had placed Commodian in the fifth century; see E. Goodspeed 1946, 46–47, and P. Courcelle 1946, 227–46. But careful analysis of the legal terminology and Commodian's discussion of Jews (ll. 671–702) as well as contemporary baptismal rites place him in the middle of the third century, K. Thraede 1959, 90–114. Courcelle, however, was surely right to declare that Commodian had no specific historic invasion in mind but rather drew together Goths and Revelation so as to mark the nearness of the end of time. On the other hand, his reference to the Goths invading must place the work after 240. Apocalyptic visions still haunted Salvianus, *De gubernatione Dei*, writing sometime after 439, but his treatment of the barbarians reflects a changed attitude toward them as Christians. Of the works of St. Augustine, see especially *De civ. Dei*, 1.2; *Sermo*, 105.10.13; *Retractiones*, 2.69.

34. Orosius, 7.38, lays the blame for Rome's demise squarely upon Stilicho, whose death freed the churches of Christ and the most pious emperor. Alaric is seen as a reasonable man leading his nation in search of peace and a place to settle but he too is tricked by Stilicho, who offered him a secret agreement but worked to be sure his pledges would not be sanctioned by the state. Orosius opens the next chapter (7.39) with Alaric's orders not to violate Christian sanctuaries and then proceeds to narrate the three days of the Gothic "sack."

35. Orosius, 7.40.2.

36. *Epis.* 123.16.

37. Socrates, *HE*, 7.10.

38. Sozomenus, *HE*, 9.6.

39. *Thiudans* was technically the closest Gothic equivalent for Βασιλεύς (emperor) but was typically seen as *rex* (king); see the discussion in T. Burns 1980, 35–50. Alaric was never *thiudans;* however, he was also not a mere prince (*reiks* in Gothic, *regulus* in Latin).

40. Orosius, 7.40.1 *nihil factum*.

41. Zosimus, 5.45.5.

42. First barbarians, Zosimus, 5.40.3, but later any whatsoever, 5.42.3. Sozomenus, *HE*, 9.7, says that especially barbarian slaves deserted to Alaric but not only barbarian.

43. Zosimus, 5.40.2.

44. Zosimus, 5.40.3–4.

45. For example, F. Paschoud 1985; E. Thompson 1944, 43–52; and J. Matthews 1970, 79–97.

46. Zosimus, 5.40.1; but Olympiodorus, frag. 7 (Photius, *Bib. Cod.* 80, p. 168).

47. Zosimus, 5.41.4–7.

48. Zosimus, 5.42.1–3.

49. Zosimus, 5.45.4.

50. *PLRE*, 2.741, Tarruntenius Maximillianus is the most likely identification. His inscription lists that he was twice sent on embassies for the Senate. On this one he was captured. Marinianus was probably *vicarius Hispaniae*, ca. 383, and a correspondent of Symmachus, if so he had been a teacher of law (*PLRE*, 1.560). Many have calculated similarly that the payment to Alaric was not unreasonable for the members of the Senate, cf. A. Jones 1964, 185.

51. Zosimus, 5.41.2–4.

52. Zosimus, 5.42.1 μὴ μόνον εἰρήνην ἀλλὰ καὶ ὁμαιχμίαν πρὸς τὸν βασιλέα ποιήσασθαι. The text is clear; the usual official terminology for concluding a military treaty is lacking. One would expect Olympiodorus and even Zosimus to have used the standard terms to describe a military alliance between two parties, συμμαχία or συμς μάχομαι from συμμαχέω. Βασιλέα, in the accusative, "emperor" makes the entire passage seem more personal and hence I prefer the more personal translation for ὁμαιχμίαν as a pledge to fight alongside of someone else. The entire sentence makes this phrase seem like a paraphrase of something Alaric himself was to have said.

53. Zosimus, 5.42.2–3.

54. As with some usurpers before, the legitimate government accepted "collegi-ality" but never took the very significant step of issuing coins as would have been cus-tomarily done with a genuine co-emperor, as, for example, when Gratian raised Theo-dosius to the purple.

55. R. Bagnall 1987, 352–53, giving all notices of the consuls for the year includ-ing the sole one for Constantine III. The young woman, Eusebia, died at age fifteen. For the full text of the inscription and discussion, see N. Gauthier 1975, v. 1, pp. 270–73 (Trèves, I.93).

56. Zosimus, 5.43.

57. PLRE, 2.1155.

58. Zosimus, 5.44.1, PLRE, 2.244–45 and F. Paschoud 1971–89 (v. 3, pt. 1), 290–91. Maximianus in Zosimus is an error or textual corruption for Maximillianus (5.45.4). Although the embassy was unsuccessful, Caecilianus was made praetorian prefect of Italy. PLRE's suggestion that he was PPO of "Italiae et Illyrici" is in error; none of the texts are addressed to him as such, nor does any concern Illyricum.

59. PLRE, 2.180–81.

60. Zosimus, 5.45.1. This force from Dalmatia may have included the four legions that had been assigned to accompany Stilicho on his mission to the court of Theo-dosius II. Otherwise, Stilicho's 4,000 men are lost to the historical record.

61. Zosimus, 5.44.2; the most recent victim was Theodorus, praetorian prefect of Italy, PLRE, 2.1087 (Theodorus 9), replaced by Caecilianus, who had arrived on the embassy from the Senate.

62. Zosimus, 5.45.6. Allobichus is the most likely candidate to have held the overall command of this force, for he was probably then comes dom. equitum.

63. Zosimus, 5.46.1.

64. Zosimus, 5.46.1; PLRE, 2.180–81 (Attalus), and 2.352 (Demetrius). Attalus succeeded Gabinius Barbarus Pompeianus, who had sought to employ the Tuscan augurs during the first siege.

65. PLRE, 2.623.

66. Zosimus, 5.47.1; PLRE, 2.61, Allobichus, a Germanic name, perhaps a relative of Ellebichus, who had been a magister a quarter century before (PLRE, 1.277).

67. Zosimus, 5.46.4; if the offending law was indeed CTh 16.5.42, addressed to Olympius, mag. off., and Valens, comes dom. equit., then the post Generidus (PLRE, 2.500) held was in the cavalry attached to the palace and commanded by the comes. There was no high command in Rome at this date; he must have been there on temporary duty when the law was passed and went into retirement. He was now recalled to duty as

comes Illyrici, not as Zosimus recorded as *mag. militum per Dalmatiam*. Dalmatia was a part of the command of the *comes*. Generidus was never a *magister militum* (contrary to F. Paschoud 1971–89 [v. 3, pt. 1], 302–6).

68. *CTh* 6.5.51.

69. Suggested by H. Wolfram 1988, 157.

70. *PLRE*, 2.623 (Iovius), and 2.61 (Allobichus); Zosimus, 5.48.1–3. Valens formerly *comes dom.*, *PLRE*, 2.1136 (Valens 1); Valens formerly *comes rei militaris* in Dalmatia and *mag. equitum* under Attalus, *PLRE*, 2.1137 (Valens 2). Turpilio became *mag. equitum* following the fall of Stilicho in 408 at Ticinum; his senior colleague at that time was Varanes, *mag. ped.* Vigilantius became *comes domesticorum equitum* at this time too. When Varanes assumed the consulship in the East in 410, Turpilio must have moved up to *mag. peditum* and Vigilantius to *mag. equitum.* Some of the confusion regarding these officers may result from a misunderstanding that Turpilio actually held the *mag. utrius mil.*, which did not exist as a functioning position in the Western hierarchy. W. Ensslin 1931, 467–502, devotes only one passage (p. 471) to these officers, but does make the point that they actually held positions other than *MVM*. "Nach Stilichos Tod folgten ihm Varanes, Turpilio, Valens und Flavius Constantius als magistri utriusque militiae in der Stelle des magister peditum praesentalis und Turpilio, Vigilantius, Allobichus, Ulphila als magistri equitum." Ensslin's lists must be clarified with the help of A. Jones 1964, 376, 609. Apparently Jovius ordered the deaths of Turpilio and Vigilantius (*PLRE*, 2.1133).

71. *PLRE*, 2.429 (Eusebius 9), probably killed in accordance with Constantius's wishes.

72. Zosimus, 5.48.3, the text actually reads both the Venetias, but officially the province was a combined province called Venetia et Histria, in the diocese of Italia. See also F. Paschoud 1971–89 (v. 3, pt. 1), 311.

73. For example, later in the century Odovacar sought to stop Theodoric there. Venetia and Histria were administered as one province.

74. On *utriusque*, Zosimus, 5.48.4; Sozomenus, *HE*, 9.7. Alaric under Attalus was one of two magisters, the other Valens (Zosimus, 6.7.2). Valens was clearly *magister equitum (mag. praes. II)* (Zosimus, 6.10.1 ὁ τῆς ἵππου στρατηγός) leaving *peditum* for Alaric. Despite the titles those officers commanded combined forces of cavalry and infantry. It should be recalled the *magister peditum praesentalis*, as reformed and centralized under Stilicho, was the highest command in the West and is so listed in the *Notitia dignitatum* (*oc.* 125–43), cf. A. Jones 1964, pp. 376, 609. In the East each of the five field armies was commanded by a *magister utriusque militiae*, although listed in the *Notitia* without the *utriusque*, since all indications in the East of *equitum* and *peditum* have ceased. Stilicho had been such a commander and found himself the sole such officer in the West after the return of all others following the death of Theodosius. He commanded the army in the West as *magister peditum praesentalis* but ruled at court as supreme commander and Honorius's principal advisor. This latter role was readily conveyed by *magister utriusque militiae.* This titular dignity evolved into the position of the Western military strongman, who ruled while the emperor reigned. Jovius's competitive bargaining strategy, whereby he started negotiations at the loftiest or most absurd level, never worked with Honorius, who was unaccustomed to striking compromises.

75. Zosimus, 5.48.4; 5.49.1.

76. So suggests R. Ridley 1982, 224, n. 173.

77. Zosimus, 5.50.1. (and F. Paschoud 1971–89 [v. 3, pt. 1], 313–15), but the oath was not alone and "on the head of the emperor" as in Zosimus, but with the chief officers and to the emperor's well being, as in Sozomenus, *HE*, 9.7.4.

78. The Huns were recognized in Valeria and Pannonia in 427; see T. Nagy 1967, 159–86, and L. Várady 1969, 278f. Zosimus, 5.50.1.

79. Zosimus, 5.50.3. εἶναί τε φιλίαν καὶ ὁμαιχμίαν αὐτῷ καὶ Ῥωμαίοις κατὰ παντὸς αἴροντος ὅπλα καὶ πρὸς πόλεμον κατὰ τῆς βασιλείας ἐγειρομένου. Used in this way ὁμαιχμίαν, especially with no personal quality really implied, since it is a relationship with "the Romans," normally means a defensive pact, and as such would have been typical of an alliance between a client beyond the frontiers and Rome. In this passage, however, I suggest that Alaric is trying to be sure that he is not left out on a limb in case Noricum is attacked, perhaps by the very Hunnic auxiliaries just called up against him once all return to their homes.

80. Zosimus, 5.51.1–2, Zosimus notes with sarcasm that what the state had really forgotten was the need for the gods' care.

81. *PLRE*, 2.181. On the second siege of the city and Attalus's policies see Zosimus, 6.6.2–3; Sozomenus, *HE*, 9.8; Socrates, *HE*, 7.10, a very brief and distorted account of Alaric and his various assaults on Rome; and Orosius, 7.42, a still briefer account that tells of Attalus's second stint as Augustus in Spain, 414–15.

82. Sozomenus, *HE*, 9.1. The Arian bishop Sigesar performed the ceremony.

83. Concerning when Galla Placidia became Alaric's hostage (see F. Paschoud 1971–89 [v. 3, pt. 2], 64–65), I concur with Paschoud that Zosimus is correct and that Galla was taken hostage in 409. The lack of any mention of her in other sources prior to 410 is the result of their jumping to conclusions. For these authors, that she was with Athaulf after the sack meant that he had taken her hostage in 410. Paschoud suggests this helps account for why Honorius was so determined not to accede to Alaric from 409 on. Honorius, however, never showed any disposition toward compromise with Alaric after the death of Stilicho.

84. Zosimus, 6.7.2, and Valens as *mag. equitum*, Zosimus, 6.10.1; thus it is clear that Alaric took *mag. peditum*, the superior post, for himself. Alaric later suspected Valens of treason and ordered his execution, Zosimus, 6.10.1

85. Sozomenus, *HE*, 9.8.2.

86. Zosimus, 6.1.2.

87. On Drumas we know only that he was a "man of proven loyalty" and that the Senate also supported sending him a little while later, *PLRE*, 2.381. For Joannes see *PLRE*, 1.459; he had been *notarius* and then *primicerius* and after Attalus's fall continued a highly successful civil career culminating with the prefectureship of Italy.

88. Sozomenus, *HE*, 9.8.5. μετὰ τῆς Ῥωμαίων καὶ βαρβάρων στρατιᾶς.

89. Olympiodorus, frag. 14 (Photius).

90. Sozomenus, *HE*, 9.8.5–6; Zosimus, 6.8.1–2 has Jovius, having returned from his embassy, announcing Attalus's counteroffer with vivid embellishment. Honorius would be exiled to an island after being maimed. The suggestion to maim Honorius is preserved in both Zosimus and Photius (Olympiodorus, frag. 14). The later reports that Jovius urged maiming upon Attalus, who strongly rejected such treatment.

91. Sozomenus, *HE*, 9.8.6, ἀμφὶ τετρακισχίλιοι στρατιῶται νύκτωρ τῇ Ῥαβέννῃ προσέπλευσαν ἐκ τῆς ἀνατολῆς.

92. Zosimus, 6.8.2–3. ἐξ τάγματα στρατιωτῶν προσωρμίσθησαν, πάλαι μὲν ἔτι

περιόντος Στελίχωνος προσδοκώμενα, τότε δὲ πρὸς συμμαχίαν ἐκ τῆς ἑῴας παραγενόμενα, χιλιάδων ἀριθμὸν ὄντα τεσσάρων. ἀνενεγκὼν δὲ ὥσπερ ἐκ κάρου βαθέος Ὀνώριος τοῖς μὲν ἐκ τῆς ἑῴας ἀφιγμένοις τὴν τῶν τειχῶν ἐπίστευε φυλακήν. Both ἀνατολῆς and ἑῴας might mean from the east, as a direction, the former originally denoting the horizon over which the sun rose, the latter, the eastern parts where the morning began. By the Late Empire, however, ἀνατολῆς could apply to the Oriens, the eastern part of the heavens, or the East, that this was the Eastern Empire. Surely the Eastern Empire is its meaning in this passage. E. Sophocles 1887, 154, 551.

93. There is universal agreement that this was a relief force dispatched by the government of Theodosius II (see F. Paschoud 1971–89 [v. 3, pt. 2], 50–52). Paschoud thinks that the diplomacy had gone on for a long time, but the present suggestion that Varanes may have gone to Constantinople to conduct it in 409 seems to be a new twist. Varanes was rewarded with the consulship, shared with Theodosius II, in 410, probably because of this diplomacy or his role in overthrowing Stilicho.

94. Olympiodorus, frag. 14 (Photius).

95. Zosimus, 6.9.1–2. The text reads literally that Jovius was influenced by Honorius's agents to defect, but this makes no sense. His backing of Alaric's recommendation of sending barbarians to fight Heraclianus, on the other hand, clearly reveals the real force at work upon Jovius. Jovius was instrumental in the deposition of Attalus in July, Olympiodorus, frag. 14 (Photius). See further F. Paschoud 1971–89 (v. 3, pt. 2), 55–56, who correctly concludes that Alaric gave up the siege of Ravenna because of the hope that Jovius could succeed diplomatically, not because of the arrival of any new forces (thus contrary to R. Ridley 1982, 229, n. 48).

96. Sozomenus, HE, 9.12.4–5, crossing the Cottian Alps and getting as far as Libarna, a city in Liguria, and was about to cross the Po. An emendation of Verona in the text to Libarna is necessary. Libarna, not Verona, is in Liguria (ed. J. Bidez, 403 to λιβερῶνα). The execution of Allobichus at court was the crucial incident that turned Constantine around (Olympiodorus, frag. 15, Photius). Allobichus may indeed have plotted to turn over the Empire to Constantine.

97. Zosimus, 6.9.3.

98. Zosimus, 6.10.2. Alaric campaigned to have Aemilia and Liguria acknowledge Attalus. On the death of Allobichus as pivotal, see Olympiodorus, frag. 15 (Photius) and Sozomenus, HE, 9.12.5.

99. Zosimus, 6.11.2, pretium inpone carni humanae (see also F. Paschoud 1971–89 [v. 3, pt. 2], 61).

100. Olympiodorus, frag. 10, 48–53 (Sozomenus, HE, 9.8); Philostorgius, HE, 12.3.

101. Zosimus, 6.12.3. Attalus's career was not over by any means (PLRE, 2.181).

102. Zosimus, 6.13.2.

103. The extant Zosimus ends with the deposition of Attalus in July 410. Sozomenus, HE, 9.8.9 and Socrates, HE, 7.10 are vague about the date of the fall. Orosius is no better, 7.39, but says that the Goths looted for three days. The accepted date is recorded by Prosper as 24 August 410, Chron. Minora, 1.465; for discussion see E. Demougeot 1951, 469, n. 153. This is sometimes called the "third siege" (for example, Bury 1923 [1958], 183), but as in the "second siege" no siege was necessary.

104. Orosius, 7.39. Saurus's raid is the last military episode recorded by Zosimus, and the other sources rarely are detailed enough or sufficiently credible to provide useful military information. Almost all the relevant sources are cited in PLRE, 2.48 (Alaricus

1) for the "Sack of Rome" and Alaric's subsequent career. Marcellinus Comes, 410, confirms that Galla Placidia was taken hostage.

105. Jordanes, *Getica*, 156–58. These included Athaulf's command; Marcellinus Comes, 410.

106. Olympiodorus, frag. 16 (Photius); Jordanes, *Getica*, 156–57.

IX. The Settlement of 418: Constantine, Constantius, Athaulf, Wallia, and Rome

1. On these offices see R. Grosse 1920, 143–51.

2. Zosimus, 5.37.1; on the various Roman offices that existed ca. 400 to command recently recruited barbarians see A. Jones 1964, 652.

3. Zosimus, 5.45.6.

4. Zosimus, 6.13.2. So too F. Paschoud 1971–89 (v. 3, pt. 2), 67.

5. J. Liebeschuetz 1992, 81–82, also notes that many slaves had joined Fritigern before the Battle of Adrianople (Ammianus, 31.6.4–7, 7.7, 15.2). On the sources for his kingship see *PLRE*, 2.177.

6. See P. Heather 1991, 32, on Jordanes and the general lack of dynastic unity among the Goths.

7. Jordanes, *Getica*, 146. J. Liebeschuetz 1992, 78, correctly stresses that for Alaric not even Isidore of Seville cared to give his ancestry and that it was Alaric himself who made the Balthi worth noting.

8. On Aelia Galla Placidia, usually just Galla Placidia, see *PLRE*, 2.888; on Attalus, see Priscus Attalus, *PLRE*, 2.180.

9. Rutilius Namatianus, *De red.* 1.39, according to whom Athaulf inflicted much destruction along the way; Jordanes, *Getica*, 160; Prosper, 412; Procopius, *BV*, 1.2.37.

10. Zosimus, 5.43.1–2.

11. *PLRE*, 2.802, Zosimus, 5.46.1. Olympiodorus, frag. 8.2 (Photius).

12. *Magister peditum (magister praesentalis I)*, on Constantius see *PLRE*, 2.321–25. He was also *comes et magister utriusque militiae*, as Stilicho had been, but in Western military terminology, which never changed, he commanded within the army as *magister peditum*. The more grandiose title of *comes et MVM* as well as *patricius* and *parens* had now combined into a complex political acknowledgment of the primary secular figure in the Western Empire. On this evolution see J. O'Flynn 1983.

13. For Constantius, *PLRE*, 2.322. Ulfilas, *magister equitum (magister praesentalis II)*, Sozomenus, *HE*, 9.14.1–2.

14. Sozomenus, *HE*, 9.13.1–15.3; Gregorius Turonensis, *Historiae Francorum*, 2.9. In 407 Edobich had defeated Sarus at Valence (Zosimus, 6.2.4–5), by 411 he had succeeded Gerontius as *MVM*. *PLRE*, 2.386.

15. Zosimus, 6.5.2. For the problems of dating these events in the early fifth century, see R. Burgess 1990, 185–95; but also M. Jones and J. Casey 1991, 211–14. Most scholars accept the redating of Honorius's letter, cited in Zosimus, to 408 or 409 rather than the traditional 410, after Constantine III had crossed to Gaul but before he had taken it entirely. S. Johnson 1980 favors 408; S. Frere 1987, 358, favors 409. On the various interpretations of this passage see F. Paschoud 1971–89 (v. 3, pt. 2), 38–42. I agree with Thompson and Bartholomew in that this letter addressed some situation

related to Constantine III's rebellion. It is fruitless to speculate on any other British developments on the basis of this letter.

16. If greater certainty were obtained for the dating of Constantine III's coinage, those examples found in Britain might suggest an answer to the degree and length of its loyalty to him.

17. He and his son Julianus were murdered on their way to Italy to stand trial. Their heads were placed on pikes and paraded across the land; Julianus's went westward at least as far as Carthagena in Spain, while Constantine's arrived in Ravenna on 18 September 411, *PLRE*, 2.316.

18. *PLRE*, 2.621, supported by various Germanic auxiliaries including Burgundian, Alamannic, Alanic, and Frankish groups. Olympiodorus, frag. 18, most prominent for their assistance was Goar, an Alan, and Guntarius, leader of the Burgundians (κατὰ σπουδὴν Γώαρ τοῦ Ἀλανοῦ καὶ Γυντιαρίου, ὃς φύλαρχος ἐχρυμάτιξε τῶν Βουρς γουντιόνων, τύραννος ἀνηγορεύθη).

19. Zosimus, 6.3–5. Although the *Notitia dignitatum*, reflecting a restoration after these events, lists eleven units of the *aux. pal.* and legions as stationed in Spain under the *comes* (most would have been in the north or in municipal garrisons along the Mediterranean), greater precision is impossible. Lusitania could not have held more than three of these units, less than a thousand men; on the units see D. Hoffmann 1970, *Beilage* "Auszug aus der Notitia dignitatum," pp. 17–18, taken from *Nd. oc.* 7. Contrary to the reading in the *PLRE*, the troops "were those infantry stationed in Lusitania" (διὰ τῶν ἐν τῇ Λυσιτανίᾳ στρατοπέδων, Zosimus, 6.4.3). The battle against Gerontius did not occur in Lusitania, as in *PLRE*, but in or near the passes of the Pyrenees (Orosius, 7.40.5–6). Lusitania must have been the primary stronghold of Honorius's supporters, including the commander of these men who followed Didymus, et al., without proper orders. The other Roman units in Spain must have stayed out of harm's way and later tried to gain Gerontius's favor by offering to defend Spain while he took his Gallic troops with him to fight Constans and Constantine. Verenianus and Didymus were two of four brothers, probably cousins of Honorius through his father, *PLRE*, 2.1155 (Verenianus) and 2.358 (Didymus). The other two brothers, Theodosiolus and Lagodius, were apparently not with the army and escaped to Italy and the East respectively. Honorius's awareness of his relatives' plight at Arles may have contributed to his partial recognition of Constantine, but their execution, which took place in 409, had actually already occurred (Zosimus, 5.43).

20. He managed to issue some coins; see A. Balaquer 1980, 141–54. And P. Grierson and M. Mays 1992, 219.

21. Olympiodorus, 17.1.

22. Orosius, 40.8–10.

23. *Nd.*, index, p. 318; Orosius, 7.40.7, in foedus recepti, that is, recruited through an official act of *receptio. Honoriaci* and *Honoriani* are interchangeable terms in the *Notitia*.

24. On the routes see M. Labrousse 1968, 572–75.

25. Sozomenus, *HE*, 9.4, related as an exemplar on the life of his last faithful bodyguard, an Alan, and particularly for the bravery of the guard's Christian wife, Nunechia. Before slaying himself Gerontius killed them.

26. Olympiodorus, frag. 20.2, from Sozomenus, *HE*, 9.15.3; on the date of Maximus's death, see A. Jones 1964, 187.

27. A. Balil 1970, 603–20, and H. Sivan 1985, 273–87.

28. Balil 1990, 618.

29. H. Sivan 1985, 285.

30. *CTh* 7.18.17, dtd. 29 February 412, issued by Constantius, *mag. mil.*, at Ravenna. His whereabouts are otherwise unknown.

31. Contrary to J. O'Flynn 1983, 71–72, who believes that "replacements could always easily be found."

32. Paulinus of Pella, *Eucharisticus*, 375, records their defection near Bazas.

33. Olympiodorus, frags. 18 and 20. The 10,000 is given in a precise manner (χιλιάδας δέκα, frag. 18, from Photius) rather than in the less critical "myriad" form, perhaps suggesting a greater degree of confidence in the figure on Olympiodorus's part. The 10,000 equates well with estimates of the size of Alaric's force of combatants given earlier and strengthens the conclusion that Athaulf took his entire force against Jovinus. Indeed, what else could he have done with them?

34. *PRLE*, 2.346, Claudius Postumus Dardanus.

35. Olympiodorus, frag. 20.

36. *PLRE*, 2.539. The sequence of cause and effect in 412–13 is lost in the conflicts and ambiguities of the sources.

37. J. O'Flynn 1983, 70.

38. *PLRE*, 2.540; Orosius, 7.42.14–17.

39. *PLRE*, 2.724.

40. Contrary to J. Liebeschuetz 1990, I do not believe that such annual single-mission use was the goal of Roman policy in the overall deployment of barbarians after the defeat at Adrianople. The case of Athaulf satisfied neither side completely and could not have been long maintained, if only because of the logistical problems that soon became obvious.

41. Olympiodorus, frag. 22.

42. Jordanes, *Getica*, 163.

43. Olympiodorus, frag. 22, delivered by Bonifatius, the future *magister* of both branches (432). He must have been just a member of the garrison at Marseilles, for he did not become a military tribune in charge of a unit of barbarian auxiliaries in Africa until 417, *PLRE*, 2.238, from Augustinus, *Epis.* 220.7.

44. Paulinus of Pella, *Eucharisticus*, ed. and tr. H. White, Ausonius, v. 2 (Loeb edition, London, 1931), ll. 330–42.

45. Ibid., 386.

46. Augustinus, *Epis.* 220.7; *PLRE*, 2.238.

47. Olympiodorus, frag. 24 (Photius). Attalus joined the poets in singing the *epithalamium;* he was made emperor again at about this time and soon deposed once more (Olympiodorus, frag. 14, from Photius), probably as a part of the conditions Constantius imposed upon Athaulf.

48. Orosius, 7.43. 4–6. Trans. I. Raymond 1936, 396.

49. Orosius, 43.1–3.

50. Prosper, 1256 (p. 467), makes it a condition of the Gothic move to Spain. He was apparently given a ship and told to leave Narbo but was captured by the blockading fleet, Marcellinus Comes, 412 (p. 71). The tradition based on Olympiodorus that he was handed over later along with Galla seems false, Olympiodorus, frag. 26.2 (Philostorgius, *HE*, 12.4–5). Orosius, 43.1–3; Jordanes, *Getica*, 163, 66.

51. Because of the swift death of his son, Athaulf could in fact never hold the title *parens*. Galla bore Constantius, her second husband, two children after their marriage on 1 January 417, a daughter, Iusta Grata Honoria, and on 2 July 419 a son, Placidus Valentinianus, the future emperor Valentinianus III; *PLRE*, 2.888. Constantius thus was *parens* first to Honorius and then later to his own son. The title is well attested for both Stilicho and Constantius, e.g., Sozomenus, *HE*, 9.13.3; J. O'Flynn 1983, pp. 66–67, and gave a clear imminence to its holder almost equal to that of a member of the imperial family itself.

52. Orosius, 7.42.9, hand; Philostorgius, *HE*, 12.5, two fingers, obviously from Olympiodorus, frag. 14 (Photius).

53. On Athaulf's son Theodosius see *PLRE*, 2.1100.

54. Olympiodorus, frag. 26.

55. Following the ideas developed by E. Thompson in several works over the years, particularly 1963, 105–26.

56. See Rousseau 1992 for laying this hypothesis to rest.

57. Jordanes, *Getica*, 163, 166; Hydatius, *Chronicon*, 49; Philostorgius, *HE*, 12.4, ὑπό τινος τῶν οἰκείων. Olympiodorus, frag. 26, tells us the assassin was a certain Dubius, a former follower of Sarus bent upon avenging his old leader's death.

58. This is a very creative and doubtless correct reading of P. Heather 1991, 79.

59. On Athaulf's death see particularly Olympiodorus, frag. 26. Hydatius, *Chronicon*, 60, notes that at his death Athaulf was engaged in discussion with his inner circle.

60. Olympiodorus, frag. 30 (Wallia), frag. 6 (Sarus). On the φύλαρχοι see also I. Shahid 1984, 513–18, who explores the evolution of the term into that of an Eastern commander of a unit of *foederati* in the sixth century.

61. *Chronica Gallica ad 452*, 78.

62. B. Bachrach 1969, 354–58.

63. Orosius, 7.43.14.

64. Olympiodorus, frag. 30; concerning this figure C. Nixon 1992, 67–68, calculates that this is about a three-months' supply for 80,000 people. However, using his same criteria, but excluding women and children since this was a military ration, produces a figure of 20,000 for one year. I prefer A. Jones 1964, 1109, n. 65, 15,000 for a year (also agreed to by P. Heather 1991, 218); in fact, this figure is but an increase of 5,000 over the sum given in Olympiodorus, frag. 18, for Athaulf's army. The system of military requisition worked on calculations of daily strength, including mounts, in a manner similar to the "morning reports" of modern armies, e.g., *CTh* 7.4.11.

65. Orosius, 7.43.15–16.

66. *PLRE*, 2.1148.

67. *Nd. oc.* 42.24–32.

68. Balil 1970, 611–19; on the dates of the *epistula* see the discussion above and H. Sivan, op. cit. Recall (ch. 5, n. 80) that in 416 Constantius was busily reordering those areas recently affected by barbarian invasions and the collapse of the rule of law (*CTh* 15.14.14). The *epistula* as well as several sections of the *Notitia* may relate to this restoration. The section of the *Nd* relating to Spain, however, also probably reflects another, even later, revision.

69. Still essentially as Balil 1970, 619, but sites not in *Nd* and with fifth-century Germanic goods may be better explained as *auxilia* rather than as a lacuna in the section on *laeti*, after *Nd. oc.* 42.44.

70. Sivan 1985, 285, thinks ca. 6,500, but this figure is based upon inflated calculations such as that of A. Jones.

71. *Epistula*, 11, attesting also to the continuance of normal payment procedures.

72. Perhaps the Sabinianus of *Epistula*, 2.

73. Salvianus of Marseille, *De gubernatione Dei*.

74. M. Rouche 1979, 19.

75. See on this theme especially W. Goffart 1988b and 1992.

76. A full discussion of the various problems associated with the settlement of the barbarians owes much to the publication of W. Goffart 1980, despite my own reservations about its applicability to Aquitaine or anywhere else. Many scholars have now staked their positions much more clearly on the settlement and on many of the related issues of Roman law and barbarian society; see, for example, the various contributions to J. Drinkwater and H. Elton 1992, the reviews, and other works cited in this chapter. The task in the current book is only to explore the military considerations that led up to the decision to settle barbarians permanently in the interior provinces. The larger question of settlement as now seen needs another book.

77. J. Drinkwater 1992, 208–17, who sees the Bacaudae as a response to the flight of refugees southward that had begun before the barbarian invasions and usurpations of the fifth century but was exacerbated by these events. On refugees see also C. Nixon 1992, 64–74, at p. 64, and R. Mathisen 1992, 228–38.

78. E. James 1977, 6.

79. H. Böhme 1985a, 76–88, 131–33, and 1988, 23–47. For a positive view of Roman capabilities see H. Elton 1992, 167–76, probably too positive for the period after the Hunnic incursions of mid-century.

80. H. Sivan 1987, 759–72, at 770, but I doubt her suggestion that the Goths were settled as veterans in 418.

81. See articles by J. Durliat 1988 and W. Goffart 1988a. Basically the entire volume is devoted to perfecting and debating the thesis first advanced by W. Goffart 1980. Contra see in particular S. Barnish 1986 and H. Sivan 1987.

82. S. Barnish 1986 in particular.

83. A. Jones 1964, 451, 457, 468. Valentinian and Valens tried unsuccessfully to take the burden of tax collection in the local communities off the shoulders of the *curiales* (town councilors).

84. The texts for the settlement of 418, given below, are too meager to state absolutely that Constantius used the precise division of later settlements (especially the thirds, *tertiae*) in the arrangement for the Gothic settlement in Aquitaine. The odds are good that he did. By the time more detailed evidence becomes available, around the middle of the fifth century, division by thirds was customary. Probably the most explicit statement on a division of land for settlement by thirds is Cassiodorus, *Variae*, 2.16, concerning the Ostrogoths.

85. *Epistula*, 16–18.

86. G. de Ste. Croix 1981, 509f.

87. Hydatius, *Chronicon*, 49 sorte ad inhabitandum sibi prouinciarum diuidunt regiones.

88. Zosimus, 6.4.3.

89. *PLRE*, 2.269. Castinus's position in 422 remains unclear. He was probably still *comes domesticorum* (probably *peditum* since his next rank was that of *magister*), the com-

mand he held against some Franks earlier (420?). In 423 the short-lived Emperor Joannes made Castinus *magister peditum (magister praesentalis I)* and consul in 424.

90. Prosper, 1250.

91. Gregorius Turonensis, *Historiae Francorum*, 2.9.

92. Prosper, 1250; Gregorius Turonensis, *Historiae Francorum*, 2.9, from Frigeridus. For the settlement of 440, *Chr. Gall.* 124 (a. 440), deserta Valentinae urbis rura Alanis, quibus Sambida praeerat, partienda tradunter. For 442, 127 (a. 442), Alani, quibus terrae Galliae ulterioris cum incolis dividendae a patricio Aetio traditae fuerant, resistentes armis subigunt et expulsis dominis terrae possessionem vi adipiscuntur. On the Alans at Bazas going over into Roman service see Paulinus of Pella, *Eucharisticus*, 375–85.

93. On the actions of 436 see *Chr. Gall.* 118 (a. 436) and Prosper, 1322. The problems of settlement from the barbarian perspective, particularly how land allotments and kin structures were interrelated, are addressed in the *Liber Constitutionum sive Lex Gundobada*, 54–55. Many aspects of the Burgundian experience are surveyed by M. Martin, et al. 1980, 224–71. For the settlement of 443, see *Chr. Gall.* 128 (a. 443); see also O. Perrin 1968, 287–330, dated in many aspects, however.

94. T. Burns 1980, 78–90, and 1984, 74–83; but see also S. Barnish 1986, 170–95, who accepts the traditional landed settlement. Note particularly his data for the common use of *tertia* as both a land unit of *hospitalitas*, p. 181, and a common division of revenues from the land, p. 173. Barnish suggests that the real burdens fell on the less wealthy property holders. This suggestion is one of the few that troubles me. I believe that the evidence for barbarian settlement in Italy and elsewhere is clear that legally the rich were expected to assume the greatest burden. Doubtless, however, Barnish is correct that they were probably able to deflect some of the burden to the poorer landowners. E. Thompson 1982, 28, similarly concludes that the burden of the settlement in Aquitaine in 418 must have fallen upon the rich, since the smaller the holding the less profitable for the barbarians and the less able to withstand "sharing."

95. Prosper, 1271. Constantius patricius pacem firmat cum Wallia data ei ad inhabitandum secunda Aquitanica et quibusdam civitatibus confinium provinciarum. "The Patrician Constantius concluded a peace with Wallia giving him Aquitanica Secunda and some civitates (cities and their environs) in neighboring provinces to dwell upon."

96. Hydatius, *Chronicon*, 69, sedes in Aquitanica a Tolosa usque ad Oceanum acceperunt. I have attempted to be neutral in translating *sedes*, rendering it and *acceperunt* as "took up settlement." I believe that *sedes* in this passage really has a much more specific translation, that of "land." The legitimacy of "land" will emerge from the discussion that follows, based particularly upon the much clearer language of the Greek sources.

97. Philostorgius, *HE*, 12.4, καὶ τὴν οἰκείαν ἀδελφὴν καὶ τὸν Ἄτταλον τῷ βασιλεῖ παρατίθενται αὐτοί, σιτήσεοί τε δεξιωθέντες καὶ μοῖράν τινα τῆς τῶν Γαλατῶν χώρας εἰς γεωργίαν ἀποκληρωσάμενοι. Compare the language to Eunapius, frag. 45.3 (n. 100 below). The verbs are the same "to receive," land is exactly the same, only here we have σιτήσεοί for supplies rather than κτήματά. The Greek is entirely consistent in both cases with the conditions of a frontier *receptio*.

98. *PLRE*, 2.181.

99. A. Jones 1964, 1109, n. 65.

100. Eunapius, frag. 45.3, from Suda Π2351, but associated with Zosimus, 4.34.4–6,

not as R. Blockley with 4.24.3–26.9. ὁ δὲ βασιλεὺς τούτους δεξάμενος· κτήματά τε αὐτοῖς καὶ χώραν ἀπένειμε...The emperor receiving (δεξάμενος) them granted them supplies (κτήματά) and land (χώραν). This is a splendid example of *receptio*, to use the Latin term for δεξάμενος, of barbarians along the frontiers.

101. G. Kaufmann 1866, 433–76, at 440, n. 1.

102. *Codico de Eurico*, 276, ed. E. Alvaro d'Ors (Madrid, 1960); H. Sivan 1987, 768. C. Nixon 1992, 71, is outspoken in rejecting the Goffart thesis as applying to the documents relating to Gaul: "that land was not given, but only the tax revenues, is ingenious, but apart from the problem that this is not what the sources say it seems peculiarly inappropriate to Gaul."

103. *CTh* 5.11,8–12, dtd. from 365 to 391; 6.2.24, dtd. 417, concerning the compulsory service of transport; 13.11.15, dtd. 417, concerning the surveying of abandoned property for exemption. Alas, 5.11.7 is almost totally lost from the manuscript. It has to do with grants of exemption (presumably since the entire surviving Title 11 deals with tax exemption on land) to veterans (*emeriti veterani*) and foreign soldiers in the army (*gentes*), dtd. 16 January 365. There were, in short, ample legal precedents for granting terms of tax exemption for those occupying deserted lands, perhaps must importantly for foreign soldiers and veterans.

104. *CTh* 7.13.16 (dated 406) permitting the slaves of auxiliaries to fight.

105. S. Barnish 1986, 192–93, rejecting arguments that all barbarian shares were necessarily tax-exempt.

106. So too concludes P. Heather 1991, 218.

107. Jordanes, *Getica*, 267, that the Goths who had followed the missionary Ulfila were still in Moesia in the mid-sixth century, essentially tending their livestock. Numerous examples of fourth-century practice have been cited in earlier chapters.

108. So too S. Barnish 1986, 192, who sees no reason to assume that the barbarians in most areas did not pay. The Vandals clearly did not, but they held their properties by right of conquest as for a few years they had in Spain.

109. A. Loyen 1934, 406–15; C. Nixon 1992, 72.

110. On the archaeological and economic continuity see R. Hitchner 1992. In general, the taxable revenues in the towns along the coast of the Mediterranean remained quite viable during this era with effective networks of distribution penetrating the interior of southern Gaul.

111. H. Sivan 1992, 132–41.

112. Hydatius, *Chronicon*, 77.

113. Ibid., 92.

114. Ibid., 97, note commentary.

115. *Chr. Gall. ad 452*, a. 433.

116. Hydatius, *Chronicon*, 115.

117. Controversy remains as to his use of Orientius, bishop of Auch, as his *legatus* to Litorius; see further the discussion by E. Thompson 1956, 64, n. 3. Hydatius is the main source for Theodoric's reign.

118. On these see J. Larsen 1955, 152, and J. Zeller 1906, 258–73.

119. R. Mathisen 1992, 236–38; for Theodoric II's own son participating in Gallic ecclesiastical politics see Mathisen 1989, 207.

120. Marius Aventicensis, *Chronica*, 456, occupaverunt terrasque cum Gallis senatoribus diviserunt.

121. E. Thompson 1969, 118–31; Wickham 1984, 20.

122. See further S. Barnish 1986, 193, n. 219, drawing upon *Nov. Theod.* 24.2 (dated 12 September 443), which is not immediate to the discussion of events as of ca. 418.

123. Hydatius, *Chronicon*, 141 (449), and note Tranoy's comment on Basil, v. 1, p. 142.

124. Surely one of the most distressing aspects of the Gothic Kingdom in Aquitaine is their virtual absence from the archaeological record; see E. James 1977, 194–201, to account for which James suggests that whatever their source of income most lived in towns, p. 198. Since 1977, however, everyone has become much more dubious about just how differently "Romans and Barbarians" dressed. There is general agreement that in northern Gaul, for example, a homogeneous population as attested archaeologically existed from the middle of the fourth century. There this was clearly a result of the Roman frontier culture (see particularly H. Böhme 1974, 200–7).

125. Areobindus, consul for 434, was *comes foederatorum* in the East as of 422, at least according to much later Byzantine sources (*PLRE*, 2.145). On the Eastern development see I. Shahid 1984, 19–24.

126. Evanthius was active in road repair in Aquitanica I in 469. He held some Roman office, either in charge of roads or probably *praeses*, provincial governor (*PLRE*, 2.403).

127. Fastes on praetorians in *PLRE*, 2.1246. On adaptations see R. Mathisen 1993.

128. S. Barnish 1986, 188.

BIBLIOGRAPHY

Primary Sources

Ambrosius, Sanctus (Bishop of Milan). *Opera omnia.* Edited by J. Migne. In *Patrologia Latina*, v. 14–17. Paris, 1845–66.

Ammianus Marcellinus. In *Römische Geschichte.* Edited by W. Seyfarth. Darmstadt, 1970–78.

———. Loeb edition. Translated by J. Rolfe. Cambridge, MA, 1935–40.

Anonymus Valesianus. *Pars prior.* Edited by T. Mommsen. In *MGH.AA*, 9 (*Chronica Minora*, 1). Berlin, 1892.

Anonymus. *De rebus bellicis* (see E. Thompson).

Augustinus. *Opera omnia.* Edited by J. Migne. In *Patrologia Latina*, v. 32–47. Paris, 1841–49.

———. *De civitate Dei libri XXII.* Edited by B. Dombart and A. Kalb. In *Corpus christianorum: Series Latina*, v. 47–48, 5th ed. Belgium, 1981.

Cassiodorus. *Variae.* Edited by T. Mommsen. In *MGH.AA*, 12. Berlin, 1894.

———. *Historia ecclesiastica tripartita.* Edited by R. Hanslik. In *CSEL*, 71. Vienna, 1952.

———. *Chronica.* Edited by T. Mommsen. In *MGH.AA*, 11 (*Chronica Minora*, 2). Berlin, 1894.

Cassius Dio. *Historia Romana.* Loeb edition. Translated by E. Cary. New York, 1914–25.

Cedrenus, Georgius. *Compendium Historiarum.* Edited by J. Migne. In *Patrologiae cursus completus*, v. 121–22. Paris, 1889.

Chronica Gallica ad CCCCLII. Trans. and commentary by T. Mommsen. In *MGH.AA*, 9 (*Chronica Minora*, 1). Berlin, 1892.

Chronicon Paschale 284–628 A.D. Edited by M. Whitby and M. Whitby. Liverpool, 1989.

Chrysostomus, Joannes. *Opera omnia.* Edited by J. Migne. In *Patrologiae cursus completus*, v. 26–34. Paris, 1842–43.

Claudianus, Claudius. *Carmina.* Loeb edition. Translated by M. Platnauer. Cambridge, MA, 1922.

Codex Euricianus. Edited by E. Alvaro d'Ors, *Estudios Visigóticos II.* Cuadernos del Instituto Juridico Español. Rome, Madrid, 1960.

Codex Iustinianus. Edited by P. Krüger. In *Corpus Iuris Civilis*, v. 2. Berlin, 1915; 12th ed., 1959.

Codex Theodosianus. Edited by P. Krüger. Berlin, 1923–6.

Codico de Eurico. Edited by E. Alvaro d'Ors. Madrid, 1960.

Commodianus. *Carmen apologeticum*. Edited by B. Dombart. In *CSEL*, 15:810–19. Vienna, 1887.

Constantius VII, Porphyrogenitus. *De Administrando Imperio*. Edited by R. Jenkins and G. Moravcsik. 2d ed. Washington, D.C., 1967.

Consularia Italica. Edited by T. Mommsen. In *MGH.AA*, 9 (*Chronica Minora*, 1). Berlin, 1892.

Consularia Constantinopolitana ad A. CCCXCV cum additamento Hydatii ad A. CCCCLXVIII. Edited by T. Mommsen. In *MGH.AA*, 9 (*Chronica Minora*, 1). Berlin, 1892.

Corpus inscriptionum latinarum consilio et auctoritate Academie litterarum regiae Borussicae editum. . . . Berlin, 1862–.

Corpus Iuris Civilis. Edited by P. Krüger. Berlin, 1915; 12th ed., 1959.

Epistolae Imperatorum Pontificum Aliorum, pt. 1. Edited by O. Guenther. In *CSEL*, 35. Vienna, 1895.

Epitome de Caesaribus. Teubner edition. Edited by F. Pichlmayer. Leipzig, 1961.

Eugippius. *Vita Severini*. Edited by R. Noll. In *Eugippius. Das Leben des heiligen Severin. Schriften und Quellen der alten Welt*, v. 11. Berlin, 1963.

Eunapius. Edited and translated by R. Blockley. In *The Fragmentary Classicising Historians of the Later Roman Empire*, v. 2. Liverpool, 1983.

Gregorius Nazianzus. *Opera omnia*. Edited by J. Migne. In *Patrologiae cursus completus*, v. 35–38. Paris, 1857–62.

Gregorius Turonensis. *Historiae Francorum*. Edited and translated by R. Buchner. In *Gregor von Tours: Zehn Bücher Geschichten*, 2d ed. Berlin, 1967.

Hieronymus. *Epistulae*. Edited by J. Labourt. In *Saint Jérôme Lettres*. Les Belles Lettres. Paris, 1933–1961.

Historia Augusta (Scriptores Historiae Augustae). Loeb edition. Translated by D. Magie. Cambridge, MA, 1921–32.

Hydatius. *Continuatio chronicorum Hieronymianorum*. In *Hydace, Chronique*. Edited and translated by A. Tranoy. Paris, 1974.

Incerti Panegyricus Constantio Caesari Dictus. Edited by E. Galletier. Paris, 1949.

Isidorus. *Historia Gothorum Wandalorum Sueborum*. Edited by C. Rodríguez Alonso. In *Las historias de los Godos, Vandalos y Suevos de Isidoro de Sevilla*. León, 1975.

Joannes Antiochenus. Edited by C. Müller. *Fragmenta Historicorum Graecorum*, v. 4. Paris 1853–1883.

Jordanes. *Romana et Getica*. Edited by T. Mommsen. In *MGH.AA*, 5. Berlin, 1882.

Leges Burgundionum. Edited by L. de Salis. *MGH, Legum*, Sectio 1.2, *Legum Nationum Germanicarum*. Hanover, Leipzig, 1892.

Leges Visigothorum. Edited by K. Zeumer. *MGH, Legum*, Sectio 1.1, *Legum Nationum Germanicarum*. Hanover, Leipzig, 1902.

Libanius. *Opera*. Teubner edition. Edited by R. Foerster. Leipzig, 1903–27.

———. *Orationes*. Loeb edition. Translated by A. Norman. Cambridge, MA, 1969.

Liber Constitutionum sive Lex Gundobada. Edited by L. de Salis. In *MGH, Legum*, Sectio 1.2.1. Hanover, 1892.

Marcellinus Comes. *Chronicon*. Edited by T. Mommsen. In *MGH.AA*, 11 (*Chronica Minora*, 2). Berlin, 1894.

Marius Aventicensis. *Chronica*. Edited by T. Mommsen. In *MGH.AA*, 11 (*Chronica Minora*, 2). Berlin, 1894.

———. *La Chronique de Marius d'Avenches* (455–581). Edited and translated with commentary by J. Favrod. Lausanne, 1991.

Mauricius, Flavius Tiberius (Emperor). *Das Strategikon des Maurikios*. Edited and translated by G. Dennis and E. Gamillscheg. In *Corpus Fontium Historicae Byzantinae*, series Vindobonesis, v. 17. Vienna, 1981.

Müller, Carl. *Fragmenta Historicorum Graecorum*. Paris, 1853–1883.

Notitia dignitatum. Edited by O. Seeck. Frankfurt, 1876. Reprint, 1962.

Novellae. Edited by P. Krüger. In *Corpus Juris Civilis*, v. 3, 12th ed. Berlin, 1915.

Olympiodorus. Edited and translated by R. Blockley. In *The Fragmentary Classicising Historians of the Later Roman Empire*, v. 2. Liverpool, 1983.

Orosius, Paulus. *Historiarum adversum paganos libri vii*. Edited by C. Zangemeister. In *CSEL*, 5. Vienna, 1882.

Pacatus. *Latini Pacati Drepanii Panegyricus Theodosio Avgvsto Dictus*. Edited by E. Galletier. In *Panégyriques Latins*, v. 3. Paris, 1955.

Panégyriques Latins. Edited by E. Galletier. Collection G. Budé. Paris, 1949–55.

Paulinus (Bishop of Nola). *Epistulae et Carmina*. Edited by G. Hartel. In *CSEL*, 29–30. Leipzig, 1894.

Paulinus of Pella. *Eucharisticus*. Edited and translated by H. White. In *Ausonius*, v. 2. Loeb edition. London, 1931.

Philostorgius. *Historia Ecclesiastica*. Edited by J. Bidez. In *Die griechischen christlichen Schriftsteller der ersten Jahrhunderte*. Leipzig, 1913. Revised edition by F. Winkelmann. Berlin, 1972.

Photius. *Bibliothèque*. Edited and translated by R. Henry. Collection G. Budé. Paris, 1959–77.

Poalino di Milano. *Vita di S. Ambrogio*. Edited by M. Pellegrino. Rome, 1961.

Procopius. *History of the Wars*. Loeb edition. Translated by H. Dewing. Cambridge, MA, 1914–40. Reprint, 1953–54.

———. *Opera omnia*. Teubner edition. Revised and edited by G. Wirth. Leipzig, 1962–64.

Prosper Tiro. *Epitoma Chronicon*. Edited by T. Mommsen. *MGH.AA*, 9 (*Chronica Minora*, 1). Berlin, 1892.

Roman Imperial Coinage. Edited by H. Mattingly et al. London, 1923– .

Rufinus. *Historia Ecclesiastica. Eusebii historia ecclesiastica translata et continuata*. Edited by T. Mommsen. In *Die griechischen christlichen Schriftsteller der ersten Jahrhunderte: Eusebius*, v. 2, pt. 1.2. Berlin, 1903–8.

Rutilius Namatianus. *De reditu suo*. Loeb edition. In *Minor Latin Poets*. Translated by J. Duff and A. Duff. Cambridge, MA, 1932.

———. *De reditu suo sive iter Gallicum libri II*. Edited by E. Doblhofer. Heidelberg, 1972.

Salvianus of Marseille. *De gubernatione Dei.* Edited by C. Halm. In *MGH.AA*, 1. Berlin, 1877.

Scriptores Historiae Augustae. Teubner edition. Edited by E. Hohl, C. Samberger, and W. Seyfarth. Leipzig, 1971.

Sextus Aurelius Victor. *Epitome de Caesaribus.* Teubner edition. Edited by F. Pichlmayr. Leipzig, 1961.

Sidonius Apollinaris. *Opera.* Text established and translated by A. Loyen. In *Sidoine Apollinaire.* Paris, 1960.

Socrates Scholasticus. *Historia Ecclesiastica.* Edited by J. Migne. In *PG*, 67. Paris, 1864.

———. *Historia Ecclesiastica.* With introduction by W. Bright. Oxford, 1878.

Sozomenus. *Historia Ecclesiastica.* Edited by J. Bidez. In *Kirchengeschichte, Die griechischen christlichen Schriftsteller der ersten Jahrhunderte,* v. 50. Berlin, 1960.

Sulpicius Severus. *Chronicon.* Edited by C. Halm. *CSEL*, 1. Vienna, 1866.

Symmachus, Q. Aurelius. *Opera.* Edited by O. Seeck. Berlin, 1883.

Synesius of Cyrene (Bishop of Ptolemais). *Opera.* Edited by J. Migne. In *PG*, 66. Paris, 1857.

———. *Opere di Sinesio de Cirene. Epistole Operette Inni.* Edited and translated by A. Garzya. Turin, 1989.

Tabula Imperii Romani. K-34. Naissus. Dyrrhachion-Scupi-Serdica-Thessalonike. Ljubljana, 1976.

———. L-32. Mediolanum. Rome, 1966.

———. L-33. Trieste. Rome, 1961.

———. L-34. Budapest. Amsterdam, 1968.

———. M-33. Castra Regina, Vindobona, Carnuntum. Prague, 1986.

———. Britannia Septentrionalis. London, 1987.

Tabula Peutingeriana. Edited by E. Weber. Graz, 1976.

Themistius. *Orationes quae supersunt.* Teubner edition. Edited by H. Schenkl and G. Downey. Leipzig, 1965–74.

———. *Orationes.* Edited by W. Dindorf. Leipzig, 1832. Reprinted Hildesheim, 1961.

Theodoretus. *Historia Ecclesiastica.* Edited by L. Parmentier. 2d rev. ed. by F. Schneiderweiler. In *Die griechischen christlichen Schriftsteller der ersten Jahrhunderte,* 44.2. Berlin, 1954.

Theophanes Homologetes. *Chronographia.* Edited by C. de Boor. Leipzig, 1883–85.

Theophylactus Simocatta. *Historiarum Libri octo.* Teubner edition, C. de Boor. Revised edition P. Wirth. Leipzig, 1972.

Vegetius (Flavius Vegetius Renatus). *Epitomae rei militaris libri IV.* Teubner edition 1855. 2d ed. by C. Lang. Reprinted Leipzig, 1967.

Zonoras. *Epitome historiarum.* Edited by T. Büttner-Wobst. In *Corpus Scriptorum Historiae Byzantinae,* v. 50. Bonn, 1897.

Zosimus. *Historia Nova.* Teubner edition. Edited by L. Mendelssohn. Leipzig, 1887.

———. *Historia Nova.* Text established and translated by F. Paschoud. Collection G. Budé. Paris, 1971–1989.

Secondary Sources

Abels, B.-U. 1983. "Die germanische Siedlung und der karolingische Friedhof von Eggolsheim, Landkreis Forchheim, Oberfranken." In *Das arch. Jahr in Bayern 1982*, pp. 98–99. Stuttgart.

——. 1984. "Eine neue germanische Befestigungsanlage auf dem Reißberg bei Scheßlitz, Landkreis Bamberg, Oberfranken." In *Das arch. Jahr in Bayern 1983*, pp. 129–30. Stuttgart.

——. 1986. *Archäologischer Führer Oberfranken. Führer zu archäologischen Denkmälern in Bayern, Franken*, v. 2. Stuttgart.

——. 1987. "Neue Fibelfunde von der Ehrenbürg bei Schlaifhausen, Gemeinde Wiesenthau, Landkreis Forchheim, Oberfranken." In *Das arch. Jahr in Bayern 1986*, pp. 103–4. Stuttgart.

Albert, G. 1984. *Goten in Konstantinopel.* Studien zur Geschichte und Kultur des Altertums, n.f. 1.2. Paderborn.

Alföldy, G. 1974. *Noricum.* London.

Arce, J. 1980. "La *Notitia dignitatum* et l'armée romaine dans le diocèse Hispaniarum." *Chiron* 10:593–608.

Archäologischer Plan von Passau in römischer Zeit. 1991. Passau.

Arnheim, M. 1972. *The Senatorial Aristocracy in the Later Roman Empire.* Oxford.

Ausbüttel, F. 1988. "Die Dedition der Westgoten von 382 und ihre historische Bedeutung." *Athenaeum* 66:604–13.

Austin, N. 1979. *Ammianus on Warfare. An Investigation into Ammianus' Military Knowledge.* Brussels: Collection Latomus 165.

Bachrach, B. 1969. "Another Look at the Barbarian Settlement in Southern Gaul." *Traditio* 25:354–58.

Bagnall, R., A. Cameron, S. Schwartz, and K. Worp. 1987. *Consuls of the Later Roman Empire.* Philological Monographs of the American Philological Association, 36. Atlanta.

Bakker, L. 1984. "Augsburg in spätrömischer Zeit." In *Geschichte der Stadt Augsburg*, pp. 34–40. Edited by G. Gottlieb et al. Stuttgart.

Balaquer, A. 1980. "Descoberta dún nou exemplar de les rares siliqiies de Màxim Tirà, atribuïdes a lec seca de Barcelona: Corpus de les emissions de Màxim." *Numisma* 30:141–54.

Baldini, A. 1984. *Ricerche sulla storia di Eunapio di Sardi: problemi di storiografia tardopagana.* Bologna.

Baldus, H.-R. 1984. "Theodosius der Grosse und die Revolte des Magnus Maximus—das Zeugnis der Münzen." *Chiron* 14:175–92.

Balil, A. 1970. "La defensa de Hispania en el Bajo Imperio." In *Legio VII Gemina*, pp. 603–20. Edited by J. Baroja. Leon.

Balla, L. 1963. "Savaria invalida: Megzegyzések a pannónia várobok Valentinianus—

kori törlénetéhez—Savaria invalida: Notes to the History of Pannonian Towns in the Time of Valentinian." *Archaeologiai Értesítö*, 90:75–80.

Balty, J. 1982. "Hiérarchie de l'Empire et image du monde. La face nord-ouest de la base de l'obélisque théodosien à Constantinople." *Byzantion* 52:60–71.

Banchich, T. 1988. "Eunapius, Eustathius, and the *Suda.*" *Am. J. Philol.* 109:223–25.

Baratte, F. 1976. "Quelques remarques à propos de lingots d'or et d'argent du Bas Empire." In *Frappes et ateliers monétaires dans l'Antiquité et au Moyen Age*, pp. 63–71. Colloque de Belgrade, 1975. Belgrad.

Barkóczi, L. 1980. "History of Pannonia." In *The Archaeology of Roman Pannonia*, pp. 85–124. Edited by A. Lengzel and G. Radan. Lexington, KY.

Barnea, I. 1967. "Themistios despre Scythia Minor." *Studii si cercetari de istorie veche* 18:563–76.

Barnes, T. 1976. "The Victories of Constantine." *Zeitschrift für Papyrologie und Epigraphik* 20:149–55.

——. 1979. "The Date of Vegetius." *Phoenix* 32:254–57.

——. 1986. "Synesius in Constantinople." *Greek, Roman and Byzantine Studies* 27:93–112.

——. 1993. "Review Article: Ammianus Marcellinus and His World." *Classical Philology* 88:55–70.

Barnish, S. 1986. "Taxation, Land, and Barbarian Settlement in the Western Empire." *Papers of the British School in Rome* 54:170–95.

Barnwell, P. 1992. *Emperor, Prefects, and Kings: The Roman West, 395–565.* London.

Barrett, J. et al., eds. 1989. *Barbarians and Romans in North-West Europe from the Later Republic to Late Antiquity.* BAR, Int. ser. 471, Oxford.

Bartholomew, P. and R. Goodburn, eds. 1976. *Aspects of the Notitia Dignitatum.* London.

Bârzu, L. 1980. *Continuity of the Romanian People's Material and Spiritual Production in the Territory of Former Dacia.* Bucharest.

Bastien, P. 1972–76. "Le Médaillon de Plomb." *Bulletin des musées et monuments Lyonnais* 5:157–76.

——. 1989. *Le Médaillon de plomb de Lyon.* Numismatique Romaine. Essais, recherches et documents, 18. Wetteren.

Bauman, V. 1983. *Ferma Romana din Dobrogea.* Bucharest.

Bayless, W. 1976. "Anti-Germanism in the Age of Stilicho." *Byzantine Studies* 3:70–76.

——. 1976b. "The Visigothic Invasion of Italy in 401." *Classical Journal* 72:65–67.

Baynes, N. 1922a. "A Note on Professor Bury's 'History of the Later Roman Empire.' " *Journal of Roman Studies* 12:217–19.

——. 1922b. "Stilicho and the Barbarian Invasion." *Journal of Roman Studies* 12:207–20.

Becatti, G. 1960. *La Colonna coclide istoriata. Problemi storici iconografici stilistici.* Rome.

Bender, H. 1981a. "Die spätrömische Siedlung von Wessling-Frauenwiese, Landkreis Starnberg, Oberbayern." In *Das arch. Jahr in Bayern 1980*, pp. 21, 146–47. Stuttgart.

———. 1981b. "Rekonstruktion der spätrömischen Anlagen auf dem Goldberg." In I. Moosdorf-Ottinger, *Der Goldberg bei Türkheim*. Münchner Beiträge, 24:132–38. Munich.

———. 1986. "Spätrömische Silbermünzen aus Bayerisch-Schwaben." In *Das arch. Jahr in Bayern 1985*, pp. 122–24. Stuttgart.

———. 1988. Habilitationsschrift [on Weßling-Frauenwiese], Universität Passau. Forthcoming.

——— and T. Burns. 1982. "Ein spätrömischer Wachturm bei Passau-Haibach." In *Ostbairische Grenzmarken* 24:55–82.

Berger, A. 1953. *Encyclopedic Dictionary of Roman Law*. Philadelphia.

Besevliev, V. 1964. *Spätgriechische und spätlateinische Inschriften aus Bulgarien*. Berlin.

Bichir, G. 1976. *Archaeology and History of the Carpi from the Second to the Fourth Century A.D.* BAR, sup. ser. 16. Oxford.

Bierbrauer, V. 1980. "Zur chronologischen, soziologischen und regionalen Gliederung des ostgermanischen Fundstoffs des 5. Jahrhunderts in Südosteuropa." In *Die Völker an der mittleren und unteren Donau im 5. und 6. Jahrhundert*, pp. 131–42. Edited by H. Wolfram and F. Daim. Vienna.

———. 1984. "Alamannische Besiedlung Augsburgs und seines näheren Umlandes." In *Geschichte der Stadt Augsburg*, pp. 87–99. Edited by G. Gottlieb et al. Stuttgart.

Biernacka-Lubańska, M. 1982. *The Roman and Early Byzantine Fortifications of Lower Moesia and Northern Thrace*. Wroclaw.

Blockley, R. 1982. "Roman-Barbarian Marriages in the Late Empire." *Florilegium* 4:63–79.

———. 1984. "The Romano-Persian Peace Treaties of A.D. 299 and 363." *Florilegium* 6:28–49.

Böcking, E. 1853. *Notitia dignitatum et administrationum tam civilium quam militarium*. Bonn.

Böhme, H. 1974. *Zur Chronologie germanischer Grabfunde des 4. bis 5. Jahrhunderts zwischen unterer Elbe und Loire*. Münchner Beiträge zur Vor- u. Frühgeschichte, 19. Munich.

———. 1985a. "Les Découvertes du Bas-Empire à Vireux-Molhain. Considérations générales." In *Le Cimetière et la fortification du Bas Empire de Vireux-Molhain, Dép. Ardennes*, pp. 76–88. Edited by J.-P. Lemant. Mainz.

———. 1985b. "Observations sur le rôle du Mont-Vireux au Bas-Empire." In *Le Cimetière et la fortification du Bas Empire de Vireux-Molhain, Dép. Ardennes*, pp. 131–33. Edited by J.-P. Lemant. Mainz.

———. 1988. "Zur Bedeutung des spätrömischen Militärdienstes für die Stammesbildung der Bajuwaren." In *Die Bajuwaren von Severin bis Tassilo 488–788*, pp. 23–37. Edited by H. Dannheimer et al. Munich.

———. 1991. "Eine Elbgermanische Bügelfibel des 5. Jahrhunderts aus Limetz-Villery (Yvelins, Frankreich)." *Archäologisches Korrespondenzblatt* 21:291–304.

Böhner, K. 1963. "Zur historischen Interpretation der sogennanten Laetengraber." *Jahrbuch d. RGZM-Mainz* 10:139–67.

Braund, D. 1984. *Rome and the Friendly King: The Character of the Client Kingship.* London.

Brennan, P. 1980. "Combined Legionary Detachments as Artillery Units in Late Roman Danubian Bridgehead Dispositions." *Chiron* 10:553–67.

———. 1984. "Diocletian and the Goths." *Phoenix* 38:142–46.

Brennecke, H. 1988. *Studien zur Geschichte der Homöer: der Osten bis zum Ende der homöischen Reichskirche.* Beiträge zur historischen Theologie, 73, Tübingen.

Brown, T. 1984. *Gentlemen and Officers.* Rome.

Bruns, G. 1935. *Der Obelisk und seine Basis auf dem Hippodrom zu Konstantinopel.* Istanbul.

Bülow, G. 1986. "Archäologische Forschungen am römischen Limes in Bulgarien." *Das Altertum* 32:78–84.

Burger, A. 1979. *Das spätrömische Gräberfeld im Somogyszil.* Budapest.

Burgess, R. 1989. "Consuls and Consular Dating in the Later Roman Empire." *Phoenix* 43:143–57.

———. 1990. "The Dark Ages Return to Fifth-Century Britain: The 'Restored' Gallic Chronicle Exploded." *Britannia* 21:185–95.

Burns, T. 1973. "The Battle of Adrianople: A Reconsideration." *Historia* 22:336–45.

———. 1978. "Calculating Ostrogothic Population." *Acta Antiqua* 26:457–63.

———. 1979. "The Alpine Frontier and Early Medieval Italy." In *The Frontier: Comparative Studies*, v. 2, pp. 51–68. Norman, OK.

———. 1980. *The Ostrogoths: Kingship and Society.* Historia Einzelschriften, no. 36. Wiesbaden.

———. 1981. "The Germans and Roman Frontier Policy (ca. A.D. 350–378)." *Arheološki Vestnik* 32:390–404.

———. 1984. *A History of the Ostrogoths.* Bloomington.

——— and H. Bender. 1982. "Ein spätrömischer Wachturm bei Passau-Haibach." *Ostbairische Grenzmarken* 24:55f.

——— and B. Overbeck. 1987. *Rome and the Germans as Seen in Coinage. Catalog for the Exhibition.* Atlanta.

———. 1994. "The Twilight of Roman Raetia: An End and a Beginning." In *Exegisti Monumentum Aere Perennius: Essays in Honor of John F. Charles.* Edited by B. Baker and J. Fischer. Indianapolis.

Bury, J. (1923) 1958. *History of the Later Roman Empire.* London.

Cameron, A. 1970. *Claudian. Poetry and Propaganda at the Court of Honorius.* Oxford.

———. 1979. "The Date of the Anonymous *De Rebus Bellicis.*" In *De Rebus Bellicis*, pt. 1, pp. 1–10. Edited by M. Hassall. BAR, 63. Oxford.

———, Long, J., with L. Sherry. 1993. *Barbarians and Politics at the Court of Arcadius.* Berkeley.

Carrié, J.-M. 1986. "L'Esercito: Trasformazioni funzionale el economie locali." In *Società romana e imperio tardoantico.* Edited by A. Giardini. Rome, 449–88.

Carson, R. 1981. *Principal Coins of the Romans*, v. 3. *The Dominate, AD 294–498*. London.

Castritius, H. 1983. "Das Ende der Geldwirtschaft im Römischen Reich am Beispiel des Donau-Alpenraumes." In *Deutscher Numismatikertag München 1981*, pp. 31–39. Edited by Bayerische Numismatische Gesellschaft e. V. Munich.

——. 1985. "Die Grenzverteidigung in Rätien und Noricum im 5. Jahrhundert n. Chr. Ein Beitrag zum Ende der Antike." In *Die Bayern und ihre Nachbarn* pt. 1, pp. 17–28. Edited by H. Wolfram and A. Schwarcz. Vienna.

——. 1988. "Die spätantike Zeit am Mittelrhein, im Untermaingebiet und in Oberhessen." In *Alte Geschichte und Wissenschaftsgeschichte. Festschrift für Karl Christ zum 65. Geburtstag*, pp. 57–78. Edited by P. Kneissl and V. Losemann. Darmstadt.

Cermanović-Kuzmanović, A. and S. Stanković. 1984. "Borđej, forteresse de la basse antiquité." *Cahiers des Portes de Fer* 2:219–20.

Cesa, M. 1984. "376–382: Romani e barbari sul Danubio." *Studi Urbinati/B3* 57:63–99.

—— and H. Sivan, 1990. "Alarico in Italia: Pollenza e Verona." *Historia* 39:361–74.

Chastagnol, A. 1970. "Le diocèse civil d'Aquitaine au Bas-Empire." *Bulletin de la Société nationale des Antiquaires de France* 272–92.

——. 1976. *La Fin du monde antique de Stilicon à Justinien (Ve siècle et début VIe)*. Paris.

Cherf, W. 1983. "The Dhema Pass and Its Early Byzantine Fortifications." Ph.D. diss. Loyola University in Chicago.

——. 1984. "Procopius, Lime Mortar C-14 Dating and the Late Roman Fortifications of Thermopylae." *American Journal of Archaeology* 88:594–98.

——. 1992. "Carbon-14 Chronology for the Late-Roman Fortifications of the Thermopylai Frontier." *Journal of Roman Archaeology* 5:261–64.

Chevallier, R. 1976. *Roman Roads*. Translated by N. Field, Berkeley.

Chichikova, M. 1983. "Fouilles du camp romain et de la ville paléobyzantine de Novae (Mésie inférieure)." In *Ancient Bulgaria*, v. 2, pp. 11–18. Edited by A. Poulter. Nottingham.

Chiriac, C. 1984. "Die *Notitia dignitatum* und einige Probleme der militärischen Flotte am skythischen Limes." *Studii si cercetari de istorie veche si Arheologie* 35:301–10.

Christiansen, P. and J. Sebesta. 1985. "Claudian's Phoenix: Themes of Imperium." *Antiq. class.* 54:204–24.

Christie, N. and A. Rushworth. 1988. "Urban Fortification and Defensive Strategy in Fifth and Sixth Century Italy: The Case of Terracina." *Journal of Roman Archaeology* 1:73–88.

Christlein, R. 1967–68. "Ausgrabung eines Gräberfeldes des 5.-7. Jahrhunderts bei Bittenbrunn, Lkr. Neuburg a. d. Donau." *Jahresbericht der bayerischen Bodendenkmalpflege* 8/9:87–103.

———. 1981. "Ein bajuwarischer Friedhof des 5.-7. Jahrhunderts von Straubing-Alburg, Niederbayern." In *Das arch. Jahr in Bayern 1980*, pp. 154–55. Stuttgart.

———. 1982a. "Die rätischen Städte Severins. Quintains, Batavis und Boiotro und ihr Umland im 5. Jh. aus archäologischer Sicht." In *Severin. Zwischen Römerzeit und Völkerwanderung*, pp. 217–53. Edited by K. Pömer. Linz.

———. 1982b. "Ostgotischer Fibelschmuck aus dem bajuwarischen Gräberfeld von Straubing-Alburg, Niederbayern." In *Das arch. Jahr in Bayern 1981*, pp. 168–69. Stuttgart.

Chrysos, E. 1972. Tὸ Βυζάντιον καὶ οἱ Γότθοι. Thessalonika.

———. 1973. "Gothia Romana: Zur Rechtslage des Föderatenlandes der Westgoten im 4. Jh." *Dacoromania* 1:52–64.

———. 1976. "Some Aspects of Romano-Persian Legal Relations." *Kleronomia* 8:1–48.

———. 1991. "Die Römerherrschaft in Britannien und ihr Ende." *Bonner Jahrbücher* 191:247–76.

Cieminski, M. 1984. "Das Militärwesen in den ostbalkanischen Gebieten während der Spätantike (von Diokletian bis Justinian)." *Ethnographisch-Archäologische Zeitschrift* 25:105–113.

———. 1986. "Zum frühbyzantinischen Festungswesen im Ostbalkanraum im 4.-6. Jh. u. Z." *Das Altertum* 32:166–173.

Ciglenečki, S. 1987. *Höhenbefestigungen aus der Zeit vom 3. bis 6. Jh. im Ostalpenraum*. Ljubljana.

Claude, D. 1970. *Geschichte der Westgoten*. Stuttgart.

———. 1988. "Zur Ansiedlung barbarischer Föderaten in der ersten Hälfte des fünften Jahrhunderts." In *Anerkennung und Integration*, pp. 13–16. Edited by H. Wolfram and A. Schwarcz. Vienna.

Cleary, S. 1989a. "Constantine I to Constantine III." In *Research on Roman Britain*, pp. 235–44. Edited by M. Todd. Britannia Monograph Series, no. 11. London.

———. 1989b. *The Ending of Roman Britain*. London.

Clemente, G. 1968. *La Notitia dignitatum*. Rome.

Clover, F. 1983. "Olympiodorus of Thebes and the Historia Augusta." In *Antiquitas*. ser. 4, 15:127–56. *Beiträge zur Historia-Augusta-Forschung*.

Courcelle, P. 1946. "Commodien et les invasions du Vᵉ siècle." *Revue des Études Latines* 24:227–46.

———. 1964. *Historie littéraire des grandes invasions germaniques*. 3rd ed. Paris.

Courtois, C. 1955. *Les Vandales et L'Afrique*. Paris.

Crees, J. 1908. *Claudian as an Historical Authority*. Cambridge.

Croke, B. 1977. "Evidence for the Hun Invasion of Thrace in AD 422." *Greek, Roman and Byzantine Studies* 18:347–67.

Crump, G. 1975. *Ammianus Marcellinus as a Military Historian*. Historia Einzelschriften, 27. Wiesbaden.

Cvjeticanin, T. 1988. "Late Roman and Early Byzantine Pottery from the Vicinity of Cacak." *Recueil des travaux du musée national* (Cacak) 18:121–30.

Czysz, W. and E. Keller. 1981. *Bedaium. Seebruck zur Römerzeit.* Munich.

Dagron, G. 1968. *L'Empire romain d'Orient au IVe siècle et les traditions politiques de l'hellénisme. Le témoignage de Thémistios.* (*Travaux et Mémoires*, 3). Paris.

Daly, L. 1972. "The Mandarin and the Barbarian: The Response of Themistius to the Gothic Challenge." *Historia* 21:351–79.

Dauge, Y. 1981. *Le Barbare: Recherches sur la conception romaine de la barbarie et de la civilisation.* Coll. Latomus, 176. Brussels.

Davies, R. 1971. "The Roman Military Diet." *Britannia* 2:122–42.

Delbrück, H. (1921) 1980. *History of the Art of War within the Framework of Political History.* Translated from 3rd German edition by W. Renfroe, Jr. Westport, CT.

Delmaire, R. 1988. "Les préfets du prétoire d'Italie de 410 à 415." *Latomus* 47:423–30.

———. 1989. *Les responsables des finances impériales au Bas-Empire romain (IVe-Ve siècles) Études prosopographiques.* Collection Latomus, 203. Brussels.

Demandt, A. 1970. "Magister militum." *Realencyclopädie der klassischen Altertumswissenschaft (R.-E.)* supplement 12:553–790.

———. 1980. "Der Spätrömische Militäradel." *Chiron* 10:609–37.

———. 1984. *Der Fall Roms. Die Auflösung des römischen Reiches im Urteil der Nachwelt.* Munich.

Demougeot, E. 1947. "Les partages de l'Illyricum à la fin du IVe siècle." *Revue Historique* 198:16–31.

———. 1948. "A propos des partages de l'Illyricum en 386–395." In *Actes du VIe Congrès international d'études byzantines,* pp. 87–92. Paris.

———. 1951. *De l'unité à la division de l'empire romain, 395–410.* Paris.

———. 1952. "Saint Jérôme, les oracles Sibyllins et Stilicon." *Revue des Études Anciennes* 54:83–92.

———. (1956) 1988. "Une lettre de l'empereur Honorius sur *l'Hospitium* des soldats." *Revue Historique de Droit Français et Étranger* 24 (1956):25–49. Reprinted in *L'Empire romain et les barbares d'Occident (IVe-VIIe siècles). Scripta Varia* pp. 75–99. Paris.

———. 1972. "Laeti et Gentiles dans la Gaule du IVe siècle." *Annales litt. de l'Université de Besançon* 34:101–12.

———. 1974a. "Constantin III, L'Empereur d'Arles." In *Hommage à André Dupont,* pp. 83–125. Montpellier.

———. 1974b. "Modalités d'établissement des fédérés barbares de Gratien et de Théodose." *Mélanges d'histoire ancienne offerts à William Seston.* Sorbonne Études 9:143–60. Paris.

———. 1979. *La formation de l'Europe et les invasions barbares. De l'avènement de Dioclétien au début du VIe siècle.* Paris.

———. 1988. *L'Empire romain et les barbares d'occident (IVe–VIIe siècle)* Paris.

Depeyrot, G. 1987. *Le Bas empire romain. Économie et numismatique (284–491).* Paris.

Diesner, H.-J. 1972. "Das Buccellariertum von Stilicho und Sarus bis auf Aëtius." *Klio* 54:321–50.

Dietz, K. 1979. *Regensburg zur Römerzeit.* Regensburg.

———. 1985. "Die Notitia dignitatum, ein Orts- und Truppenverzeichnis." In *Die Römer in Schwaben: Jubiläumsausstellung 2000 Jahre Augsburg*, pp. 274–75. Arbeitshefte des Bayerischen Landesamtes für Denkmalpflege 27. Munich.

Doise, J. 1949. "Le Commandement de l'armée romaine sous Théodose et au début des règnes d'Arcadius et d'Honorius." *Mélanges d'archéologie et d'histoire d'École Française de Rome* 61:183–94.

Domaneantu, C. and A. Sion. 1982. "Die spätrömische Festungsmauer von Histria. Versuch einer Chronologie." *Studii si cercetari de istorie veche si Arheologie* 33:377–394.

Donini, G. and G. Ford, trans. 1970. *Isidore of Seville's History of the Goths, Vandals, and Suevi*. 2d ed. Leiden.

Downey, G. 1965. "The Perspective of the Early Church Historians." *Greek, Roman and Byzantine Studies* 6:57–70.

Drack, W. and R. Fellmann. 1988. *Die Römer in der Schweiz*. Stuttgart.

Drinkwater, J. 1992. "The Bacaudae of Fifth-Century Gaul." In *Fifth-Century Gaul: A Crisis of Identity?* pp. 208–17. Edited by J. Drinkwater and H. Elton. Cambridge.

Drinkwater, J. and H. Elton, eds. 1992. *Fifth-Century Gaul: A Crisis of Identity?* Cambridge.

Duncan, G. 1993. *Coin Circulation in the Danubian and Balkan Provinces of the Roman Empire, 294–578*. London.

Duncan-Jones, R. 1978. "Pay and Numbers in Diocletian's Army." *Chiron* 8:541–60.

Durliat, J. 1988. "Le salaire de la paix sociale dans les royaumes barbares (V^e–VIe siècles)." In *Anerkennung und Integration*, pp. 21–72. Edited by H. Wolfram and A. Schwarcz. Vienna.

Eadie, J. 1982. "City and Countryside in Late Roman Pannonia." In *City, Town and Countryside in the Early Byzantine Era*, pp. 25–41. East European Monographs, 120, Byzantine series, no. 1. Edited by R. Hohlfelder. New York.

Ehrhardt, A. 1964. "The First Two Years of the Emperor Theodosius." *Journal of Ecclesiastical History* 15:1–17.

Elbern, S. 1987. "Das Gotenmassaker in Kleinasien (378 n. Chr.)." *Hermes* 115:99–106.

Elmer, G. 1935. "Exkurs über die römischen Goldbarren aus Sirmium (Naissus und Thessalonice) und ihre Datierung." *Numismaticar* 2:3–21.

Elton, H. 1992. "Defence in Fifth-Century Gaul." In *Fifth-Century Gaul: A Crisis of Identity?* pp. 167–76. Edited by J. Drinkwater and H. Elton. Cambridge.

Engemann, J. and C. Rüger, eds. 1991. *Spätantike und Frühes Mittelalter. Ausgewählte Denkmäler im Rheinischen Landesmuseum Bonn*. Cologne, Bonn.

Ensslin, W. 1930. "Zum Heermeisteramt des spätrömischen Reiches." *Klio* 23:306–25; 24 (1931):102–47, 467–502.

Fischer, H. 1981. "Archäologische Funde der römischen Kaiserzeit und der Völkerwanderungszeit aus der Oberpfalz (nördlich der Donau)." *Verhandlungen des Historischen Vereins f. Oberpfalz und Regensburg* 121:349–89.

———. 1984. "Ein germanisches Gräberfeld der jüngeren Kaiserzeit aus Berching-Pollanten." In *Das arch. Jahr in Bayern 1983*, pp. 123–28. Stuttgart.

———. 1987. "Passau im 5. Jahrhundert." *Anzeiger des Germanischen Nationalmuseums*. 89–104.

———. 1988a. *Römer und Bajuwaren an der Donau*. Regensburg.

———. 1988b. "Römer und Germanen an der Donau." In *Die Bajuwaren von Severin bis Tassilo 488–788*, pp. 39–45. Edited by H. Dannheimer et al. Munich.

——— and H. Geisler. 1988. "Herkunft und Stammesbildung der Baiern aus archäologischer Sicht." In *Die Bajuwaren von Severin bis Tassilo 488–788*, pp. 61–68. Edited by H. Dannheimer et al. Munich.

——— and S. Rieckhoff-Pauli. 1982. *Bavaria Antiqua. Von den Römern zu den Bajuwaren. Stadtarchäologie in Regensburg*. Munich.

——— and K. Spindler. 1984. *Das römische Grenzkastell Abusina-Eining*. Führer zu arch. Denkmälern in Bayern. Niederbayern, 1. Stuttgart.

Fitz, L. 1983. *L'Administration des provinces pannoniennes sous le Bas-Empire romain*. Collection Latomus, 181. Brussels.

Fitzgerald, A. 1930. *Essays and Hymns of Synesius*. London.

Fontaine, J. 1983. *Isidore de Seville et la culture classique dans l'Espagne wisigothique*. 2d ed. Paris.

Fornara, C. 1992a. "Studies in Ammianus Marcellinus—I: The Letter of Libanius and Ammianus' Connection with Antioch." *Historia* 41:328–344.

———. 1992b. "Studies in Ammianus Marcellinus—II: Ammianus' Knowledge and Use of Greek and Latin Literature." *Historia* 41:420–38.

Fotion, A. 1988. "Recruitment Shortages in Sixth-Century Byzantium." *Byzantion* 58:65–77.

Frere, S. 1987. *Britannia. A History of Roman Britain*. 3rd rev. ed. London, New York.

Freshfield, E. 1922. "Notes on a Vellum Album Containing Some Original Sketches of Public Buildings and Monuments, Drawn by a German Artist Who Visited Constantinople in 1574." *Archaeologia* 72:87–104.

Fulford, M. 1985. "Roman Material in Barbarian Society c. 200 BC–c. AD 400." In *Settlement and Society: Aspects of West European Prehistory in the First Millennium BC*, pp. 91–108. Edited by T. Champion and J. Megaw. Leicester.

Gabler, D., ed. 1989. *The Roman Fort at Ács-Vaspuszta (Hungary) on the Danubian Limes*. BAR, Int. ser. 531. Oxford.

Gabričević, M. 1986. "Rtkovo-Glamija I, une forteresse de la basse antiquité, fouilles de 1980." *Cahiers des Portes de Fer* 3:71–94.

Garbsch, J. 1970. *Der spätrömische Donau-Iller-Rhein-Limes*. Stuttgart.

———. 1975. "Neues vom spätrömischen Pons Aeni." *Archäologisches Korrespondenzblatt* 5:87–91.

——— and P. Kos. 1988. *Das Spätrömische Kastell Vemania bei Isny I*. Münchner Beiträge zur Vor- u. Frühgeschichte, 44. Munich.

Gaupp, E. 1844. *Die germanischen Ansiedlungen und Landtheilungen in den Provinzen des römischen Westreichs*. Breslau.

Gauthier, N. 1975. *Recueil des Inscriptions Chrétiennes de la Gaule,* 1. Paris.

Geanakoplos, D. 1982. "The Second Ecumenical Synod of Constantinople (381): Proceedings and Theology of the Holy Spirit." *Greek Orthodox Theol. R.* 27:407–29.

Geisler, H. 1987. "Das Gräberfeld Straubing-Bajuwarenstraße." In *Germanen, Hunnen und Awaren. Schätze der Völkerwanderungszeit,* pp. 608–22. Edited by W. Menghin. Nuremberg.

Gerlach, S. 1991. "Ein völkerwanderungszeitliches Metalldepot aus Zell a. Main, Landkreis Würzburg, Unterfranken." In *Das arch. Jahr in Bayern 1990,* pp. 137–40. Stuttgart.

Gibbon, E. (1776–88) 1897–1902. *The History of the Decline and Fall of the Roman Empire,* 2d ed. Edited by J. Bury. London.

Giorgetti, D. 1983. "Rataria and Its Territory." In *Ancient Bulgaria,* pp. 19–39. Edited by A. Poulter. Nottingham.

Gluschanin, E. 1989. "Die Politik Theodosius I und die Hintergründe des sogenannter Antigermanismus im oströmischen Reich." *Historia* 38:224–49.

Goffart, W. 1974. *Caput and Colonate: Towards a History of Late Roman Taxation.* Toronto.

———. 1980. *Barbarians and Romans* A.D. *418–584: The Techniques of Accommodation.* Princeton.

———. 1988a. "After the Zwettl Conference: Comments on the 'Techniques of Accommodation.' " In *Anerkennung und Integration.* Edited by H. Wolfram and A. Schwarcz. Vienna.

———. 1988b. *The Narrators of Barbarian History (AD 550–800): Jordanes, Gregory of Tours, Bede, and Paul the Deacon.* Princeton.

Goodspeed, E. 1946. "The Date of Commodian." *Classical Philology* 41:46–47.

Gottlieb, G. 1984. "Ausdehnung der römischen Herrschaft." In *Geschichte der Stadt Augsburg,* pp. 18–22. Edited by G. Gottlieb et al., Stuttgart.

———. 1989. "Spätrömische Zeit und Ende der römischen Herrschaft." In *Geschichte der Stadt Kempten,* pp. 63–64. Edited by V. Dotterweich. Kempten.

Grattarola, P. 1986. "L'usurpazione di Procopio e la fine dei Constantinidi." *Aevum* 60:82–105.

Greensdale, S. 1945. "The Illyrian Church and the Vicariate of Thessalonika, 378–95." *Journal of Theological Studies* 46:17–24.

Grierson, P. and M. Mays. 1992. *Catalogue of Late Roman Coins in the Dumbarton Oaks Collection and in the Whittemore Collection, from Arcadius and Honorius to the Accession of Anastasius.* Washington, D.C.

Grigg, R. 1977. "*Symphonian Aeido tes Basileias:* An Image of Imperial Harmony on the Base of the Column of Arcadius." *Art Bulletin* 59:469–82.

Grosse, R. 1920. *Römische Militärgeschichte von Gallienus bis zum Beginn der byzantinischen Themenverfassung.* Berlin.

Grumel, V. 1951. "L'Illyricum de la mort de Valentinian Ier (375) à la mort de Stilicon (408)." *Revue des études byzantines* 9:5–46.

Haberl, J. 1976. *Wien-Favianis und Vindobona. Eine archäologische Illustration zur Vita Severini des Eugippius.* Leiden.

Härtel, G. 1983. "Zur Problematik in der Niedergangsperiode des Imperium Romanum im 5. Jahrhundert an den *praefectus praetorio per Illyricum* gerichteten Gesetze anhand des *Codex Theodosianus* und des *Codex Iustinianus.*" *Klio* 56:405–12.

Haldon, J. 1984. *Byzantine Praetorians. An Administrative, Institutional, and Social Survey of the Opsikion and Tagmata, c. 580–900.* Bonn.

Hall, J. 1988. "Pollentia, Verona and the Chronology of Alaric's First Invasion of Italy." *Philologus* 132:245–257.

Hamerow, H. 1987. "Anglo-Saxon Settlement Pottery and Spatial Development at Mucking, Essex." *Rijksdienst voor het Oudheidkundis. Berichten van de Rijksdienst voor het Oudheidkundis Bodenonderzoek* 37:245–73.

Hammond, N. 1972. *A History of Macedonia,* v. 1. Oxford.

Hampel, J. 1905. *Die Alterthümer des frühen Mittelalters in Ungarn.* Braunschweig.

Harries, J. 1984. "Prudentius and Theodosius." *Latomus* 43:69–84.

Hartranft, C. 1890. *The Ecclesiastical History of Sozomen.* In *Nicene and Post Nicene Fathers,* v. 2. New York.

Heather, P. 1991. *Goths and Romans 332–489.* Oxford.

Heering, W. 1927. *Kaiser Valentinian I. (364–375 n. Chr.).* Magdeburg.

Heger, N. 1988. "Das Ende der römischen Herrschaft in Alpen- und Donauraum." In *Die Bajuwaren von Severin bis Tassilo 488–788,* pp. 14–22. Edited by H. Dannheimer et al. Munich.

Heinen, H. 1985. *Trier und das Trevererland in römischer Zeit. 2000 Jahre Trier,* v. 1. Trier.

Hendy, M. 1972. "Aspects of Coin Production and Fiscal Administration in the Late Roman and Early Byzantine Period." *Numismatic Chronicle* 12:117–39.

———. 1988. "From Public to Private; The Western Barbarian Coinages as a Mirror of the Disintegration of Late Roman State Structures." *Viator* 19:29–78.

Henning, J. 1987. *Südosteuropa zwischen Antike und Mittelalter. Archäologische Beiträge zur Landwirtschaft des 1. Jahrtausends u. Z.* Schriften zur Ur.- und Frühgeschichte, 42. Berlin.

Herrmann, J. 1986. "Iatrus und die frühe Geschichte Bulgariens." *Das Altertum* 32:69–77.

Hill, P., J. Kent, and R. Carson. 1960. *Late Roman Bronze Coinage.* London.

Hind, J. 1984. "Whatever Happened to the Agri Decumates?" *Britannia* 15:187–92.

Hitchner, R. 1992. "Meridional Gaul, Trade and the Mediterranean Economy." In *Fifth-Century Gaul: A Crisis of Identity?* pp. 122–31. Edited by J. Drinkwater and H. Elton. Cambridge.

Hitzinger, P. 1855. "Der Kampf des Kaiser Theodosius gegen den Tyrannen Eugenius am Flusse Frigidus." *Mittheilungen des Historischen Vereins für Krain* 10:81–85.

Hoddinott, R. 1975. *Bulgaria in Antiquity. An Archaeological Introduction.* New York.

Hodgson, N. 1991. "The Notitia dignitatum and the Later Roman Garrison of

Britain." In *Roman Frontier Studies*, pp. 84–92. 15th Int. Congress of Roman Frontier Studies, 1989, Canterbury. Edited by V. Maxfield and M. Dobson. Exeter.

Höckmann, O. 1896. "Flotten und Legionstruppen im Schiffsdienst an Donau und Save nach der *Notitia dignitatum.*" *Jahrbuch d. RGZM-Mainz* 33:369–416.

Hoepffner, A. 1936. "Les 'Magistri militum praesentales' au IVe siècle." *Byzantion* 11:483–98.

Hoffmann, D. 1970. *Das spätrömische Bewegungsheer und die Notitia dignitatum.* Düsseldorf.

——. 1973. "Die Gallienarmee und der Grenzschutz am Rhein in der Spätantike." *Nassauische Annalen* 84:1–18.

——. 1978. "Wadomar, Bacurius und Heriulf: zur Laufbahn adliger und fürstlicher Barbaren im spätrömischen Heere." *Museum Helveticum* 35:307–18.

Holum, K. 1982. *Theodosian Empresses: Women and Imperial Dominion in Late Antiquity.* Berkeley.

Horn, H. 1930. *Foederati: Untersuchungen zur Geschichte ihrer Rechtsstellung im Zeitalter der römischen Republik und des frühen Principats.* Frankfurt.

Iordache, R. 1983. "La confusion 'Gètes-Goths' dans la 'Getica' de Jordanes." *Helmantica* 34:317–37.

Isaac, Benjamin. 1990. *The Limits of Empire. The Roman Army in the East.* Oxford.

James, E. 1977. *The Merovingian Archaeology of South-West Gaul.* BAR, Int. ser. 25. Oxford.

——. 1988. *The Franks.* Oxford.

James, S. 1984. "Britain and the Late Roman Army." In *Military and Civilian in Roman Britain. Cultural Relations in a Frontier Province*, pp. 161–86. Edited by T. Blagg and A. King. BAR, Brit. 136. Oxford.

" 'Jerinin Grad'—Belica (Explorations in 1987)." *Glasnik* 5 (1989):82–86. No author given.

Johnson, S. 1980. *Later Roman Britain.* London.

——. 1983. *Late Roman Fortifications.* Totowa, NJ.

Jones, A. 1964. *The Later Roman Empire, 284–602: A Social, Economic and Administrative Survey.* Norman, OK.

Jones, M. and J. Casey. 1991. "The Gallic Chronicle Exploded?" *Britannia* 22:212–15.

Jovanović, A., M. Korać, and Đ. Janković. 1986. "L'embouchure de la rivière Slatinska reka." *Cahiers des Portes de Fer* 3:378–86.

Judeich, W. 1891. "Die Schlacht bei Adrianople." *Deutsche Zeitschrift für Geschichtswissenschaft* 6:1–17.

Kaegi, W. 1968. *Byzantium and the Decline of Rome.* Princeton.

——. 1981a. "Constantine's and Julian's Strategies of Strategic Surprise Against the Persians." *Athenaeum* 59:209–13.

——. 1981b. *Byzantine Military Unrest 471–843.* Amsterdam.

Kahane, A., L. Threipland, and J. Ward-Perkins. 1968. "The Ager Veientanus, North and East of Rome." *Papers of the British School at Rome* 36:1–218.

Kähler, H. 1975. "Der Sockel des Theodosiusobelisken in Konstantinopel als Denkmal der Spätäntike." *Acta ad archaeologiam et artium historiam pertinentia. Institutum romanum Norvegiae* 6:45–55.

Kasser, R. 1975. *Yverdon. Histoire d'un sol et d'un site avec la cité qu'ils ont fait natre* (Eburodunum 1). Yverdon.

Kaufmann, G. 1866. "Ueber das Foederatverhältniss des tolosanischen Reichs zu Rom." *Forschungen zur deutschen Geschichte* 6:433–76.

———. 1872. "Kritische Untersuchungen zu dem Kriege Theodosius des Großen mit den Gothen 378–382." *Forschungen zur deutschen Geschichte* 12:411–38.

Keller, E. 1971. *Die spätrömischen Grabfunde in Südbayern*. Münchner Beiträge zur Vor- u. Frühgeschichte, 14. Munich.

———. 1977. "Germanische Truppenstationen an der Nordgrenze des spätrömischen Raetien." *Archäologisches Korrespondenzblatt* 7:63–73.

———. 1979. *Das spätrömische Gräberfeld von Neuburg an der Donau*. Materialhefte zur bayerischen Vorgeschichte, A40. Kallmünz.

———. 1985. "Germanische Fremdenlegionäre in Raetien: Der Bruderkrieg an der Grenze." In *Die Römer in Schwaben: Jubiläumsausstellung 2000 Jahre Augsburg*, pp. 252–55. Arbeitshefte des Bayerischen Landesamtes für Denkmalpflege 27. Munich.

———. 1986. "Germanenpolitik Roms im bayerischen Teil der Raetia Secunda während des 4. und 5. Jahrhunderts." *Jahrbuch d. RGZM-Mainz* 33:575–92.

Kellner, H. 1978. "Das Kastell Schaan und die Spätzeit der römischen Herrschaft." *Helvetia archaeologica* 9:187–201.

———. 1981. "Die Zeit der römischen Herrschaft." In *Handbuch der Bayerischen Geschichte*, 2d ed., v. 1, pp. 65–100. Edited by M. Spindler. Munich.

Kent, J. 1956. "Gold Coinage in the Later Roman Empire." In *Essays in Roman Coinage Presented to Harold Mattingly*, pp. 190–204. Edited by R. Carson. London.

———. 1979. "The End of Roman Britain: The Literary and Numismatic Evidence Reviewed." In *The End of Roman Britain*, pp. 15–22. Edited by P. Casey. BAR, Brit. 71. Oxford.

——— and K. Painter. 1977. *Wealth of the Roman World, AD 300–700*. London.

Kienast, D. 1966. *Untersuchungen zu den Kriegsflotten der römischen Kaiserzeit*. Bonn.

Kiilerich, B. and H. Torp. 1989. "Hic est: hic Stilicho. The Date and Interpretation of a Notable Diptych." *Jahrbuch des Deutschen Archäologischen Instituts* 104:319–71.

———. 1956. "Kaiser Valens vor Adrianopel." *Südost-Forschungen* 15:53–69.

———. 1960. "Fritigern, Athanarich und die Spaltung des Westgotenvolks am Vorabend des Hunneneinbruchs." *Südost-Forschungen* 19:34–51.

King, C. 1987. "Fifth Century Silver Coinage in the Western Roman Empire: The Usurpations in Spain and Gaul." In *Mélanges de Numismatique offerts à Pierre Bastien*, pp. 285–96. Edited by H. Huvelin, M. Christol, and G. Gautier. Wetteren, Belgium.

Klein, K. 1951. "Der Friedensschluss von Noviodunum: Zur Vorgeschichte der Schlacht von Adrianopel." *Anzeiger für die Altertumswissenschaft der Österreichischen humanistischen Gesellschaft* 4:189–192.

Kondić, V. 1973. "Two recent acquisitions in Belgrade Museums." *Journal of Roman Studies* 63:47–49.

———. 1984. "Les formes des fortifications protobyzantines dans la région des Portes de Fer." In *Villes et peuplement dans l'Illyricum protobyzantin*. Actes du colloque organisé par l'Ecole française de Rome, pp. 131–61. Rome.

Kos, P. 1986. *The Monetary Circulation in the Southeastern Alpine Region, ca. 300 BC–AD 1000*. Situla, 24. Ljubljana.

Koschik, H. 1983. "Schutzmaßnahmen auf der vor- und frühgeschichtlichen Höhensiedlung Gelbe Bürg bei Dittenheim, Landkreis Weißenburg-Gunzenhausen, Mittelfranken." In *Das arch. Jahr in Bayern 1982*, pp. 57–59. Stuttgart.

Kovrig, I. 1959. "Nouvelles trouvailles du Ve siècle découvertes en Hongrie." *Acta Archaeologica* 10:209–225.

Kraft, K. 1978. "Die Taten der Kaiser Constans und Constantius II." In *Kleine Schriften*, v. 2, pp. 87–132. Darmstadt.

Kubitschek, W. 1909. *Ausgewählte römische Medaillons der kaiserlichen Münzensammlung in Wien*. Vienna.

Kuhnen, H.-P. 1988. "Zwiebelknopffibeln aus Palaestina und Arabia. Überlegungen zur Interpretation einer spätrömischen Fibelform." *Zeitschrift des deutschen Palästina-Vereins* 10:92–124.

Labrousse, M. 1968. *Toulouse antique des origines à l'établissement des Wisigoths*. Paris.

Ladner, G. 1976. "On Roman Attitudes Toward Barbarians in Late Antiquity." *Viator* 7:1–26.

Lafaurie, J. 1953. "La Chronologie des monnaies de Constantin III et de Constant II." *Revue Numismatique* 15:37–65.

———. 1987. "Les dernières émissions impériales de Trèves au Ve siècle." In *Mélanges de Numismatique offerts à Pierre Bastien*, pp. 297–323. Edited by H. Huvelin, M. Christol, G. Gautier. Wetteren, Belgium.

Larsen, J. 1955. *Representative Government in Greek and Roman History*. Berkeley.

Larson, C. 1970. "Theodosius and the Thessalonian Massacre Revisited—Yet Again." In *Studia Patristica* 10, Texte und Untersuchungen 107, pp. 297–301. Edited by F. Cross. Berlin.

Lemerle, P. 1954. "Invasions et migrations dans les Balkans depuis la fin de l'époque romaine jusqu'au VIIIe siècle." *Revue historique* 211:263–308.

Lieb, H. and R. Wüthrich. 1967. *Lexicon Topographicum der römischen und frühmittelalterlichen Schweiz*, v. 1: *Römische Zeit, Süd- und Ostschweiz*, Antiquitas I. 15. Bonn.

Liebeschuetz, J. 1986. "Generals, federates and buccelarii in the Roman Armies around AD 400." In *The Defense of the Roman and Byzantine East*, pp. 463–73. Oxford.

———. 1990. *Barbarians and Bishops. Army, Church and State in the Age of Arcadius and Chrysostom*. Oxford.

———. 1992. "Alaric's Goths: Nation or Army." In *Fifth-Century Gaul: A Crisis of Identity?* pp. 75–83. Edited by J. Drinkwater and H. Elton. Cambridge.

Lippold, A. 1968. *Theodosius der Grosse und seine Zeit.* Stuttgart.

———. 1980. *Theodosius der Grosse und seine Zeit.* 2d ed. Munich.

Lörincz, B. 1989. "The Structural Sequence. The Fort in the Pannonian *limes*, A Historical Survey." In *The Roman Fort at Ács-Vaspuszta (Hungary) on the Danubian limes.* Edited by D. Gabler. BAR, Int. ser. 531. Oxford.

Loyen, A. 1934. "Les débuts du royaume wisigoth de Toulouse." *Revue des Études Latines* 12:406–15.

Lund, A. 1985. "Ist 'Decumates agri' eine Textverderbnis (Tacitus, Germania, 29.3)." *Latomus* 44:336–50.

Luttwak, E. 1976. *The Grand Strategy of the Roman Empire.* Baltimore and London.

MacCormack, S. 1981. *Art and Ceremony in Late Antiquity.* Berkeley.

McCormick, M. 1986. *Eternal Victory. Triumphal rulership in late Antiquity, Byzantium and the Early Medieval West.* Cambridge.

MacMullen, R. 1963. *Soldier and Civilian in the Later Roman Empire.* Cambridge, MA.

———. 1980. "How Big Was the Roman Imperial Army?" *Klio* 62:451–60.

———. 1988. *Corruption and the Decline of Rome.* New Haven.

Maenchen-Heflen, J. 1973. *The World of the Huns.* Berkeley.

Maier, L. 1968. "The Giessen, Parma and Piacenza Codices." *Latomus* 27:96–141.

———. 1969. "The Barberinus and Munich Codices of the 'Notitia dignitatum omnium.'" *Latomus* 28:960–1035.

Mann, J. 1976. "What Was the Notitia dignitatum for?" In *Aspects of the Notitia dignitatum,* pp. 1–8. Edited by R. Goodburn and P. Bartholomew. BAR, sup. ser. 15. Oxford.

———. 1977. "Duces and Comites in the 4th Century." In *The Saxon Shore,* CBA Research Report, No. 18, pp. 11–15. Edited by D. Johnston. London.

———. 1991. "The Notitia dignitatum—Dating and Survival." *Britannia* 22:215–19.

Martem'yanov, A. 1986. "The Roman Villa in Thrace and Lower Moesia." *Vestnik drevnei istorii* 177:2.162–74.

Martin, M. 1979. "Die spätrömisch-frühmittelalterliche Besiedlung am Hochrhein und im schweizerischen Jura und Mittelland." In *Von der Spätantike zum frühen Mittelalter,* pp. 411–46. Edited by J. Werner and E. Ewig. Sigmaringen.

——— et al. 1980. "Burgunden." In *Reallexikon der germanischen Altertumskunde,* v. 4, pp. 224–71. Edited by H. Beck. Berlin.

Martindale, J. et al. 1971, 1980. *The Prosopography of the Later Roman Empire.* Cambridge.

Maspero, J. 1912. "Φοιδεράτοι et Στρατιῶται dans l'armée byzantine au VIᵉ siècle." *Byzantinische Zeitschrift* 21:97–109.

Mathisen, R. 1979. "Resistance and Reconciliation: Majorian and the Gallic Aristocracy after the Fall of Avitus." *Francia* 7:597–627.

——. 1981. "Epistolography, Literary Circles, and Family Ties in Late Roman Gaul." *Trans. Am. Philological Assoc.* 111:95–109.

——. 1989. *Ecclesiastical Factions and Religious Controversy in Fifth-Century Gaul.* Washington.

——. 1992. "Fifth-Century Visitors to Italy: Business or Pleasure?" In *Fifth-Century Gaul: A Crisis of Identity?* pp. 228–38. Edited by J. Drinkwater and H. Elton. Cambridge.

——. 1993. *Roman Aristocrats in Barbarian Gaul: Strategies for Survival in an Age of Transition.* Austin.

Matthews, J. 1970. "Olympiodorus of Thebes and the History of the West (407–425)." *Journal of Roman Studies* 60:79–97.

——. 1975. *Western Aristocracies and Imperial Court, A.D. 364–425.* Oxford.

——. 1986. "Ammianus and the Eastern Frontier in the Fourth Century: A Participant's View." In *The Defense of the Roman and Byzantine East*, pp. 549–64. Edited by P. Freeman and D. Kennedy. BAR, Int. ser. 297. Oxford.

——. 1989. *The Roman Empire of Ammianus.* London.

Mattingly, H., et al., ed. 1923–. *Roman Imperial Coinage.* London.

Mazzarino, S. 1942. *Stilicho.* Rome.

Menestier, C. 1702. *Description de la belle et grande colonne historiée dressée à l'honeur de l'empereur Theodose dessinée per G. Bellin.* Paris.

Menghin, W. 1990. *Frühgeschichte Bayerns. Römer und Germanen, Baiern und Schwaben, Franken und Slaven.* Stuttgart.

Mészáros, G. 1970. "A Regölyi Korai Népvándorlá Fejedelmi Sír." *Archaeologiai Értesítö* 97:66–93.

Middleton, P. 1983. "The Roman Army and Long Distance Trade." In *Trade and Famine in Classical Antiquity*, pp. 75–83. Edited by P. Garnsey and C. Whittaker. Cambridge.

Miller, M. 1975. "Stilicho's Pictish War." *Britannia* 6:141–45.

Miteva, N. 1979. "The Goths and the Late-Ancient Civilization in the Balkan Peninsula." *Études historiques* 9:7–21.

Mladenova, Y. 1969. "La villa romaine d'Ivajlovgrad." *Congrès international des études balkaniques et sud-est européenes.* 2:527–34.

Mócsy, A. 1970. *Gesellschaft und Romanisation in der römischen Provinz Moesia Superior.* Amsterdam.

——. 1974a. "Ein spätantiker Festungstyp am linken Donaufer." In *Roman Frontier Studies*, pp. 191–96. 8th Int. Congress of Roman Frontier Studies, 1969, Cardiff. Edited by E. Birley and B. Dobson. Cardiff.

——. 1974b. *Pannonia and Upper Moesia.* London.

Moosdorf-Ottinger, I. 1981. *Der Goldberg bei Türkheim.* Münchner Beiträge zur Vor- u. Frühgeschichte, 24. Munich.

Mossé, C., ed. 1977. *Armées et fiscalité dans le monde antique.* Paris.

Muhlberger, S. 1984. "The Copenhagen Continuation of Prosper: A Translation." *Florilegium* 6:71–95.

Nagy, T. 1967. "Reoccupation of Pannonia from the Huns in 427 (Did Jordanes Use the Chronicon of Marcellinus Comes at the Writing of the Getica?)." *Acta Antiqua* 15:159–86.

Naudé, C. 1958. "Battles and Sieges in Ammianus Marcellinus." *Acta Classica* 1:92–105.

Nehlsen, H. 1984. "Codex Euricianus." *Reallexikon der germanischen Altertumskunde*, v. 5, pp. 42–47. Edited by H. Beck. Berlin.

Nesselhauf, H. 1938. *Die spätrömische Verwaltung der gallisch-germanischen Länder 2.* [Abhandlungen der Preussischen Akademie der Wissenschaft]. Berlin.

Niermeyer, J. 1976. *Mediae Latinitatis Lexicon Minus.* Leiden.

Nikolov, D. 1976. *The Thraco-Roman Villa Rustica near Chatalka, Stara Zagora, Bulgaria.* BAR, sup. ser. 17. Oxford.

Nischer, E. 1923. "The Army Reforms of Diocletian and Constantine and Their Modifications up to the Time of the Notitia dignitatum." *Journal of Roman Studies* 13:1–55.

Nixon, C. 1983. "Coin Circulation and Military Activity in the Vicinity of Sirmium, A.D. 364–378, and the Siscia Mint." *Jahrbuch für Numismatik und Geldgeschichte* 33:45–55.

———. 1987. *Pacatus. Panegyric to the Emperor Theodosius.* Liverpool.

———. 1990. "The Use of the Past by the Gallic Panegyrists." In *Reading the Past in Late Antiquity*, pp. 1–36. Edited by G. Clarke. New York.

———. 1992. "Relations between Visigoths and Romans in Fifth-Century Gaul." In *Fifth-Century Gaul: A Crisis of Identity?* pp. 64–74. Edited by J. Drinkwater and H. Elton. Cambridge.

Nuber, H. 1988. "Sontheim und Brenz in frühgeschichtlicher Zeit. Römische und frühmittelalterlicher Besiedlung." In *Person und Gemeinschaft im Mittelalter. Karl Schmid zum fünfundsechzigsten Geburtstag.* Edited by G. Althoff, D. Geuenich, O. Oexle, and J. Wollasch. Sigmaringen.

O'Flynn, J. 1983. *Generalissimos of the Western Roman Empire.* Edmonton, Alberta.

Oost, S. 1968. *Galla Placidia Augusta.* Chicago.

Overbeck, B. 1982 and 1973. *Geschichte des Alpenrheintals in Römischer Zeit auf Grund der archäologischen Zeugnisse.* Münchner Beiträge zur Vor- u. Frühgeschichte, 20–21, v. 1 (1982) and v. 2 (1973). Munich.

———. 1988. "Eine spätrömische Silbermünze von der 'Römerschanze' bei Grünwald, Landkreis Mnchen." In *Das arch. Jahr in Bayern 1987*, pp. 143–44. Stuttgart.

———. 1990. "Eine spätrömische Siliqua von Burghöfe. In *Das arch. Jahr in Bayern 1989*, pp. 147–48. Stuttgart.

———. 1991a. "Eine weitere spätrömische Siliqua von Burghüfe." In *Das arch. Jahr in Bayern 1990*, pp. 135–36. Stuttgart.

———. 1991b. "Siliqua von Constantinus III von Gelbe Bürg bei Dittenheim, Unterfranken." To appear in *Jahrbuch f. Numismatik u. Geldgeschichte*, 41.

——— and M. Overbeck. 1985. "Zur Datierung und Interpretation der spätantiken Goldbarren aus Siebenbürgen anhand eines unpublizierten Fundes von Feldioara." *Chiron* 15:199–210.

—— and L. Wamser. 1983. "Ein Schatzfund spätrömischer Münzen von der völker-wanderungszeitlichen Befestigung in der Mainschleife bei Urphar, Markt Kreuzwertheim, Landkreis Main-Spessart, Unterfranken." In *Das arch. Jahr in Bayern 1982*, pp. 96–97. Stuttgart.

Pabst, A. 1986. *Divisio Regni: der Zerfall des Imperium Romanum in der Sicht der Zeitgenossen*. Habelts Dis. Reihe alte Gesch., v. 23. Bonn.

Palanque, J.-R. 1929. "Sur l'usurpation de Maxime." *Revue des Études Anciennes* 31:33–36.

——. 1951. "La Préfecture du prétoire de l'Illyricum au IVe siècle." *Byzantion* 21:5–14.

Parović-Peškan, M. 1984. "Ljubičevac-Glamija I, fouilles de 1980." *Cahiers des Portes de Fer* 2:141–44.

Paschoud, F. 1971–89. *Zosime. Histoire nouvelle*. Collection G. Budé. Paris.

——. 1975. *Cinq études sur Zosime*. Paris.

——. 1983. "Le rôle du providentialisme dans le conflict de 384 sur l'autel de la Victoire." *Museum Helveticum* 40:197–206.

——. 1985a. "Le début de l'ouvrage historique d'Olympiodore." In *Studia in honorem Iiro Kajanto*, pp. 185–96. Helsinki.

——. 1985b. "Eunapiana." *Bonner Historia Augusta Colloquium 1982/83*. Antiquitas 17, pp. 239–93. Bonn.

Paunier, D. 1978. "Un refuge du Bas-Empire au Mont-Musiège (Haute-Savoie)." *Museum Helveticum* 35:295–306.

Pavan, M. 1964. *La politica gotica di Teodosio nella pubblicistica del suo tempo*. Rome.

——. 1979. "La battaglia di Adrianopoli (378) e il problema gotico nell'impero romano." *Studi romani* 27:153–65.

Pearce, J. 1933. *The Roman Imperial Coinage*, v. 9. *Valentinian–Theodosius I*. London.

——. 1938. "Gold Coinage of the Reign of Theodosius." *Numismatic Chronicle* 98:205–46.

Penella, R. 1990. *Greek Philosophers and Sophists in the Fourth Century A.D. Studies in Eunapius of Sardis*. Arca, v. 28. Leeds.

Périn, P. 1987. *Les Francs*. Paris.

Perrin, O. 1968. *Les Burgondes*. Neuchatel.

Petrikovits, H. von. 1971. "Fortification in the North-Western Roman Empire from the Third to the Fifth Centuries." *Journal of Roman Studies* 61:178–219.

Petrović, P. 1980. "Les Forteresses du Bas-Empire sur le limes Danubien en Serbie." In *Roman Frontier Studies*, pt. iii, pp. 757–73. 12th Int. Congress of Roman Frontier Studies, University of Stirling. Edited by W. Hanson and L. Keppie. Oxford.

Pharr, C. 1952. *The Theodosian Code*. Princeton.

Piganiol, A. 1972. *L'Empire Chrétien (325–395)*. Paris.

Pillinger, R., ed. 1986. *Spätantike und frühbyzantinische Kultur Bulgariens zwischen*

Orient und Okzident. Schriften der Balkankommission. Antiquarische Abt., 16. Vienna.

Poisote, L. 1982. "Le consul de 382 Fl. Claudius Antonius fut-il un auteur antipäien." *REL* 60:273–82.

Popescu, E. 1973. "Das Problem der Kontinuität in Rumänien im Lichte der epigraphischen Entdeckungen." *Dacoromania* 1:69–77.

Popović, V. 1987. "Die süddanubischen Provinzen in der Spätantike vom Ende des 4. bis zur Mitte des 5. Jahrhunderts." In *Die Völker Südosteuropas im 6. bis 8. Jahrhundert. Südosteuropa Jahrbuch* 17, pp. 95–139. Edited by B. Hänsel. Berlin.

Poulter, A., ed. 1983a. *Ancient Bulgaria.* Nottingham.

———. 1983b. "Town and Country in Moesia Inferior." In *Ancient Bulgaria,* pp. 74–118. Edited by A. Poulter. Nottingham.

———. 1983–84. "Roman Towns and the Problem of Late Roman Urbanism." *Hephaistos* 5–6:109–32.

———. 1988. "Nicopolis ad Istrum, Bulgaria: An Interim Report on the Excavations 1985–87." *The Antiquaries Journal* 68:69–89.

Prammer, J. 1982. "Das spätrömische Gräberfeld Straubing-Azlburg, Niederbayern." *Das arch. Jahr in Bayern 1981,* pp. 154–55. Stuttgart.

———. 1986. "Das spätrömische Gräberfeld Azlburg II." In *Das arch. Jahr in Bayern 1985,* pp. 117–19. Stuttgart.

———. 1987. "Neue Forschungen zum Spätrömischen Straubing. Die Gräbergelder Azlburg I und Azlburg II." *Vorträge des 5. Niederbayerischen Archäologentages* pp. 133–42. Munich.

Press, L., W. Szubert, and T. Sarnowski. 1982. "Novae in 1979—West Sector." *Klio* 64:471–83.

Pröttel, P. 1988. "Zur Chronologie der Zwiebelknopffibeln." *Jahrbuch d. RGZM-Mainz* 35:347–72.

Pryor, J. 1989. "The Voyage of Rutilius Namatianus: From Rome to Gaul in 417, C. E." *Mediterr. Hist. R.* 4:271–80.

Randsborg, K. 1990. "Between Classical Antiquity and the Middle Ages: New Evidence of Economic Change." *Antiquity* 64:122–27.

Rankov, J. 1987. "Satio Cataractarum Diana." *Cahiers des Portes de Fer* 4:16–36.

Rankov, N. 1983. "A Contribution to the Military and Administrative History of Montana." In *Ancient Bulgaria,* pp. 40–73. Edited by A. Poulter. Nottingham.

Raymond, I., trans. 1936. *Seven Books of History against the Pagans. The Apology of Paulus Orosius.* New York.

Reece, R. 1984. "Mints, Markets, and the Military." In *Military and Civilian in Roman Britain,* pp. 143–60. Edited by T. Blagg and A. King. BAR, Brit. 136. London.

Ridley, R. 1969–70. "Eunapius and Zosimus." *Helikon* 9–10:574–92.

———, trans. 1982. *Zosimus. The New History.* In Australian Association for Byzantine Studies, Byzantina Australiensia 2, Sydney.

Robertson, A. 1982. *Roman Imperial Coins in the Hunter Coin Cabinet.* Oxford.

Rodgers, B. 1981. "Merobaudes and Maximus in Gaul." *Historia* 30:82–105.

Roques, D. 1983. "Synésios de Cyrène et les migrations berbères vers l'Orient (398–413)." *Académie des Inscriptions et Belles-Lettres.* Comptes-rendus des séances, November–December: 660–77.

Rosenstock, D. 1984. "Eine prachtvolle römische Emailscheibenfibel und weitere Erzeugnisse römischen Kunstgewerbes aus der germanischen Siedlung von Frankenwinheim, Landkreis Schweinfurt, Unterfranken." In *Das arch. Jahr in Bayern 1983,* pp. 120–22. Stuttgart.

———. 1985. "Völkerwanderungszeitliche Körpergräber aus Dettingen, Gemeinde Karlstein, Landkreis Aschaffenburg, Unterfranken." *Das arch. Jahr in Bayern 1984,* pp. 128–30. Stuttgart.

Rouche, M. 1979. *L'Aquitaine des Wisigoths aux Arabes (418–781). Naissance d'une région.* Paris.

Rousseau, P. 1992. "Visigothic Migration and Settlement, 376–418: Some Excluded Hypotheses." *Historia* 41:345–61.

Rowell, H. 1937. "Numerus." *Realencyclopädie der klassischen Altertumswissenschaft* 17:1327–41.

Ryan, N. 1988. *Fourth-Century Coin Finds from Roman Britain. A Computer Analysis.* BAR, Brit. 183. Oxford.

Sabbah, G. 1978. *La Méthode d'Ammien Marcellin: Recherches sur la construction du discours historique dans les Res Gestae.* Paris.

Sablayrolles, R. 1984. "Bibliographie sur l'Epitoma rei militaris de Vègéce." *Armée Romaine et Provinces* 3:139–45.

Sacce, C. 1958. *Die Constitutio Antoniniana.* Wiesbaden.

Sage, W. 1984a. "Frühes Christentum und Kirchen aus der Zeit des Übergangs." In *Geschichte der Stadt Augsburg,* pp. 100–14. Edited by G. Gottlieb et al. Stuttgart.

———. 1984b. *Das Reihengräberfeld von Altenerding in Oberbayern.* I Germ. Denkmäler d. Völkerwanderungszeit, A14. Berlin.

Salamon, Á. and L. Barkóczi. 1970. "Bestattungen von Csákvár aus dem Ende des 4. und dem Anfang des 5. Jahrhunderts." *Alba Regia* 11:35–80.

Salway, P. 1981. *Roman Britain.* Oxford.

Sarnowski, T. 1983. "La forteresse de la légion I Italica à Novae et les limes du sud-est de la Dacie." *Eos* 71:265–76.

———. 1985. "Die legio I Italica und der untere Donauabschnitt der Notitia dignitatum." *Germania* 63:107–27.

Šašel, J. 1971a. Claustra Alpium Iuliarum pt. 1 Fontes. Ljubljana.

———. 1971b. "The Struggle between Magnentius and Constantius II for Italy and Illyricum." *Živa Antika* 2:205–16.

———. 1979. "Antiqui Barbari: Zur Besiedlungsgeschichte Ostnoricums und Pannoniens im 5. und 6. Jahrhundert nach den Schriftquellen." In *Von der Spätan-*

tike zum frühen Mittelalter, pp. 125–39. Edited by J. Werner and E. Ewig. Sigmaringen.

Scharf, R. 1991. "Praefecti Practorio Vacantes—General quartiermeister des spätrömischen Heeres." *Byzantinische Forschungen* 17:223–33.

Schlumberger, J. 1974. *Die Epitome de Caesaribus. Untersuchungen zur heidnischen Geschichtsschreibung des 4. Jahrhunderts n. Chr.* Munich.

Schmidt, L. 1941. *Die Ostgermanen.* Munich.

Schneider-Schnekenburger, G. 1980. *Churrätien im Frühmittelalter auf Grund der archäologischen Funde.* Münchner Beiträge zur Vor- u. Frühgeschichte, 26. Munich.

Schönberger, H. 1980. "Recent Research of the Limes in Germania Superior and Raetia." In *Roman Frontier Studies*, pp. 541–52. 12th Int. Congress of Roman Frontier Studies, University of Stirling. Edited by W. Hanson and L. Keppie. Oxford.

Schwarz, K. 1972–73. "Regensburg während des ersten Jahrtausends im Spiegel der Ausgrabungen im Niedermünster." *Jahresbericht d. bayerischen Bodendenkmalpflege* 13/14:20f.

Scorpan, C. 1980. *Limes Scythiae. Topographical and Stratigraphical Research in the Late Roman Fortifications on the Lower Danube.* BAR, Int. ser. 88. London.

Seeck, O. 1919. *Regesten der Kaiser und Päpste für die Jahre 311 bis 476 n. Chr. Vorarbeit zu einer Prosopographie der Christlichen Kaiserzeit.* Stuttgart.

———. (1921, 1920–22), 1966. *Geschichte des Untergangs der antiken Welt*, v. 1, 4th ed., v. 2–6, 2d ed., reprint Stuttgart.

——— . ed. (1876) 1962. *Notitia dignitatum.* Frankfurt.

——— and G. Veith. 1913. "Die Schlacht am Frigidus." *Klio* 13:451–67.

Seibt, W. 1982. "Wurde die Notitia dignitatum in 408 von Stilicho in Auftrag gegeben?" *Mitteilungen des Instituts für österreichische Geschichtsforschung* 90:339–46.

Shahîd, I. 1984. *Byzantium and the Arabs in the Fourth Century.* Washington, D.C.

Shelton, K. 1981/83. "Usurpers' Coins: The Case of Magnentius." *Byzantinische Forschungen* 8:211–35.

Shennan, S. 1989. "Introduction: Archaeologial Approaches to Cultural Identity." In *Archaeological Approaches to Cultural Identity*, pp. 1–32. Edited by S. Shennan. London.

Simpson, C. 1988. "*Laeti* in the *Notitia Dignitatum.* 'Regular' Soldiers vs. 'Soldier-Farmers.' " *Revue belge philol. hist.* 66:80–85.

Sinnigen, W. 1963. "Barbaricarii, Barbari and the Notitia Dignitatum." *Latomus* 22:806–815.

Sivan, H. 1985. "An Unedited Letter of the Emperor Honorius to the Spanish Soldiers." *Zeitschrift für Papyrologie und Epigraphik* 61:273–87.

———. 1987. "On foederati, hospitalitas, and the Settlement of the Goths in AD 418." *American Journal of Philology* 108:759–72.

———. 1992. "Town and Country in Late Antique Gaul: The Example of Bordeaux." In *Fifth-Century Gaul: A Crisis of Identity?* pp. 132–43. Edited by J. Drinkwater and H. Elton. Cambridge.

Slabe, M. 1987. "Settlement Structure in the South-East Pre-Alpine Territory in the Fifth and Sixth Centuries A.D." *Balcanica* 18–19:195–201.

Sophocles, E. 1887. *Greek Lexicon of the Roman and Byzantine Periods.* New York.

Soproni, S. 1978. *Der spätrömische Limes zwischen Esztergom und Szentendre.* Budapest.

———. 1985. *Die letzten Jahrzehnte des Pannonischen Limes.* Munich.

Speidel, M. 1983. "Exploratores. Mobile Elite Units of Roman Germany." *Epigraphische Studien* 13:63–78.

Spindler, K. 1981a. *Die Archäologie des Frauenberges von den Anfängen bis zur Gründung des Klosters Weltenburg.* Regensburg.

———. 1981b. "Ein spätrömisches Kastell auf dem Frauenberg bei Weltenburg, Landkreis Kelheim, Niederbayern." *Das arch. Jahr in Bayern 1980,* pp. 148–49. Stuttgart.

———. 1985a. "Archäologische Aspekte zur Siedlungskontinuität und Kulturtradition von der Spätantike zum frühen Mittelalter im Umkreis des Klosters Weltenburg an der Donau." *Archäologische Denkmalpflege in Niederbayern.* Arbeitshefte des Bayerischen Landesamtes für Denkmalpflege 26:179–200.

———. 1985b. "Germanenfunde der Völkerwanderungszeit in Nordbayern. Bemerkungen zur Keramik vom Typ Friedenhain-Prest'ovice." *Arch. Korrespondenzblatt* 15:235f.

Springer, M. 1982. "Haben die Germanen das weströmische Reich erobert?" *Klio* 64:179–87.

Srejović, D. 1985. "Felix Romuliana, Le Palais de Galère à Gamzigrad." *Starinar* 36:51–67.

Stallknecht, B. 1969. *Untersuchungen zur Römischen Aussenpolitik in der Spätantike (306–395 n. Chr.).* Bonn.

Stančeva, M. 1980. "Témoignages archéologiques sur les Thraces pendant la Basse Antiquité." *Thracia* 5:235–42.

de Ste. Croix, G. 1981. *The Class Struggle in the Ancient Greek World.* London, Ithaca.

Stein, E. (1941) 1968. *Histoire du Bas-Empire.* Edited by J.-R. Palanque. Amsterdam.

Stertz, S. 1976. "Themistius: A Hellenic Philosopher-Statesman in the Christian Roman Empire." *Classical Journal* 71:349–58.

Steuer, H. 1990. "Höhensiedlungen des 4. und 5. Jahrhunderts in Südwestdeutschland. Einordnung des Zähringer Burgberges, Gemeinde Gundelfingen, Kreis Breisgau-Hochschwarzwald." In *Archäologie und Geschichte des ersten Jahrtausends in Südwestdeutschland,* pp. 139–205. Edited by H. Nuber, K. Schmid, H. Steuer, and T. Zotz. Sigmaringen.

Stevens, C. 1933. *Sidonius Apollinaris and His Age.* Oxford.

———. 1957. "Marcus, Gratian, and Constantine." *Athenaeum* 35:316–47.

Straub, J. 1943. "Die Wirkung der Niederlage von Adrianopel auf die Diskussion über das Germanenproblem in der spätrömischen Literatur." *Philologus* 95:255–86.

Stribrny, K. 1989. "Römer rechts des Rheins nach 260 n. Chr. Kartierung, Struk-
turanalyse und Synopse spätrömischer Münzreihen zwischen Koblenz und
Regensburg." *Bericht der Römisch-Germanischen Kommission.* 70:351–506.

Stroheker, K. 1965. *Germanentum und Spätantike.* Zürich.

———. 1970. *Der senatorische Adel im spätantiken Gallien.* 2d ed. Darmstadt.

Svoboda, B. 1963. "Zum Verhältnis frühgeschichtlicher Funde des 4. und 5. Jahrhunderts aus Bayern und Böhmen." *Bayerische Vorgeschichtsblätter* 28:97–116.

Teichner, F. 1990. "Abschluß der Ausgrabungen im Bereich der völkerwanderung-
szeitlichen Siedlung mit Gräberfeld bei Kahl a. Main, Landkreis Aschaffenburg." In *Das arch. Jahr in Bayern 1989*, pp. 149–51. Stuttgart.

Teillet, S. 1984. *Des Goths à la nation Gothique. Les Origines de l'idée de nation en
Occident du Ve au VIIe siècle.* Paris.

Teja, R. 1971. "Invasions de godos en Asia Menor autes y después de Adrianopolis
(275–382)." *Hispania Antiqua* 1:169–77.

Thompsen, H. 1959. "Athenian Twilight: A.D. 267–600." *Journal of Roman Studies*
79:61–72.

Thompson, E. 1944. "Olympiodorus of Thebes." *Classical Quarterly* 38:43–52.

———. 1952. *A Roman Reformer and Inventor, Being a New Text of the Treatise De
rebus bellicis.* Oxford.

———. 1956. "The Settlement of the Barbarians in Southern Gaul." *Journal of
Roman Studies* 46:65–76.

———. 1963. "The Visigoths from Fritigern to Euric." *Historia* 12:105–26.

———. 1966. *Visigoths at the Time of Ulfilas.* Oxford.

———. 1969. *The Goths in Spain.* Oxford.

———. 1980. "Barbarian Invaders and Roman Collaborators." *Florilegium* 2:71–88.

———. 1982. *Romans and Barbarians. The Decline of the Western Empire.* Madison.

Thraede, K. 1959. "Beiträge zu Datierung Commodianus." *Jahrbuch für Antike und
Christentum* 2:90–114.

Tolkin, C. 1953–57. "The Battle of the Goths and the Huns." *Saga-Book of the
Viking Society* 14:141–63.

Tomović, M. 1986. "Mihojlovac-'Blato'—Une forteresse de la Basse Antiquité."
Cahiers des Portes de Fer 3:401–31.

———. 1987. "Les Tours fortifiées de la basse antiquité sur le limes es Portes de
Fer." *Archaeologia Iugoslavica* 24:91–100.

Tudor, D. 1960. "Contributii privatore l'armata de la Dacia Ripensis." *Studii si cercetari de istorie veche* 11:335–60.

Ulbert, T. 1979. "Zur Siedlungskontinuität im südöstlichen Alpenraum (vom 2. bis
6. Jahrhundert n. Chr.). Dargestellt am Beispiel von Vranje (ehem. Untersteier-
mark)." In *Von der Spätantike zum frühen Mittelalter*, pp. 141–57. Edited by
J. Werner and E. Ewig. Vorträge and Forschungen, 25. Sigmaringen.

———. 1981. *AD PIRVM (Hrusica). Spätrömische Passbefestigung in den Julischen Al-
pen.* Münchner Beiträge zur Vor- u. Frühgeschichte, 31. Munich.

Van Dam, R. 1987. *Leadership and Community in Late Antique Gaul*. Berkeley.

Vanags, P. 1979. "Taxation and Survival in the Late Fourth Century: The Anonymous' Programme of Economic Reforms." In *De Rebus Bellicis*, pt. 1, *Aspects of the De Rebus Bellicis*, pp. 47–57. Edited by M. Hassal. BAR, 63. Oxford.

Vanderspoel, J. 1989. *Themistius and the Imperial Court*. Ph.D. diss. University of Toronto.

Várady, L. 1969. *Das letzte Jahrhundert Pannoniens, 376–476*. Amsterdam.

Vasić, M. 1978. "A IVth and Vth Centuries Hoard of Roman Coins and Imitations in the Collection of the National Museum in Belgrade." In *Sirmium VIII*, pp. 113–32. Edited by D. Bosković, N. Duval, V. Popović, and G. Vallet. Numismatique: Trésors, lingots, imitations, monnaies de fouilles (Collection de l'École Française de Rome, 29/2). Rome-Belgrade.

———. 1988. "The Circulation of Bronze Coinage at the End of the 4th and Beginning of the 5th Centuries in Moesia Prima and Pannonia Secunda." In *Studia Numismatica Labacensia. Alexandro Jelocnik Oblata*, pp. 165–84. Edited by P. Kos and Z. Demo. Ljubljana.

Velkov, V. (1955) 1980. "Svedeniata na Themistius za Trakia." In *Serta Kazaroviana* 2 (1955):245–60. Translated into English, "Themistius as a source of information about Thrace." In *Roman Cities in Bulgaria, Collected Studies*, pp. 171–98. Amsterdam.

———. (1958) 1977. "La construction en Thrace à l'époque du Bas-Empire (d'après les écrits)." *Archeologia* 10 (1958):124–38. In *Cities in Thrace and Dacia in Late Antiquity (Studies and Materials)*, pp. 263–75. Amsterdam.

———. (1961) 1980. "Ein Beitrag zum Aufenthalt des Kaisers Theodosius I. in der Provinz Skythien im Jahre 386 im Lichte neuer Erkenntnisse." *Eunomia* 5 (1961):49–62. Reprinted in his *Roman Cities in Bulgaria*, pp. 215–28. Amsterdam.

Vercauteren, F. 1934. "Note sur la ruine des villes de la Gaule." *Bruxelles université libre. Institute de philologie et d'histoire orientales. Annuaire* 2:955–63.

Vetters, H. 1950. *Dacia ripensis*. Österreichische Akademie der Wissenschaften in Wien: Schriften der Balkankommission 11.

Vulić, N. 1916. "Illyricum," in *Realencyclopädie der klassischen Altertumswissenschaft* (R.-E.), 9.1085–87.

Vulpe, R. 1957. *Le Vallum de la Moldavie inférieure et le "mur" d'Athanaric*. The Hague.

Waas, M. 1965. *Germanen im römischen Dienst im 4. Jahrhundert*. Bonn.

Wagner, M. 1967. *Getica: Untersuchungen zum Leben des Jordanes und zur frühen Geschichte der Goten*. Berlin.

Walford, E. 1855. *The Ecclesiatical History of Sozomen*. London.

Wamser, L. 1982. "Eine völkerwanderungszeitliche Befestigung im Freien Germanien: die Mainscheife bei Urphar, Markt Kreuzwertheim, Landkreis Main-Spessart, Unterfranken." In *Das arch. Jahr in Bayern 1981*, pp. 156–57. Stuttgart.

Wanke, U. 1990. *Die Gotenkriege des Valens. Studien zu Topographie und Chronologie im unteren Donauraum von 366 bis 378 n. Chr.* Europäische Hochschulschriften, s. 3, v. 412. Frankfurt.

Wardman, A. 1984. "Usurpers and Internal Conflicts in the Fourth Century A.D." *Historia* 33:220–37.

Weber, G. 1989. "Das spätrömische Cambodunum." In *Geschichte der Stadt Kempten*, pp. 56–62. Edited by V. Dotterweich. Kempten.

Weinlich, E. 1985. "Eine germanische Siedlung des 4./5. Jahrhunderts n. Chr. bei Treuchtlingen-Schambach, Landkreis Weißenburg-Gunzenhausen, Mittelfranken." In *Das arch. Jahr in Bayern 1984*, pp. 126–27. Stuttgart.

———. 1991. "Ausgrabungen in einem neuentdeckten germanischen Gräberfeld des 4./5. Jahrhunderts n. Chr. bei Forchheim, Stadt Freystadt, Landkreis Neumarkt i. d. Opf, Oberpfalz." In *Das arch. Jahr in Bayern 1990*, pp. 136–37. Stuttgart.

Weiser, W. 1987. "Felicium Temporum Reparatio." *Schweizer Numismatische Rundschau.* 66:161–74.

Welsby, D. 1982. *The Roman Military Defense of the British Provinces in Its Later Phases.* BAR, Brit. 101. Oxford.

Wenskus, R. 1961. *Stammesbildung und Verfassung. Das Werden der frühmittelalterlichen Gentes.* Cologne.

Werner, J. 1969. *Der Lorenzberg bei Epfach. Die spätrömischen und frühmittelalterlichen Anlagen.* Münchner Beiträge zur Vor- u. Frühgeschichte, 8. Munich.

———. 1980. "Der goldene Armring des Frankenkönigs Childerich und die germanischen Handelenkringe der jüngeren Kaiserzeit. Mit einem Anhang von L. Pauli." *Frühmittelalterliche Studien* 14:1–49.

———. 1984. *Der Grabfund von Malaja Pereščepina und Kuvrat, Kagan der Bulgaren.* Munich.

Whittaker, C. 1983. "Late Roman Trade and Traders." In *Trade in the Ancient Economy.* Edited by P. Garnsey et al. Berkeley.

———. 1989. *Les frontières de l'empire romain.* Paris.

Wickham, C. 1984. "The Other Transition: From the Ancient World to Feudalism." *Past and Present* 103:3–36.

Wilkes, J. 1969. *Dalmatia.* London.

Wirth, G. 1967. "Zur Frage der föderierten Staaten in der späteren römischen Kaiserzeit." *Historia* 16:231–51.

Wolfram, H. 1977. *Die Schlacht von Adrianopel.* Veröffentlichungen der Kommission für Frühmittelalterforschung, Bd. 1. Vienna.

———. 1979. *Geschichte der Goten.* 2d ed. Munich.

———. 1988. *A History of the Goths.* Berkeley.

——— and W. Pohl, eds. 1990. *Typen der Ethnogenese unter besonderer Berücksichtigung der Bayern.* Denkschriften der Österreichischen Akademie der Wissenschaften, phil.-hist. Kl. 201. Vienna.

—— and A. Schwarcz, eds. 1988. *Anerkennung und Integration. Zu den wirtschaftlichen Grundlagen der Völkerwanderungszeit 400–600.* Vienna.

Zaharia, E. and N. Zaharia. 1975. "La Nécropoles des IVe-Ve siècles de Botosani-Dealul (Caramidariei)." *Dacia* 19:201–226.

Zahariade, M. 1983. "Ammianus Marcellinus (27.5.2), Zosimus (4.11) et la campagne de Valens de 367 contre les Goths." *Studii si cercetari de istorie veche* 34:57–70.

——. 1988. *Moesia Secunda, Scythia, and the Notitia dignitatum.* Biblioteca de arheologie, 49. Bucharest.

Zeller, J. 1906. "Concilia provincilia in Gallien in der späteren Kaiserzeit." *Westdeutsche Zeitschrift für Geschichte und Kunst* 25:258–73.

INDEX

Abundantius, 155

Adrianople, Battle of: civilian life in Thrace after, 35–42; historiography on, 1; reconstruction of tactical development of, 306n.139, 307n.156; Roman military policies before, 2–23; Roman military policies following, 72, 280–84; Valens and conduct of, 29–35

Aequitius, 8, 296n.35

Aetius, 107, 119, 227, 274–75, 276, 284

Agilo, 5

agriculture: evolution to less labor-intensive crops in West, 202; in Raetia and Noricum Ripense in late 4th century, 123–24, 126; rural life in Danube provinces after Battle of Adrianople, 40–42; and soldiers of frontier garrisons, 184

agri deserti, 272

Alamanni, 9, 117, 145, 298n.52, 305n.138

Alans, 94, 261–62, 269–70

Alaric: battle of the Frigidus, 106, 110, 111; from battle at Verona to deposition and death of Stilicho, 183–223; campaign in Greece, 157–59, 339n.33; death of, 245; kingship of, 176–77, 232, 342n.63; march to Italy in 401, 107, 364n.32; sack of Rome, 224–46; Stilicho and Roman politics, 151–82, 282

Alatheus, 30, 61–63

Alavivus, 23

Alburg, excavation site, 332–33n.47

allies, use of term, 327n.65

Allobichus, 236, 237, 238, 249–50, 369n.96

Alps: Roman fortifications in, 107–108. *See also* Noricum Ripense; Raetian provinces; Rhine

Altenerding, 146

Amantius (bishop of Iovia), 62

Ambrose (bishop of Milan), 33, 93, 94, 98

Ammianus Marcellinus: on Athanaric, 179; on barbarians on Rhenish frontier, 117; on Battle of Adrianople, 1, 29, 30, 31, 32, 33, 34, 35; on Goths in Thrace, 38, 39–40, 41, 185; reliability of as source, xvi,

294n.6; on rebellion in Britain in 367–368, 9–11; on Valens and Goths, 16

Anaolsus, 274

Anatolius, 159, 161, 172, 175–76, 348n.125

annonae, system of, 350–51n.3

Anthemius, 195

Antiochus, 157–58, 342n.64

Aoricus, 15

Aquitaine, settlement of 418, 263–74, 281, 283, 374n.84, 375n.94, 377n.124

Arbitio, 105

Arbogastes (388–94), 54, 75, 96, 98, 104–107, 135, 283

Arcadius, xv, 154–55, 159, 171, 173, 204, 215, 348n.123

archaeology, xvii. *See also* coinage; specific sites

Ariaricus, 15

Arinthaeus, 15

aristocracy, Roman: anti-barbarian ideology of, 221–23; conflict with military leadership prior to Battle of Adrianople, 19; hostility between civilian and military, 230–31

Armenia, partition of, 92

Armorica, 275

army, Roman: from Battle of Verona to deposition of Stilicho, 183–223; civil wars and barbarian recruits in late 4th and early 5th centuries, 92–111; conclusion of Gothic wars in late 4th century, 73–91; Gothic settlement of 418, 247–79; military policy before Battle of Adrianople, 2–23; and movement of Goths across Danube, 23–42; and Roman politics at end of 4th century, 148–82; sack of Rome, 224–46; Stilicho and recruitment of barbarians in transalpine region, 112–47; Theodosius and military policy following Battle of Adrianople, 43–72, 280–84

Arsacius, 224, 238

Asding Vandals, 261–62, 269

Athanaric: arrival of in Constantinople, 74,

408

91; crossing of Danube by Goths, 70; death of, 80, 283; as king of Goths, 16, 197; as successor to Fritigern, 318–19n.16; Theodoius and, 56, 57, 72; as *thiudans*, 179

Athaulf: establishment of Gothic government within Western Empire, 247–79; Roman politics and, 282; as successor to Alaric, 227, 232–33, 236, 241

Attalus, 235, 236, 237, 241–42, 243, 244, 246, 247, 248–49, 258, 366n.64, 372n.47

Attila, 276

Augsburg (Augusta Vindelicum), 119, 330n.17

Augustine, Saint, 128, 137, 187, 231, 257

Aurelianus, 171–72, 178, 344–45n.93, 345n.94, 345n.100, 346n.106, 346n.107, 349n.132

Ausonius, 83

Austin, N., 306n.143

Auvergne (Gaul), siege of, 44

auxilia, use of term, 281, 327n.65, 328n.73

Auxonius (praetoian prefect of Orient), 15, 18

Azlburg, 144–45

bacaudae, 18–19

Bacurius, 106, 107, 110, 150, 151, 328n.75

Bagnall, R., 349n.132

Balkans. *See* Danube provinces

Balzers (Raetia Prima), 122

barbarians: conclusion of Gothic wars in late 4th century, 73–91; limited-contract theory of recruitment, 337n.8; political collapse of Roman Empire in final years of 4th century, 92–111; Raetian provinces and Noricum Ripense as recruitment areas in late 4th century, 113–47; Roman military policy before Battle of Adrianople, 2–23; Roman military policy following Battle of Adrianople, 280–84; Roman military policy under Theodosius and Gratian, 43–72; settlement of 418, 247–79. *See also* specific ethnic groups

barbaricum, 117

Barnish, S., 375n.94, 376n.108

Bastarnae, 103

Batavians, 299n.58

Bathanarius, 217

Bauto, 75, 159, 324n.9

Bavaria, Elbgermans in, 134

Baynes, N., 209, 358–59n.97

Becatti, G., 347–48n.118

Bedaium (Seebruck), 126

Bede, 209, 358n.97

Belisarius, 206

Berching-Pollanten, 130

Blockley, R., 153, 351n.6

Bohemia, Elbgermans in, 134

Boiotro, Roman camp of, 336n.97

Bonaduz (Raetia), 122–23

Bonafatius, 257–58

Boulogne, 210

Bregenz Oberstadt (Brigantium), 122

Britain: Honorius and independence of, 251; *laeti* and *limitanei* in, 360n.113; rebellion of 367–368, 9–11; Stilicho's regime and revolts of 406–407, 208–10, 359n.99. *See also* Constantine III; Magnus Maximus

buccellarii, 199

Bulgaria, urban life in, 39

Burgundians, 269, 276, 337n.8

Burns, T., 302n.103

Bury, J., 346n.108, 362n.140

Caecilianus, 235, 236, 366n.61

Caesarius, 171, 174, 344–45n.93, 345n.99, 346n.107

Caligula, 149

Cameron, Alan, 154, 339n.25, 339n.26, 340n.45, 343n.83, 344n.84, 345n.97, 346n.107, 346n.108, 348n.123

Caracalla, 298n.54

Carausius (286–93), 359n.98

Carpi, 58, 306n.149

Carpodaces, 56, 57, 58, 328n.85

Carrié, J.-M., 356n.61

Cassiodorus (ca. 519), 60, 61, 80

Castinus, 274, 374–75n.89

Celts, 355–56n.49, 356n.55

Chariobaudes, 216, 217, 362n.140

Cherf, W., 302n.102

chiliarch, 324n.8

Christianity: Alaric and, 229–30, 232; anti-barbarian ideology of contemporary historians, 221–23; and barbarians of late 4th century, 231; and Goths in Danube provinces, 25; and Goths in Scythia, 16–17, 300n.78; historiography on Stilicho,

Christianity—(continued)
220, 230, 364n.18, 365n.34; indictment
of late imperial politics, 230–231
Chur (Raetia Prima), 122, 331n.25
Chrysostom. See John Chrysostom
civil war: Alaric's sack of Rome as, 245;
military and political disintegration of
Roman Empire in final years of 4th century, 92–111; Theodosius and recruitment of barbarians, 326n.44. See also
Constantine III
Claudian (poet), 102, 103, 114, 152–54, 156,
165, 176, 180–81, 189, 191, 326n.50,
339n.31
Claudius Dardanus, 256
Clearchus, 203, 353n.31
Codex Spirensis, 334n.80
Codex Theodosianus, 47, 52, 321n.52
coinage: archaeological sites in Unterfranken, 133; of Constantine III, 126–28,
137, 212, 214; distribution of Roman in
upper Rhine, 330n.15; "hut-type"
bronze, 11–12; iconography of victory
over barbarians, 298n.50; issued in Constantinople (ca. 378–83), 85; of Magnus
Maximus, 93, 95; as source of information, xvii; Theodosius's sphere of administration, 49–50, 323n.66; of Thessalonica
and Siscia, 311n.27, 311n.28, 312n.31
Colias, 26, 65
coloni, 13, 41
comes, 293n.1
comes domesticorum, 296n.36
comitatenses, 112
Commodianus, 365n.33
Constans (337–50), 117
Constans (son of Constantine III), 253–54
Constantine the Great (307–37), 31, 281
Constantine III (407–11): coinage of, 126–
28, 137, 212, 214; crossing into Gaul in
407, 208–10; as general, 334n.80;
Honorius and, 235, 240, 241, 243, 245,
249; rebellion of, 212–17; surrender and
death of, 250, 251–55
Constantinople: Athanaric's formal entry
into, 57; Gothic siege of after Battle of
Adrianople, 34–35; massacre of Goths in
400, 172–73, 178, 346–47n.109
Constantius II (337–61), 2, 4, 12, 117
Constantius III (ca. 411), 250, 257, 259, 261,
262, 263–74, 277, 281, 335n.80

Consularia Constantinopolitana, 77
Courcelle, P., 365n.33
Courtois, C., 358n.90
Croke, B., 355n.44
Cvjeticanin, T., 352n.13
Czechoslovakia, Elbgermans in, 134

Dacia. See Danube provinces
Dagron, G., 320n.34
Daly, L., 301n.90
Danube provinces: conclusion of Gothic
wars in late 4th century, 73–91; crossing
of Danube by Goths in 376–378, 23–42;
and Roman military policy before Bat-
tle of Adrianople, 19–23; and Roman
military policy following Battle of Adri-
anople, 43–72
dediticii, 12–13, 86, 281, 298n.54, 354n.37
deditio, 298n.55
Demetrius, 237
Demougeot, E., 46, 60–61, 314n.56, 354n.34
De rebus bellicis (anon., ca. 368–376), 18, 19
Didymus, 254
Dietz, K., 334n.74
diocese, as civil administrative unit, 9
Diocletian (284–305), 31, 306n.149, 356n.62
Doise, J., 325n.38
Downey, G., 314n.52
Drinkwater, J., 374n.77
Drumas, 368n.87

Eastern Empire: fixing of boundaries in
392, 164; Gaïnas and politics of, 171–73;
Hellenism in, 84; information on in Notitia dignatum, 297n.37; military policy after 418, 284; military reorganization of
in final years of 4th century, 100–101,
325–26n.38; Stilicho's death and restoration of cooperation with West, 246; territorial jurisdiction of Illyricum, 46–52,
88, 150–51, 158, 161, 164–65, 177–78,
179–80, 310n.10, 310–11n.27, 338–
39n.22, 354n.34
Ecdicius, 44, 250
economics: Danube provinces in 4th century, 20; importance of army to Late
Empire, 356n.61; military pay and taxable resources in 5th century, 200–202;
Valentinian I and activity along Rhine
and Upper Danube, 112. See also agriculture; taxation

Edobich, 250
Edobinchus, 214
Eining (Abusina), 140
Elbgermans, 130, 134, 135–36, 146, 186,
    335n.83
Ensslin, W., 367n.70
Epiphanius Scholasticus, 314n.52
Eruilf, 65, 68
ethnicity: of Alaric's army, 187–88; compos-
    ite nature of late Roman units in
    Raetian provinces, 133–34; usage of
    terms for Germanic tribes in 4th cen-
    tury, 116–17. See also Goths; specific
    groups
Eucherius, 218, 219, 221, 224, 230, 363n.146
Eudoxia (daughter of Bauto), 159, 175,
    348n.123
Eugenius (392–394), 54, 104–107
Eugippius, 330–31n.21
Eunapius of Sardis, 17, 18, 37, 41, 57, 58,
    150, 153, 155, 158, 300n.80, 343n.82,
    364n.25
Euric (466–84), 273, 283
Eusebius, 238
Eutropius, 47–48, 155, 157, 159, 169–70
Eutychianus, 171, 172, 345n.98, 346n.108
Evanthius, 377n.126
Evodius, 93

fabricae, use of term, 350n.143
familiae, translation of term, 351n.3
Farnobius, 305n.133
federate (foedus) policy: development and
    results of, xiii–xxi; and receptio program,
    14–15; after settlement of 418, 277. See
    also foederati
fibulae, military, 333n.53, 335n.81
Fischer, H. Thomas, 134, 313n.46, 336n.97
foederati, 293–94n.4, 300n.73, 317n.2. See
    also federate policy
Frankenwinheim (Germany), 132
Franks: abandonment of hill forts in early
    6th century, 333n.51; battle of the
    Frigidus, 106; as laeti along lower Rhine,
    31, 42, 64, 295n.14; Pacatus on, 325n.28
Fravitta, 65, 68, 170–82, 345n.97, 346n.107,
    348n.120
Friedenhain, 144
Frigeridus, 27, 28, 29, 304n.125
Frigidus, battle of (ca. 394), 104–107, 110,
    111, 151

Fritigern, 25, 26, 28, 31, 35, 60, 61, 65, 77,
    304n.122, 305n.131, 305n.134
Fullofaudes, 11

Gabinius Barbarus Pompeianus, 366n.64
Gaïnas: battle of the Frigidus, 105–106, 107;
    death of, 347n.115; and Eastern system
    of command, 150; exile of Aurelianus,
    345n.94; as general of Goths, 151–82,
    283, 338n.17, 343n.83; Tribigild revolt
    and, 343n.80, 344n.84, 344n.88
Galla Placidia, 244, 245, 248, 258, 261, 271,
    368n.83
Gallienus, 294n.11
Gamzigrad, imperial villa at, 307n.160
Garbsch, J., 329n.4
Gaudentius, 363n.11
Gaul: from 409 to settlement of 418, 251–
    63; Gothic settlement of 418, 263–78;
    population of northern in mid-4th cen-
    tury, 377n.124; Stilicho's regime and re-
    volts of 406–407, 208–10
Geiseric (king of the Vandals, 428–77), 206
Gelbe Bürg, 130–31
generalships, Roman equivalents of mod-
    ern, 293n.1
Generidus, 192, 194, 196, 237, 313n.45, 366–
    67n.67
Germanic tribes: and Roman military in
    Raetia and Noricum Ripense, 113–47.
    See also specific ethnic groups
Gerontius, 90–91, 157–58, 214, 253–55,
    316n.85, 342n.64
Gibbon, Edward, xviii, 204, 207, 293n.3
Gildo, 159, 161
Goar, 269–70, 371n.18
Godigisclus, 206, 357–58n.79
Gomoarius, 3, 295n.12
Goths: conclusion of Gothic wars in late
    4th century, 73–91; crossing of Danube
    (376–378), 23–42; establishment of gov-
    ernment within Western Empire, 247–
    79; ethnic identity of Alaric's army,
    187–88; Gaïnas as Roman general of,
    151; massacre of in Constantinople (400),
    172–73, 178, 346–47n.109; names of
    groups at end of 4th and early 5th centu-
    ries, 303–304n.117, 315n.73; in Raetia in
    late 4th century, 139; relations with
    Huns, 110; revolt of Procopius, 8–9; role
    in war against Magnus Maximus,

Goths—(continued)
322n.62; Roman military policy after
Battle of Adrianople, 43–72; settlement
of 418 in Aquitaine, 263–74, 281, 283,
374n.84, 375n.94, 377n.124; Tribigild
and, 168; Valens and campaigns against in
Danube provinces, 366–369, 15–17
Grasgasse, 143–44
Gratian: and Battle of Adrianople, 26–27,
29, 32, 33–35; conclusion of Gothic wars
in late 4th century, 73–91; death of,
316n.79; Roman military policy after
Battle of Adrianople, 43–72; territorial
jurisdiction of Illyricum, 310n.10, 310–
11n.27; at Viminacium, 321–22n.54
Gratian (usurper, 406–407), 209, 210–12
Greece, Alaric's campaign in, 157–59,
339n.33
Gregory of Tours, 269, 360n.107
Greutungi, 168, 303n.112, 315n.73
Grumel, V., 47, 337n.5
Gunderic, 205, 207, 357n.69
Guntarius, 371n.18

Hadrian, 326n.45
Heather, P., 300n.69, 300n.76, 303n.117,
317n.106, 318n.15, 319n.19, 321n.54,
324n.23, 326n.44, 339n.27, 356n.52
Heliocrates, 224
Hellenism, in Eastern Empire, 84
Hendy, M., 312n.31
Heraclianus, 230, 243–44, 256–57
Hesperius, 47, 48
Hierax, 174
Hill, P., 311n.27
historiography: on Battle of Adrianople, 1;
image of Stilicho, 220, 230; image of
Theodosius, 314n.54
Hodgson, N., 360n.113
Hoepffner, A., 325n.38
Hoffman, D., 303n.116, 315n.73, 325n.38,
334n.76
Honoriani, 149, 254
Honorius: British independence and, 251;
Constantine III and, 235, 240, 241, 243,
245, 249, 251–55; death of in 423, xv; let-
ter to Arcadius in 404, 195; marriage to
daughters of Stilicho, 159, 214; palace
coup of Olympius, 217–18; proclamation of as consul, 93; sack of Rome, 224–
46; Stilicho and Alaric, 282

Hormisdus, 59
hospitalitas, 264, 267–68, 273
Huns: battle of the Frigidus, 107; death of
Gaïnas, 347n.115; Eutropius's campaign
against (397–98), 155–56; incursions of
425 in Raetia and Noricum, 313n.45;
service in Roman military in late 4th
century, 110; Theodosius's victories over,
328n.85; westward expansion in late 4th
century, 23
Hydatius (ca. 470), 79–80, 81–82, 268–69,
270–71, 277–78

Iatrus (Danube), 20
Illyricum: Alaric and command of, 167;
continuity of urban settlement through
mid-fifth century, 196–97; Stilicho and
territorial jurisdiction of, 150–51, 158,
161, 164–65, 177–78, 179–80, 354n.34;
Theodosius I and territorial jurisdiction
of, 46–52, 88, 310n.10, 310–11n.27, 338–
39n.22
Ingenuus, 294n.11
ingots. See coinage
Innocent I (Pope), 234, 236
Isidore of Seville (ca. 625), 80–81, 277
Italy: Alaric's invasion of in 401, 178–79,
180–81, 364n.32. See also Rome
iudex, use of term, 300n.73
Iuthungi, 117
Ivajlovgrad (Thrace), 40

Jacobus (401–2), 338n.17
James, E., 377n.124
James, S., 360n.113
Jason, 363n.11
Jerome, Saint: on Athaulf, 258; on Battle of
Adrianople, 1, 33; on Goths, 37, 62, 63,
64, 231; on Stilicho, 220, 229; on Vandals,
203–204
Joannes Antiochenus, 158, 174, 327n.65,
328n.71
John Chrysostom (bishop), 19, 104, 169,
173, 326n.54, 346n.109
Jones, A. H. M., 30–31, 212, 271, 303n.116,
307n.156, 325n.38, 334n.76, 339n.31,
341n.62
Jordanes: on Alaric, 176, 179; on Athaulf,
247–48, 257, 260; on death of Athanaric,
80; on Gothic leaders, 61, 318–19n.16; on

Theodosius's military policy, 50, 52, 57, 58, 60; on Vandals, 205
Jovianus (363–364), 3, 301n.81
Jovinus, 10, 249, 251, 256
Jovius, 196, 203, 236, 237, 238, 239–40, 242, 243, 249, 363n.11, 369n.95
Julian (355–63), 2, 4, 17, 117, 299n.58, 329n.3
Julius, 8, 23, 34
Justina (mother of Valentinian II), 93
Justinianus, 214, 361n.122

Kalyopius, 50, 311n.30
Keller, E., 313n.43, 333n.53, 335n.81, 336n.85
Kempten-Lindenberg (Cambodunum), 119, 122
Kent, J., 311n.27, 323n.3
king: Alaric as, 176–77, 232, 342n.63; Athaulf as, 249; concept of within Roman empire, 182, 197, 232, 276, 278; Gothic use of term, 179, 283
Klein, K., 306n.143
Kos, P., 329n.4
Krüppel (Lichtenstein), 294n.4

laeti: Franks along lower Rhine as, 31, 42, 64, 295n.14; late Roman auxiliaries compared to, 281–82; and Roman military policy before Battle of Adrianople, 4–5, 13
Lampadius, 215
land: Gothic settlement of 418 in Aquitaine, 264–68, 272; as payment to Roman military recruits, 199, 318n.15; resettlement of by barbarians along frontiers, 184; tax exemption for occupation of deserted, 376n.103. *See also* agriculture
languages, of Raetia and Noricum Ripense in late 4th century, 118
Lentienses, 298n.55
Leo, 170, 343n.83
Libanius, 63, 73, 87
Liebeschuetz, J., 345n.94, 345n.100, 348n.118, 372n.40
Limenius, 217
limes: in Raetia and Noricum Ripense, 117–18; use of term, 299n.65
Limigantes, 298n.53
limitanei, 102
Litorius, 275

Long, J., 340n.45, 343n.83, 344n.84, 345n.97, 346n.107, 346n.108, 348n.123
Lupicinus, 24–25, 26, 33
Luttwak, E. N., xx
Lyon, tetrarchic medallion of, 13, 14, 156

Macedonia, 75. *See also* Danube provinces
MacMullen, R., 351n.5
magister militum, 9
magister peditum, xv, 293n.1
magister utriusque militiae, xv–xvi, 293n.1, 326n.38, 367n.74
magistri, 99, 293n.1
Magnentius (350–53), revolt of, 3–4, 117, 294n.11
Magnus Maximus (388), 54, 89, 92–11, 322n.62, 324n.9
Maiorianus, 316n.92
Mallobaudes (Frank), 132
Mann, J., 334n.79, 359n.99
Marcellinus Comes, 80, 81, 82, 166, 167, 338n.16, 342n.63
Marcianopolis (Thrace), 36, 37–38, 302n.108, 304n.121
Marcomanni, 185, 352n.18
Marcus (usurper, 406–407), 208–209, 210, 358–59n.97
Maria, empress (daughter of Stilicho), 159
Marinianus, 365n.50
Marinus, 257
Mascezel, 159
Matthews, J., 294n.6, 349–50n.140
Maurice (ca. 600), 199
Maximillianus, 234, 236
Maximus (*dux Sythiae*), 24, 25
Maximus (praetorian prefect of Gauls, 371–376), 58
medieval era, transition to in Raetia and Noricum Ripense, 126
Melta (Thrace), 37
Menghin, W., 329n.4, 333n.48, 333n.51, 334n.74, 335n.83
Merobaudes (Flavius), 82–83, 324n.11
military policy. *See* army, Roman
military tribunes, 106
Miller, M., 359n.99
Mócsy, A., 63, 316n.86, 322n.56
Modares, 54, 65, 313n.48
Montana (Thrace), 36
München-Aubing, 146

Naissus, 311n.30
Nanninus, 305–306n.138, 360n.107
navy, Roman, Danubian fleet in late 4th century, 35
Nebiogastes, 214, 361n.122
Nebridius, 5
Nectaridus, 10
Neuburg an der Donau, 138–40, 335n.83
Nicopolis ad Istrum (Thrace), 37
Niedermünster, 143–44
Nischer, E., 325n.38
Nixon, C., 319n.19, 351n.3
Noricum Ripense: Hunnic incursions of 425, 313n.45; Roman military occupation in late 4th century, 113–47; Roman town life in 5th century, 44–45
Notitia dignitatum: problems of dating in, 149, 303n.115; reliability of as source, 98–99, 296–97n.37
Novae (Danube), 20, 39

obelisk, of Theodosius I (Constantinople), 89, 91, 323n.65, 323n.66
Oberfranken (Germany), 131–32
Odotheus, 89, 96
Odovacar, 201, 332n.44
Olybrius, 47
Olympiodorus of Thebes, 153, 198, 208, 209, 233, 260, 293n.4
Olympius, 217–19, 221, 224, 236, 247, 249
Orientus (bishop of Auch), 376n.117
Orosius (Paulus): on Athanaric, 55, 57, 58; on Athaulf, 258; on Battle of Adrianople, 1; myth of Gothic nobility, 187; on sack of Rome, 244; on Stilicho, 194, 207, 220, 221, 228–29, 363n.146; on Theodosius, 55, 57, 58, 79, 81, 314n.54
Ostrogoths, 30, 270. See also Goths; Visigoths
Overbeck, B. & M., 311–12n.31

Pacatus, 52, 77–79, 96, 101–102, 312n.33, 319n.17
pactum, use of term, 301n.81
paganism: barbarians of late 4th century, 231; easing of legislation against in early 5th century, 237–38; legislation against under Honorius, 364n.18; Stilicho and charges of, 220, 230; Theodosius I and suppression of, 95
Palanque, J.-R., 341n.62
Pamphylia, 170

Pannonia. See Illyricum
parens, title of, 373n.51
Paschoud, F., 313n.48, 314n.49, 322n.62, 354n.34, 361–62n.130, 364n.32, 368n.83, 369n.93, 369n.95
Patrick, Saint, 359n.97
Paulinus of Nola, 16–17, 199
Paulinus Pelleus (ca. 415), 257, 274, 276
Pearce, J., 49–50, 311n.27, 323n.3
Persia: fortified towns on Roman frontier of, 308n.182; and partition of Armenia in 387, 92–93; and Roman military policy in 4th century, 3, 17
Pharr, C., 351n.3
Philippopolis (Thrace), 36
Philostorgius, 168, 271, 342n.70, 344n.88
Photius, 364n.25
Picts, 209, 359n.99
politics, Roman: anti-barbarian ideology of contemporary historians, 221–23; disintegration of Western Empire in final years of 4th century, 92–111. See also Eastern Empire; Stilicho
Pompeianus, 234
Pons Aeni (Pfaffenhofen), 126
Popescu, E., 300n.78
Popovic, V., 355n.46
praetorian prefect, 8
princeps religiosus, 320n.33
Procopius (365–366), revolt of, 3–5, 8–9, 18, 296n.35
Procopius (ca. 550), 205, 206
Profuturus, 27
Promotus (ca. 388), 89, 102, 103–104, 322n.60, 322n.62, 326n.50, 327n.54
Prosper of Tiro, 269, 270
Pröttel, P., 333n.53
pseudocomitatenses, 112

Quadi, 296n.35, 298n.52
Quintinus, 360n.107

Radagaisus (ca. 405), 128, 195, 197–98, 353n.33
Raetian provinces: Constantine III's influence in, 214; excavation of Roman fortifications in, 336n.85; Hunnic incursions of 425 in, 313n.45; Roman military occupation of in late 4th century, 113–47
Ratiaria (Thrace), 38–39

receptio program: continuation of in late 4th century, 108, 146; development of as Roman military policy, 12–15, 280; as goal of Goths, 64; and Goths in Danube provinces, 25, 28, 42, 91; Stilicho and recruitment of barbarians, 156; transfer and integration of new recruits, 59

recruitment, of barbarians. *See* army, Roman; barbarians; Goths; specific regions and tribes

Regensburg, 140, 142, 143–44

Respendial, 269–70

Rhine: pattern of barbarian settlement in late 4th and early 5th centuries, 185–86; Vandals and crossing of in 406, 203–204

Richomeres, 27, 30, 31, 32, 33, 304n.125, 305n.126, 307n.154

Ridley, R., 313–14n.49, 354n.34, 361n.127

road systems: Danube provinces in late 4th century, 76–77; and reconstruction of military campaigns, 302n.100, 306n.139

Roman Empire. *See* army, Roman; Eastern Empire; politics, Roman; specific emperors

Rome, sack of city, 224–46

Rufinus, 103, 153, 154, 155–56, 166–67, 328n.73

Rutilius Namatianus, 229

Salvian (bishop of Marseilles), 262, 365n.33

Salway, P., 360n.117

Saphrax, 30, 61–63

Saracens, cavalry, 28–29

Sarmatians, 309n.2

Sarus, 214, 216, 218, 244, 256, 361n.122

Sasel, J., 316n.84

Saturninus, 28, 33, 82–83, 84, 85, 86, 87, 171, 305n.134, 307n.154

Saul, 106, 150, 151

Saxons, 298n.52, 325n.28, 359n.97

Scots, 209

Scythia: taxation of after Battle of Adrianople, 38; Themistus on barbarians in Macedonia, 321n.50; Valens and Gothic wars in, 16–17

Sebastianus, 28, 29, 32, 33, 256, 305n.134

sedes, translation of, 375n.96

Seeck, O., 309n.2, 327n.57, 346n.108, 348n.126

Seguntienses, 192

Seibt, W., 334n.79

Serdica (Thrace), 36

Serena (wife of Stilicho), 224, 230, 363n.146

Severinus, St., 45

Severus, 10, 296n.36

Sidonius Apollinaris (Bishop), 44, 119, 316n.92

Silings, 261–62, 269

Singeric, 260

Sirmicum, 311n.27

Siscia, coinage of, 311n.27, 312n.31

Socrates (5th century historian), 55, 101, 231, 327n.65, 342n.70, 343n.80, 343n.82

Soproni, Sándor, 53, 313n.45, 355n.45

Sozomenus, 46, 55, 203, 208, 231, 310n.10, 310–11n.27, 343n.82

Spain: from 409 to settlement of 418, 251–63, 371n.19, 372n.50; settlement of Vandals in 411, 268–69

Sribrny, K., 333n.49

Stein, E., 338n.10

Steuer, H., 329n.3

Stevens, C., 209, 359n.98

Stilicho: Alaric and, 228, 282; battle of the Frigidus, 105; Britain and regime of, 208–10, 359n.99; Christianity and, 220, 230, 364n.18, 365n.34; on death of Promotus, 326n.50; deposition and death of, 183–223, 361n.129, 363n.146, 364n.18; and Fravitta, 348n.120; purge of supporters after death of, 224–25; rise of as military officer, 95, 100; and Roman politics at end of 4th century, 148–82; and territorial jurisdiction of Illyricum, 150–51, 158, 161, 164–65, 177–78, 179–80, 354n.34; transalpine recruitment areas for, 113–47

Straubing, 144–45

Stribrny, K., 329n.3

Succi Pass (Haemus Mountains), 4–5, 295n.14

Sueridus, 26

Sueves, 261–62, 269

Svoboda, B., 134

Syagrius (380–82), 317n.108

Symmachus, 350n.140, 362n.140

Synesius of Cyrene, 161–63, 340–41n.52, 344n.84, 344n.93, 345n.100, 346n.109

Szilágysomlyó, treasure of, 62, 65

Tacitus, 339n.26

Tarruntenius Maximillianus, 365n.50

taxation: in Balkans after Battle of Adrianople, 38; decline in taxable resources and military spending in 5th century, 199–202; exemption for occupation of deserted lands, 376n.103; and Gothic settlement of 418 in Aquitaine, 264–65, 267; government oppression and civil unrest before Battle of Adrianople, 18

Teillet, S., 320n.29

Terentius, 224, 238

Tervingi, 303–304n.117, 315n.73

tetrarchic medallion of Lyon, 13, 14, 156

Themistius (ca. 317–85), 17–18, 19, 77, 82, 83–87, 300n.69, 320n.34, 320–21n.46, 321n.50

Theodoretus, 169, 347n.111

Theodoric I (418–51), 262, 274, 275, 276–77, 283

Theodorus, 159, 161

Theodosius I (379–382): as Christian hero, 314n.54; and conclusion of Gothic wars, 73–91; cost containment policies of, 201; death of in 395, xv, 148; and legislation on rural labor force, 41; military policy of following Battle of Adrianople, 43–72, 284; military and political disintegration of Roman empire at end of 4th century, 92–111; recruitment of barbarians for civil wars, 326n.44; and suppression of rebellion in Britain, 9–11; and territorial jurisdiction of Illyricum, 164; Vandals recruited by, 205; Zosimus on, 318n.7

Theodosius II, 35

Theophanes, 355n.44

Thermantia (daughter of Stilicho), 214, 224, 230

Thermopylae, fortifications at, 339n.29

Thessalonica, coinage of, 311n.27, 311n.28

Thessaly, 75

thiudans, use of term, 179, 300n.73, 365n.39

Thompson, E., 308n.177, 375n.94

Thrace: civilian life after Battle of Adrianople, 35–42; diocesan structure in 4th century, 22; permanent assignment of strategic forces to, 25; revolt of Procopius, 5, 8; Stilicho and civil government of, 165. See also Danube provinces

Timasius, 103, 150, 152, 155

Tolkin, C., 328n.84

Tomovic, M., 312n.42

Traianus, 27, 28, 33

treaties, terminology of, 301n.81. See also federate (foedus) policy

Treuchtlingen-Schambach, 130

Tribigild, revolt of (398–99), 168–71, 324n.8, 342n.70, 343n.80, 344n.88

tribute payments, from Romans to barbarians, 67

Turpilio, 224, 238, 367n.70

Uldin, 347n.115

Uldis, 110

Ulfilas, 31, 37, 250, 376n.107

units, use of term, 328n.74

Unterfranken, archaeological sites in, 132–33

Vadomarius, 5, 295n.19

Valens (364–78), 2–23, 306n.154

Valens (5th century), 238

Valentinian I (364–75), 2, 8, 9, 11–12, 112, 117, 294n.4, 296n.35

Valentinian II, 93, 98, 99, 104

Valentinianus III, 373n.51

Valentinus, 3, 11

Vallatum, 143

Vandals, 203–208, 252–55, 268–69

Várady, L., 60, 62–63, 316n.91

Varanes, 219–20, 224, 243, 367n.70

Vegetius, 35, 98, 202

Veith, G., 327n.57

Vercauteren, F., 358n.90

Verenianus, 254

Verona, battle of (402), 180, 181, 191–223, 350n.141

veterans, legislation on, 301n.92. See also army, Roman; land

Vetranio, 4

vexillationes, 337n.8

Victor, 32, 45

Vigilantius, 224, 238, 367n.70

villae rusticae, 40, 124, 126

Viminacium (Moesia I), 87–88, 321–22n.54, 322n.56

Vincentius (ca. 408), 217, 338n.17

Vireux-Molhain, site of, 335n.85

Visigoths, 23, 30, 303n.117, 304n.122, 315n.73. See also Goths; Ostrogoths

Vitalianus, 56, 58, 59, 64, 65, 71

Wallia, 260–62, 276, 278, 283

Wamser, L., 333n.62

Wanke, U., 302n.103, 302n.108, 304n.121, 304n.122, 304n.125, 306n.139
Weßling-Frauenwiese, 124
Weltenburg, 140, 142–43

Zeno, 67
Zosimus: on Alaric's march into Italy, 364n.32; on Battle of Adrianople, 45–46; chronology of, 55; on death of Gaïnas, 347n.115; Eunapius of Sardis and Olympiodorus of Thebes as sources of, 309–10n.8; on Goths and Danube frontier, 16; on Greece in late 4th century, 338n.11; reliability of as source, 98; on revolt of Marcus, 208; on sack of Rome, 233–34; on Stilicho, 194, 229; on Theodosius, 56, 58, 59–60, 96, 318n.7; use of terms "auxiliaries" and "allies," 327n.65

THOMAS S. BURNS is Samuel Candler Dobbs Professor of History, Emory University. He is the author of *A History of the Ostrogoths*, *The Ostrogoths: Kingship and Society*, and (with Bernhard H. Overbeck) *Rome and the Germans as Seen in Coinage*.